Copyright 2009, 2010 Don K. Preston D. Div.
All rights reserved
No part of this publication may be reproduced, stored in a retrieval system, or transmitted by any means, electronic, mechanical, photocopy, or otherwise, without the prior permission of Don K. Preston, except for brief quotations in critical reviews or articles.

Unless otherwise noted, all scripture citations are from the New King James Translations of 1983 1985, 1990, Thomas Nelson, Nashville, TN.

ISBN: 978-0-9799337-5-2

Produced by:
JaDon Management Inc.
1405 4th Ave. N W. #109
Ardmore, Ok. 73401

Original Cover Art by
James Kessler and *Because of Him* Art Ministries
P.O. Box 52
Everson, Pa 15631
e-mail: becauseofhim@zoominternet.net
(724) 887-0804

Adaptation of Art Work for Cover by Kim Lester
Graphic Designs by Kim
P. O. Box 33741
Amarillo, Tx. 79120
(806)-622-8399

TABLE OF CONTENTS

PAGES 1-3
Introduction and an Examination of the Presuppositions Underlying the Traditional Interpretation of 1 Thessalonians 4:13-14

PAGES 4-46
Establishing Four Critical Preliminary Contextual Facts:
1.) 1 Thessalonians 4 is the Restoration Of The Life Lost In Adam
2.) 1 Thessalonians 4 as the Fulfillment of God's Promises to Israel
3.) 1 Thessalonians 4 as the Dedication of the Messianic Temple
4.) 1 Thessalonians 4 as the Wedding (Re-Marriage) of Israel

PAGES 47-62
Establishing the Context of 1 Thessalonians 4 / An Examination of 1 Thessalonians 1:10, 3:1-3, and 3:13, and 2 Thessalonians 1 and 2.

PAGES 63-80
"This We Say to You By The Word of the Lord" / An Examination of the Source of Paul's Discourse in 1 Thessalonians 4. A Special Study of the Parallels Between the Olivet Discourse and Thessalonians / Establishing the Unity of the Olivet Discourse

PAGES 81-103
"Those Who Have Fallen Asleep In Christ Shall God Bring with Him" / An Examination of the Doctrine of the Resurrection As It Relates to 1 Thessalonians 4 / The Unseen Nature of the Resurrection / The Resurrection as The Last Days Hope of Israel / Now Is the Acceptable Time, Today Is The Day of Salvation

PAGES 104-117
Those Who Died *In* Christ, Or Those Who Died *Through* Christ? / Were the Dead Saints in Thessalonica Martyrs?: An Important Question / Matthew 23, Hebrews 11 and Thessalonians: A Firm Framework for Interpretation

PAGES 118-124
The Lord Himself Shall Descend From Heaven / A Comparison of Thessalonians Texts / Is The Coming of the Lord in 1 Thessalonians 4 the Same as His Coming in Chapter 2? / A Comparison of 1 Thessalonians 4 and 2 Thessalonians 1 / The issue of Martyr Vindication and 1 Thessalonians 4 / Discerning the *Purpose* of the Parousia

PAGES 125-129
With The Voice of The Arch-Angel / An Often Ignored Interpretive Key / Who Is The Arch-Angel / Daniel's Definitive Data About The Arch-Angel

PAGES 130-140
With the Sound of the Trump / An Examination Of The Key Texts That Discuss The Great Trump / The Restoration of Israel, The Resurrection, And The Sounding Of The Trumpet / Are The Trumpets Literal, Or Metaphoric? / What About The First Six Trumpets?

PAGES 141-164
We Shall *Meet* Him In the Air: A Theological Atom Bomb! / A Special Word Study– "Apantesis": What Did It Mean to "Meet" the Lord / The Hellenistic and Jewish Background to this Special "Meeting" / Turning The Modern Eschatologies On Their Ear!

PAGES 165-170
We Shall Meet Him In The *Air*? / Is The Air The Atmosphere, Or The Spiritual Realm? / In The Air And On The Clouds

PAGES 171-193
"So Shall We Ever Be with the Lord." More on the Resurrection, and a Special Study of the "Gathering" of 1 Thessalonians 4 / What Is the "*Episunagogee*"? / What Is the "*Harpdazo*"? / What About Heaven And Eternal Life?

PAGES 194-238
We Who Are Alive and Remain Until the Coming of the Lord" / "When the Lord Jesus Shall Be Revealed" / Establishing the Time for the *Parousia* / What Did Paul Mean? / The Present Tense Reality Of The Resurrection In The First Century / Does Time Mean Anything To God?

PAGES 239-244
The Coming of the Lord Shall Be *As A Thief In The Night* / A Brief Examination of Christ's Thief Coming / The Unity of the Olivet Discourse Proven by the Thief Coming! / Jeremiah 2-7 and Christ's Thief Coming

PAGES 245-250
Then Sudden Destruction Comes On Them, *As a Woman In Travail* / A Simple Illustration or *Crux Interpretum*? / The Old Testament Background of Paul's Illustration– The Illustration of A Woman In Travail Meant Impending National Judgment / The Messianic Woes and the Coming of Christ

PAGES 251-273
1 Thessalonians 4 and the End of the Age / A Deeper Look At A Critical Issue / Will the Christian Age Ever End? / What Age Was to End? / Daniel 9, The Seventy Weeks, and the End of the Age / Daniel 12, 1 Corinthians 15, And The End Of The Age

PAGES 274-309
Special Study: Do Expectations Demand A Rapture?: A Refutation of the AD 70 Literal Rapture Doctrine / Did the Early Christians Expect to be Removed From Earth at the *Parousia*? / Arguing From Silence / What Does "Gather? Mean? / Matthew 13: Look Who Is Gathered! / Luke 19- Why Does The King Come? / Romans 13 and Living In "The Day" / Do We Have Any Early References to Christ's AD 70 Coming? / What About the 144,000? / 2 Thessalonians 1, A Death Blow to the Rapture Doctrine

PAGES 310-336
Special Study: A Look At The Dispensational Rapture Doctrine / The Doctrine of Imminence and the Rapture / Rapture or Second Coming, Two Comings or One / Who's On First / "With" or "For," "For" or "With," Or Is It Both? / John 14 and the Rapture / John 14 and the New Temple of God / What About Heaven? / Signs, Signs, Everywhere a Sign, Or, *Maybe Not*! / Did the Early Church Believe in Two Future Comings of the Lord? / Gaps in the Gap Theory: A Special Study of Daniel 9 and the Dispensational Gap Theory / One Taken, One Left, What Does This Really Mean?

PAGES 337-348
Comings and More Comings: An Examination of Partial Preterism / Does Thessalonians Predict More Than One *Parousia*? / A Question of Hermeneutic / An Examination And Refutation of Kenneth Gentry's Partial Preterist Arguments on Thessalonians

PAGES 349-351
SUMMARY AND CONCLUSION

FOREWORD

This book is for serious Bible students, and specifically for students of eschatology. In the evangelical world of today, there is a "New Reformation" taking place in regard to the doctrine of the "last days." The movement called preterism, or *Covenant Eschatology* is growing and changing lives. Along the way it is challenging the long standing traditions of the day. As a result, prominent theologians such as John MacArthur, popular prophecy pundits like Tim LaHaye, Grant Jeffrey, Thomas Ice and others have leveled the charge of heresy, Hymenaeanism, etc, against those who believe that Jesus kept his word to return in the first century.

Preterism is the view that all prophecy of the end times, the Judgment, Second Coming, and Resurrection were fulfilled in the events surrounding the fall of Jerusalem in AD 70. In that event, the Old Covenant world of Israel came to an end, as the New Covenant World of Jesus and his church was fully established. This view holds that Biblical eschatology is not about the end of history, but the end of Israel's Covenant World, thus, *Covenant Eschatology*, not *Historical* Eschatology.

Standing at the heart of this controversy is 1 Thessalonians 4:13-18. Our dispensational friends believe this passage is the key to proving a yet future rapture at the end of the Christian age. Our amillennial and postmillennial friends believe Thessalonians is about the end of the church age as well, but are opposed to the millennial view of things. The millennialist, the amillennialist and the postmillennialist all stand together in claiming that 1 Thessalonians 4 refutes the idea that Jesus returned in the events of AD 70.

The purpose of this book is to present some of the evidence that 1 Thessalonians 4:13-18 applies to the end of the Old Covenant world of Israel in AD 70, and not the end of the Christian age. It is my intent to keep this book to a manageable size so that understanding of this passage is enhanced. I am going to present some of the more salient evidence to establish the case. I know that I will not answer every question that could be asked. Nonetheless, I will present enough evidence to aid the inquisitive student to pursue the topic further, and to realize that there is strong reason for seeing that Thessalonians does not describe a future event.

So, keep in mind as you read that I am not trying to answer every question that could be raised. What I will strive to do is to provide you the reader with a framework of understanding, a context into which you can securely, safely, *scripturally* place this text. By providing this framework you can then proceed to ferret out the answers to the finer details of the text that I will probably not address.

I ask only that you enter this investigation with an open mind and an open Bible. Join with me and countless other Bible students who are beginning to see the Scriptures in a "new" way, unfettered from the creedalism, traditionalism, and prejudice that can, and does, so often blind us to what the Scriptures meant to the original readers.

I have attempted to present a positive exegesis of the text. However, I feel compelled to also compare that exegesis with the dominant and popular views of the day. This means that at times my presentation is somewhat polemic. I mean no disrespect for any of the representatives of the respective paradigms that I cite. My purpose is not in any way to impugn motives, but to critically examine the issues. My personal motto, which is on both of my websites, is "Dialogue When Possible, Debate When Necessary, At All Times Charity." Christian dialogue, indeed, Christian debate is an honorable thing when conducted with mutual respect. I do my best to live up to that standard and always welcome such exchanges.

I must acknowledge my proof readers, Steve Temple, Jack Gibbert, Natalie Murray and of course, my ever diligent wife, Janis. All of these sharp eyed readers have contributed to make this work as accurate as possible. Naturally, all remaining *errata* are strictly my own doing.

In addition, a very special thanks goes to Sam Dawson who is a highly talented technical person. His willingness to do what I could not do in this regard is deeply appreciated.

Finally, I was almost ready to send this book to the printer when I became aware that Kenneth Gentry and Keith Mathison had published two new works: *He Shall Have Dominion* (Gentry), and *From Age To Age, The Unfolding of Biblical Eschatology* (Mathison). The *Dominion* book is an extensive revision of Gentry's 1992 work and includes an in-depth attack on Covenant Eschatology, i.e. true preterism. Wanting to provide the readers of this work with the very latest in thinking, I have incorporated a number of interactions with Gentry and Mathison's works herein. Quite frankly, I am convinced that many Bible students will be shocked at some of the radical changes in both Mathison and Gentry's positions, not to mention their amazing logical fallacies.

I want to say that due to my great respect for both men and their past works, I hesitated before adding this final thought about *journalistic integrity*. When you read their works you will see that when citing the scholars, even those with whom they differ, both men are scrupulous about giving proper journalistic attribution and bibliographic references. Lamentably, this is *not* the case when they make claims about what preterists believe.

I have gone through the entire bibliography in Mathison's massive work, and unless I missed it, he does not list the work of a single preterist author. All that he does is refer to his own, *When Shall These Things Be?* to urge his readers to examine that work. This is *not* proper attribution! *This is not journalistic integrity.*

Gentry is little better, only listing John Noe (p. 159, 293), Sam Frost (p. 277), and Ed Stevens (p. 302). Neither man mentions Max King who wrote a massive, influential and scholarly work, *The Cross and the Parousia, The Two Dimensions of One Age-Changing Eschaton* (1987–available from me).

Make no mistake, both men are *fully aware* of King and his work. Neither man lists– *although they are familiar with them*-- any of the works by myself, although to my knowledge I have written more books than any other preterist author, some fifteen titles.

Both men make many claims about what true preterists believe or don't believe, and they roundly condemn us. Yet, they do not offer their readers the customary, ethical, journalistic attribution to document their claims. One can only conclude that this is a *purposeful omission* on the part of these men. After all, they properly attribute and reference dispensational authors that they consider guilty of false doctrine. They fully document their claims about what amillennialists believe. Yet, when they comment on what preterists believe, they give little to no documentation.

How do their readers know if true preterists are being represented accurately? How would Gentry and Mathison react if those who interact with their works never gave proper attribution? Worse, how would they feel if authors *misrepresented their views*– as Gentry does the preterist hermeneutic– and said, "This is what postmillennialists believe" and yet, did not document that claim? In point of fact, if in this work I made claim after claim about what these men believe, and never gave documentation, both men would undoubtedly say that I was being unscholarly and unethical. And rightly so.

There may well be a distinct reason why these men refused to properly reference true preterist works. Both men, but especially Gentry, have been challenged, *repeatedly*, to meet me in formal public debate. Both have consistently refused. It may well be, to speculate a bit, that they refuse to give the normal, ethical journalistic attribution of preterist authors because to do so opens them up to further challenges. After all, if you "name names" by way of condemnation, does not *honor* suggest that you allow the accused to defend themselves? Even the pope allowed Luther to publically defend himself against the charges of heresy!

Now, this may indeed be speculation. What is *not* speculation is the fact that neither man gives the normal, ethical, journalistic attribution that one has every right to expect. From my side of the fence this is lamentable, revealing and improper.

WE SHALL MEET HIM IN THE AIR
The Wedding of The King of kings

A STUDY OF 1 THESSALONIANS 4:13-18

Don K. Preston D. Div

WE SHALL MEET HIM IN THE AIR!:
A STUDY OF 1 THESSALONIANS 4:13-18

Will one day, very soon, millions of believers suddenly and mysteriously disappear? Will planes fall out of the sky as their pilots, faithful Christians, are raptured by the Lord? Will the most sensational event in the history of the world snatch countless believers off of the world, ushering in a period of unparalleled tribulation? Our dispensational premillennial friends tell us that this doctrine is taught in 1 Thessalonians 4:13f.

On the other hand, our amillennial and postmillennial friends tell us that Thessalonians is about the end of time, the destruction of the cosmos, as Jesus descends from heaven on the clouds, with the literal blast of a heavenly trumpet. Every corpse, of every person who has ever lived is re-constituted, restored, and raised out of the ground!

Without question, 1 Thessalonians 4:13-18 is one of the most popular "end times" passages in all of the Bible.

> "But I would not have you to be ignorant, brethren, concerning them which are asleep, that ye sorrow not, even as others which have no hope. For if we believe that Jesus died and rose again, even so them also which sleep in Jesus will God bring with him. For this we say unto you by the word of the Lord, that we which are alive and remain unto the coming of the Lord shall not prevent them which are asleep. For the Lord himself shall descend from heaven with a shout, with the voice of the archangel, and with the trump of God: and the dead in Christ shall rise first: Then we which are alive and remain shall be caught up together with them in the clouds, to meet the Lord in the air: and so shall we ever be with the Lord. Wherefore comfort one another with these words."

The purpose of this book is to establish the truth that 1 Thessalonians 4 speaks of the coming of Christ in the destruction of Jerusalem at the end of the Old Covenant world of Israel in AD 70. To those not familiar with this view, this will of course sound entirely non-traditional, and I understand the consternation, and even shock that such a view might cause.

I was raised in the amillennial tradition (fifth generation) and was convinced that Thessalonians is about a future "end of the world." I discovered however, that this view is untenable. And so, while the great majority of Bible students posit 1 Thessalonians 4 in the future, I suggest that we must leave the future (interpretation) behind, and look to the past for our proper understanding of the text.

EXAMINING THE PRESUPPOSITIONS

The first thing we want to take a look at is the basic presupposition that lies behind the traditional interpretation of Thessalonians. That presupposition is that it is about the end of the Christian age. Remember that the dispensationalist says Thessalonians is about the rapture. Thomas Ice says: "The purpose of the rapture is to bring the church age to an end so that God may return and complete His program with Israel. This would be impossible if the church and Israel are combined."[1] The problem is that the Bible *never* speaks about the end of time, and most assuredly never addresses the end of the Christian age.[2]

When the angel spoke to Mary about the birth of her son he promised that God would give him the throne of his father David, and, "of his kingdom there will be no end" (Luke 1:32-33). According to Peter on the day of Pentecost Jesus had been enthroned on the throne of David, as promised (Acts 2:29-36). The Hebrews writer said that the first century saints were in the process of receiving the kingdom (i.e. the church, Hebrews 12:20f) that is unshakable, i.e. indestructible (Hebrews 12:28). This goes back to the promise of Daniel 2:44 and 7:13-14, where God said that the kingdom of Jesus would never pass away. It could never be destroyed. Further, Paul affirms that the church is an *age without end* (Ephesians 3:20-21).

If Christ sits on the throne of his kingdom to rule *without end,* and if the church, thus, the church age, has *no end*, then how can anyone say Thessalonians speaks of *the end of the church age?* You really have to see the power of this seemingly overlooked issue. Every futurist view of eschatology, the doctrine of the last days, says that one day the Christian age will end. But that is not what the Bible says!

If the Christian age has no end it does not matter what you think 1 Thessalonians 4 means, it can't be at the end of the Christian age!

> **If the current Christian age has no end, then no matter what you think 1 Thessalonians 4 means, it can't apply to a future rapture, *or any other event*, at the end of the Christian age! Without end means, *without end!***

It will be rejoined that the New Testament does speak of the end of the age, and of course this is undeniable. The great question is, *what age did the New Testament writers believe was coming to an end?* The pivotal passage is Matthew 24:1-3.

As Jesus and his disciples walked out of the splendid edifice at Jerusalem, the disciples showed Jesus the size and beauty of the stones. They were huge and beautiful! Jesus' response shocked the disciples: "Do you not see all these things? Verily I say unto you, not one stone shall be left standing here upon another, that shall not be thrown down." This prediction elicited the following question: "Tell us, when shall these things be, and what shall be the sign of your coming and the end of the age?"

There is no doubt that the disciples associated the fall of the temple with the end of the age.[3] But again, the question is, the end of what age? Here is a simple question, and yet, virtually no one is asking this question: What age was associated with the Temple? What age did that temple represent? Was it the Old Covenant age of Israel, or was it the New Covenant age of Jesus?

Isn't it clear that the disciples associated the temple in Jerusalem with the Old Covenant age of Moses? The New Covenant had not been revealed, and furthermore, *the New Covenant would have no relationship to the Temple!* See Jesus' comments in John 4:20f. Why then would the disciples associate the fall of the Temple, the symbol of the Old Covenant age, with the end of the Christian age? That is anachronistic to say the very least.

There is something critical to understand:

First, The Jews only believed in two ages, and Jesus and the New Testament writers concurred in that belief and doctrine. The Jews believed in "this age" and "the age to come."

Second, Their "this age" was the age of Moses and the Law, and the "age to come" was the age of Messiah and the New Covenant.

Third, The age of Moses and the Law was to end, while the age of Messiah and the New Covenant was to be eternal (see Matthew 24:35).

As we have already seen, the New Testament says that the age of Jesus and his New Covenant will never end. His New Covenant age, the current age of the church, was "the age to come" from the Old Testament perspective. With the passing of "this age," the age of Moses and the Law in the destruction of the Temple, Jesus' "age to come" was fully established and confirmed.

Let me say again how important this is in our study of 1 Thessalonians 4. All futurist views of 1 Thessalonians 4 place it at the end of the Christian age. Yet, as we have seen, albeit ever so briefly, *the Christian age has no end.* Thus, we say again, the basic presupposition that underlies the majority view of Thessalonians is fundamentally flawed. If the Christian age has no end, then no matter what you think Thessalonians means, it does not apply to a future end of the Christian age.

There are four other preliminary facts that we want to present as *critical* to understanding and interpreting 1 Thessalonians 4. As I present these issues I am cognizant that if you are an amillennialist or postmillennialist, or for that matter, if you are a premillennialist, you may not be aware of these critical tenets. The failure to honor, or even be aware of these facts is to my mind, demonstrative of how far the modern church has departed from the proper foundation for proper Biblical interpretation.

FACT #1: 1 THESSALONIANS 4 AS THE RESTORATION OF THE LIFE LOST IN ADAM
THE DEATH OF ADAM– THE LIFE OF CHRIST

Few Bible students would deny that 1 Thessalonians 4 is about the resurrection, the resurrection from the death introduced by Adam. In fact, the focus of eschatology is to restore the life lost in Adam: "As in Adam all men die, even so in Christ, shall all be made alive" (1 Corinthians 15:22).

If Thessalonians is about restoring the life lost in Adam is this not somewhat contradictory of our emphasis on Thessalonians as the fulfillment of God's promises to Israel? After all, Adam, his sin, and his death, predated the Torah. Thus, the promise of overcoming the death of Adam can be, it is claimed, delineated from God's promises to Israel. This overlooks several facts however.

> **If you wrongly identify the death of the Garden, you will of necessity wrongly identify the nature of the resurrection in 1 Thessalonians 4, and the rest of the New Testament. If your *protology* (doctrine of the beginning) is wrong, your *eschatology* (doctrine of the end) is destined to be misguided.**

First and foremost is the undeniable fact that Paul, when considering the resurrection from the death of Adam, posited that resurrection as the fulfillment of *God's promises to Old Covenant Israel.*[4] He directly cites Isaiah 25 and Hosea 13, not to mention the fact that he indirectly alludes to Daniel 9, Daniel 12, the Psalms and other O.T. prophecies (1 Corinthians 15:54-56). This means that the promise of the resurrection made in the Garden *is incorporated into YHVH's promises to Old Covenant Israel.* So, the story of the Garden becomes the story of *Israel.*

What we intend to do now is to demonstrate that the death of Adam, which is the focus of Christ's end time resurrection work, has nothing to do with biological death, but with the loss of spiritual fellowship with God. The implications of this study are profound, for, if you mis-identify the death of the Garden, you will of necessity wrongly identify the nature of the resurrection in Thessalonians and all other New Testament passages. If our protology (the story of the beginning) is in error, our eschatology is likewise wrong. So, what death did Adam and Eve die?

IN THE DAY THAT YOU EAT, YOU WILL SURELY DIE!
"And the LORD God commanded the man, saying, 'Of every tree of the garden you may freely eat; but of the tree of the knowledge of good and evil you shall not eat, for in the day that you eat of it you shall surely die.'" (Genesis 2:16-17)

It is widely admitted that a simple reading of the text of Genesis would indicate that Adam and Eve were to die the very day that they ate the forbidden fruit. However, what is amazing to me is that so few people give serious thought to the problems of the traditional views. Here is what I mean.

God said the day that you eat, you will surely die. Satan on the other hand, said "you will not surely die." Allow me an anecdotal illustration of the problems confronting the traditional view. For several years, I have been privileged to have a booth at a major Christian University. I have interacted with literally thousands of Bible students, professors, ministers, etc.. One of the questions we ask of those who come by our booth is: "Did Adam and Eve die the day that they ate the forbidden fruit?" By far, and I mean, *it is not even close*, but by far the vast majority of those who respond say, "No, Adam and Eve did not die the day they ate the forbidden fruit." Interestingly however, when we point out that God said they would die that day, and that Satan said they would not die that day, there is an immediate recognition that their view has a serious problem! The denial that Adam and Eve died the day they ate the fruit makes Satan the one who told the truth, and YHVH becomes the one who was, after all "a liar from the beginning." This conundrum, is very real. Who really told the truth, God, or Satan?

It will be readily admitted that the term "day" can be used metaphorically. In fact, in Genesis 2 we find such an example: "This is the history of the heavens and the earth when they were created, *in the day* that the LORD God made the earth and the heavens" (Genesis 2:5). How do we know that "the day" here is not a single, twenty-four hour day? It is because Genesis 1 delineated the creation of "the heavens and the earth" in six days. In other words, the previous discussion undeniably defined the day of Genesis 2:5.

However, while this metaphoric use of "the day" is unmistakable, we can go back to Genesis 1:14 and learn that the "normal" definition of the day, must be defined as that for which God created the sun, moon and stars, i.e. as signs and markers of days, weeks, months and years. That is, therefore, the normal definition of "the day." Preconceived ideas must bow to that. Only context can determine what "the day" means in any given text. Do we have any contextual help for understanding what "the day" means in Genesis 2:15f? We do indeed.

Note that YHVH told Adam and Eve, "In the day that you eat thereof, you will surely die." When Satan confronted Eve, he told her, "You will not surely die, but, God knows that *in the day* you eat of it your eyes will be opened, and you will be like God, knowing good and evil" (Genesis 3:5). Notice the direct correlation between *"in the day you eat* you will surely die" and, *"in the day you eat*, you will know good and evil."

Of course, Adam and Eve ate the forbidden fruit. The question therefore is, in what day did they come to know good and evil? Was that knowledge imparted *900 years later*? Did they continue in their innocence for several more centuries? The answer is obvious, is it not? They knew good and evil *in that very day*, the day marked by the sun, moon, and stars, a twenty-four hour day.

The identical term "in the day" is used to say they would die, and they would come to know good and evil. Where is the contextual evidence that "in the day that you eat you will surely die," can be extrapolated into almost a millennium, yet that identical term cannot, *under any circumstances* be extended beyond the limits of a normally defined twenty-four hour day?

Consider the grammatical problem of saying Adam and Eve did die spiritually that day, but they did not die physically for hundreds of years. This means that the same identical term, in the same verse, has two totally disparate, contradictory, definitions. We are told that "in the day that you eat, you will surely die," means that in that very same twenty-four hour period, they would lose their fellowship life with YHVH and be cast out of His presence. But then, that same identical statement, within the same verse, meant you will die physically hundreds of years from now! What rule of grammar, of linguistics, of semantics, of hermeneutic, allows the identical term, in the identical verse, to mean two totally different things? It appears from our vantage point that only a preconceived idea of the nature of the death of Adam can force this kind of meaning onto the text.

One of the most common objections to the above is based on the case of Shimei in 1 Kings 2. This scoundrel had cursed David as he fled from the insurrection of Absalom (2 Samuel 16:5f). After Absalom was killed, David was in the process of restoring order. Shimei came groveling before David asking for mercy. David, counter to the advice of his counselors, graciously granted Shimei a pardon of sorts. However, when David, before he passed away, was giving Solomon final instructions he reminded Solomon of Shimei and instructed him to watch him closely.

Solomon called Shimei in and gave him the conditions of his pardon:
"Then the king sent and called for Shimei, and said to him, 'Build yourself a house in Jerusalem and dwell there, and do not go out from there anywhere. For it shall be, on the day you go out and cross the Brook Kidron, know for certain you shall surely die; your blood shall be on your own head'" (1 Kings 2:36f).

It is argued that we have here a parallel to the story of the Garden. However, a closer reading will dispel that argument. Notice that the text does not say, "in the day that you cross Kidron, you will surely die." What it says is, "on the day that you cross Kidron, *know that you will die.*" What would happen the day Shimei crossed Jordan was the certain knowledge that he would die. It is *the knowledge of certain death* that would come the day he crossed, *not necessarily* his death. As Solomon said, "your death will be on your own head." This is totally different from the Garden! In the Garden YHVH did say, "in the day you eat, you will surely die." He did not say, "In the day that you eat, *know for certain* that you will die." There is a distinct difference between the two situations, and we must honor that distinction.

A more precise parallel to the language of Genesis is found in Numbers 30:5f.

"Or if a woman makes a vow to the LORD, and binds herself by some agreement while in her father's house in her youth, and her father hears her vow and the agreement by which she has bound herself, and her father holds his peace, then all her vows shall stand, and every agreement with which she has bound herself shall stand. But if her father overrules her on the day that he hears, then none of her vows nor her agreements by which she has bound herself shall stand; and the LORD will release her, because her father overruled her. If indeed she takes a husband, while bound by her vows or by a rash utterance from her lips by which she bound herself, and her husband hears it, and makes no response to her on the day that he hears, then her vows shall stand, and her agreements by which she bound herself shall stand. But if her husband overrules her on the day that he hears it, he shall make void her vow which she took and what she uttered with her lips, by which she bound herself, and the LORD will release her."

We have here the same construction. I think it will be admitted that it is impossible to make "in the day" of this passage refer to an extended period of time. By the very nature of the case it must refer to a twenty-four hour day.

So, when we examine the nature of the death of Adam based on the explicit statements of Genesis we find no justification for identifying that death as physical death. Thus, the resurrection at Christ's coming, the resurrection of 1 Thessalonians 4, is not focused on biological death and resurrection. When we examine *the death of Christ* in relationship to the death of Adam we find positive confirmation that the death of the Garden could not be physical death.

CHRIST THE FIRST FRUIT

"Therefore, having obtained help from God, to this day I stand, witnessing both to small and great, saying no other things than those which the prophets and Moses said would come— that the Christ would suffer, that He would be the first to rise from the dead, and would proclaim light to the Jewish people and to the Gentiles" (Acts 26:21f).

I believe one of the best ways to define and identify the death of Adam is to take a look at the death and resurrection of Jesus. This is true because in Paul's writings, there is a powerful presentation of what is known as the Two Adam doctrine. Adam was the first "Adam," Jesus was the second Adam (1 Corinthians 15:45). Christ, the second Adam, came to reverse what was done by the first Adam.

Paul makes a clear-cut, unambiguous declaration that Christ was *the first to be raised from the dead*. This is an important fact when one considers the question of the death of Adam, and the resurrection of 1 Corinthians 15. Let me state it as succinctly as possible:

Christ was the first to be raised from the dead, from the death of Adam (1 Corinthians 15:19f).

But, Christ was not the first to be raised from physical death (many people were raised from physical death prior to Jesus' resurrection).

Therefore, the death of Adam, from which Christ was the first to be raised, was not physical death.

What must be kept in mind when we examine the physical resurrection of Jesus is that it is distinctly, and repeatedly, called a sign (See Matthew 12:39; 16:2f; John 20:30f). Now, a sign never signifies itself, but something else, and something greater. A stop sign at an intersection is not the be all, do all, end all, is it? That stop sign is a visual symbol of the law of the land that far transcends the metal and paint on that pole.

The fact that Jesus' physical resurrection is called a sign in no way mitigates or depreciates the significance or reality of that event. Without that physical, visible event, we would not know of the transcendent reality that it signified and confirmed. But, the fact remains that the physical event was still a *sign*, and signs do not point to themselves, but to greater realities. Just read the gospel of John, and the seven miracles / signs of Jesus recorded there. Would it be argued that the miracles themselves pointed to greater identical miracles? I know of no commentator that has ever so argued.

So, when we examine the physical death of Jesus, that Jesus was the first to be raised from the dead, that his physical resurrection was a sign, and realize that he was not the first to be raised from physical death, we are confronted with the absolute necessity of re-examining the nature and identity of the death of Adam. Jesus' physical resurrection pointed to the greater spiritual reality that he was the first to be raised from the death of Adam, *from alienation from YHVH!*

A note here on whether Jesus actually suffered the death of Adam, i.e. alienation from the Father. I increasingly hear, especially in polemic encounters, that Jesus did not actually suffer alienation from the Father. In March 2008, in a formal public debate with Mac Deaver (amillennialist) he argued that Jesus did not experience, for even one moment, separation from the Father.[5] It seems to me-- to state it as kindly as possible-- that those who make this claim have not thought about what such a claim means.

Here is what we know of Jesus' death. We know that he was "made to be sin for us" (2 Corinthians 5:21). We know that he became a curse (Galatians 3:13). Consider then the following:

If physical death is the death of Adam as virtually all commentators contend, then to argue that Jesus did not experience the curse of Adam says that he did not actually die physically. Or, it argues that physical death does not separate man from God. Or, it argues, after all, that physical death is not the death of Adam. But if this is the case, how could physical death be, in any sense, the enemy of man and thus, need to be destroyed as is normally argued? To argue that Christ did not experience the curse of Adam removes physical death from the entire discussion of the resurrection of the dead in 1 Corinthians 15 and 1 Thessalonians 4.

> If physical death is the death of Adam, as most commentators contend, then to argue that Jesus did not experience the Curse of Adam says that he did not actually die **physically**!

You cannot logically say that the Curse of Adam was physical death, that Christ died physically, and yet claim that Christ did not experience the Curse of Adam. Nor can you say that the Curse of Adam was spiritual alienation from the Father, but that Jesus was not separated from the Father, without saying that Christ did not experience the Curse of Adam. No matter how you define the death of Adam, if Jesus did not experience that Curse, then he could not be the first fruit from the death of Adam. Let me express it as simply as possible.

The death (Curse) of Adam was physical death (most commentators).
Jesus died physically.
Therefore, Jesus died the death (Curse) of Adam.

Put another way, consider this:
The death (Curse) of Adam was (included) alienation from God.
Jesus was not alienated from God (we are told).
Therefore, Jesus did not die the death (Curse) of Adam.

If spiritual alienation is at least *included* in the death of Adam, as all commentators admit, then if Jesus was not separated from YHVH because he bore our sins, and became a curse, then *what death did he die?* If he did not die the death of Adam-- and if the death of Adam was spiritual alienation-- could he then be the first fruit from (Greek *ek*, which means "out from among") the death of Adam? If he was not raised from the death of Adam, then the Two Adam doctrine of Paul is negated.

The bottom line is that if Jesus was not alienated from the Father- more on this below-- because he bore our sins, because he was made to be a curse, because he tasted death for every man, and because, "Christ died for the ungodly," then *his death is unrelated to the death of the Garden* and Adam. Adam *was* alienated / separated! We have to ask then, *if Christ was not separated from the Father,* what death did he die?

> You cannot logically say that the Curse of Adam was physical death, that Christ died physically, and yet, that Christ did not experience the Curse of Adam. Nor can you say that the Curse of Adam was spiritual alienation from the Father, but that Jesus was not separated from the Father, without saying that Christ did not experience the Curse of Adam. No matter how you define the Death of Adam, if Jesus did not experience that Curse, then he could not be the first fruit from the Death of Adam.

Related to this issue is another critical issue, the substitutionary death of Christ. Let's take a look at that.

CHRIST'S SUBSTITUTIONARY DEATH

I recently did a Google search on the substitutionary death of Christ. It was no surprise to me to discover that I could not find a website that denied this tenet of Christianity. There were even some sites dedicated to defending claims that they, or other noted scholars did deny the substitutionary sacrifice, but I did not find one that overtly denied that Christ died in the place of man. Now, I must admit that I did not look at all of the gazillion sites that addressed the topic, but I did look at a good number.

The scriptures seem clear that Jesus died in the place of man. One could present a host of passages, but just a few will suffice to prove this.

ISAIAH 53:4-6

"Surely He has borne our griefs And carried our sorrows; Yet we esteemed Him stricken, Smitten by God, and afflicted. But He was wounded for our transgressions, He was bruised for our iniquities; The chastisement for our peace was upon Him, And by His stripes we are healed. All we like sheep have gone astray; We have turned, every one, to his own way; And the LORD has laid on Him the iniquity of us all."

ROMANS 5:6F

"For when we were still without strength, in due time Christ died for the ungodly. 7 For scarcely for a righteous man will one die; yet perhaps for a good man someone would even dare to die. 8 But God demonstrates His own love toward us, in that while we were still sinners, Christ died for us."

2 CORINTHIANS 5:21

"For He made Him who knew no sin to be sin for us, that we might become the righteousness of God in Him."

GALATIANS 3:13

"Christ has redeemed us from the curse of the law, having become a curse for us (for it is written, 'Cursed is everyone who hangs on a tree'),"

1 PETER 3:18

"For Christ also suffered once for sins, the just for the unjust, that He might bring us to God, being put to death in the flesh but made alive by the Spirit,"

These verses are but a small sampling of many that could be brought forth to demonstrate that Jesus died a substitutionary death. This tenet of Christianity is virtually undisputed, so far as I can tell, among serious Bible students.[6] So, how does this basic Biblical truth relate to the identity of the death of Adam? It establishes that the death of Adam, which is the focus of the eschatological resurrection, *could not be physical death*.

If Christ died in the place of man, so that those in him would not have to die (for it is surely *"in him"* that the benefit of his death is applied) then consider what it means if the physical death of Christ, and the physical death of man is the focus of his substitutionary death.

If Christ died physically,[7] so that man– those in the power of his death– would not have to die (physically) then two things are abundantly clear:

Either

➤ Jesus' substitutionary death itself has been *totally ineffective,* since every man since Jesus died his substitutionary death, to the present generation has experienced physical death. Furthermore, all men will die physically.

Or,

➤ No man since Jesus died his substitutionary death has truly entered into the power and benefit of Christ's substitutionary death.

It will not solve the problem to say that all men will one day be *raised from the dead*. That is not, *not dying* as a result of Christ dying *in man's place*. Consider again Romans 5:6 which affirms that Christ died for the ungodly. Let me illustrate.

Think of a prisoner condemned to die. He is guilty of heinous crimes and has the death penalty on him. However, his brother, never convicted of any crime, under no condemnation steps forward, and offers to die for the "ungodly" brother. The governor grants the brother the right to die for his brother and sentence is carried out. The innocent brother is executed.

Then, the executioner turns to the (*supposedly*) pardoned brother and says, "You are next!" The horrified brother responds, "No, that can't be, my brother just died for me!" The executioner responds however, "Well, just because he died for you, does not mean you don't have to die anyway!"

In the illustration, did the innocent brother really die for his brother? Did he die a *substitutionary death?* For whom, and *why*, did he die, if his brother had to die anyway? To say that he died *on his behalf* is merely semantical gymnastics. There would be no benefit from the innocent brother's death since the guilty brother had to pay the full penalty for his crimes after all.

To say that Christ died a substitutionary death is to agree with scripture. However, to say that the focus of Christ's substitutionary death was his *physical death* is to effectively say that his substitutionary death is ineffective, or it says that no one has ever entered into the benefit of his death.

However, if one takes the (correct) view, that the substitutionary death of Christ was separation from the Father, i.e. *spiritual alienation,* there is no such problem. This properly identifies the death of Adam.

When Jesus died on the Cross, he cried out: "Eli, Eli, lama sabachthani?' that is, 'My God, My God, why have You forsaken Me?'" (Matthew 27:46). This is a direct quote from Psalms 22.

It will be admitted by virtually everyone that Jesus' words sound like he felt that the Father had turned His back on him. However, there are some who claim that Jesus was not actually forsaken by the Father. They affirm that what David says in the Psalm is that while it might *appear* that YHVH had forsaken him, in reality he was never forsaken at all. So, we are told that Jesus' words on the Cross *only seemed* like a lament of anguish that the Father had forsaken him, due to the fact that he had been made a curse. In reality however, his cry was a cry of triumph. I find no justification for this view of Psalms 22.

Psalms 22 clearly affirms that David had been forsaken. Read verses 1-2, 7-8, 13-18. David's problems were real, not imagined. He knew that his troubles were the result of sin (see Psalms 41:11, and remember his offense with Bathsheba, Psalms 51) a violation of Torah, and the Law of Blessings and Cursing (Deuteronomy 28-30).

However, David did express full confidence that YHVH was with him because he was a man of tender, repentant heart. While YHVH *temporarily* deserted him due to sin, that desertion led to reunion, reconciliation, and joy! David knew that because he cried out to the Lord in humility and repentance, the Lord would not finally turn His face from him (cf. v. 24). In other words, the alienation was very real, painful and traumatic, but it was only *temporary.* Thus, Jesus' lament from Psalms 22 does not say that he was not forsaken by the Father. It affirms that while the alienation was very real-- because he bore our sins– he knew that it was for only a moment!

So, if the physical death of Christ cannot be the focus of his substitutionary death, then what of the alienation from fellowship? I suggest that this is the *only* answer that fits.

If Christ died a substitutionary death as scripture affirms, and if that death was so that man *would not have to die*, then those in Christ and the power of his substitutionary death would not have to be separated from him. This is precisely what Jesus affirmed. Take a look at just a few of the passages in John and the promise that those in Christ will never die.

John 3:15- "Whoever believes in Him should not perish but have eternal life. (16) For God so loved the world that He gave His only begotten Son, that whoever believes in Him should not perish but have everlasting life."

John 3:36- "He who believes in the Son has everlasting life; and he who does not believe the Son shall not see life, but the wrath of God abides on him."

John 6:50- "This is the bread which comes down from heaven, that one may eat of it and not die."

John 8:51- "Most assuredly, I say to you, if anyone keeps My word he shall never see death. (52) Then the Jews said to Him, 'Now we know that You have a demon! Abraham is dead, and the prophets; and You say, 'If anyone keeps My word he shall never taste death.'"

John 10:28- "And I give them eternal life, and they shall never perish; neither shall anyone snatch them out of My hand."

John 11:25-26- "Jesus said to her, 'I am the resurrection and the life. He who believes in Me, though he may die, he shall live. 26 And whoever lives and believes in Me shall never die. Do you believe this?"

Do you notice all of the times that Jesus said that those who follow him *will never die?* Do you catch the *power* of that? *They will never die!* Now, every single person who heard those words of Jesus, from that day to the present, has, or will, died physically. Has no one ever truly believed in him? *Has no one ever entered into the power of his life and substitutionary death?*

If Jesus was *in any way* speaking of physical death we are faced with an insurmountable conundrum, are we not? Commentators see the problem acutely. So, they tell us, in these texts Jesus was speaking of spiritual life but in other texts he is speaking of physical life. This cannot be justified contextually and exegetically.

So, when we consider the substitutionary death of Jesus as it relates to the identification of the death of Adam we are virtually forced to admit that the nature of Christ's substitutionary death was not physical death, nor could it be. Christ's substitutionary death is the direct counterpart to the death of Adam. It must be to fit Paul's Two Adam paradigm. Since Christ's substitutionary death was spiritual alienation from the Father, this means that the death of Adam– the focus of the eschatological resurrection of 1 Thessalonians 4– was spiritual death, i.e. alienation from fellowship. This is corroborated by a look at another aspect of Christ's work.

CHRIST'S ATONEMENT
"The wages of sin is death, the gift of God is eternal life."
(Romans 6:23)

As in the Garden, Paul informs us that the law of sin and death is "you sin, you die." Likewise, Paul says that he had, as all men,[8] experienced that death: "I was alive once, without the Law, but the commandment came, sin revived, and I died" (Romans 7:7-9). The apostle was patently not speaking of biological demise. He had experienced the death of Adam![9] However, Paul exults that the work of Christ would result in deliverance– at the resurrection– in deliverance from that "body of death" (Romans 7:25-8:1-3). Notice that Paul could say, although the work of Atonement was not yet fully completed- more on that momentarily- that Christ, "has set me free from the law of sin and death" (Romans 8:1-3). Consider that if one is free from the law of sin and death then he cannot die, correct? If the law of sin and death does not apply, if it has been abrogated in Christ, then those in Christ and the power of "the Law of the Spirit of life in Christ"are not subject to death! Once again, it is abundantly clear that biological death cannot be the focus of Paul's discussion. This is not, in the words of Sam Frost, "a tissue issue."[10] The idea of the Atonement is forgiveness not the deliverance from biological demise. And, the Atonement is inextricably related to the substitutionary death of Christ.

In the Hebrew scriptures, the Day of Atonement was a most auspicious occasion. It was, in one sense, the high point of the entire year. Leviticus 16:21f gives us the fullest discussion of that Day, and the significance of the High Priestly actions:

"Aaron shall lay both his hands on the head of the live goat, confess over it all the iniquities of the children of Israel, and all their transgressions, concerning all their sins, putting them on the head of the goat, and shall send it away into the wilderness by the hand of a suitable man. The goat shall bear on itself all their iniquities to an uninhabited land; and he shall release the goat in the wilderness."

Take particular note that the goat would *bear the sins of the people*. The sins of the people were laid on it. He stood in their place. He was the substitute for them![11]

Hebrews 9:24-28 sets forth the doctrine of Christ's atoning work in fulfillment of the typological actions of the Old Covenant High Priest on the Day of Atonement. Notice the chart that sets forth the direct typological parallels between the Old Covenant High Priest's actions on the Day of Atonement, and Jesus' atoning work.

Old Covenant High Priest	*Jesus the High Priest*
Killed the Sacrifice	*Offered Himself*
Entered the MHP	*Entered the MHP (V. 24)*
Came out to Announce Salvation (cf. Leviticus 9:22f)	*To Those Who Look for Him He Shall Appear a Second Time for Salvation*

| No Entrance (Salvation) to MHP While O.T. Stood Valid | Salvation (Entrance to MHP) at His Coming |

Under the Old Covenant the blessings of the atonement were not declared and "administered" until the High Priest came out of the Most Holy Place and "blessed the people." This is critical because in direct parallel, Jesus would bring salvation at his second coming (Hebrews 9:28).[12]

The point of this discussion of course, is that Christ's work was the work of the Atonement. He was to pay the penalty of sin. As the scape goat bore the sins of the nation, Christ was to bear the sin of the people (See Isaiah 53 again). This critical fact, that Christ died to pay the penalty of sin to take that awful price on himself, *so that man would not have to pay the penalty*, is what helps us identify the nature of the death of Adam.

Consider the following:

Christ took on himself the penalty of sin– he died to make the Atonement-- so that those in him would not have to pay the penalty of sin.

Those in Christ do not have to pay the penalty of sin– since they receive the benefit of the Atonement.

Therefore, those in Christ do not have to die.

As in the case of the substitutionary death of Christ, it is patently and painfully clear that the focus of Christ's atoning work *cannot* be physical death. If Christ took on himself the penalty of sin, i.e. physical death we are told, so that those in him do not have to pay the penalty, then...

Either

➤*Jesus' atoning work–paying the penalty of sin-- has been, so far, totally ineffective. Every man has or will die, since Christ died. Thus, every man since Christ has or will pay the penalty for his own sin if physical death is the penalty for sin!*

Or,

➤No man, since Jesus performed the work of Atonement has truly entered into the power and benefit of Christ's substitutionary death. As we noted above in regard to the substitutionary death of Jesus, it will not do to say that man will one day be raised from the dead. This argument simply evades or ignores the fact that to argue that man will be raised from the dead, essentially argues that man still has to pay the penalty of death for his sin. To be raised from the dead is not the same as *not dying* due to the atoning work of Christ, who (ostensibly) paid the penalty for our sin *so that we would not have to die.*

Christ's atoning work was to pay the penalty of sin for man for those in him so that those in him *would not have to die.*

Yet, at the risk of being redundant, we say again that it is painfully clear that every man, regardless of faith, dies physically.

Therefore, either the focus of Christ's atoning work was not physical death, or, Christ's atoning work is totally ineffective.

The problem is solved however, when we realize that Christ's atoning work was to restore man to fellowship, it was to overcome the death of Adam for sure, and bring man back into the presence of his God. Although I am not sure he comprehended the implications of what he wrote, I concur with Goppelt's assessment of the death of Adam and the life of Christ in Paul's theology:

"It is clear that for Paul the difference between the original Adam and the fallen Adam is not so much in the transformation of his physical nature as in a change in his relationship to God. Accordingly, the fall of the first Adam and the subsequent sinning by all is not set aside by any natural process, but by the obedience of the second Adam and by reconciliation (cf. Colossians 1:18f)."[13]

Do you see the problem with identifying the death of Adam, the death that was the focus of Christ's atoning work, and the death that is the focus of the resurrection of 1 Thessalonians 4, as *physical death?* By seeking to identify the death of Adam as physical death and by making the physical death of Jesus the focus of his atoning work we essentially *deny the efficacy of his death* and place the burden of Atonement on every man. Everyone must die (physically) no matter what Jesus died to accomplish. This forces us to consider the topic of forgiveness.

> The wages of sin is physical death, so we are told concerning the death that Adam introduced. Christ died to make the Atonement so that man would not have to pay the penalty of sin. Yet, every man, to the present generation since Jesus died has died physically. Does this not mean that every man has paid the penalty for his own sin? If every person's physical death is the price of atoning for his own sin, then why was the death of Christ necessary? Why do all men still pay the penalty of physical death for their own sin, if Jesus' death was to make Atonement so that man would *not* have to pay the penalty?

Let me offer the following thoughts:
The wages of sin is death (Romans 6:23).

Those in Christ are forgiven of sin– they have no sin.

Therefore, those in Christ do not receive the wages of sin, i.e. death.

Do we not have the right, indeed, the responsibility, to ask, does the child of God actually, objectively possess the forgiveness of sin today, through the power of the blood of Christ? If man does in fact possess the forgiveness of sin today– if forgiveness is not just a "someday" promise– then does it not follow that man, forgiven of sin, should not die? Let me put it this way:
The wages of sin is death.

Forgiveness removes all sin– the cause of death.

Thus, those forgiven of sin do not receive the wages of sin, i.e. they do not die.

Many exegetes see the problem here so they admit that in Romans especially, Paul is indeed focused on spiritual alienation, but in other texts he is focused on physical death. This is especially true, we are told, in Romans 6 where Paul discusses death, burial and resurrection of the believer in baptism. While it is admitted that Paul uses powerful resurrection language, we are told that since he has a futuristic expectation of resurrection (Romans 6:5) he is contrasting the spiritual resurrection with the physical.

However, to divide Romans 6 into a discussion of two deaths and two resurrections is unwarranted. This says, in effect, that physical death was originally the wages of sin– since Adam died physically due to sin– but now, man will die physically *no matter if he sins or not*.[14] And this in spite of the fact that he is forgiven of the sin that originally brought physical death! However, this is not what Romans 6 says.

Furthermore, this view demands that we ask: if physical death is no longer the result of sin, then how can it be called the *curse of sin*? Likewise, if physical death is not the curse of sin, then why did Paul say– per the traditional view of 1 Corinthians 15-- that the resurrection is the time of the deliverance from sin (1 Corinthians 15:54-56)?

The issue of resurrection really is the Atonement, forgiveness and death. And in this light, we need to address another related topic.

If Adam's sin brought about an instantaneous physiological change in the material body of Adam and Eve– as must be the case in the futurist view of death and resurrection[15]– then why does not forgiveness bring about an equal but contrastive change in the believer's physiology? Why does the believer not begin, *at the very moment of faith*, to become immortal and incorruptible *biologically*?[16] Let me emphasize what we have already stated above, and that is that the traditional view of resurrection will not fit into the idea of sin-death-forgiveness and life.

Remember, sin brings death– and this was, we are told, *physical death*.

But, in Christ the believer has the forgiveness of sin. Thus, if it is the case that sin brings death, and forgiveness removes sin, then the believer should never die *physically*.

It must be emphasized at this juncture that Paul positively posits the resurrection as the time of *the removal of sin* (1 Corinthians 15:55-56). So, there is no question about the relationship between sin-death-life. Furthermore, Paul definitely linked forgiveness with resurrection in the same chapter (1 Corinthians 15:17). For Paul, being raised out of sin death was in fact resurrection (Colossians 2:11-13). There is no doubt that sin-death-forgiveness-resurrection are all inextricably connected. For our purposes in identifying the death of Adam, this connection positively identifies the death of Adam as loss of fellowship, not the loss of physical life.

So, the *parousia* and resurrection of 1 Thessalonians would restore the life lost in Adam. But, if the *parousia* of Thessalonians is to complete the Atonement, then man today does not truly possess forgiveness–and cannot do so until the *parousia*.

If man is forgiven today then the Atonement is completed and the *parousia* has occurred. In other words, whereever and whenever you posit the *parousia, it is there that you place forgiveness*. Unless the Atonement is perfected, there is no forgiveness. If there is objective forgiveness today, then Christ's *parousia* and the resurrection of 1 Thessalonians 4 have occurred. You cannot possess forgiveness without the *parousia* to consummate the Atonement.

If the Atonement is completed, and man (those in Christ) possesses forgiveness, not just judicially, not just forensically, not just potentially, *then man should not die!* Yet man- even those in Christ -- do die (physically). Thus, we say again that if physical death is the focus of Christ's atoning work, then the fact that all men– even the most faithful- continue to die, is a testimony to the utter failure of Christ's atonement! If every man must die, as is patently clear, then man makes atonement for his own sin. He (we) all pay the penalty for our own sin, we make our own atonement.

It is only when we acknowledge that the focus of Christ's atoning work was not physical death that we can solve this conundrum. Jesus did not die to deliver man from physical death. Jesus died to make the Atonement to reconcile man to his God, to break down the barrier of alienation, to bring together all things in heaven and earth.[17]

This is the focus of 1 Thessalonians 4 and every other resurrection text in the Bible. To wrongly identify the death of Adam is to wrongly construct eschatology. To wrongly identify the nature and focus of Christ's substitutionary, atoning work is to mis-interpret Thessalonians and the story of redemption. We must place our understanding of 1 Thessalonians and all eschatological passages within the proper context and framework or we are doomed to miss and/or misconstrue their message.

Fact #2– 1 THESSALONIANS AS THE HOPE OF ISRAEL

One of the most ignored, but critical issues that must be taken into consideration in any attempt to understand Thessalonians is that whatever Paul is saying, it is an expression of *the hope of Israel,* found in the Old Testament promises made to her. This is true not only of Thessalonians, however. It is true of all New Testament eschatological texts. I want you to read what I am about to say very carefully. *All New Testament prophecy is the reiteration of the Old Covenant promises made to Israel.* We will establish this by examining some key texts of what we will call the big three, Peter, Paul and John.

However, before we look at the "big three", we need to look at the big One, Jesus. It is undeniably true that Jesus' mission was the fulfillment of God's promises to Israel, and this includes the eschatological promises. The implications of this fundamental fact are profound.

☞ The Source of Jesus' Eschatology

It is commonly believed, especially in the amillennial world, that Jesus removed the Old Law at the Cross, and that God was through with Israel at that time.[18] However, this misguided view fails to honor what Jesus said of his ministry and mission.

Matthew 5:17-18–

> "Do not think that I came to destroy the Law or the Prophets. I did not come to destroy but to fulfill. For assuredly, I say to you, till heaven and earth pass away, one jot or one tittle will by no means pass from the law till all is fulfilled."

Notice that Jesus said he came to fulfill prophecy as well as Torah.[19] Jesus did not say that only some prophecy had to be fulfilled. He said *all* had to be fulfilled. Furthermore, Paul said that Jesus, "became the servant to the circumcision to confirm the promises made to the fathers" (Romans 15:8).

So, did Jesus' mission– which was *not* limited to his Incarnation-- include the eschatological promises made to Israel? It did.

Jesus said his mission was to gather together the children of God scattered abroad (John 11:50-51). He said his mission was to gather, "the lost sheep of the house of Israel" (Matthew 15:21). This re-gathering is the time of Israel's *salvation*. There is *nothing* more eschatological than the promise of the re-gathering / salvation of Israel!

Israel was to be re-gathered / saved by Messiah in the Second Exodus (Isaiah 11:10f).

Israel was to be re-gathered / saved in the day of the Resurrection and Messianic Banquet (Isaiah 24-25:6-9).

Israel was to be re-gathered / saved at the sounding of the Great Trumpet, in the Day of the Lord (Isaiah 27:9-13).

Israel was to be re-gathered / saved in the Day of Salvation, the Acceptable Time (Isaiah 49:6f) at the coming of the Servant of YHVH.

Israel was to be re-gathered / saved at the time of her "re-marriage" Hosea 1-3; Isaiah 61:2-12) at the coming of the Lord in judgment.

Israel was to be re-gathered / saved at the time of the New Creation, when the Lord would come in flaming fire (Isaiah 65-66:15f).

This is just a small sampling of the Old Testament prophecies of the re-gathering and salvation of Israel. So, Jesus said that he came to fulfill the Law and to re-gather and save the lost sheep of the house of Israel. The re-gathering and salvation of Israel is linked in prophecy with the eschatological coming of Messiah– *it cannot be limited to his Incarnation*. It is patently clear therefore, that Jesus' eschatological hope was *nothing but the hope of Israel*. His mission to fulfill that hope *included his coming in judgment.*

The significance of seeing that Jesus' mission was inseparably bound up with the promises to Israel is that his apostles were given the task of proclaiming that message and continuing his ministry, until it was consummated at the aforementioned *parousia*. In other words, Jesus' apostles did not have a different ministry and message than Jesus. Let's demonstrate that now, as we turn to consider the big three of the New Testament writers.

☛ The Source of Peter's Eschatology

Note three passages from Peter that demonstrate that his eschatology was nothing but the hope of Israel.

Acts 3:21-24 -- Peter says that the "restoration of all things" to be completed at the *parousia* of Christ would be the fulfillment of all the prophets from Samuel forward, "yea, all who have ever written." Peter was not proclaiming a postponed hope of Israel. Nor a hope transferred to the church, taken from Israel. He was not preaching an eschatological hope different from that promised to Israel.

1 Peter 1:9-12 – 1 Peter (of many passages that could be adduced) Peter was looking for the "ready to be revealed" salvation at Christ's coming. He specifically tells us that the Old Testament prophets foretold that salvation at the *parousia*. Furthermore, if we are sensitive to it, Peter's epistle is full of references to the Old Covenant last days prophecies.

2 Peter 3:1-3, 13 – Peter informs us in no uncertain terms that his hope of the New Heaven and Earth at the Day of the Lord was "according to His promise" i.e. the Old Covenant promises found in the prophets who had spoken before.

When one reads the literature, there is virtually no disagreement that Peter is citing, and even directly quoting from Isaiah's prediction of the New Creation. (There are other O.T. texts lying behind 2 Peter 3 such as Daniel

9 and Isaiah 50f, but Isaiah 65-66 are the ones that come most easily to mind).

So, from these three texts from the pen of Peter it is easily established that his eschatological hope, his gospel, was nothing but the reiteration of the Old Testament promises made to Israel.

☛ The Source of John's Eschatology

It is sometimes argued that John's gospel is not overly eschatological, because it contains no explicit statements such as, "The kingdom of heaven has drawn near," like Matthew and Mark. Also, whereas Matthew, Mark and Luke all contain parallel accounts of the Olivet Discourse, John's gospel is quiet about that account. However, this does not mean that John's gospel[20]– not to mention the Apocalypse– is not eschatological. Consider a few passages.

"Jesus said to her, 'Woman, believe Me, the hour is coming when you will neither on this mountain, nor in Jerusalem, worship the Father. 22 You worship what you do not know; we know what we worship, for salvation is of the Jews. But the hour is coming, and now is, when the true worshipers will worship the Father in spirit and truth; for the Father is seeking such to worship Him.'" (John 4:21f)

When understood *within its prophetic background and context*, this passage is tremendously eschatological. Jeremiah 3:14f had foretold the time– *when Israel was restored*– when men would no longer go to Jerusalem to worship,[21] and the Ark of the Covenant would lose its covenantal significance.[22] The restoration of Israel is inseparably linked with the time of the kingdom, the coming of Messiah in judgment, resurrection and every other major eschatological tenet. So for Jesus to say that the hour had arrived when men would no longer worship in Jerusalem was to say that the time for Israel's salvation had come, the kingdom was near!

In chapter 5:24-28, Jesus spoke of the resurrection:
"Most assuredly, I say to you, the hour is coming, and now is, when the dead will hear the voice of the Son of God; and those who hear will live. For as the Father has life in Himself, so He has granted the Son to have life in Himself, and has given Him authority to execute judgment also, because He is the Son of Man. Do not marvel at this; for the hour is coming in which all who are in the graves will hear His voice and come forth—those who have done good, to the resurrection of life, and those who have done evil, to the resurrection of condemnation."[23]

The prophetic background for Jesus' discourse here is Ezekiel 37 and Daniel 12. Both passages promised the resurrection of Israel, in the last days, at the end of the age, and the establishment of the kingdom. There are of course other eschatological references in John, particularly to the resurrection. As we have demonstrated, the resurrection was clearly the Old Covenant hope of Israel.

It should go without saying that John's Apocalypse is based squarely upon Israel's Old Testament promises. Virtually every scholar agrees that Revelation reiterates the prophecies of Daniel for instance. But, it is not only Daniel that John draws from. Revelation draws heavily from Isaiah, Zechariah, Ezekiel, and other Old Testament prophecies as well. John specifically tells us that the fulfillment of his vision would be when, "the mystery of God foretold by the prophets" would be fulfilled (Revelation 10:7).

It is a great theological tragedy when Bible students seek to understand, interpret and teach Revelation without an appreciation and understanding of the Old Testament background and source of Revelation. There is no possible way to properly understand and interpret Revelation without keeping it within its proper context and that as the fulfillment of God's promises to Israel. John's eschatological hope was nothing but the hope of Israel.

> **The failure to interpret Revelation as the final fulfillment of God's promises to Old Covenant Israel is a guarantee of a false interpretation of the book. The failure to honor this context of Revelation is surely one of the great theological failures of all time.**

☞ The Source of Paul's Eschatology

At the risk of redundancy, we will give again here what Paul said about the source and nature of his eschatology.

Acts 24:14-15: "But this I confess to you, that according to the Way which they call a sect, so I worship the God of my fathers, believing all things which are written in the Law and in the Prophets. I have hope in God, which they themselves also accept, that there will be a resurrection of the dead, both of the just and the unjust."

Acts 26:5f: "According to the strictest sect of our religion I lived a Pharisee. And now I stand and am judged *for the hope of the promise made by God to* *our fathers.* To this promise our twelve tribes, earnestly serving God night and day, hope to attain. For this hope's sake, King Agrippa, I am accused by the Jews. Why should it be thought incredible by you that God raises the dead?" (My emphasis)

Acts 26:21f: "Therefore, having obtained help from God, to this day I stand, witnessing both to small and great, *saying no other things than those which the prophets and Moses said would come*— that the Christ would suffer, that He would be the first to rise from the dead, and would proclaim light to the Jewish people and to the Gentiles."

Acts 28: 19f: "But when the Jews spoke against it, I was compelled to appeal to Caesar, not that I had anything of which to accuse my nation. For this reason therefore I have called for you, to see you and speak with you, because for the hope of Israel I am bound with this chain."

Romans 8:23-9:4: "Not only that, but we also who have the first-fruits of the Spirit, even we ourselves groan within ourselves, *eagerly waiting for the adoption*, the redemption of our body... I tell the truth in Christ, I am not lying, my conscience also bearing me witness in the Holy Spirit, 2 that I have great sorrow and continual grief in my heart. 3 For I could wish that I myself were accursed from Christ for my brethren, my countrymen according to the flesh, *4 who are Israelites, to whom pertain the adoption,* the glory, the covenants, the giving of the law, the service of God, and the promises."

Now, if Paul said that his gospel, his eschatology, was *nothing* but what Moses and the prophets said, then this means that when we read 1 Thessalonians 4, we are reading Paul's take on Israel's eschatological hope. When we read 1 Corinthians 15, it is the hope of Israel being discussed.[24] When we read Revelation, or Acts, or Galatians, *it does not matter*, we are reading about *God's promises to Israel.* The New Testament writers not only proclaimed that their eschatological hope was the hope of Israel, but they never, and we emphasize this, they *never* say that the fulfilment of God's promises to Israel had been postponed, delayed, or altered.

Dispensationalism insists that although Christ came to establish the kingdom, due to Jewish unbelief, "it became impossible to establish the kingdom."[25] Consequently, Christ postponed the kingdom and established the church instead. The church, per millennialism, is a direct result of the failure of Israel to enter into her promises. The church however, was never predicted by the Old Testament prophets. Dispensationalist John F. Walvoord wrote: "The present age (of the gathering of the church by the blood and Spirit of Jesus Christ) is a parenthesis or a time period not predicted by the Old

Testament and therefore not fulfilling or advancing the program of events revealed in the Old Testament fore view.[26] LaHaye and Ice claim, "The church was an unforeseen mystery in the Old Testament."[27] Pentecost says, "The concept must stand that this whole age with its program was not revealed in the Old Testament, but constitutes a new program and a new line of revelation in this present age....It has been illustrated how this whole age existed in the mind of God without having been revealed in the Old Testament."[28]

The problem for the millennial view is that as we have just seen the New Testament writers tell us that they were experiencing and writing about was directly from and based on God's Old Covenant promises made to Israel. Paul tells us that his proclamation of the mystery of God– Jew and Gentile equality in the church, the body of Christ– was directly from the Old Testament prophets.

> "Now to Him who is able to establish you according to my gospel and the preaching of Jesus Christ, according to the revelation of the mystery kept secret since the world began but now made manifest, and by the prophetic Scriptures made known to all nations, according to the commandment of the everlasting God, for obedience to the faith– to God, alone wise, be glory through Jesus Christ forever. Amen" (Romans 16:25-27).

Ask yourself this question: If the mystery of God, Jew and Gentile equality in the church, was not foretold by *any* of the Old Testament prophets as affirmed by the dispensationalists, *how could Paul preach the mystery of God from the Old Testament prophets?*

If the mystery of God, Jew and Gentile equality *in the church*, was not foretold anywhere, by any of the Old Testament prophets, as affirmed by the dispensationalists, how was it possible for Paul to preach the mystery of God *from the Old Testament prophets?* Did Paul pervert the Old Testament prophets to say something they never predicted?

Likewise, when Peter stood up on Pentecost and proclaimed the gospel of grace to the Jews that day he did so in full conviction that what was happening was in fulfillment of God's promises to Israel and the blessings promised to her for the last days:

> "But Peter, standing up with the eleven, raised his voice and said[29] to them, 'Men of Judea and all who dwell in Jerusalem, let this be known to you, and heed my words. 15 For these are not drunk, as you suppose, since it is only the third hour of the day. 16 But this is what was spoken by the prophet Joel: 17 'And it shall come to pass

in the last days, says God, That I will pour out of My Spirit on all flesh; Your sons and your daughters shall prophesy, Your young men shall see visions, Your old men shall dream dreams.'" (Acts 2:15-17)

Joel said that in the last days, YHVH would pour out the Spirit on Israel, and salvation– the salvation of the remnant– would be the result. The Spirit was poured out on the day of Pentecost. Peter said that what was happening was in direct fulfillment of Joel's promise, "This is that which was spoken by the prophet Joel." There could not be any clearer, more emphatic words found anywhere. But, what was happening on the day of Pentecost was the establishment of the church. Therefore, Joel's prediction included the establishment of the church.

Our point in all of this, and much more could be said, is that the New Testament writers not only tell us that they were looking for the fulfillment of the Old Testament promises to Israel, they tell us that what was happening in their day and in their ministries, was the *fulfillment of* God's promises to Israel. There was no postponement, no alteration of God's plan.[30] All was on schedule, as planned. Israel's unbelief was not unforeseen, but predicted. Israel's recalcitrance did not postpone anything; it was the prophesied means for God to offer salvation to all men. As Nanos says: "We are thus prepared to recognize that for Luke the commencement of the gentile mission was based not on Israel's rejection, but on the belief that her promised restoration had begun, with the inherent obligation to proclaim this message to all the nations (Acts 15:13-18)" (*Mystery*, 269).

In other words, the Gentile mission and the establishment of the church, the body of Christ, was not the sign of the failure of Israel's promises it was the *fulfillment* of Israel's promises.

In light of the facts set forth above, no matter what else it might be, Paul's eschatology in Thessalonians is his iteration of *the hope of Israel*!

All futurist eschatologies, including the dispensational paradigm posit 1 Thessalonians 4 in the future at the end of the current *Christian age*. However, let me frame my introductory argument like this:

1 Thessalonians 4 predicted the resurrection.

But, the resurrection of the dead was the hope of Israel after the flesh, and found in and based on, "Moses and the prophets" (Acts 24:14f; Romans 8:23-9:5).

Therefore, the resurrection of the dead as taught in 1 Thessalonians 4 was the hope of Israel after the flesh, and found in and based on, "Moses and the prophets."

The fact that Paul's entire eschatology is drawn from the O.T. prophecies made to Israel seems all but lost on most students of eschatology, particularly those of the amillennial and postmillennial views.[31] The common view in both schools is that God was essentially through with Israel at the Cross, and that beginning on Pentecost, He started all over as it were, with a new set of promises to the church divorced and separate from Israel.

It must be kept in mind that Paul was actually accused of preaching a doctrine different from, and divorced from Israel: "Men of Israel, help! This is the man who teaches all men everywhere against the people, the law, and this place; and furthermore he also brought Greeks into the temple and has defiled this holy place" (Acts 21:28). He was accused of preaching against Israel and her covenant promises! What was Paul's response to that: "And they neither found me in the temple disputing with anyone nor inciting the crowd, either in the synagogues or in the city. *Nor can they prove the things of which they now accuse me*" (Acts 24:13f, my emp.).

Since Paul affirms in the clearest terms that his gospel, his eschatology, his hope of the resurrection, was from Moses and the prophets, it should go without saying that any interpretation of 1 Thessalonians 4 that one might wish to offer must first of all be found in the O.T. prophecies made to Israel. In other words, if one cannot find the modern concept of the nature, framework, and time of the eschaton in the O.T., then that demonstrates *prime facie* the inherent fallacy of that given eschatology. That includes the idea of the end of the Christian age, the end of time, a literal, bodily, visible Day of the Lord, the idea of a literal rapture, whether at the end of the Christian age or in AD 70, etc.. In other words, any eschatological teaching not found in the O.T. promises made to Israel is not true.

Thus, when we come to Thessalonians we have every right, indeed, the obligation to ask where in the Old Testament

> *If a given interpretation of 1 Thessalonians 4 cannot be found in the O.T. prophetic hopes of Israel that interpretation is false. Paul said his eschatological doctrine was nothing other than what was promised in Moses and the prophets.*

do we find the prophecy of the events of Thessalonians, as interpreted by most modern exegetes? In other words, where do we find the O.T. prediction of the literal rapture of the church at the end of the Christian age? Amazingly, the dispensationalists openly state that the Torah never foretold such a thing. As we have just seen, the millennialists do not believe that the church was foretold in the O.T..

Here is what we have. The millennialists say that 1 Thessalonians 4 is about the rapture of the church at the end of the Christian age. They claim that the O.T. never predicted the events of 1 Thessalonians 4. Yet Paul, in discussing his eschatological hopes, i.e. including Thessalonians of course, said that he taught nothing but what was foretold in Moses and the prophets. Thus, unless Paul was mistaken the events of Thessalonians were in fact foretold in the O.T.. But if that is true the foundation of dispensationalism crumbles.

> The millennialists say that the rapture was not prophesied in the Old Testament. Yet, Paul said his eschatology was nothing other than what the O.T. prophets foretold! This means that Thessalonians is, after all, based on the O.T., and millennialism is falsified!

The amillennial paradigm fares no better. As noted, generally speaking, amillennialists claim that God was through with Israel at the Cross, and from Pentecost onward, God was not concerned with the Old Covenant people or His Old Covenant promises.[32] Personally, as a former amillennialist, I can relate that *not once* did I *ever* hear any amillennial preacher so much as indicate that he was even remotely aware that Thessalonians was supposed to be viewed through the spectrum of God's promises to Israel or Torah. Yet, if Paul's eschatology, including Thessalonians, was nothing but the hope of Israel, based on and drawn from the Old Testament, then there is something fatally wrong with the amillennial doctrine.

FACT#3: 1 THESSALONIANS 4 AS THE ARRIVAL OF THE NEW TABERNACLE

Fully consistent with what we just presented on Thessalonians as the fulfillment of God's promises to Israel, consider this:

The *parousia* of Christ in 1 Thessalonians 4 is the *parousia* of Christ in John 14:1-6 and Revelation 21.

The *parousia* of Christ in John 14 and Revelation 21 was the coming of the Messianic Temple foretold by the Old Testament prophets.

The Messianic Temple foretold by the Old Testament prophets was not the removal of man–or the church-- from the earth but the restoration of God's presence with man on earth.

Therefore, the *parousia* of Christ in 1 Thessalonians 4 was the coming of the Messianic Temple for the restoration of God's presence with man on earth.

I want to establish this argument by examining first of all the Old Testament prophecies of the Messianic Temple, and then I want to examine John 14 and Revelation 21.

I WILL PUT MY TABERNACLE AMONG THEM

1 Thessalonians 4 and John 14 speak of the same event, the coming of Christ. Further, there is no question that both speak of the same purpose of the coming of Christ the gathering of the elect to dwell with Christ. There is another fact that is too often ignored, and that is that the coming of the Messiah to dwell with his people is directly related to the Old Testament promise of the Messianic temple or the new tabernacle.

I will only develop *some* of the O.T. promises of the new temple. However, it is important to realize that in all of the promises of the new temple there is one central theme: the idea of God establishing (re-establishing) His dwelling among men. Not one of them posit the removal of man from earth. It follows therefore, that if John 14 speaks of the fulfillment of the Old Testament promises of the new temple, then this proves that John 14 is not about the removal of man from the earth in a rapture, but the re-establishment of God's presence among men.

ISAIAH 2-4

"Now it shall come to pass in the latter days That the mountain of the LORD'S house Shall be established on the top of the mountains, And shall be exalted above the hills; And all nations shall flow to it. Many people shall come and say, 'Come, and let us go up to the mountain of the LORD, To the house of the God of Jacob; He will teach us His ways, And we shall walk in His paths.' For out of Zion shall go forth the law, And the word of the LORD from Jerusalem.... In that day the Branch of the LORD shall be beautiful and glorious; And the fruit of the earth shall be excellent and appealing For those of Israel who have escaped. And it shall come to pass that he who is left in Zion and remains in Jerusalem will be called holy—everyone who is recorded among the living in Jerusalem. When the Lord has washed away the filth of the daughters of Zion, and purged the blood of Jerusalem from her midst, by the spirit of judgment and by the spirit of burning, then the LORD will create above every dwelling place of Mount Zion, and above her assemblies, a cloud and smoke by day and the shining of a flaming fire by night. For over all the glory there will be a covering. And there will be a tabernacle for shade in the daytime from the heat, for a place of refuge, and for a shelter from storm and rain. (Isaiah 2:2-3; 4:2-6)

The first passage to be noted is one of the most famous of all O.T. prophecies. This prophecy can be outlined briefly:

1.) It foretold the events of the last days (2:2f).
2.) It foretold the establishment of the kingdom among men, on earth (2:2f).
3.) It foretold the coming of the Lord in judgment of Old Covenant Israel (2:10f, 19-21; 3:1-3, 13-24; 4:2f).
4.) It would be when Jehovah judged Israel for her blood guilt (4:4).
5.) At this time, "there shall be a tabernacle[33] of shade for the daytime from the heat, for a place of refuge, and for a shelter from storm and rain" (4:6).

There is no hint of a removal of man from the earth in the text. The language demands that the new tabernacle is among men *on earth* as a glorious shelter and dwelling with Jehovah.

Now unless John 14 and 1 Thessalonians 4 speak of a different Day of the Lord from that promised in Isaiah 2-4,[34] since Isaiah says not one word about a removal of man from earth one cannot force John 14 and Thessalonians into a discussion of a removal of man from earth.

EZEKIEL 37

"Moreover I will make a covenant of peace with them, and it shall be an everlasting covenant with them; I will establish them and multiply them, and I will set My sanctuary in their midst forevermore. My tabernacle also shall be with them; indeed I will be their God, and they shall be My people" (Ezekiel 37:26f).

Like Isaiah 2-4, Ezekiel 37 is a familiar passage. It's bearing on our discussion is great since the N.T. writers often not only allude to it but make extensive commentary on it (e.g. Ephesians 2:2 Corinthians 3-6).

For brevity we can outline the constituent elements of the prophecy.

1.) God would reunite the two houses of Israel (37:15f). The reunification would be the resurrection out of their "graves" (37:10-14). The referent is not to physical graves however, but to the death and grave of alienation from God.
2.) The reunification would be under Messiah (v.22-24).
3.) The reunification would involve a New Covenant (v. 26). This is the time of the wedding promised in Hosea (cf. Hosea 2:18).
4.) The reunification would involve a new tabernacle "in their midst forever" (v. 26). See my discussion of Ezekiel 11 and 37 for more on this.[35]
5.) The reunification, focused around the new tabernacle, would result in God's dwelling with the people, "My tabernacle shall be with them; indeed I will be their God, and they shall be my people. The nations also will know

that I, the Lord, sanctify Israel, when my sanctuary is in their midst forevermore" (v. 27-28).

Ezekiel was not predicting a removal of men from the earth. God's tabernacle would be *among the people*. He would be "in their midst forevermore." Furthermore, by the presence of this tabernacle, this dwelling with His people, "the nations will know that I, the Lord, sanctify Israel." This demands that the saints be on earth as shining examples of Jehovah's grace and presence among them. The nations would observe God among His people and glorify Him through them. This would hardly be possible if the saints were removed from the earth.

We have *prima facie* proof that Ezekiel was being fulfilled in the first century, in the body of Christ.

We will have more to say about 2 Corinthians 3-6 below, but for now note that Paul contrasts the temples of idols with the church, the temple of God (2 Corinthians 6:14-16). Paul then says, "you are the temple of the living God, as God has said, 'I will dwell in them and walk among them. I will be their God and they shall be My people.'" Notice Paul's emphatic "you are, as God has said." The "you are" that he identifies them as being is the temple / tabernacle promised in Ezekiel 37! The Messianic temple promised to Israel was becoming a reality. Israel was being restored. Since the promise of Ezekiel was that God would dwell with man, and that man would see His presence via the temple (His *people* –not a building-- in 2 Corinthians) then it is hardly logical to suggest that God would *remove* that temple so that the nations could know Him. It was to be through the temple and God dwelling among His people that the nations would come to know Him. Paul saw that new temple as under construction, comprised of living people, the followers of Jesus (Ephesians 2:19f; 4:16f).

Peter likewise believed that the Messianic temple foretold by the Old Testament prophets– Ezekiel's Messianic Temple-- was under construction. Peter's first epistle is intensely eschatological and exudes a sense of the imminent *parousia*. What is more, and this is often overlooked by the commentators, 1 Peter is focused on *the restoration of Israel*. It is common among some commentators to say that Peter is actually addressed to a Gentile audience even though he utilizes language that was normally descriptive of Israel. This is what I was personally taught in seminary. In my 2008 formal debate with amillennialist John Welch he insisted that Peter was writing to Gentiles who were unconcerned with God's O.T. promises to Israel.[36] I believe this is misguided. We will establish our premise by quickly noting some of the salient issues in 1 Peter.

➢ Peter was the apostle to the *circumcised* (Galatians 2) those whose history and promises were in the Old Testament that he quotes. He is writing to "his audience." Just like Paul the "apostle to the gentiles" wrote to his audience, Peter, "apostle to the circumcision" was writing to his audience.

➤ The geographical locations that Peter mentions are some of the very locations mentioned in Acts 2. There we are told that Jews from "every nation under heaven" had gathered. Did these "Jews" not go back to their home after hearing Peter speak to them about their Messiah on that momentous day? This alone is sufficient to understand that Peter truly was addressing Israel scattered abroad.

➤ Peter specifically addresses "the *elect*, those *scattered* throughout Pontus, Galatia, Cappadocia, Asia and Bithynia, etc." A bit more accurately, he says, "to the chosen sojourners of the dispersion..." These terms, i.e. the *elect*, *sojourners* (cf. 1:17; 2:12) and the *diaspora* are virtually technical terms for the ten northern tribes, i.e. Israel scattered abroad. Many commentators acknowledge that *diaspora* was, "a technical term among Greek speaking Jews for members of their race dwelling outside Palestine."[37]

➤ Further proof that Peter is addressing the *diaspora* of Israel– albeit *now Christians of the diaspora*– is that he speaks of them being "elect according to the foreknowledge of God." Paul makes it clear in Romans 9-11 that it was Israel that was foreknown. It was Israel that was elected. It was Israel to whom the promises of the election were made (Romans 9:3f; 11:1-3).

➤ Throughout his epistle Peter uses language reminiscent of Israel's bondage and exodus. The terms "strangers and sojourners" recall the Exodus. He also says that they had been "redeemed" (1 Peter 1:18). This word carried strong connotations of deliverance from bondage. It is used of deliverance from Egyptian and Babylonian captivity (Isaiah 43:3-7; 48:20).[38]

➤ Throughout his epistle Peter cites Old Covenant prophecies of Israel's last days restoration under Messiah. He draws heavily from Isaiah 40-66 which is recognized as a set of prophecies predicting the Second Exodus, Israel's eschatological deliverance into the New Creation.

➤ Peter quotes verbatim from Hosea 1:9-10; 2: 23 which is the prediction of the restoration of the ten tribes: "who once were not a people but are now the people of God, who had not obtained mercy but now have obtained mercy." As Dubis cogently notes, according to Hosea and the other prophets, "it is only when God regathers Israel and Judah to the promised land[39] that they are once again called 'Sons of the Living God....Thus, when 1 Peter 2:10 takes up the language of Hosea 1:6, 9, 2:25 (LXX) and says that those who were formerly called 'Not a people' (*ou laos*) are now called 'People of God' (*laos theou*) and that 'Not pitied' (*ouk eleemenoi*) has now received pity (*nun...eleethentes*) this is tantamount to saying that Israel's restoration from exile has taken place."[40]

➤ Peter tells his audience, *experiencing the restoration promised by Hosea*, that, "you also, as living stones, are being built into a spiritual house" (1 Peter 2:4). Just like Paul who said that the Ephesians were, "being builded together for an habitation of God", i.e. "An holy temple in the Lord" (Ephesians 2:20-21). Also like Paul, Peter says his audience was built on the foundation– the Rejected Stone– Jesus Christ (1 Peter 2:5f, cf. Ephesians 2:20).

Remember that the promise of Hosea and Ezekiel was that when Israel was restored under Messiah and the New Covenant, He would establish His temple among them. Now, here is the apostle to circumcision addressing the people to whom the promises were made long ago, citing those promises and telling them that they were the living stones of that promised Messianic temple! For ease of understanding I would form the thoughts like this:

✚ Hosea and Ezekiel foretold the restoration of Israel under Messiah.

✚ Ezekiel said that when Israel was restored under Messiah the Messianic Temple would be constructed and YHVH would dwell among His people (Ezekiel 37:26-27).

✚ Peter says that the restoration of Israel promised in Hosea (and thus in Ezekiel) was taking place through Christ and the church when he wrote (1 Peter 2:9-10).

✚ Peter likewise affirmed that his audience was part of the construction of the promises temple. They were the living stones of that promised temple and Messiah himself– in fulfillment of Israel's promises-- was the foundation stone of that promised temple.

✚ Therefore, for Peter, God's dwelling place among men, the Messianic Temple promised to Israel was being fulfilled in Christ and the church.

As Dubis notes, "Peter has transferred[41] first century expectations of an eschatological temple to the Christian community (2:5). Thus, the OT images of a gloriously restored temple are ultimately realized in the church for 1 Peter....According to 1 Peter 2:5 the restoration of the temple has already begun– the temple is already 'being built' (*oikodomeisthe* is present tense)" (*Woes*, 2002, 55).

I cannot develop it here, but Peter's extended discussion of the Rejected Stone (1 Peter 2:5f) shows that Peter was positively affirming the fulfillment of God's promises to Old Covenant Israel concerning the temple. God had foretold the rejection of His Messiah (Psalms 2; Isaiah 53; Daniel 9:26) but that rejection would be the ground and foundation of the enthronement of Messiah in his temple. Of course, this means that the Cross did not postpone *anything*. It was *The Plan* all along. It is just that *"The Plan"* was not understood or appreciated by Israel.

Thus, Peter's declaration that his audience was being built up as a spiritual temple, built on the promised Rejected Stone was showing that

Israel's promises had not failed. However, there was a dark side to that discussion of the Rejected Stone for those who rejected him were about to be crushed by him.[42]

➤ Peter's focus on the suffering of his audience suggests that he believes that the Birth Pangs of Messiah– see our discussion below– were being experienced by his audience. And as Peter affirms, since the Messianic Woes were present, the end was near (1 Peter 1:4f; 4:5, 7, 17-19). Jesus had foretold the suffering being experienced by Peter's audience and referred to them as the beginning of the birth pangs (Matthew 24:8f).

➤ Peter's repeated and emphatic declarations of the nearness of the consummation falsifies any attempt to remove the fulfillment of those Old Testament promises beyond his generation. His emphasis on the then present fulfillment of God's promise of the Messianic Temple shows that for Peter– as for Paul– the promise of the temple did not entail the removal of man from the earth, but the restoration of God's fellowship with man.

➤ Peter's use of the Shepherd motif (1 Peter 2:25; 5:1f) is a clear echo of the Old Covenant promises of Messiah (Isaiah 40; 49). We would note that the other New Testament writers clearly affirm the first century fulfillment of those promises, since John the baptizer was the voice in the wilderness (cf. Mark 1:1-3) preparing the Way for the Lord, the Great Shepherd (Isaiah 40:10-11). Likewise, as we will see below the Great Shepherd would lead Israel to salvation, "in the acceptable time, the day of salvation" (Isaiah 49:6-12). He would lead them to the living waters. Paul affirms that the anticipated day of salvation had arrived (2 Corinthians 6:1-2).

Ezekiel's promise of the Messianic Temple not only did *not* entail the removal of man from the earth, but, the New Testament writer's application of Ezekiel's promise shows that Ezekiel's promise was being fulfilled in Christ and the church. So if, as we propose, 1 Thessalonians 4 has to do with the coming of Christ to "dedicate" the Messianic Temple this is highly suggestive, if not determinative, that the *parousia* of Thessalonians was not for the purpose of removing man from earth.

EZEKIEL 40-48

The description of the temple in Ezekiel has been and continues to be one of the most enigmatic passages in scripture.[43] However, one thing is certain, and that is that it is the same tabernacle /temple as chapter 37, and since we have established that the dwelling place of God established by the construction of that temple is on earth, that demands that this is the case with chapters 40-48. The soteriological temple of Ezekiel does not represent the removal of man from earth. The establishment of the temple of God among man meant that God was restoring His presence with man. The relationship severed in the Garden was now being restored. And let me repeat this important point: It was to be through the temple and God dwelling *among His people*, that the nations would come to know Him.

DANIEL 9

Another OT text that foretold the arrival and construction and completion of the Messianic Temple is Daniel 9:24-27:

> "Seventy weeks are determined For your people and for your holy city, To finish the transgression, To make an end of sins, To make reconciliation for iniquity, To bring in everlasting righteousness, To seal up vision and prophecy, And to anoint the Most Holy. "Know therefore and understand, That from the going forth of the command To restore and build Jerusalem Until Messiah the Prince, There shall be seven weeks and sixty-two weeks; The street shall be built again, and the wall, Even in troublesome times. 26 "And after the sixty-two weeks Messiah shall be cut off, but not for Himself; And the people of the prince who is to come Shall destroy the city and the sanctuary. The end of it shall be with a flood, And till the end of the war desolations are determined. 27 Then he shall confirm a covenant with many for one week; But in the middle of the week He shall bring an end to sacrifice and offering. And on the wing of abominations shall be one who makes desolate, Even until the consummation, which is determined, Is poured out on the desolate."

Note that in verse 24, one of the six constituent elements promised to Israel was "to anoint the Most Holy." There are some who hold that this predicted the anointing of Jesus at his baptism (Matthew 3) when the Spirit descended and the Father said "This is My beloved Son." There is a problem with this linguistically, however, as Farrar noted years ago: "Holy of Holies (In the Hebrew of Daniel 9, DKP) is never once used of a person, though it occurs forty-four times."[44] Furthermore, an examination of the various translations on the Internet,[45] reveals that the great majority of translations favor the "most holy *place*" rendering. So, the favored rendering and meaning of "to anoint the most holy" would definitely seem to be referent to the anointing of the Messianic Temple.

Daniel gives us some very clear evidence for our understanding of the Messianic Temple.

☛ It is concerned with the fulfillment of God's promises to Israel. Daniel is not concerned with the end of time or the end of human history. The prophecy concerned the holy city and the people, i.e. Old Covenant Israel / Judah: "Seventy weeks are determined on your people and on your city..." (Daniel 9:24).

☛ The fulfillment of the prophecy lies within the framework of the seventy weeks and the terminus of that seventy weeks can be no later than the destruction of Jerusalem promised in v. 27. That occurred in AD 70.[46]

☛ The fulfillment of the promised Messianic Temple therefore, lies within the crucial seventy weeks of Daniel 9. This becomes important for our understanding of 1 Thessalonians 4 and other New Testament texts.

If, as we are suggesting, 1 Thessalonians 4:13f is the prediction of the completion and anointing of the Messianic Temple in fulfillment of the O.T. prophecies, then Daniel 9 gives us some unmistakable parameters into which we must place the Thessalonian text.

Let me express my thoughts as succinctly as possible:

The anointing of the Most Holy of Daniel 9:24-27 is the establishment (re-establishment) of God's presence among men in and through the Messianic Temple.

But, the *parousia* of Christ predicted by 1 Thessalonians 4:13-18 is the establishment (re-establishment) of God's presence among men (1 Thessalonians 4:17-18; 5:10).

Therefore, 1 Thessalonians 4:13-18 is the establishment (re-establishment) of God's presence among men in and through the Messianic Temple.

Now, let me follow that with this:

1 Thessalonians 4:13-18 is the establishment (re-establishment) of God's presence among men in and through the Messianic Temple– in fulfillment of Daniel 9:24-27.

But, the Messianic Temple of Daniel 9:24-27 would be anointed within and no later than the completion of the seventy weeks ending no later than AD 70 and the destruction of the Old Covenant Temple.

Therefore, 1 Thessalonians 4:13-18 would be fulfilled within the seventy weeks and ending no later than AD 70 and the destruction of the Old Covenant Temple.

If the Thessalonian text is inextricably related to Daniel's prophecy and the other predictions of the establishment of the Messianic Temple it is clear that we must take a different view of Thessalonians than is normal in evangelical exegesis. The parameters established by Daniel 9 for the anointing of the Most Holy Place and the establishment of God's dwelling with man, demand that we take a fresh look at a number of Biblical prophecies, not the least of which is John 14.

JOHN 14:1-6 AND THE MESSIANIC TEMPLE

Jesus said: "In my Father's house are many dwelling places...I go to prepare a place for you, and if I go and prepare a place for you, I will come again and receive you to myself; that where I am, there you will be also." The problem with the common view of the text is that it assumes that Jesus was going to go away, prepare a place, return, *remove his followers from earth*, and take them to the prepared place. In actuality, *Jesus was promising to bring the prepared place with him so that he and the Father would dwell with man!* Another problem with the traditional view of John 14 is that normally the prophetic background of the gospel– i.e. the prophecies just examined– is virtually ignored! It is as if Isaiah, Ezekiel and Daniel said nothing of God's tabernacle, nothing of God's re-establishment of His presence among His people, nothing of His promises to Old Covenant Israel.

The gospel of John is full of new temple imagery. The gospel begins by telling us that the Word became flesh and "tabernacled among us" (John 1:14). Jesus puzzled and perplexed the temple audience, "Destroy this temple and in three days I will raise it again" (John 2:19f). Over and over again, John's gospel sets before the observant reader the idea that Jesus was in the process of building the Messianic Temple. In John 14 the terms that Jesus used reflected idioms of the day that referred to the Temple.

Bryan shows that Jesus' allusion to many rooms (*not mansions*, DKP) may well reflect a commonly held belief of the day. In the Dead Sea Scrolls, the Temple Scroll, Bryan shows that there was the belief that in the Messianic Temple would have rooms *for all twelve tribes*. In other words, "All Israel will be gathered. Here, the people of God as a whole enjoy unprecedented access to the presence of God, in rooms that have been prepared for them."[47]

Likewise, Jesus' reference to "my Father's house" is a term well known in first century Judaism to refer to the temple. Bryan, shows that, "references to the temple as God's house are frequent in Jewish literature."(*Temple*, 22). He even shows that the term "place" that Jesus used in v. 2 "I go to prepare a place for you" is also a "term frequently found in Jewish literature in reference to the temple" (*Temple*, 26).[48]

It is virtually axiomatic in the evangelical world that John 14 predicted the coming of Christ *to remove believers from the earth*. The amillennialist and postmillennialists both believe that John 14 will be fulfilled at the end of the Christian age. The millennialist believes that John 14 is about the rapture at the end of the Christian age. But, all of these views overlook the fact that John 14 is about the establishment of the Messianic Temple and that this mitigates any "removed from this world" interpretation.

As Coloe[49] has noted: "Against this 'heavenly' dwelling place, it must be noted that the subject of the verb *meno*, throughout chapter 14, is not the *believer* but *God*. The action therefore, is not the *believers* coming to dwell in God's heavenly abode, but the *Father, the Paraclete and Jesus* coming to dwell with the believers. It is a 'descending' movement from the divine realm to the human, not an 'ascending' movement from the human to the divine."[50] Likewise, Bryan concurs with this assessment, "Jesus' words, however, are not so much concerned with the removal of his followers from earth to heaven as they are about the dissolution of the divide between heaven and earth; God's earthly house is no longer separate from his heavenly house. Jesus displaces the earthly dwelling place of God and also goes to the Father to prepare the heavenly dwelling of God to be the dwelling place of his people. It is thus through union with Jesus that the followers of Jesus ultimately enjoy the continual experience of God presence" (*Temple*, 39).

There is no question that in John 14, the issue is Christ's coming to dwell with man. In John 14:19f the disciples, after hearing of Jesus' promise to come, ask him how it is that they will see Jesus manifested (*emphanizo*). Jesus' answer is determinative for the correct view of verses 1-6: "Jesus answered and said unto him, 'If a man love me, he will keep my words; and my Father will love him, and we will come unto him, and make our abode with him.'" Here is the promise of the coming of Christ. It is the coming to dwell with man. It is not the removal of man to heaven. It is the Father and the Son coming to man in sweet fellowship!

To put it another way, John 14 is not about man leaving the earth, it is about Christ bringing God's presence to man so that man and God could dwell together. (See Ephesians 1:9-10). The rapture view of John 14 turns the text 180 degrees out. It is not about the disciples going, *it is about Christ coming!*

REVELATION 21

Our thesis is verified when we compare John 14, the theme of the Temple, and Revelation.

In Revelation 19-21 we find the coming of Christ in judgment and the consequent establishment of the New Creation. What is the purpose of that New Creation? Is it to remove man from the earth? Not at all! Read Revelation 21:3: "I heard a loud voice from heaven, saying, 'Behold, the tabernacle of God is with men, and He shall dwell with them, and they shall be His people and God himself shall be their God.'" The question of course is, is this the removal of man from earth? The answer is no, for the previous verse is definitive: "I, John, saw the holy city, New Jerusalem, coming down out of heaven from God, as a bride adorned for her husband."

So, what we have is the New Jerusalem comes down out of heaven from God and as a result of that coming out of heaven from God, "The tabernacle of God is with men!"

The "tabernacle of God" is nothing less than the "my Father's house" in John 14.[51] In John, Jesus said he was going away to *prepare* (from *hetoimasai*) a place, a dwelling place, in his Father's house so that at his *parousia* his disciples could dwell with him and his Father. In Revelation, John sees the tabernacle of God (the "Father's house") coming down out of heaven as a Bride prepared (*hetoimasmenen*, literally, "having been prepared") and God and man dwell together.

It cannot go unnoticed that Revelation 21 is a direct allusion to Ezekiel 37. We have already established that Ezekiel cannot be a referent to a removal of man from earth. Ezekiel foretold the re-establishment of fellowship between God and man on earth.

The Old Testament predicted the coming of the Lord and the establishment of the new temple of God so that man and God could dwell together. Yet, no Old Testament reference foretold the removal of man from earth so that man could dwell with God in that new temple. Unless Jesus was predicting a different dwelling of man with God from that foretold in the Old Testament prophecies of the new temple, then his prediction to come again so that man could dwell with the Father is ruled out by those Old Testament predictions. This means that John 14 does not predict a rapture of man from the earth, in the first century, or today.

The argument would go like this:

The coming of Christ foretold in John 14, for man and God to dwell together, is the same coming as in Revelation 19-21.

But the coming of Christ foretold in Revelation 21 is the coming of Christ for man and God to dwell together on earth (Revelation 21:2-3).

Therefore, the coming of Christ foretold in John 14 is the coming of Christ for man and God to dwell together on earth.

This argument brings us back full circle to what we presented at the first of this section:

The *parousia* of Christ in 1 Thessalonians 4 is the *parousia* of Christ in John 14:1-6 and Revelation 21.

The *parousia* of Christ in John 14 and Revelation 21, was the coming of the Messianic Temple foretold by the Old Testament prophets.

The Messianic Temple foretold by the Old Testament prophets was not the removal of man–or the church-- from the earth, but the restoration of God's presence with man on earth.

Therefore, the *parousia* of Christ in 1 Thessalonians 4 was the coming of the Messianic Temple for the restoration of God's presence with man on earth.

So, what we find in John 14, and thus 1 Thessalonians 4, is the establishment (re-establishment) of God's *Living Presence* among men. It is the restoration of the Garden fellowship. It is resurrection to be sure, but it is not the resuscitation and raising of a biological body. It is the raising of man back into the presence of a loving God.

FACT #4: 1 THESSALONIANS 4 AS THE TIME OF THE *REMARRIAGE* OF ISRAEL

Having established that Christ's *parousia* would be to dedicate the Messianic Temple and restore the fellowship between God and man on earth, we can now turn to a similar theme. It is often overlooked that the establishment of the new temple, God's dwelling with man, is also the fulfillment of God's promise to *remarry Israel*. The marriage and the new temple are inextricably connected: "I John, saw the holy city, New Jerusalem, coming down out of heaven from God, prepared as a bride adorned for her husband. And I heard a loud voice from heaven saying, 'Behold, the tabernacle of God is with men, and He will dwell with them, and they shall be His people, and He Himself shall be their God" (Revelation 21:2-3).

See the connection? *Wedding and temple go together!* They are clearly synchronous with one another.

In Hosea's marvelous living parable the prophet was told to marry "a wife of harlotry" (Hosea 1:2). As time progressed it became apparent that Gomer, his wife, was becoming increasingly unfaithful. Finally, through God's revelation the last child born to the union was named "Lo-Ammi," meaning, "Not my people" (Hosea 1:9). As a result of this unfaithfulness, this adultery, Hosea divorced Gomer.

Hosea's experience was a living parable of YHVH's relationship with Israel, specifically the ten northern tribes. As Hosea divorced Gomer, likewise, YHVH divorced Israel: "Bring charges, bring charges: For she is not my wife, nor am I her husband!"[52] (Hosea 2:2).

It is critical right here to understand what this divorce meant to Israel. The divorce meant that YHVH was not only going to divorce her, *she was going to die!* After all, according to Torah, a woman guilty of adultery was to be killed (Leviticus 20:10). And this is precisely what YHVH did to Israel.

In Hosea 5:15, the Lord said He was going to "tear them and go My way." This tearing imagery is of a lion killing its prey. Also, in 6:1-2, Israel laments, "He has torn, but He will heal, He has stricken, but He will raise us up...that we may live in His sight." YHVH is quite clear that *He had killed His adulterous wife* (cf. 6:5; Also, Israel had "died" when she committed adultery, Hosea 13:1-2. See also Isaiah 27:9f where the Lord said He had slain Israel by sending her away. We have here a *corporate concept of death and resurrection* that is critical to understanding the New Testament doctrine of resurrection.)

So, Israel violated her marriage covenant and as a result YHVH divorced her. He killed her.

However, shining through the despair, the pathos, and the tragedy of the unfaithfulness and severance of that "divorce and death," YHVH made a wonderful promise for the last days:

"Therefore, behold, I will allure her, Will bring her into the wilderness, And speak comfort to her. I will give her her vineyards from there, And the Valley of Achor as a door of hope; She shall sing there, As in the days of her youth, As in the day when she came up from the land of Egypt. And it shall be, in that day, Says the LORD, That you will call Me 'My Husband,' And no longer call Me 'My Master,' For I will take from her mouth the names of the Baals, And they shall be remembered by their name no more. In that day I will make a covenant for them With the beasts of the field, With the birds of the air, And with the creeping things of the ground. Bow and sword of battle I will shatter from the earth, To make them lie down safely. I will betroth you to Me forever; Yes, I will betroth you to Me In righteousness and justice, In loving kindness and mercy; I will betroth you to Me in faithfulness, And you shall know the LORD" (Hosea 2:14-18).

What an incredible, wonderful expression of the grace of a loving God! I want to take note of a few things here.

1.) God would remarry Israel. However, Israel would not be "re-married" in her Old Covenant form, for YHVH was going to bring that to an end (Hosea 1:4-5): "I will bring to an end the kingdom of the house of Israel." God would sweep away the Old Covenant feast days, Sabbaths, and sacrifices, when He remarried her, and made the New Covenant with her (Hosea 2:11-18). So, while YHVH was going to graciously re-marry Israel, she was going to be transformed by means of a New Covenant, with a new form, with a new cultus. Jeremiah hinted at this later when he said that the New Covenant– and thus the New People– would not be, "like the covenant that I made with you when I took you out of the land of Egypt" (Jeremiah 31:30f).

Instone-Brewer observes that the remarriage of Israel would demand that she be remarried in a different form: "Israel who has had many lovers is not the same Israel who is reconciled...God does not remarry exactly the former wife...she becomes a new wife in unification with Judah" (2002, 42).

This transformation would be necessary for several reasons. Among them is the fact that according to YHVH's own Torah, *it was "unlawful" to retake a wife that had been divorced* (Deuteronomy 24). Jeremiah 3 appeals to this law stating that if YHVH were to accept Israel back as before, "would not the land be defiled?" (Jeremiah 3:1-2). So, Israel would be transformed and Jeremiah 3 proves this by foretelling that when the reconciliation / re-marriage takes place, God's people would no longer travel to Jerusalem, and no longer "remember"[53] the Ark of the Covenant! This is a transformation of the most radical sort.

Of course, it cannot go un-noted that in John 4 Jesus directly echoes Jeremiah 3 by telling the Samaritan woman that the hour had come in which men would, "no longer worship in this mount or in Jerusalem" (John 4:20-24). Judah was about to undergo the necessary transformation that would–like Israel– be the metamorphosis[54] into the body of Christ.

So, when we come to 1 Thessalonians 4 *which is the parousia of King Jesus for the wedding* by the consensus of virtually all commentators, we must interpret the text in the light of the fulfillment of God's promises to Old Covenant Israel to remarry her in the last days. To fail to honor this fundamental context– which is what 99.9% of all commentators do– is to guarantee a mis-application of the text.

2.) God would make a new covenant with Israel (Hosea 2:18). The idea of *remarriage demands a new covenant*. To the Jewish mind marriage was, pre-eminently, entrance into *covenant*. So, YHVH's promise to restore Israel in the last days and at that time to make a covenant of peace with her *is* the promise of the remarriage. It is misguided to seek to divorce (pun intended) the ideas of new covenant and remarriage.

What this means in the New Testament is that when Jesus spoke of the wedding feast, we must see those promises in the context of God's remarriage of Israel. Of course, the Wedding Feast was one of Jesus' favorite parable themes (Matthew 22, 25, Luke 14). What tragically happens in most exegesis of these parables however, is that the modern reader fails or even refuses to keep the parable within the context of the fulfillment of God's promises to Israel, and the making of the New Covenant with her, as He transformed her into the New Bride. In the amillennial[55] and post millennial views, Matthew 25 is seen as the *parousia* of Christ to marry the *church*– completely divorced from Israel and her promises.

This divorcing of Jesus' teaching on the wedding is a tragedy in light of the fact that Paul tells us Jesus came to confirm the promises made to the Fathers, i.e. the Old Covenant fathers (Romans 15:8). So, when we read Jesus' wedding feast parables, and see other references to the New Covenant (Matthew 26:26f) we must realize that these texts, and Jesus' focus, is on the restoration of Israel in fulfillment of God's promises to her.

3.) God would raise Israel from the dead (Hosea 6:1-3; 13:14f). The observant reader will have noticed the corollary between the *divorce* of Israel and the *death* of Israel. So when YHVH promised to remarry Israel, He was promising to raise her from the dead! Patently, we are not discussing the raising of dead human corpses. Is this not clear in chapter 5-6 where *living humans* say they have been *slain*, but will be raised to live in presence of God? This is Israel, as a *corporate body*, alienated from God through sin. She was divorced, slain by her sin. Yet through Messiah, she is reconciled, remarried, raised from that death of alienation.[56]

So, again, when we read 1 Thessalonians 4 and its promise of the resurrection, we must keep in mind that the resurrection was the hope of Israel found in her Old Covenant promises. That resurrection was to take place through, and *by the means of the making of the New Covenant, the remarriage* of Israel! It is not about the raising of dead human corpses. It is about the restoration of fellowship lost through sin.

4.) All of the above would be accomplished when, "the children of Israel shall return and seek the Lord their God, and David their king. They shall fear the Lord and His goodness in the latter days" (Hosea 3:4).

5.) Finally, this restoration of Israel would occur at the "return" of the Lord, when Israel was raised from the dead (Hosea 5:15-6:1-3). In other words, the restoration, the resurrection and the re-marriage of Israel are all *synchronous*, almost synonymous concepts to occur at the "return" of the Lord.[57] Now in Hosea, YHVH is depicted as "leaving" (forsaking) Israel: "I will return to my place until they acknowledge their sin" (Hosea 5:15). It should strike us that YHVH was not bodily or visibly present. He was present through His *covenantal blessings and approval*. Thus, the coming of the Lord for the resurrection and the remarriage would be through the making of the New Covenant and His covenantal approval and presence! (Hosea 2:18f)

The resurrection of 1 Thessalonians 4, to occur at the *parousia* of Christ, must therefore, be viewed as the fulfillment of God's resurrection / *parousia* promise to Israel. Remember that Paul said his eschatology was nothing but the hope of Israel found in Moses and the prophets. It is fundamentally important therefore, *critical to proper exegesis*, that we harmonize 1 Thessalonians 4 with God's Old Covenant promises to remarry Israel.

Why have we spent so much time establishing these issues? It is because today, when most people read 1 Thessalonians 4 they approach the text with certain presuppositions that either ignore, deny, or overlook these facts.

The amillennialists approach Thessalonians with the conviction that it has *nothing to do with God's Old Covenant promises made to Israel*. It is believed that Paul was speaking of the church, New Covenant promises and the end of the Christian age.

To a great extent, the postmillennialists approach Thessalonians with the same presuppositions maintaining that it is about the end of human history as we know it, and the fulfillment of God's promises to the church.

The premillennialists hold that 1 Thessalonians predicts the rapture of the church out of the world, an event unknown and un-prophesied in the Old Testament. The church is removed from the world so that God can resume His dealings with Israel. In Paul's view however, Thessalonians is all about God's promises to Israel! Thus, any view of Thessalonians that removes it from the framework of God's promises to Israel is misguided.

By establishing the underlying framework and context of Thessalonians as the Old Covenant promises made to Israel, we have exposed an inherent fault in the modern attempts to understand Thessalonians. It is time for a fresh look at 1 Thessalonians, an examination that honors the proper prophetic and covenant context and framework.

So, we have examined several preliminary issues that are vital to a proper understanding and exegesis of Thessalonians 4. Yet, in the majority of commentaries, these issues are all but ignored. Let me repeat these keys here, to keep them before us:

√ We must interpret Thessalonians within the framework and context of the proper identification of the death of Adam. We must interpret 1 Thessalonians as the triumph *over* the death of Adam. We have shown that the death of Adam was not biological death, but *alienation from God*. Thus, since Thessalonians is about the restoration of fellowship with God, it is relevant to ask why God would have to destroy earth, end time, and remove man from earth to restore a fellowship that man had, on earth, in time? This means that whatever else we might understand, we must realize that Thessalonians is focused on the restoration of spiritual fellowship between man and God.

✓ We must interpret 1 Thessalonians in light of the fact that it is the reiteration of God's Old Covenant promises to Israel. All New Testament eschatology is based on, and taken from, the Old Testament.

✓ 1 Thessalonians 4 must be seen as the fulfillment of the O.T. promises that God would establish (re-establish) His presence among men in and through the Messianic Temple. This is not the removal of man from the earth. It is, "the tabernacle of God is among men!" (Revelation 21:3)

✓ 1 Thessalonians 4:13f must be seen as the fulfillment of God's Old Testament promise to *remarry Israel*. This remarriage, this radical transformative marriage, would come when *Judah* was destroyed nationally, just as Israel was destroyed (Hosea 1; Amos 5) and YHVH remarried "the tribes of Jacob," and invited all men into the blessings of that New Covenant relationship (Isaiah 49:6-8).

✓ We must interpret Thessalonians within the framework and context of the substitutionary death of Christ.

✓ We must interpret Thessalonians within the framework and context of Jesus' work of atonement.

In light of the above, even at this early stage of our investigation, it is evident that there is something fundamentally wrong with the modern view of Thessalonians.

THE CONTEXT OF THE TEXT

With these preliminary facts before us, it will be helpful now to consider the passages prior to 1 Thessalonians 4 that speak of the Day of the Lord. If the previous passages can give us insight into our text then we are ahead in our study. For brevity, we can only do a short examination of each of these passages. However, what we find in the previous verses is definitely helpful.

1 THESSALONIANS 1:9-10

"For they themselves declare concerning us what manner of entry we had to you, and how you turned to God from idols to serve the living and true God, and to wait for His Son from heaven, whom He raised from the dead, even Jesus who delivers us from the wrath to come" (NKJV).

There are a couple of significant points that need to be made.

First, it is clear that the coming of the Lord under consideration was something the Thessalonians expected in their lifetime. This is clear.

I cannot develop it fully here, but in my book *Into All The World, Then Comes The End*,[58] I demonstrate that in the Olivet Discourse, in the section that both amillennialists and postmillennialists admit applies strictly to the AD 70 coming of Christ, there is a pattern that is likewise found in the rest of the New Testament. That pattern, briefly stated is this:

☞ *Preaching*-- Jesus told his disciples to preach the gospel into all the world before the coming of the end (Matthew 24:14).[59]

☞ **Persecution**– Jesus told his disciples that as they preached they would be persecuted (Matthew 24:9f; Mark 13:9f)

☞ **Power**– Jesus promised his disciples divine power to guide them during their persecution (Mark 13:11). This divine inspiration would confound their enemies (See Acts 6-7 and the story of Stephen).

☞ *Parousia*– Jesus promised his disciples that he would come in their generation in vindication of their suffering and judgment of their persecutors (Matthew 24:29f).

Remember that each of these tenets is found in the section of the Olivet Discourse that amillennialists and postmillennialists say predicted the AD 70 coming of Christ (i.e. Matthew 24:4-34). This is significant because we find this exact same pattern throughout the N.T. even in passages that are normally applied to a yet future coming of Christ.

In 1 Thessalonians 1, notice that we find this same pattern:
V. 5,8– The **preaching** of the gospel to and by the Thessalonians.
V. 6 – The **persecution** of the Thessalonians as a result of preaching.

V. 5– The **power** in the proclamation of the gospel and in the midst of the suffering.

V. 9-10– The *parousia* was promised and was their expectation.

The question is, if these four elements from the Olivet Discourse must be kept within the first century and find fulfillment in Jesus' AD 70 coming what is the basis for severing these exact elements in Thessalonians from their Olivet source? In other words, what is the justification for seeing a different *parousia* in Matthew from that in Thessalonians? This is a particularly pressing question when we realize that Paul tells us that his gospel was received from Jesus. Paul draws from the Olivet Discourse.

The perfect parallel between the Olivet Discourse and 1 Thessalonians 1 demands that we keep Thessalonians within the first century context.

Second, Jesus had delivered "us," that is that contemporary generation from "the wrath to come." There is not a word here about a yet future Great Tribulation to occur after a rapture. Whatever wrath was coming Paul said Jesus had delivered *the Thessalonians* from it (cf. Revelation 3:10). It is not good hermeneutic to divorce the people to whom Paul was writing from the things he was writing about, especially when he uses the personal pronouns that directly linked them with those events.

Third, consider "the wrath to come." Where does this idea come from? It comes from John the Baptist. As John was baptizing in the Jordan the multitudes came out to him. Even the Pharisees and Sadducees came to be baptized. He immediately warned them, "Who has warned you to flee from the wrath that is about to (from *mello*) come" (Matthew 3:7).

Notice the urgency of his warning. He said, "the axe is already at the root" (v. 10). He told them Jesus already had the winnowing fork in his hand (v. 12). This later reference would have brought to mind Jeremiah 15, and the prophets warning of impending judgment on Jerusalem in the prophet's day. The image of the winnowing fork was not a promise of blessing. It was the promise of wrath about to come.

John the Baptist is one of the most significant yet ignored eschatological figures in the New Testament.[60] Most folks forget him the moment he is beheaded. It likewise seems that most see him as the proclaimer of Jesus' *incarnate* work. This is a lamentable oversight. John, citing Isaiah 40, said he was, "the voice of one crying in the wilderness, prepare the way of the Lord." What is often overlooked is that the coming of the Lord for which John was the "voice" was none other than the coming of the Lord in judgment (Isaiah 40:10-11). In the words of Jesus, John was the anticipated Elijah who was to come as a herald of the Day of the Lord (Matthew 11:13f; 17:11f). Now, if John was the herald and sign of the Day of the Lord, and he said that the Day of Wrath was about to come then this definitely means that the Day of the Lord was near. Why is John such a forgotten figure in studies of New Testament eschatology?

Here is something important. John was Jehovah's messenger proclaiming wrath that was about to come against Israel. He was the messenger *to Israel* to call them *to obedience to the Law of Moses* (Malachi 4:5-6). He said the Day of wrath was near. Yet, that Day had not yet come when Paul wrote the book of Thessalonians. The question therefore is, if John proclaimed the imminent wrath to come and it had not yet come when Paul proclaimed the wrath to come, why is Thessalonians not predicting the same *wrath to come as John*? Would not that wrath to come be nearer when Paul wrote than when John warned that it was "about to come"? Where is the disconnect between these discussions?

It might be rejoined that John indeed was a messenger to Israel but that Paul was writing to Gentiles in Thessalonians. Why would the Thessalonians be concerned with wrath coming on the Jews?[61] Well, there were many reasons but there was one especially pressing reason.

The Thessalonian Christians were being persecuted and the Jews were the movers and shakers, indeed, the actual participants in that persecution. (See Acts 17:1f). As a direct result of this Jewish persecution against the Thessalonian church Paul addressed the issue of the wrath about to come:

> "For you brethren, became imitators of the churches of God which are in Judea in Christ Jesus. For you also suffered the same things from your own countrymen, just as they did from the Judeans, who killed both the Lord Jesus and their own prophets, and have persecuted us; and they are contrary to all men, forbidding us to speak to the Gentiles that they might be saved, so as always to fill up the measure of their sins; but wrath has come upon them to the uttermost." 1 Thessalonians 2:14-16)

So, John proclaimed wrath that was about to come on Israel. Paul also proclaimed wrath about to come on Israel. John's "wrath about to come" had not yet come when Paul wrote. Why then was Paul's "wrath about to come" not John's "wrath about to come?" If this connection is valid then the very first referent to the Day of the Lord in Thessalonians is the impending Day of Wrath that occurred in the fall of Jerusalem in AD 70.

In an enlightening read Wright notes that 1 Thessalonians 2:14f anticipated the judgment, "warned of by Jesus himself, on that city and the people that had rejected their Messiah. Indeed, when he grieves over his fellow Jews in Romans 9-11, I think part at least of that grief is his conditioned awareness that they are living under the shadow of impending disaster" (*Paul*, 56). However, Wright delineates between 1 Thessalonians 4 and chapter 2 claiming that chapter 4 must be some kind of final, dare I say *physical*, revelation of Christ to live on earth.

Here is what is so inexplicable about this as we read Wright's otherwise probing and insightful work (s).

1.) Wright does a fine job demonstrating the metaphoric nature of the "end of the world" language of the gospels especially. He shows that the Jews of Jesus' day simply did not anticipate the end of human history.[62]

2.) Wright likewise affirms that when Christ spoke of his coming on the clouds of heaven that neither he nor the Jews would ever have imagined a literal descent of a human form riding on a cumulus cloud: "We can say that the coming of the son of man does not refer to the *parousia* in the modern scholarly and popular sense of a human figure traveling downwards towards the earth on actual clouds" (*Victory*, 361). Wright chides Schweitzer who understood these texts literalistically, and proclaimed that since Jesus said he was coming soon, but didn't, that therefore Jesus was wrong (*Victory*, 365).

However, in *Paul* (p. 55) Wright says 1 Thessalonians 4 speaks of a literal reign on the earth. Why should we believe that Paul spoke of the *parousia* as a literal appearance of Jesus, when Jesus, who spoke of the same *parousia* never had such a coming in mind, per Wright? This is especially pertinent when we realize that according to Paul he got his doctrine directly from Jesus. Did Jesus change the meaning of his own predictions of the *parousia*?

3.) Wright does an excellent job of demonstrating that in Paul's pnuematology, eschatology and soteriology he was proclaiming the hope of Israel now identified as fulfilled in the body of Christ. It is certainly true that the message he preached was not what Israel expected or wanted however: "One of the central tensions in Paul's thought, giving it again and again its creative edge is the clash between the fact that God always intended what has in fact happened, and the fact that not even the most devout Israelite had dreamed that it would happen like this" (*Paul*, 54).

One of the profound things that Wright does, that has a direct implication for the interpretation of 1 Thessalonians 4, is to show that for Paul, the presence of the Spirit meant that God was establishing the promised Messianic Temple. The temple was now identified, not according to the traditional eschatological hopes of Israel, but as Christ and his body. This is precisely what we are arguing in this book, i.e. that passages like John 14 and 1 Thessalonians 4 speak of the dedication of that new temple. As such it has nothing to do with a literal descent of Christ out of heaven at all, but God "tabernacling among men."

Now, if Wright can so clearly see and communicate that the *parousia* has nothing to do with a literal descent of Christ out of heaven then why impose that concept–in whatever manner-- on 1 Thessalonians? If Christ spoke of the re-establishment of the Sovereignty of God over His Creation why does that necessitate the physical presence of Jesus on earth?

Christ's coming in 1 Thessalonians 4 was to be "in the glory of the Father." This meant, not that he was coming back to earth as a man to be a man among men but that he was to be revealed as King of kings and Lord of lords. Jesus was to judge as the Father had judged. And this meant that his *parousia*, though it would be his "coming" to dwell among men for sure, would be the manifestation of his deity, not the re-manifestation of his humanity.[63] The Transfiguration (Matthew 17) should put an end forever to the idea that Jesus was coming back as a five foot five Jewish man![64]

4.) This inconsistency in Wright is exemplified in his examination of 2 Thessalonians 2 which he applies to the Judean catastrophe that Paul knew was coming soon. Wright argues that since some of the Thessalonians believed that the Day of the Lord had already occurred this demands that they could not have believed it was, "the royal presence of the Lord in 1 Thessalonians 4 or 1 Corinthians 15, still less to the end of the space-time universe, which the Thessalonians themselves would presumably have noticed" (*Paul*, 56).[65]

This, in my mind, contradicts much of what Wright says elsewhere about the two-sided nature of the Day of the Lord, i.e. *the Day was both judgment and salvation*. Furthermore, how does one delineate between the *parousia* of 1 Thessalonians 4 and the *parousia* of 2 Thessalonians 2?

See our discussion below of the attempts by some to see two different comings in Thessalonians based on the use of different words. In these two texts, however, the same word *parousia* is used. So, again, how does Wright argue that 1 Thessalonians 4 must refer to a yet future event involving a literal bodily presence of Jesus, but that 2 Thessalonians 2 must refer to the AD 70 *parousia*? How does he square his thoughts on the *parousia* of 1 Thessalonians 4 and Jesus' prediction and concept of his *parousia* found in the gospels? Did Paul, as some scholars have argued, not understand the non-literal, Old Testament based concept of the Day of the Lord and invent a new, literalistic idea?

The problem is compounded in Wright's assignation of 1 Thessalonians 2:14f and 2 Thessalonians 2:1-2 to what he calls "an interim judgment, warned of by Jesus himself, on the city and the people that had rejected their Messiah" (*Paul*, 56). However, as noted, he applies 1 Thessalonians 4 to a yet future *parousia*. Just exactly how we are to delineate between these different comings Wright is not clear. Interestingly, Wright does not mention 2 Thessalonians 1 in his *Paul* and only alludes to it with no exegesis in *Victory*. If 1 Thessalonians 2:14f must be assigned to the impending *parousia* of Christ in judgment against Judea then surely 2 Thessalonians 1 must be assigned to that event as well since it describes the same reason and purpose for the *parousia*: the vindication of the suffering of the saints.

The *parousia* of 2 Thessalonians 1 was also to be the time of Christ's glorification among his saints and the fulfillment of the prophecy of Isaiah 2-4, as we shall see. The *parousia* of 1 Thessalonians 4 was to be Christ's coming to gather his saints to him. What is the great rift between these two passages? What is the exegetical sword that cuts a line of demarcation revealing that one of these *parousias* was "interim," but the other "ultimate"? How do we determine that one of these parousias is in the same nature as the Old Covenant comings, but that 1 Thessalonians must, after all, be a prediction of a human form descending out of heaven? Wright never tells us why we are to see that Paul on the one hand incorporated Jesus' non-literal concept of the *parousia*, and then essentially invented a totally different concept of the *parousia* in 1 Thessalonians 4.

1 THESSALONIANS 3:3-4

"That no one should be shaken by these afflictions; for you yourselves know that we are appointed to this, For, in fact, we told you before when we were with you that we would suffer tribulation, just as it happened and you know."

The reason this verse is important is because of its link to chapter 2:15-17, and the persecution instigated by the Jewish countrymen of the Thessalonians, and of course the impending judgment against them. Also, take note that Paul said he had told them when he was with them that they were appointed to tribulation. A good question to ask is, where did Paul get the idea that persecution was appointed to them, and what is the connection to the Day of the Lord?

The answer to the first question is found in Matthew 24. As we have seen, the disciples asked Jesus about a sign of the end of the age and his *parousia* (his *presence*). Notice what Jesus told his disciples: "They will deliver you up to tribulation and kill you and you will be hated by all nations for my name's sake" (Matthew 24:9). So, Jesus told his first century disciples that they would be persecuted before the end of the age. And he told them that the end would be in their generation (Matthew 24:34).

Paul reminded the Thessalonians that he had warned them that to follow Jesus was to bring tribulation (*thlipsis*) on themselves. Jesus said his followers would be persecuted (*thlipsis*). Paul was writing to Jesus' followers reminding them that the persecution they were enduring was foretold by Jesus. (As a side bar, John, in Revelation was likewise experiencing precisely what Jesus predicted in Matthew 24 (Revelation 1:9) and he said that the end was near. This has a profound impact on the dating of Revelation.)

Of course, the point cannot be missed that the tribulation of Matthew 24 was to occur prior to, and as a sign of the end of the Mosaic age that came with the destruction of the temple in AD 70. Paul was writing in approximately AD 50-51 encouraging the church to remain faithful because they knew that what was happening was *appointed*. What was happening in Thessalonica was the fulfillment of Matthew 24. This is highly suggestive that the Day of the Lord being anticipated was the end of the Mosaic age that came in AD 70.

1 THESSALONIANS 3:13

"So that he may establish your hearts blameless in holiness before our God and Father at the coming of our Lord Jesus Christ with all his saints."

It is widely acknowledged that this verse is a direct allusion to Zechariah 14:5: "Thus, the Lord will come and all the saints with You." So, we have Paul who proclaimed the hope of Israel, speaking of the coming of the Lord with his saints, and appealing to Zechariah 14. What does this mean?

Zechariah 14:1f predicted the time when Jerusalem would be destroyed: "Behold the day of the Lord is coming, and the spoil will be divided in your midst For I will gather all the nations to battle against Jerusalem; the city shall be taken, the houses rifled, and the women ravished." Zechariah's prophecy had not been fulfilled when Paul wrote Thessalonians. Jerusalem still stood. The Lord had not yet come with his saints. But Paul, writing just a few years before the destruction of Jerusalem cited Zechariah's prediction of the Lord's coming in the destruction of Jerusalem.

There has always been widespread belief that Zechariah 14 predicted the AD 70 *parousia* of Jesus. Early Christian writers applied this chapter to Jerusalem's demise.[66] The Second Coming Bible says Cyril and Theophylact held the view.[67] Hengstenberg also cites Jerome, and "several others, particularly of the fathers," who applied Zechariah "to the captivity by the Romans."[68] Merrill Unger, millennial writer, acknowledged that Zechariah's prophecy was applied to AD 70 by "many early writers."[69] Adam Clarke said, "This appears to be a prediction of that war in which Jerusalem was finally destroyed, and the Jews scattered over the face of the earth."[70] Terry says Zechariah spoke of the AD 70 coming of the Lord.[71]

If the prophecy of Zechariah had not yet been fulfilled and had nothing to do with the coming of the Lord that Paul was thinking of in 1 Thessalonians 3:13, *why would he cite that prophecy?* Why refer to the prophecy of one event when you have in mind a totally different kind of coming at a totally different time, for a totally different purpose?

WHEN THE LORD JESUS IS REVEALED FROM HEAVEN
2 Thessalonians 1:4-12

We move now to consider Paul's eschatological teaching in his second epistle. We find there the identical thoughts as in the first epistle. We will look first at 2 Thessalonians 1:4f.[72] This passage contains emphatic declarations about when Christ was to return in aid and comfort of the Thessalonians, and yet its declarations are ignored by many Bible students.

> "So that we ourselves glory in you in the churches of God for your patience and faith in all your persecutions and tribulations that ye endure: Seeing it is a righteous thing with God to recompense tribulation to them that trouble you; And to you who are troubled rest with us, when the Lord Jesus shall be revealed from heaven with his mighty angels, In flaming fire taking vengeance on them that know not God, and that obey not the gospel of our Lord Jesus Christ: Who shall be punished with everlasting destruction from the presence of the Lord, and from the glory of his power; When he shall come to be glorified in his saints, and to be admired in all them that believe (because our testimony among you was believed) in that day" (KJV).

We need to take note of several facts:

First, the Thessalonians were currently undergoing intense persecution. Paul uses the word *thlipsis* as well as *pasxo* (suffering) to describe what they were enduring. Paul was not speaking of the church throughout the ages. He was writing to living, breathing humans being persecuted in their home town. Nor was Paul referring to the mundane human existence as *thlipsis*. He was not referring to heart disease, cancer, financial difficulties, or even problems with teenage children! He was speaking of persecution for believing in the name of Jesus.

Second, Paul promised the Thessalonians *rest* (from *anesis*, which means relief from pressure[73]) from their persecution.

Third, Paul said *their persecutors would become the persecuted* at the same time that the Thessalonians received relief (v. 6-7). He said, "it is a righteous thing with God to repay with tribulation, those who are troubling you" (2 Thessalonians 1:6). In other words, the tables would be turned. The persecutors would become the persecuted. What is somewhat amazing is that few commentators ask the question: *Who was persecuting the Thessalonian Christians when Paul wrote to them?* If we are to properly interpret 2 Thessalonians 1 and by extension 1 Thessalonians 4, the question of the identity of those persecutors is critical.[74]

Many commentators see that Paul is expressing the *Lex Talianos* principle (we would call it the "eye for an eye" principle). As Perriman says,

"What Paul envisages here is a quite literal repayment: the society that persecutes the church will itself be the victim of aggression. Whether he would have regarded the eventual fall of Rome to the invading Goths and Huns in the fourth and fifth centuries AD as adequate fulfillment of this expectation is impossible to know; but, he would surely have seen some justice in the fact that the city which sent an army to besiege and destroy Jerusalem was itself sacked by an invading force" (*Coming*, 159).

I think Perriman is right to question any application of Thessalonians to the fall of Rome hundreds of years away. The suggestion that the judgment of Jerusalem is in Paul's mind is, in my view, spot on.
Let me explore this a bit.

◆ Paul said God would repay with tribulation (*thlipsis*) "those who are troubling (*thlipsis*) you." Notice the present tense verbs. As the old saying goes, "timing is everything." Who was persecuting the Thessalonians, or for that matter the rest of the churches in the year AD 51? One thing is certain *it was not Roman persecution*. Nor was Paul discussing some future unknown persecutor or persecution.

When Jesus foretold the persecution of his disciples he said it would be the Jews behind the animosity: "they will deliver you to councils (*sunedria*– i.e. sanhedrins) and you will be beaten in the *synagogues*" (Mark 13:9; cf. Matthew 23:34f). Remember where Paul got his "letters of authority" to persecute the saints (Acts 21)? Gentry says, "Throughout Acts, Jerusalem is portrayed as the persecutor and Rome as the protector of Christianity."[75] See the extensive list of texts from Acts cited by Gentry in support of his comments (*Before*, p. 380, n. 38).

The record of Acts shows that even when the disciples were brought before kings and governors the Jews were behind that persecution (Cf. Acts 18, 24:13f, etc.). As Harnack noted sometime ago: "Unless the evidence is misleading, they (the Jews, DKP) instigated the Neronic outburst against Christians; and as a rule, whenever bloody persecutions were afoot in later days, the Jews are either in the background or the foreground."[76] Stuart said that the Jews were the chief almost exclusive persecutors of the church in the first century and also applies 2 Thessalonians 1:3-6 to Jews.[77] Virtually all historians concur in this assessment.

Historians are clear that Nero was the first of the Roman emperors to persecute the church *and that persecution did not begin until AD 64.*[78]

Paul was writing to and about Christians in severe trial of persecution *in approximately AD 51 well before any kind of imperial persecution manifested itself*. So, while commentators somehow inject Rome or the Roman Catholic church, or a future restored Babylon into Paul's prediction of coming judgment on the persecutors in Thessalonica, the chronology of the text demands that the focus of this promise of judgment against the persecutors is centered on Jerusalem.

◆ Paul said that at Christ's coming, "those who are troubling you" would be *cast out of the presence of the Lord* (2 Thessalonians 1:9). The question is, who does the Bible describe as having a relationship with YHVH, but due to the persecution of the Chosen Seed, they would be cast out? The answer is found in Galatians 4:22-32.

The apostle tells his famous allegory of Abraham's two wives, Sarah and Hagar. The two sons of the two women represented the two seeds, the natural seed of Abraham and the spiritual seed. The spiritual seed was the body of Christ. These two women and their sons represented the two covenants, the Mosaic Covenant and the New Covenant of Messiah, and the two seeds. The children of the flesh was Old Covenant Israel. The children of promise were the followers of Messiah, the seed of Abraham by faith (Galatians 3:6f).

In Paul's allegory he calls to mind how Ishmael persecuted Isaac and said, "as the children of the flesh then persecuted the children of promise, even so it is now" (Galatians 4:29). He then poses the question: "What says the scripture? Cast out the bondwoman and her children" (Galatians 4:30).

So, the children of the flesh, Old Covenant Israel, dwelt in the presence of God. However, when Paul wrote she was persecuting the children of the promise, the true seed of Abraham. Consequently, Paul said the children of the flesh were to be cast out of the presence of God![79] Nisbet sounded the right cord centuries ago, "Destruction from the presence of the Lord, and from the glory of his power' appear to me to have a singular propriety in them, when applied to the ruin of the Jewish nation; for God's presence was the peculiar privilege of that people; which they could only forfeit by their wickedness, and their forsaking of the covenant of their God."[80]

Galatians 4 is a direct commentary on 2 Thessalonians 1 yet this connection is mostly ignored. This situation fits what Paul said perfectly, "It is a righteous thing with God to repay with tribulation... those who are troubling you" (2 Thessalonians 1:5-6).

◆ The question to ponder now is this: When would Israel– "those who are troubling you" be judged– *cast out per Galatians 4*-- for persecuting the seed of Messiah? The answer, *the definitive answer*, is found in Matthew 23:

"Therefore, indeed, I send you prophets, wise men, and scribes: some of them you will kill and crucify, and some of them you will scourge in your synagogues and persecute from city to city, that on you may come all the righteous blood shed on the earth, from the blood of righteous Abel to the blood of Zechariah, son of Berechiah, whom you murdered between the temple and the altar. Assuredly, I say to you, all these things will come upon this generation" (Matthew 23:34-36).

Jesus leaves no doubt, no room for controversy. Israel was to be judged in a climactic, consummative judgment for persecuting the saints. And that was to be in his generation.

When we consider these facts it is difficult to see how it can be suggested that Paul was contemplating a far distant judgment of some unknown persecutor of the church in some unknown city. Paul was addressing living humans experiencing very real persecution in their city. He promised that "those who are troubling you" would be judged and cast out of the presence of the Lord at His *parousia*. Jesus definitively posited the time for those events in the judgment of Jerusalem in his generation. Let me summarize.

The Thessalonians were experiencing the persecution foretold by Jesus (1 Thessalonians 3:3f).

They were experiencing that persecution at the hands of the ones that Jesus said would be the persecutors– the Jerusalem authorities.

Paul promised the Thessalonians the very thing that Jesus promised them, vindication and relief.

Paul said the promised vindication and relief would come "when the Lord Jesus is revealed from heaven" (v. 7-8).

Israel was judged for shedding the blood of the saints in Paul's generation, just as Jesus foretold.

Those who were troubling the Thessalonians became the persecuted just as Paul foretold.

Paul's prophecy of the coming of the Lord was fulfilled.

Let's continue now with our look at the text.

Fourth, it will be helpful to focus on *what Paul did not say*:

✖ *He did not say* the Thessalonians would receive relief from their persecution by *dying*. Their relief would come when the Lord came.

✖ He *did not say* that the *church* thousands of years later would eventually receive relief from persecution. He said that the *Thessalonians*, those who were being persecuted when he wrote, would receive relief from their current persecution. Thessalonians is an "occasional letter" which means that a specific historical situation prompted Paul to write to them. It was that urgent crisis that prompted Paul's promise of relief from that very real, very personal, very contemporary occasion.

Our choices here are limited:

First, the Thessalonians are either still alive and being persecuted if the Lord has not come, or they are dead. It is safe to say they are dead.

Second, if the Thessalonians are dead then the Lord either came in their lifetime and gave them relief from their persecution, or he did not come in their lifetime and give them the promised relief.

Third, if the Lord did not come in the lifetime of the Thessalonians and give them relief from their persecution, Paul's prediction failed.[81]

Fourth, if Paul's promise/prediction failed then he was a false prophet and the inspiration of scripture is destroyed.

So, just as Paul said in 2 Thessalonians 1 the persecutors would become the persecuted and the Christians would receive relief. In other words, Jesus did come in judgment of the persecutors (Israel) and gave relief to the persecuted brethren.

We will show below that the coming of 1 Thessalonians 4 and the coming of 2 Thessalonians 1 are the same event. (Some say that these are two different times and events.) However, when it is seen that the coming of the Lord in 1 Thessalonians 4 and that of 2 Thessalonians 1 is the same, the promise of 2 Thessalonians unequivocally places the *parousia* of Christ at the end of the Old Covenant age in AD 70. Jesus came in judgment of the city that had slain the prophets, killed Jesus, and was now guilty of killing his apostles and prophets.

The temporal parameters and constraints of all of the texts above cannot be ignored. If we have not been taught that Christ was to come in the judgment of Israel, instead of the end of the Christian age, what we have shown thus far may be disturbing and challenging. I understand that, *believe me*. Nonetheless, we must candidly confront the inspired Word and what it says about when Jesus was to come in judgment and reward. And there is no denying that it was to be in the first century.

LET NO ONE DECEIVE YOU....
THAT THE DAY OF THE LORD HAS ALREADY COME
2 THESSALONIANS 2:1-2

2 Thessalonians 2:1-2 poses a daunting challenge to any concept of a time ending, earth burning *parousia*. Do you catch the true power of what was going on in Thessalonica? Some actually believed that *Christ had already returned!* Like those in Ephesus, this means that they believed that the resurrection had already occurred (2 Timothy 2:18).

In 1992 I wrote a book entitled *How Is This Possible?* In that work, recently revised and enlarged, I pose the following question: "If the Day of the Lord is an earth burning, time ending, cosmos destroying event, when every human who has ever lived comes out of the grave, how could anyone convince anyone that it had already occurred?" Furthermore, how could anyone convince you that time had ended *by sending you a letter*, as Paul suggests had been done? Do you see the problem?

Since we have an extended discussion of 2 Thessalonians 2:1-2 below in our discussion of the rapture doctrine, we will not dwell long here. But we do want to note this: If the Day of the Lord that Paul taught was in any way at all what evangelical Christianity teaches today, how could anyone convince anyone that it had already happened?

Could anyone convince you that the earth had burned up yesterday?

Could anyone convince you, *by sending you a letter*, that every dead person who had ever lived had been raised out of the dirt?

Could anyone convince you that "every eye" had seen Jesus descend out of heaven on the clouds?

Undeniably, there is no way to convince anyone that any of these things had literally, visibly, physically occurred. The only way that anyone could be convinced that the Day of the Lord had already happened was if they believed in the Old Covenant concept of the Day of the Lord. And since Jesus said that his coming was to be "in the glory of the Father" (Matthew 16:27-28) meaning that he was going to come as the Father had come many times before, then this is precisely the kind of coming that Paul had in mind.

Jesus did say that he was going to come "in the glory of the Father." And, he said that coming would be in the lifetime of his first century audience: "there are some standing here that shall not taste of death until the see the Son of Man coming in his kingdom" (Matthew 16:28).[82]

2 THESSALONIANS 2:3F: THE MAN OF SIN

Whoever the enigmatic Man of Sin, the son of perdition was, and we emphasize *was*, we can be certain of a number of facts that militate against any future appearance.

→ Paul emphatically says "the spirit of lawlessness works already" (2 Thessalonians 2:7). Thus, the Man of Sin was already alive. Since the Man of Sin would be the very expression of that spirit of lawlessness, this is *prima facie* demonstration that the Man of Sin was already alive.

→ The restrainer, or the restraining thing, whichever it truly was, and it may have been both, was already restraining the Man of Sin (v. 6).[83] It is impossible to restrain something or someone that is not present!

→ The Man of Sin would sit in the temple of God. This means that whoever he was, he operated within the context of the Old Covenant nation of Israel. Some try to say that the temple of God that Paul refers to here is the church, and of course, in this scenario, the Man of Sin is taken to be a future person that leads the church into the depths of the apostasy mentioned in 2 Thessalonians 2:3. This is untenable however, and overlooks several facts.

A.) There is no doubt that Paul does refer to the church as the temple of God (e.g. 1 Corinthians 3; 6; 2 Corinthians 6:16; Ephesians 2, etc.). However, I am unaware of a single text in which Paul refers to the temple of God, when he had the church in mind, in which he did not clearly contextually identify the church as his subject. He does nothing like that in 2 Thessalonians 2.

B.) There is in Paul a constant conflict between the Old Covenant temple, Old Covenant Jerusalem, the Old Covenant world. Davies has well noted that in Paul's writings, Old Covenant Israel, her cultus, her city, etc., all still hold a vitally important role in the eschatological schema.[84]

The apostle posits an on-going conflict between the Old Covenant world and the New and he sees Old Covenant Jerusalem–which would include the temple– as the source of the persecution (Galatians 4:22f). This fits the imagery of 2 Thessalonians 2 where the Man of Sin, sitting in the temple of God, is the source of corruption and the cause of apostasy.

Jesus said that as result of the increase of lawlessness and persecution–Jewish instigated--the love of the majority would grow cold (Matthew 24:9-12).[85] In 2 Thessalonians 2 Paul is drawing from Jesus' discourse. DeMar has adduced at least nine direct parallels between the Olivet Discourse and 2 Thessalonians 2.[86] The parallels demonstrate that this conflict was Jewish motivated. To overlook this background of Paul's discussion is to miss the interpretive key of 2 Thessalonians.

So, Paul's referent to the fact that the Man of Sin would sit in the temple of God, and that the Man of Sin was *already alive* and *being restrained*, places 2 Thessalonians within the context of the first century.

→ This first century context is confirmed when we examine the idea of the Abomination of Desolation. Virtually all commentators agree that the appearance of the Man of Sin leads directly to the Abomination of Desolation. What seems to be missing in these discussions is the fact that if the locus of the Man of Sin and Abomination of Desolation is the Jerusalem Temple, then it cannot be denied that the Abomination of Desolation must be viewed as a horrid violation of *Torah*, and the resultant Great Tribulation must be seen as *the application of Mosaic Covenant Wrath*.

Pitre astutely lists three facts about the Abomination in Daniel which of course is the source of Matthew 24:15f and Thessalonians 2:

1.) It always refers to a profanation of the Jerusalem temple, and this profanation "is carried out by means of the forced cessation of the sacrifices."

2.) The profanation is always carried out by a royal figure, "he shall cause the sacrifice to cease."

3.) The profanation of the Temple, "brings about the destruction of the temple and the city of Jerusalem" (Daniel 9:27). "It is such an egregious sacrilege that it calls down divine wrath and destruction on both the temple and the city."[87]

So, from Pitre's perspective, and I think he is spot on, an Abomination of Desolation is something committed by "insiders", i.e. by the Jews, that leads to judgment from YHVH at the hands of pagans in accordance with covenantal provisions. This fits well with the Law of Blessings and Cursings (Deuteronomy 28-30) where Israel's sin leads to God's wrath on them.[88]

One thing is certain, and that is that Biblically, YHVH never allowed, or brought, pagan desecration and desolation unless Israel had violated Torah. This is expressed in a number of passages, but just two will suffice to demonstrate the validity of what we are saying.

2 Chronicles 6:24– "If your people Israel are defeated before an enemy because they have sinned against you..."

Psalms 41:11– "By this I know that you are well pleased with me, when my enemy does not triumph over me."

Solomon and the Psalmist expressed the same sentiment. Israel's sin would lead to Israel's judgment. So, Biblically, judgment on Israel came as a direct result of Torah transgression and the application of covenantal wrath from YHVH. This is where the millennial concept is skewered. Here is why.

The millennial view essentially holds that during the Tribulation period following the rapture, Israel is, for all practical purposes the "innocent victim" of the Man of Sin. She has blindly signed a peace treaty with him, and he has turned on her. The Man of Sin sets up the Abomination in the Temple and mercilessly persecutes Israel.

If the modern view of the Abomination of Desolation and Man of Sin is correct it demands that Torah is still binding today and will be in the Tribulation period. Yet, even the millennialists admit that the Law of Moses has been removed in Christ.[89] This is a problem of huge proportions.

If the Law of Moses has been forever fulfilled and removed in Christ, then the postulated Man of Sin and Abomination of Desolation schema of the millennialist is invalidated. Everything that Paul–and Jesus in the Olivet Discourse– predicted belongs to a time when Torah would still be binding. And this demands a first century fulfillment of 2 Thessalonians 2.

The amillennialist and postmillennialist have an equal problem with 2 Thessalonians 2. It is common for these two camps to see in 2 Thessalonians 2 a prediction of the papacy destroyed at the *parousia*, due to his awful outrages against the church.[90] But this is not the contextual use of the temple of God. And it certainly violates what we have just seen about the Torah being binding during the time of the Man of Sin. *You cannot divorce 2 Thessalonians 2 from a historical context when Torah was binding.* We must honor these contextual indicators that tell us that 2 Thessalonians 2 is dealing with first century people, problems and fulfillment.

So, in Thessalonians, every one of the references to the coming of the Lord applied to the end of the Old Covenant age of Israel that came in the fall of Jerusalem in AD 70. It is fair to ask therefore, upon what basis one would change that application in chapter 4. Should we not find some mark of delineation that demands such a change in understanding? Clearly there is no suggestion that the coming in chapter 4 is different from that in the rest of Paul's Thessalonian epistles. This all but demands that the coming of the Lord in 1 Thessalonians 4 has to be, in spite of all the traditional presuppositional teaching about it, the coming of the Lord in AD 70.

Our brief survey of the Thessalonian epistles finds a unified, harmonious doctrine of the *parousia* of Christ. Every text leading up to- and after- 1 Thessalonians 4 reveals the following:

☛ Paul was preaching the same message as John the Immerser of the impending *wrath to come*. But this impending wrath was not a time ending, earth burning event. It was the end of the Old Covenant age.

☛ Paul was reminding the Thessalonians that their suffering had been predicted by Jesus as part of the end times scenario of the Olivet Discourse, therefore, they should not be shaken in their faith.

☛ Paul directly cites an O.T. prophecy of the Day of the Lord against Israel (Zechariah 14:5–> 1 Thessalonians 3:13).

☛Paul unequivocally taught that the *parousia* of 1 Thessalonians 4 was near. The Thessalonians would "remain until" that great day.

☛ Paul taught– based on the O.T. prophecies– that Christ's coming to avenge the suffering of the saints was to occur while they– the Thessalonians- were under persecution. This is *prima facie* proof that the *parousia* cannot be a yet future event. The Thessalonians had to be alive, under persecution, at the time of the *parousia*. I think it is safe to say that those Thessalonians are not alive today, under persecution.

☛ Paul taught that the Man of Sin, and thus the apostasy,[91] was already present, but being restrained.

These contextual facts force us to re-evaluate the traditional interpretations of 1 Thessalonians 4. If this chapter speaks of a Day of the Lord different from the first century event found in the other texts in Thessalonians, where is the evidence? What are the indicators that Paul is radically departing from what he says in every other passage in the book? As good students of the Word, it behooves us to look beyond creeds, tradition, prejudice and presuppositions, and base our interpretations on text, context and proper hermeneutics.

THIS WE SAY TO YOU BY THE WORD OF THE LORD
1 THESSALONIANS 4:15
A DEMONSTRATION OF THE UNITY OF THE OLIVET DISCOURSE: THE SOURCE OF PAUL'S DISCOURSE

The next thing we want to examine is taken from verse 15 of 1 Thessalonians 4: "For this we say to you by the word of the Lord, that we who are alive and remain until the coming of the Lord will by no means precede those who are asleep." What did Paul mean when he said, "This we say to you by the word of the Lord"? There are two views of this:

Paul was saying that he was reminding the Thessalonians of the teaching of Jesus given during Jesus' earthly ministry.

It is believed by some that Paul was saying, "What I am saying to you, I received directly from the Lord by inspiration." In this case it is argued that Paul was not necessarily reminding them of anything from Jesus' personal teaching, but delivering "new" revelation.

There is no need to dichotomize between the two choices. Paul *was* reminding the Thessalonians of what Jesus had taught during his personal ministry. Gentry concurs, stating: "Most commentators agree that the Olivet Discourse 'is undoubtedly a source of the Thessalonian Epistles.'" (Citing D.A. Carson, with approval).[92] Weima says Paul is referring, "to an authoritative teaching of the Jesus Christ."[93] Likewise, Beale says, "Paul is recollecting the words of the earthly Jesus and paraphrasing him. This is apparent from noticing that 4:15-5:7 has numerous parallels[94] that demonstrate a high probability that Paul is dependent on Jesus' teaching on the last things."[95]

Paul was simply reiterating the content of the Olivet Discourse. The parallels between the Olivet Discourse and Paul's Thessalonian epistles are precise. Even if Paul was not previously cognizant of the Olivet material (and we cannot imagine that he wasn't) it still remains true that what Jesus was now revealing to him was the Olivet material. We want now is to establish the correspondence between Matthew 23-25 and Thessalonians. This is important to establish the points to be made later so we will present quite a bit of material here.

Our argument is simple. If the Olivet Discourse (Including Matthew 23, which serves as the intro to the Discourse) is parallel to Thessalonians then since the subject of the Olivet Discourse is the judgment on Jerusalem that occurred in AD 70 this will establish the topic of Thessalonians.

I understand that my millennial friends will object to our statement that the Olivet Discourse is about the fall of Jerusalem in AD 70. We also understand that the amillennial and postmillennial views divide the Discourse into two topics, the fall of Jerusalem (Matthew 24:4-34) and the "end of time" (v. 36-25:46).[96] I will try to respond to both criticisms as we proceed.

First, if we demonstrate that the Olivet Discourse is not divided then the amillennial and postmillennial views fall apart. This will be demonstrated shortly.

Second, if it is proven that the Olivet Discourse and 1 Thessalonians 4 are the same topic then millennialism falls as well. Millennialists believe that Matthew 24 speaks of the Second Coming. They hold that 1 Thessalonians 4 speaks of the rapture that occurs 7 years *before* the events of Matthew 24:29f. We will examine the rapture doctrine later.

So, let us establish the unity of the Olivet Discourse. It must be remembered that the amillennial and postmillennial views deny that any of Matthew 24:36-25:46 applies to first century events.[97] If, therefore, we can prove that any portion of the Discourse after 24:36 does refer to AD 70, then the amillennial and postmillennial view is negated. As a matter of fact, it can be proven that Matthew 25 is directly related to the fall of Jerusalem.

To prove this, let's look first at the wedding parable of Matthew 22. A man made a great wedding feast for his son. The time came for the wedding and those who had been previously invited were summoned. However, they mistreated the messengers and killed them: "When the king heard about this, he was furious. And sent out his armies destroyed those murderers, and burned their city." The wedding then took place as planned with the addition of other guests.

> **The parable of the 10 Virgins proves the unity of the Olivet Discourse beyond a doubt.**

There is virtually unanimous consent in the evangelical world that this parable refers to the events leading up to the fall of Jerusalem in AD 70. Postmillennialist Gentry says, "The destruction of Jerusalem by Rome is providential destruction 'by His armies' (Matthew 22:7)" (*Dominion*, 1992, 472). So in Matthew 22 the wedding of the Son takes place when Jerusalem is destroyed. Now to the Olivet Discourse.

In Matthew 25 Jesus told the parable of the 10 Virgins. What is the story about besides the obvious concept of readiness? *It is about the time of the wedding!* Is this a different wedding from chapter 22? Is it a different "Son" getting married? Is a different "Bride" involved? Unless the wedding of chapter 25 is a different wedding, at a different time, to a different partner, then since the wedding of chapter 22 is clearly within the context of AD 70 this means that Matthew 25 must apply to that time and event as well. By this single parable then the unity of the Olivet Discourse is established.

Yet Gentry holds that the parable of the Virgins is proof of a yet future, literal coming of Christ at the end of human history. He says that since

Matthew 25 and the parable of the Virgins posits a delay in the coming of the Groom, that this speaks of a long (2000 years so far!) delay in the Wedding / parousia.[98] Gentry insists that since the Virgins were having to watch for the bridegroom, just as the servants of the absent master were to watch for his return, that, "Watchfulness implies delay" (*Dominion*, 2009, 437).

Gentry fails to explain or give any evidence as to why we must understand "Watchfulness" as demanding a delay of 2000 years. Where is the logic of such a claim? Where is the *evidence* for this bold assertion? If I were to call a friend and tell him that I was going to visit him next spring, but I do not give the day or the hour of my visit, will my friend not watch for my coming? Will he think that because he does not know the day or the hour of my visit that I will not be coming in his lifetime? As winter passes, and spring approaches, will he not watch for me? How exactly does his watchfulness demand that I will not come for many, many years? But Gentry has worse problems yet with the parables. Let me illustrate with the following points:

The resurrection of Revelation 20 is at the end of the millennium (Gentry).

The resurrection of Revelation 20 is the resurrection of 1 Cor. 15 (Gentry).

The resurrection of 1 Corinthians 15 would be the fulfillment of Hosea 13:14 (1 Corinthians 15:55f).

The resurrection of Hosea 13 would be at the marriage (remarriage) of Israel (see our discussion of this).

But, the marriage (remarriage) of Israel was in the first century i.e. AD 70 (Matthew 22 / Revelation 21; Gentry).

Therefore, the resurrection of Revelation 20– unless it is a different resurrection from 1 Cor. 15, or a different marriage from that of Matthew 22, or Matthew 25– was in the first century, i.e. AD 70.

Does Gentry believe in two weddings, of two grooms, or, that Jesus will marry the church twice? No, at least we have not found that in his writings. This means that if the story of the wedding in the NT (not to mention the OT) is a harmonious unity, then the wedding of Matthew 25 was in AD 70. This means that Gentry's argument concerning a 2000 year delay is falsified. And, we have Gentry's own words to help us here.

In Revelation 18-19 we find the story of the impending destruction of the city called *Babylon*. This is the city, "Where the Lord was slain" (Revelation 11:8). Can there be any serious doubt about what city that was? Gentry vigorously advocates the identity of Babylon in Revelation as none other than Old Covenant Jerusalem (2009, 382+). Commenting on the descent of the New Jerusalem as the Bride adorned for her husband, Gentry says that in Revelation 21:1f, "John sees the New Jerusalem coming down out of heaven to earth in the establishment of Christianity (Revelation 21:1-2). This was the heavenly city that Abraham ultimately sought beyond the temporal (and typical) Promised land (Hebrews 11:10, 16) (2009, 147). He adds: "The Heavenly Jerusalem is the bride of Christ that comes down from God to replace the earthly Jerusalem (Rev 21:2-5) in the first century (Rev 1:1, 3; 22:6, 10). With the shaking and destruction of the old Jerusalem in AD 70, the heavenly (recreated) Jerusalem replaces her" (2009, 367). He insists: "It seems clear from the time statements in Revelation following the New Jerusalem imagery that this must come to pass not long after John wrote (Revelation 22:6, 7, 10)" (2009, 147, n. 44).

So, for Gentry the wedding was a first century event, and I think it helpful to note that Jesus told the church at Sardis, "If you will not watch, I will come up on you as a thief, and you will not know the hour that I come upon you" (Revelation 3:3).

It should be noted that in his excellent tome, *Before Jerusalem Fell*, Gentry applied Revelation 3:3 to Jesus' first century judgment coming.[99] Thus, *in his own writings* Gentry has falsified his argument that watchfulness demands a delay of 2000 years. If he can posit a first century fulfillment of the thief coming of Revelation 3:3 with its attendant demand for *watchfulness* because *they did not know the hour* of that coming, then there is no exegetical or logical reason for saying that Matthew 25 must include a delay of 2000 years because the virgins-- or the servants of the absent master-- were told to watch because they did not know the hour of the coming of the groom / master. But there is even more from Gentry.

In Revelation 10:7 we find this: "But in the days of the sounding of the seventh angel, when he is about to sound, the mystery of God would be finished, as He declared to His servants the prophets." Gentry says that the sounding of the seventh trump indicated:

> "The angel is clearly Christ, as we see in comparing Revelation 10:1 with 1:13-16. He declares that Israel's time is up: 'There should be no more delay' (Rev 10:6). This answers the plea from the martyred souls at heaven's altar (Rev. 6:10). As he declares no more delay he proclaims that 'the mystery of God is finished' (Rev 10:7). By this

we understand that God finally, forever and fully accepts the Gentiles as He removes the temple with its 'separating wall' (Eph 2:14; Rev 11:1-2). The end of the temple economy and national Israel is near (1 Co 10:11; 1 Th 2:16; Heb 1:2; 9:26; 12:26-27; 1 Jn 2:18)" (*Dominion*, 2009, 408).

Here are a few thoughts to consider.

The sounding of the seventh trump is the end of Israel's Old Covenant age (Gentry, Revelation 10:6f).

The end of Old Covenant Israel's age was at the destruction of Babylon (Gentry, Revelation 18-19).

The wedding of Christ would be at the destruction of Babylon (Revelation 19:6-8).

But, there was to be "no more delay" in the sounding of the seventh trump (Revelation 10:6-7).

Therefore, there was to be no more delay in the *wedding*.

Building on what we just saw, let me follow that with this:

There was to be no more delay in the *wedding*– the time for the wedding was truly imminent in Revelation.

But, the time of the wedding is the time of the coming of the groom in Matthew 25:1-13, i.e. the second coming of Christ.

Therefore, there was to be no more delay in the time of the second coming of Christ.

These facts demonstrate the unity of the Olivet Discourse. They prove the unity of the wedding theme in the NT. They prove that the "delay" of the parousia in the parables in Matthew 25 was a delay only in relationship to the first century. It was not a delay of 2000 years! Let me succinctly outline Gentry's problem when it comes to the wedding theme.

Matthew 22– Gentry says the wedding was in AD 70.

Matthew 24:29f– Gentry says that Christ's coming in AD 70 was for the wedding.

Matthew 25:1-13– Gentry says this is a yet coming of Christ. But of course if this is true, *then the wedding was not truly in AD 70 afer all!* How then can Gentry say that the bride of Christ fully supplanted the old bride in AD 70?

Revelation 19-22– Gentry says the wedding of Revelation 19-21 was fulfilled in AD 70.

The burden of proof is patently on Gentry to prove definitively that the wedding of Matthew 25 *cannot* be the wedding of chapter 22 or of Revelation. However, note that in Matthew 25 the call, "Behold the bridegroom comes!" was not made *until the bridegroom was truly imminent*. In Revelation, "The Spirit and the Bride say come" and Jesus' emphatic, "Behold I come quickly" are undeniable declarations that the time of the wedding was at hand. Thus, the so called "delay" of Matthew 25 was now at an end in Revelation.

How can Gentry divorce Matthew 25 from these declarations that he himself places as fulfilled in AD 70? How can Gentry say that the bride of Christ fully supplanted Israel in AD 70 unless the groom came to marry his bride, just as described in Matthew 25? There is no justification for divorcing Matthew 25 from these other declarations about the wedding. Since Gentry unequivocally posits the wedding of Matthew 22 and Revelation 19-21 as AD 70, this demands that the wedding of Matthew 25 was likewise in AD 70.

All of this has profound implications for understanding New Testament eschatology. Yet Gentry claims that even if the Olivet Discourse is proven to be concerned only with the Lord's AD 70 judgment that, "Orthodox preterists[100] see no doctrinal problem arising if we apply all of Matthew 24 (and thus, Matthew 25, DKP) to AD 70." This is an incredibly naive, not to mention false, statement. Few scholars would agree with him on this.

If the New Testament doctrine of the wedding is a united theme, and if 1 Thessalonians 4 is about Christ's coming for his bride, then to suggest that a united Olivet Discourse would present no doctrinal problems for the postmillennial paradigm is nothing other than a denial of reality.

Note again that Gentry admits that virtually all scholars agree that Paul is drawing from the Olivet Discourse in 1 Thessalonians 4:13f. Let me frame a few thoughts for your consideration:

1 Thessalonians 4:13f is drawn from the Olivet Discourse (Gentry).

But, all of the Olivet Discourse may well be discussing only one topic, the coming of the Lord in AD 70 (Gentry).

Therefore, 1 Thessalonians 4 is drawn from a discussion of only one topic, the coming of the Lord in AD 70.

And we are supposed to believe that this would pose "no doctrinal problem" for Gentry and other futurists? That would be all the same as saying that there would be no doctrinal problem if all of 1 Corinthians 15 discussed the coming of Christ in AD 70. If Thessalonians is drawn from a discussion of Christ's AD 70 parousia, then *of necessity* Thessalonians (and

1 Corinthians 15) is about that event as well. That is, unless Gentry can find some way to divorce the discussion of Thessalonians from the Olivet Discourse, or claim that although Paul is in fact utilizing the Olivet Discourse, he has something totally different in time and nature in mind.

There is no indication whatsoever in Thessalonians that Paul was changing the application either in time or nature from what Jesus said in the Discourse. On the contrary, Paul emphasizes that he is simply reiterating what Jesus said. I suspect that Gentry is seeking to deflect attention from what is a major theological problem for postmillennialism and futurism.

Some postmillennialists are openly abandoning the idea of a divided discourse. Mathison now holds that the entire Discourse discusses but one topic, Christ's AD 70 parousia.[101] This is a *dramatic* change from his earlier position of a divided discourse.[102] This clearly puts him at odds with noted postmillennial scholars of the past, not to mention the creeds which he claims are the arbiters of orthodoxy. Back to our discussion of the wedding.

Are we to believe that the wedding of Matthew 22 and Revelation are the same but that Matthew 25 speaks of a different wedding?[103] If so, who are the different parties involved? If there are two weddings who are the two sons? Who are the two brides? Based on the information above we offer the following argument:

The marriage of the son would take place at the destruction of Jerusalem in AD 70 (Matthew 22, Revelation 18-19).

But the wedding of Matthew 25 is the marriage of the son.

Therefore, the marriage of the son in Matthew 25 would take place at the destruction of Jerusalem in AD 70.

It cannot be over-emphasized how important this is. The fact that Matthew 25 discusses the same topic as Matthew 22 is undeniable. But since the topic of Matthew 22 is AD 70, this means that Matthew 25 is also AD 70. This means that the Olivet Discourse cannot be divided into two topics. There is no "continental divide" between a discussion of the fall of Jerusalem and the end of the Christian age. And I must interject just a comment or two here about Gentry's view of Matthew 24:36 and his claim that a United Discourse would pose no difficulty for his eschatological views.

While Gentry claims that a united Discourse would present no doctrinal difficulty for the postmillennial view, his use of Matthew 24:36, and the parables of the "delayed" parousia, belie that claim. Gentry references Matthew 24:36 several times to prove that we cannot know the day or the hour of Christ's second coming. Furthermore, he refers to the delay parables repeatedly, insisting that the delay of the groom and the absent master demands a delay of so far 2000 years. There is no question that for Gentry Matthew 24:36 is a pivotal text.

So what happens if, as Mathison contends (2009, 379) Matthew 24:36 means that they could not know the day or hour of Christ's coming in judgment of Jerusalem? *It means that Gentry's reliance on Matthew 24:36 to negate the imminence of the parousia in other texts is negated!* And what happens if, as we demonstrate in this book, that the "delay" of the coming of the bridegroom and absent master was only a delay within that generation? It would mean that Gentry's paradigm would suffer a severe blow, in spite of his protestations. Without a "delayed parousia" Gentry's postmillennialism is virtually dead. The Olivet Discourse is *the key text* for Gentry's doctrine of a delayed coming. Very clearly then Gentry's claim that a united Discourse would present no doctrinal problems for the postmillennial view is a desperate attempt to derail the oncoming train.

Okay, back to a demonstration of the unity of the Olivet Discourse.

A second demonstration of the unity of Matthew 24 is the parable of the talents in Matthew 25. Jesus told of a master that went on a journey.[104] He first called his servants in, and dispensed responsibilities and authority among them. When the master left the servants began to use their respective moneys. Some gained great gain, but the man with the least amount "dug in the ground and hid his lord's money" (Matthew 25:18). When the master returned, the servants were judged according to their faithfulness.

Jesus told another parable of talents that has virtually the identical point. The information provided in the other parable helps us determine the framework of the judgment under consideration. In Luke 19 Jesus told the story of, "a certain nobleman who went into a far country to receive for himself a kingdom and to return" (Luke 19:12). Before he left he entrusted his servants with responsibilities and privileges, just as the master did in Matthew 25. He told them to take care of business until he returned, just as the master did in Matthew.

In Luke, we have some additional information. Luke tells us, "His citizens hated him, and sent a message after him, saying, 'We will not have this man to reign over us'" (Luke 19:14). There is a well known historical situation behind this story.

When Herod the Great died his sons were to receive the kingdom. However, as the custom was in the Roman Empire, before this could happen, the sons, in this case Archaelus, had to travel to Rome and there receive his inheritance from the Caesar. This demonstrated the superiority of Rome as well as showed that the Roman power stood behind this new ruler. When Archaelus traveled to Rome however, the Jews, fearful of a replay of Herod's atrocities and cruelty, sent an ambassage to Rome asking that Archaelus not be appointed king over them. It did not work as they had planned, however.

When Archaelus was acknowledged by Rome and returned to Judea there was an awful price to pay.

That historical situation stood as a stark and foreboding background to Jesus' parable. Remember that Jesus told this parable in the context of the Pharisees' expectation that the kingdom was about to come *immediately* (Luke 19:11, from *paraxrama mellei*). It should be noted that in Matthew 25 Jesus introduced the parable of the absent master and the talents with "the kingdom of heaven is like" (Matthew 25:14f).

In both parables we have a master leaving. Both parables are about the kingdom. Both parables deal with the entrusting of servants with talents. Both parables are about the time of judgment of the servants. Luke informs us that the return of the master in Luke 19 is the time when the servants who said, "We will not have this man to rule over us" were going to be judged and destroyed: "But those mine enemies, which would not that I should reign over them, bring hither, and slay them before me" (Luke 19:27). The parallels are direct.

Is there any doubt about who it was that said, "We will not have this man to rule over us!"? In the words of Lightfoot, "This parable of the pounds hath for the general the same scope with that of the talents (Matthew 25). That nobleman or king that went into a far country to receive for himself a kingdom is Christ in his gospel, going forth to call in the Gentiles to his obedience: returning, he cuts off the nation of the Jews that would not have him to reign over them (v. 27)."[105]

To negate the correlation between Matthew and Luke one has to prove some things:

1.) It must be proven that the parable in Matthew 25 and that in Luke are not parallel.

2.) It must be proven that the returning master in Matthew is a different master, or returns at a different time, or judges a different group than the absent master in Luke.

3.) It would have to be proven that the parable in Luke is not concerned with the time of the judgment of Israel, i.e. those who would not have him rule over them. However, the problem here is that the consistent theme of many of Jesus' parables is that it was Israel that was rejecting his Lordship, not the nations or men in general. *It was Israel*. Remember the words of the leaders of Israel at Jesus' trial, "We have no king but Caesar!" As a result, it was Israel that was to be judged.

If it be admitted that Matthew 25 and Luke 19 are the same parable, and if it be admitted that Luke 19 speaks of Christ's return in the judgment of Israel in AD 70, then this effectively proves that Matthew 25:14f is about the return of Christ in AD 70. Of course, if the parable of the talents in Matthew

25 is about Christ's coming in AD 70 then all theories about a divided Olivet Discourse are falsified.

The belief that the Olivet Discourse speaks of two events, the fall of Jerusalem (v. 4-34) and the so called "end of time" (24:36-25:46) is in many respects the foundation of the amillennial and postmillennial eschatology. Although as just seen, some leading postmillennialists are now abandoning the argument of a divided discourse claiming that it does not matter if the Discourse is about AD 70 after all. In spite of these claims, the demonstration that Matthew 25 discusses the Lord's coming in AD 70 is a devastating refutation.

In identifying the time of the wedding as the time of the fall of Jerusalem in AD 70, and thus placing Matthew 25 in that context, the dispensational view is also falsified. This is true because the millennial view normally places Matthew 25 immediately before the millennium after the rapture.

In summary, our argument is this. In Thessalonians Paul said that he was only reminding his readers of what the Lord said. His source is the Olivet Discourse. But the Olivet Discourse refers to the events leading up to and consummating in the fall of Jerusalem in AD 70. Therefore, Thessalonians must be about the Lord's coming at the end of the Old Covenant world of Israel in AD 70.

To prove that the Discourse is truly the same as Thessalonians, we now turn our attention to the direct parallels between them. We have provided a rather lengthy list of these parallels here. We will follow up with a simplified list of parallels that powerfully demonstrate that these texts truly are parallel. Take a look now at the longer list of parallels.

Temple Sermon and Olivet Discourse	Thessalonians
1.) Matthew. 23:29f- Jews had slain the prophets	1 Thessalonians. 2:15- Jews had slain the prophets
2.) 23:34- Would kill Jesus' "prophets."	1:2:15- Had killed Jesus' prophets.
3.) 23:32- Would fill the measure of their sin by persecuting	1:2:15-16- Were filling the measure of their sin by persecuting.[106]
4.) 23:36- Judgment would come in that generation (cf. Lk. 21:23)	1:2:16- Wrath has come on them to the uttermost.

5.) 24:9- Shall deliver you to be afflicted-(thlipsis) (first section)	1:1:6- Received the word in much affliction-(thlipsis, cf. 2:1:5-7)
6.) 24:10-12- Apostasy (v. 12) love of *most people* will grow cold, (NASB) (first section)	2 Ths. 2:3- *The* apostasy. Paul had told them of this when he was with them (v. 5). Paul is basing his prediction on the Olivet Discourse.
7.) Lawlessness (*anomia*) will abound (24:12:	Spirit of lawlessness (*anomia*) is already at work (2 Ths. 2:5)
8.) 24:14- Gospel mission	1 Thessalonians. 1:8- Gospel mission being fulfilled
9.) Mark 13:11- Miraculous presence of Spirit	1 Ths. 1:5; 5:19f- Miraculous presence of Spirit
10.) Matthew 24:15- Abomination of Desolation (first section)	2 Ths. 2:3f- Man of Sin. (Jesus said the appearance of the apostasy and the Man of Sin were signs of the end. Paul says the same thing. See #11)
11.) Matthew. 24:24-27- False prophets saying Christ had come. (first section)	2 Ths. 2:2- Some saying day of the Lord had come.[107]
12.) 24:31-32- When you see these things come to pass know it is near, at the door (first section)	2 Ths. 2:2f- That day will not come except there come first the apostasy, and the Man of Sin.[108]
13.) Matthew. 24:24- Working of false miracles (first section)	2 Ths. 2:9- Working of false miracles

14.) Matthew 24- Coming of Christ, v. 3- *parousia*[109] v. 27- *parousia* v. 30- *erchomai* v. 39- *parousia* v. 42- *erchomai* v. 44- *erchomai*	Thessalonians- Coming of Christ, 1 Ths. 3:13- *parousia* 4:15- *parousia* 5:2- *erchomai* 5:23- *parousia* 2 Ths. 1:10- *erchomai* 2 Ths. 2:1, 8- *parousia* Jesus two favorite words in the Olivet Discourse are the words Paul used the most in Thessalonians.
15.) 24:30- Coming with shout (first section)	4:16- Coming with shout
16.) 24:30- With clouds	4:17- With clouds
17.) 24:30- With power and great glory.	2 Ths. 1:9-10- Coming to be glorified (cf. vs. 9, power and glory).
18.) 24:30, 37-51; 25:31f- Judgment of the wicked	2 Ths. 1:7f- Judgment of the wicked
19.) 24:31- Coming with angels 25:31- Coming with angels	4:16- Coming with angels; 2 Ths. 1:7-8 coming with angels- (draws from both sections!)
20.) 24:31-Trumpet	4:16-Trumpet
21.) 24:31- Believers gathered (*episunagogee*)	4:17- Believers gathered; 2 Ths. 2:1-concerning the gathering, (*episunagogee*)
22.) 24:34-This generation shall not pass till all fulfilled	4:15,17- We who are alive and remain until the coming (cf. 5:23.)[110]
23.) Believers can *know* when it is *near* (24:32-33)	5:4- "Ye, brethren are not in darkness"
24.) 24:36- Day and hour unknown (second section)	1 Ths. 5:1-2- Times and seasons unknown.

25.) "That day" (v. 36) Lk. 21:34-"that day."	5:4- "that day," "that day" (2:1:10) "that day" 2:2:2-3
26.) 24:38- Marrying and giving in marriage--i.e."peace and safety" (second section).	1 Ths. 5:3- "Peace and safety."
27.) 24:37-39- Unbelievers unaware.	5:3- Unbelievers unaware.
28.) 24:43- Coming as a thief (cf. Lk. 21:34-36)[111]	5:3- Coming as a thief[112]
29.) 24:42- Call to watch	5:6- Call to watch.
30.) Believers *escape* (Luke 21:36).	5:3- Believers *escape*.
31.) 24:47- Warning against drunkenness (cf. Luke 21:34f).	5:7- Warning against drunkenness
32.) 25:31-32- Time of *separation*; (*24:31*-gathering of elect implies separation! First and second sections say same thing.)	2 Ths. 1:7-10- Time of *separation* (1 Ths. 4:13f is the *gathering*, also 2 Ths. 2:1) Draws from both sections!
33.) 25:41, 46- Depart from me; everlasting punishment	2 Ths. 1:9- Everlasting destruction from the presence of the Lord

This is an impressive list of parallels. These comparisons show that Paul is indeed referring to the Olivet Discourse when he says, "This I say to you by the word of the Lord." These parallels directly falsify Mathison's attempt to say that Thessalonians is not taken from the Discourse.

Mathison appeals to what is known as "progressive revelation" claiming, "Jesus himself may have said very little about the second coming (2009, 365 n. 92,). Paul, according to this view, is the one that received later (progressive) revelation about Jesus' end of history parousia, and that is what we have in Thessalonians and 1 Corinthians 15. This is more than a little remarkable, not to mention specious.

Furthermore, as we have seen, Paul said that his gospel, his *eschatology* was nothing other than that found in Moses and the prophets. Paul did not say that he was receiving something not taught in the prophets; he taught *nothing* but what the prophets said! Would it not be more than a little remarkable that Jesus came to confirm the promises made to the fathers (Romans 15:8) that Paul got his gospel from Jesus, the gospel that was nothing but what the Old Covenant prophets said, and yet, Paul, per Mathison, did say something radically different from what Jesus and the prophets foretold? So, Jesus' eschatology was a confirmation of the OT prophets. Paul's eschatology was from the OT. Yet, per Mathison, Paul's eschatology was in fact different from the OT eschatology and different from Jesus' eschatology.

In point of fact, Mathison does believe that Jesus spoke of his final coming. He believes that Jesus' first parable, and the parallel ones in Matthew 13 refer to the end of history (2009, 361+). He fails to mention that Matthew 13:43 is a citation of Daniel 12:3, and that he believes that Daniel 12's prophecy of the resurrection is likewise a prediction of the "end of history." But all of this compounds Mathison's problems.

Mathison tells us that the Son of Man eschatological prophecies are from Daniel 7 and foretold the events limited to the period from Christ's ascension to AD 70. Yet, Matthew 13 is an eschatological Son of Man passage! Why does it not apply to AD 70?

Mathison's application of Daniel 12 to an end of time event is false. Daniel 12 predicted *the destruction of the holy people*. Yet Daniel is emphatic that the Messianic kingdom will never be destroyed (Daniel 2:44; 7:13f). Furthermore, Daniel 7, just like Daniel 12, foretold *the Great Tribulation* (Daniel 7:21f). Mathison posits the Great Tribulation for the first century. This demands a first century fulfillment for the resurrection since Daniel 12:2 emphatically posits the resurrection at that time.

I suggest that the *only* reason Mathison would take such a position is theological, not exegetical. He understands that the OT and Jesus delimited their eschatological predictions to the end of the OT age. If he grants that the Olivet Discourse or the OT is the true source of Thessalonians, his futurism is falsified.

Paul is emphatic that he received his gospel directly from Jesus (Galatians 1:11-2). So, per Mathison, we are to believe that although Jesus spoke of his coming extensively during his ministry, that those discussions had nothing to do with his "real" coming. This demands that what Peter, James and John all heard from Jesus had little or nothing to do with Jesus' final coming, and that what Paul heard was different–*radically* different-- from what they were taught! Yet Paul said that he and the other apostles taught the same gospel (Galatians 2:7-9).

To suggest that Thessalonians is distinct from the Olivet Discourse is untenable. Now, let me simplify the list to focus on 1 Thessalonians 4:13-18 and to show that it is parallel with Matthew 24:29f.

Matthew 24:29-31	1 Thessalonians 4:13-18
Coming of the Son of Man	Coming of the Son of Man
With the angels (v. 30-31)	With the angels (v. 16)
With the Trumpet (v. 31)	With the Trumpet (v. 16)
Coming in the clouds (v. 30)	Descend from heaven, in the air (v. 16, 17)
Gathering of the redeemed (v. 31)	Gathering of the redeemed (v. 17)
This generation shall not pass until all these things are fulfilled (v. 34)	"We who are alive and remain until the coming of the Lord" (v. 15, 17)

The parallels between Matthew 24:29f and Thessalonians are undeniable. The themes and motifs are the same, the terms are the same, the time indicators are the same. This not simply similar sounding language. This means that if Matthew 24:29-31 refers to the judgment of Israel in AD 70, then that is what Thessalonians refers to as well. Without preconceived ideas no one would think differently.[113]

Paul says he is reiterating the word of Christ and the word of Christ that contains *every element* listed by Paul is the Olivet Discourse, specifically Matthew 24:29-31. Is this not powerful evidence that the Olivet Discourse is Paul's source? Furthermore, and this is almost definitive: nowhere else in the Olivet Discourse do we find the prediction of the coming on the clouds, the angels, the trump and the gathering of the elect.[114] Those elements are found *exclusively* in verses 29-31 and chapter 25:31f. But as we have seen one cannot divide chapter 25 from chapter 24 because of the wedding. The wedding of Matthew 25 is married, excuse the pun, to Christ's coming in Matthew 24:29f!

The elements of Matthew 25:31f are identical to 24:29f. So, if/since Paul is reiterating the Discourse, then since *the only place* in the Discourse that contains the elements that Paul gives is 24:29-31 this means that Paul is reiterating Matthew 24:29-31 in 1 Thessalonians 4:13f. Yet, remember that per Gentry, Mathison, and most postmillennialists, Matthew 24:29f speaks exclusively of Christ's coming in AD 70!

It is likewise significant that Mathison now holds to a united Olivet Discourse.[115] Thus, he sees the parallels between Matthew 24:29f and 25:31 as determinative of identicality. So, Paul affirms that he is drawing from Jesus' eschatological discourse. The only place in all of Jesus' eschatological teachings that we find every element that Paul uses is the Olivet Discourse (24:29-31; 25:31f). These are texts that Mathison insists refer to AD 70. Yet per Mathison, we are not to see any link between Thessalonians and the Discourse. This is clearly illogical and untenable.

To delineate between Matthew 24 and Thessalonians therefore, one must prove that the elements of Jesus' discourse really are different from Paul's teaching in Thessalonians.[116] If the elements are the same and the timing is the same then the topic is the same.[117] This is not mere "similar language" as Mathison and Gentry affirm. But if the topic is the same in Matthew and Thessalonians then the traditional futurist views of eschatology are called into question to say the least.

Millennialists insist that Matthew 24:29-31 speaks of a visible, bodily descent of Jesus out of heaven on cumulus clouds seven years after the events of Thessalonians, i.e. the rapture. They believe that Thessalonians speaks of a silent, invisible event that transpires in a dimension beyond the time space continuum. What is the contextual justification for such a dichotomy? Where does Jesus say that the event he is describing would be optically visible but Paul said his would be invisible?[118] Where does Paul say that the Trumpet would be silent for the rapture but audible for the *parousia* in Matthew. Both Matthew 24 and Thessalonians are speaking about the *parousia* and the chart above shows how Paul used the words used by Jesus interchangeably in Thessalonians. This powerfully suggests that there is no distinction in the nature of the events.

Neither Jesus nor Paul delineated between the events they were predicting and neither should we. This is important. Matthew 24 and 1 Thessalonians describe the same time and event. Since Jesus said the events of Matthew 24 were limited to his generation, and since Paul said that some of the Thessalonians would live until that event then any modern application of either text is misplaced.

In order to apply Thessalonians to an event other than that found in Matthew one must decide that Matthew 24 does not, after all, apply to AD 70. Or, it must be shown that Matthew 24:29-31 and Thessalonians are indeed different types of comings at two different times. This is what Mathison is attempting now to do. (*Age*, 2009, 379f).

However, take a look at the short chart again and ask yourself where the differences might be. What makes the coming of one text spiritual (providential) and the other literal and bodily? What makes the angels in Matthew *preachers of the gospel*, but the angels in Thessalonians *angelic beings*? What makes the Trumpet silent or metaphoric in Matthew, but *audible* in Thessalonians? What makes the descent from heaven on the clouds in Matthew a typical prophetic description of the action of God in history, but in Thessalonians it is a literal descent *to put an end to history?*

What is the difference between, "this generation shall by no means pass," and, "those of us who are alive and remain until the coming of the Lord?" The truth is that there is *not one thing* in the context of either passage that forces us to draw a distinction between the two texts. On the contrary, given the *identical time restrictions* in each passage and given the identical nature of the language, consistency would demand that we admit that both passages speak of the same time and event.

Let me close this section with a summary of what it would mean for Gentry and virtually all futurists if the Olivet Discourse is a united discussion of Christ's AD 70 coming.

1.) 1 Thessalonians 4 is drawn from the Olivet Discourse. Gentry admits that virtually all scholars believe this. So, if the Discourse speaks only of the AD 70 redemptive event, this demands that this is what Thessalonians is about as well. Needless to say, this would not only give Gentry doctrinal problems, it would falsify virtually all futurist paradigms!

2.) If Matthew 24-25 is strictly about Christ's AD 70 parousia, then Gentry loses his key argument, based on Matthew 24:36 about not knowing the day or the hour.

3.) If Matthew 24-25 is strictly about Christ's AD 70 parousia then Gentry loses his key argument that the delay of the bridegroom and the absent master in chapter 25 demands an event different from the Lord's AD 70 coming. Having to apply the "delay of the parousia" texts in the Discourse to AD 70 virtually demands that he apply the "delay of the parousia" in 2 Peter 3 to AD 70, since Peter emphatically says that his teaching in 2 Peter 3 is taken from the Lord's teaching. Where in Jesus' teachings do we find reference to the delay of the parousia if it is not the Discourse? The Olivet Discourse (Matthew 25) is Gentry's *key text* of appeal for the delay of the parousia.

4.) If Matthew 24-25 is strictly about Christ's AD 70 parousia, then Gentry loses his key argument about Christ's thief coming having to be an end of time event. Surrendering this argument would demand that he likewise apply Christ's thief coming in 1 Thessalonians 5 and 2 Peter 3 to AD 70. Such an abdication would be fatal to Gentry's postmillennialism.

5.) If Matthew 24-25 is strictly about Christ's AD 70 parousia, then Gentry loses his key argument that there are no signs of Christ's coming.

6.) If Matthew 24-25 is strictly about Christ's AD 70 parousia, Gentry loses his key argument about the millennium having to be a period of a tremendously long period of time, i.e. so far 2000 years. It is undeniably true that the Great Judgment of Matthew 25:31f is the Great White Throne Judgment of Revelation 20:10f of *which follows the millennium!* Thus, if the judgment of Matthew 25:31f is AD 70, then the millennium of Revelation 20 ended in the first century!

It would be interesting to see Gentry's attempt to dichotomize between Matthew 25:31f and Revelation 20:10f. His *only* resort would be to his untenable hermeneutic that says just because one text includes– or excludes– some tenet of another text that this demands different topics. See our examination of this hermeneutic under the heading: **COMINGS AND MORE COMINGS: A BRIEF EXAMINATION OF PARTIAL PRETERISM**. This hermeneutic is false.

As you can see, a United Discourse does in fact give Gentry and all futurist eschatologies severe problems. As we stated, Gentry's claim that a United Discourse would cause no doctrinal problems for futurists is a totally naive statement intended to deflect attention away from the *incredible significance* of a United Discourse. And Mathison's attempt to deflect the problem will not work, as we demonstrate in this book.

Mathison and Gentry, indeed most commentators, approach the Olivet Discourse understanding that it addresses the fate of the temple and the end of Israel's age. Then however, as suggested already, they approach Thessalonians divorced from that context, because they believe that Thessalonians is about the fulfillment of *God's promises to the church,* divorced from Israel. Instead of framing their interpretation within the context of the fulfillment of God's promises to Israel– the source of Paul's gospel and eschatology– they create an interpretation that has *nothing to do with Israel*, nothing to do with the fulfillment of *Old Testament prophecy.* This is misguided.

Let's summarize what we have seen in this section.

We have seen that the Olivet Discourse cannot be divided into two topics. It is a united discourse about the judgment coming of Christ against Israel in AD 70.

We have seen how Paul says that he is reiterating what Jesus had to say about his coming.

We have seen that *the only place* in all of Jesus' teaching that contains every element that Paul describes is Matthew 24:29-31. This amounts to proof that Thessalonians must be discussing the same thing as the Olivet Discourse. Since the Olivet Discourse is a discussion of the coming of Christ in judgment (and the *kingdom* and *salvation,* Luke 21:28-32) of Israel in AD 70, this means that 1 Thessalonians is about the coming of Christ in AD 70.

THOSE WHO HAVE FALLEN ASLEEP IN CHRIST SHALL GOD BRING WITH HIM
(1 Thessalonians 4:14)

Paul is dealing with the resurrection of the dead in 1 Thessalonians 4. It is normally taken for granted, by everyone except the millennialists, that Thessalonians must be speaking of a visible event at the end of the Christian age. This is not the case at all. In this section we want to establish a couple of points.

We want to show that the resurrection was to be an unseen event.

We want to show the relationship between the resurrection and the time of the vindication of the martyrs. By so doing we will establish beyond doubt the *time* and *context* of the resurrection.

We want to establish that the anticipated and predicted time of the resurrection was the first century.

Turning then to the resurrection, we want to establish the unseen nature of that event. We are fully cognizant of church history that teaches, as I personally taught for years, that the time of the resurrection is associated with the end of time, and the destruction of material creation. However, there are several things that establish the resurrection as an unseen event.

First is the association of the ascension of Jesus with the "descent." Not many Bible students seem to think of this in any substantive manner. However, consider Ephesians 4:8, "When he ascended on high, he led captivity captive, and gave gifts to men." For our purposes, we want to focus on the ascension and the fact that it says "he led captivity captive."

The background for this statement is Psalms 68 and Judges 5. In both instances the context is that the enemies of God had taken members of God's people captive, see especially Judges 5. However, Jehovah fought for the people and defeated the enslaving enemy, setting the captives free, leading them home in triumph. This context of the passages cited helps us understand Ephesians a bit better.

While there is some controversy about exactly what, "he led captivity captive" means, we suggest that the thought is this: At his ascension, Jesus took the souls of the righteous that were in Hades, (i.e. the *captives*) and took them into the heavenly realm with him, and placed them "under the altar" (Revelation 6:9f) to await the imminent answer to their prayer for vindication and vengeance against their persecutors, when the wrath of God would be finished (Revelation 15:8 16:17f).

We recognize this is a very brief explanation of Ephesians 4, but hold that it is the best explanation for the text.[119] Furthermore, this work is not dependent on this explanation. We simply find it corroborative of the rest of the evidence presented herein. With this in mind, let me make my point.

If it is true that, "when he ascended up on high, he led captivity captive," refers to Christ's actions in the Hadean realm at his ascension my question is, *Who saw it?* Did the disciples on the Ascension Mount see the souls of the righteous dead ascend with Jesus? If they did, we don't have a word about it. Did anyone see the dead ascend with Jesus? The easy answer is, No.

What this means is that if, "when he ascended up on high, he led captivity captive," does

> **If the ascension with the dead was an *unseen event*, then why would the descent *with the dead* not be of the same nature?**

refer to Christ's actions involving the Hadean realm at the ascension, then since that was an unseen event, since Paul in 1 Thessalonians 4 is dealing with the dead coming with Christ at his *parousia*, there is no justification for believing that 1 Thessalonians 4 is dealing with an event in the visible dimension! If the ascension with the dead was an unseen event, why would the descent with the dead not be of the same nature? By the nature of the case, we are dealing here with the Hadean realm, the realm of the unseen. In fact, the Bible is quite clear that the resurrection was to be in the unseen realm, yet this fact is either virtually ignored or unknown by the majority of Bible students.

We need to establish a few facts. Among them is that *the time of the resurrection is the time of the coming of the kingdom.* This is established by several passages, but we want to take note of just a few.

1.) Matthew 13:24-30; 37-43- Jesus told the parable of the time of the harvest at the end of the age, and the *parousia* of the Son of Man. He said "the kingdom of heaven is like." Thus, the kingdom, harvest, *parousia* and the end of the age are all inseparable tenets.

In 1 Corinthians 15, Paul says that Jesus was the first fruit of the *harvest* (v. 20) and he said that the *end* (v. 24) would come at the *parousia (23-24) and links it with entrance into the kingdom (v.50).* The time of the resurrection is, therefore, linked with the coming of the kingdom.

2.) Matthew 25:31f- Jesus told of the gathering of the nations before the Great Judgment Seat. It would be the time, "when the Son of Man shall sit (not *quit!* DKP) on the throne of his glory," and the righteous would, "enter the joys of the kingdom prepared since the foundation of the world." Unless one is prepared to place this gathering, judgment and kingdom in a totally different context from that of Matthew 13 and 1 Corinthians 15, we have here a definite connection between Christ entering into the full exercise of his sovereign kingdom authority and the resurrection.

3.) 2 Timothy 4:1- Paul urged Timothy to preach the word as he should in light of the fact that Jesus was, "about to (from *mello*) judge the living and the dead at his appearing and kingdom." The connection between the kingdom and resurrection is explicit and undeniable.

4.) Revelation 11:15-18- John saw his vision of when the martyred prophets were to be rewarded (v. 18) and said, "The kingdoms of this world have become the kingdoms of our Lord and of His Christ" (v. 15). That vindication was to be at the judgment of the city "where the Lord was slain" (Revelation 11:8).

So, once again, scripture links the arrival of the kingdom with the time of the resurrection, and of course judgment. This means that in 1 Thessalonians 4, Paul, while mentioning the resurrection specifically, was also anticipating the arrival of the kingdom. What does this mean for our study of 1 Thessalonians 4? It means that the resurrection, since it was the time of the coming of the kingdom, was to be "without observation." See also our discussion of the connection between resurrection and the arrival of the kingdom in Thessalonians, and Daniel 7 below.

In Luke 17:20f, the Pharisees approached Jesus demanding to know when the kingdom was to come. They thought it was to come immediately (*paraxama*). It is clear that they had a literalistic concept of the kingdom, just as those did in John 6, when Jesus flatly rejected the national zealotry of the crowd that tried to make him their king (John 6:1-15).

When he was asked about the coming of the kingdom, Jesus responded with words that still need to be grasped and accepted today: "The kingdom does not come with observation, nor will they say, 'Lo, here!' Or 'Lo, there!' For indeed, the kingdom of God is within you." The Jews definitely wanted the kingdom to come with observation. They wanted a king on the literal throne of David to re-establish the national glory. They wanted the geographical boundaries of the land restored. They wanted to be able to point to the kingdom as a tangible, socio-politico-religious-military reality. This is *precisely* the kind of kingdom the modern premillennialist is wanting today, by the way. Yet, it is the very kind of kingdom Jesus rejected.

Notice that Jesus said the kingdom "does not come with observation." Virtually all futurist eschatologies have the kingdom coming with observation because they envision that, in one way or another, the "final" coming of the kingdom takes place in a cataclysmic, cosmos destroying event at the end of time. Would that be *observable* or not?

Jesus however, said that the kingdom would not be an entity that you could point to or observe with human optics. The kingdom is an inward reality, "the kingdom of God is within you."

Since the kingdom would not come with observation, and since the coming of the kingdom would be the coming of the resurrection, does it not follow that *the resurrection would not come with observation?* If not, what is the difference? What makes the *kingdom* "not with observation," but the resurrection has to be with observation, i.e. visible?

The fact is that Paul also taught that the resurrection would not be an optically visible event. In 2

> **If the kingdom does not come with observation, and if the resurrection is synchronous with the kingdom, it therefore follows that the resurrection does not come with observation!**

Corinthians 4-5, the apostle spoke at length of the resurrection, the change *from the outer to the inner man*, from the mortal to the immortal, from the "earthly house of this tabernacle," to the "house of God, eternal in the heavens."[120] What did Paul have to say about this resurrection change? His words are virtually ignored but vital: "We do not look at the things that are seen, but at the things that are unseen. For the things that are seen are temporal, but the things that are unseen are eternal."

What are the unseen things that Paul was referring to? It is what he called *the inward* man, "we know that if the outward man perish, the inward man is being renewed day by day." The *inward* man was the unseen man[121] that was being transformed from being un-manifested, to being manifested in incorruptibility. To properly understand this one has to return to 2 Corinthians 3 and Paul's discussion of covenantal transformation "from death to life" (v. 6f) and from "glory to glory" (v. 18). This was the transformation from the Old Covenant to the New Covenant.

So, Paul emphatically says that this change was "unseen." If Paul's discussion is resurrection change, and if he says, "we do not look on the things that are seen," then shouldn't we stop looking for the things that are seen?

The same goes for the corollary doctrine of Christ's coming, which of course, along with the resurrection, is the heart of 1 Thessalonians 4:13f. Notice what Paul says in the same context of 2 Corinthians 4-5: "Even though we have known Christ according to the flesh, yet now we know him thus no longer" (2 Corinthians 5:16).

One of the fundamental concepts of all futurist views is that Jesus is coming back in a physical body, the same–yet glorified--body that came out of the tomb. It is assumed that the body that came out of the tomb was a glorified, immortal, and incorruptible body (After all, we are told, he passed through walls after his resurrection, right?[122]) The trouble with this view is that Jesus' resurrection body was indeed *the same body that went into the tomb*. It was *not* a glorified, immortal body![123] Our point is that the argument is made that Jesus will come back bodily, *in the flesh*. However, this is the diametric opposite of what Paul says in 2 Corinthians 5! The apostle said they had known him after the flesh, *but that Christ would not be known after the flesh anymore!* If Jesus were to come back in the flesh, wouldn't that be knowing him after the flesh again?

So what we have is this: 1 Thessalonians 4:13f is about the resurrection at Christ's *parousia*. Paul says that at the ascension Jesus took the righteous that were in Hades with him. This occurred outside the dimension of human sight. And, Paul tells us that at the *parousia* Jesus would bring the dead with him. If the *taking* of the dead with him was unseen, where do we get the idea that *bringing* the dead with him would be seen?

We have seen that the time of the resurrection is the time of the kingdom. However, Jesus said that the coming of the kingdom would not be "with observation" (Luke 17:20-21) men would not be able to point to it as an observable event! Thessalonians is about the time of the resurrection. The time of the resurrection is the time of the kingdom. But the kingdom would not come with observation. It therefore follows that the resurrection of 1 Thessalonians would not come with observation.

Paul, in discussing the resurrection transformation said, "we do not look on the things that are seen." The resurrection, the event that is the focus of 1 Thessalonians 4, would be "unseen."

When discussing the coming of Christ at the time of the resurrection and judgment, the focus of Thessalonians, Paul said that Christ would no longer be known after the flesh. This is a categoric rebuttal of the concept that the coming of Christ must be bodily and fleshly.

We should mention here, that just prior to his passion, Jesus said, "A little while, and the world will see me no more, But you will see me; because I live, you will live also. At that day you will know that I am in the Father, and you in me, and I in you... Judas (not Iscariot) said to him, Lord, how is it that you will manifest yourself to us, and not to the world? Jesus answered and said to him: If anyone loves me, he will keep my word, and My Father will love him, and we will come and make our home with him."

The significance of this passage is greatly overlooked. Jesus said *the world would not see him anymore*! Judas wanted to know how it was that the world would not see him, but that he would be manifested to them. Jesus said he would be "seen" by those who live by faith and obedience. Both the Father and the Son would manifest themselves in the heart and life of the believer in an unending fellowship with them! (John 14:22-23 is a direct commentary on John 14:1-6.) What we need to see is that resurrection and the *parousia* is all about *relationship*. (Cf. 1 Thessalonians 5:10). It is not about physical resuscitation of rotting corpses!

We close this section with a brief examination of the correlation of 1 Thessalonians 4 and the Garden of Eden. Briefly stated, God told Adam that if he ate the forbidden fruit, he would die that very day (Genesis 2:15-17).[124] They ate. They died. It should be clear that they did not die physically that day. However, they did lose spiritual fellowship with God that very day, and that is the point. They lost fellowship. They experienced "sin-death," separation from God caused by sin.

Eschatology is the story of God's work to restore to man what was lost in Adam: "As in Adam all men die, even so in Christ shall all men be made alive" (1 Corinthians 15:22). This is the "nutshell" story of God's Scheme of Redemption to be perfected at the *parousia* and resurrection. At the *parousia* and resurrection, God would restore man, and destroy Satan.

Thessalonians encapsulates the story of Redemption. It is the story of resurrection, and Biblically, this is the time of the defeat of Satan.[125] Jehovah told Satan and Eve that the time was coming when He was going to destroy Satan and his work through the Seed of woman (Genesis 3:15f). So, here is our argument:

The time of the resurrection would be the time when Satan was destroyed (Revelation 20:10f). [126]

But 1 Thessalonians 4 is about the time of the resurrection.

Therefore, 1 Thessalonians 4 is about the time of the destruction of Satan.

With this in mind, let's take a look at Romans 16:20: "And the God of peace will crush Satan under your feet shortly." The words of Dunn are appropriate. He says that Paul's words:

"Reflects the eschatological expectation which seems to have been characteristic of the Christian movement from the beginning–of the final power of God already pushing back the frontiers of evil, of a victory already being won and soon ("speedily") to be completed. Above all, the slogan, with its echo of Genesis 3:15, effectively ties together the whole sweep of salvation-history: God's purpose is nothing less than the complete destruction of the evil which has grown like a large malignant cancer within the body of mankind and the restoration of his creation to the peace and well-being he originally intended for it."[127]

Dunn patently sees that for Paul, the final defeat of Satan as promised in Genesis was near. Gentry also sees the connection between Romans 16 and the Genesis *protoevangelium*, the first promise of the gospel: "In the New Covenant itself, we discover continuity with the preceding covenants. Romans 16:20 hearkens back to the Adamic Covenant" (*Dominion*, 1992, 113).

Dunn and Gentry see that the defeat of Satan hearkens back to the Garden and the promise of the eschatological consummation. Interestingly, Gentry, in his writings and debating insists that we must honor the temporal indicators of scripture. He rightly notes that the indications of the imminent *parousia* in the New Testament refer to Christ's AD 70 coming to bring in the New Creation. Yet, here in Romans, Paul was affirming that the promised defeat of Satan–which is nothing less than the resurrection of Thessalonians– was coming soon.

The Greek term that Paul uses to describe the nearness of that defeat of Satan is *en taxei*. Commenting on this term in Revelation 1:1, Gentry takes note of the commentators who deny the objective nearness of the fulfillment of Revelation saying that the proper key to understanding the book is the temporal expectation of John. Gentry shows that this term does not mean "with speed" or "suddenly," but, "quickly, at once, without delay."

Gentry says, "One of the most helpful interpretive clues in Revelation is at the same time one of the most generally overlooked among lay students of Scripture and one of the most radically reinterpreted by evangelical scholars. This clue is the contemporary expectation of the author regarding the fulfillment of the prophecies. John clearly expected the *soon* fulfillment of his prophecy."[128] (His emphasis)

Furthermore, in his debate with Thomas Ice, Gentry emphasized that you cannot make these imminence statements mean *nothing*. You cannot elasticize them into meaning that the predicted at hand event was going to be thousands of years away. He poses the following question: "In that John is dealing with real churches in a time of dire Tribulation (Revelation 1:9) why would he inform them that judgment will fall rapidly some two thousand years later? Such would be wholly irrelevant to their circumstances...The relief must be soon, not amazingly fast though two thousand years (or more!) later" (*Tribulation*, 184). Well said, but destructive to Gentry's futurist view.

Now if, as Gentry (correctly in our view) insists, John was expecting the soon coming fulfillment of his prophecy, why does this not demand that Paul was likewise expecting the soon fulfillment of his prophecy, the defeat of Satan, i.e. *the resurrection*, in Romans 16:20?

With these thoughts in mind, let me present my thoughts:

The time of the resurrection– the resurrection of 1 Thessalonians 4:13f– would be the time of the crushing of Satan.

But, Paul affirmed that the crushing of Satan would happen soon (Romans 16:20).

Therefore, the resurrection– the resurrection of 1 Thessalonians 4:13f– would happen soon. (We will comment more on the destruction of Satan below)

There are only a few possible ways to counter this.

First, one could prove that Satan was going to be crushed (destroyed) on more than one occasion. But of course, this raises the issue of why something that has been destroyed needs to be destroyed again? And, if he was *destroyed*, then how did he revive from that destruction? Paul was not saying that God was simply going to wound Satan. Paul was promising the victory of Genesis 3:15 and that was the ultimate victory over Satan.

Second, a person could prove that the destruction of Satan is not related to resurrection. This is of course, impossible. Revelation 20 is too clear.

Third, you could prove that "shortly" in Romans 16:20 does not actually mean soon. However, linguistically and contextually this is untenable as well. This Greek term *en tachei* is used only a few times in scripture and *never* refers to rapidity of action as opposed to nearness of occurrence[129] (See Luke 18:8 and compare with Matthew 23:34-36; Acts 12:7, 22:18, 25:4, etc.) All translations agree that *en tachei* means soon, quickly, without delay.

The crushing of Satan is the time of the resurrection. Satan was only going to be destroyed *one time*. And "shortly" does mean soon. Our argument stands and this proves that the fulfillment of 1 Thessalonians 4;13-18 was near when Paul wrote Romans 16:20. It is therefore inappropriate to place the fulfillment of 1 Thessalonians 4:13-18 at the so-called end of the Christian age, or at the end of time. Unless Paul was wrong[130] when he said that the destruction of Satan was near, then that consummative event did occur in the first century at the end of the Old Covenant age of Israel.

I want now to demonstrate that the *parousia* of Christ as foretold in Thessalonians was not to be a literal, bodily, visible descent of the human body of the man named Jesus. Now, make no mistake. *I am affirming the coming of Christ in no uncertain terms.* I am simply seeking to set forth the proper understanding of the *nature* of Christ's coming.

Jesus said that he was coming "in the glory of the Father" (Matthew 16:27-28). See my *Like Father Like Son, On Clouds of Glory* for a fuller discussion of the significance of this prediction. Suffice it to say that Jesus said that his coming in judgment was going to be his coming in the same manner as the Father had come. Likewise, in John 5:19f, Jesus said the Father had committed all judgment to the Son. Henceforth the Son would judge as he had seen the Father judge. Patently, the Son had never seen the Father manifest Himself bodily and visibly by literally descending out of heaven on the clouds. The Father had manifested His majesty and glory by His sovereign use of one nation to judge another nation, within history.

This coming of Christ in the glory of the Father would, by all accounts, be to bring in the New Creation foretold by Isaiah 64-66. For brevity, I am going to present here an edited and abbreviated form of material from my *The Elements Shall Melt With Fervent Heat*, to illustrate that Christ's *parousia*, the coming of 1 Thessalonians 4, was to be an event not optically visible to the human eye. I urge that you read that work for a more in-depth analysis of the argument.

Notice Isaiah 64:1f:

"Oh that thou would rend the heavens, that thou would come down, that the mountains might flow down at thy presence, As when the melting fire burns, the fire causes the waters to boil, to make thy name known to thine adversaries, that the nations may tremble at thy presence! When thou did terrible things which we looked not for, You came down, the mountains flowed down at Your presence."

It is strange to realize how little attention this text receives in discussions of eschatology. Most commentators spend their time on the New Creation itself, and virtually ignore what Isaiah has to say about the nature of the Day of the Lord that would bring in the New World. Yet Isaiah definitively defines the nature of the Day of the Lord that would bring in the New Creation. And don't forget that the coming of the Lord to bring in the New Creation of Isaiah is the *parousia* of Christ in Thessalonians. So, if we determine the nature of the Day of the Lord in Isaiah we have therefore identified the nature of Christ's *parousia*.

In this passage leading to the promise of the new creation (65:17f; 66:15f) Israel longed for her salvation. She prayed for Jehovah to come. She prayed for El Shaddai to reveal Himself by rending the heavens and melting the mountains.

Now notice, Israel was praying for Jehovah to come *as He had come in the past*. "*When you came down*, the mountains flowed at your presence!" Here is a clear-cut demonstration that the Day of the Lord language was metaphoric and never intended to be taken literally. Jehovah had come in the past. Israel wanted God to come again *as He had come in the past*. Therefore, since Jehovah had never literally, bodily, visibly come in the past, Israel was not asking God to come literally, visibly, bodily. Here is our argument then in application of Isaiah to Thessalonians.

The coming of Christ of 1 Thessalonians 4 is the coming of Christ to bring in the New Creation foretold by Isaiah 64-66.

The coming of the Lord foretold by Isaiah, to bring in the New Creation, would be a coming of the Lord similar in nature to previous comings of the Lord (Isaiah 64:1-3).

> But, previous comings of the Lord had been "in history" events in which YHWH had manifested His sovereignty by using one nation to judge another nation. (The previous Days of the Lord had never been a literal, visible, bodily appearing of the Lord.)
>
> Therefore, the coming of Christ in 1 Thessalonians 4, to bring in the New Creation foretold by Isaiah 64-66, would be an "in history" event in which Jesus (judging as he had seen the Father judge, John 5:19f) would manifest His sovereignty by using one nation to judge another nation. (It would not be a literal, visible, bodily appearing of the Lord.)

The connection between Isaiah and Thessalonians is seldom explored. Yet the goal of 1 Thessalonians 4 will be admitted to be the New Creation foretold by Isaiah. This being true, since Isaiah specifically foretold a Day of the Lord of the same nature as previous Days of the Lord, then this is *prima facie* demonstration that the *parousia* of Christ in Thessalonians was not intended to be understood as a bodily, visible, descent of Jesus out of the sky.

THE RESURRECTION:
THE HOPE OF ISRAEL IN THE DAY OF SALVATION

To establish that the resurrection foretold by the prophets and anticipated by the New Testament writers was to occur in the first century, we want to explore a couple of the key texts predictive of the resurrection and discover how they are used by the New Testament writers.

In 2 Corinthians 3-7, Paul gives a "*midrash*" (i.e. commentary) on Ezekiel 37, one of the pivotal prophecies of the last days resurrection of Israel. Every constituent element foretold by Ezekiel, the Messiah, the New Covenant, the resurrection through the work of the Spirit,[131] the new temple, etc. is found in 2 Corinthians 3-7.[132] Notice that in 2 Corinthians 6:14-16, Paul urges the Corinthian saints to holiness by contrasting the worship of the contrasting "temples." He tells them to be holy because, "you are the temple of God, as it is written." He cites Ezekiel 37:26f.

So, for Paul the Corinthian church was the fulfillment of what was promised in Ezekiel. This is *incredibly* significant. Ezekiel said that Israel's resurrection would be when the Messianic temple was established. Paul said the church was the temple foretold by Ezekiel. This demands that the time of the resurrection was present.

Paul also said, "Israel has not obtained that for which she sought, but the elect has obtained it, and the rest were blinded" (Romans 11:7f). No matter what our concepts of the New Covenant Temple, the "hope of Israel," or the kingdom for which she sought, *or the resurrection* might be, we must come to grips with Paul's declaration that the elect, the righteous remnant of his day, were entering into the fulfillment of what was promised. Now, to be sure, as Wright notes, "One of the central tensions in Paul's thought, giving it again and again its creative edge is the clash between the fact that God always intended what has in fact happened, and the fact that not even the most devout Israelite had dreamed that it would happen like this."[133]

Jesus' declaration of the *nature* of the kingdom was not what was imagined and expected. Likewise, Paul's declaration that the church was what Ezekiel predicted about the restoration of Israel and the Messianic temple was undoubtedly part of "the offense of the Cross." We know for a fact that as Paul taught the kingdom of God, that the Pharisees wanted to kill him for his doctrine of the *resurrection* (Acts 24:13-15). Just as the Jews rejected Jesus' message of the nature of the kingdom, the Pharisees rejected Paul's message of the kingdom and resurrection.

It is obvious that Paul's words, "you are... as it is written," cannot be construed to mean that the church was not what was promised. To add to this, let's examine Isaiah 49 one of the key prophecies of the restoration (the resurrection!) of Israel in the day of salvation.

NOW IS THE ACCEPTABLE TIME, TODAY IS THE DAY OF SALVATION

Note in 2 Corinthians 6:1f: "We then, as workers together with Him also plead with you not to receive the grace of God in vain. For He says: 'In an acceptable time I have heard you, and in the day of salvation I have helped you.' Behold, now is the accepted time; behold, now is the day of salvation."

Paul's words are unequivocal and remarkable. He quotes directly from one of the most emphatic promises of the restoration of Israel, the New Covenant, the restoration of the "earth" (*eretz*, land) the calling of the nations, and says, "Now is the acceptable time, now is the day of salvation."

Isaiah 49 is one of those texts whose eschatology is somewhat ignored. Scholars understand that, "Paul (In 2 Corinthians 6, DKP) is claiming that prophecy has been fulfilled."[134] Likewise, Harris says that Paul, in good *pesher* style, "applies the OT text to the contemporary situation."[135] While scholars see that Paul affirmed the present fulfillment of Isaiah 49, the one thing missing in their comments is the realization that *Isaiah 49 foretold the resurrection*. Thus, for Paul to affirm the contemporary fulfillment of Isaiah 49 was to declare that the time of the resurrection had arrived. Let's take a closer look then at Isaiah 49 and establish that it did predict the resurrection.

> "Indeed He says, 'It is too small a thing that You should be My Servant To raise up the tribes of Jacob, And to restore the preserved ones of Israel; I will also give You as a light to the Gentiles, That You should be My salvation to the ends of the earth.'" Thus says the

LORD, The Redeemer of Israel, their Holy One, To Him whom man despises, To Him whom the nation abhors, To the Servant of rulers: "Kings shall see and arise, Princes also shall worship, Because of the LORD who is faithful, The Holy One of Israel; And He has chosen You." Thus says the LORD: "In an acceptable time I have heard You, And in the day of salvation I have helped You; I will preserve You and give You As a covenant to the people, To restore the earth, To cause them to inherit the desolate heritages; That You may say to the prisoners, 'Go forth,' To those who are in darkness, 'Show yourselves.' "They shall feed along the roads, And their pastures shall be on all desolate heights. They shall neither hunger nor thirst, Neither heat nor sun shall strike them; For He who has mercy on them will lead them, Even by the springs of water He will guide them" (Isaiah 49:6-10).

Isaiah 49 had a profound impact on the New Testament authors. The prophecy speaks eloquently of the Suffering Servant who would restore the tribes of Israel and offer salvation to the Gentiles. He would make– he would *be*!– the New Covenant with the people. In his day, the "acceptable time, the day of salvation," the "earth" (*eretz*, land) would be restored. YHVH would lead His people to living waters and they would never hunger and thirst. Isaiah 49, like Isaiah 65, foretold the creation of a new people (cf. v. 20-21) and this would be in the day when the Lord set up a *standard* (Strong's #05251) for the gathering of His people (v. 22). This standard is the "banner" of Isaiah 11:10-12 which Paul said had been set up. *It was Jesus the Christ*, and the people, including the nations were being gathered to him in the first century (Romans 15:8-12).

Paul's statement in Romans 15 that the nations were being gathered in fulfillment[136] of Isaiah 11 forces us to posit Isaiah 49 and the gathering of the people in the first century. But again, we want to focus on the reality that Isaiah 49 foretold the resurrection.

Let me state my thoughts:

The time of the resurrection of the dead, the resurrection of 1 Thessalonians 4 and 1 Corinthians 15, is the time of the salvation of Israel (Isaiah 25:8-9).

But, the time of the salvation of Israel is "the acceptable time, the day of salvation" (Isaiah 49:6-8).

Therefore, the acceptable time, the day of salvation, is the time of the resurrection of 1 Thessalonians 4 and 1 Corinthians 15.

Now, consider this in light of Paul's words:
The acceptable time, the day of salvation (the salvation of Israel) is the time of the resurrection.

But, Paul said, "Now is the acceptable time, today is the day of salvation" (2 Corinthians 6:1-2).

Therefore, the time of the resurrection (the salvation of Israel) had arrived at the time of Paul's ministry in the first century.[137]

You cannot make Paul's, "Now is the acceptable time, today is the day of salvation," mean that the day of Israel's salvation was *not* present. You cannot make, "Now is the day of salvation" mean, "one of these millennia the day of salvation will finally come."

The only way to discount this is to sever the relationship between Isaiah 25 and Isaiah 49. It would have to be argued that the salvation of Israel in Isaiah 25 is of a different nature, and would occur at a different time from the salvation of Israel foretold in Isaiah 49. But is this tenable? We think not. Let me demonstrate the unity between Isaiah 25 and 49, and then show the unity between both of these passages and the Apocalypse.

Isaiah 25	Isaiah 49
The salvation of Israel (v. 9)	The salvation of Israel (v. 6-8)
The resurrection	
The day of salvation (v. 9)	The day of salvation (v. 8)
It is the resurrection of 1 Corinthians 15 / Revelation 20-22	To be demonstrated momentarily
This resurrection leads to the River of Life (Rev. 22)	The salvation leads to the waters of life (10)

This comparison establishes the parallelism of the two texts. And we have more commentary on the two prophecies in the book of Revelation. John conflates the two chapters from Isaiah in his discussion of the salvation of Israel (the 144,000) in Revelation 7:15-17:

" And I said to him, 'Sir, you know.' So he said to me, 'These are the ones who come out of the great tribulation, and washed their robes and made them white in the blood of the Lamb. Therefore they are before the throne of God, and serve Him day and night in His temple. And He who sits on the throne will dwell among them. They shall neither hunger anymore nor thirst anymore; the sun shall not strike them, nor any heat; for the Lamb who is in the midst of the throne will shepherd them and lead them to living fountains of waters. And God will wipe away every tear from their eyes."

Beale and Carson agree that John is drawing directly from Isaiah 49 (2007, 1108f). John's reliance on Isaiah 49 can be seen clearly in the chart:

Isaiah 49	Revelation 7
Salvation of the 12 Tribes (6f)	Salvation of the 12 Tribes
Followers of the Suffering Servant who Shepherds them (v. 10)	Followers of the *Lamb* who Shepherds them (7:14, 17)
They are inscribed on God's Palm (v. 16)	God's seal is on their forehead (7:3f)
They shall never hunger or thirst (v. 10)	They shall never hunger or thirst (7:16)
They come out of the Tribulation[138]	They come out of the Great Tribulation (7:14)
They are led to living waters (v. 10)	They are led to living waters– The River of Life at the resurrection! (Chapters 20-22)
Restoration of "the earth" (eretz– land, v. 8)	New Heaven and Earth (21:1-3)

In light of these comparisons let me offer the following:

The salvation of the tribes of Israel in Isaiah 49 is the salvation of the 144,000 (the tribes of Israel) in Revelation 7-22.

The salvation of the 144,000 in Revelation would occur at the resurrection resulting in access to the River of Life.

Therefore, since the salvation of the 144,000 occurs at the time of the resurrection– the resurrection of Isaiah 25– this proves that Isaiah 25 and Isaiah 49 are parallel prophecies.

John did not see a disconnect between Isaiah 49, the resurrection promised in Isaiah 25 and his discussion of the salvation of Israel. Isaiah 49 and 25 are the *source* of his hope. In light of this, consider the 144,000 and their salvation a bit more.

The time of Israel's salvation, the salvation of the 144,000, is when she would be led to the living waters (Isaiah 49:10).

The time of Israel's salvation is the resurrection (Isaiah 25:6-9).

Thus, the time when Israel would be led to living waters is the time of Israel's salvation, i.e. the resurrection.

Consider then:
The time when Israel would be led to living waters is the time of *no tears* Revelation (Revelation 7:14).

But the time of no tears is the time of the resurrection (Isaiah 25:6-8).

Thus, the time of living waters is the time of the resurrection.

Consider then:
Isaiah 49 is The Day of Salvation– Israel's Salvation.

The Day of Israel's Salvation is the time of the resurrection– Isaiah 25

The time of the fulfillment of Isaiah 25 and Isaiah 49 is the time of the salvation of the 144,000– Revelation 7, 14.

But, the time of the salvation of the 144,000 would be in the first century. (They are the firstfruit, experiencing the Great Tribulation in the first century, and their reward would be at the end of that time, Revelation 14:2f).

Therefore, the resurrection– the Day of Salvation of Israel– would be in the first century.

Let me bring together now an additional element to demonstrate that the context of the fulfillment of these promises was the end of the Old Covenant era in the AD 70 fall of Jerusalem, by bringing in Isaiah 65 and the New Creation. I will do this as succinctly as possible, without a lot of additional comment.

The time of *no tears* is the time of the resurrection, the time of Israel's salvation (Isaiah 25:6-8).

The time of no tears and Israel's salvation is the time of the New Creation of Isaiah 65:17f.

But, the time of the New Creation of Isaiah 65 is the New Creation of Revelation 21f.

Therefore the time of the resurrection, the time of Israel's salvation is the time of the New Creation of Revelation 21f.

Now consider three facts:
✱ Israel's salvation, the time of no tears, would be when the city of confusion (OT Jerusalem) would be destroyed and the temple turned over to foreigners (Isaiah 25:1-8).
✱ The New Creation, the time of no tears, would be when Old Covenant Israel was destroyed (Isaiah 65:13f).
✱ The New Creation, the time of no tears, would be at the destruction of Babylon, the city where the Lord was slain (Revelation 11:8; 18-22).

Bringing these facts together leads us to this:
The time of no tears in the New Creation, Israel's salvation at the resurrection, would be at the time of the destruction of Old Covenant Jerusalem, i.e. Babylon.

But, the time of the destruction of Babylon was at hand when John wrote (Revelation 14:6f; 18; 21:10-12).

Therefore, the time of no tears in the New Creation, Israel's salvation at the resurrection, was at hand when John wrote.

Several things are apparent from these facts.
☛Revelation is about the consummation of God's promises to Israel. As the promise of the salvation of Israel in fulfillment of Isaiah 25 and 49– not to mention the rest of the Old Covenant prophecies cited– it is wrong to posit the fulfillment of Revelation in any other context.
☛The implications for the dating of Revelation are profound.
☛It is unjustified to extrapolate the fulfillment of Revelation into a distant time.
☛Paul's, "Now is the acceptable time, today is the day of salvation," coupled with the emphatic temporal statements of the nearness of the consummation

must be honored. Jesus declaration, "Behold, I come quickly and my reward is with me," is taken directly from Isaiah 40:10f, and 62:10 and the promise of the marriage of Israel.

☛ The implications for the context and time of *the end of the millennium* are tremendous.

☛ This means that the *parousia* of 1 Thessalonians– the time of the wedding of the King of kings, belongs to the end of the Old Covenant age of Israel.

Early in his ministry Jesus confirmed that the fulfillment of Isaiah's prophecy of Israel's salvation had arrived. In Luke 4:18 Jesus stood up in the synagogue and read from Isaiah 61:1-6:

"The Spirit of the Lord GOD is upon Me, because the LORD has anointed Me to preach good tidings to the poor; He has sent Me to heal the brokenhearted, to proclaim liberty to the captives, and the opening of the prison to those who are bound; to proclaim the acceptable year of the LORD, And the day of vengeance of our God; To comfort all who mourn, to console those who mourn in Zion, to give them beauty for ashes, the oil of joy for mourning, the garment of praise for the spirit of heaviness; That they may be called trees of righteousness, The planting of the LORD, that He may be glorified. And they shall rebuild the old ruins, they shall raise up the former desolations, And they shall repair the ruined cities, The desolations of many generations. Strangers shall stand and feed your flocks, And the sons of the foreigner shall be your plowmen and your vinedressers. But you shall be named the priests of the LORD, they shall call you the servants of our God. You shall eat the riches of the Gentiles, and in their glory you shall boast."

Our millennial friends tell us that because Jesus stopped reading after "the acceptable year of the Lord," this means he was excluding the proclamation of the day of vengeance from his ministry and generation. This claim is false on two accounts.

First, it is a violation of Jewish hermeneutical practice. As Perriman has noted, "generally speaking, when Old Testament quotations or allusions occur in the N T., they should be allowed to bring into focus the wider narrative or argumentative context from which they have been drawn."(*Coming*,125). Likewise, Watts says: "In the absence of chapter and verse divisions, part-citations were apparently used as short hand references to larger contexts. The same could reasonably be expected of allusions."[139] Holland adds that the early church knew the O.T. so well that when NT writers used a key word or two, "the theology of the O.T. passage that the text (or words) was originally in was brought over into the passage in which it was now quoted."[140]

What these writers are saying is profoundly important in light of Jesus' citation of Isaiah 61. Jesus did *not* exclude the proclamation of the day of vengeance when he stopped his reading as he did. He included it! His listeners would automatically have known that the day of vengeance was in Jesus' mind. The millennial claim that Jesus' "short reading" of Isaiah excludes the day of vengeance is a violation of the Jewish hermeneutic.

Second, it is undeniable that Jesus did proclaim the day of vengeance in his ministry. Not only so, he said that all things written concerning that day of vengeance would be fulfilled in his generation! Read Luke 21:20f:

"But when you see Jerusalem surrounded by armies, then know that its desolation is near. Then let those who are in Judea flee to the mountains, let those who are in the midst of her depart, and let not those who are in the country enter her. For these are the days of vengeance, that all things which are written may be fulfilled. But woe to those who are pregnant and to those who are nursing babies in those days! For there will be great distress in the land and wrath upon this people. and they will fall by the edge of the sword, and be led away captive into all nations. And Jerusalem will be trampled by Gentiles until the times of the Gentiles are fulfilled."

Significantly, millennialists admit that Luke 21:20-24 refer to the events leading up to and ending in AD 70. Ice says: "Those first century days are called the 'days of vengeance' for Jerusalem is under the divine judgment of covenantal sanctions recorded in Leviticus 26 and Deuteronomy 28. Luke notes that God's vengeance on His elect nation 'is in order that all things that are written may be fulfilled.' Jesus is telling the nation that God will fulfill all the curses of the Mosaic Covenant because of Israel's disobedience. He will not relent and merely bring to pass a partial fulfillment of His vengeance. Some of the passages that Jesus says will be fulfilled include the following: Leviticus 26:27-33; Deuteronomy 28:49-63; 1 Kings 9:1-9; Jeremiah 6:1-6; 26:1-9; Daniel 9:26; Hosea 8:1-10:15; Micah 3:12; Zechariah 11:6."[141] This is more than a little remarkable, and fatal.

Millennialists say the Mosaic Covenant was removed at the Cross. Yet Ice says the fall of Jerusalem was the fulfillment of the Mosaic Covenant.

Millennialists say God's Old Covenant promises to Israel were suspended and that after Pentecost no Old Covenant promises made to Israel were being fulfilled. Yet Ice says AD 70 was the fulfillment of many Old Testament prophecies concerning Israel.

Millennialists say the day of vengeance of Isaiah 61 was not proclaimed by Jesus. Yet Ice says that AD 70 was the fulfillment of all of the curses of the Mosaic Covenant, not a partial fulfillment. (The day of vengeance of Isaiah is based on the Law of Blessings and Curses).

Jesus did proclaim the day of vengeance and his prophecy was fulfilled.

Of course, the millennialists tell us that while Jesus did say the kingdom was near in the first century, due to Jewish unbelief that promise was withdrawn and the kingdom was postponed. However, the millennial take on Isaiah 61, and Jesus' application of it, presents some daunting obstacles to the millennial view of things.

⊃ Isaiah's prediction of the acceptable time in chapter 61 is parallel to the prediction of the acceptable time of Isaiah 49. Both passages predicted the restoration of Israel, giving liberty to the captives, etc.. There is no disjunction between the two prophecies.

⊃ Jesus affirmed the first century fulfillment of Isaiah (Luke 4:16f). He was thus affirming that the time for the fulfillment of Isaiah 49 was present.

⊃ The millennialists however, claim that Isaiah 49 speaks of the restoration of Israel and that this has been postponed. But if Isaiah 49 and Isaiah 61 are parallel *there was no postponement of the kingdom plan.*

⊃ One of the main tenets of millennialism is that the Old Testament never predicted the establishment of the church. Keep this critical fact in mind in light of the next fact.

⊃ Tim LaHaye and Thomas Ice actually claim that Isaiah 61 *did* foretell the establishment of the church and the church age! This astounding and fatal admission seems to have escaped the notice of many commentators. In their *Charting the End Times*, (P. 28) commenting on Isaiah 61 they say: "The phrase 'proclaim the acceptable year of the Lord' (KJV) refers to the fulfillment of Jesus' prophecy in Matthew 16:18-19 to build his church, which would be victorious over 'the gates of Hades.'" On page 30 of the same work, Ice and Lahaye say of Isaiah 61 and the acceptable year of the Lord: "That's a reference to the church age, often called the age of grace."

So, on the one hand we are told that the Old Testament never predicted the establishment of the church age. The church was an

> **On the one hand the millennialists tell us that the church was not foretold anywhere in the Old Testament. On the other hand, they tell us Isaiah 61 foretold the church! This is an unreconcilable contradiction.**

unknown, unpredicted mystery. On the other hand, Isaiah 61 was a prediction of the church age! This is an unreconcilable contradiction.

If Isaiah 61 foretold the establishment of the church then one of the foundational pillars of millennialism crumbles. If Isaiah 61 is a prediction of the establishment of the Messianic Kingdom, and of course it is, and if it is parallel with Isaiah 49, then we have definitive proof that the kingdom was not postponed.[142] Here is why.

The acceptable time of Isaiah 49 is the acceptable time of Isaiah 61. We not only have Jesus affirming that the time of fulfillment had come, but Paul, writing years after the supposed postponement of the kingdom, says, "Now is the acceptable time!" Luke 4 and 2 Corinthians 6 serve as an inspired bookend commentary on Isaiah 49 and 61. Jesus', "This day is the scripture fulfilled," is directly parallel with Paul's, "Now is the acceptable time." If the millennial view of the postponed kingdom is correct, Paul could not affirm that the time for the anticipated salvation of Israel had arrived. He should have said that the Day of Salvation will come some day when the church is raptured and God resumes His dealings with Israel to give them the blessings of the acceptable day.

Paul's, "Now is the day of salvation" must also be allowed full interpretive influence on his, "We who are alive and remain until the coming of the Lord" (1 Thessalonians 4:15, 17). The resurrection and the salvation of Israel are linked by Paul *to his generation.* There is therefore, no justification for saying that Paul was speaking in some timeless, ambiguous manner when he said, "we who are alive and remain until the parousia."

> **Paul's "Now is the Acceptable time," must be allowed its full interpretative force on his "we who are alive and remain until the coming of the Lord."**

In spite of the congruity and power of the comments above, and the emphatic declarations concerning the chronology of fulfillment, there still is the question of exactly how the promises of the restoration of Israel, the New Covenant, new temple, resurrection from sin-death, etc. was to give great comfort to the *Gentile Christians* at Thessalonica? Aren't those prophecies somewhat dry, abstract, theological doctrines?

The saints at Thessalonica had experienced the loss of their loved ones, probably through persecution. They wanted desperately to know if their dead brethren were going to "miss out" on the blessings of Christ and the kingdom. They weren't concerned about God's promises to Old Covenant Israel, *were they*? So, again, how would the fulfillment of God's promises to Israel give comfort to the *Gentile*, Thessalonian Christians?[143] Furthermore, many might ask, how does the fulfilling of God's Old Covenant promises to Israel give comfort to us *today*? After all, Paul said, "Comfort one another with these words." Just how does that work for us *today*, if Thessalonians is about the fulfillment of God's Old Covenant promises made to Israel?

It all goes back to the Garden and God's promise there (Genesis 3:15) which was reiterated to Abraham, and carried through Israel, to restore man to Him and give him eternal life. As we suggested at the outset of this work, we must see Thessalonians within the context of the restoration of the life lost in the Garden. Contrary to some, among them (seemingly) Wright and others, I am not convinced that YHWH intended for man to live endlessly on planet earth. I am convinced, along with many others, that physical death was not the curse of the Garden, but that loss of spiritual fellowship with all of its implications is the focus of Biblical eschatology.

With the sin of Adam, "heaven and earth" were separated. The barrier between God and man was set in place, and the blood of bulls and goats could never bring man back into the presence of the loving God. As long as the Old Covenant system stood valid there could be no entrance (back) into the presence of God (Hebrews 9:6-10). But, throughout the Old Testament, we find the promise of the coming of the New Creation, a world of righteousness, a world of fellowship restored. And that time of restored fellowship, that time of resurrection life, is invariably posited at the end of the Old Covenant age, when the ministry of death engraven in stones (2 Corinthians 3:6ff) which epitomized and exacerbated the problem of sin and death (Romans 5:21) would be removed.

Paul believed that it was God's eternal purpose to reunite heaven and earth in one body in Christ (Ephesians 1:8-10). And he said that it was God's purpose to do His reuniting work in "the fullness of time." And make no mistake, the apostle believed that Christ had appeared in the appointed "fullness of time." He said that the goal of all previous ages had arrived (1 Corinthians 10:11). Christ appeared at the crucial appointed time. He was "born of a woman, made under the Law," *in the fullness of time* (Galatians 4:4). Likewise, he said that in the fullness of time, i.e. at just the right time, Christ died to bring about the reunification and reconciliation (Romans 5:6f; see also 1 Timothy 2:6).

This is the nature of the "gathering" that Paul has in mind in Thessalonians. It is the re-gathering out of *alienation* which Israel personified and epitomized through her violation of Torah. As we will see in our investigation of *episunagogee*, a geo-centric, physical re-gathering of a specific blood line is not the focus of Biblical eschatology. To refer to Romans 11:7 again, Paul said that the elect remnant was, when he wrote, receiving the hope of Israel: "Israel has not obtained that for which she sought, but the elect has, and the rest were blinded." There can be no doubt that a re-gathering to a geographically defined land had nothing to do with Paul's discussion. Whatever the true, prophetic hope of Israel may be *perceived* to be, we must confess that Paul, who knew that hope better than anyone, said that it was being realized by the remnant in the first century.

Was literal, physical Israel being re-gathered back into the confines of the promised land? Patently not. Were the 12 tribes once again living in harmony under a physical king?[144] No. Yet both Peter and James wrote to the diaspora and spoke of their unity in Christ, *in fulfillment of God's promises to restore Israel* (James 1:1f; 1 Peter 1:1; 2:9f)!

Perriman sees the problem with the traditional paradigm and offers a solid solution, "It would not strain the sense of Jesus' words (In Matthew 24:29f, DKP) to suppose that this gathering of the elect is fulfilled, first, in the establishment of a renewed people of God, a messianic community, embracing Gentiles, circumcised in the heart rather than in the flesh (cf. Romans 2:28-29; 2 Corinthians 3:15-18) who worship in the power of the Holy Spirit on Mount Zion, the 'city of the living God, the heavenly Jerusalem' (Hebrews 12:22)" (*Coming*, 75). But, back to our question about how all of this would comfort the saints in Thessalonica.

Perriman sees that the issue is not a re-gathering to a certain patch of dirt. It is about a spiritual re-gathering into fellowship with God. If you will notice he says that this gathering is concerned with "embracing the Gentiles." The fact is that God had to restore Israel– including the ten northern tribes– before offering salvation to the rest of the nations. Take note of one such passage among many that could be offered.

Acts 15:14f

"Simon has declared how God at the first visited the Gentiles to take out of them a people for His name. And with this the words of the prophets agree, as it is written: After this I will return and will rebuild the tabernacle of David that is fallen down; I will rebuild its ruins and I will set it up: so that the rest of mankind may seek the Lord, Even all the Gentiles who are called by My name."

In Amos 9, YHVH vowed to destroy the ten northern tribes: "The virgin daughter of Israel is fallen, and will never rise again," and yet, a remnant would be saved (Amos 5:1-3). This is the same promise as in Hosea. The Lord said He was going to cause the house of Israel to cease (Hosea 1:5f) and yet, one day betroth a remnant to Him again (1:19; 2:20f). But notice that in Amos, that restoration and salvation of the remnant would be when the Lord raised again the tabernacle of David.[145] And, not only would He restore the ten tribes, He would do *so that all men might call on Him*!

In Acts 15 Peter rehearsed his journey to the house of Cornelius. James then stood up and said that what had happened was in fulfillment of Amos 9:11! But notice again that he says that the tabernacle of David had to be restored, "so that all men might call on the Lord." In other words, until Israel was restored to her God through the Messiah and New Covenant the Gentiles could not receive their salvation. The story of the gospel is invariably, "To the Jew first, then to the Greek" (Romans 1:16-17). This is what Jesus said to the Samaritan woman, "Salvation is of the Jews" (John 4:20f).

So, why would the Thessalonians– hundreds of miles from Jerusalem-- be concerned with the story of Israel and the fulfillment of God's promises to her? It is because fulfillment of God's promises to Israel meant that the saints who had died in Thessalonica were about to receive their eternal reward. It meant that entrance into the "heavenly city and country" longed for by Abraham and the faithful worthies (Hebrews 11) was now open to their loved ones. And, it means that men *today* may call on the name of the Lord regardless of nationality. It means that fellowship with God is not limited to one socio-religious, ethnically centered, geo-centric people. Fellowship in Christ is now through faith and grace, not race. It means that although a man die "he shall live" (postmortem– the concern of the Thessalonians) and if he believes in Christ, "he shall never die" (John 11:25f).

Would not these promises be of comfort to the Thessalonians? Would the assurance that when God had perfected His work with Israel, in faithfulness to Abraham, not mean something *wonderful* and *comforting* to those of faith like Abraham? Should not the realization that God has kept His word, all of it, bring true comfort and assurance to believers today?

It is sad that today the evangelical community is so far removed from understanding the relationship between Gentile salvation and the salvation of Israel that this doctrine is actually rejected as all but heretical. Max King wrote a small book some time ago, entitled *Old Testament Israel, New Testament Salvation*.[146] In this excellent work, King demonstrates in a powerful manner that salvation for the world was dependent on the salvation of Israel. So, in reality it is not a question of how fulfillment of God's Old Covenant promises at Christ's *parousia* would give comfort to the Thessalonians, hundreds of miles removed from Rome, Athens, Corinth, Thessalonica. The real question is, how did the modern church get so far removed from understanding that unless God did keep His promises to Israel, those Gentile saints– nor we– could find comfort in Paul's words!

The *real question then*, is *not* how the Gentile Christians in Thessalonica, Rome, Athens, etc, could find comfort in the fulfillment of God's OT promises to Israel. The *real question is* how did the modern church get so far removed from understanding the relationship between Israel's promises and Gentile salvation?

THOSE WHO HAVE FALLEN ASLEEP *IN* CHRIST, OR THOSE WHO DIED *THROUGH* CHRIST?
1 Thessalonians 4:14

We now come to consider more closely Paul's words, to use the New King James rendering, "those who sleep in Christ" (v. 14). This is a controversial rendering of the Greek text.[147] The normal and correct word to translate "in" is the word "en." But, that is not the word that Paul uses, and it has caused perplexity among the translators, who freely acknowledge this difficulty. As A. T. Robertson notes, the text is, 'literally through, or by means of Jesus."[148]

It should, perhaps, be noted that the term "in Christ" (*en Christos*) was one of Paul's favorite terms. He used that term some 69 times in his epistles. Thus, the fact that Paul did not use his normal *en Christos* term, but rather, used a term that has perplexed the commentators is significant. Paul evidently had a purpose in using "*dia Christos*" and not "*en Christos*."

What might that purpose be? I suggest that what Paul is saying in 1 Thessalonians 4:14 is what he said in 2 Thessalonians 1: the time of Christ's *parousia* would be the time of the rewarding and the vindication of the martyrs. When he spoke of those who had fallen asleep *through Christ*, he was speaking of those who had died due to their faith in Christ.

Persecution is part of the warp and woof of both Thessalonian epistles. Lenski's confident assertion: "These dead Thessalonians were not martyrs, they had died a natural death," can hardly be given credence. Bruce, commenting on the difficulty of the grammar of this verse rejects the idea that Paul has in mind the vindication of the martyrs: "the references in both 1 and 2 Thessalonians to the 'afflictions' endured by the Christians of Thessalonica scarcely give the impression that positive martyrdom was involved."[149] Other commentators note the difficulty of the grammar of verse 14.[150]

The great majority of commentators acknowledge that Christ's coming in 1 Thessalonians 4 is the same as the coming in 2 Thessalonians 1. They expound on the fact that 2 Thessalonians 1 posits the *parousia* of Christ for the purpose of the *vindication of the martyrs.* Yet, they nonetheless, like Bruce, deny that martyrdom is in Paul's mind in 1 Thessalonians 4! We freely admit that Paul is specifically concerned with the post mortem reward of the dead. However, just why this would mean that he was not speaking of that within the context of the vindication of the martyrs is not clear. It is likewise not clear how this concern would exclude Paul's promise to the living, "we who are alive..." from being an implicit promise of vindication. After all, it would be a dangerous hermeneutic indeed to say that because 1 Thessalonians 4 is focused on post mortem reward, and that because 2

Thessalonians 1 is centered on actual relief from persecution, that the two texts cannot be speaking of the same time and same event.

So, when we see 1 Thessalonians 4 within the context of the vindication of the martyrs, as promised by Paul in 2 Thessalonians 1 (and, we might add, in light of 1 Thessalonians 2:14f) this positively establishes the parameters for the fulfillment to the first century.

If in fact, 1 Thessalonians 4 must be seen within the context of the avenging of martyrs then we can directly relate it to not only Matthew 23, but to Luke 18:2-8 as well. Notice the parable of the Importunate Widow.

"There was in a certain city a judge who did not fear God nor regard man. Now there was a widow in that city; and she came to him, saying, 'Get justice for me from my adversary.' And he would not for a while; but afterward he said within himself, 'Though I do not fear God nor regard man, yet because this widow troubles me I will avenge her, lest by her continual coming she weary me.' Then the Lord said, 'Hear what the unjust judge said. And shall God not avenge His own elect who cry out day and night to Him, though He bears long with them? I tell you that He will avenge them speedily. Nevertheless, when the Son of Man comes, will He really find faith on the earth?"

Note that in Luke 17:25f Jesus said that he must suffer– in his "this generation"-- before the establishment of the kingdom that would come without observation. He said the days were coming in which his disciples would long to see the halcyon days of the Son of Man. In other words, times of persecution were coming and his disciples must share in his sufferings to fill up the measure of suffering (Matthew 23:32f). They would long to see the peaceful days when Jesus was still among them. Lamentably, those peaceful days would not be seen. Thus, the Lord told them the parable of the Widow to teach them perseverance and the power of prayer. He also told them that their prayers would not go unheeded. Relief and vengeance (*ekdekeesis*) would come quickly.

I think it will be admitted that the suffering saints in Thessalonica would qualify to be included among those saints who would "cry out day and night" for vindication and relief. Mathison admits that, "While not stated explicitly, the death of the Thessalonian believers may very well have been at the hands of those who were persecuting them." (2009, 511, n. 62). I am convinced this is true. But this establishes a direct connection with 2 Thessalonians 1 and the promise of imminent vindication and relief at Christ's coming.[151]

It is no accident that in 2 Thessalonians 1:8, Paul said the Lord would be revealed from heaven "taking vengeance (*ekdekeesis*) on them that know not God" i.e. the persecutors of the Thessalonians. Paul was promising the

Thessalonian Christians, crying out to the Lord for relief and vindication, that the vindication (*ekdekeesis*) promised by Jesus was coming and that meant it was coming quickly.

We will demonstrate below that Matthew 23:29f is the fountain from which 2 Thessalonians 1 flows. But, Matthew 23 and Luke 18 promised the same thing: judgment on the persecutors, vindication and relief for the suffering saints. Matthew 23:34f promised that judgment and vindication in the judgment of Jerusalem in the first century generation. Luke 18 promised that vindication was coming quickly (*en tachei*). Paul promised living, suffering saints that relief and vindication was coming when, "those who are troubling you," would be given tribulation at the *parousia* of Christ, "taking vengeance on those that know not God."

Let me frame my thoughts like this:

The coming of Christ in 1 Thessalonians 4 is when he would come with those who had died through him, i.e. who had died for their faith. They were martyrs.

The coming of Christ of 1 Thessalonians 4 is the same coming of the Lord as 2 Thessalonians 1, his coming in vindication and relief of the suffering saints.

The coming of the Lord in 2 Thessalonians 1 is the coming of Christ of Luke 18 in response of the suffering saints crying for vindication and relief.

But, the coming of the Lord of Luke 18 was to be quickly ("he will avenge them quickly, Luke 18:8).

Therefore, the coming of the Lord in 1 Thessalonians 4, being the coming of the Lord to avenge the martyrs, was to occur quickly.

Now, again, it is admitted that the translation of "through the Lord" has some grammatical issues. We are not resting our argument on this translation. However, the translation of "those who have fallen asleep *through* Christ," lends itself perfectly to the idea found throughout both of the Thessalonian epistles, and that is that Paul was deeply concerned with the coming of Christ to vindicate the suffering saints, to give them relief from that persecution, and to reward those saints who had already died the martyr's death.

Furthermore, for those like Bruce who seek to delineate between the motif of the vindication of the martyrs and 1 Thessalonians 4, it would have to be proven that 2 Thessalonians 1 (where it is universally admitted that martyr vindication and relief is of paramount concern) is a different *parousia* from that in 1 Thessalonians 4. This is untenable as we will show. There is no temporal disconnect between the Lord's coming in 1 Thessalonians 4 and that predicted in 2 Thessalonians 1. Furthermore, there is no disjunction between Thessalonians and Matthew 23 or Luke 18.

So, what we are saying is that the purpose of Christ's *parousia* in 1 Thessalonians 4 is for the same purpose as his coming in 2 Thessalonians 1. While there are different nuances of emphasis in the two texts this does not mean that different times or events are in focus. Furthermore, as we will develop more in-depth below, the correlation between these two texts and 1 Thessalonians 2:14f firmly establishes the time and framework for the fulfillment of 1 Thessalonians 4.

HEBREWS 11 AND THOSE WHO FELL ASLEEP THROUGH CHRIST

It is fascinating how few commentators see– or at least comment on– the connection between 1 Thessalonians 4 and the great chapter of faith, Hebrews 11. Beale does not list Hebrews 11 in his entire discussion of the Thessalonian text (2003, 129+). Nor does Bruce, Wright, Perriman, Lane,[152] or others. I suggest that these two chapters are inseparably linked.

The Thessalonians were focused on the fate of their personal loved ones. It is important to see the connection with these dead ones and the fate of those in the roll call of faith in Hebrews 11. After all, when Abraham, Isaac, Jacob and the other worthies were given the promise of "the reward" (Hebrews 11:26) they understood that it was far off and not for their day (Hebrews 11:13f; see also 1 Peter 1:10f). They longed to see the time of fulfillment (John 8:56) and Jesus said they saw it and were glad. Jesus said that many prophets and wise men had desired to see the realization of the things they predicted but did not see it. However, his disciples and his generation were witnessing what had been foretold (Matthew 13:17f). All of this language is highly suggestive that the great "cloud of witnesses" in Hebrews 12:1-2– the great ones of faith in chapter 11– were being given the opportunity to witness what was taking place in the crucial last days. In Jesus' ministry and that of the apostles the things once far off were now being fulfilled, for, "all the prophets from Samuel forward, spoke of these days" (Acts 3:21-24).

To help us explore the relationship between Thessalonians and Hebrews 11 notice the comparative chart. The comparisons are impressive.

1 Thessalonians 4	Hebrews 11
Time of reward	The Great Reward / Inheritance promised (v. 11f)
Resurrection hope	They longed for "the better resurrection" (v. 36)
Involved postmortem reward	"The reward"– Not earthly reward– heavenly country
Involved vindication for martyrdom (2 Ths 1-Rev. 6)	Involved vindication for martyrdom (11:32-37)
Involved the living and the dead	Involved the living and the dead- i.e. "they, (the dead) could not be made perfect without us" (11:39)
Thessalonians were suffering *for the cause of Christ*	The worthies endured *"the reproach of Christ"* (v. 26)
They were suffering for the kingdom (2 Thessalonians 1:5)	Saints were suffering for the kingdom that was being delivered (12:26-28)
The reward of the physically dead.	Promise to dead Abraham (et. al.) about to be fulfilled
We who are alive and remain	Saw the fulfillment far off-But it was now near– the reward in a very, very little while (10:35-37)

In Hebrews 11:26, it says Moses endured the "reproaches (*oneidismois*) *of Christ*." The Hebrews likewise were suffering the same "reproaches" (*oneidismois*, 10:33). It may seem strange to the modern reader to think that Moses *suffered for Christ*, since Jesus would not come for a millennium and a half after Moses. Yet, to the Hebrews writer– to the New Testament writers– there was a corporate, organic unity between the suffering of God's people no matter when they suffered. The writer's point in Hebrews is that if they were sharing in those sufferings– just like Moses their esteemed law giver-- and if he endured knowing that the reward was *far off*, then how much more should they endure knowing that the time of the reward was *near* (10:32-37)? The connection with Thessalonians should be clear.

Paul is ever mindful of the suffering on the part of the Thessalonian saints, for they "received the word in much affliction," and were now experiencing the afflictions that Paul said were "appointed" (1 Thessalonians 1:6; 3:3). He, as in Hebrews, urged his readers not to be shaken from their faith due to this persecution.

Interestingly, in 1 Thessalonians 2:14-16 we find a recapitulation of Matthew 23 and Jesus' rehearsal of Israel's internecine history. We find the past martyrdom of the prophets, Jesus, and his apostles and prophets. This is to some great extent a precursor to the lengthy discussion of the history of the martyrs found in Hebrews 11. In Hebrews 11:32f the author recounts the killing of the martyrs. In chapter 12:1-2, he brings up the death of Jesus, and in chapter 10:33f, he had already discussed how their suffering made them partners together with him in his, "reproaches (*oniedismois*) and tribulations (*thlipsis*)."

These connections between Thessalonians and Hebrews help us exegetically to establish the framework and time frame for the fulfillment of Paul's eschatological discourse in Thessalonians.

Note again that Abraham and the worthies saw the fulfillment of YHVH's promises to them as being "far off" i.e. not near. But remember that Peter in Acts 3, as well as in 1 Peter 1:10f, reminds us that while those O.T. worthies were told that fulfillment of God's promises was not for their day, it *was* for Peter's day (Acts 3:21-24; 1 Peter 1:10f). Likewise, Jesus said the prophets and angels longed to see and experience what his first century audience was privileged to see– the fulfillment of the prophet's hope. There can be no doubt that the time of fulfillment was in the first century, in the "fullness of time" (Galatians 4:4) since, "the goal of the previous ages has arrived" (1 Corinthians 10:11, my translation).

If the resurrection of 1 Thessalonians 4 is the "better resurrection" longed for by the ancient worthies in Hebrews 11:36, and surely it is, then the fact that the fulfillment of the Abrahamic promise was near in Hebrews demonstrates *prima facie* that the fulfillment of Thessalonians was near. Let me frame it like this:

The time of the rewarding of the faith of Abraham, Isaac, Jacob, and the ancient worthies of faith through the "better resurrection" is the time of the resurrection of 1 Thessalonians 4:13f.

But, the time of the rewarding of the faith of Abraham, Isaac, Jacob, and the ancient worthies of faith through the "better resurrection" was coming "in a very, very little while," and "without delay" (Hebrews 10:37) the time of the "great reward" (Hebrews 10:35-39).

Therefore, the fulfillment of the resurrection in 1 Thessalonians 4:13f was coming in a "very, very little while," and "without delay."

Since the Hebrews writer tells us that what the faithful were longing for was the heavenly city and country, not a reward to be given to them during their earthly lifetime, then the postmortem nature of their reward is firmly established.

The Abrahamic promise of the heavenly city and country– with all of its implications for postmortem reward– lies behind Paul's thought in Thessalonians. Due to the forced brevity of his stay in Thessalonica he had not been able to fully share with those saints the fullness of teaching concerning these things. Thus, they were uncertain as to the fate of their loved ones who died before those promises were consummated at the *parousia*.

The elements of the Abrahamic promise are the promises of Thessalonians. After all, Abraham looked for the heavenly city and country, and this can scarcely be anything but the New Heaven and Earth, including the New Jerusalem. He likewise looked for the "better resurrection"(Hebrews 11:35) and this is the resurrection promise of Thessalonians. So, when the author of Hebrews assured his audience that, "you have come to Mt. Zion, the city of the living God, the heavenly Jerusalem" (Hebrews 12:21f) he was telling them that the time for the fulfillment of the promises to Abraham had arrived! They were in fact in the process of, "receiving the kingdom that cannot be shaken" (Hebrews 12:28). Needless to say, this forces us to honor Paul's statement, "We who are alive and remain until the *parousia*" as a legitimate, objective statement concerning the imminence of the *parousia*. Here is what we are saying, in simplified form:

Abraham looked for a heavenly city and country, the better resurrection.

The Hebrews writer said that his first century audience had arrived at the time of fulfillment of the promise of the heavenly city promised to Abraham.

Therefore, the time for the fulfillment of the resurrection promise made to Abraham had arrived in the first century.

Let me express it another way:

The better resurrection of Hebrews 11:35 is the time when Abraham, Isaac, Jacob and all the faithful worthies would receive their reward the promise of the heavenly city and country.

The better resurrection of Hebrews 11:35, the time of receiving the reward and the promise made to the ancient worthies of faith, is the time of the resurrection of 1 Thessalonians 4:13f.

But, the writer of Hebrews said that the time for receiving the promise, the reward, was coming in "a very, very little while" (Hebrews 10:35-39).

Therefore, the time for the better resurrection of 1 Thessalonians 4:13f was coming in "a very, very little while."

Undeniably, the city and country at the resurrection, that Abraham longed for is the heavenly city that Hebrews said they had now approached, and were in fact receiving the kingdom represented by those realities.

Clearly, a lot of the focus in Hebrews 11 is on the postmortem aspect of the promise. After all, the author is discussing all of the ancient worthies who died in faith, "not having received the promise." And yet, the author likewise is saying that there was a pre-mortem (is that a word?) historical aspect to those promises, because the living saints were already receiving the eternal kingdom. This is illustrative of the work of Christ to reunite "heaven and earth" as stated in Ephesians 1:10. It shows that in the author's view there is "one family in heaven and earth" (Ephesians 3:14) and that the work of Christ to reunite heaven and earth stood on the cusp of fulfillment. This is not the removal of living saints from the earth, but the promise of the New Creation where man is once again in the presence of a loving God. It is the restoration of the Edenic fellowship.

The correspondence between Thessalonians and Hebrews chapters 10-12 is powerful. Paul is speaking of the rewarding of those "who have fallen asleep through Christ."[153] Hebrews is speaking of all the faithful who through the ages had suffered the reproaches of Christ, longing for the better resurrection. Unless the rewarding of the dead ones of Thessalonians had no relationship with the rewarding of the faithful dead in Hebrews, then the fact that Hebrews posited the time of fulfillment as having arrived, this becomes determinative for our understanding of Thessalonians. The connection between Thessalonians and Hebrews cannot be severed. Furthermore, there are other connections that help us understand Thessalonians.

We will have more to say in this work about the relationship between Matthew 23 and 1 Thessalonians 4. Few commentators make the connections, or if they do they gloss over the significance of the connections, because of their preconceived ideas of how Thessalonians must be fulfilled.

We have just established the parallel between Thessalonians and Hebrews. But, to help us understand the framework and context of the fulfillment of Thessalonians, I want to explore the relationship between Matthew 23, Thessalonians and Hebrews.

Matthew 23	Hebrews 10-11
Jesus discussed the martyrs	Hebrews discusses the martyrs
Discusses the past suffering of the saints	Discusses the past suffering of the saints
Martyrs beginning with *Abel*	Begins his discussion at *Abel* (11:4)
Martyrs including *Zecharias*	Martyrs including *Zecharias*[154]
Martyrs include the prophets	Martyrs include the prophets (11:32f)
Discusses the coming suffering of the saints (23:34f)	Discusses the *present* suffering of the saints (10:33f)
Judgment of persecutors / vindication / reward promised (v. 34-36)	Better resurrection– Abrahamic promise of the heavenly city and country; vindication at the judgment (10:35-39)
Judgment of living and dead (34-36)	Judgment of living and dead
This generation (23:36)	In a very, very little while (10:37)

Just as Jesus spoke of all of the blood shed on the earth all the way back to *Abel*, Hebrews 11 begins with *Abel*. Jesus discussed the martyrdom of the *prophets*. Hebrews 11 likewise focuses on the blood of the *prophets*. Jesus foretold the suffering of his *apostles*. The Hebrew brethren were partners in the suffering of the apostles (Hebrews 10:33f). The direct parallels between Jesus' martyr discourse in Matthew 23 and Hebrews 11 cannot be denied.[155]

It is significant that the author of Hebrews not only lists the very martyrs listed by Jesus i.e. prophets, Jesus, apostles, but he does so in the context of the imminent vindication of those martyrs just as Jesus promised. Jesus said vindication of the martyrs would take place in the judgment of Old Covenant Jerusalem in his generation (Matthew 23:36). The writer of Hebrews said that promised vindication was coming "in a very, very little while." Furthermore, the Hebrew author had already stated that the judgment of the persecutors and the time of the rewarding of the faithful, was coming in fulfillment of Deuteronomy 32 (Hebrews 10:33-37)! More on this later. Suffice it to say that the promise of the vindication of the martyrs was to occur in Israel's last days (Deuteronomy 32:20, 29, 43).

Given all of these parallels, let me make my point in regard to Thessalonians.

The promise of the vindication and rewarding of the martyrs in Hebrews 11 would be fulfilled at the time of the "better resurrection."

But, the vindication and rewarding of the martyrs in Hebrews 11 is the same promise of the vindication of the martyrs in Matthew 23.

The vindication of the martyrs in Matthew 23 was to be fulfilled in Jesus' generation (Matthew 23:36).

Therefore, the "better resurrection" of Hebrews 11:35 was to be fulfilled in Jesus' generation.

Let me make the connection with Thessalonians.

The better resurrection of Hebrews 11:35 is the resurrection of 1 Thessalonians 4 (and 1 Corinthians 15 of course).

The "better resurrection" of Hebrews 11:35 was to be fulfilled in Jesus' generation (Matthew 23/ Hebrews 11).

Therefore, the resurrection of 1 Thessalonians 4 (and of course 1 Corinthians 15) was to be fulfilled in Jesus' generation.

Notice the more specific parallels and argument:

The vindication and rewarding of the martyrs, *all the way back to Abel*, would be at the "better resurrection" of Hebrews 11:35.

But, Jesus said that the vindication of all the martyrs, *all the way back to Abel*, would be in his generation.

Therefore, the "better resurrection" of Hebrews 11:35 would be in Jesus' generation.

This agrees perfectly with the promise of Hebrews 10:37, as already noted, that judgment at Christ's coming was to be "in a very, very little while" (*hosan, hosan micron*) and without delay.

Unless the salvation of the dead saints in Thessalonians has *nothing* to do with the time and context of the salvation of the martyrs in Hebrews, and unless the vindication and rewarding of the saints in Hebrews has *nothing* to do with Jesus' promise in Matthew 23, then we have before us *prima facie* proof that Thessalonians was to be fulfilled in the first century generation.

Modern commentators are inconsistent in regard to Hebrews and the promises to Abraham. Mathison chronicles the promises listed in Hebrews 12:21f and insists: "Under the New Covenant we *have come* to Mt. Zion. We *have come* to the heavenly Jerusalem. We *have come* to the church of the firstborn. We *have come* to Jesus, the mediator of this glorious New Covenant.... That which the Old Testament believers looked for in faith has come, and they have now received what was promised" (*Hope*, 1999, 135-his emphasis). However, in the very next paragraph Mathison affirms, "the fullness of the blessing is yet future, because we await the consummation."

It seems not to have dawned on Mathison– or the contributors to his book, *When Shall These Things Be?*, that if the promises of Hebrews 11-12 have become a reality and the Old Covenant faithful, "have now received what was promised," that this *demands* that *the resurrection has occurred.* How the Old Covenant saints could have already "received what was promised" and yet, are still awaiting what was promised, Mathison does not explain. This is a contradiction of terms. Do the O.T. saints "almost" have what was promised? Have they partially entered into the promised heavenly city and country? Have they received part of the "better resurrection"? To say, "Have received what was promised," is not the same as "we await the consummation."[156]

To say that *they* received what was promised, but that *we haven't* turns Hebrews 11:39f on its head. The writer affirmed: "They without us should not be made perfect." So, if the faithful of Hebrews 11 have received the reward of what was promised, yet modern believers are still awaiting the consummation this demands that either the Old Covenant faithful have not yet in fact received what was promised, or, it means that they have entered their reward "without us."

The resurrection would occur on "Zion" per Isaiah 25:6f?[157] It was this resurrection that the faithful worthies longed for (Hebrews 11:35). Thus, if the faithful Old Covenant saints have indeed received what was promised, and Hebrews says that the first century church had arrived at Zion, then of necessity the resurrection occurred in the first century.

The heavenly city and country promised to Abraham in Hebrews 11:13f is the New Creation promised in 2 Peter 3 and Revelation 21. If then the Abrahamic promise is fulfilled, as Mathison affirms, and Christians today have what was promised to those worthies, then 2 Peter 3 and Revelation 21–not to mention 1 Thessalonians 4-- stand fulfilled.

Does Mathison not know that the heavenly Jerusalem promised to Abraham is the New Jerusalem promised in Isaiah 65 and Revelation 21:1f, and that this heavenly city would only come after *the resurrection*?

You cannot divorce the heavenly city and country promised to Abraham from the better resurrection. After all, in prophecy the resurrection and Zion the promised city, go hand in hand (Isaiah 24:20-25:8). These are inseparable elements of the same promise. So, for Mathison (and other postmillennialists and amillennialists) to affirm the fulfillment of Hebrews 12 is tantamount, logically to an affirmation of the fulfillment of the resurrection.

Consider now the Abrahamic promise in light of Matthew 8:11f:
"And I say to you that many will come from east and west, and sit down with Abraham, Isaac, and Jacob in the kingdom of heaven. But the sons of the kingdom will be cast out into outer darkness. There will be weeping and gnashing of teeth."

In this text the kingdom and the Messianic Banquet is presented as the goal of the Abrahamic promise. Almost all commentators recognize that the concept of Abraham at the Banquet is the story of the *resurrection*. It is the "better resurrection" of Hebrews 11:35. This fits Isaiah 25:6f perfectly, for the time of the Messianic Banquet is posited there as the time when YHWH would destroy death.

Note then the argument:

Abraham would sit at the Messianic Banquet at the time of the resurrection– the resurrection of 1 Thessalonians 4:13f.

The time when Abraham would sit at the Messianic Banquet would be when the sons of the kingdom, "you yourselves"(Luke 13:28f) were cast out.

Therefore, the time of the resurrection– the resurrection of 1 Thessalonians 4:13f– would be when "the sons of the kingdom" were cast out.

Significantly, Gentry posits the fulfillment of Matthew 8 in AD 70 (2009, 234, 342). He emphasizes that the sons of the kingdom were cast out at that time calling it a "dramatic redemptive-historical event." He claims however, without a word of corroborative proof, that, "AD 70 points to the end of history itself" (2009, 342).

What Gentry fails to honor is that the sitting at the table by Abraham and the faithful is in fact the Messianic Banquet of Isaiah 25– one of Paul's sources for his resurrection doctrine in 1 Corinthians 15:55-56! So, if Abraham sitting at the table would occur when the sons of the kingdom were cast out in AD 70, per Gentry, and if Abraham sitting at the table is the time of the resurrection foretold by Paul (given that the Messianic Banquet is the time of the resurrection foretold by Paul) then very clearly, Gentry cannot argue that AD 70 pointed to *anything* else! Just exactly what other resurrection did Abraham anticipate? What other Messianic Banquet did Isaiah predict?[158] The promise of sitting at the Messianic Banquet is the promise of the eschatological end of the age resurrection, not the anticipation of another resurrection at the end of another age! Since Gentry is clearly positing the Messianic Banquet at AD 70– as he does the wedding– this logically demands that the resurrection was in AD 70.

Let me express it like this:

The time when Abraham would sit at the table in the kingdom would be in AD 70 (Gentry).

Abraham sitting at the table is the time of the Messianic Banquet of Isaiah 25:6f.

The Messianic Banquet of Isaiah 25:6f would be established at the time of the resurrection– when death would be destroyed (Isaiah 25:6-8).

Therefore, the time of Abraham sitting at the Messianic Banquet would be at the time when death would be destroyed.

Let me build on that with this:

The time of Abraham sitting at the Messianic Banquet would be when death would be destroyed.

But, the time of Abraham sitting at the Messianic Banquet was in AD 70, when the sons of the kingdom were cast out (Gentry).

Therefore, death was destroyed- the resurrection of Isaiah 25 occurred– in AD 70.

Notice now, that it is for this kingdom– the kingdom (salvation and resurrection) of Matthew 8-- that the Thessalonians were suffering (2 Thessalonians 1:5). This is, as we will show, the promise of Daniel 7 the time when the martyrs would be vindicated at the judgment of the persecuting power (Daniel 7:21f). But when would Abraham, Isaac and Jacob sit down at the Messianic Banquet? Notice again Matthew 8:11: "But the sons of the kingdom will be cast out into outer darkness. There will be weeping and gnashing of teeth." The time when Abraham would sit at the Messianic Banquet– *the time of the resurrection*– would be *when the sons of the kingdom would be cast out!*[159]

We will have much more to say below about the theme of the vindication of the martyrs as it relates to 1 Thessalonians 4. However, I think it can be seen that 1 Thessalonians 4 cannot be severed from that discussion. This means that no matter what our concept of Thessalonians might be we must accept the fact that Jesus, Paul and the entirety of the New Testament posited the vindication and rewarding of the martyrs at the *parousia* of Christ in the first century, at the time of the removal of the Old Covenant world.

Thessalonians is permeated with the pathos of persecution and Paul's concern to comfort his beloved brethren. It is exegetically wrong to divorce Paul's predictions from what is said in the rest of the Biblical corpus about the time and context of the avenging of the suffering of God's elect. As we have seen, the correlation between 1 Thessalonians, Hebrews 11 and Matthew 23 is undeniable. And yet as noted, the commentators are virtually silent about these connections.

This failure on the part of the commentators is lamentable. It is time to honor what these great chapters have to contribute to the story of eschatology. We well understand that the story told by these connections, the implications of accepting these arguments, is a great challenge to modern paradigms. But, that does not mean that our arguments are not sound or that the connections are not valid. And, it does not mean that we should not pursue the trail of Truth no matter how unsettling to our traditional paradigms.

THE LORD HIMSELF SHALL DESCEND FROM HEAVEN
"For the Lord Himself will descend from heaven with a shout, with the voice of an archangel, and with the trumpet of God. And the dead in Christ will rise first" (1 Thessalonians 4:16).

1 Thessalonians 4 is a direct commentary on 2 Thessalonians 1, and *vice versa* in purpose and design. Commentators mostly see these as parallel passages.[160] However, what is missing is the correlation of the texts in regard to *the stated purpose of the parousia*. Perriman is correct to note: "The Lord does not descend arbitrarily or for no particular reason; he descends into the turmoil of history to deal with a situation that actually threatens either the security or the sanctity of his people. If Paul re-uses this prophetic idea, it is because he has in view not a remote end-time state of affairs but an actual (present or impending) situation that requires a similar intervention."[161] It is this distinct purpose of the *parousia* in both Thessalonian epistles that we want to explore.

In 1 Thessalonians 4, Paul is concerned with giving the living Christians comfort and assurance that their loved ones, either Christian relatives or members of the body, will not lose out on their promised salvation because they have died before the *parousia*. So, the focus of 1 Thessalonians is on the assurance of salvation of the dead, *and thus, in the unseen realm*.

As we have noted however, in verse 14, Paul seems to be saying that those who had fallen asleep in Christ were *martyrs*, for they had fallen asleep "through (Greek, *dia*) Christ." It was because of their relationship with Christ that they had died. This comports well with 2 Thessalonians 1.

In 2 Thessalonians 1 however, the focus is slightly different, although the common thread of martyrdom and suffering is very much in the fore. In 2 Thessalonians 1 Paul is not focused on those who have *already* suffered death for Christ. He is concerned with giving the living, suffering saints assurance that they are about to receive *relief* from their tribulation. They stand in need of that Divine intervention into history by YHVH on their behalf, as mentioned by Perriman. Of course, in the New Testament it is Jesus that would come, "in the glory of the Father" (Matthew 16:27) i.e. as the Father had previously come.[162] The Father had now committed all judgment to the Son (John 5:19f) and the Son would engage in judgment in the stead of the Father. Witherington has this to say,

> "It has often been conjectured, probably rightly, that Paul has taken over the 'Day of the Lord' phrase from the Septuagint, and instead of using it to refer to Yahweh he now predicates it of Christ. That such a transfer has been made is clear from comparing 1 Thessalonians 4:14-17 to 5:2. Whether Paul is the first to make this transfer of the *Yom Yahweh* language is uncertain. However, this

usage is perfectly logical in view of the early Christian confession 'Jesus is Lord,' which Paul takes up and uses. It is simply a matter of pursuing the logic of the confession to its end. The Christological importance of this transfer of the titles of Yahweh to Christ should not be minimized as it means that, for Paul, Christ is to be confessed and worshiped as in some sense God. In the use of the *Yom Yahweh* language, however, the focus is on Christ taking over the functions of Yahweh, bringing in the final judgment and redemption that is predicated of Yahweh in the Old Testament."[163]

So, the *Day of YHVH* in the Old Testament becomes the *parousia* of Christ in the New Testament. This alone should inform us that the coming of the Lord in 2 Thessalonians was not to be an end of history event.

In sum then, 1 Thessalonians 4 and 2 Thessalonians 1 can be summarized as this:

1 Thessalonians 4 promised *Reward* and Vindication.
2 Thessalonians 1 promised *Relief* and Vindication.

So, while the specific focus in the two texts is different, one centered on *post mortem salvation* the other on pre-death *relief from persecution*, the common thread running through both is martyrdom and suffering for Christ.

Not only would those who had died the martyrs' death prior to the *parousia* receive their *reward* at the *parousia*, they would likewise receive their desired *vindication*. Consider Thessalonians 4 in the light of Revelation 6:9-11:

"When He opened the fifth seal, I saw under the altar the souls of those who had been slain for the word of God and for the testimony which they held. And they cried with a loud voice, saying, 'How long, O Lord, holy and true, until You judge and avenge our blood on those who dwell on the earth? Then a white robe was given to each of them; and it was said to them that they should rest a little while longer, until both the number of their fellow servants and their brethren, who would be killed as they were, was completed."

Is the suffering and martyrdom of those who had died "through the Lord" (1 Thessalonians 4:14; 2 Thessalonians 1) in Thessalonica to be divorced from the filling up of the measure of suffering (and of sin on the part of their persecutors) in Revelation? Do they have no connection to what Jesus spoke of in Matthew 23? How could we dichotomize Paul's discussion in Thessalonians from the discussion of Matthew 23 in light of 1 Thessalonians 2:14f? What is the justification for delineating between these discussions? How would we exclude the Thessalonians?[164]

In Revelation, the martyrs were told that they must rest only a little while before their vindication at the Day of the Lord, while the number of their brethren who had to die for their faith was fulfilled, i.e. filled up. This agrees perfectly with what Paul said in 1 Thessalonians 2:14-16:

> "For you, brethren, became imitators of the churches of God which are in Judea in Christ Jesus. For you also suffered the same things from your own countrymen, just as they did from the Judeans, who killed both the Lord Jesus and their own prophets, and have persecuted us; and they do not please God and are contrary to all men, forbidding us to speak to the Gentiles that they may be saved, so as always to fill up the measure of their sins; but wrath has come upon them to the uttermost."

This likewise agrees with Jesus' statements in Matthew 23:29f:
> "Woe to you, scribes and Pharisees, hypocrites! Because you build the tombs of the prophets and adorn the monuments of the righteous, and say, 'If we had lived in the days of our fathers, we would not have been partakers with them in the blood of the prophets.' "Therefore you are witnesses against yourselves that you are sons of those who murdered the prophets. Fill up, then, the measure of your fathers' guilt. Serpents, brood of vipers! How can you escape the condemnation of hell? Therefore, indeed, I send you prophets, wise men, and scribes: some of them you will kill and crucify, and some of them you will scourge in your synagogues and persecute from city to city, that on you may come all the righteous blood shed on the earth, from the blood of righteous Abel to the blood of Zechariah, son of Berechiah, whom you murdered between the temple and the altar. Assuredly, I say to you, all these things will come upon this generation."

Jesus said that he was going to send his own prophets and wise men, and apostles (cf. Luke 11:49f) and the Jews were going to persecute them until the measure of suffering and sin was filled up. Paul said the Jews were in the process of filling that number by their persecution of the apostles and prophets, as he wrote. The Thessalonians were partaking in and sharing in that suffering predicted by Jesus. Paul has these themes and promises in mind in his discussion of Christ's *parousia* even in 1 Thessalonians 4. Let me frame my argument like this. (We will see this argument again below).

The coming of Christ in 1 Thessalonians 4:13-18 is the same coming of Christ in 2 Thessalonians 1.

The coming of Christ in 2 Thessalonians 1 is the coming of Christ to vindicate the suffering saints, give them relief from their persecution, and bring judgment on their persecutors.

But, the time of the judgment of the persecutors of the Thessalonians– and thus the relief of the Thessalonians– was near (1 Thessalonians 2:14-16).

Therefore, the coming of Christ in 1 Thessalonians 4:13-18 was near.

To mitigate this argument one would have to prove that Paul is not concerned with the rewarding of the martyrs, the vindication and relief of the living saints or the judgment of the persecutors in 1 Thessalonians 4. One would have to show that 2 Thessalonians 1 is discussing a different persecution, a different persecuting entity, a different church being persecuted and entirely different judgment from what he discusses in 1 Thessalonians 2:14f. I fail to see how this can be established.

If the persecution in 1 Thessalonians 2:14f is the same persecution as in 2 Thessalonians 1 then the connection of 1 Thessalonians 2 and 1 Thessalonians 4 is firmly established. One thing is certain, in both passages (1 Thessalonians 2:14f and 2 Thessalonians 1) Paul is concerned with the then present, contemporary persecution of the Thessalonian church. This amounts to virtual *prima facie* proof that 1 Thessalonians 4 must have some relationship to the AD 70 judgment.

I am suggesting that 1 Thessalonians 4 must be seen in the light of not only the rewarding of the dead saints with their eternal reward of everlasting life (cf. 2 Timothy 4:6-8; Hebrews 9:15f; 11; Revelation 2:10) but the *vindication* of those dead martyrs as promised in Matthew 23, Luke 18; 1 Thessalonians 2:14f, Revelation 6, etc.. As Revelation shows that vindication through the judgment of their oppressors would be played out "on the earth" (Revelation 6:11). This is, after all, what Paul taught in 2 Thessalonians 1:

> "We are bound to thank God always for you, brethren, as it is fitting, because your faith grows exceedingly, and the love of every one of you all abounds toward each other, so that we ourselves boast of you among the churches of God for your patience and faith in all your persecutions and tribulations that you endure, which is manifest evidence of the righteous judgment of God, that you may be counted worthy of the kingdom of God, for which you also suffer; since it is a righteous thing with God to repay with tribulation those who trouble you, and to give you who are troubled rest with us when the Lord Jesus is revealed from heaven with His mighty angels, in flaming fire taking vengeance on those who do not know God, and on those who do not obey the gospel of our Lord Jesus Christ. These shall be punished with everlasting destruction from the presence of the Lord and from the glory of His power, when He comes, in that Day, to be glorified in His saints and to be admired among all those who believe, because our testimony among you was believed."

There is something important here. The martyred saints cried out for vindication. That vindication would be played out "on those on the earth"–not after the earth is destroyed In other words, just as 2 Thessalonians 1 predicted, *the persecutors would become the persecuted*. However, in both Thessalonians and in Revelation, that vindication would be at the *parousia* the Great Day of the wrath of God (Revelation 16:15f). This demonstrates that the Day of the Lord, the "wrath to come" (1 Thessalonians 1:10) that Paul anticipated should be seen as, "a judgment upon the world that opposed the preaching of Christ's lordship and persecuted those who professed his name. The deliverance that would take place at the *parousia* of the Lord then, would also be an event within history: the church would not be finally overcome by the world, nor would it be swept away in the destruction that was to come" (Perriman, *Coming*, 174).

The historical judgment of the persecutors of the early church was the *visible sign* of the Day of the Lord. For the righteous who knew the Lord, believed His word, and knew of the prophecies of that coming vindication, the historical events stood as the vindication of their identity as the children of God. It stood as the *visible* vindication of the word they had been proclaiming for a generation. We see here the fulfilment of Isaiah 26:9-11:

"With my soul I have desired You in the night, yes, by my spirit within me I will seek You early; for when Your judgments are in the earth, the inhabitants of the world will learn righteousness. Let grace be shown to the wicked, yet he will not learn righteousness; In the land of uprightness he will deal unjustly, And will not behold the majesty of the LORD. LORD, when Your hand is lifted up, they will not see. But they will see and be ashamed For their envy of people; Yes, the fire of Your enemies shall devour them."

Isaiah foretold the time of the *resurrection*, when YHVH "comes out of His place," and avenges the blood of the saints (v. 19-21). These are the very elements that Paul foretold in Thessalonians. However, what we see in Isaiah is that this predicted Day of the Lord was not to be an earth-burning, time-ending event.

Isaiah says that when Jehovah would come out of His place to shake the earth and avenge the blood of the martyrs, that the righteous would see it and "learn righteousness." However, although the wicked would see *the same event*, they would, "see but not see" (v. 10-11). They would not see the majesty of the Lord being revealed as they should. They would not see the righteousness of God at work as they should. They would *see events* occurring in their world to be sure. However, they would refuse to *see* that it was God at work. *Do you catch the power of that?*

Isaiah predicted one event. It would be an event witnessed by both believers and unbelievers. When the *believers* saw it they would see that it was YHVH's coming in judgment. In contradistinction, the wicked would see the same event, but they would not "get it." They would not recognize it as the Day of the Lord until it was too late.

If the language of the text is taken literally and Jehovah will literally come out of heaven on a cloud, the earth will split, and physical bodies come out of the ground, how could *anyone*, no matter how unrighteous, and no matter how skeptical, not realize that God was manifesting His glory? Let's face it, I don't care how hardened or skeptical a person might be, if Isaiah's prediction began to unfold in a woodenly literalistic manner, all skepticism would vanish, "in a moment, in the twinkling of an eye"!

Our point is that the Day of the Lord was to be an event that involved historical realities and when it occurred it took *wisdom* to comprehend that He was at work. To see the events themselves one might think that it was just history at work. But for the observant it was the Day of the Lord. This is what Paul predicted in Thessalonians.

Paul said that the tables would be turned at the coming of the Lord. *The persecutors would become the persecuted.*[165] As Wanamaker notes, Paul, "expresses God's decision with regard to those who afflict the Thessalonians and the Thessalonians themselves as those who are afflicted (v. 7)." He says that the Greek words that Paul uses, "state the principle of retribution, the *lex talionis* associated with the day of the Lord in such passages as Isaiah 66:6 where recompense is promised to the enemies of God."[166] Just as Jesus predicted in the Olivet Discourse, his disciples would be persecuted by the Jews (Mark 13:9f). But, their persecutors would become the persecuted (Matthew 23:34f; 24:15f[167]). This is precisely what happened in the Jewish War of AD 66-70.

Paul was writing just 20+ years after the Olivet Discourse. This was of course, prior to the fulfillment of Jesus' prediction that all of the blood shed on the earth would be avenged and judged in his generation in the judgment of Old Covenant Judah.

We know that the persecution of the Thessalonians was instigated, initiated and motivated by the Jewish unbelievers in Thessalonica (Acts 17). This is just as Jesus predicted, that it would be the leaders of Jerusalem who would lead the movement against his disciples.

In light of the above, the question is: what is the basis for divorcing the *parousia* of Christ in 1 Thessalonians 4 and 2 Thessalonians 1 from that historical judgment predicted in Matthew 23, Jesus' promise to avenge the suffering of the martyrs? When Paul wrote to the Thessalonians they were living in the shadow of that coming judgment. Since he tells us that the purpose of Christ's coming in 2 Thessalonians 1 is the same purpose of the judgment of Matthew 23, how do we divorce 2 Thessalonians 1 from that context? *This purpose– the avenging of the blood of the martyrs and judgment of the persecutors-- for Christ's parousia in 1 Thessalonians 4 cannot be ignored.* Once the vindicatory purpose of Christ's *parousia* in 1 Thessalonians 4 is acknowledged to be the time frame and context of that coming is firmly established by Jesus' Temple Discourse in Matthew 23.

WITH THE VOICE OF AN ARCHANGEL
1 THESSALONIANS 4:16

Paul's referent to the accompaniment of the *parousia* with "the voice of an archangel" may on first blush not seem overly important. In fact, many scholars see little significance to Paul's mention of the archangel. Bruce is all but dismissive and simply mentions the Jewish tradition that there were seven archangels.[168] Likewise, Robertson mentions the archangel but makes no attempt to explore the meaning.[169] This is surprisingly common.

I would suggest that like so much else in Thessalonians (and the New Testament prophetic corpus as a whole) this allusion needs to be unpacked. The problem with most modern readings of Biblical texts however, is that a lot of Bible students do not want to go to the trouble of unpacking the Hebraic expressions and thought. In fact, in-depth study of the Old Testament is even discouraged in some circles,[170] if not overtly, then no doubt subtly. Brinsmead has taken note of this problem in modern studies,

"For various reasons we Christians have neglected or discarded the art of preaching Christ out of the Old Testament as the apostles did. Marcion, the great heretic of the second century, wanted to discard the Old Testament entirely. Although the church rejected Marcion, the Marcionian tendency has persisted. The church has not always been comfortable with the Old Testament. Christians often have not known what to do with it. And to the extent that we have neglected the God-given framework of the gospel, we have had to invent frameworks of our own."[171]

Paul did not write in a vacuum and he did not just "make up" the imagery he incorporated in Thessalonians. We dare not invent "frameworks of our own" for our understanding of what Paul says. Paul's terminology, his symbols, his expressions, were "stock in trade" from the Old Testament apocalyptic literature. His references to the Day of the Lord, the gathering of the saints, the coming on the clouds, the coming with fire, the shout and the trumpet are all taken directly from the Old Covenant prophetic language, and in predictions of the last days. This is true of his statement that the archangel would be a participant in the end times resurrection.

Biblical allusions to the archangel or Michael as archangel are few, but eschatologically significant. The term *archangel* itself only appears in Thessalonians 4 and Jude 9. Jude informs us that Michael is indeed the archangel (*michael ho archaggelos,* Michael *the* archangel). *Michael* as chief angel, or chief of the princes or archangel appears a total of five times.[172]

The references in Daniel 10-12 relate to the prophet's vision that extended to the time of the end, the time of the resurrection (Daniel 12:4, 9).

Michael was seen as playing a "behind the scenes" role in the providence of YHVH (10:13, 21). Then, "the great prince" would stand up on the behalf of the people of God, the elect, to deliver them, at the time of the Great Tribulation and resurrection (Daniel 12:1-2). So, in Daniel's vision of the end times we see a period of persecution against the saints, the appearance of Michael the archangel and the resurrection. These are the elements of Thessalonians.

The Thessalonians– the elect people of God (1 Thessalonians 1:4; 2 Thessalonians 2:13)-- were being persecuted. Some had died in that severe tribulation. Yet, Paul– who preached nothing but the hope of Israel as found in the O.T. prophets– promised that at the *parousia* the dead martyrs would be rewarded, the living saints vindicated and given relief from their suffering. All of this at the time of the resurrection when the arch-angel sounded forth. This is no mere coincidence or vague similarity.

It is clear that when Paul alludes to the archangel he is drawing on the O.T. corpus. Biblical references to the archangel are sparse, being limited in the Old Testament to Daniel's prophecy of the end times and resurrection. This is virtually *prima facie* evidence that Paul's allusion to the archangel in Thessalonians is an echo of Daniel.

Daniel 12 is explicit in positing the actions of Michael, the arch-angel, at the time of the end, at the resurrection:

"At that time Michael shall stand up, the great prince who stands watch over the sons of your people; and there shall be a time of trouble, such as never was since there was a nation, even to that time. And at that time your people shall be delivered, every one who is found written in the book. And many of those who sleep in the dust of the earth shall awake, some to everlasting life, some to shame and everlasting contempt. Those who are wise shall shine like the brightness of the firmament, and those who turn many to righteousness like the stars forever and ever. But you, Daniel, shut up the words, and seal the book until the time of the end; many shall run to and fro, and knowledge shall increase. Then I, Daniel, looked; and there stood two others, one on this riverbank and the other on that riverbank. And one said to the man clothed in linen, who was above the waters of the river, 'How long shall the fulfillment of these wonders be?' Then I heard the man clothed in linen, who was above the waters of the river, when he held up his right hand and his left hand to heaven, and swore by Him who lives forever, that it shall be for a time, times, and half a time; *and when the power of the holy people has been completely shattered, all these things shall be finished.'"* (My emphasis)

Daniel tells us that the work of Michael, "one of the chief princes" (Daniel 10:13) "the great prince" (Daniel 12:1) at the time of the end and the resurrection would be, "when the power of the holy people is completely shattered." For ease of understanding and clarity, I would offer the following.

The resurrection and end of the age would be accompanied by the archangel (1 Thessalonians 4:16).

But, the resurrection and end of the age accompanied by the archangel, Michael, was to be, "when the power of the holy people is completely shattered" i.e. at the judgment and destruction of Old Covenant Jerusalem in AD 70.

Therefore, the resurrection and end of the age accompanied by the archangel, was to be, "when the power of the holy people is completely shattered" i.e. at the judgment and destruction of Old Covenant Jerusalem in AD 70.

Unless Paul has a different archangel, a different resurrection, at a different time of the end, from what Daniel was predicting we must keep our interpretation of Thessalonians within the framework and time established by Daniel.

Revelation 12 likewise sets the same context for our understanding of the end times, and Michael's role.

"Then the woman fled into the wilderness, where she has a place prepared by God, that they should feed her there one thousand two hundred and sixty days. And war broke out in heaven: Michael and his angels fought with the dragon; and the dragon and his angels fought, 8 but they did not prevail, nor was a place found for them in heaven any longer. So the great dragon was cast out, that serpent of old, called the Devil and Satan, who deceives the whole world; he was cast to the earth, and his angels were cast out with him. Then I heard a loud voice saying in heaven, 'Now salvation, and strength, and the kingdom of our God, and the power of His Christ have come, for the accuser of our brethren, who accused them before our God day and night, has been cast down. And they overcame him by the blood of the Lamb and by the word of their testimony, and they did not love their lives to the death. Therefore rejoice, O heavens, and you who dwell in them! Woe to the inhabitants of the earth and the sea! For the devil has come down to you, having great wrath, because he knows that he has a short time.'" (Revelation 12:6f)

To help us visualize the similarities, as well as a significant contrast, let me present a chart comparing Daniel's visions (7, 12) with Revelation 12.

Daniel 7, 10-12	Revelation
In the days of the fourth empire (Rome-Daniel 7:7f)	In the days of the fourth empire (Rome- Revelation 13)
Persecuting little horn	The beast that empowered "Babylon" (10:6f; 13; 17-18)
Persecution for time, times, half time (7:21f; 12:6--1260 days)	Persecution for 1260 days (12:6)
Time of the end (12:4)	Time of the end
Michael the prince stands up for the saints (12:1)	Michael the prince fights for the saints (12:7)[173]
Michael's defeat of the enemy results in the kingdom, and resurrection (7:21f; 12:2f)	Michael's defeat of the enemy results in the kingdom, and resurrection (cf. Revelation 11:15f with 12:10)
Fulfillment confined to the days of the fourth empire (Rome)	Fulfillment confined to the days of the fourth empire (Revelation 13, 17, 22:10-12)
Fulfillment consummated, "when the power of the holy people is completely shattered" (12:7)	Fulfillment in the judgment of the city "where the Lord was slain," Babylon, the city guilty of shedding all the blood shed on the earth (Matthew 23:34f; Revelation 18:20-24)
Daniel told to *seal the book*, the time was not near (12:4, 9)	John was told, *"do not seal the book*, for the time is at hand" (22:10)
Fulfillment was *not near* when Daniel wrote (Spanned four kingdoms; long time away, not near, Daniel 10:4, 14; 12:4)	Fulfillment was not a long time away; "these things must shortly come to pass"(22:6, 10-12); "Satan knows that he has but a short time" (12:12)

Patently, John has Daniel in mind. Just as Daniel and John posit the kingdom and resurrection within the context of persecution, vindication and the work of Michael the archangel, Paul discusses the persecution of the saints, the kingdom, vindication and the resurrection. Like Daniel and John, Paul says the archangel attends the end time events.

Daniel confines the fulfillment of his vision to the days of the fourth empire, Rome, and specifically at the time of the resurrection. He says the close of the age would be, "when the power of the holy people is completely shattered."

John likewise, writing during the days of the fourth beast posits the consummative resurrection at the time of the judgment of the city, "where the Lord was slain" (Revelation 11:8, 15f) when the kingdom of YHVH and His Messiah is manifested (11:15f).

Paul, in full agreement says that judgment of the persecutorial power was just at hand– indeed, had already begun[174] (1 Thessalonians 2:14f). The living saints would receive relief at Christ's *parousia*. They were suffering on the behalf of the kingdom. It was through that tribulation that they would enter the kingdom. The archangel would attend the resurrection at the time of the end, just as foretold.

Paul's assurance to the Thessalonians was that these events were not far off. Herein lies the major contrast between Daniel and the New Testament writers. Daniel was emphatically told that fulfillment was far off and not near. Paul on the other hand, promised the Thessalonians relief from their contemporary persecution at the *parousia*. Indeed, his repeated, "we who are alive and remain until the *parousia*," and, "to those who are being troubled, rest, when the Lord Jesus is revealed,"[175] promises, unless one's theological presuppositions interfere, clearly communicated the promise of imminent vindication, imminent relief, imminent reward.

So, in 1 Thessalonians 4:16, in an often overlooked reference to the archangel we find an interpretive key to understanding the passage. The Bible is not vague nor ambiguous about the time and framework for the end time work of the archangel. It was to be in the days of Rome. More specifically, at the judgment of Old Covenant Jerusalem.

WITH THE SOUND OF THE TRUMPET
"For the Lord Himself Shall Descend from Heaven...With the Sound of a *Trump*."
1 Thessalonians 4:16

Virtually all commentators at least *mention* the sounding of the trump in the verse before us. Yet, while some of those commentators acknowledge that Paul is drawing from the Old Testament[176] few indeed seem to see the framework– *and the result*[177]-- established by the Old Covenant for the sounding of the Great Trump. I suggest however, that as in the case of the archangel, an examination of the concept of the sounding of the trump sets the stage for a proper understanding of the time and nature of the *parousia* and gathering of the elect in 1 Thessalonians.

Since Paul constantly reminds us that his eschatological hope is drawn from the Old Covenant hope of Israel we should be able to find the promise of the Day of the Lord, the gathering of the elect, the resurrection and the sounding of the Trumpet in those Old Covenant promises.

Wright acknowledges that Paul's discourse is drawn directly from Israel's prophetic world, and some of the implications of that.

"It is uncontroversial to point out that this (1 Thessalonians 4:13f, DKP) is Paul's reworking of the Jewish 'Day of the Lord' traditions; but it is highly controversial to point out, as I did...that for Paul, 'the Day of the Lord' by no means denoted the end of the world. Just as in Amos or Jeremiah the really appalling thing about the Day of YHWH was that there would be another day after it–had it been the actual end of the world it would have been a shame, but there wouldn't have been anybody around to worry about it after it had happened–so in Paul the Day of the Lord is clearly something which might well happen during the continuing lifetimes of himself and his readers. It is something you might hear about in a letter. ...I have no hesitation in saying that, had Paul been alive in the year we call AD 70, when the convulsions in Rome during the Year of the Four Emperors were quickly followed by the destruction of Jerusalem, he would have said, 'That's it. That's the Day of the Lord" (Wright, *Paul*, P. 141).

Likewise, Perriman is correct when he says that 1 Thessalonians 4:16, "must owe something to the 'great trumpet' of Isaiah 27:12-13, which is blown on the day when the lost sons of Israel are gathered (*sunagagete*) from the nations of the world to 'worship the Lord on the holy mountain at Jerusalem'" (*Coming*, 155). In Isaiah 27:12-13 Jehovah promised:

"And it shall come to pass in that day that the Lord will thresh, from the channel of the River to the Brook of Egypt; and you will be gathered one by one, O you children of Israel. So it shall be in that day that the great trumpet will be blown. They will come, who are about to perish in the land of Assyria, and they who are outcasts in the land of Egypt, and shall worship the Lord in the holy mount of Jerusalem."

Isaiah says the trumpet of God would sound and the outcasts of Israel would be gathered. There are some important facts to be noted here.

First, Isaiah is simply reiterating his earlier promise of the re-gathering of the scattered people of God, i. e. the remnant. This is a prominent concept of the Messianic predictions.

In Isaiah 11 the priestly prophet spoke of the day when the ensign would be raised, Gentiles would be saved and, "It shall come to pass in that day that the Lord shall set his hand again the second time to recover the remnant of his people who are left from Assyria, and Egypt, from Pathros... He will set up a banner for the nations and will assemble the outcasts of Israel, and gather together the dispersed of Judah from the four corners of the earth" (v. 11f). The dispersed would come for, "There will be a highway for the remnant of his people who will be left from Assyria, as it was for Israel in the day that he came up from the land of Egypt" (v. 16).

Second, it is vital to understand that in the imagery of the prophets, those who were scattered abroad were *dead*. They were not physically dead to be sure, but *dead because of separation from God's presence in the holy land!* Israel's sin had *separated* between her and God (Isaiah 59:1-2). When He drove them into the foreign countries they were dead because "life" for Israel only existed in fellowship with God in their land, city and temple. *Death– just as in the Garden-- is separation.*

This is found in a study of the wider context of Isaiah 27, as we explore elsewhere in this study. In chapter 24 God views creation as destroyed because Israel had "transgressed the laws..., broken the everlasting covenant" (v. 5f). In spite of the punishment, there is promise of deliverance; a great banquet will be prepared for the faithful and He will destroy the veil of destruction, "He will swallow up death forever, And the Lord God will wipe away tears from all faces; the rebuke of His people he will take away from all the earth" (25:6-8). If the death is alienation due to covenantal violation, then resurrection is the restoration of that relationship, is it not?

Chapter 26 offered peace to the repentant. It is said His enemies are dead and will not arise, yet of God's *dead* it is said, "Your dead shall live; together with my dead body they shall arise. Awake and sing, you who dwell in the dust" (v. 19). These *dead* are those taken into captivity by the invaders. This is confirmed in chapter 27:7, when he asks, "Has he struck Israel as he struck those who struck him? Or has he (Israel, DKP) been slain according to the slaughter of those who were slain by him?" So, God had "killed" Israel. How had He killed her? The answer is, "By sending her away" (Isaiah 27:8f). Israel, carried into captivity was seen as *dead*. The sounding of the Great Trump was to "raise the dead" from that alienation back into the Presence of YHVH.

This same motif is depicted in Ezekiel's famous vision of the valley of dry bones in chapter 37. The vision is set in the context of Judah's Babylonian captivity. In verse 11, God interprets the vision: "these bones are the whole house of Israel. They indeed say, 'Our bones are dry, our hope is lost, and we ourselves are cut off.'" But God promised: "Behold, O my people, I will open your graves and cause you to come up from your graves, and bring you to the land of Israel" (v. 12). Once again Israel's return from captivity is depicted as the resurrection from the dead because they are being returned to God's fellowship in His land.

This then is the concept of Isaiah 27:13. The Great Trumpet of God was to sound and gather God's elect, in the "grave" of alienation because of the sin of the nation, back to life and fellowship with Jehovah. In the New Testament the sounding of the trumpet of God is also for the raising of the dead from captivity to be gathered to life with God.

This concept of resurrection is somewhat foreign to the Western reader. We have been trained to think of a biological body raised from the ground when we think of resurrection. However, it is being increasingly recognized that this was not the Hebraic view of resurrection, and certainly not the Biblical view of things. Levenson comments on the Hebraic view of resurrection:

> "The sources in the Hebrew Bible, as we have seen, have a definition of death that is broader than ours. That is why they can see exile, for example, as death and repatriation as life, in a sense that seems contrived (to state it negatively) or artful (to put it positively) to us but probably did not seem so to the original authors and audiences. In part, this is because the ancient Israelites, altogether lacking the corporealist penchant of thought so powerful in modernity, did not conceive of death and life as purely and exclusively biological phenomena. These things were, rather, *social* in character, (his emp) and could not, therefore, be disengaged from the historical fate of the subjects of whom they are predicated. Or, to put it differently, death and life in the Hebrew Bible are often best seen as relational events and are for the selfsame reason inseparable from the personal circumstances of those described as living or as dead. To be alive in this frequent biblical sense of the word inevitably entailed more than existing in a certain physical state."[178]

So, when we read of resurrection in the Old Testament prophets Levenson– and many others– are urging that we understand that the Hebrew concept of resurrection was not focused on physical death and the raising of decomposed bodies out of the ground. The concept of resurrection in the Torah dealt with relationship, with covenant, with fellowship.

What we see then is that the sounding of the Great Trump of God signaled the end of exile for Israel and a return to covenantal fellowship. It signaled the gathering of the elect from the four winds. It signified the resurrection. But, there is far more linked with the concept as well.

I want to demonstrate that this theme, the resurrection as the restoration of Israel to covenantal life and fellowship at the sounding of the Trump of God, has profound implications for understanding the resurrection and gathering in Thessalonians. In showing the relationship between the sounding of the Great Trump and the salvation of Israel in the last days, it will be shown that the resurrection at the sounding of the Great Trump would result in a New Covenant world on earth, in time, and could not possibly relate to the end of human history as we know it.[179]

Here is my premise: The sounding of the eschatological Trump of God is inextricably linked with the resurrection of Israel, dead through sin. That restoration is inseparably tied chronologically to other eschatological elements. When we examine the other elements that are tied to the restoration of Israel we will soon realize that the restoration at the sounding of the trump precludes a restored *terra firma*. It precludes a biological resurrection at the end of human history. It precludes any application whatsoever of Thessalonians to a future end of the Christian age.

For brevity let me express it like this:

The Trump of God would sound to raise Israel out of "death," i.e. alienation and separation from God (Isaiah 27:12-13); this is the restoration of Israel.

The time of the restoration of Israel would also be the time of the New Covenant, the inclusion of the Gentiles, the re-marriage of Israel, the establishment of the new temple, etc..

But, the time of the New Covenant, the inclusion of the Gentiles, the re-marriage of Israel, the establishment of the new temple, etc., are all constituent elements of the New Covenant world of Christ in the church, on earth and in time. (They are not elements of a post "end of time" world).

Therefore, the Trump of God to raise Israel out of "death" and to restore Israel, would signal, not the end of the world or time, but the full establishment of the New Covenant world of Jesus the Messiah, in the church on earth, and in time.

Let me flesh this out a bit. The re-gathering (resurrection) of Israel foretold in Isaiah 27:13 is the same gathering of Israel foretold in Isaiah 11:10f at the time of the Second Exodus: "The Lord shall set His hand again the second time to recover the remnant of His people who are left, From Assyria and Egypt, from Pathros and Cush." Isaiah 27 is reiterating the promise of chapter 11. But, it is virtually unanimously agreed that Isaiah 11 is not predictive of the "end of time," but of the establishment of the kingdom of Messiah. Isaiah said this would be done when YHVH erected an ensign for the calling of the nations (v. 10, 12). Paul quotes from Isaiah 11 saying it was being fulfilled in his ministry to the Gentiles to present them as an acceptable sacrifice to God (Romans 15:9f). And remember, Paul preached nothing but the hope of Israel.

Note again that Isaiah said that "at that time," the time of the establishment of the kingdom, the gathering of the dispersed from all the earth, God would set up that ensign. Paul said the nations were being called through his Gentile ministry *in fulfillment of Isaiah*. But remember, the dispersed of Israel and the nations were to be gathered *at the sounding of the Great Trump*.

Paul affirms that Isaiah's promise of the gathering of Israel and the calling of the nations was being fulfilled in his ministry, in his generation. Israel was to be gathered at the sounding of the trump. It therefore follows that the trump cannot in any way be considered a literal, audible Trumpet blast at some imaginary end of time. The gospel call bringing Jew and Gentile together in Christ was the "trump" of God that had been, and was blowing.[180] That trump would also sound to signal the consummation of God's Scheme of Redemption, as Paul says in Thessalonians.

Let me see if I can express it in a simplified manner that will perhaps seem a bit redundant, but I think necessary manner.

✔The sounding of the Great Trump would be for the restoration / re-gathering / resurrection of Israel (Isaiah 27:13).

✔The time of the restoration / re-gathering of Israel is also the time of the wedding (Re-marriage) of God and Israel (Hosea).

✔The time of the restoration / re-gathering of Israel is also the time of the New Covenant between God and Israel (Ezekiel 37; Hosea 2:18).

✔The time of the restoration / re-gathering of Israel is also the time of the New Covenant Temple of God dwelling with His people, among the nations (Ezekiel 37:26f).

✔The time of the restoration / re-gathering of Israel is also the time of the restoration of the earth (Isaiah 49:6-8).

✔ The time of the restoration / re-gathering of Israel is also the time of the New Heaven and Earth (Isaiah 65-66).

✔ The time of the restoration / re-gathering of Israel is also the time of the salvation offer to the nations (Isaiah 49:6-8).

Each of these tenets is linked to the sounding of the Great Trumpet at the resurrection. And yet, the popular view is expressed by Strimple who comments on the "last trump" of 1 Corinthians 15: "Surely the Greek term *eschatos* (last) must here be given its full eschatological force (compare Paul's reference to death as the 'last enemy' in v. 26). This final, eschatological trumpet sounds the passing away of the present order of reality–'the end' *(to telos)* announced in verse 24– and the arrival of 'a new heavens and new earth, the home of righteousness'" (2 Peter 3:13)" (*WSTTB*, 345).

But, take a close look at each of these constituent elements above that are linked to the sounding of the trump. Not one of them describes an "end of time" scenario as posited by Strimple. They each have to do with the restoration of covenantal fellowship in the presence of YHWH. Keep in mind that all of the elements are part and parcel of the theme of the restoration of Israel, *at the sounding of the Great Trump.* Strimple acts as if there is no connection between the sounding of the trump for the resurrection in 1 Corinthians and Thessalonians, and the sounding of the trump for the resurrection in Isaiah. Yet, 1 Corinthians emphatically tells us that the resurrection at the sounding of the Trumpet would be in fulfillment of Isaiah 25f, *where the resurrection would be at the sounding of the Trumpet*!

Let's apply some of what we have seen to the sounding of the Great Trumpet.

Israel's salvation would be at the time of the sounding of the Great Trump (Isaiah 27:13).

But, Paul said the time of Israel's salvation in fulfillment of Isaiah 49:6-8 was present at the time of his ministry in his generation.

Therefore, the sounding of the Great Trumpet must be linked to the time of Paul's ministry and his generation.

Keep in mind that the salvation of Israel was the resurrection of the dead (Isaiah 25:6-10) *at the sounding of the last trump* (1 Corinthians 15:52). This salvation would be at the sounding of the Great Trump (Isaiah 27:13). So, when Paul wrote of Christ's *parousia*, the resurrection and the sounding of the Trumpet of God how do we divorce Thessalonians from the hope of Israel? How do we deny Paul's statements that he and they were living in the promised time of fulfillment?

Notice again the connection between Thessalonians and Corinthians in regard to the resurrection as the hope of Israel and the end of Israel's Old

Covenant age. In Paul's extended discourse on the resurrection in 1 Corinthians 15, he says that the anticipated resurrection would be the fulfillment of Isaiah 25:8f– the time of Israel's salvation (v. 9). He says the resurrection would be "at the last trumpet" (1 Corinthians 15:52). It is no mere coincidence that Isaiah's prediction of the resurrection also foretold the resurrection at the sounding of the Great Trumpet in chapter 27:13. It is all one context, one prediction. And Paul's declaration that the time of Israel's salvation was present is *prima facie* proof that the time of the resurrection was present.

Revelation likewise posits the resurrection at the sounding of *the last trump*, at the time of the judgment of Old Covenant Israel.

Notice Revelation 11:8-17, and the discussion of the two witnesses:

"And their dead bodies will lie in the street of the great city which spiritually is called Sodom and Egypt, where also our Lord was crucified. Then those from the peoples, tribes, tongues, and nations will see their dead bodies three–and–a–half days, and not allow their dead bodies to be put into graves. And those who dwell on the earth will rejoice over them, make merry, and send gifts to one another, because these two prophets tormented those who dwell on the earth. Now after the three–and–a–half days the breath of life from God entered them, and they stood on their feet, and great fear fell on those who saw them. And they heard a loud voice from heaven saying to them, 'Come up here.' And they ascended to heaven in a cloud, and their enemies saw them. In the same hour there was a great earthquake, and a tenth of the city fell. In the earthquake seven thousand people were killed, and the rest were afraid and gave glory to the God of heaven. The second woe is past. Behold, the third woe is coming quickly. Then the seventh angel sounded: And there were loud voices in heaven, saying, 'The kingdoms of this world have become the kingdoms of our Lord and of His Christ, and He shall reign forever and ever!'"

Is this the time of the resurrection? Patently so. Is it the time of the sounding of the last trumpet, i.e. the seventh trump? Undeniably. Is it the time of the rewarding of the dead? There is no question. Is it not also the time of the reception of the kingdom by the suffering saints, just as Daniel 7 foretold? Yes. Is it not also the time of the judgment of the city "where the Lord was slain"? Who could deny that?

The resurrection of Revelation 11 presents a daunting challenge to the postmillennial and futurist paradigms. Gentry posits Revelation 10-11 as fulfilled in the end of the Jewish age in AD 70 (*Dominion*, 1992, 407f). Yet, he fails to discuss the connection with the resurrection and rewarding of the dead in fulfillment of Daniel 12, in Revelation 11:15f! Likewise, Gentry and virtually all postmillennialists, while positing Revelation 11 as a discussion of the end of the Old Covenant age in AD 70, ignore the connection between the last trump and resurrection in 1 Corinthians and the seventh, i.e. last, trump and the resurrection in Revelation. (They also ignore the fact that Daniel 12 emphatically places the resurrection at the time when "the power of the holy people is completely shattered." It is more than remarkable to see how virtually all futurist eschatologies see Daniel 12 as predictive of the "final resurrection" but ignore what Daniel was told about when it would occur).

In a book written to refute Covenant Eschatology, i.e. preterism, three of the contributors to that book cite Daniel 12 as predictive of an end of time resurrection.[181] Mathison, editor of that work, posits Daniel 12 at the end of time (*WSTTB*, 161, also see his latest work[182]). *Yet Mathison posits Revelation 11 as fulfilled in the war of AD 66-70!*[183] There can be little doubt that Revelation 11 is based on Daniel 12. Daniel predicted the time of the end, the resurrection when the prophets would be rewarded (Daniel 12:2-13). Revelation is about the time of the end, the resurrection and the rewarding of the prophets.

It should be noted that there are changes happening in the postmillennial world in regard to Daniel 12. While Gentry has historically applied Daniel 12:2 to the "end of the world"[184] he now says, "Daniel appears to be presenting Israel as a grave site under God's curse; Israel as a corporate body is in the dust (Daniel 12:2; cp. Ge. 3:14, 19). In this he follows Ezekiel's pattern in his vision of the dry bones, which represents Israel's 'death' in the Babylonian dispersion (Ezekiel 37). In Daniel's prophecy many will awaken, as it were, during the great tribulation to suffer the full fury of divine wrath, while others will enjoy God's grace in receiving everlasting life" (*Dominion*, 2009, 538).

So, Gentry now applies Daniel 12 to AD 70. This is, needless to say, a *radical* change from his earlier view, and yet he has given no indication noting that change.[185] This likewise puts him at odds with the huge majority of scholarship, church history and the creeds. One can but wonder if the on-going controversy with what Gentry disparagingly calls "hyper-preterism" has spawned Gentry's "conversion." He now takes the preterist view of Daniel 12, while condemning preterists for their views. I suppose one could also wonder if Mathison will now castigate Gentry for his non-creedal view.

In Revelation 11 we have the resurrection and rewarding of the prophets at the sound of the seventh, i.e. *the last trump*. Leading postmillennialists posit Revelation 11 as fulfilled in AD 70. Yet, Revelation 11 anticipated precisely what 1 Corinthians 15 predicted. This is, needless to say, a major problem. Let me express it simply:

The resurrection of 1 Thessalonians 4:13f at the sounding of the Trump of God is the resurrection of 1 Corinthians 15 at the sounding of the Trump of God.

The resurrection of 1 Corinthians 15 is at the sounding of the *Last Trump* (1 Corinthians 15:52).

The resurrection of Revelation 11:15-17 is at the sounding of the Seventh, i.e. *the Last Trump*.

But, the sounding of the Seventh, Last Trump of Revelation 11 occurs at the time of the judgment of the city, "Where the Lord was slain" (Revelation 11:8f).

Therefore, the resurrection of 1 Thessalonians 4:13f occurs at the time of the judgment of the city, "Where the Lord was slain."

The correlation between Thessalonians, Corinthians and Revelation in regard to the resurrection and the sounding of the trump is undeniable.

As a not insignificant point, one can but wonder about the consistency of the modern paradigms in regard to the trumpet of God.

The postmillennial and amillennial view is that 1 Corinthians 15 and Thessalonians are "end of time" predictions. The final trump is a literal blast of the heavenly trump. Hendrickson says the trumpet blast promised in Thessalonians must be literal and audible, "a reverberating sound will actually pervade the universe."[186] If so, then do we not have the right to ask when *the previous six trumpets will sound*? Will the blast of the previous trumpets also be a literal blast of the heavenly musical instrument? If not, then how can it be insisted that the *last trump* will be the blowing of a literal heavenly musical instrument?

Most postmillennialists and amillennialists say that there are no signs of Christ's end of time coming at the resurrection. Yet, if the resurrection is at the last trumpet as

> **If the sounding of "the last trumpet" at the resurrection is a literal, audible sounding of a heavenly trumpet, then that means that *there must be six literal, audible trumpets of God sounded before the end of time!* I am unaware of anyone that teaches this.**

Corinthians says, and if the last trumpet is the trumpet blown at the resurrection of Revelation 11 then a couple of things are virtually undeniable.

First, as just seen, it means that prior to the end of time the previous six trumpets have to be sounded, literally, audibly.

Second, it means that there would positively be signs of the end for if six audible heavenly trumpets sound before the end, then those previous six trumpets would be undeniable signs of the end.

This may seem to some a trivial question, but it is not insignificant. This question raises a serious hermeneutical question. If the sounding of the trumpet in Corinthians and Thessalonians is to be understood as a literal blast of a heavenly trumpet, this demands that previous to that climactic trumpet there should be the sounding of *six other literal trumpets!* Yet, I am unaware of any amillennialists or postmillennialists who believe this.

It is interesting that some commentators seem to realize that a literal interpretation of the trumpet presents a daunting challenge for the interpretation of Thessalonians. Beale hesitates to take a woodenly literal view of Thessalonians, all the while insisting nonetheless on a, well, literal fulfillment. He says, "The resurrection of the dead (1 Thessalonians 4:16) should not be conceived as a physical rising upward from the grave, but a transformation of an old-worldly body into a new creational body that can inhabit the dimension of the new world in Christ's and God's presence" (2003, 139f). He then goes on to say, "The figurative nature of the language is also pointed to by reference to the trumpet call of God (1 Thessalonians 4:16) which is like the blowing of the trumpets in Revelation...Revelation's vision that are certainly figurative. Paul's reference to the trumpet, points further to a figurative understanding, since the trumpet sound at Sinai did not emanate from a literal trumpet" (2003, 140). So, we are to expect a literal end to human history, a literal resurrection, at a literal coming of the Lord,[187] and yet, it is not actually a physical rising upward from the grave, at the sounding of a literal trumpet. It truly makes one wonder how one can demand a literal fulfillment of Thessalonians when the spiritual nature of the event is being emphasized after all.

All of this gives insight into the spiritual nature of the fulfillment of Corinthians, Thessalonians and all eschatological prophecies. It shows that the commentators recognize the danger of literalization and yet their personal theologies demand some sort of literal fulfillment. This challenges all prevailing eschatologies. While our Grecian, literalistic concept of the resurrection at the sounding of the trump is challenged by Paul's declarations concerning the salvation of Israel, we must come to terms with *his* interpretation of both the time and the nature of the prophetic scriptures.

So, our investigation of the trumpet of God in 1 Thessalonians leads us inexorably to the end of the Old Covenant age in AD 70, and the judgment of Old Covenant Israel. We cannot divorce the sounding of the trumpet in Thessalonians from its prophetic fountain, and the hope of Israel. Nor can we divorce it from the rest of the New Testament testimony, especially Matthew 24 and Revelation which in clear terms restrict the sounding of the trump to the first century judgment of Jerusalem and the old age.

WE SHALL *MEET* HIM IN THE AIR
An Examination of *Apantesis*
1 Thessalonians 4:17

We come now to consider what is to me a critical aspect of our study. The implications of this study are profound. In fact, if what I am suggesting is correct, *all futurist eschatologies are falsified*. What I will present is in fact a theological atomic bomb and some representatives of the various eschatologies are aware of this. The millennialists are fully, acutely aware of the potential problem as we will see. They seek, sometimes desperately, to defuse this issue. I think unsuccessfully. What is the issue? What is the potential theological atomic bomb in Thessalonian text?

Paul uses a word that, *when taken in its normal technical sense* as used and understood in the first century world, negates the idea of a removal of Christians from the earth. It negates the idea of an end of time. Here is why. The terms *parousia* and *apantesis* as technical terms, were used in the ancient world to speak of a king or royal dignitary that was making a visit to a given city. As he approached that city for his visit (his *parousia*) the citizens of that city, being watchful for him, would, when his entourage was sighted, leave their city and go out to "meet" (*apantesis*) him. *They would then escort him back to their city*. The city was the destination of the dignitary. It was the location of his *parousia*. He was not coming to *remove* the citizens of the city. *He was coming to visit them.*

These two words, *parousia* and *apantesis*, are often companion words in the *koine* (common) Greek language of Paul's world. The ancient reader of these two terms when used together would immediately have a mental picture of events, but those events are not what the modern reader sees in the text.

Needless to say, if *parousia* and *apantesis* are being used in Thessalonians in their technical sense then Paul was not predicting the coming of Christ to take the church off of the earth. Rather, he was coming to be with his saints. This would mean that Thessalonians was predictive of the re-establishment of fellowship between heaven and earth (Ephesians 1:10). "Eden" would be restored. It would mean that, "The tabernacle of God is with men!" (Revelation 21:3).

Our purpose therefore, in this section is to explore what Paul meant when he said "we shall *meet* him in the air." Did he envision the rising of human bodies into the atmosphere to literally, bodily meet Christ in the clouds? Or, was Paul using typical, well understood terminology that in its historical context meant no such thing?

The real question, the *crux interpretum*, is, did Paul intend for his readers, and us, to understand *apantesis* (meet) in its formal, technical definition, or was he using this word in a mundane, non-technical sense? One thing is virtually certain in the literature, and that is that *parousia* and *apantesis*, when *used together*, have a technical significance. So, if these companion words could and did have such a technical usage, the only question then is upon what basis do we reject that meaning in Thessalonians.

We suggest that the evidence is strongly in favor of understanding 1 Thessalonians 4 in the technical sense. If this claim is substantiated, needless to say, the traditional eschatologies that see in Thessalonians a prediction of the removal of the church from the earth, whether in an unseen rapture in AD 70, or at any time in the future, are misguided.

Keep in mind that while we will focus on *apantesis*, we are arguing that *when coupled with parousia*, in the context of *a royal visit*, that the technical sense is virtually demanded.[188] In addition, we will see that even in instances when *parousia* is not present *apantesis* can be used in the technical sense. We will present our case here under four headings:

Apantesis in the Lexicons and Grammars
Apantesis In the Commentators
Apantesis in the New Testament
Apantesis in Josephus

We turn first of all to consider the lexical evidence.

THE LEXICONS AND *APANTESIS*

◆ Balz and Schneider, in the *Exegetical Dictionary of the New Testament*, acknowledges that *apantesis* had a technical usage, but says that whether this technical definition should be applied to Thessalonians should be, "left to the exegesis of the respective contexts."[189] They seem to understand the landmine lying in the road if one applies the technical meaning for they speak of the, "far reaching deductions regarding the *parousia* of the *kurios* to the miniature apocalypse of 1 Thessalonians 4:16 ('caught up...in the clouds to *meet* the Lord'; —> *harpazo*) or the delayed coming of the *numphios* (groom, DKP) of Matthew 25:1-13." To say that the technical application of *apantesis* has far reaching implications is a profound understatement!

◆ Bauer's Arndt and Gingrich likewise gives only a brief definition, with several non-Biblical references, among them a technical referent to bringing in the goddess of the Romans to her resting place.[190]

◆ Bullinger's Critical Lexicon says of *apantesis*, "To come or go from a place towards a person, and so to meet face to face from opposite directions; especially to meet and come back with the person met."[191] You will note that Bullinger precedes Peterson, whom we will note below. Peterson is often cited as the originator of the idea of the technical sense of *apantesis*, but Bullinger clearly preceded him.

◆ Kittel's (TDNT) says of *apantesis* (ἀπάντησις) "The word is to be understood as a technical term for a civic custom of antiquity whereby a public welcome was accorded by a city to important visitors."[192] Unfortunately, Kittel's does not develop this, nor offer much other information. However, it is significant that they recognize the technical meaning of the word.

◆ Liddell and Scott, give only the briefest of definitions, "to come, or to go to meet, to encounter, whether as friend or foe."[193]

◆ Louw and Nida give this, "to come near and to meet, either in a friendly or hostile manner."[194]

◆ Moulton and Milligan says, "The word seems to have been a kind of technical term for the official visit of a newly arrived dignitary."[195] They add, "This connotation points toward our rising to meet Christ in order to escort Him immediately back to earth."

◆ Thayer gives an abbreviated definition of *apantesis*, with virtually no comment: "a meeting."[196]

◆ Vine says of *apantesis*, "It is used in the papyri of a newly arriving magistrate. It seems that the special idea of the word was the official welcome of a newly arrived dignitary" (He cites Moulton's, *Greek Testament Grammar,* Vol. 1, p. 14, as a source).[197] In other words, Vines sees *apantesis* in a technical sense.

From the above, it seems that some lexicons are almost reticent about offering much information on *apantesis*. Some comment on the background and context of the word, others offer no comment on its history and social usage. Those lexicons that do offer comment on the historical use emphasize the technical definition. Others emphasize that only the context of a given usage can determine whether *apantesis* is being used in its technical sense. We agree with this, and are convinced that Thessalonians demands the technical understanding of *apantesis*. Let's turn now to examine what the commentators say.

THE COMMENTATORS AND *APANTESIS*

Before examining the commentators, perhaps it would be good to be reminded of what Cosby says, "Increasingly, biblical scholars are articulating the decisive role played by their own presuppositions in exegesis. Instead of appealing to the long discredited myth of objectivity still prevalent in some circles, scholars are expressing their personal agendas that lead to particular understandings."[198] Without doubt, the personal theological "bent" of commentators influences how they interpret the scriptures. We are all human beings, and very much want the scriptures to support what we believe.[199] This is not dishonest, it is humanity!

I make no claims to being totally free of presuppositions or prejudices. However, I am not interested in what I have been taught. My personal journey has caused me to jettison many of the theological beliefs handed to me by my forefathers. In other words, I did not come to the Thessalonian text with a predisposition that *apantesis* means to meet and bring in. I was raised believing and teaching that Paul was describing in literal terms the removal of the church from the earth. I was, in fact, *stunned* to see the definition of *apantesis* in the literature and embarked on an extensive investigation into its usage before taking a position on it.

Peterson, in 1930, is sometimes credited with being the first to emphasize the technical use of *apantesis*. He argued that Paul was indeed using *apantesis* in its technical sense and that this meant that Paul was presenting the idea that, "at the coming of the Lord from heaven, the faithful go up to bring him into their earthly city."[200] Clearly, Peterson was not the first however, for Bullinger's Lexicon, (1908) presented that view much earlier than Peterson.

Plevnik notes that Peterson's view was "enthusiastically received" for a good while and actually held sway in the scholarly world for a good while before losing favor. He says that Peterson's view is not now the accepted norm and presents some of the reasons why. Cosby however, says that the technical sense is, "the dominant scholarly understanding of *apantesis*" (1994, 28). Both Plevnik and Cosby wrote articles rejecting the technical definition of *apantesis* in Thessalonians. We will address Cosby's article below, as well as another recent attempt to reject the technical definition.

In its normal use in the first century, as noted by Wanamaker, "The expression *eis apantesin* was a technical expression in Hellenistic Greek for the departure from a city of a delegation of citizens to meet an arriving dignitary in order to accord the person proper respect and honor by escorting the dignitary back to the city. Whether this technical application should be taken in a literal sense in v. 17 to suggest that the Lord and those with him return to earth, as Marshall (131) conjectures. seems unlikely."[201]

Do you notice what Wanamaker says? The *normal* technical meaning of *apantesis* was that a delegation from the *destination* of the visiting dignitary, went out to meet him and then *escorted him onto his destination*. The ones greeting the dignitary belonged to the destination city. Wanamaker does not tell us *why* it is unlikely that *apantesis* is not being used with its normal technical meaning in Thessalonians. However, what is apparent is that the reason for taking that view is his theological paradigm which posits the *parousia* of Christ for the removal of the church from the earth at the end of time. Since *apantesis* in its technical sense violates that presupposition then as Cosby noted above, the presuppositions of the commentator take precedence.

Frame takes note of Moulton who says that *apantesis* is, "the official welcome of a newly arrived dignitary," but suggests that the idea is of Christians leaving earth, meeting Christ in the air, and then proceeding on to heaven.[202] He emphasizes the meeting in the air, in a literal sense, and ignores the fact that Paul could be using air (*aer*) to refer to the spiritual realm, per Ephesians 2 and 6.

Simply stated, if we apply the normal technical definition of *apantesis* to 1 Thessalonians 4:17, it means that the believers were to be caught up (*harpazo*) to meet Christ, "in the air," and then *escort him back to earth to dwell with him forever.* Earth is the destination! This agrees with Revelation 21:3, 10, and the New Jerusalem, "descending out of heaven from God," and God dwelling with man, "The tabernacle of God is with men."

Eadie states the case clearly, "The Lord is descending to the earth, they are caught up on His progress to meet Him, and thus God 'brings them with Him' (v. 14)."[203] Likewise Bruce, although he hesitates to apply the technical use of the word consistently, nonetheless says, "When a dignitary paid an official visit (*parousia*) to a city in Hellenistic times, the action of the leading citizens of going out to meet him and escort him back on the final stage of his journey was called the *apantesis.*"[204] Wright says the language of 1 Thessalonians 4,

"Evokes the scene, familiar from much Hellenistic and Roman writing, of a king or emperor paying a state visit to a city or province. As he approaches, the citizens come out to meet him at some distance from the city, not in order then to hold a meeting out in the countryside, but to escort him into the city. 'Meeting the Lord in the air' is not a way of saying 'in order then to stay safely away from the wicked world'. It is the prelude to the implied triumphant return to earth where the Messiah will reign, and his people with him, Lord, Savior and judge. And in that context parousia means what it means in imperial rhetoric: the royal presence of the true Lord, or emperor" (*Paul*, 55+).

The point of course is that if we allow *apantesis* to have its normal technical definition in 1 Thessalonians 4:17, the passage teaches precisely the *opposite* of most futurist paradigms. As Waldron notes, "Pretribulationalists assume that statement (meet the Lord in the air, DKP) implies that after this meeting, Christ and the church return together to heaven. Actually this is neither stated, nor implied. In fact, the word in the original (*apantesis*) implies exactly the opposite."[205]

Perriman says *apantesis:*

"is characteristically used with reference to what happens when people go out from a town or city to meet someone who is approaching. Luke describes how believers in Rome came out of the city as far as the Forum of Appius and Three Taverns to meet (eis *apantesin*) Paul's party (Acts 28:15). ...The parousia of Christ in the Roman world, then, was Christ coming to play part in people's lives that the emperor and imperial cult would otherwise have played: the parousia of the Son of man supersedes the parousia of the man of lawlessness. The language is a direct challenge to the prevailing theology– it both mimics and subverts– and if we disconnect the prophecy from its political context, we render it vacuous" (*Coming*, 163).

Perriman then goes on to connect the *apantesis* with *harpazo* (translated as "caught up") and suggests that the idea is, "the idea of deliverance or salvation from the affliction they were experiencing" (*Coming*, 164) and sees a direct connection with 2 Thessalonians 1. We do not reject this,[206] but we would add that the *harpazo* that Paul has in mind is in direct connection also with the gathering together into the entourage of the Bridegroom, the King of kings.[207] And this brings us back to the consideration of the link between Thessalonians and the Olivet Discourse, and the connection between *apantesis, harpazo*, and *episunagogee*. See that discussion.

We could of course, multiply the quotes from the commentators many times over. This brief survey reveals a couple of things, however.

☛ Virtually all scholars admit that *apantesis* did have a technical usage in the first century, when used in stories of the visit of royalty.

☛ Virtually no scholar attempts to reject the technical sense of *apantesis* in Thessalonians on linguistic grounds. This is important.

☛ Virtually all scholars who seek to reject the technical usage of *apantesis* in Thessalonians do so on presuppositional *theological grounds*. In other words, they believe that the purpose of Christ's *parousia* is to remove the church from the earth, and to put an end to human history. But, to allow *apantesis* its technical meaning falsifies that theology, therefore, the technical definition is rejected. This is patently a misguided hermeneutic. Theology should not define words. Context, not presuppositional dogma should be our guide, not the traditions of creeds or churches.

APANTESIS IN THE NEW TESTAMENT

The question is, does Paul use *apantesis* in its normal, technical sense in 1 Thessalonians 4:17.[208] To help us answer this we must ask how, or if, Jesus used the word, and in what contexts, in order to see how Paul may have intended the word to be understood. We must not lose sight of the fact that

Paul said that his eschatology was received from and was a reminder of the words of Jesus, and was the Old Covenant Hope of Israel. So, if Jesus used *apantesis* that should give us insight into how Paul intended us to understand what he meant.

Apantesis is used by Jesus and in an eschatological text that has a direct relationship to 1 Thessalonians 4. In Matthew 25:1-13, we find the story of the virgins and their wait for the bridegroom. The wise virgins went out to *meet* (*apantesis*) the bridegroom. History and tradition tell us that the bridegroom was on his way to the father's house,[209] and the virgins would have met him and escorted him the rest of the way to his destination.

On the other hand, Noland (*NIGTC*, Matthew, 1004) says, "We have little knowledge of the specifics of wedding customs among first century Jews, and we do not know how fixed the various customs were. The present story, however, seems to work best if we imagine the bride is already at the bridegroom's destination and as sending out her maidens to welcome him in." Whether one sees that the bride was already at the Father's house, or at another destination is not, as Noland observes, clearly stated or understood. The point is, in the parable, there was no meeting him and then turning around and going back to where he had been.

The wedding must be placed within the context of the judgment of Old Covenant Judah in AD 70. The wedding promise of scripture belonged to Israel (Hosea 1-2) for her last days. This critical fact is often overlooked by exegetes, but is normative for our understanding of the wedding motif in the N.T..

When we bring our understanding of the promise of the Wedding– i.e. 1 Thessalonians 4-- in line with Hosea's promise of the "return" of YHVH, it helps clarify our understanding of Paul's promise. In Hosea, YHVH divorced the ten northern tribes for her adulterous ways. But, as we have seen, He promised to remarry her in the last days. *That remarriage is also cast in the terms of the resurrection.* And we must never lose sight of the fact that this resurrection foretold by Hosea is the basis of Paul's resurrection doctrine in 1 Corinthians and Thessalonians.

Take note that in Hosea, this marriage and resurrection theme is also posited in the context of *the return of YHVH*. In Hosea 5-6 we find the slaying of Israel, the desertion of Israel (i.e. YHWH *leaves*) the resurrection of Israel, and *the return of YHVH*.

"For I will be like a lion to Ephraim, and like a young lion to the house of Judah. I, even I, will tear them (Israel dies, DKP) and go away; I will take them away, and no one shall rescue. I will return again to My place (The departure of YHVH, DKP) till they acknowledge their offense. Then they will seek My face; In their affliction they will earnestly seek Me. 'Come, and let us return to the LORD; for He has torn, but He will heal us; He has stricken, but He will bind us up. After two days He will revive us; on the third day He will raise us up (The resurrection, DKP) that we may live in His sight. 3 Let us know, let us pursue the knowledge of the LORD. His going forth is established as the morning; He will come to us like the rain, like the latter and former rain to the earth" (The "return" of YHVH, DKP) (Hosea 5:14-6:1-3).

What should be clear from this paradigmatic text is that the absence of YHVH, His departure, was *the loss of covenantal fellowship*. Likewise, the "return of YHVH" at the time of the resurrection, as depicted in Hosea, was *the restoration of fellowship*. The text and the promise have nothing to do with a "physical" absence, or of a literal bodily return of some sort. It refers to YHVH's *covenantal presence*– i.e. of dwelling before His face. (In the Greek Old Testament, the LXX, the word that most often speaks of dwelling in the *presence* of the Lord is *prosopon*, which literally means "face").

I am suggesting in regard to Matthew 25:1-13, and thus 1 Thessalonians 4:13f, that since these texts deal with the theme of the wedding, that they echo and comment on the promise of Hosea. The wedding was, as we have established earlier, the hope of Israel. So, in the parable of the wedding, with its use of *apantesis*, we find the story of the *YHVH's return to covenantal fellowship*, not the story of the removal of man from the earth. YHVH was returning to His people! Where had He dwelt with man? It was not in some place removed from the time-space continuum. YHVH had dwelt with man on earth, in time. And His promise was to return and restore that fellowship at the time of the resurrection and marriage.

This theme of the return of YHVH is continued in Matthew 25:14f, the story of the absent Master and his return to judge the servants to whom he had entrusted the Talents. Notice that the master does not remove even the wise servants from their abodes. He blesses them where they are, and where he had left them. He was "simply" returning to his home, his dwelling place, and judging those servants to whom he had entrusted his "kingdom." What is lamentably missing in many commentaries is a cognizance that Jesus' promise here is related to the Old Covenant promises of the return of YHVH to His people, as promised in Hosea. Wright is one of the few who develop this significant theme.

"I propose that this parable (Matthew 25:14f, DKP) should be seen as a key explanatory riddle for Jesus' own action. He saw his journey to Jerusalem as the symbol and embodiment of YHWH's return to Zion. ...so YHWH was returning to his people, his city and his temple. But, who would abide the day of his coming?" (*Victory*, 639– See page 640 also)

Over and over in the Old Testament, YHVH left His people due to their sins. Yet, His gracious promise was that in the last days, He would return as King, in salvation of His people (cf. Isaiah 59; 62). Now to be sure, that return of their king would not be in the manner that Israel had hoped for. As Wright cogently observes, Jesus radically redefined Israel's hope and her promises:

"Throughout the teaching, story telling and career of Jesus, this message rang out again and again, in word and in deed. Israel was being redefined; and those who failed to heed Jesus' warnings would discover themselves in the position that they had thought was reserved for the pagan" (*Victory*, 329).

YHVH would do "a strange thing," "a marvelous work and wonder," His "awesome work," with very negative connotations (Isaiah 28:21; 29:14; Compare Acts 13:40f). Yet, while there was a negative, destructive aspect of the return of YHVH there was also the positive side, and that was remarriage, resurrection, the New World promised in the prophets. This was to be the greatest, "I have some good news, and I have some bad news" story ever told.

To fail to see Paul's use of *parousia* and *apantesis* within the context of this story of the return of YHVH is to mis-define the words. There could have been no greater "royal visit" depicted than the return of YHVH. There could be no greater expression of the *presence* of the God of Israel who was keeping His promise to dwell with His people. The story of the wedding– and its use of *apantesis* (*hupantesin*, Matthew 25:1; *apantesin*, v. 6) with its undeniable connection to Thessalonians, with Hosea as the backdrop, gives no credence to the idea that Jesus was coming to remove anyone from the earth. He was coming to re-establish YHVH's fellowship with man, the fellowship lost in the Garden.

Let me express it as succinctly as I can.

The *parousia* (presence) of Christ and the meeting in the air, (*apantesis*) is the time of the wedding of Christ in Matthew 25:1-13.

The time of the wedding of Christ in Matthew 25:1-13 is the time of the "return of YHVH," as promised in Hosea 5-6.

But, the time of the return of YHVH– the time of the wedding (Hosea 2:19f)– would be the time of the restoration of covenantal fellowship– not the time of a literal, visible return of YHVH.

Therefore, the *parousia* of Christ and the meeting in the air *apantesis*-- at the wedding promised in Hosea– would be the time of the restoration of covenantal fellowship– not the time of a literal, visible return of YHVH.

As we have seen, in the wedding parable of Matthew 22, the Master made a wedding for his Son. Those who had been invited to the wedding spurned the invitation and killed the servants sent to bid them to the wedding. The Master sent out his armies and burned the city of the recalcitrant citizens. There can be little doubt as to what this refers to. So, the temporal and theological context and framework for that wedding, for the going out to meet the Bridegroom is established. And as just noted, history and tradition shows that the virgins did not go out to meet the bridegroom and then go back to where he had been. They escorted him the rest of his way to his destination.

There is, therefore, perfect agreement between Matthew 25 and 1 Thessalonians 4. The meeting was not a leaving of earth, or snatching away from the earth and travel to another destination. It was a meeting "in the air" to accompany the Bridegroom to his destination, his tabernacling among men!

When we couple the technical usage of *apantesis* with the *episunagogee* (gathering) study later in this work (p. 171f) there is little support for the idea of a removal from earth, but rather a gathering into covenantal, spiritual relationship. This gathering and meeting may in fact have direct implications for the "other worldly" dimension, and we would in fact suggest that very thing. However, the focus and definition of the words is not on a physical gathering.

Let me repeat an argument made earlier since we are comparing Thessalonians and Matthew 25. It is widely admitted that the passages speak of the same *parousia* of Christ. That being the case, please note:

The wedding of the Son in Matthew 25:1f is the time of the coming of Christ in 1 Thessalonians 4:13f.

The wedding of the Son in Matthew 25:1f is the same wedding of the Son in Matthew 22:1f.

The wedding of the Son in Matthew 22 would occur at the time of the destruction of the wicked servants who had killed the prophets sent to them, i.e. Old Covenant Judah.

Therefore, the coming of Christ in 1 Thessalonians 4:13f being the same coming for the wedding as Matthew 25:1f, and the same wedding as Matthew 22, would occur at the time of the destruction of the wicked servants who had killed the prophets sent to them, i.e. Old Covenant Judah.

Unless the coming of Christ in 1 Thessalonians 4 is a different coming of Christ from Matthew 25, and unless the coming of the Son in Matthew 25 is for a different wedding from that in Matthew 22, then this argument is unassailable and the *parousia* of Christ occurred in the judgment of Jerusalem in AD 70.

Apantesis is also used by Jesus in a text that while it is not eschatological–it nonetheless shows that the word does not carry with it the idea of meeting someone and then going back to where he had been. Instead, it suggests the idea of meeting someone and continuing with him to the point of destination. That text is Mark 14:13: "So he sent out two of his disciples and said to them, 'Go into the city, and a man will meet you carrying a pitcher of water, follow him."

The natural sense of the context suggests that the man was on his way to his house with the water he had drawn. The disciples were to meet (*apantesis*) him, and go with him to his destination. So, once again, the idea is meeting a person and going with him to his *destination*.

Likewise, in Luke 17:12, Jesus was traveling to a certain village. As he began to enter he was met (*apantesan*) by ten lepers. It will be admitted that the lepers cannot enter the city as they wished, but they were nonetheless meeting him with the idea of association with him as much as possible. They were not going to go with him back to where he had been.

Acts 28:15 uses *apantesis*, and it is suggestive. Paul was on his way to Rome to stand trial for his faith. As he traveled to Rome as a prisoner, "when the brethren heard of us, they came to meet us as far as Appii Forum, and the three taverns: whom when Paul saw, he took courage. And when we came to Rome, the centurion delivered the prisoners to the captain of the guard." So, once again we find a journey to a given destination, and the traveler is met by an entourage and escorted on. They *traveled with him on his journey to his destination.*

These instances of *apantesis* in the N.T. suggest that the word carries with it more than a simple meeting. Each of these contexts indicate that the meeting was for the purpose of then escorting the "met" person to his destination-- as Bullinger suggested -- where ever that might be.

While a person can– as Plevnik does– suggest that there are instances in which *apantesis* is used of a simple meeting, this does not negate the idea that Paul is using the word in its technical sense in Thessalonians. Here is why we believe this is valid.

➤We are not arguing that the word *apantesis* alone must be understood in its technical sense.

➤We *are arguing* that when used *with parousia*, which itself is considered by many sources to be a technical term,[210] that *apantesis* must be taken in its technical sense.[211] In other words, we have two words that are admitted by virtually all sources to be technical terms. So again, the fact that Paul uses these two words together as he does is highly suggestive that he did not intend a simple "meeting." Rather, he was using the words to conjure up the mental image contained in those highly loaded terms.

▶ The third thing that seems all but conclusive is that when *parousia* and *apantesis* are used together to speak of the visit of *a royal dignitary*, there is little question that they are used to speak of *escorting the visiting king into the city of his destination.* Why is this so conclusive? The answer is that in scripture, Christ's *parousia* is his revelation as the King of kings and Lord of lords. His *parousia* is his "royal visit."

Notice 1 Timothy 6:14f:

"I urge you in the sight of God who gives life to all things, and before Christ Jesus who witnessed the good confession before Pontius Pilate, that you keep this commandment without spot, blameless until our Lord Jesus Christ's appearing, which He will manifest in His own time, He who is the blessed and only Potentate, the King of kings and Lord of lords, who alone has immortality, dwelling in unapproachable light, whom no man has seen or can see, to whom be honor and everlasting power. Amen."

> No one would deny that Paul is describing the "royal visit" of Christ as King of kings and Lord of lords. But, this admission, in conjunction with *parousia* and *apantesis*, virtually demands the technical application of these words. And this means that Christ was not coming to remove the church, but to dwell with man forever!

Likewise, Revelation 19:14f posits Christ's *parousia* as a royal procession of the King of kings and Lord of lords:

"And the armies in heaven, clothed in fine linen, white and clean, followed Him on white horses. 15 Now out of His mouth goes a sharp sword, that with it He should strike the nations. And He Himself will rule them with a rod of iron. He Himself treads the winepress of the fierceness and wrath of Almighty God. And He has on His robe and on His thigh a name written: KING OF KINGS AND LORD OF LORDS."

Would anyone deny that Thessalonians is about the "royal visit" of Christ as King of kings and Lord of lords? Thus, we have in Thessalonians all of the elements necessary to understand *apantesis* in its technical sense. We have the use of *parousia*, the royal visit of the king, and the *meeting* of that King. With all of these elements present what would be the basis for denying the technical use of *apantesis* in the text? The fact is that in first century (and before) descriptions of *royal visits* and *apantesis*, there is little if any evidence to deny the idea of going out to meet, and escort back.

There is no snatching away of the church from the earth. There is no destruction of earth. There is no end of time. Instead, the Garden relationship is restored. There is the wedding. There is the anointing of the Messianic Temple to re-establish the intimate fellowship between heaven and earth. There is the visit of the King of kings to dwell with His citizens. Paul is using well known language of his day to conjure up the mental images of the spiritual realities that were to take place at Christ's royal visit. To turn Paul's language into a prediction of the end of time, the removal of man from earth, and a crassly literal description of events is to entirely miss– and mis-apply– what Paul was saying.

JOSEPHUS AND *APANTESIS*

I want now to introduce a rather lengthy citation from Josephus, who of course was a contemporary of Paul. The context of this section of Josephus has the conquering Alexander the Great approaching Jerusalem. The high priest was naturally fearful of the situation and decided to seek to appease Alexander, and avoid disaster. To do so, he decided to "meet" Alexander in royal apparel and attendant splendor. The scene is typical of the Greek (as well as Roman and Jewish) use of *apantesis* and *parousia*.

> "Now Alexander, when he had taken Gaza, made haste to go up to Jerusalem; and Jaddua the high priest, when he heard that, was in an agony, and under terror, as not knowing how he should meet (*apantesis*) the Macedonians, since the king was displeased at his foregoing disobedience. .... whereupon God warned him in a dream, which came upon him after he had offered sacrifice, that he should take courage, and adorn the city, and open the gates; that the rest should appear in white garments, but that he and the priests should meet (*hupontesis*) the king in the habits proper to their order ... According to which dream he acted entirely, and so waited for the coming (*parousia*) of the king.... 5. And when he understood that he was not far from the city, he went out in procession, with the priests and the multitude of the citizens. ... for Alexander, when he saw the multitude at a distance, in white garments, while the priests stood clothed with fine linen, and the high priest in purple and scarlet clothing, with his mitre on his head, having the golden plate whereon the name of God was engraved, ... I believe that I bring this army under the Divine conduct, and shall therewith conquer Darius, and destroy the power of the Persians, ... and had given the high priest his right hand, the priests ran along by him, and he came into the

city. And when he went up into the temple, he offered sacrifice to God, according to the high priest's direction, and magnificently treated both the high priest and the priests. And when the Book of Daniel was showed him (23) wherein Daniel declared that one of the Greeks should destroy the empire of the Persians, he supposed that himself was the person intended."[212]

This story demonstrates that for hundreds of years before the time of Paul– and to the very time of Paul and Josephus his contemporary-- *apantesis* and *parousia* were companion words used in a technical sense. It shows that to go out to meet a royal visitor did not mean to go out to meet him and go back to where he had been. It shows that *apantesis* meant to go out *and to bring the royal visitor into the destination city.*[213]

Josephus also records the reception of Vespasian into Rome as the new emperor. The dignitaries of Rome, "impatient of awaiting him, hastened to a great distance from Rome to be the first to greet (*apantesis*) him." He then describes the entrance into the city of that royal entourage.[214] Clearly, Josephus is using *apantesis* in its technical sense here.

According to Cosby, Josephus employs some form of *apantesis* 92 times, but only uses the term 10 times of "formal receptions."[215] What Cosby does not note is that in many of those references, while a royal visit is not discussed, the idea of meeting and escorting back is present.

So, this gets back to the point we are making, and that is that *apantesis* can be used of mundane meetings. However, even though the word can be used in non-technical examples there is no question that even in many incidents, the idea of meeting and bringing in is present. Also, Cosby acknowledges that the word is used to describe the royal visitations and bringing in of the royal personage. This is the core of our argument.

So, Josephus' description of royal *parousias*, utilizing *apantesis*, is suggestive that this was the common understanding of the terms when Paul wrote. Of course, this does not *demand* that Paul was using *apantesis* in a technical sense, but it assuredly supports that idea.

Our study of *apantesis* has been, we think, productive. We have shown that when the lexicons discuss the history and background of the word that they emphasize the technical use of the word.

We have shown that among the commentators, there is little, if any, doubt that *apantesis* was used in a technical sense in the first century world. Many commentators, as we have seen, nonetheless reject the technical meaning of *apantesis* in Thessalonians, but they do not do so because of context, linguistics or grammar. They do so on theological grounds, i.e. because they reject the idea that the purpose of Christ's *parousia* would be to restore man to fellowship without the destruction of material creation, the end of time and human history.

We have shown that while there are examples where *apantesis* can and does have a non-technical application– just as the technical term *parousia* does— that in the New Testament scriptures, there is support for the technical definition and use.

We have shown that Josephus lends support to the technical understanding of *apantesis*, by giving examples from the period before the first century and the first century, contemporary world of Paul.

What we have emphasized in this study is this:

➜ *Parousia* is normally considered to be a technical term for Christ's judgment coming, although there are admittedly examples where it does not carry that meaning. This does not forbid us from understanding that it is a technical term, as virtually all scholars agree.

➜ *Apantesis* is unequivocally considered to be a technical term, when describing the visit of a royal dignitary, although, like *parousia*, there are examples where the technical connotation does not apply.

➜ 1 Thessalonians 4 is undeniably describing the visit of Jesus as King of kings and Lord of Lords.

These three facts are virtually indisputable. It seems therefore, that *the combination of these three elements* in the text of 1 Thessalonians 4, demands that *apantesis* is being used in its technical sense. And this being true, the dominant eschatology of modern evangelicalism, that holds that Paul was predicting the coming of Christ to remove the church from the earth at the end of the Christian age, is falsified. Paul had nothing of the sort in mind. He was speaking of the Day of the Lord, when Jesus would come, "in the glory of the Father" (*as the Father had come before*, Isaiah 64:1-3) to restore the fellowship lost in the Garden. What Abraham had longed to see, but had never received, was about to become a reality. He and the faithful worthies were about to receive their reward of the heavenly city and country, and those still alive would be restored into the covenantal presence of the faithful God. The accuser of man was about to be defeated and that meant that Jesus was coming to meet the saints in the *air*.

A LOOK AT THE OBJECTIONS

Make no mistake, the dispensationalists are well aware of the implications if the technical meaning of *apantesis* is established. In short, if the technical definition of *apantesis* is established in 1 Thessalonians 4 the millennial doctrine of the rapture is falsified.

Cosby's article has become the ground for the dispensational denial of the technical definition of *apantesis* in Thessalonians. Thomas Ice claims that

Cosby's article proves "beyond a shadow of a doubt" that the technical definition of *apantesis* is to be rejected.[216] Ice's dependence on Cosby's article is a prime example of what Cosby had to say about theological bias impacting interpretation. Ice even implies that any other conclusion is not honest. It is clear that if the technical sense of *apantesis* is confirmed this would have a devastating impact on dispensationalism, not to mention virtually all futurist paradigms. We believe Ice's promotion of Cosby's article is not well grounded.

Cosby came to reject the technical sense because, he claimed, certain elements present in other descriptions of *apantesis*, are not present in Thessalonians. Cosby claimed that the following essential elements of the technical *apantesis* are missing from Thessalonians:

➡ Cosby claims that in contrast to the *parousia* of a visiting monarch, Paul posits the coming of Christ as unexpected and unannounced. As Gundry notes however, in an article responding to Cosby,[217] this simply is not true. Paul emphatically said that Christ's *parousia* would be unexpected *by the unbelievers,* not the believers (1 Thessalonians 5:1-3). See my *He Came As a Thief* for a fuller discussion of this issue.

➡ Cosby somewhat surprisingly claims that there is no referent to the waiting throngs putting on special garments as they anticipated the coming of the Sovereign, as in normal examples of *apantesis*. While it is admitted that special garments are not mentioned in Thessalonians, it certainly cannot be denied that this is a part of the story of the coming of Christ. Revelation 19 tells of the bride being adorned for her husband and the wedding– which as we have shown is intrinsically a part of Thessalonians-- and the saints being clothed with white garments, which is their righteousness.

➡ Cosby claims that in normal examples of *apantesis*, the crowds shouting a greeting to the approaching visitor, whereas in Thessalonians the saints are not said to shout or exclaim at the *parousia*. Gundry seems to think that this is true, although not altogether unexpected, "in view of the need for supernatural action in the raising of the deceased Christians and in catching of them and the living Christs up to meet the Lord in the air" (1996, 40). I would argue that this is not a legitimate, albeit partial, concession, on the part of Gundry. In 2 Thessalonians 1 Paul speaks of Christ's coming as the time "when he comes to be glorified in his saints" (2 Thessalonians 1:9f). Are we to suppose that this glorification does not qualify as the spiritual equivalent of the shouting crowds depicted in some of the historical accounts? On the contrary, I would argue that this imagery is suggestive of the acclaim offered to the visiting king.

➡ It was normal for the citizens of the destination city to offer gifts and sacrifices to the visiting royalty, notes Cosby. This is in contrast to

Thessalonians where there is no mention of gifts being offered to the King. Gundry correctly rejoins that in regard to Christ's *parousia*, the aim is to "present every man perfect to Christ," and that the church might be presented "as a chaste virgin unto Christ" (Colossians 1:27; 2 Corinthians 11:2). Furthermore, I think it should be worthy of note that Paul, in anticipation of the *parousia*, urged the Romans to present "their bodies as living sacrifices unto Christ" (Romans 12:1). So, the idea of the presentation of gifts is not as removed from Thessalonians as Cosby imagines.

➡ Cosby claims that the idea of judgment at the *parousia* that is dominant in 2 Thessalonians 1 does not fit the traditional concept of *apantesis*. This is an interesting, and perhaps contrived, contrast since as Gundry observes, Cosby himself lists several examples of visiting sovereigns exacting judgment on criminals upon their visit. As a result, Gundry says that this "contrast" offered by Cosby, "looks like an assertion having little or no probative value" (1996, 41).

➡ The final contrast offered by Cosby is the assertion that Paul makes no mention of the custom of visiting dignitaries offering sacrifices upon their visit. However, Gundry is certainly correct in pointing out that as Cosby himself admitted Jesus had already offered himself as the ultimate sacrifice.

Gundry concludes his examination of Cosby's claims:
"On the whole, then, Paul's description of the Parousia in 1 Thessalonians 4:15-17 comes closer to what we know of Hellenistic receptions than Cosby allows. True, *apantesis* does not by itself connote a reception of that kind. But, the Thessalonian context, the *autos* which calls special attention to Jesus' dignity as Lord or Emperor (the 'Lord himself'–1 Thessalonians 4:15) the remarkable fact that only here in the N.T. are Christians said to be 'caught [up]... to meet the Lord in the air" (1 Thessalonians 4:17, though cf. Matthew 25:1, 6) and the appearance of the elements of Hellenistic formal receptions also in other Pauline mentions of the Parousia all combine to favor such a connotation for *apantesis*."

In addition to Cosby, in December of 2008, at the "17th Annual Pre-Trib Study Group Conference" in Dallas, Texas, Kevin Zuber presented a paper seeking to discount the technical definition of *apantesis*.[218] Although he actually admits to what he calls "a limited technical meaning" of *apantesis*, he rejects what he calls "the full technical meaning" (P. 2).

In addition to repeating Cosby's analysis, Zuber offers some objections to the "full technical meaning" of *apantesis*.

✱ He says, "the interpretive picture drawn by advocates of the "full technical meaning" of apantesis, a) confuses the Rapture of the Saints with the Second

Coming (a very typical mistake by advocates of a non-pre-tribulational views) and b) leaves the several texts that do speak of the Rapture, as well as the Lord's relationship with the church rather disconnected" (p.2). This is one of Zuber's key objections.

✱ Zuber takes note of N. T. Wright, Witherington and others who appeal to the well attested first century use of *apantesis*, and who claim that Paul is using "imperial cult language" and "anti-imperial rhetoric" as a counter to the Roman cult. Zuber says, "I frankly find this sort of 'scholarship' tiresome" (P. 8). He says that an appeal to the "imperial cult language" of *apantesis* would demand an ability to understand a "coded" message known only to insiders.

✱ Zuber claims that the technical definition of *apantesis* is mitigated because the context and background of 1 Thessalonians 4 is the wedding, and he claims that the Bride is "retrieved" by the Groom. He correlates John 14 with this motif insisting that there must be a removal of the Bride.

✱ Zuber notes that there are some instances in which *apantesis* is used in which there is no escorting back into the city. In other words, there are exceptions to the technical usage.

Since we have already taken note of the last point this is not a determinative objection. The issue is not whether *apantesis* is sometimes used in a "mundane" sense. The question is, are the elements that indicate the technical definition present in Thessalonians and the resounding answer is that they are. Zuber notes that *parousia* is sometimes used in a non-technical sense, but, he likewise admits that it is used in a technical sense to speak of Christ's coming. This alone mitigates his objection.

I want to focus on Zuber's objections in regard to the rapture versus the Second Coming, and his argument about the wedding, but let me make a brief observation in regard to his hermeneutic.

Zuber says that he finds it "tiresome" to suggest that the modern student must understand the way language was being used in the first century. He rejects the contention by Wright, Witherington and others who seek to understand the "audience relevance" of the language that Paul uses, arguing that if we have to understand these things it demands a secret decoder. I find this to be distressing, not to mention self-defeating. And as we are about to see, *Zuber contradicts his own hermeneutic* by appealing to the first century understanding of Paul's language.

Is this not theology driving definition? Would this kind of argument be made about *any other piece of literature*? Do we approach Shakespeare with a presuppositional modern understanding of his language, his metaphors, his idioms? Is it important to understand the Roman world as we read Suetonius, Pliny, Tacitus, et. al.? What kind of literary nightmare would it create to suggest that we ignore the true context of *any* literature?

It does not take a secret decoder ring to understand the language of the Bible. What it does take is a knowledge of the way language was used in the first century world. It takes putting aside preconceived literary ideas and determining through research what *that* world, what *that* culture and society meant when it used those words, terms, phrases, symbols and metaphors. As we have seen, the Bible is a Jewish book, written about God's promises to Israel and written to audiences intimately familiar with the Old Covenant, as well as intimately familiar with the Greco-Roman world that they lived in. To seek to interpret the Bible in isolation from that *sitz em leben*– the real life situation– of those audiences is misguided, self-defeating and unscholarly.

THE RAPTURE VERSUS THE SECOND COMING

Since we deal with this objection somewhat below, I will keep this brief. However, Zuber, citing Paul Benware, gives four supposed contrasts between the rapture and the Second Coming. I will present these in chart form:

	The Rapture	**The Second Coming**
Place	The Lord comes in the air; returns to the Father's house	The Lord descends to the Mt. of Olives; remains on earth
Purpose	The Lord comes to gather, unite and bless His church; glorified bodies	The Lord comes to judge the unbelievers, wrath; no glorified bodies
Result	No mention of establishing the kingdom; believers removed from the earth	The Lord comes to establish the kingdom; believers remain on the earth.
Time	Imminent, any time!	After the Tribulation (*Meaning*, p. 15)

These contrasts are arbitrary and untenable.

By way of response, let me first of all repeat what we have noted already. Paul said he preached *nothing* but the hope of Israel (Acts 24-28; Romans 16:25f). *Nothing*! This means that no matter what else we might think about 1 Thessalonians 4 it is about *the fulfillment of God's Old Covenant promises made to Israel*

This means that the millennial claim– upon which Benware's chart is based– that the church and Israel must be delineated, is false. Paul was not discussing the church in isolation from God's promises to Israel. He was discussing God's promises to Israel! This fundamental fact cannot be ignored in any discussion of 1 Thessalonians 4, and yet, *it is precisely that fact that the millennialists reject*! Let me illustrate this as I respond to each of these points.

Place– Benware's (Zuber's) delineation between Christ returning to the Father versus remaining on earth is based in large part to the idea that Thessalonians is about the church, while Zechariah's promise concerning the Mt. of Olives has to do with God's promises to Israel. As just seen, this is a false distinction, therefore the objection falls.

Purpose– The presuppositional idea behind this "contrast" is the idea that Christ comes *for* the saints at the rapture, but then comes *with* the saints at the Second Coming. See our discussion of Matthew 13 and 24 and the discussion of "With or For, or For or With" below.

Note that Benware says the wicked are judged at the Second Coming, not the rapture. Matthew 13:39f is supposedly the rapture. But at the coming of Christ in Matthew 13 the wicked are gathered (judged!) *first and thrown into the fire*! Likewise, see our discussion below of 2 Thessalonians 1. Paul says that the *church* would receive relief from Tribulation at the Second Coming. These are *fatal contradictions* of millennial dogma.

Result– We will discuss the hermeneutical principle that lies behind this claim below. What Benware and Zuber are doing is assuming that because some eschatological tenets are mentioned in one text but not in another that this demands that different comings at different times are in view. This is a tenuous hermeneutic.

Time– Be sure to read our in-depth analysis below of the millennial claim that imminent does not mean near. Thomas Ice and the millennialists have invented a new definition of imminent.

Note that imminent supposedly does not mean near. Also, per the millennial view, the early church was not looking for the Second Coming but were eagerly looking for the rapture. But again, 2 Thessalonians 1 was written to and about the first century church. Paul assured them that Christ was coming soon to give them relief from that tribulation. This is a *prima facie* falsification of the millennial claim.

So, every contrast suggested by Benware and Zuber is shown to be presuppositional and false. The New Testament knows nothing of the millennial doctrine of the rapture and the Second Coming. Let's look now at Benware's suggestion that lying behind 1 Thessalonians 4 is the idea of the wedding, and that the wedding must be seen as a removal of the church from the earth.

THE WEDDING: WHOSE PROMISE IS THIS?

I just suggested that one of the fundamental flaws in the millennial doctrine is the attempt to delineate between the promises to the church and the promises to Israel. Thessalonians is seen as a promise relating to the church to be fulfilled at the end of the Christian age. According to the millennial view the church has (temporarily) replaced Israel. (Yes, dispensationalists do teach a Replacement Theology.[219]) However, at the rapture the church is finally married to her Groom as Jesus comes and sweeps her off to heaven. After the rapture the Lord resumes his currently interrupted relationship with Israel as she is restored and the millennium begins. It is at the Second Coming that God's Old Testament promises to re-marry and restore *Israel* are fulfilled.

As can be readily seen, this scenario demands that the Bible teaches *two Weddings of two Brides*. Per the millennialists, the promise of the wedding at the rapture must be the church. It cannot be Israel. And yet, they insist that at the Second Coming there is *another wedding*. So, there is a wedding of the church at the rapture (Zuber, *Meaning*, 15-16) and there is a wedding of Israel at the Second Coming.[220]

Let me remind you of what we have seen earlier in regard to the source of all New Testament eschatology. We have established beyond doubt that *all* New Testament doctrine of the coming of Christ is based and taken from God's Old Covenant promises to Israel. In spite of this claim: "Dispensational premillennialists hold that Israel and the church are two separate and distinct entities throughout all of history, including the millennium" (Ice/Demy, *Prophecy Watch*, 241). However, the Bible is clear that there are *not* two separate programs, two separate sets of promises.

To reiterate what we have already seen, Paul informs us that he had one message, one hope (Ephesians 4:4f) and that hope was the hope of Israel found in Moses and the prophets. The millennial contention that the Old Testament never foretold the church, and therefore never foretold the wedding of Thessalonians is directly contrary to Paul's emphatic words.

So, if Paul preached nothing but the hope of Israel then the promise of the coming of Christ for the wedding in Thessalonians is from the Old Covenant promises to Israel. You cannot make Paul teach something that he said he did not teach and he said he had only one gospel message. He taught that gospel message from the Old Covenant prophets (Romans 16:25-26).

There is something ironic here, however. As we have noted Zuber says that he grows tired of the kind of scholarship that seeks to understand the historico-grammatical world in which a text was written. He says this would demand a secret decoder ability. However, in his attempt to negate the technical meaning of *apantesis*, he sets forth what he claims was the normal practice of the groom in retrieving his bride. He then says: "Understanding key aspects of this metaphor (the coming of the bridegroom, DKP) *requires a knowledge of ancient wedding customs with which the disciples and early church would have been assuredly been acquainted*" (*Meaning*, 15, My emphasis, DKP).This is more than a little remarkable.

According to Zuber, it is "tiresome" to investigate the metaphor of meeting a royal dignitary, a metaphor– to borrow Zuber's terminology-- that, "requires a knowledge of visits of a royal dignitary, customs with which the disciples and early church would have been assuredly been acquainted." And yet, he insists that it is *required* to understand the wedding customs that were prevalent and well understood in the ancient world.

If it is important that we understand the wedding customs of the ancient world in order to understand the metaphor of the coming of the Bridegroom, why is it not likewise as important to know the meaning behind the metaphor of a royal visit?

I reject Zuber's claims concerning the wedding customs of the first century for several reasons, but I will only list two.

❧First, as the hope of Israel, the *parousia* of Christ in 1 Thessalonians 4 is the wedding (remarriage) of Israel foretold in Hosea. YHVH was married to Israel. *Israel, the Bride, was on earth in that marriage relationship.* God *divorced* her, and *went away (Hosea 5:15).* But, He would *return* and *marry* her again (Hosea 2:19; 6:3). This remarriage would not be the removal of Israel from the earth, but a New Marriage Covenant with Israel, transformed to be sure, into the body of Christ.

Matthew 25 (as is Matthew 22:1f) is the depiction of that promised wedding. *The coming of Christ is the return of YHVH for the wedding.* Since the marriage relationship had been on earth before, where is the indication that the marriage relationship would now only exist in heaven, with Israel removed from earth? As Ephesians 1:10 indicates, God's intent was to reconcile heaven and earth in Christ (cf. Ephesians 3:14f).This establishes the technical meaning of *apantesis* in Matthew 25 and thus in 1 Thessalonians 4. God was "returning" to earth to be in a restored covenantal relationship with man.

❧ A related reason for rejecting Zuber's claims is taken from Revelation 21, where, as we have seen the New Jerusalem comes down out of heaven as a bride adorned for her husband. When the wedding takes place, we have the pronouncement, "The Tabernacle of God is with man!" This is not the removal of man from the earth. It is the fulfillment of Ezekiel 37 and God's promise to restore fellowship between Himself and man.

We have examined Zuber's key points in his efforts to mitigate the technical meaning of *apantesis*. His arguments are based on false presuppositions and faulty logic. Interestingly, he admits that *apantesis* sometimes does have a technical definition. As we have argued throughout this study, *apantesis*, when used in the context of a royal visit, in conjunction with *parousia*, virtually demands the technical application. These are the elements of 1 Thessalonians 4. It is this combination of elements that Zuber and the dispensational world ignores. Zuber's arguments are less than convincing.

There is a final bit of irony here as well. Zuber and the dispensationalists are zealous to reject the technical meaning of *apantesis*. Yet interestingly enough, the dispensationalists actually believe in the principle of *apantesis*! In other words, *apantesis* suggests the coming of Christ to establish his fellowship presence among men. The millennialists says this cannot be so. Yet, what does the dispensationalist believe about Christ's second coming? They believe *it is his coming to dwell on earth in fellowship with man.* They posit for the second coming that which *apantesis* implies! Why not grant the proper definition of *apantesis* in the first place?

A FINAL OBJECTION BRIEFLY CONSIDERED

While the dispensationalist clearly has a lot to lose if the technical meaning of *apantesis* is granted, they are not alone. The amillennialist and postmillennialists also have much– virtually all!– to lose if the technical meaning of *apantesis* is allowed.

Intrinsic to both of these paradigms is the view that at the end of human history as we know it material creation is destroyed. 2 Peter 3 is taken as a prediction of the end time and the cosmos. Thus, the objection would be that you cannot posit 1 Thessalonians as predictive of the restoration of fellowship between heaven and earth at the *parousia* since earth will be destroyed when Christ comes.

We clearly do not have space to do an exhaustive examination of this objection. See my *The Elements Shall Melt With Fervent Heat*,[221] for an in-depth analysis of 2 Peter 3 showing that it is not speaking of the end of time. There are a number of quick thoughts to consider, however.

As Perriman (2005, 123) and a host of other scholars point out, the more accurate translation of 2 Peter 3:10 is that the earth[222] would be "discovered," "exposed," etc., not *destroyed*.[223] Middleton notes that the traditional translations are based on inferior Greek manuscripts but that there is virtually no longer any support, other than theological bias, to support the translation of "shall be dissolved."[224]

The "elements" that Peter speaks of are not the basic elements of material creation but the elemental doctrines of Old Covenant Israel. Again, see my *Elements* book for an in-depth study.

Revelation 5:5 shows that the triumphant saints, "shall reign on the earth" in the everlasting kingdom that was, even when Thessalonians was written, being delivered (Hebrews 12:28). The reception of this kingdom– the time of the New Jerusalem that would come, "down from God out of heaven," would be at the judgment of the city, "where the Lord was slain (Revelation 11:8-17). This could hardly be possible if the earth is to be burned up.

So, let me summarize what we have seen, including in our summary some of the issues covered earlier in this work. Here are the reasons why *apantesis* must be given its proper technical definition:

● The coming of Christ in 1 Thessalonians 4 is to restore what was lost in the Garden. Man was in fellowship with God. Man sinned. The story of eschatology is the story of *the restoration of that fellowship*. It is not the story of the end of human history or the removal of man from the earth.

● We have established that Thessalonians is the dedication of the Messianic Temple promised in the Old Covenant. This is definitive proof that Thessalonians is not about the end of human history, the destruction of earth, or any of the other proposed schemas of traditional eschatologies. It is the realization of the New Covenant presence of YHWH among His people.

● Thessalonians is about the remarriage of God and Israel resulting in salvation being offered to the nations, with all of the attendant implications. When YHWH was married to Israel this was not manifested in a bodily presence, but through covenantal relationship. He had divorced her, but promised to remarry her, and this is what Thessalonians is about, *the marriage of the King*!

● The lexical evidence supports the technical definition of *apantesis*.

● The Greek commentators support the technical definition of apantesis.

● When used with its companion technical word, *parousia*, in context of a royal visit, as in Thessalonians, the technical definition *of apantesis* is virtually demanded.

● So, the bottom line is that when *apantesis* is given its proper technical definition as the evidence demands, then the idea that 1 Thessalonians 4 predicted the destruction of earth and the removal of man from the earth is falsified. This is the theological atom bomb of 1 Thessalonians 4.

WE SHALL MEET HIM IN THE *AIR*
Is the *Air* the Atmosphere– Or the Spiritual Realm
1 THESSALONIANS 4:17

Paul said, "we shall meet him in the *air*" (Greek, *aer*). This is one of those pregnant Biblical statements that has to be unfolded to be understood, and not simply viewed in a woodenly literal manner. While much could be said about this, we will limit our comments.

In Paul's first century thought world, Satan was "the ruler of this world" (John 12:31; 2 Corinthians 4:4). He was also *the ruler of the air* (Greek word *aer*, Ephesians 2:2).[225] The conflict between God and Satan was a spiritual conflict "in the heavenly places" (2 Corinthians 10:1f; Ephesians 6:12). As King cogently remarks on 1 Thessalonians 4: "Air is the symbol of the heavenly or spiritual realm wherein the government of God is exercised. Concerning Satan (before he was cast out) it was said that he was the prince of the power of the air. But Christ conquered Satan and cleansed the 'air' and restored man to his rightful dominion of life and righteousness."[226]

The Tyndale Commentary observes: "The air was usually thought to be the abode of all manner of evil spirits (cf. Ephesians 2:2) and it is thus a measure of the complete supremacy of the Lord that He should meet His saints in such a region."[227] Likewise, Morris says, "There may be significance in the meeting place being 'in the air.' In the first century the air was often thought of as the abode of demons (Satan is described as the 'ruler of the kingdom of the air,' (Ephesians 2:2). That the Lord chooses to meet his saints there, on the demon's home ground so to speak, shows his complete mastery over them."[228]

Strimple (*WSTTB*, 342f) scoffs at the idea that *aer* might be indicative of the spiritual realm, simply pointing out some texts that do not have that definition. Interestingly, Strimple actually offers up Ephesians 2:2f as a refutation of the preterist contention that *aer* does not mean heaven. It hardly devastates preterism however, to cite a text that actually proves the very thing being affirmed, that the *aer* is not heaven, but the spiritual realm!

This concept is important, and while *many* commentaries take note that the "air" was the realm of wickedness, they then ignore the fact that the realm of wickedness was in the *unseen dimension*! If therefore, the spiritual realm of "the prince of the power of the air" was the unseen realm, and Christ was to come "in the air" in triumph, upon what basis does one posit *a visible appearance of Christ*?

So, for Paul to say "we shall meet him in the air," is a *paeon* of triumph over Satan. It is to say that Satan had been defeated and man was now being restored to that position of fellowship he had with God before he fell. What

Paul would later write: "The God of Peace shall crush Satan under your feet shortly" (*en tachei*) is anticipated here by the apostle.

Thessalonians is about the consummation of the battle begun at the Cross where Christ triumphed, "over the principalities and powers, making an open spectacle over them in it" (Colossians 2:14f). Now, at his *parousia*, "the prince of this world" was to meet his fate just as Jesus promised (John 12:31f) "now shall the god of this world be cast out, now shall the god of this world be judged." The "god of this world" ruled in the "air." So, Christ was going to meet his saints "in the air" to manifest his total victory.

Paul's statement, taken literally, misses the entire point. 1 Thessalonians 4:17 is not about the atmosphere or clouds. It is about the victory of Christ over the rulers of spiritual high places.

It seems not to have dawned on most exegetes that the traditional views of Thessalonians pose a severe problem. Paul said, "we shall meet him in the air, and so (*kai houtos*) shall we ever be with the Lord." What is the problem?

Well, remember that the traditional view of 1 Thessalonians 4 is that it occurs when, "the earth and the elements that are therein shall be burned up" (2 Peter 3:10). According to this literalistic view of things, *the air is one of the basic elements to be burned up!*

So, the problem is that if the air is one of the elements to be incinerated, how would it be possible for the saints to meet Christ in the air and be with him forever, *in the air*? Per the traditional view of things the air no longer exists after the *parousia*! How could the saints dwell with Christ in the air– which is what Paul clearly expresses, if the air is destroyed? As a friend Jim Gunter noted to me in an email, the same problem applies to the clouds. The clouds on which Jesus is supposed to ride are comprised of the "elements." Yet, again, the elements are to be totally burned up! Are we supposed to believe that Jesus will come riding on clouds that are literally burning up as he rides them? This is not an attempt at being facetious. It is taking the literalism of the traditional views at their word and demonstrating the fallacies therein.

So far as I have been able to ascertain, the word *aer* is never a synonym for heaven, and this is important. But, whatever *aer* meant to Paul, it was to be the realm of being with Christ forever, "and so shall we ever be with the Lord." If therefore, *aer* is not heaven, and it cannot be one of the basic elements of material creation, does this not demand that Paul's discussion is about the spiritual realm, as we have discussed above?

ON THE CLOUDS OF HEAVEN

There is, it can hardly be doubted, a relationship between the coming of Christ "in the air," and the predictions that he was coming on the clouds of heaven. Go back and look again at the direct parallels between Matthew

24:29f and 1 Thessalonians 4. Where Matthew posits Jesus coming on the clouds of heaven, Paul (who says he is reiterating Jesus' teaching) says Christ was to be met in the air. These are the moral equivalents of each other, even though there may be different nuances within each. When we examine this concept of the coming on the clouds, i.e. in the air, we must once again look to the Old Testament– the source of Paul's eschatology– for help in understanding this idea. And when we do we find that the idea of God coming on the clouds never refers to a literalistic, visible, bodily descent out of heaven. There were always visible events to be sure, but the faithful, the discerning, would see in those events the majesty and sovereignty of YHWH, not His bodily form.

Take note of just a few of the Old Testament passages of the many that could be brought forth.

★Psalms 18:11f– When David described the coming of the Lord to vindicate and save him from Saul's murderous intent, here is how he described YHWH's actions: "He made darkness His secret place; His canopy around Him was dark waters and thick clouds of the skies. From the brightness before Him, His thick clouds passed with hailstones and coals of fire."

★ Psalms 68:4– In expressing the majesty and glory of the actions of God, *within history*, the Psalmist said: "Sing to God, sing praises to His name; extol Him who rides on the clouds, by His name YAH, and rejoice before Him."

★Psalms 97:2– In a chapter full of references to God's manifestation of His sovereignty the Psalmist says: "Clouds and darkness surround Him; righteousness and justice are the foundation of His throne."

★ Psalms 104:3– In this Psalm, the writer speaks of the clouds as the chariots of God. And yet, patently, he did not have a literal appearance of God in mind. "He lays the beams of His upper chambers in the waters, who makes the clouds His chariot, who walks on the wings of the wind."

★ Ezekiel 30:3f– In describing the impending Day of the Lord in judgment of Egypt at the hands of Nebuchadnezzar, here is how the son of man described that event: "For the day is near, even the day of the LORD is near; it will be a day of clouds, the time of the Gentiles."

★ Isaiah 31:4f– In describing the imminent destruction of the Assyrians it said, "So the Lord of Hosts will come down."

★ Micah 1:3-- "Behold, the Lord is coming out of His place; He will tread on the high places of the earth, the mountains will melt under His feet." This was a prediction of the eighth century judgment of Samaria and Jerusalem at the hands of the Assyrians.

★Nahum 1:3– In describing the judgment of Nineveh that was to come at the hands of the Babylonians, the prophet described YHWH's actions: "The LORD is slow to anger and great in power, and will not at all acquit the wicked. The LORD has His way in the whirlwind and in the storm, and the clouds are the dust of His feet."

★ Zephaniah 1:15– This prophet predicted the Day of the Lord against Jerusalem at the hands of the Chaldeans (1:12f). He describes that Day of the Lord: "That day is a day of wrath, a day of trouble and distress, a day of devastation and desolation, a day of darkness and gloominess, a day of clouds and thick darkness."

There are three nuances to the idea of coming on the clouds. First, there is the idea of the majesty of YHVH. Second, there is the Messianic concept found in Daniel 7:13f, which we have commented on. This concept includes the time of judgment on the persecutors. That is the third concept: the idea of judgment. What is important is that not one of these nuances demands or even *suggests*, a literal, visible manifestation of God on literal clouds. All of these passages describe the actions of YHVH *within history*.

The language is graphic and taken literally would demand a literal coming of God on literal clouds. Yet, this language is never used of such a coming of the Lord. The language of Christ's coming on the clouds must be interpreted in light of this well established OT metaphoric usage.

The famous commentator Milton Terry commented on the "coming on the clouds" and similar language: "Whatever the real nature of the *parousia*, as contemplated in this prophetic discourse, our Lord unmistakably associates it with the destruction of the temple and city, which he represents as the signal termination of the pre-Messianic age. The coming on clouds, the darkening of the heavens, the collapse of elements, are, as we have shown above, are familiar forms of apocalyptic language, appropriated from the Hebrew prophets."[229]

The noted postmillennialist Marcellus Kik, commenting on Matthew 24:30, says: "Many commentators have taken it for granted that the expression 'coming in the clouds' refers to a visible coming of Christ. A careful study of the Scriptures, however, reveals that that is not a necessary interpretation."[230] The popular "Bible Answer Man," Hank Hanegraaff, commenting on Luke 21:25f and Christ's prediction of his coming on the clouds, says that the language: "has nothing to do with physically riding on a moving cloud."[231] Likewise, Gentry says: "Beyond these spiritual comings and in addition to the bodily second advent, there is another sort of coming. This is the providential coming of Christ *in historical judgments on men*. (His emp). In the Old Testament, clouds are frequently employed as symbols of divine wrath and judgment. Often God is seen as surrounded with foreboding clouds which express His unapproachable holiness and righteousness. Thus, God is poetically portrayed in certain judgment scenes as coming in the clouds to wreak historical vengeance upon His enemies" *(Dominion, 1992, 273f)*.

This kind of quote could be multiplied many times over. The legitimate hermeneutical question is posed by Ladd. After examining the common metaphoric use of the language of the Day of the Lord in the Old Testament, and its use in the New Testament, he asks: "Does this not give us the reason to interpret all such language about the eschatological shaking of the world, collapse of the heavens, etc. as poetical language?"[232] Brown, taking note of the undeniable metaphoric use of the coming on the clouds language, says that the key to "this generation" in Matthew 24:34 is to recognize this well attested apocalyptic language of v. 29-31.[233]

What these authors are suggesting is eminently logical and valid. They are suggesting that we allow the scriptures to define their own terms. But, interestingly, with few exceptions they then violate their own hermeneutic. Here is what happens in the commentaries:

☞ It is recognized that the O.T., is the source for the Day of the Lord language.

☞ It is recognized that in the O.T., the language of the Lord coming out of heaven on the clouds is strictly metaphoric, and was never intended to be taken literally. Instead, the language described historical manifestations of the sovereignty of God.

☞ It is recognized that in Matthew 24:29f Jesus is employing that demonstrably metaphoric language to describe the impending judgment of Israel in AD 70.

☞ It is even recognized that Paul was a Jew, trained in the O.T. and that he said that his eschatology was taken from Moses and the prophets.

☞ It is even recognized that in Thessalonians, Paul is drawing directly from the Olivet Discourse and Jesus' use of the well attested metaphoric language of the Old Testament prophets.

HOWEVER....

☞ When the exegetes then begin to interpret Paul's Thessalonian discourse it is argued that he is predicting a literal descent out of heaven on literal cumulus clouds! The question is however, if we should honor the metaphoric nature of the coming on the clouds language in the Old Testament and in Matthew 24, as Gentry, Brown, Hanegraaff, et. al. say we must, then in light of the fact that Paul tells us that his eschatology is drawn from the Old Testament, what is the hermeneutical key for informing us that we must now take the language literally in Thessalonians? And to repeat, this is especially pertinent given the fact that Paul says his Thessalonian discourse, in addition to being drawn from the Old Testament, was a reiteration of Jesus' Olivet

Discourse. In other words, why must we understand Matthew 24:29f as a metaphoric description of Christ's judgment against Old Covenant Israel, and yet we must take that *identical language*, that Paul tells us he is repeating from the Olivet Discourse, and demand that when Paul uses it, it is a description of a literal coming of Christ on literal cumulus clouds?

All of this evidence is in perfect harmony with the Thessalonian concept of the manifestation of Christ's royal majesty. It is the coming of Christ as King of kings and Lord of lords, his *parousia*. It is in keeping with the well attested Old Testament usage of the "coming on the clouds" language, and the symbolic, spiritual significance of meeting him in the "air."

So, what we are saying is that the concept of Christ coming on the clouds of heaven, coupled with the meeting in the *air*, is so firmly established in scripture as metaphoric language, that it is a violation of usage to demand that Paul is using the language to describe literal clouds, a visible, bodily coming of Jesus.

SO SHALL WE EVER BE WITH THE LORD
1 Thessalonians 4:17
THE *GATHERING* AND THE *SNATCHING*

The tendency of many is to ask, "Okay, it was supposed to happen in that generation, but exactly what is '*it*' that they were looking for? It is not enough to simply say they were looking for the end of the age and Christ's *parousia*. What was the *it* that the Thessalonians were concerned that their loved ones would miss since they had died prior to the coming of Jesus?" As just suggested, *it* was life, *eternal life in relationship with God*.

To demonstrate this, we return to the issue introduced above and that is the parallel between Thessalonians 4 and the Olivet Discourse. For convenience sake, we re-introduce the comparative chart that shows the parallels between Matthew 24 and 1 Thessalonians 4.

Matthew 24:29-31	1 Thessalonians 4:13-18
Coming of the Son of Man	Coming of the Son of Man
With the angels (v. 30-31)	With the angels (v. 16)
With the Trumpet (v. 31)	With the Trumpet (v. 16)
Coming in the clouds (v. 30)	Descend from heaven, in the air (v. 16, 17)
Gathering of the redeemed (v. 31)	Gathering of the redeemed (v. 17)
This generation shall not pass until all these things are fulfilled (v. 34)	"We who are alive and remain until the coming of the Lord" (v. 15, 17)

Remember that Paul said, "This I say to you by the word of the Lord." He was reiterating what Jesus had said. And, the only place in the entirety of Jesus' ministry where we find every element mentioned by Paul in Thessalonians is Matthew 24:29-31. We want to focus here on point #5, *the gathering of the elect*. To help us in our study, we return to Matthew 23:37.

As Jesus stood in the temple he gave his poignant cry, "O Jerusalem, Jerusalem, the one that kills the prophets and stones those who are sent to her! How often I wanted to gather your children together, as a hen gathers her chicks under her wings, but you were not willing!" It is important to note that when Jesus spoke of his desire to "gather" Israel that he used a distinctive Greek word *episunagogee*. This is a compound word based on the word *synagogos*. The prefix *epi* is affixed to the basic word, which, as Chilton observes, "intensifies the meaning of the original word."[234] There are a couple of things we want to take note of in regard to what Jesus was saying here, and its significance to what we shall see later.

First, it must be remembered that Jesus was sent, "to gather together (synagogue) the children of God that were scattered abroad" (John 11:52).

Second, Jesus' work of gathering together the elect was the object of Old Testament prophecy. God had promised that He would gather Israel: "If your outcasts are at the ends of heaven, from there the Lord your God will gather (synagogue) you, and from there he will take you" (Deuteronomy 30:4, LXX, i.e. the *Septuagint*).

Third, prophetically the gathering of Israel was the time of the *resurrection*. This is critical, especially in light of Matthew 24:31. Ezekiel 37:12 foretold the time when God would resurrect Israel, "I will open your graves and cause you to come up from your graves." It is clear from the context of Ezekiel 37 that the resurrection under consideration *is not a physical resurrection from biological death*. The context is that Israel was in bondage due to her sin. She was in *"sin-death"* because of her violation of the covenant. In other words, Israel's promise of resurrection was not a promise of physical resurrection from biological death. It was the promise of the restoration of fellowship with God through the forgiveness of sin. (See Paul's comments in Acts 26:17-18, in light of the fact that all he proclaimed was Israel's hope of resurrection).

The resurrection promised by Ezekiel was to occur when Israel's Messiah came, established the New Covenant and his temple in their midst (Ezekiel 37:22-27). Significantly, Paul cites Ezekiel's prophecy in 2 Corinthians 3-6. He specifically says that the body of Christ in Corinth was the fulfillment of God's promise to build His tabernacle among His people: "You are the temple of the living God, as God has said, 'I will dwell in them and walk among them. I will be their God, and they shall be my people'" (2 Corinthians 6:16).

If the inspired apostle Paul, who preached *nothing* but the resurrection hope of Israel said that the body of Christ in Corinth was the fulfillment of God's promise *to resurrect Israel* then we today have no right to say he was wrong or to look for a different kind of resurrection.

Israel was being raised from the dead by coming into the body of Christ and there finding the forgiveness of her sin, the sin that had killed her in the first place. Notice that Paul told the Corinthians, "You are what God promised." He *did not say* you are living proof that one day God will keep His promises to Israel. He did not say that the church was a foretaste of God's work for Israel in a later time. He did not say that the church was a *type* of the coming fulfillment of His promises to Israel. He said, "You are the temple of the living God, As God has said" (2 Corinthians 6:16). There could hardly be a clearer affirmation that the resurrection promises of God made to

Israel were being fulfilled. It is also clear that the resurrection in view is not a resuscitation of biologically dead physical bodies. It was the restoration to *fellowship*, the restoration to *relationship*.

Isaiah also foretold this resurrection and gathering of Israel in reference to the northern tribes. And Isaiah's prophecy actually serves as the source for Jesus' prediction in Matthew 24:31. The prophet spoke of the time when Israel's guilt for shedding innocent blood would be required of her (Isaiah 26:20-21) at the coming of the Lord in vengeance.[235] There can be no doubt that Jesus set the time for this judgment as his generation (Matthew 23:34-36). *Yet, this would also be the time of the resurrection (Isaiah 26:19f)!*

The prophet lamented the fact that Jehovah had "slain" Israel for her sin (Isaiah 27:7) yet would ultimately also offer salvation. The dual themes of judgment and salvation are found here. There would be judgment for the guilty and salvation for the righteous. The promise of salvation, the promise of resurrection, is found in Isaiah 27:13: "So shall it be in that day: the great trumpet will be blown: They will come, who are about to perish in the land of Assyria, and who are outcasts in the land of Egypt, and shall worship the Lord in the holy mountain of Jerusalem."

An important note. In v. 8-9, Jehovah promised salvation to Israel, yet that promised salvation would come, "When He makes all the stones of the altar like the chalk stones that are beaten to dust." The idea is that Israel would be saved *through* judgment, *not*, as the millennialists would have it, saved *from* judgment. Wright expresses the thought well: "There was a belief, hammered out not in abstract debate, but in and through poverty, exile, torture and martyrdom, that Israel's sufferings might be, not merely a state *from* which she would, in YHWH's good time, be redeemed, but paradoxically, under certain circumstances and in certain senses, part of the means *by* which that redemption would be effected"[236] (His emphasis).

Isaiah 27:9 is also one of the verses Paul cites in his promise of Israel's salvation in Romans 11:26-27. Thus, while that text promised salvation for Israel, implicit in that promise was also the threat of judgment and the reality that the salvation would come through judgment.

For brevity we want to note that Isaiah promised that in the day when Israel's blood guilt would be required (yet salvation offered) God would sound the blast of *the Great Trumpet* and gather the dead together out of their bondage. (Compare Hosea 13:1-2, 13-14, where the prophet spoke of the resurrection of the ten tribes from the identical kind of death, i.e. sin-death).

This passage is the fountain for Matthew 24:31: "And he will send His angels with the great sound of a trumpet, and they will gather together His elect from the four winds, from one end of heaven to the other."

Notice the parallels between Isaiah 26-27 and Matthew 23-24. Both deal with the time when Israel would be judged for her bloodguilt (Isaiah 26:21/

Matthew 23:34f). Both deal with the time of salvation and judgment (Isaiah 26:8-9/ Matthew 23:34f, 24:31). Both deal with the coming of the Lord (Isaiah 26:21/ Matthew 24:30). Both deal with the time when the Trumpet would sound (Isaiah 27:13/ Matthew 24:31). Both deal with the sounding of the Trumpet to gather the elect. In Isaiah the elect to be gathered are the dead (Isaiah 26:19; 27:13). Thus, since Matthew 24:31 is taken from Isaiah 27 then Matthew 24:31 is nothing less than a prediction of the resurrection. Of course, Jesus said that all of the things he was predicting would occur in his generation at the fall of Jerusalem (Matthew 24:34). This means that the resurrection was also to occur at that time.

So, let's take a look at the argument in simplified form:

The time of the resurrection would be when the blood of the martyrs was avenged at the coming of the Lord (Isaiah 26:19-21).

But the time when the blood of the martyrs was to be avenged was to be in Jesus' generation (Matthew 23:34-36).

Therefore the time of the resurrection at the coming of the Lord was to be in Jesus' generation.

In order to separate Matthew 24 from 1 Thessalonians 4 one must show that Matthew 24:31 is not related to the resurrection promise of Isaiah. Or it must be shown that the resurrection promise of Isaiah is not the time of the vindication of the blood of God's martyrs. This failing, one must accept the fact that the promise of the resurrection found in Isaiah is placed by Jesus within the context of his judgment coming against Jerusalem in AD 70. Since 1 Thessalonians 4 is dealing with the resurrection then Thessalonians must be placed within the context of Jesus' coming in AD 70. With these issues in mind, we want to return to our examination of the key concept of the gathering of the elect. And the reason is simple.

With the connection between Matthew 24:31 and Isaiah 27 established, it is clear that Matthew 24:31 was predicting the resurrection. Since 1 Thessalonians 4 is patently about the resurrection, the connection between Matthew and Thessalonians is undeniable. Since Jesus said in Matthew 24:34 that the events he was predicting were to occur in his generation, this demands that the events of Thessalonians had to occur in his generation as well. Of course, the temporal indicators of Matthew 24:34 and 1 Thessalonians 4:15, 17 should be enough to establish this fact. However, now that we have established that both texts speak of the resurrection the parallel between the two texts is undeniable. So, let's take a closer look at Jesus' desire and promise of the *gathering*.

Notice again that in Matthew 23:37, Jesus said that he had desired to gather together Israel to him. The question is, what kind of gathering did Jesus have in mind when he used that distinctive Greek word *episunagogee*? Did Jesus have in mind a spatial, that is, a *geographical* gathering of people, or was Jesus speaking of his desire to gather Israel into *fellowship* with him? Patently, Jesus was not speaking of his desire to gather Israel into a geographical location. His cry, "Come unto me," was not, and is not, a call to gather to a centralized location. It is a call to fellowship and life in him.

However, Israel would not heed the invitation to be gathered to Jesus. As a result Jesus said, "Your house is left unto you desolate" (Matthew 23:38). Israel's refusal to be gathered into fellowship with him would find her centralized Zion desolated. The Temple, the focal point of Israel's fellowship with Jehovah for centuries would now be annihilated. The time was rapidly approaching when, "You will neither in this mountain, neither in Jerusalem worship the Father" (John 4:21) because that Old Synagogue would be removed by YHVH. Israel's refusal to heed the voice of the prophet "like unto Moses" would bring the curse of being "cut off from the people" (Acts 3:24f).

God would not summarily remove that Old Synagogue without first extending a gracious invitation to enter the New, and proclaiming a warning about the impending removal of the Old. Thus, as Jesus warned that Jerusalem would be judged in that generation, as he and the disciples left the Temple, the disciples showed him the size and beauty of the temple stones. His response was ominous to be sure: "Do you not see all these things? I tell you that the hour is coming in which there shall not be one stone standing on another that shall not be cast down." The disciples were clearly impressed and inquired: "Tell us when shall these things be, and what shall be the sign of thy coming and the end of the age?" (Matthew 24:2-3)

As we have seen the disciples had every right to associate the fall of Jerusalem with the end of the Old Covenant age of Moses and the Law. That is the age that the temple and city represented. Jesus' words in Matthew 24:2 are simply a reiteration, with additional clarification in chapter 24, of what he had said in chapter 23. It is a mistake to delineate between the subject of chapter 23 and that of chapter 24. Chapter 24 is the fuller discussion of what was predicted in chapter 23.

In response to the disciples' questions, Jesus told them: "This gospel of the kingdom must be preached into all the world for a witness to the nations, then comes the end" (Matthew 24:14). What end have they asked about? The end linked with the destruction of the Temple. The end of the *temple age*, if we may coin a term. The only end that had been asked about was the end of the temple age and that has nothing to do with the end of the Christian age.

What this means is that in Matthew 23:37, Jesus declared that Jerusalem and the temple, the center of the Old Synagogue fellowship, was going to be desolated. However, before God would completely abandon the Old Synagogue, He was going to send the message of its doom to all of its adherents inviting them into the New Synagogue, and to the wedding (cf Matthew 21). In addition, the invitation was also going to be extended to anyone and everyone to join this New Synagogue. This New Assembly would not be simply for the physical descendants of Abraham. God was going to raise up children of Abraham by faith (Galatians 3:26-29).

In the preaching of the gospel, it was always extended "to the Jew first, then to the Greek" (Romans 1:16-17). Why is this? Read our discussion below on this and ask, why did Paul, *the apostle to the Gentiles*, always go to the Jews first? It was because, "Salvation is of the Jews" (John 4:22) and, "It was necessary (Greek *dei, a divine necessity*) that the word of God should be spoken to you first; but since you count yourselves unworthy of everlasting life, behold, we turn to the Gentiles" (Acts 13:46). So, Paul said it was God's plan that the gospel should be preached to the Jews first, even though he was the apostle to the Gentiles. The reason has already been suggested. God would not reject and desolate Israel's Old Synagogue until she had been given full opportunity to come into the Synagogue of her Messiah. Only when Israel had rejected that invitation would God's justice be fully justified in dismantling that Old House.

In the fourth century, Eusebius made the following comments:

"Christ sojourned in this life, and the teaching of the New Covenant was borne to all the nations, and at once the Romans besieged Jerusalem, and destroyed it and the Temple there. At once the whole of the Mosaic law was abolished, with all that remained of the Old Covenant, and the curse passed over to those who became lawbreakers because they obeyed Moses' law, when its time had gone by, and still clung ardently to it, for at that very moment the perfect teaching of the New Law was introduced in its place.'"[237]

Eusebius has captured the thought well. Jesus foretold the demise of the Old Synagogue, but the warning of its destruction had to be sent to all of its members to abandon it and enter the New Synagogue. Those who refused to abandon that Old House would find themselves, like the temple itself, abandoned.

While that Old Synagogue was doomed to be desolated because she had refused to be "synagogued" to Jesus, the Messiah was determined to have his Synagogue. So, as we have seen, the message of invitation went out to call Israel and all nations into the New Assembly, as the New Synagogue was "under construction."

The New Testament is clear that from Pentecost onward, the new temple of God was indeed under construction. This is why Jesus was going away "to prepare a place" (John 14:1-3). Paul wrote to the Ephesians to remind them that they, Jew and Gentile alike, "are being built together for a dwelling place of God in the Spirit" (Ephesians 2:22).

We cannot develop this at length here, but in Ephesians 2, we find the elements of Ezekiel 37 once again. As Jehovah promised to make the two houses of Israel one again, under the Messiah in the New tabernacle, Paul says that Christ was making "one new man" of the two, Jew and Gentile, in Christ, and building the new temple of God. The ten northern tribes had "dwelt among the Gentiles" to such an extent that they were assimilated into them: "Israel is among the Gentiles, they are swallowed up" (Hosea 8:8). Thus, the salvation of the Gentiles was, in the mind of Paul, in some manner, considered to be the salvation of the ten tribes. By the way, the ten tribes were never *lost*! See James 1:1; 1 Peter 1:1. If the ten tribes were lost how could James and Peter be writing to them?

The point is, the Bible does present the idea of a new temple that was under construction in the first century generation. Peter said, "You also, as living stones, are being built up a spiritual house, a holy priesthood, to offer spiritual sacrifices acceptable to God through Jesus Christ" (1 Peter 2:5).[238] Notice the present tense "are being built up."

So, both Paul and Peter present the idea of the temple of God being under construction in the first century. However, Matthew 24 also presents the picture of the dedication of the completed temple at the *parousia* of Christ "to anoint the Most Holy" in fulfillment of Daniel 9. Matthew presents the descent of the *Shechinah* glory cloud to gather the elect into the New Assembly of God, through the imagery of the sounding of the trumpet. To understand this thought, we must turn to the Old Testament tabernacle and temple for the background ideas.

In Exodus 25-40, Jehovah gave specific and detailed instructions for the construction of the tabernacle. With painstaking care, Moses constructed the tabernacle according to the pattern showed him in the Mount (Hebrews 8:4-5). The work of construction was finally finished, and when it was, "The cloud covered the tabernacle of meeting, and the glory of the Lord filled the tabernacle" (Exodus 40:34). At the dedication of the tabernacle God descended in the glory cloud and He entered the Most Holy Place to dwell among His people.

Later, when Solomon built his magnificent Temple, on the day of the dedication, "It came to pass, when the priests came out of the holy place, that the cloud filled the house of the Lord, so that the priests could not continue ministering because of the cloud; for the glory of the Lord filled the house of the Lord" (1 Kings 8:10-11).

So, in the Old Testament, on the two occasions of the dedication of the tabernacle and temple, God descended in the Shechinah glory cloud to anoint the completed edifice and to make His dwelling there. Likewise, in the New Testament, the foundation of the apostles and prophets with Jesus as the cornerstone, was laid. Just like with the building of the tabernacle, when God anointed special men with special abilities and talents for the work of construction (Exodus 31:1-7) Jesus gave gifts to men, "to equip the church for the work of the ministry" (Ephesians 4:8f) so that, "the whole body, joined and knit together by what every joint supplies, according to the effective working by which every part does its share, causes growth of itself in love" (Ephesians 4:16).

From Pentecost onward the new temple was "under construction" working toward completion when Jesus would anoint the Most Holy Place. In Matthew 23, we find the picture of the abandonment of one temple followed by the promise of a new temple, the new synagogue, and the promise of Christ descending in the glory cloud to gather together his people that have been invited to enter the new synagogue.

> *The Messiah would anoint the new Most Holy Place by his coming in the clouds of heaven with power and great glory.*

This is exactly what Daniel 9 foretold. That prophet said, "Seventy weeks are determined for your holy people and your city...to anoint the Most Holy" (Daniel 9:24). Daniel foretold the coming of the Messiah and the destruction of the old city (Daniel 9:26). The people of the Old temple, and the Old temple itself, would be destroyed because of their rejection of the Messiah, just like Jesus said in Matthew 23. However, the Messiah would also anoint the Most Holy of the new temple. Thus, we have the destruction of one Temple and the establishment of another. (Zechariah 6:12-13 said the Messiah would build the Temple). *The Messiah would anoint the new Most Holy Place by his coming in the clouds of heaven with power and great glory.*[239] The Shechinah glory cloud of Jesus, coming in the glory of the Father, would fill the new temple. The destruction of the old temple would be the sign of the Son of Man in heaven and the "true tabernacle that God built, and not man" (Hebrews 8:1f).[240]

So, while Old Israel refused to be gathered (*episunagogee*) to Jesus, and as a result her Old Synagogue was to be desolated, Jesus was going to construct a New Synagogue, and come to gather (*episunagogee*) those who believed on him into this new assembly (Matthew 24:31). Gentry has touched on this idea: "With the coming destruction of Jerusalem and the Temple, Christians would henceforth "be gathered together" in a *separate* and *distinct* 'assembly' (*episunagoge*; the church is called a *synagoge* in James 2:2)" (*Dominion*, 386, his emphasis).

Chilton also has some excellent comments on the significance of Matthew 23:37 and 24:31. He calls attention to Israel's refusal to be "gathered" in 23:37 and then says:

"Because Jerusalem apostatized and refused to be synagogued under Christ, her temple would be destroyed, and a New Synagogue and temple would be formed; the church. The new temple was created of course, on the Day of Pentecost when the Spirit came to indwell in the church. But the fact of the new temple's existence would only be made obvious when the scaffolding of the old temple and Old Covenant system was taken away" (*Paradise*, 104).

The problem with Chilton (at the time he wrote)[241] and Gentry is that they see the gathering of Matthew 24:31 as a process that was to *begin* with the destruction of Jerusalem, instead of seeing it as the climax of a process begun on Pentecost. The coming of Christ on the clouds to gather the elect must be seen as *the dedication of the New Synagogue*, not as the beginning of the gathering. The gospel call had been made for a full generation to come into the New Synagogue, and now the sounding of the Trumpet (Matthew 24:30) was the call to the *dedication* of God's New Synagogue.

This should in no wise be construed to mean that there would no longer be a call into the New Synagogue. After all, what happened in the Old Covenant when Israel was called to the dedication of her new tabernacle and temple? Were the doors closed when the dedication was completed or did the dedication mean that those edifices were now "open for business?" Clearly the latter is true. Likewise, the sounding of the trumpet to gather for the dedication of the New Synagogue did not signify the termination of the call, it signified the perfection of the temple of God. That building was dedicated and, "The Spirit and the Bride say come!" (Revelation 22:17).

What Gentry and most commentators miss is the correlation between Matthew 23:37, 24:31 and 1 Thessalonians 4. They see that Jesus was calling Israel into fellowship with him and that Israel refused. Consequently, she was to be destroyed and a New Synagogue, the church, was constructed. They even suggest that the gathering of 24:31 is a spiritual gathering into the body of Christ. This much is good. However, they miss the connection between Matthew 23 and 24:31 and 1 Thessalonians 4:13f.

Clearly, Matthew 23:31-37 is the time of the resurrection. It was to be the time of the judgment of the *living,* "upon *you* will come," and the *dead*, "all the righteous blood shed on the earth."[242] *The time of the desolation of Israel's Old Synagogue (Matthew 23:37) was to be when the martyrs were vindicated (23:33-36) and that is nothing less than the time of the resurrection (Revelation 11:15f).*

As corroborative proof of the connection between Matthew 23 and Thessalonians, it is probable that the dead Thessalonians of chapter 4 were *martyrs*. We have shown that the church was undergoing intense persecution (1 Thessalonians 1:6; 2:15-17). In 2 Thessalonians 1:4f, Paul uses the present participial form of *thlipsis,* translated *tribulation,* to speak of what they were enduring. This is a strong word for persecution and often involved martyrdom (Matthew 24:9). He promised them relief from that persecution at the coming of Christ in judgment of their persecutors (2 Thessalonians 1:7-10). Paul's promise that the persecuted Thessalonians were to be vindicated and given relief at the *parousia* is the same as Jesus' promise that the *martyrs of God were to be vindicated in his generation* (Matthew 23:34-36; Luke 18:8). This is strong proof that Jesus' *parousia* in 1 Thessalonians 4 was to be in the first century and is related to the judgment of Israel.

We would form the argument like this: If the dead Christians in 1 Thessalonians 4 were *martyrs* (1 Thessalonians 2:15f; 2 Thessalonians 1:4-6) and if the martyrs of God were to be vindicated at the time of the judgment of Israel in AD 70 (Matthew 23:33-36) then it must be true that the dead Christians in 1 Thessalonians 4 were to be vindicated in AD 70. The dead Christians of 1 Thessalonians 4 were to be vindicated in AD 70. But, the dead Christians of 1 Thessalonians 4 were to be vindicated at Christ's coming, and the resurrection (1 Thessalonians 4:15-17). Therefore, Christ's coming and the resurrection was to be in AD 70.

We have already established that Matthew 24:30-31, with its reference to the sounding of the trumpet to gather the elect has (at least[243]) two motifs behind it, the dedication of the New Synagogue and the resurrection, since it is a direct allusion to Isaiah 26-27. So, Matthew 24:31 is speaking of the gathering of the "dead" at the coming of Christ. 1 Thessalonians 4 also speaks of the gathering of the dead. Therefore, unless one can delineate between the nature of the "dead," and the time of the occurrence of Matthew and Thessalonians, since Jesus unequivocally placed the gathering in his generation (Matthew 24:34) that means that the gathering of the "dead" in Thessalonians was to occur in Jesus' generation as well.

The point we want emphasize is that the nature of the gathering in Matthew 23-24, and thus, in Thessalonians cannot be construed as a literal, bodily, geographical gathering of physically dead (or living) people. Since Jesus uses *episunagoge* as bookends in his discourse it would be highly unusual and discordant to use the identical word in two radically different senses in the same discussion. Jesus wanted to gather Israel into *spiritual fellowship* with him. But they refused. In spite of that refusal Jesus was going to gather *(episunagoge)* men to him (24:31). It would take some powerful evidence to suggest that the second gathering was to be literal.

EPISUNAGOGEE AND HARPAZO

It might be rejoined that Paul said the Christians were going to be "caught up together with him in the air," and that the Greek word translated "caught up" (*harpazo*, ἁρπάζω) demands a literal physical snatching way. However, while it can mean that, for instance in Acts 8 and the catching away of Phillip after the baptism of the Eunuch, it does not have to mean a literal snatching away. (Compare John 10:28, 29, Jude 23). It is far more contextual to correlate *harpazo* with *episunagogee*, and with 1 Corinthians 15:52. Paul said, "In a moment, in the twinkling of an eye...we shall all be changed." This *transformation, the change,* is the focus. Paul's focus is not the physical removal of man from earth but the change from corruption, the fallen man, to the state of eternal life in Christ.

Furthermore, I suggest that Paul is using typical prophetic language in his description of the gathering and being "caught up." As we have already noted, Paul's eschatological hope was nothing but the hope of Israel found in Moses and the prophets. So, the challenge for those who espouse a literal rapture *is to find that doctrine in the Old Testament.*

The dispensationalist is loathe to even try since they do not believe that the church is foretold in the Old Testament scriptures. This fact alone falsifies the millennial paradigm:

Paul's doctrine of the "rapture of the church" (His eschatology) in 1 Thessalonians is from the Old Testament scriptures (Paul preached nothing but the hope of Israel found in Moses and the prophets--Acts 24:14f; 26:21f).

But, millennialism says that the church was not foreseen or predicted in the Old Testament scriptures.

Therefore, Paul and the millennial doctrine are at odds since Paul said his eschatology was from the Old Testament scriptures.

The point is that if you posit a "literal" bodily rapture in Thessalonians, you should be able to produce an Old Testament prophecy that foretold such an event. But, where in the Old Testament do we find the prediction of a literal rapture?

Furthermore, as suggested, Paul's use of the language in Thessalonians is so typically figurative that it should immediately raise caution flags when a literal, physical event is suggested.

Remember that in Thessalonians, Paul is dealing with a church experiencing severe persecution. They are hated, despised, pursued. Paul is writing to remind them that their suffering was part of the predetermined end time scenario. He had warned them it would happen when he converted them

(1 Thessalonians 3:1-3). Within this framework, Paul had plenty of Old Testament passages full of metaphoric, hyperbolic language to convey his message of comfort and to express himself as a thoroughgoing Jewish prophet. One of those Old Testament passages, Psalms 18:3-17, contains language and thought that is similar to Thessalonians.

"I will call upon the LORD, who is worthy to be praised; so shall I be saved from my enemies. The pangs of death surrounded me, and the floods of ungodliness made me afraid. The sorrows of Sheol surrounded me; the snares of death confronted me. In my distress I called upon the LORD, and cried out to my God; He heard my voice from His temple, and my cry came before Him, even to His ears. Then the earth shook and trembled; the foundations of the hills also quaked and were shaken, Because He was angry. Smoke went up from His nostrils, and devouring fire from His mouth; coals were kindled by it. He bowed the heavens also, and came down With darkness under His feet. And He rode upon a cherub, and flew; He flew upon the wings of the wind. He made darkness His secret place; His canopy around Him was dark waters and thick clouds of the skies. From the brightness before Him, His thick clouds passed with hailstones and coals of fire. The LORD thundered from heaven, and the Most High uttered His voice, hailstones and coals of fire. He sent out His arrows and scattered the foe, lightnings in abundance, and He vanquished them. Then the channels of the sea were seen, the foundations of the world were uncovered at Your rebuke, O LORD, at the blast of the breath of Your nostrils. He sent from above, He took me; He drew me out of many waters. He delivered me from my strong enemy, From those who hated me, for they were too strong for me."

Note that David, God's elect, was being pursued by Saul. David prayed to YHWH to deliver him and the Psalm is David's recounting of that story. It goes without saying, *does it not,* that the entire creation was not destroyed when the Lord delivered David? The Lord did not literally, visibly, audibly, bodily "come down" out of heaven, in flaming fire, hailstones, with a thunderous shout and the angelic hosts, causing the literal creation to pass away. (Does any of this language sound familiar as we read Thessalonians?) Clearly, God did not lift David up from the earth literally, bodily, physically, and deliver him in a cosmos destroying event.

The parallels of thought and theme between Psalms and Thessalonians are remarkable. Like Moses, David is mentioned in Hebrews as one of the great martyrs of God who suffered "the reproach of Christ" (Hebrews 11:26-32). David was being persecuted by his own countryman, just as the Thessalonians. The Thessalonians, as part of the organic unity of the body of the saints, were likewise enduring that suffering. David, like the

Thessalonians, cried out for deliverance. The Lord, in response to his prayer was "seen" as He came down out of heaven, in flaming fire, with the angels, with a shout, and creation was destroyed. YHWH lifted David up in deliverance by destroying his persecutorial enemy.

Likewise, the Thessalonians were promised that Jesus was coming (in the glory of the Father, Matthew 16:27) out of heaven, on the clouds, with a shout, in flaming fire (2 Thessalonians 1:7f) with the angels, and they would be lifted up (*harpazo*) in deliverance from their persecutorial enemies.

This literary background from the O.T. is what informed and formed Paul's prophetic thought. Are we to suppose that even though Paul tells us that his eschatology was from the OT prophets, who consistently used metaphoric language to describe God's actions in judgment and deliverance, that he now becomes a strict literalist in his description of God's work? Where did he, where would he, have gotten the idea of a literal, visible, bodily coming of Christ?

Everywhere we turn in the Old Testament, as Wright correctly notes, the language used by Paul in Thessalonians is metaphoric, non-literal. In fact, commenting on Jesus' use of the Day of the Lord language, Wright says: "It is crass literalism, in view of the many prophetic passages in which this language denotes socio-political and military catastrophe, to insist that this time (in the teaching of Jesus, DKP) the words must refer to the physical collapse of the space-time world" (1996, 361). We would only add that if it is crass literalism to make Jesus' use of this language woodenly literal, then it is likewise crass literalism to demand that Paul was predicting a literal descent of Christ out of heaven. Even Beale, acknowledging Wright's work, admits: "There is some question whether or not Jesus will literally come down out of heaven (4:16)" (*Thessalonians*, 2003, 138).

Unless it can be proven that *harpazo* and *episunagogee* are being used in totally different ways, then the correlation between the two words, and then the indisputably "spiritual" meaning of *episunagogee* demands that we view *harpazo* in the light of the spiritual gathering into the life of Christ. When we couple this with the significance of meeting Christ "in the air" which has nothing to do with physical air, but exaltation and victory over the forces of evil, we have a powerful testimony that Paul was not speaking of a physical removal of man from earth.

Here is the summary of our argument:
- ✓ Matthew 23:31f, 24:29-31 and Thessalonians 4:13-18 are parallel in thought, words, motifs, subject and time.
- ✓ Matthew 23 speaks of the *gathering*, using a distinctive word (*episunagogee*) that does not refer to a physical geographical gathering. .
- ✓ Israel's refusal to be gathered to Jesus would result in the desolation of the Old Synagogue (Matthew 23:37).

- ✓ The message of that destruction would be proclaimed into all the world as a warning as well as an invitation to enter the New Synagogue that Messiah was to build (Matthew 24:14).
- ✓ As the message of invitation and warning went out, the foundation of the New Temple was laid and the New Temple was under construction (Ephesians 2:19f; 1 Peter 2:5).
- ✓ When the gospel had been fully proclaimed, with invitation and warning, the time of the judgment would come in AD. 70.
- ✓ At the destruction of the Old Synagogue, Jesus would come in the glory of the father, in judgment of the old and in dedication of the New, gathering into the New Synagogue those who had heard and believed (Matthew 24:29-31).
- ✓ Since the gathering desired by Jesus (Matthew 23) was not a geographical gathering then the gathering of 24:31 was not a geographical literal gathering, but a gathering (restoration) into spiritual fellowship.
- ✓ Since Matthew 24:29f is parallel with Thessalonians, and Matthew 24 speaks of *a spiritual gathering into fellowship*, then it must be true that Thessalonians is not speaking of a geographical gathering, but a gathering into spiritual fellowship.
- ✓ *Jesus was going to do at his coming what Israel refused: bring man into fellowship with him.* What had been lost in Adam, *fellowship with God*, would now be restored. By the nature of the case the restoration of fellowship would not, and did not demand the end of time, destruction of earth and removal of man from planet earth.
- ✓ The *episunagogee* of Matthew 23 is the *harpazo* of 1 Thessalonians 4. But, the *episunagogee* cannot be construed as a physical gathering, therefore, the *harpazo* of 1 Thessalonians 4 cannot be construed as a literal snatching of man from earth. The *episunagogee* and the *harpazo* was the transformation from the Old Creation to the New Covenant temple of the Messiah.

The judgment scene of Matthew 25:31f also fits this scenario. The nations of the world to whom the message of the impending passing of the Old Synagogue went (Matthew 24:14) were called into account. Those who accepted the message and the messengers were invited to enter the *kingdom*, the New Synagogue, the New Fellowship. But, those who insisted on tenaciously holding onto the Old Kingdom and persecuted the messengers of the New, were cast out. The messengers of the kingdom, the New Assembly, were persecuted as they proclaimed the message (Mark 13:9f) but their reward, and the reward of those who accepted their message, was inclusion into the New Synagogue of the Messiah: "enter thou into the joys of the kingdom, prepared for you since the foundation of the world" (Matthew 25:34).

The gathering of the elect in Thessalonians is the consummation of God's scheme of redemption, i.e. the restoration of what was lost in Adam. Thus, the correlation with the "gathering" desired by Jesus in Matthew 23, but spurned, and then promised in chapter 24, must be seen as that promised consummation. When we couple the promise of Paul in Romans 16:20 (see our discussion) this connection is confirmed and the time frame and framework of that consummation is also established. The fulfillment of God's promise in Genesis 3 would be fulfilled in Christ's coming at the end of the Old Covenant age of Israel in AD 70.

Unless it can be proven that the gathering of 24:31 is literal–as opposed to 23:37-- or that 24:31 is different from Thessalonians, then the correlation between 23:37➜ 24:31➜ 1 Thessalonians 4 proves that Thessalonians cannot be a literal, physical, bodily gathering.

Furthermore, to return to an earlier point, since Matthew 23 speaks about the time of the vindication of the martyrs, and 1 Thessalonians 4 includes martyred saints, then since Jesus placed the vindication at the time of his coming in judgment of Israel in AD 70, this means that the *parousia* of 1 Thessalonians 4 had to have been in A. D. 70.

The only way to counter this argument is to prove:

A.) That none of the dead in 1 Thessalonians 4 were martyrs, or,

B.) You would have to prove that the vindication of the martyrs promised by Jesus in Matthew 23 is yet future.

C.) You would have to prove that the coming under consideration in Thessalonians, since it supposedly did not include the vindication of *Thessalonian* martyrs-and thus is unrelated to Matthew 23-was not related in *any way at all* to the coming of Christ to vindicate God's martyrs.

D.) You would have to prove that there is another vindication of the martyrs different from that foretold by Jesus in Matthew 23, and different from that foretold by Paul in Thessalonians. Undeniably, both Matthew 23 and 2 Thessalonians predicted the vindication of the suffering saints and both passages posit that vindication within that generation. Therefore, if there is a yet future vindication of the martyrs different from either Matthew 23 or Thessalonians, you must prove that to be the case.

You cannot prove point A that the dead in 1 Thessalonians were not martyrs because the word used to describe the *tribulation* (*thlipsis*) they were enduring is a word that included martyrdom (Matthew 24:9). You cannot prove that the vindication of Matthew 23 (point B) is yet future without denying the words of Jesus. He undeniably placed that vindication in his generation (Matthew 23:36).

In regards to point C, only if the coming of Thessalonians 4 has no relationship to the coming of the Lord in vindication of the martyrs can you delineate Thessalonians from the promise of Matthew 23. However, if you make the claim that 1 Thessalonians is unrelated to the time of the vindication of the martyrs, then you are thereby saying that the future coming you are seeking to prove is itself unrelated to the vindication of God's martyrs. To prove point C is therefore to disprove point D.

If you seek to divorce a yet future coming of the Lord from the doctrine of the vindication of the martyrs this means that you cannot appeal to 2 Thessalonians 1:7-10 as a yet future coming of Christ for that passage is patently about the vindication of God's suffering saints.

So, the connection between Matthew 23-24 and Thessalonians is two-fold, the vindication of the martyrs, (the time of the resurrection) and the gathering. In both connections, Jesus emphatically said that the vindication of the martyrs would occur in his generation (23:36). He said the gathering of the elect would occur in his generation (24:34). Since the vindication of the martyrs and the gathering of the saints are the motifs and theme of 1 Thessalonians 4 then the coming of Christ in Thessalonians was to occur at the time of the judgment of Israel in A..D. 70. But there is even more here.

Again, take note of the fact that Jesus promised vindication of the martyrs and judgment of the persecutors in his generation, in the judgment of Israel (Matthew 23). This is almost universally admitted. However, Paul reiterated that theme in 1 Thessalonians 2:15-17, and except for those scholars who believe that these verses are a later Christian invention it is admitted that Paul was following Jesus in predicting the judgment of A. D. 70. What is often missed is the direct correlation with 2 Thessalonians 1.

1 Thessalonians 4 and 2 Thessalonians 1 are addressed to the same church. It sounds almost facetious to state that, but it is important to keep in mind. Not only was Paul addressing the same church he was speaking of the identical problem, persecution. Not only was he addressing the same people about the same problem, he made *the same promise*. And that promise was that the vindication of their suffering and the judgment on their persecutors was near: "To you who are (being) troubled, rest with us, when the Lord Jesus is revealed from heaven, in flaming fire taking vengeance on those who know not God" (2 Thessalonians 1:7f).

In Matthew 23:33f Jesus spoke of the past suffering of the saints and foretold further, future suffering of his own apostles and prophets (Luke 11:49) at the hands of Israel. In chapter 24 he predicted that all who followed him would be subject to that same persecution before the time of the end (Matthew 24:9f). That future suffering would fill up the measure of eschatological suffering. As a result, God's judgment would come against the persecutor, Israel, in that first century generation (Matthew 23:34; 24:15-34).

Likewise, in 1 Thessalonians 2:15f, Paul rehearses how the Thessalonians were suffering at the hands of "your own countrymen," and this persecution was without question not only instigated but executed by the Jews (Acts

17:1f).²⁴⁴ The apostle recounts what Jesus had said in Matthew 23: the Jews had killed the prophets, had killed Jesus, and were now guilty of persecuting the apostles and prophets sent to them by Jesus. As a result of this long history of persecution judgment was now about to fall. Israel's cup of sin was now all but full.²⁴⁵

In 2 Thessalonians 1 the apostle is addressing that same congregation enduring the same suffering he had written about only a year or so earlier. The persecution had not abated; it had grown worse it seems. Were the persecutors now a different group? Had the Jews stopped their persecutorial ways? We know for certain that the judgment of the persecutors foretold in 1 Thessalonians 2 had not yet fallen on Israel.

> **The coming of Christ in 2 Thessalonians 1 would be in judgment of "those who are troubling you." That could not be the Romans, or the Roman Catholic church, or a yet future anti-christ. It was Israel and Israel alone that was their contemporary persecutor. It is anachronistic to inject any other persecutor into the text.**

So, in 2 Thessalonians 1, Paul was addressing the same church as in the first epistle and they were still enduring the tribulation addressed in the first epistle. We have no reason whatsoever to believe that the Jews had ceased their persecution and that a different group had picked up the sword. The Romans did not begin their persecution of the church for almost fifteen years. And since Paul promised that judgment was coming very soon against "those who are troubling you" (the persecutors in 1 Thessalonians 2) does this not demand that the judgment of 2 Thessalonians 1 was coming very soon?

What makes this chain of association so certain is that in 2 Thessalonians 1 Paul quotes from Isaiah 2-4 in his prediction of the Lord's coming in judgment of the persecutors. We can only develop this briefly here, but see my book *Who Is This Babylon?* for a full discussion. Here is the point.

Isaiah 2-4 predicted the last days and the establishment of the kingdom (2:2f). Consummating that last days period would be the Day of the Lord (2:10f; 19-21) when men would flee to the mountains, "from the terror of the Lord and the glory of His majesty" (2:10, 19, 21). The reader needs to know that 2 Thessalonians 1:9 is a *direct quote* of the LXX (the Greek translation of the Hebrew Old Testament) of Isaiah! In other words, Paul was anticipating the fulfillment of Isaiah's prophecy of the Day of the Lord. What is so significant about that, and what does it have to do with our study? *Everything*!

You see, the Day of the Lord in Isaiah cannot be a time ending, earth-burning event, *because men could escape it by fleeing to the mountains!* That hardly agrees with the traditional idea that the coming of the Lord destroys the earth "in a moment, in the twinkling of an eye!" Furthermore, this Day of the Lord would be a time of famine (Isaiah 3:1-2) and a time when God would judge Israel (3:14f) in the time of "the war" (3:18-24). It would also be when Jehovah would, "purge the blood of Jerusalem by the spirit of fire and the spirit of burning" (4:4). In other words, Isaiah's Day of the Lord would be when God judged Israel for her guilt of killing the innocent!

In Luke 23:28-31 Jesus was being led to his death. The women who loved him followed, crying and wailing. Jesus turned to them and said: "Daughters of Jerusalem, weep not for me, but weep for yourselves and for your children. For indeed the days are coming...then they will say to the mountains, 'Fall on us' and to the hills, 'Cover us!'" In this passage, Jesus was citing Isaiah 2 (parallel Hosea 10:8) and undeniably applying it to the upcoming judgment of Jerusalem.

So, Jesus applied Isaiah's prediction of the Day of the Lord against Israel, for shedding innocent blood, to the fall of Jerusalem in AD 70. This means that when Jesus predicted that Israel would be judged for shedding innocent blood in his generation in Matthew 23, he was actually predicting the fulfillment of Isaiah's prediction of the Day of the Lord. In other words, the judgment of Israel in AD 70 would be the Day of the Lord! Notice how this applies to 1 and 2 Thessalonians.

In 1 Thessalonians 2:15-17 Paul was predicting judgment on Israel for shedding the blood of God's saints. Paul was reiterating what Jesus had predicted. Jesus foretold the AD 70 judgment in fulfillment of Isaiah 2-4. But this means that Paul was anticipating the fulfillment of Isaiah's prophecy of the Day of the Lord against Israel, the Day when men would flee, "from the terror of the Lord and the glory of His majesty" in fulfillment of Isaiah 2-4. But if 1 *Thessalonians 2* is a prediction of the fulfillment of Isaiah 2-4, since it predicted the time of the judgment of Israel for shedding the blood of the saints, then since Paul *directly quotes Isaiah 2* in 2 Thessalonians 1, his prediction of the Day of the Lord against the persecutors of the saints, this is *prima facie* evidence that 2 Thessalonians 1 is a prediction of the AD 70 Day of the Lord against Israel.

How could it be argued that 1 Thessalonians 2 predicted the judgment of Israel in AD 70, in fulfillment of Isaiah, and then claim that although Paul specifically cites Isaiah's prophecy in 2 Thessalonians 1 that he did not have the same judgment as 1 Thessalonians 2 in mind? Jesus said the AD 70 judgment of Israel's blood guilt would be the fulfillment of Isaiah. 1 Thessalonians 2 predicted that judgment in A. D. 70. Since Paul quotes from the Isaiah text that Jesus applied to AD 70, are we not bound to apply Paul's passage to AD 70?

So, here are the points we have made:

☞ 1 Thessalonians 4 is the same Day of the Lord as 2 Thessalonians 1.

☞ The Day of the Lord in 2 Thessalonians 1 would be the fulfillment of the prophecy of Isaiah 2-4, the prophecy of the Day of the Lord when God judged Israel for shedding the blood of the saints.

☞ Jesus applied the prophecy of Isaiah 2-4 to the judgment of Jerusalem in AD 70 (Luke 23:28f).

☞ Therefore, since Jesus applied Isaiah 2-4 to the Day of the Lord against the persecutors of the saints to A. D. 70, and since Paul quotes from Isaiah 2-4 in his prediction of the Day of the Lord against the persecutors of the saints, this means that 2 Thessalonians 1 must be applied to the judgment of Israel in AD 70. How could anyone argue that Paul was applying Isaiah 2-4 in a totally different way, to a dramatically different event, to a time far removed, from what Jesus applied that prophecy?

☞ But, since 2 Thessalonians 1 is the same coming as 1 Thessalonians 4 this demands that the coming of 1 Thessalonians 4 must be the Day of the Lord of AD 70.

To posit 2 Thessalonians 1 in our future one must delineate between the persecution and the promise of vindication and judgment in 1 Thessalonians 2 and that in 2 Thessalonians 1. But where is the distinction? It is undeniable that in 1 Thessalonians 2 and 2 Thessalonians 1, Paul is writing to the *same church*, about the *same problem*, and gives the *same promise*.[246] Their persecutors were about to be judged. In 1 Thessalonians 2 the judgment of the persecutors was so near that Paul could say it had "come upon them to the uttermost." In 2 Thessalonians 1, the apostle told the suffering church that they would receive relief (*anesis*) from their tormentors, and their persecutors- "those who are troubling you"- would receive tribulation (*thlipsis*) "when the Lord Jesus is revealed from heaven."

To make 2 Thessalonians 1 a yet future event one must divorce it from the very passage that Paul quotes, Isaiah 2-4, and from Jesus' application of Isaiah. *How is that possible?* But if one cannot divorce 2 Thessalonians 1 from Isaiah neither can you divorce 1 Thessalonians 4 from Isaiah. 2 Thessalonians 1 and 1 Thessalonians 4 are the same event.

We cannot extrapolate that relief and judgment promised in 2 Thessalonians 1 into the distant future far removed from that first century context. Paul was writing to living breathing humans undergoing very real persecution at the hands of first century murderers. He was promising relief from that then on-going persecution, and judgment on those persecutors, "when the Lord Jesus is revealed from heaven." Now to our point.

Few commentators believe that the *parousia* of 1 Thessalonians 4 is a different event from that foretold in 2 Thessalonians 1.[247] With that consensus in mind, here is our argument:

The coming of the Lord of 1 Thessalonians 4 is the same coming of the Lord in 2 Thessalonians 1.[248]

But the coming of the Lord in 2 Thessalonians 1 would be the fulfillment of Paul's prediction of judgment on the Jews for persecuting the church (1 Thessalonians 2:15-17).[249]

Therefore, the coming of the Lord in 1 Thessalonians 4 would be the coming of the Lord in judgment of Israel for persecuting the church.

Let me put it another way:

Jesus was going to come in judgment of the persecutors of the church in his generation (Matthew 23).

But the coming of the Lord in 2 Thessalonians 1 was to be the judgment of the persecutors of the church and was going to occur in the lifetime of the Thessalonians (2 Thessalonians 1:4-10).

Therefore, the coming of the Lord of 2 Thessalonians 1 was to be the coming of Christ in judgment of Israel for persecuting the church.

There are a limited number of ways to mitigate our argument here:
1.) You would have to prove that the coming of 1 Thessalonians 4 and 2 Thessalonians 1 are different comings. This is untenable.
2.) You would have to prove that the persecution of 1 Thessalonians 2:15-17 is a different persecution from that of 2 Thessalonians 1. Yet, there is only a space of a year or so between the two epistles. There is no contextual indication in either epistle that the apostle had two different persecutions, at the hands of two different persecutors at two totally different times, in mind.
3.) You would have to prove that the persecution and the promised vindication/judgment of 2 Thessalonians 1 is unrelated to the promise of Jesus in Matthew 23. Yet, what was happening in 2 Thessalonians 1 is the direct fulfillment of Jesus' prophecy that his disciples were to be persecuted before the end (Cf. 1 Thessalonians 3:1-3). What Paul was promising was what Jesus promised, vindication and judgment in that generation.
4.) You would have to prove that although Jesus applied Isaiah 2-4 to AD 70, and that although Paul quoted *from the same verses* that Jesus applied to AD 70, that Paul was not predicting what Isaiah predicted, that Paul was ignoring Jesus' application of Isaiah. This is a tenuous position.

Since none of these things can be proven the association between Matthew 23, 1 Thessalonians 2, 1 Thessalonians 4 and 2 Thessalonians 1 stands. And this being true, this proves that 1 Thessalonians 4 is inextricably linked with the judgment of Israel in AD 70.

WELL, WHAT ABOUT HEAVEN, WHAT ABOUT ETERNAL LIFE?

We want to address an important issue. Some might conclude, incorrectly, that since Thessalonians, John 14, etc. are not a removal of man from earth that we are suggesting that there is no heaven after death for the faithful.[250] This could not be further from the truth! We are simply demonstrating that in Scripture, Christ's coming is not to remove man from earth or to bring history to an end. So, does the Bible promise a glorious life after death? *I firmly believe so!*

Paul affirmed that it was God's eternal purpose for man to have eternal life with him (Titus 1:2).

Paul anticipated his own death in Philippians 1:19f, and believed that what awaited him was "far better" than even the blessings of this life. Likewise, in 2 Timothy 4, he believed that through Christ's coming, his own death was to result in a crown of life just as Jesus promised those at Smyrna, "Be thou faithful until death, and I will give thee a crown of life" (Revelation 2:10). There was something, *eternal life*, awaiting them if they suffered martyrdom.

What is the promise of *life* and *immortality* that has been brought to life through the gospel (2 Timothy 1:9f) if it does not include life after physical death? The work of Christ has brought life and immortality to light through the gospel! Well, if, after we die physically there is *nothing*, then there is no life and immortality in Christ or his gospel! So what would be the point? What did he accomplish? Do the writers of the Bible not affirm that it is God's desire for man to live with Him (Titus 1:2)?

The gospel of John abounds with Jesus' discussion of eternal life. Those passages lead us to believe that God has something wonderful in store for His saints.

There are at least nine passages in the gospel of John that affirm that those in fellowship with Christ through faith in him "will never die," "will not perish," or similar language.[251] Patently, these texts could not be speaking of physical death, or else no one has ever believed in him since there is a 100% physical death rate from Jesus to the present! There are no less than 24 passages that say, in varying terms that the gift of God is eternal life.[252]

To this writer, these verses offer solid assurance of eternal life with Christ. They not only offer assurance of fellowship with him *now* in this dimension, but life with him that physical demise does not diminish, does not destroy!

Hebrews 9:15f is a text that virtually demands a doctrine of "life after death" promise and assurance: "And for this reason He is the mediator of the new covenant, by means of death, for the redemption of the transgressions under the first covenant, that those who are called may receive the promise of the eternal inheritance." The writer sets forth the efficacy of Christ's death to provide remission of sin for those who lived and died under the first covenant. Think about that! If there is no life after death then forgiveness and redemption are moot, meaningless issues!

So, the writer affirms that through the efficacy of Jesus' sacrifice, redemption for those under the first covenant would become a reality at the *parousia* (Hebrews 9:24-28) when the power of Christ's atoning work would be perfected. His work "to put away sin" in fulfillment of Daniel 9:24f would be finished.

Notice that the writer also calls that inheritance to be received by those who could not receive redemption (i.e. Life, Galatians 3:21) under Torah, "the eternal inheritance." This is undoubtedly the gift of "never dying" promised by Jesus in John. It is the "crown of life" promised to those about to die a martyr's death in Revelation 2:10f.

The Abrahamic promise abounds with assurance of life– real life– after this earthly existence. Abraham looked for a heavenly city and country and that promise stood on the brink of fulfillment when Hebrews was written (Hebrews 11:13f, 39f; 12:21f). What is so important for this discussion is that Abraham was informed that the fulfillment of God's "land- city- country" promises to him were, *from the moment of promise* "far off," and were indeed heavenly and spiritual.

Some adversaries of Covenant Eschatology claim that a first century fulfillment of Christ's *parousia* destroys hope and essentially destroys Christianity. Do you think Abraham would see the fulfillment of his hope as the nullification of his faith? When he would finally sit down at the Messianic table in the kingdom (Matthew 8:11) *which is nothing less than the promise of resurrection* (cf. Isaiah 25:6f) do you think he would cry, "Foul, my hope is destroyed!"?

The fact that the Hebrews writer affirms that the promises to Abraham were, after such a long time, on the verge of fulfillment speaks eloquently to Jesus' words concerning his Father, "He is not the God of the dead, but of the living."If there is no life after death then there was to be no heavenly city, no heavenly country, no spiritual and eternal inheritance for Abraham. But Hebrews confidently affirms that God's faithfulness to Abraham, Isaac and Jacob was about to be fulfilled. This demands that the promises involved life beyond, life after, life that transcended the physical realm.

In Revelation 14:13, the angel announced that as a result of the *parousia* of Christ, "Blessed are the dead, who die in the Lord from henceforth, for they shall rest from their labors."[253] There was to be, and is, a state of blessedness for those dying in the Lord, since his coming, that did not exist prior to his coming. Now, if man–if the righteous-- are simply like the old dog rover, and are "dead all over" when they die, then there is no difference in their state of being before or after Christ's coming.

So, the purpose of Christ's *parousia* was not a removal of man from the earth at a supposed rapture or end of history. However, his coming would establish (re-establish) an eternal relationship between man and God that physical death cannot sever. There is life, eternal, un-ending life for those in Christ! This is truly "good news!"

WE WHO ARE ALIVE AND REMAIN UNTIL THE COMING OF THE LORD: THE FIRST CENTURY NEARNESS OF THE *PAROUSIA*
1 Thessalonians 4:15, 17

Before we conclude the exegetical aspect of this work we need to address a vitally important issue, the issue of timing. Regardless of what else we might believe about 1 Thessalonians 4 there is no doubt that the passage deals with the topic of the coming of the Lord in the context of imminence. In other words, the Thessalonians–and Paul-- believed that the Lord was coming back in their generation. The question is, were they right?

In verses 15 and 17, Paul said, "those of us who are alive and remain until the coming of the Lord." Notice the "us" references, and the "remain until" statements. The most natural, the *most literal*, way to understand this is to see that Paul was saying the Thessalonians, i.e. that generation, would remain until Christ's coming. This is confirmed by the fact that all futurist commentators spend considerable time seeking to mitigate the force of the language. If, "we who are alive and remain until the coming of the Lord" does not naturally convey the idea that Paul was affirming the first century fulfillment, no need would be felt by those who deny the first century fulfillment, to explain the words away.

Strimple scoffs at the preterist emphasis on the words of Paul in Thessalonians and the similar words in 1 Corinthians 15:51-52:

"Hyper-preterists insist, of course, that when Paul writes that 'we will not all sleep, but we will all be changed,' he is teaching definitively that some of those to whom he is writing will be alive at the Parousia, a clear pointer to the fact that the coming took place in the first century. The hyper-preterist cannot claim that we includes Paul, because Paul suffered martyrdom at Rome prior to AD 70. But, as Sproul observes, if 'we' simply implies that some of those who receive the apostle's teaching would be alive at the Second Coming, 'then it is likewise possible that the 'we who are alive' can be even more inclusive and refers to any reader of the Corinthians text in the future.' All we have to keep in mind when reading such alleged 'imminency' statements in the New Testament is that none of the apostles knew when the Lord would return (Matthew 24:36); so how else would we expect them to write of that great event?"(*WSTTB*, 344)

The problem with Strimple's objection is that it has no contextual, scriptural support. Furthermore, Gentry, one of his fellow authors in WSTTB, has actually provided us with an excellent refutation of Strimple.

Gentry takes note of the oft stated argument of the dispensationalists that "this generation" in Matthew 24:34 simply means "the Jewish race." Citing Ridderbos, Gentry observes that, "It would mean that Israel will not pass away until all these things happen to Israel. But in the dispensational view, Israel will never pass away. So the statement would be irrelevant as a means of identifying any prophetic time context." (*Dominion*, 2009, 347). However, apply Gentry's logic to the Thessalonian and Corinthian statements.

If "we who are alive and remain" and "we shall not all sleep" "simply implies that some of those (i.e. *Christians of any age*, dkp) who receive the apostle's teaching would be alive at the Second Coming" then Ridderbos' (Gentry's) argument is applicable.

The church– and thus, Christians– *will never pass away*. So, per Gentry's appeal to Ridderbos, this means that Paul was simply saying that Christians will not all die until Christians see these things happen! This is a tautology, and is borderline facetious.

The traditional understanding of the coming of Christ is of a bodily, visible descent out of heaven on a cloud. Since that did not happen the language of *when it was to happen* is denied. Or, it is said that Paul was using the "editorial we," the "royal we," or the "covenantal we." What is meant by this is that Paul was speaking of the church timelessly, saying that, "The Christians that are alive when the Lord finally comes, whenever that is, will not precede those who have died." However, this violates the text.

First, notice Paul's use of "we" throughout the epistle. We can't examine each occurrence of "we," or "us," in the book, but urge you to do so. You will find that Paul was definitely using the term in a manner to refer to the Thessalonians personally. Take a look however, at the immediate context. In verse 13, Paul says "*we* do not want you to be ignorant brethren." Who is Paul's "we" here? Is it a timeless, editorial, royal "we"? Clearly not. It refers to Paul's apostolic group, his contemporaries. If Paul uses "we" in such a personal contemporary manner where is the authority for dramatically shifting gears to an abstract timeless definition *in the same text?*

Notice Paul's continued use of "we" in verse 15: "This *we* say to you by the word of the Lord." Who is this "we?" Was it Paul and the apostolic group, or was it the church timeless, as suggested by Strimple and Sproul? There is no doubt, it was Paul's contemporary group. So, if Paul's, "*we* say unto you," is to be applied contemporaneously, then it would be incongruous to insist that his, "we who are alive and remain," *in the same verse*, did not include his contemporary audience as well.

Further, all commentators agree that what prompted Paul's epistle to the Thessalonians was that some of the beloved members of the church had died before Christ returned. The church was unprepared for this since they believed so fervently that Jesus was coming back in their lifetime. This discouragement– see again 1 Thessalonians 3:1-3-- caused them to contemplate the fate of their loved ones. Paul wrote to console them by telling them that the death of their loved ones before the *parousia* (Christ's presence) would not deprive their loved ones of their reward.

We must honor the reality of the death of the Thessalonian Christians in regard to Paul's reference to, "those of us who are alive and remain until the coming of the Lord." The "we who are alive" reference is in direct contrast to those members of the Thessalonian church that had died. When Paul said, "we who are alive" he was saying, "We who are *still alive*, in contrast to our loved ones that have already died." And it meant, "We who are alive *right now*." This is not a reference to 10th, 15th, or 21st century Christians! Paul *did not say*, "*Those* who are alive centuries from now and remain until the Lord's coming." He did not say, "The Christians who are alive at the time of the *parousia*." Paul's "*we* who are alive," are the ones that he said could, "remain until the coming of the Lord."[254] *Paul's then living ones were the remaining ones!* The important thing to see is that the "remaining" is in direct contrast to the dead *Thessalonians* of the first century. Once we honor this connection, there is no justification for divorcing Thessalonians from its first century context, and this demands that Paul taught that Christ's coming would occur in that generation.

For emphasis of this point, consider the words of Jesus:

"For the Son of Man will come in the glory of His Father, with His angels and then he will reward each according to his works. Assuredly I say to you, there are some standing here who shall not taste death till they see the Son of Man coming in his kingdom" (Matthew 16:27-28).

The coming of the kingdom is the time of the resurrection (2 Timothy 4:1; Revelation 11:16f) so in reality, Jesus was predicting the time of the resurrection.[255] Needless to say this is involved in 1 Thessalonians 4. When did Jesus say it would occur? The challenging, yet undeniable answer is: "Assuredly I say to you, there are some standing here who shall not taste death till they see the Son of Man coming in his kingdom."

What is the difference between, "there are some standing here that shall not taste of death until they see the Son of Man coming," and, "those of us who are alive and remain until the coming of the Lord?" There is no difference. Both are assertions that the then living generation would witness the events being foretold.

This is the case in 1 Corinthians 15:51 as well. Corinthians discusses the resurrection, and of course, this is involved in Thessalonians. When did Paul say it would occur? Verse 51 has the answer: "Behold, I tell you a mystery: We shall not all sleep, but we shall all be changed." The apostle was addressing the *same generation* of living, breathing human beings as in Thessalonians. In Thessalonians he said, "those of us who are alive and remain until the coming." In Corinthians he tells the members of that congregation that not all of them would die. (The word *sleep* is used as a euphemism for physical death). This is precisely what Jesus told the multitude in Matthew 16! Thus, in three key texts, we have the unequivocal testimony of Jesus and his inspired apostle, that Jesus' coming and the resurrection would occur in the lifetime of the first century generation.

There is a tremendous amount of corroborative evidence for the expectation of the resurrection in the first century. Consider the following. **The time of the resurrection, inclusive of 1 Thessalonians 4:13-18, would be the time when the martyrs of God would be judged and vindicated (Revelation 11:16f).**

But the time of the judgment and vindication of the martyrs of God was to be the time of the judgment of Israel in the first century generation (Matthew 23:29-39).

Therefore, the resurrection, inclusive of 1 Thessalonians 4:13-18, was to be the time of the judgment of Israel in the first century generation.[256]

The text in Matthew 23 is critical, and yet in eschatological studies is mostly ignored. It is widely admitted to be speaking about the events of AD 70, but the actual content of the text seems to have escaped the notice of the commentators. Jesus said that *all of the blood of all of the martyrs of God all the way back to creation* would be judged and vindicated in his generation! Isn't the vindication and judgment of the dead the time of the resurrection? Of course it is! Well, in Matthew 23 Jesus said, "Verily I say unto you, all these things shall come upon this generation."

It is almost impossible to find a commentator that does not admit Jesus was referring to the coming judgment of Israel. So, the time of the vindication and judgment of the martyrs is the time of the resurrection. Jesus said the vindication and judgment of the martyrs was to take place in the judgment of Jerusalem. This is an unequivocal statement that the resurrection was to take place in the judgment of Jerusalem.

Finally, consider the testimony of 1 Peter that agrees perfectly with Matthew 23. The Christian saints were suffering the persecution foretold by Jesus in Matthew 23:34 (1 Peter 1:5f; 2:20f; 4:1-2, 12-17). Jesus said that the persecution of his saints would result in Israel filling up the measure of her sin (Matthew 23:32). Remember that Paul said Israel was indeed persecuting the saints, and was filling up the measure of her sin (1 Thessalonians 2:15-17). Jesus said that judgment of *the living persecutors,* and vindication of the *dead,* thus *the judgment of the living and the dead,* would occur in his generation (Matthew 23:36). Peter, writing amidst the predicted persecution, tells his suffering audience that they will only have to suffer their persecution "for a little while" before the revelation of their salvation at the coming of Jesus (1 Peter 1:5-7). Jesus was "ready to judge the living and the dead" (1 Peter 4:5).

The word translated ready is *hetoimos*, and means not only prepared but on the point of doing. The *Expositors Greek Testament* says that the Greek reader of the text would understand Peter to be referring to "the imminent judge"[257] (See Acts 21:13; 2 Corinthians 12:14, etc.) Some commentators seek to mitigate the nearness of the judgment in this verse by saying that Peter was simply saying that Jesus was prepared to judge, not that the judgment was near. However, this word *hetoimos*, while containing the meaning of *prepared*, certainly contains the idea of nearness. This is the word used when the wedding preparations were all completed and the announcement made, "All things are now ready" (*hetoimos*, Matthew 22: 4, 8). Would anyone argue that once the *preparations* are completed that the wedding is *not near*? In Revelation, it says: "Let us be glad and rejoice and give him glory, for the marriage of the Lamb has come, and His wife has made herself ready" (Revelation 19:7). Notice the connection between, "the time has come for the wedding," and, "the bride is prepared." When a bride is all dressed up and *ready* for the wedding, is the wedding simply *prepared*, or is the wedding *at hand?*

The point is, Jesus said the judgment of *the living and the dead, i.e.* the resurrection, was to occur in his generation. Peter, writing later in that same generation said Jesus was then, "ready to judge the living and the dead." However, Peter did not stop there. He also said, "the end of all things has drawn near" (1 Peter 4:7). Peter was not referring to the end of time or he was patently wrong, and disqualified as a prophet of God.

Further, Peter said, "The time has come for the judgment to begin at the house of God" (1 Peter 4:17). Notice that Peter said, "the time has come." It is important to note that Peter uses a distinctive word for *time*, kairos, and it means more than just time broadly considered. The Greeks had a generic word for time, *chronos*. That should sound familiar to you.

According to the lexicons, "*Chronos* designates a 'period of time' in the linear sense, while *kairos* frequently refers to 'eschatologically filled time, a time for decision.'"[258] To put it another way, "Chronos is time, contemplated as such, the succession of moments." However, *kairos* refers to, "the joints and articulations in these times, the epoch-making periods foreordained by God."[259] In other words, *chronos* is the generic word for time broadly considered, but *kairos* means a certain time, an appointed time. What this means is that Peter was saying that the appointed time for judgment had come. But this is not all he said. See our critique of Gentry's claims about *chronos* and *kairos* on page 231f.

Peter also said the appointed time for "the judgment" had arrived. The apostle did not say the appointed time for "a judgment" or simply,"the time for judgment has come." He said "the appointed time for "the judgment" (Greek, *to krino*) had come. He used the definite article to speak of the judgment. When one considers the normal use of the definite article this is powerful proof that Peter was affirming the nearness of the resurrection.

In the Greek, the definite article is *anaphoric* in the great majority of cases. This simply means that the article normally refers back to a previous reference. Thus, when Peter said the time for "*the* judgment" had arrived he was referring back to the judgment mentioned earlier. What judgment was that? It is in verse 5 that says Christ was, "ready to judge the living and the dead." If the article of verse 17 is anaphoric, and the preponderant use of the article is anaphoric, this *demands* that the judgment of verse 17 is the judgment of verse 5. Peter was affirming in no uncertain terms that the time for the resurrection had arrived.[260] (Interestingly, Gentry ignores 1 Peter 4:17, and Mathison offers only the vaguest of comments, although he admits that 1 Peter 4:7 probably does refer to Christ's AD 70 coming, *Age*, 2009, 632).

The judgment under consideration was one that his audience knew had been "appointed by God," and it involved the judgment of "the living and the dead," and "the end of all things." What judgment might that be?

In Acts 17:30-31, Paul gave his marvelous sermon on Mars Hill: "Truly the times of ignorance God overlooked, but now commands all men everywhere to repent, for He has appointed a day on which He will judge the world in righteousness by the Man whom He has ordained. He has given assurance of this all by raising Him from the dead."

The word *appointed* is from the Greek word *istemi*, and means to "make stand, to set" and thus to appoint or designate.[261] Thus, God designated the Day of Judgment. When Jesus was on earth he said that only the Father knew the day and hour of that Day (Matthew 24:36). As noted, Strimple believes this nullifies all later New Testament statements of imminence. Gentry likewise hinges his concept of a delayed parousia on this text (2009, 437). Simply stated, this view effectively negates the reality of *the revelatory Spirit* as promised by Jesus.

When Jesus ascended, the Father gave him the Spirit to send to the apostles to "shew you things

> **An appeal to Matthew 24:36, to mitigate the apostolic statements of the nearness of Christ's coming is an implicit denial of the inspiration of the apostles. It was the Father– who knew the day and hour– who sent the Spirit to the apostles, to "show you things to come." Thus, all apostolic declarations of the nearness of the end were, in fact, statements from the Father!**

to come" (John 16:7). Thus, when we read the statements of imminence in the New Testament, and realize that those statements were inspired by the Spirit, sent from the Father, to show them things to come, this completely falsifies all claims that the New Testament writers did not know whether the *parousia* was near or not. This simple, yet critical fact is either ignored, overlooked, or denied by Strimple and the other contributors to *When Shall These Things Be*, not to mention virtually all futurist commentators.

Thus, when the New Testament writers, by inspiration of the Spirit, said the Day was near they were *speaking what the Father had revealed.* It is improper to say that the New Testament writers could not have said the Day was actually near because Jesus did not know the time *when he was on earth*. Jesus himself said that after his return to the Father the Spirit would be sent to reveal things to come. Part of what the Spirit revealed to those disciples was, "the end of all things has drawn near," and, "the time has come for the judgment to begin" (1 Peter 4:7,17). If the disciples were writing by inspiration of the Spirit who was revealing this from the Father, then either the end truly was near, or the Father did not reveal the truth to the disciples, or the Spirit did not communicate properly what the Father was revealing.

The Spirit was truthfully revealing the truth about the day of judgment to Jesus' disciples. Paul said God had appointed the day of judgment (the time of the resurrection). Peter said *the appointed time for the judgment* had come. We are forced therefore to accept the fact that the Bible does indeed teach that the resurrection, which involves 1 Thessalonians 4:13-18, was to occur in the first century.

Paul actually indicated that the judgment was near when he delivered his Mars Hill sermon. When he said, "he has appointed a day in which he will judge the world," he used a Greek word, *mello*, that means, "to be about to, to be on the point of."[262] So, Paul actually said that God was *about to judge the world* when he gave his sermon.

There is a tremendous amount of additional testimony to demonstrate that the time of Christ's coming and the resurrection predicted in 1 Thessalonians 4 truly was near in the first century and was to occur with the end of the Old Covenant age, in the fall of Jerusalem in AD 70. Let's take a look at some more evidence under four headings.

✱ Point #1– The Old Testament Prophets Foretold the Coming of the Kingdom, The Resurrection, The End of the Age, The New Heavens and Earth, The Destruction of Satan, The Avenging of the Martyrs– All of the Eschatological Tenets Found in the New Testament Writings.

We will keep this brief. However, this point is critical.

1.) Deuteronomy 32:43– Foretold the avenging of the martyrs in the last days, in *Israel's* last days.

2.) **Isaiah 2-4**– Isaiah foretold that *in the last days* (2:2f) YHVH would establish His kingdom, *at the Day of the Lord* (2:10-21) when the blood guilt of Israel was judged and purged by the spirit of fire and judgment (4:4f) and the tabernacle of God's living presence was established (4:5).

3.) **Isaiah 24-27; Hosea 6:1-3; 13:14; Daniel 12**– All foretold the resurrection.

4.) **Isaiah 62**– Foretold the coming of Christ in judgment at the time of the Wedding– one of Jesus' favorite themes.

5.) **Isaiah 65-66**– Foretold the New Heaven and Earth.

6.) **Ezekiel 37, Zechariah 6:12f**– Foretold the Messianic Temple.

7.) **Daniel 12:2-4, 9f**– Foretold the end of the age at the time of the resurrection.

There are, of course, other constituent elements but this brief list establishes that the Old Covenant prophets did predict every constituent element of the eschatological hope proclaimed by the New Testament writers.

✱ **Point #2– The Old Testament Prophets Clearly Say That the Anticipated End Was *Not* Near When They Wrote, But, They Said That When the Last Days Arrived, Fulfillment Would Be at Hand, and Come Quickly.**

This is an *important point* that is often overlooked by commentators. The Old Testament prophets were told, sometimes clearly, sometimes not so specifically, that the fulfillment of their eschatological promises was not near, but was for another time far removed from them. Let's take a look at some of those texts.

➡ **Numbers 24:17**-- "I see Him, but not now; I Behold Him, but not near; A Star shall come out of Jacob; A Scepter shall rise out of Israel, and batter Moab and destroy all the sons of tumult."[263]

Balaam foresaw the coming of the Messiah. Was he told that time statements from YHVH mean nothing, or that they are so vague, elastic, or ambiguous as to be virtually meaningless? No. Was he told that Messiah *could come* at any moment? No. Was he told that since God does not see time like man, that what he was being told meant nothing? No.

Balaam was told, very clearly, that the coming– the judgment coming- of Messiah was far off. It was not near. It was not at hand.

Likewise, other Old Covenant prophecies show that the prophets did not expect, or say, that the fulfillment of their end time hopes was near, but was in fact a long time away in their future.

➡ **Daniel 2, 7, 10-12**-- Daniel's prophecies spanned four kingdoms (Daniel 2; 7; 10-12) beginning at Babylon and extending to Rome.[264] Note that in Daniel, the prophet specifically outlined the span of fulfillment, showing that it would begin with Nebuchadnezzar and Babylon, and extend through the history of four kingdoms. He then said that the ultimate fulfillment belonged to the last days, during the time of the fourth empire (Rome– Daniel 2:28f). Daniel knew therefore, that the final fulfillment– the time of the establishment of the kingdom of God– was not near. It was in fact far off.

This same sequence of kingdoms and events is reiterated in chapter 7, where the coming of the Lord destroys the persecutorial little horn, and the kingdom is possessed by the saints (v. 21f). There is no expression of urgency, no expression that these events could happen at any moment, no statement that, "the kingdom of heaven has drawn near." On the contrary, a reading of the text patently communicates that Daniel and all those who read the prophecy knew those events were far removed from their days.

Daniel 10-12 picks up after the fall of the Babylonian kingdom and is in the early stages of the Persian (Daniel 10:1). Daniel was given a vision that extended all the way to the Roman empire and the time of the end, the time of the resurrection (Daniel 12:1-9f). Notice what Daniel wrote: "In the third year of Cyrus king of Persia a message was revealed to Daniel, whose name is Belteshazzar. The message was true, but the appointed time was long; and he understood the message, and had understanding of the vision" (Daniel 10:1).[265]

Note that Daniel was told emphatically that the vision was not for his day. It was a long time off. See also 10:14, where this is reiterated: "the vision refers to many days yet to come." In Daniel 12:4, 9, Daniel was told, twice, that the fulfillment of his vision was for the time of the end, it was far off. Consequently, Daniel was to seal the prophecy. There could hardly be a clearer expression of the *non-imminence* of fulfillment than these words.

➡ **Hebrews 11:13f**– Even the New Testament writers tell us that the Old Covenant figures were told that the fulfillment of their end times hope was far removed from them.

"These all died in faith, not having received the promises, but having seen them afar off were assured of them, embraced them and confessed that they were strangers and pilgrims on the earth. 14 For those who say such things declare plainly that they seek a homeland. 15 And truly if they had called to mind that country from which they had come out, they would have had opportunity to return."

This text tells us that Abraham, Isaac and their descendants were promised, looked for, and longed for, the heavenly country and city. This is undoubtedly the New Creation promise that was carried through as Israel's hope in Isaiah 65-66. However, those Old Testament worthies were told that the fulfillment of their hope was not near. They knew that fulfillment was "afar off." Of course, this language demands that we reject the idea that time statements mean nothing to God. He clearly communicated in an understandable way that the New Creation was not imminent.

We have established then that the Old Testament prophets foretold the last days and the Day of the Lord. They were told that the consummation was not near. Let me reiterate this; it is important. The Old Testament writers *never say* that the kingdom had drawn nigh. They *never say* that the end of the age had come upon them. They *never say* that the last days had arrived, or that they were living in the last days.

However, what the Old Covenant writers do say is that *when the last days arrived* the eschatological consummation would be near.[266] They tell us that when the appointed time finally came, YHVH would consummate things quickly, without delay. Let's take a look at some of these passages.

First however, it is at this point that we find another contradiction in the postmillennial camp. Gentry is emphatic that a "distinctive" of the postmillennial view is that the end is *not imminent* (*Dominion*, 2009, 343). On the other hand, Mathison, although he insists that we honor the NT statements of the temporal imminence of the AD 70 parousia, nonetheless also affirms that the final coming of the Lord must be considered as always imminent (*Age*, 2009, 638). It is difficult to determine what the *real* postmillennial position now is supposed to be. On the one hand, postmillennialism never affirms the imminence of the end, per Gentry, but on the other hand, per Mathison, postmillennialism affirms the *perpetual imminence of the end!* Such confusion could be avoided if we honor the fact that the Old Testament never affirms the nearness of the end of the age, while the New Testament invariably says the end had now drawn near.

There is another irony here that should not go unnoticed. Gentry often condemns the full preterist paradigm based on the unbroken testimony of the early church fathers about a future coming of the Lord. Gentry condemns preterists for challenging this unbroken chain of testimony. (Of course, it does not bother Gentry to take a view of Revelation that is not found in the patristics or the creeds! He openly admits that his views are not traditional or creedal "no other church fathers suggest it" in reference to the identity of Nero as the beast of Revelation (*Beast*, 2002, 44). Gentry asks for an open mind in light of the "flood of evidence becoming a 'river that no man can cross'" (*Beast*, 2002, 18). Here is the irony of Gentry's position.

On the one hand, Gentry appeals to the patristics and their virtual unanimous belief in a future coming. He says that preterists must honor this testimony. What Gentry fails to tell his readers is that not only do the patristics believe in a future coming, they are almost as unanimously in agreement *that the end was near!* In fact, commenting on the constant dispensational claims of the nearness of the end, Gentry cites Tertullian (AD 160-220) Cyprian (AD 195-258) and others who said that the end was very near. And yet, Gentry says that the distinctive of postmillennialism is that the coming of Christ is not imminent! Clearly then the patristics did not hold to the postmillennial "distinctive."

➜ **Joel 2:28-chapter 3**– In Joel 1-2, we have repeated statements that the Day of the Lord was near (1:15; 2:1, 10). However, take careful note of chapter 2:28: "It shall come to pass afterward." This can only mean that after the Day of the Lord that was imminent in Joel's day, "in the last days" there would come *another* Day of the Lord. There is a marked contrast between the two Days of the Lord. One was at hand, one was *not* near. Only confusion can result if we fail to honor what the text emphatically says as it delineates between the near Day and the far Day.

Furthermore, take note of the fact that in chapter 3:1, the inspired author continues, "It shall come to pass that in *those days* and at *that time*..." The antecedent referent is the last days and Day of the Lord of 2:28f. When one compares the earlier discussion of the near Day, we find no language of projection into a different time. In the previous discussion, all is near, everything is virtually happening at that time. There is no such discussion in 2:28f. Everything is for the last days, and "in those days, and at that time."

However, note that when the author speaks of "in those days and at that time" he then says, "The Day of the Lord is near in the Valley of Decision" (Joel 3:14). We must emphasize again that he is *not* saying that the Day of the Lord of 3:14 was near *when he wrote*. He was projecting himself– or the Spirit was projecting him– into the last days to speak of the consummative Day of the Lord. What he is saying is that when the last days arrived, then, and only then, would the Day of the Lord be at hand.

The failure to honor this projection into the future has caused some students to claim that Joel's language of imminence cannot be taken seriously. It is claimed that Joel speaks of the last days and the Day of the Lord as near *when he wrote*. Here is the argument that is given.

Joel said the last days and Day of the Lord was near.

But, Peter said Joel was being fulfilled on Pentecost (Acts 2:15f– "This is that which was spoken by the prophet Joel...") hundreds of years removed from Joel.

Therefore, Joel's at hand statement spanned hundreds of years, and the Biblical language of imminence is elastic and nebulous.

This argument fails to honor the language of Joel. To illustrate the problem take note of Luke 21:8.

When Jesus' disciples asked him about the end of the age (Matthew 24:2) Jesus began to explain the events that had to happen before that consummative event. However, he warned them that before the end would come there would be false signs and false prophets saying the end was near when it was not actually near: "Take heed that you not be deceived. For many will come in My name, saying, 'I am He,' and, 'The time has drawn near.' Therefore, do not go after them."

Notice that Jesus was warning his disciples that they were to reject premature declarations of the nearness of the end. Jesus told his disciples that *fellow believers* would say the end had drawn near, when in fact it had not (Luke 21:8). He told his apostles to reject those false prophets. However, he then gave them the signs by which they could themselves know the end was near (Matthew 24:32-33). And of course, *those very apostles began to declare that the end was near.*

Compare Jesus' warnings about making premature declarations of the end with the claim that the Old Testament writers– in this case Joel– said that the end was near hundreds of years before Jesus ever came. Would this not make the Old Testament writers false teachers? Would this not mean that the Old Covenant prophets were making premature declarations of the nearness of the end? If Joel was making a premature declaration of the nearness of the end, was he not a false prophet?

Jesus' warnings against believing or making premature declarations of the nearness of the end must be taken seriously, and when we do, it will be quickly realized that Joel was not, and could not be saying that the end had drawn near, hundreds of years before Jesus even came the first time. Such a claim makes Joel, and all other Old Covenant prophets, to be the very false prophets that Jesus warned about.

Furthermore, consider what Peter had to say:

"Of this salvation the prophets have inquired and searched carefully, who prophesied of the grace that would come to you, 11 searching what, or what manner of time, the Spirit of Christ who was in them was indicating when He testified beforehand the sufferings of Christ and the glories that would follow. 12 To them it was revealed that, not to themselves, but to us they were ministering the things which now have been reported to you through those who have preached the gospel to you by the Holy Spirit sent from heaven—things which angels desire to look into. 13 Therefore gird up the loins of your mind, be sober, and rest your hope fully upon the grace that is to be brought to you at the revelation of Jesus Christ" (1 Peter 1:10f)

Peter wrote of the salvation to come at the Day of the Lord (1 Peter 1:3-5) and said it was "ready to be revealed." Of particular significance is that he says the Old Covenant prophets wrote of that coming salvation. And remember, Joel did! But, Peter says that while the Old Covenant prophets predicted the Day of the Lord, he says that they were told that *it was not for their day*! It was not near. However, Peter says while they were told that it was not for their day, it was being revealed in Peter's day, and that is why Peter told them to gird up the loins of their mind and to look eagerly for the *parousia*, which, he said, had now drawn near (1 Peter 4:7).

One cannot help but note the irony of 1 Peter 4:5, 7, 17, in light of Jesus' warnings in Luke 21:8. Again, Jesus told his disciples– Peter being present when Jesus spoke– to not believe or thus make, premature declarations of the end. He told them, however, that when they saw the signs of the end that they could know that the end was near. And now, here is Peter, fully cognizant of the warnings against making premature declarations saying, "the end has drawn near," He confidently proclaims, "The end of all things has drawn near!"

Had Peter forgotten Jesus' warnings? Was Peter wrong? Was he deluded? Was Peter one of the false teachers that Jesus warned against? And to the point, was Joel a false prophet?

The answer to this question is an unequivocal no. Joel was not a false prophet, because he did not make a premature declaration of the nearness of the end, in spite of the modern claims to the contrary. Joel, as we have seen, predicted a Day of the Lord that was near, but he also predicted the Great and Terrible Day of the Lord that was *not* near– in full harmony with what Peter said in 1 Peter 1:10.

So, Joel foretold an imminent Day of the Lord and a far off Day of the Lord. However, Joel said that *when the last days arrived* the Day of the Lord would be near. As we have seen from 1 Peter 1 this comports precisely with what the New Testament writers tell us.

➜ **Isaiah 60:22**– This great chapter is another example of Old Testament prophets foretelling the events of the last days, and saying that when the predicted time came, it would be fulfilled quickly.

"A little one shall become a thousand, And a small one a strong nation. I, the LORD, will hasten it in its time."

The promise of the prophecy was that Jerusalem would be restored, and the description is the source for John's prediction of the New Jerusalem in Revelation 21. The gates of the city would be open forever (v. 11–>cf. Revelation 21:25); there is no need of the sun, moon, stars (v. 19–>cf. Revelation 21:23). The nations flow into the city (v.11–> Revelation 21:26). There are many other parallels, but these are sufficient to show that Isaiah is indeed John's source text for the description of the New Jerusalem.

Note then that in verse 22, YHVH said, "in its time, I will hasten it."[267] In other words, when the time for fulfillment arrived, fulfillment would be at hand and come quickly. Isaiah did not say the New Creation was at hand, coming quickly or shortly at the time he wrote.

So, what we see in these verses, and there are others,[268] is that in the Old Testament, the prophets foresaw things to come, wonderful things. However, they were told that the fulfillment of their predictions was not near. In fact, they were told that fulfillment was far off, and would only come after the rise and fall of several kingdoms. There is no parallel to this kind of language *anywhere* in the New Testament.

It is not proper therefore, for modern exegetes to appeal to the Old Testament prophets and claim that they, just like the New Testament prophets, said the end was near, and coming soon. They never said any such thing. They *knew* fulfillment was not near. However, the New Testament prophets had a different view of the time of the end than did the Old Covenant prophets, and to that investigation we turn.

Point #3– As Fully Demonstrated Above, the New Testament Writers Were Almost All Jews,[269] Who Tell Us Repeatedly That Their Eschatological Hope Was *Nothing* but the OT Prophecies Made to Israel. Whereas this truth was once actually denied among scholars, that has now changed. Nanos correctly says, "Where NT scholarship is concerned, the literature (The NT., DKP) can now be read as Jewish correspondence, written by and for Jews and gentiles concerned with the Jewish context of their faith in Jesus as the Jewish Messiah. Simply put, we can now read the NT as a Jewish book."[270] Holland concurs: "It is now increasingly being recognized that Paul's gospel can only be understood in Jewish terms."[271] To fail to honor this context of the New Testament teaching– including 1 Thessalonians 4-- is to doom ourselves to a wrong understanding of its message.

We will not belabor the point here, but ask that you please keep this vital fact in mind.

Point #4– Jesus and the New Testament Writers All Affirm That They Were Living in the Days Foretold by the Old Testament Prophets. They Say the End Was Near. The Day of the Lord Was at Hand. The Resurrection Was Near, Etc.

Having established the first three points, we now turn to the establishment of the fact that the New Testament writers affirm, indisputably, that the end– the time of fulfilment of God's promises to Israel– was near. The time had come. And let me remind you that the Old Testament writers never affirmed this. As a matter of fact, even dispensationalist Thomas Ice says, "A survey of the New Testament enables one to realize that there is an expectancy regarding the return of Christ and the consummation of His plan not found in the Old Testament."[272]

This sense of urgency of the imminent end is what the German scholars called the *Naherwartung*. This sense of the soon coming end permeates virtually every book of the New Testament. It is at this juncture that we must comment on the glaring inconsistency of Gentry in regard to the temporal framework of NT eschatology.

On the one hand, Gentry castigates the millennial claims that turn the imminence statements of the NT into vague, generic meaningless words: "If imminency can stretch out for 2000 years (so far!) then imminency is not imminency. How can 2000 years be called 'soon-ness'? We cannot reasonably stretch imminency over a 2000 year period." (*Dominion*, 2009, 334). Well stated.

However, Gentry then claims, "Orthodox preterists, however, hold that passages specifically delimiting the time-frame by temporal indicators (such as 'this generation,' 'shortly,' 'near' and similar wording) *must* apply to AD 70, but similar sounding passages may or may *not*" (*Dominion*, 2009, 528, his emphasis).

So, on the one hand Gentry says that language of imminence *must* mean soon, but, on the other hand, language of imminence may *not* mean soon! This is a *glaring, illogical inconsistency*. Gentry does not offer any proof for his claims, but of course the real reason is his *theology*. He cannot make the argument based on linguistics or grammar. I must quickly take note of how Gentry's hermeneutic backfires on him, however.

Gentry says that "at hand" "quickly" "shortly" time indicators *must* apply to AD 70. Consider then that in 1 Peter we have several of these powerful imminence statements. See below.

If Gentry honors his own hermeneutic, this demands that when Peter said that Christ was "ready to judge the living and the dead" (1 Peter 4:5) that "the end of all things has drawn near" (1 Peter 4:7) and "the time has come for the judgment to begin" (1 Peter 4:17) these passages must refer to AD 70. In *Dominion*, however, Gentry is strangely silent about these texts. Be that as it may, we can match Gentry's hermeneutic with Peter's statements, and see that Peter was anticipating Christ's soon coming judgment on Israel. Now notice how this impacts Gentry's view of 2 Peter 3.

Gentry spends considerable time seeking to prove that 2 Peter 3 speaks of a yet future, "refashioning of the earth as the saints eternal abode" (*Dominion*, 2009, 300f–Incidentally, *once again*, this is not a universally held creedal position). But, Gentry overlooks (or ignores) 2 Peter 3:1-2: "Beloved I now write to you this second epistle (in both of which I stir up your pure minds by way of reminder) that you may be mindful of the words which were spoken before by the holy prophets."

Note that Peter says both epistles that he wrote teach the same thing, and specifically about what the OT prophets, Jesus and the other apostles spoke. For our purposes, please note the following argument:

2 Peter 3 is a reiteration of what 1 Peter said about the Day of the Lord, as foretold by the OT prophets.

But, 1 Peter said that the Day of the Lord, the time of the end and the appointed time of the judgment was very near (1 Peter 4:5,7, 17).

Therefore, the Day of the Lord of 2 Peter 3 was very near.

So, Gentry insists that the time statements that delimit the coming of the Lord to an imminent time frame must refer to his coming in AD 70. 1 Peter emphatically posits the time of Christ's revelation (1 Peter 1:5f) as ready to be revealed, and says the end "has drawn near" (1 Peter 4:7, literal rendering). Since 2 Peter 3 is simply a reminder of what Peter said in 1 Peter then of necessity, the Day of the Lord in 2 Peter had drawn near. It was imminent and to use the words of Gentry, "If imminency can stretch out for 2000 years (so far!) then imminency is not imminency. How can 2000 years be called 'soon-ness'? We cannot reasonably stretch imminency over a 2000 year period." Gentry's own hermeneutic, applied consistently, demands an AD 70 application of 2 Peter 3.

What we want to do now is to present just some of the evidence that proves that the New Testament authors and speakers taught as doctrine, not merely their personal hope, but as truth, that the end was near, the time anticipated by the prophets was now upon them. We will develop this thematically, returning to and expanding on Point #1, that the Old Testament prophets foretold every eschatological tenet found in the New Testament.

☆ The Time Is Fulfilled

Matthew 3:2; Mark 1:15– "Repent for the kingdom of heaven has drawn near," "The time is fulfilled, repent, for the kingdom has drawn near." Both John and Jesus proclaimed that the kingdom was at hand, literally had drawn near. Bruce comments on Jesus' statement: "the time is fulfilled" in Mark 1:15: "These words express, among other things, the assurance that an ardently desired new order, long since foretold and awaited. was now on the point of realization."[273]

Remember that Daniel– foreseeing the kingdom– was told that it was not near. It would come after three kingdoms had come and gone, and it would be in the last days. And now, both John and Jesus proclaim that the time had come! The temporal contrast could not be clearer. Of course, it cannot be overlooked that Jesus appeared in the days of that appointed fourth kingdom (Luke 3:1f) which was indeed "just the right time" for the establishment of the predicted kingdom.

☆ The Prophets Have Desired To See What You See

"But blessed are your eyes for they see, and your ears for they hear; for assuredly, I say to you that many prophets and righteous men desired to see what you see, and did not see it, and to hear what you hear, and did not hear it" (Matthew 13:16-17).

This passage seems to get little notice in the literature, and yet, it is important. This is especially true in light of the verses just cited. Not only did Jesus say the time was fulfilled, Jesus now says that the time the prophets longed to see, but did not see, was now being experienced by his disciples.

The temporal context of Jesus' statement is important when it is realized that according to the millennialist, Matthew 12 is the time at which the kingdom offer was postponed, and Jesus began to plan for the church. That means that Jesus should have been telling his disciples that what the prophets foretold, which *should* have been fulfilled in their days, was now postponed. It was now delayed! Instead of proclaiming the privileged position of his disciples, Jesus should have been telling them how *sad* it was that they did not– after all– get to see what the prophets predicted.

The fact that Jesus, at a time when he should have been speaking of postponement and failure, instead spoke of the fulfillment of the prophets, speaks eloquently to the fact that there was no delay in God's scheme. No postponement of the kingdom. The last days, the time of fulfillment, had arrived and his disciples were participants in that critical end times drama.

☆ It Shall Come to Pass in the *Last Days*

The Old Testament prophets posited all of their eschatological predictions for the Last Days. The New Testament writers all say that the predicted last days had arrived!

Acts 2:15f– As just seen above, Peter quoted Joel's promise that in the last days, God would redeem Israel, and offer salvation to the Gentiles. Peter's declaration, "this is that which was spoken by the prophet Joel," simply cannot be distorted, manipulated, and perverted into meaning that Pentecost was not the initiation of the fulfillment of Joel.

Hebrews 1:1-2– The Hebrews writer says that Jesus appeared "in these last days." Furthermore, Galatians 4:4 tells us that Jesus appeared in the fullness of time. Romans 5:6 and 1 Timothy 2:6 likewise tell us that Christ appeared "at the right time." It should be noted that in both of these texts Paul uses the word *kairos* for time. This word does not mean time broadly considered. It means *appointed* or *designated* time.[274] So, the last days in which Jesus appeared were the appointed last days.

James 5:3-6-- James accosts the rich of his day for their abuse of the poor. The contemporary nature of his diatribe against the corrupt rich cannot be denied. He is not projecting himself to a far distant future. He is speaking of the abuses taking place in his world:

> "Come now, you rich, weep and howl for your miseries that are coming upon you! 2 Your riches are corrupted, and your garments are moth–eaten. 3 Your gold and silver are corroded, and their corrosion will be a witness against you and will eat your flesh like fire. You have heaped up treasure in the last days."

Not only does James speak of his time as the last days, he then turns to the oppressed and persecuted saints and says, "Be patient therefore brethren, until the coming of the Lord... the coming of the Lord has drawn near" (James 5:6-8).

1 Peter 1:5, 20– The prophets foretold the salvation to come in the last days, at the Day of the Lord (1 Peter 1:5-12). Peter said that predicted salvation was "ready to be revealed" and that Jesus had been revealed "in these last times" (1:20).[275] Remember that Peter tells us that the prophets knew they did not speak of their own times, but of Peter's day (1:10-12). Again, it must be realized that Peter uses the word *kairos*, appointed time. Thus, his statement that Christ was ready to be revealed, at the appointed time, emphasizes the true nearness of the predicted events.

So, the Old Covenant prophets foretold the coming of the last days. The New Testament writers said they were living in the last days foretold by the OT prophets..

It should not be overlooked that in some New Testament texts the writers do speak of the last days in what appears to be a futuristic sense (e.g. 1 Timothy 4:1f; 2 Timothy 3:1f; 2 Peter 3:3f). However, keep in mind that these writers have already told us that their discussions of the last days is the reiteration of the Old Testament prophecies. In other words, when the New Testament writers speak of the last days they are hearkening back to what the Old Covenant writers predicted. An excellent example of this is 2 Peter 3.

We have already seen that Peter specifically informs us that his eschatological discourse is a reminder of what the Old Covenant prophets foretold. And yet, he speaks of the coming of the scoffers in the last days. So, we should be able to find in the Old Covenant prophets the prediction of the coming of scoffers before the Day of the Lord to destroy "heaven and earth." And in fact, we find exactly that in Isaiah 28:21-22.

> "For the LORD will rise up as at Mount Perazim, He will be angry as in the Valley of Gibeon—That He may do His work, His awesome work, And bring to pass His act, His unusual act. Now therefore, do not be mockers, Lest your bonds be made strong; For I have heard from the Lord GOD of hosts, A destruction determined even upon the whole earth."

We have here a prediction of the coming of the Lord, the destruction of the "whole earth" in the day that the Lord would lay the foundation stone in Zion,[276] and bring salvation (v. 16f).[277] And yet, the scoffers would deny that coming Day.

Here is the source of Peter's last days prediction. And of course, what is so significant is that Isaiah was predicting the time when Israel would be judged and destroyed. While she *thought* she had a covenant with death that would spare her from judgment and destruction (28:15) YHVH said, "Your covenant with death will be annulled, and your agreement with Sheol will not stand; when the overwhelming scourge passes through, you will be beaten down" (v. 18).

The point is, again, that Peter was not contemplating a far distant time, or events. He was anticipating the fulfillment of Isaiah, and Isaiah's prophecy is specifically posited at the time of the destruction of the Old Covenant world! Peter's prediction of the last days period was predicted by the Old Testament prophets.

So, the Old Testament prophets said the fulfillment of their eschatological hopes would take place in the last days. They said that when the last days arrived fulfillment would come quickly. The New Testament writers, appealing to those Old Testament prophecies, said the last days had arrived and the end was near.

☆ The End of the Ages Has Come Upon Us

Daniel 12 foretold the time of the end, the end of the age. The New Testament writers believed and taught that the end of the age was near and would come in their generation.

Matthew 24:2-3, 34– "And Jesus said to them, 'Do you not see all these things? Assuredly, I say to you, not one stone shall be left here upon another, that shall not be thrown down. Now as He sat on the Mount of Olives, the disciples came to Him privately, saying, 'Tell us, when will these things be? And what will be the sign of Your coming, and of the end of the age?'"... "Assuredly, I say to you, this generation will by no means pass away till all these things take place."

One thing is certain, in the mind of the disciples, Jesus' prediction of the destruction of the temple was tantamount to a prediction of his coming and the end of the age. This belief was common in the Judaism of Jesus' day.[278] While it is commonly believed that the disciples were confused or simply wrong to draw this connection,[279] that claim is patently false.

In Matthew 13:39-51 Jesus spoke of the end of the age. He cited the prophecy of Daniel 12 (Matthew 13:43) and then asked the disciples if they understood what he was saying. They responded, "Yes." So, the disciples *said they understood* what Jesus meant by the end of the age, when he appealed to Daniel's prediction that the power of the holy people would be completely destroyed at the time of the end. It therefore seems the height of arrogance for modern exegetes to say that they really didn't.

We clearly do not have space to present a full commentary on the Olivet Discourse. However, our comments above show that it did predict the AD 70 coming of Christ in judgment of Old Covenant Jerusalem, and has nothing to do with a supposed end of time. Jesus' declaration in verse 34 is therefore an undeniable prediction that the end of the age would be in that first century generation. That prediction agrees perfectly with what Paul wrote to the Corinthians.

1 Corinthians 10:11– "Now all these things happened to them as examples, and they were written for our admonition, upon whom the ends of the ages have come."

This passage is significant because Paul does not simply say that the end of the age had arrived. While the "end of the age" is present, Paul uses the word *telos* (for end). This word carries with it the idea of *goal*, the completion of what is lacking, filling something to its perfection.

Paul also uses the word *katantao*, for "have come." The latter word carries with it the idea of the arrival at a destination. In addition, Paul does not say that the end of the age, singular, had come. He says the end of the *ages* plural had come.

So, Paul was saying that all the previous ages had arrived at their anticipated destination, their *goal*! Considering that Paul preached nothing but the hope of Israel, and that the kingdom and salvation life through resurrection was the goal of Israel's expectation, this is a stunning text. This means of course, that there had been no delay in God's plan. It means that the church was God's plan and promise in the previous ages. It means that the first century generation was the generation to see that consummation and perfection.

Not only did Paul say that the end (goal) of the previous ages had arrived, he said that the time remaining had been *shortened*, and the world was passing away. In 1 Corinthians 7:29, the apostle said, "This is what I mean, the appointed time (*kairos*, dkp) has grown very short" (English Standard Version). One can hardly fail to hear the echo of Matthew 24:22 in Paul's words. Paul then said, "The present form of this world is passing away" (1 Corinthians 7:31). Notice the present tense verbs.

Perriman says, "These statements must imply a restricted outlook on the future. There is a tendency for interpreters to universalize what Paul has to say about the immediate circumstances faced by the Corinthians, so that his teaching in this chapter acquires a more existential than an eschatological character. ...But, Paul's whole argument presupposes an exceptional and limited period of distress, not the general open-ended condition of the church's existence" (*Coming*, 113+).

Perriman is certainly correct. Paul's references to the shortened time and the present tense passing of the fashion of the world demanded certain ways of living that do not characterize the entirety of Christian living. There was a *contemporary crisis* like that in 2 Thessalonians 1, that demanded exceptional but *temporary* actions (doing without a wife/husband) before the end. Those exceptional drastic actions are not applicable to the span of Christianity throughout the ages. They were necessary due to "the present distress" (1Corinthians 7:26) of Paul's day. Thus, we must take seriously Paul's emphasis on the impending "end of the world."

The full significance of 1 Corinthians 10 in light of these earlier verses is beginning to be appreciated by commentaries. This is an incredibly meaningful text.[280]

1 Peter 4:7– "But the end of all things is at hand; therefore be serious and watchful in your prayers."

Let's be candid, shall we? The only way to avoid the emphatic declaration of Peter is to deny the meaning of words. To say that Peter was not saying that the end was near (literally had *drawn near*) in fulfillment of God's promises to Israel is to distort the meaning of his words.

As we have seen, Peter knew that no one was to make premature declarations of the nearness of the end. He knew full well that Jesus did not want generation after generation making false predictions that the end had drawn near, in order to keep the church "on the tiptoe of expectation."

John MacArthur, noted author, claims that God caused the Bible writers to say things like this because, "He desired to keep His people on the tiptoe of expectation, continually looking for Him."[281] On the other hand, he insisted that, "It is not that He desires each succeeding generation to believe that He will certainly return in their lifetime, for He does not desire our faith and our practices to be founded on error, as, in that case, the faith and practice of all generations except the last would be. But it is a necessary element of the doctrine concerning (the Second Coming of Christ) that it should be possible at any time, that no generation should consider it improbable as theirs (Archbishop Trench)." This is the same author who wrote: "James, Peter, John and Paul, and the writer of Hebrews all believed Christ's return was very near--'at the door' (James 5:9); 'at hand' (Philippians 4:5; 1 Peter 4:7); 'approaching' (Hebrews 10:25); 'coming quickly' (Revelation 3:11; 22:7)" (*Coming*, 56).[282]

The problem is, these were not statements of *hope* or mere *expectation*. They were statements of fact, of *doctrine*. You cannot have these writers expressing imminence in such certain, unambiguous manner, without the sense of failure when the soon expectation fails.

MacArthur takes note of the fact that skeptics have used the NT teaching on the imminence of the *parousia* to discount inspiration: "The enemies of the faith have seized upon these very statements to show that the apostle Paul (and the other apostles, DKP) was in error, that he wrote by unaided human wisdom, that he merely recorded in his epistles his own beliefs, and that in some of these he was clearly mistaken. But such an objection is quite pointless to the saints who believe that, 'All Scripture is given by inspiration of God.'" (*Coming*, p. 204). What is so remarkable, is that the skeptic and the futurists say virtually the identical thing!

MacArthur cites one skeptic who wrote, "Paul himself, showed... that he was among those who awaited the imminent return of Christ" (p.57). MacArthur agrees as to what Paul believed, "So real was the hope of the Redeemer's return to the heart of the apostle Paul and so imminent did this event appear to him that we find *he included himself* among those who might not fall asleep but be among the living saints when the assembly shout would be heard" (*Coming*, P.204). Thus, *the skeptic and MacArthur agree* that Paul believed that the *parousia* was to occur in his lifetime.

The skeptic continues, "As the history of that era clearly shows, all was for nought. No Messiah appeared" (*Coming*, p. 57). MacArthur must concur, "Eighteen hundred years have run their weary course since then, *and He has not yet returned*!" (*Coming*, p. 211, his emp.). Thus, *the skeptic and MacArthur agree* that Jesus and the apostles taught that Christ's appearing was to occur in the first century, and *they both agree that it did not happen*. The futurists have inadvertently given the skeptics plenty of ammunition with their argumentation.

This lamentable situation must cease in the light of the current attacks on the inspiration of scripture and the Deity of Christ. Christianity is under a full frontal assault, and admissions like that of MacArthur's demonstrate the utter inability of the futurist paradigm to confront the challenge. It *is true* that the Bible writers affirmed the nearness of the end, as Peter's words patently prove. It is *not true* that their hopes were dashed and disappointed. As the Proverb writer expressed it: "Hope deferred makes the heart sick" (Proverbs 13:12). It is time for modern apologists for the faith to communicate the reality of fulfillment, not the failure of the prophetic hope.

Of course, the point is that Peter was saying that what the Old Testament authors said was far off, not for their day, had drawn near. This temporal contrast between the Old Testament hope, and the New Testament inspired statements demands that we honor the imminence of the texts.

✡ Will God Not Avenge The Elect Who Cry Out To Him? I Tell You That He Will Avenge Them Speedily!

The theme of the avenging of the blood of the martyrs and the need for it, begins in Genesis, when, after Cain had killed his brother, YHVH said to him: "The voice of your brother's blood cries to me from the ground" (Genesis 4:10). Throughout the OT the cry, "How long" is repeated over and over by the righteous, oppressed and persecuted.[283] As we have seen, God promised that in the last days, He would indeed avenge the blood of His saints at the Day of the Lord.

Matthew 23:29-36–

"Woe to you, scribes and Pharisees, hypocrites! Because you build the tombs of the prophets and adorn the monuments of the righteous, and say, 'If we had lived in the days of our fathers, we would not have been partakers with them in the blood of the prophets.' "Therefore you are witnesses against yourselves that you are sons of those who murdered the prophets. Fill up, then, the measure of your fathers' guilt. Serpents, brood of vipers! How can you escape the condemnation of hell? Therefore, indeed, I send you prophets, wise men, and scribes: some of them you will kill and crucify, and some of them you will scourge in your synagogues and persecute from city to city, that on you may come all the righteous blood shed on the earth, from the blood of righteous Abel to the blood of Zechariah, son of Berechiah, whom you murdered between the temple and the altar. Assuredly, I say to you, all these things will come upon this generation."

Millennialists, who normally deny the objective meaning of the language of imminence in the New Testament admit that this text was fulfilled in the AD 70 judgment on Jerusalem. Ice, commenting on Jesus' prediction that "all of these things shall come upon this generation" says, "The use of 'this generation' in all other contexts is *historical*, but 24:34 (Matthew 24:34, DKP) is *prophetic*.[284] In fact, when one compares the historical use of 'this generation' at the beginning of the Olivet Discourse in Matthew 23:36 (which is an undisputed reference to AD 70) with the prophetic usage in 24:34, a contrast is obvious" (*Tribulation*, 103).

If it is admitted that Matthew 23:36 is an undeniable referent to the judgment of AD 70, notice what this means.

The Old Testament prophets foretold the avenging of the blood of the martyrs in the last days of Israel (Deuteronomy 32:43; Isaiah 2-4; Isaiah 26:19f).

The blood of the martyrs was avenged in the judgment of Jerusalem in AD 70 (Matthew 23:34-36).

Therefore, the last days of Israel were in existence in the judgment of Jerusalem in AD 70.

The significance of this is great. Remember that the millennialists claim that Israel's last days were postponed somewhere around Matthew 12. *By no means were the last days of Israel supposed to be present and counting in AD 70!* And yet, again, it was in Israel's last days when the blood of the martyrs was to avenged, and Jesus said that all the martyrs' blood all the way back to creation would be avenged in the judgment of Jerusalem in his generation. The eschatological implications of this fact are indeed profound. It means indisputably, that the end was near, and came, in the first century.

Luke 18:1-8–

"Then the Lord said, Hear what the unjust judge said. And shall God not avenge His own elect who cry out day and night to Him, though He bears long with them? I tell you that He will avenge them speedily.[285] Nevertheless, when the Son of Man comes, will He really find faith on the earth?"

Jesus' use of the widow in Luke 18 to illustrate the long standing cry of the martyrs is loaded with eschatological significance. It hearkens back to the story of Cain and Abel. It echoes the story of all of those who: "had trial of mockings and scourgings, yes, and of chains and imprisonment. They were stoned, they were sawn in two, were tempted, were slain with the sword. They wandered about in sheepskins and goatskins, being destitute, afflicted, tormented— of whom the world was not worthy. They wandered in deserts and mountains, in dens and caves of the earth. And all these, having obtained a good testimony through faith, did not receive the promise" (Hebrews 11:36-39). It not only echoes their stories and their cry for vindication, it positively promises that their vindication was coming in Jesus' generation.

Jesus' promise that the prayer of the martyrs would be answered in his generation and shortly must be given its full eschatological import. This is true because in Isaiah 26:19f, the vindication of the martyrs' blood is posited *at the Day of the Lord and the resurrection*. For Jesus to say that the vindication of the martyrs' was to be in his generation was nothing less than an unequivocal statement that the *resurrection* was to be in his generation.

2 Thessalonians 1:4f--

"We ourselves boast of you among the churches of God for your patience and faith in all your persecutions and tribulations that you endure, which is manifest evidence of the righteous judgment of God, that you may be counted worthy of the kingdom of God, for which you also suffer; since it is a righteous thing with God to repay with tribulation those who trouble you, and to give you who are troubled rest with us when the Lord Jesus is revealed from heaven with His mighty angels, in flaming fire taking vengeance on those who do not know God, and on those who do not obey the gospel of our Lord Jesus Christ. These shall be punished with everlasting destruction from the presence of the Lord and from the glory of His power, when He comes, in that Day, to be glorified in His saints and to be admired among all those who believe, because our testimony among you was believed."

We have already addressed this text above. There can be no doubt that on a straightforward reading of the text, Paul was writing to living humans, being persecuted for their faith, and he promised them relief[286] from that persecution, at the *parousia* of Christ. This dovetails perfectly with Matthew 23 and Luke 18. In fact, we are perfectly justified in asking, what is the contextual justification for divorcing Thessalonians from Jesus' promise that all of the blood shed on the earth– including the blood of his personal apostles and prophets that would be slain– was to be avenged and judged in his generation?

As Perriman says, "In the Thessalonian letter the revelation of the Lord Jesus from heaven is described twice: it comes first as a response to the suffering of the church (2 Thessalonians 1:4-10) secondly in reaction to the specific threat posed by the revelation of the man of lawlessness (2:8-10). In both cases it is linked directly to the actual circumstances of the community of the Thessalonica, not to some inconceivable event beyond the historical horizon of the early church" (*Coming*, 157).

Revelation 6:9f–
"When He opened the fifth seal, I saw under the altar the souls of those who had been slain for the word of God and for the testimony which they held. And they cried with a loud voice, saying, 'How long, O Lord, holy and true, until You judge and avenge our blood on those who dwell on the earth?' Then a white robe was given to each of them; and it was said to them that they should rest a little while longer, until both the number of their fellow servants and their brethren, who would be killed as they were, was completed."

Beale is correct to note that "the saints petition that God 'vindicate their blood' is a desire that God demonstrate before the whole world that they were in the right and their persecutors were wrong. This is to be done by God's justifying them in the heavenly court by overturning the wrong verdict on them rendered by the earthly courts (cf. Luke 18:8). And this takes place when God judges the persecutors."[287] What Beale and most other commentators fail to honor is that Jesus places that vindication at the judgment of Old Covenant Jerusalem in his generation, as we have seen in Matthew 23. Note the parallels between Matthew and Revelation.

Matthew 23	Revelation
Jewish persecution of the elect (v. 29f)	Jewish persecution of the elect (3:9f)
Had killed the prophets	Babylon: Killer of the prophets (16:6f)
Would kill Jesus (Matthew 21:33f)	Babylon: "Where the Lord was slain" (11:8)
Would kill Jesus' apostles and prophets (23:34f)	Babylon: Killer of Jesus' apostles and prophets (18:20, 24)
Would fill the measure of their guilt by killing Jesus' disciples (23:32)	The measure of suffering and guilt was to be filled up (6:11)
All of the blood shed on the earth would be avenged (v. 35-36)	All of the blood shed on the earth would be avenged (1:20-24)
The judgment of the persecutors and the vindication of the martyrs would be in Jesus' generation (v. 36)	"They were given white robes and told to rest for a little while"; "Behold, I come quickly, and my reward is with me" (6:11; 22:12).[288]

Beale, like many commentators, ignores these connections. In fact, in his discussion of Revelation 6:9f, Beale says *not one word* about Matthew 23! Nor does Beale take note that the persecutors in Revelation, and the idea of vindication, is posited within the context of *Jewish persecution of the saints*. Notice particularly Revelation 3:9f, where Jesus addresses the church at Philadelphia: "Indeed I will make those of the synagogue of Satan, who say they are Jews and are not, but lie—indeed I will make them come and worship before your feet, and to know that I have loved you. Because you have kept My command to persevere, I also will keep you from the hour of trial which shall come upon the whole world, to test those who dwell on the earth."

Here is Jewish persecution of the saints. Here is vindication of the suffering saints. Here is the promise of imminent vindication. Virtually every element of Matthew 23, and Revelation 6:9f, is found here, and yet, Beale and other commentators ignore it, as if it were irrelevant.

While the saints cry out for vindication, in Revelation 6:12f John is given heaven's visionary response; it is the Day of the Lord. This Day of the Lord in which the martyrs would be vindicated would be in fulfillment of Isaiah 2-4, the promise of YHVH that in Israel's last days (Isaiah 2:2f) He would "purge the blood guilt of Jerusalem by the spirit of fire and the spirit of judgment" (Isaiah 4:4). Revelation 6:12f directly cites Isaiah's prophecy.[289]

The Day of the Lord described in Isaiah (2:10f; 19f) cannot by any stretch of the imagination be a time-ending, earth-burning event, since men could and would run to the mountains to escape it. It would be a time of famine (3:1f) when YHVH would judge Israel (3:18f).

This promise that in the last days (*Israel's* last days, Deuteronomy 32:19f, 29) at the Day of the Lord, the martyrs would be avenged, is the reiteration of the promise of Deuteronomy 32:43:[290] "He will avenge the blood of His saints." Revelation 19 follows the judgment of the persecutorial Babylon and the angels declare, "He has avenged the blood of his saints" (19:2).

Our point, again, is that the Old Testament prophets foretold these events. The Old Testament prophets knew that fulfillment was far off, and not for their days. Yet, the New Testament writers affirmed that the time for fulfillment had arrived, and the end was coming soon. Thus, Beale's assertions that the time statements of Revelation are so nebulous as to mean nothing must be discounted.

If we honor, as we should, Jesus' definitive didactic in Matthew 23, and place that within the context of the fulfillment of God's Old Covenant promises to Israel, then the eschatological teaching of the New Testament, and particularly Revelation, is brought sharply into focus. It is not about the end of the world. It is not about the end of time. It is the time of the avenging of the blood of the martyrs,[291] that Jesus undeniably said would occur in his generation, in the judgment of Old Covenant Jerusalem.

☆ The Coming of the Lord Has Drawn Near

"For the Son of Man will come in the glory of His Father with His angels, and then He will reward each according to his works. Assuredly, I say to you, there are some standing here who shall not taste death till they see the Son of Man coming in His kingdom" (Matthew 16:27-28).

While many efforts, some of them desperate, are made to avoid the clear meaning of Jesus' prediction, these words stand inviolate.[292] Jesus said his coming in judgment and the kingdom was to be in his contemporary generation.

Jesus did not say that "some people" would be alive to see his coming; he said some of *that contemporary audience* would see Him coming in judgment and the kingdom.[293] He did not say that some of that audience would live only six days and see a vision of his coming, as proposed by those who say the Transfiguration fulfilled Jesus' prediction. As we have shown conclusively above, Mark 9:1, the parallel with Matthew 16, shows that some standing there that day would live *until* the *parousia*. They would live *through* the *parousia*. They would live *beyond* the *parousia*, and look back and realize what had occurred. Jesus did not say that only some of that audience would live six days, see a vision, and then look back on that vision and realize that they had seen a vision! This view is specious at best.

Hebrews 10:35-39--
"Therefore do not cast away your confidence, which has great reward. For you have need of endurance, so that after you have done the will of God, you may receive the promise: For yet a little while, And He who is coming will come and will not tarry. Now the just shall live by faith; But if anyone draws back, My soul has no pleasure in him. But we are not of those who draw back to perdition, but of those who believe to the saving of the soul."

Remember that in 1 Peter 1, we saw that Peter was anticipating the revelation of the "salvation of your soul," which was to be revealed at the *parousia* of Christ. That salvation- "ready to be revealed"- was foretold by the Old Covenant prophets. Now, in Hebrews, the author speaks of the salvation of the soul, at the coming of Christ, and said that Jesus was coming "in a very, very little while" (The Greek of the text is *hosan, hosan micron*, v. 37, and literally means "how, how little," or "very, very little"). He insisted that Jesus "will not tarry."

There is no ambiguity in the Hebrews text. There is no elasticity, no vagueness. There is simple assertion that Christ's *parousia*, to bring salvation (the salvation of Hebrews 9:28) was coming, very, very soon.

James 5:7-9--
"Therefore be patient, brethren, until the coming of the Lord. See how the farmer waits for the precious fruit of the earth, waiting patiently for it until it receives the early and latter rain. You also be patient. Establish your hearts, for the coming (*parousia*) of the Lord is at hand."

There are more than a few remarkable things about this text.

James is writing *during the last days*, as we have already seen. It should also be noted and emphasized that James is writing "to the twelve tribes scattered abroad" (James 1:1) so, we are on firm ground to affirm that he is discussing "the hope of Israel" as he promises the coming of Christ and the attendant salvation.

James is writing to Jewish Christians being persecuted for their faith (James 2:4f; 5:1-6).

James promises them that the judgment of their persecutors– and thus, their own vindication and relief– was near.[294]

James does not invoke images of delay, postponement, and protraction. He does urge them to be patient, but he assures them that their vindication and relief is near. Literally he says "the *parousia* of the Lord has drawn near (*eggeken*, the perfect tense of *engus*).

Revelation 22--

Verse 7- "Behold, I am coming quickly! Blessed is he who keeps the words of the prophecy of this book."

Verse 12- "And behold, I am coming quickly, and My reward is with Me, to give to every one according to his work."

Verse 20- "He who testifies to these things says, 'Surely I am coming quickly.' Amen. Even so, come, Lord Jesus!"

It strikes one as significant that in a book in which numbers are so significant, that Jesus says *three times*– the number of perfection-- that he was coming quickly. This tri-fold repetition of his prediction would not have been lost on his first century audience, but lamentably, it is seemingly lost on modern audiences bent on ignoring his emphasis on when he was coming.

We want to take note of one of the most compelling temporal contrasts to be found anywhere.

Remember that in Daniel 12, in speaking of the time of the end, the Great Tribulation, the end of the age and the resurrection, Daniel was told, twice, to seal the book. The fulfillment was a long way off; it was not near. In fact, Daniel would die. It was patently not for his day.

However, in Revelation, which as we have seen is the reiteration of Daniel's prophecies, John was told: "Do not seal the sayings of the prophecy of this book: for the time is at hand."

Could there be a clearer proof that Revelation was to be in John's generation? Could there be any more positive demonstration that Biblical time statements were meant to be taken seriously? Could there be a clearer statement that Christ's coming was truly near?

This emphatic and impressive contrast between the "far off," "not at hand" *OT prophecies*, and the New Testament affirmations of the nearness of the end must be given its full force.

☆ The Time Has Come For The Judgment
Matthew 16:27-28--

"For the Son of Man will come in the glory of His Father with His angels, and then He will reward each according to his works. Assuredly, I say to you, there are some standing here who shall not taste death till they see the Son of Man coming in His kingdom."

We offer Matthew 16:27-28 again because we want to emphasize that the concepts of judgment and kingdom are synonymous concepts.

Daniel 7 is one of the prophetic fountains from which Matthew 16:27-28 flows.[295]

In Daniel we find the prediction of events- eschatological events- to transpire in the last days (Daniel 2:28f) the days of the fourth world empire– Rome (Daniel 7:3f).

In the days of that fourth empire, the little horn would arise and persecute the saints (Daniel 7:8-11f).[296]

While the saints would be persecuted, the Ancient of Days would come and vindicate their suffering (Daniel 7:21f).[297]

At the judgment of the persecutorial little horn and vindication of the suffering saints, "the kingdom and dominion, and the greatness of the kingdoms under the whole heaven shall be given to the people, the saints of the Most High, His kingdom is an everlasting kingdom" (Daniel 7:27). In Matthew 16:27-28, at *the coming of the Son of Man* judgment is accomplished and the saints are given the kingdom.[298]

Mathison is clearly desperate in his attempts to explain, and to explain away, the "Coming of the Son of Man" predictions. He resorts to an interpretation *unknown in the creeds which he claims determine orthodoxy*, but worse, which is in violation of the very texts that he appeals to.

Mathison says it is possible that Matthew 16:27 refers to Christ's Second Coming, "without mentioning the amount of time that might elapse between them" (i.e. the events of v. 27 as opposed to v. 28, DKP). This is grammatically untenable, however. Verse 28 begins with the Greek term "*amen lego humin*."[299] This term *never* breaks a topic and never introduces a new topic. It is always stated to *emphasize something already under discussion*. This means that verse 27 is the prediction of *what* was to happen, the coming of the Son of Man, and verse 28 is the emphasis of *when* it would occur. These are not two events separated by millennia. Verse 28 emphatically *does mention* the amount of time that might elapse between the two events (actually *one* event). The coming of the kingdom is the coming of Christ (Daniel 7:23-25). It would occur before that first century audience would all pass away.

Mathison claims that the coming of the Son of Man of verse 27 is the fulfillment of Daniel 7:9-10, but that it speaks of "a *heavenly judgment* of the beast/nations" (*Age*, 366). This sounds amazingly like the Adventist doctrine of the heavenly Sanctuary Doctrine. The problem is that Mathison cannot contextually or correctly say that the judgment took place in heaven. I can only briefly outline the problem for Mathison's view.

✸ The coming of the Son of Man of Daniel 7:21-24 (which is the *interpretation* of the vision of v. 10f) would be in vindication of the suffering saints, and the judgment of the "little horn" who persecuted them.

✸ Revelation 6:9-11 depicts the saints, persecuted by "Babylon" and "the beast" crying out: "How long O Lord, do you not avenge us on those who dwell on the earth?" *The judgment of the persecutor would play out on the earth, manifested in the destruction of the city Babylon.* It was not a simple "heavenly judgment."

✸ Revelation 11:15f depicts the fulfillment Of Daniel 7: "Then the seventh angel sounded: And there were loud voices in heaven, saying, "The kingdoms of this world have become the kingdoms of our Lord and of His Christ, and He shall reign forever and ever! 16 And the twenty-four elders who sat before God on their thrones fell on their faces and worshiped God, 17 saying: "We give You thanks, O Lord God Almighty, The One who is and who was and who is to come, Because You have taken Your great power and reigned." This is an undeniable echo of Daniel 7 (not to mention Daniel 12). And this judgment of the persecuting entity– the city where the Lord was slain, (11:8)-- and the vindication of the saints resulted in the reception of the kingdom. Note again that all of this is precisely what is discussed in 1 and 2 Thessalonians.

✸ The judgment against the persecuting city Babylon would occur at the coming of the Son of Man (Revelation 19).

✸ Mathison claims that the vision of Daniel 7:10f was fulfilled at Christ's ascension, and that this is when the "heavenly judgment" occurred. However, this is clearly falsified by the fact that the "little horn"–which Mathison sees as Rome-- had not persecuted the saints prior to the Ascension! How could Rome be judged and destroyed– remember that Revelation demands that *this judgment took place on earth*– before Rome ever persecuted a single saint?[300]

Our point of course is that Mathison creates an almost unprecedented theology regarding the coming of the Son of Man and imposes it on Matthew 16:27, not to mention the other "Son of Man" texts. His thesis backfires on him however, for his arguments all demand fulfillment in AD 70 for Thessalonians since Paul's epistles are concerned with the fulfillment of Daniel's Son of Man prophecies. Furthermore, the imminence of the very texts that Mathison appeals to demand that application.

Mathison's problems in regard to Daniel 7 and Matthew 16:27f are compounded by the fact that Matthew 16:27f is undoubtedly the time of God's remarriage with Israel, an issue Mathison does not so much as mention in his discussion of Matthew 16:27. Jesus is drawing on Isaiah 40 and Isaiah 62 in his predictions of his coming with his reward. See our discussion of the significance of this above. As a prediction of the consummation of God's dealings with Old Covenant Israel, Matthew 16:27f must be seen within the context of covenantal fulfillment, not the climax of world history, or, for that matter, a prophecy of God's dealings with Rome.

So, in Daniel, we find a vision of the *parousia*, the time of the judgment and the kingdom. It clearly was not near in Daniel's day, but Jesus affirmed that the time for what the prophets desired to see, and did not, had now come. He affirmed that his living contemporaries would live to see the fulfillment. The judgment truly was near.

Consider the implications for 1 Thessalonians 4 in light of the motifs from Daniel: The days of Rome, the persecuting power, the *parousia* of Messiah, judgment of the persecutor, vindication of the martyrs, the entrance into the kingdom..

Let me remind you that Paul's eschatology is drawn from Moses and the prophets. And the prophets, specifically Daniel for our purposes, limited fulfillment to a given time frame.

☆ "It Is The Last Hour!"

"Little children, it is the last hour; and as you have heard that the Antichrist is coming, even now many antichrists have come, by which we know that it is the last hour."

John's declaration that the last hour was upon his audience is nothing less than a declaration of the impending resurrection.

Notice John 5:25-29:

"Most assuredly, I say to you, the hour is coming, and now is, when the dead will hear the voice of the Son of God; and those who hear will live. For as the Father has life in Himself, so He has granted the Son to have life in Himself, and has given Him authority to execute judgment also, because He is the Son of Man. Do not marvel at this; for the hour is coming in which all who are in the graves will hear His voice and come forth—those who have done good, to the resurrection of life, and those who have done evil, to the resurrection of condemnation."

Jesus said that the hour for the resurrection was present: "The hour is coming and *now is*"! Unfortunately, many commentators seek to dichotomize Jesus' discussion into two different kinds of resurrections, separated in time by two millennia so far. This is unjustified. The "contrast" in the text is between "now is" and "is coming," between "some" and "all," and life now for some, versus life versus condemnation for some in the future. It was the judgment of condemnation that is the focus on the "is coming." There is no contrast in the *nature* of the death, or the graves.[301]

Gentry seeks to deflect the power of the text before us by arguing that, "though Scripture refers to 'last days' and 'the last day,' it does not refer to 'hours' leading up to 'the last hour.' Thus, John's 'the last hour' differs from the singular 'last day,' and stands for the whole period of time from Christ's advent to his second, emphasizing the unity of the period which is introduced by the arising of the first century antichrists." (*Dominion*, 2009, 325, n. 68).

I should point out that Gentry blatantly contradicts himself in regard to 1 John 2:18. Commenting on Revelation 10:6 he says: "The end of the temple economy and national Israel is near (1 Co 10:11; 1 Th 2:16; Heb 1:2; 9:26; 12:26-27; *1 Jn 2:18)*" (2009, 408, my emphasis). He also says that the antichrists of 1 John 2:18, "are not harbingers of a distantly future Antichrist, for their presence is the signal that 'the last hour' has already come (*gegonasin*)" (2009, 377).

Just how can 1 John 2:18 signal that, "the end of the temple economy and national Israel is near," and yet at the same time mean that the Christian age will last for who knows how many thousands or millions of years? Gentry offers no explanation or proof. Just assertions. But these are two irreconcilably contradictory positions.

Mathison insists that John was basically saying, "The final end, therefore, always remains imminent and could occur at any time" (*Age*, 2009, 638). This puts him at odds with Gentry who says the "distinctive mark" of postmillennialism is that the end is *not* considered to be always imminent! And we should point out that Gentry *thought* Mathison agreed with this! He quotes Mathison as saying: "Scripture simply does not teach the dispensational doctrine of the 'imminent' return of Christ.'" (2009, 332, citing Mathison's *Postmillennialism*, 206).[302]

I must say in all candor that Gentry's remarks smack of desperation. He is essentially saying that because the plural term "hours" is never used in other contexts to speak of the time leading up to the consummation, that John (i.e. the Holy Spirit) was therefore unable to speak of the eschatological climax as the last hour! Upon what journalistic principle does Gentry base his claim? Upon what hermeneutical principle or rule can it be said that John must be limited in his vocabulary and journalistic expression?

Gentry's hermeneutic is wrong. While it is true that there are no terms such as "hours before the hour" specifically used in the scripture, what we do have is Jesus' use of "the hour is coming and now is," and, "the hour is coming." It must be kept in mind that for Gentry, the "hour" that Jesus said was coming is "the last hour" of the final resurrection! In other words, for John, the last hour was the time of the resurrection.

So, Gentry does in fact believe that "the last hour" is the hour of the eschatological consummation. But, to admit that John was saying the last hour was actually so critically imminent–as he does in spite of himself--

falsifies Gentry's paradigm, so he imposes an artificial journalistic and hermeneutical demand on the Spirit.

In fact, it is possible to argue that scripture does speak of the last hour and the last day in reference to AD 70. Remember that Gentry believes that Matthew 24:29-31 speaks of the Day (singular) of the Lord. That Day was the end of the age (1 Corinthians 10:11, *Dominion*, 2009, 324). So, that Day of the Lord had "days" leading up to it (Matthew 24:21f). That Day was the end of the age. So, that final Day was *the last day of the Old Covenant age*, was it not? And since Gentry has already told us that the OT prophets actually foresaw the age to come, the resurrection, etc. as fully arriving at the end of the Old Covenant age, then what we have in Matthew 24 is the prediction of the last day of the old age, ushering in the age to come and the resurrection, i.e. the last hour! But let's discuss the antichrists a bit more.

To emphasize Gentry's problem consider this: John said, "You have heard that the Antichrist is coming." *Where had they heard this?* They "heard" it from the Olivet Discourse, and significantly, they "heard" it from the section that Gentry admits speaks of the events prior to and terminating in Christ's AD 70 parousia: "And Jesus answered and said to them: 'Take heed that no one deceives you. For many will come in My name, saying, 'I am the Christ,' and will deceive many'" (Matthew 24:4-5; cf. also Luke 21:8). Of course, Mathison now posits the entire Discourse as fulfilled in AD 70.

In 1 John the apostle reminds his audience of Jesus' words. Jesus said that antichrists would come before his appearing in judgment against Jerusalem. John said that the predictions of the appearing of the antichrist before the end were being fulfilled when he wrote. Therefore, Christ's AD 70 coming was very near.[303] (Remember that Gentry applies 1 John 2:18 to AD 70).

To mitigate this argument it has to be proven that the prophecies of the antichrist to which John alludes are not the words of Jesus in the Olivet Discourse. For Gentry, this is particularly problematic since he agrees that Paul's prediction of the antichrist in 2 Thessalonians 2 is drawn from the Olivet Discourse and was a prediction of events prior to and consummating in AD 70, as we have seen. So, unless Gentry can demonstrate, definitively, that John was drawing on some unknown to us prophecy of the appearing of the antichrists before the so-called end of the world, it is far safer to conclude that John was simply reminding his audience of the words of Jesus in the Olivet Discourse. And this means that the "last hour" really was near. It means that the hour of the resurrection had arrived.

☆ In the Days of the Fourth Beast

Need we note that Paul, in Thessalonians, was living and ministering in the days of the fourth empire of Daniel? Remember what we have just seen from Daniel 7 and 12.

The prophet foretold the coming of the Son of Man against the persecutor of the saints. The suffering saints are vindicated through the reception of the kingdom. In Thessalonians, Paul is addressing the saints suffering for the kingdom, and promises them vindication and relief at the coming of the Lord in judgment "of those who are troubling you." See just below for more.

As we have seen above, the New Testament writers affirm repeatedly that the predicted last days had arrived. Jesus came in the days of that fourth empire to fulfill the promises made to the fathers (Luke 3:1f; Romans 15:8). There is no question that what Daniel foretold was being played out in the first century church.

☆ The Suffering of the Saints

Jesus told his disciples that if they would follow him, they would be persecuted (Matthew 16:24f). The suffering that Jesus predicted (see also Matthew 24:9) was present in the Thessalonians.

In Thessalonians one of the dominant themes is the suffering of the saints. Thus, the predicted persecutor was very much present.[304] Paul certainly believed that the restrainer of the man of sin, and thus, the man of sin, were already alive (cf. 2 Thessalonians 2:5f).

In chapter 1:6 the Thessalonians received the word in much affliction" ("severe suffering" NIV– from *thlipsis*).

Paul had preached the gospel among the Thessalonians, "in spite of strong opposition" (2:2).

In chapter 2:14f Paul reminded them that they had, "suffered from your own countrymen."

In chapter 3:1-3 Paul urged them not to be shaken in their faith because of their trials, because he had warned them that they, "were destined for them." In fact, when we were with you we kept telling you that we would be persecuted. And it turned out that way" (NIV).

Vindication and Relief From Persecution:

Jesus promised to come, in the lifetime of his contemporary audience, in vindication of their suffering (Matthew 16:27-28). Likewise, in the midst of their (predicted) suffering, Paul promised that vindication and relief was near, and coming soon, at the coming of the Lord Jesus Christ– *the Son of Man* (1 Thessalonians 2:14f; 2 Thessalonians 1:4f).

Suffering For the Kingdom

Not only did Paul promise judgment on the persecutors of the Thessalonians, he reminded them that they were suffering on the behalf of, and in hopes of, *the kingdom*.

1 Thessalonians 2:12–
"You know how we exhorted, and comforted, and charged every one of you, as a father does his own children, that you would walk worthy of God who calls you into His own kingdom and glory."

2 Thessalonians 1:4f–
"We are bound to thank God always for you, brethren, as it is fitting, because your faith grows exceedingly, and the love of every one of you all abounds toward each other, 4 so that we ourselves boast of you among the churches of God for your patience and faith in all your persecutions and tribulations that you endure, which is manifest evidence of the righteous judgment of God, that you may be counted worthy of the kingdom of God, for which you also suffer"

As we have seen, when Paul initially went to Thessalonica, he warned them that they would be persecuted for following Jesus. He did this because the prophetic source of his gospel, the Old Testament prophets, informed him that the faithful would be persecuted in the last days before the bestowal of the kingdom. So, Paul proclaimed, "We must, through much tribulation, (*thlipsis*) enter the kingdom" (Acts 14:22). Paul believed that the reign of the saints in the kingdom lay on the other side of the period of tribulation:[305] "If we endure, we shall reign with him" (2 Timothy 2:11). Here are clear echoes of Daniel 7 and the promise of vindication and the kingdom at the time of the end. As Perriman says, "The kingdom that the Thessalonians were suffering for, is precisely the kingdom promised in Daniel 7" (*Coming*, 142). Also see Pitre, *(Tribulation, 2005)* cited above, for an excellent discussion of this.

In Thessalonians then we find every motif found in Daniel's prediction of the last days and the consummation. Thus, *no matter what our concept of the kingdom, the parousia, or the resurrection, it must be kept within the framework of the days of the Roman empire!*

☛There is no "Revived Roman Empire" in Daniel.
☛There is no postponed kingdom in Daniel.[306]
☛There is no way that one can extrapolate Daniel's prophecy 2000 years beyond the days of the fourth empire.
☛There is no way that one can apply Daniel 7, the judgment and reception of the kingdom to the day of Pentecost.

If Daniel's prophecy (prophecies) lie behind Paul's thought in Thessalonians, as is evident, this means that his discussion of the coming of Christ must be seen as the coming of the Son of Man in Daniel 7. But if this is true, you cannot contextually, textually or logically extend the *parousia* and resurrection of Thessalonians beyond the days of the fourth empire. We cannot fail to note how this negatively impacts Mathison's view of Thessalonians. Let me put it this way:

Daniel 7 predicted the coming of the Son of Man.

Daniel's prediction of the coming of the Son of Man is not a prediction of the end of human history, but was fulfilled beginning at Christ's ascension and extending to AD 70. (Mathison, *Age*, 2009, 380).

The predictions of the coming of the Son of Man in the NT, being based on Daniel's prophecy, do not speak of the end of redemptive history (i.e. the end of human history.

But, 1 Thessalonians 4 is a prophecy based on the prophecy of Daniel 7, the coming of the Son of Man (virtually all scholars agree).

Therefore, the prophecy of 1 Thessalonians 4, being a prophecy based on the prophecy of Daniel 7, does not speak of the coming of Christ at the end of human history.

The only way for Mathison to negate this conclusion is to demonstrate that while Daniel foretold the suffering of the saints and the inheritance of the kingdom, and although Paul, who says he preached nothing but the OT hope of Israel found in the OT prophecies, said that the Thessalonian saints were suffering for the kingdom into which they were being called, that in fact, Paul has something totally different in mind from what Daniel foretold. I fail to see how this is possible.

Whereas Daniel knew that fulfillment of his prophecy extended for a long time, and was not near, Paul nowhere projected fulfillment of his prediction beyond his lifetime. This is why he spoke of, "those of us who are alive and remain until the coming of the Lord." The judgment truly was near.

> **If Daniel 7 serves as part of the source of Paul's eschatology in Thessalonians, and few scholars doubt this, then you cannot extrapolate the *parousia* and resurrection of 1 Thessalonians 4 beyond the days of the fourth world empire, i.e. Rome!**

Let me summarize my thoughts as succinctly as possible:

The judgment coming of the Son of Man in Matthew 16:27-28 is the judgment coming of the Son of Man in Daniel 7:21f.[307]

The judgment coming of the Son of Man in Matthew 16:27-28 is the coming of Jesus in 1 Thessalonians 4:13-18.

But, the judgment coming of the Son of Man of Daniel 7:21f was to occur in, and not beyond the time of, the fourth world empire, the Roman empire.

Therefore, the coming of Jesus of Matthew 16:27-28 and 1 Thessalonians 4:13-18 was to occur in, and not beyond the time of, the fourth world empire, the Roman empire.

Since we have spent so much time developing the relationship between Daniel and Thessalonians in regard to the judgment, we cannot discuss other texts in-depth. Suffice it to say that other New Testament texts– all other New Testament texts– posit the judgment as coming soon.

James 5:9–
"Do not grumble against one another, brethren, lest you be condemned. Behold, the Judge is standing at the door!" Even Mathison, who is growing increasingly vague[308] in his defense of the objective imminence in the NT language admits that this is referent to Christ's AD 70 coming (*Age*, 627).

1 Peter 4:17–
"The time has come for the judgment to begin at the house of God..."

This text is extremely difficult to mitigate or ignore. Peter said that "the time" literally, "the appointed time" (*ho kairos*) for "*the* judgment" (*to krino*) had arrived. The definite articles are present. And, the word *kairos* means designated, appointed time.

Compare Gentry's self contradiction on *kairos*. On the one hand he argues that *kairos*, along with *chronos*, are "the two broadest words in Hellenistic Greek for 'time'" (2009, 332, citing Bloomberg). On the other hand, he admits that *kairos* indicates "the fateful and decisive point" that demanded imminent fulfillment (2009, 218).

Neither *chronos or kairos* indicate or demand a broad span of time. Gentry's remarkable claim that, "*Chronos* indicates a long period of time of uncertain duration" (2009, 332) *is patently false. While chronos is a generic word for time, it* does *not of itself* indicate whether the time under consideration is short or long. Only context determines the duration of the *chronos* under consideration. *Chronos* demands a *contextual qualifier* that indicates the duration of time in view. Can *chronos* mean a long time? *Yes*. Does it *automatically mean* "a long period of uncertain duration"? *No*. To say otherwise is unjustified.

Chronos, according to the Greek Concordance,[309] is used some 55 times. There are only a small *fraction* of instances in which *chronos* refers to a period of time longer than a man's life![310]

There are eleven instances in which *chronos* is said to be "long."[311] However, in *each of those instances* the context limits the duration of the "long time" to the lifetime, the generation in view! In some instances, the "long time" is referent to what is in fact a relatively *short* period of time (e.g. John 14:9; Acts 8:11; 14:3, 28). See Acts 27:9 that refers to Paul's time on the ship as he journeyed to Rome.

There are several instances in which *chronos* speaks of a *short* period of time. Luke 1:57 refers to the "full time" of Elisabeth's pregnancy. In 1 Peter 1:17 *chronos* is used to speak of a person's lifetime. In Hebrews 11:32 the author says, "time (*chronos*) would fail me" to tell of all the faithful men and women of faith. Note that in Revelation 6:11 the martyrs under the altar would only suffer for "a little while (*chronon micron*)." Gentry says that this "little while" was fulfilled in the AD 70 judgment of Jerusalem. Finally, although there are other examples, in Revelation 10:6 the angel said there should be "no more time" (*chronos*) in the fulfillment of the seventh trump. *Gentry affirms that this means "there will be no more delay" and was fulfilled in AD 70!*

Very clearly, Gentry's attempt to read 2000 years into *chronos* in Acts 1[312] and 1 Thessalonians 5 is specious at best. Gentry has *badly misrepresented the linguistic evidence.*

Neither does *kairos* mean an extended period of time. *Kairos* means a special, *designated* time *within chronos*. Trench emphatically shows that *kairos* is a specially designated, appointed time, and is *not* time broadly considered.[313] See also Bauer's Lexicon, Thayer's, and any of the lexicons.

The point of course is that Peter's words speak eloquently and powerfully of a positive expectation of the imminent consummation. There is no vacillation. There is no vagueness. There is no delay. The "appointed time for the judgment" had arrived.

☆ The God of Peace Shall Crush Satan Under Your Feet Shortly

"And the God of peace will crush Satan under your feet shortly. The grace of our Lord Jesus Christ be with you. Amen" (Romans 16:20).

In Genesis 3:15f the destruction of Satan is the first word of the gospel, the *proto-evangelium*. It is this victory over the Adversary that is the focus of all Biblical eschatology (1 Corinthians 15; Revelation 20). While Satan is not mentioned in 1 Thessalonians 4, the concept cannot be divorced from the text. The resurrection is when Satan, the Old Serpent, would be vanquished (Revelation 12, 20).

Isaiah predicted the final victory over the Serpent, Leviathan: "In that day the LORD with His severe sword, great and strong, will punish Leviathan the fleeing serpent, Leviathan that twisted serpent; And He will slay the reptile that is in the sea" (Isaiah 27:1).

We would remind ourselves that Peter said the Old Testament prophets knew that fulfillment of their prophecies were not near. Like Daniel, Isaiah gives no indication that he believed ultimate fulfillment was imminent. What Isaiah does do however, is provide the context and framework for that fulfillment, and it is the time of the judgment of Old Covenant Jerusalem!

Note that Isaiah 27 said the destruction of Leviathan would be "in that day." What is the antecedent "day"? It is the Day of the Lord when "the LORD comes out of His place to punish the inhabitants of the earth for their iniquity; The earth will also disclose her blood, And will no more cover her slain" (Isaiah 26:21). As Cline says,

> "The final proclamation of the resurrection in 26:21 depicts it not only as a redemption of believers from the prison of death (v. 21d) but as a vindication of the martyrs against these Satanic persecutors: 'The earth shall disclose her blood' (v. 21c). The cry of the martyrs' blood will be heard. At the resurrection they will have their day in court. [35] For the Lord will come forth 'to punish the inhabitants of the earth for their iniquity' (v. 21ab). Vindication of the Lord's people will not stop short of taking vengeance on their primeval adversary, the serpent-devil (27:1)."[314]

While Cline sees clearly that Isaiah was predicting the time of the vindication of the martyrs at the Day of the Lord, what he *misses* is that Isaiah is not speaking of biological revivication of corpses, but the restoration of the *"body of Israel"* (Isaiah 25-26:16f). Furthermore, he ignores Jesus' paradigmatic words in Matthew 23 about when the martyrs' blood, all the blood shed on the earth, would be avenged: in the AD 70 judgment of the slayer of the prophets and righteous. Isaiah's prophecy fully concurs with Jesus' prophecy.

In Isaiah 24, the prophet foretold the time of the kingdom, the destruction of the earth, and YHVH's rule established in "Zion." He posits all of this at the time when the "city of confusion" in the midst of "the land" inhabited by "the people" is destroyed (24:10f).

In Isaiah 25 the prophet predicted the time when death would be swallowed up in victory– the source of Paul's resurrection doctrine in 1 Corinthians 15. What few commentators notice is that verses 1f of chapter 25 plainly give us the framework for that resurrection: "O LORD, You are my God. I will exalt You, I will praise Your name, For You have done wonderful things; Your counsels of old are faithfulness and truth. For You have made a city a ruin, A fortified city a ruin, A palace of foreigners to be a city no more; It will never be rebuilt." Isaiah is positing the resurrection at the time when the city– this is the city of confusion of 24:10f, i.e. Jerusalem / Zion– was destroyed and the temple turned over to foreigners!

Likewise, in chapter 27, in predicting the destruction of Leviathan, (the resurrection) Isaiah tells us when this would be accomplished:

"Therefore by this the iniquity of Jacob will be covered; And this is all the fruit of taking away his sin: When he makes all the stones of the altar like chalk stones that are beaten to dust, Wooden images and incense altars shall not stand. Yet the fortified city will be desolate, The habitation forsaken and left like a wilderness; There the calf will feed, and there it will lie down And consume its branches. When its boughs are withered, they will be broken off; The women come and set them on fire. For it is a people of no understanding; Therefore He who made them will not have mercy on them, And He who formed them will show them no favor. And it shall come to pass in that day That the LORD will thresh, From the channel of the River to the Brook of Egypt; And you will be gathered one by one, O you children of Israel. So it shall be in that day: The great trumpet will be blown; They will come, who are about to perish in the land of Assyria, And they who are outcasts in the land of Egypt, And shall worship the LORD in the holy mount at Jerusalem" (Isaiah 27:9-13).

So, Isaiah not only predicted the resurrection and destruction of Satan, Leviathan, but *three times* he tells us that those events would be when Jerusalem and the temple were destroyed.[315] It would be when YHVH would no longer have mercy on the people whom He had created. It would be when the temple was turned over to foreigners, the altar turned to dust.

Thus, when we come to the New Testament and we find that Paul promises, "The God of peace shall crush Satan under your feet shortly," there is no excuse for extending Paul's prophecy beyond his generation. The judgment on Jerusalem was truly coming shortly when he wrote Romans and that is where Isaiah placed the resurrection and vindication of the martyrs at the Day of the Lord, when the great serpent would be defeated.

Of course, this dovetails with Paul's promise to the Thessalonians about "we who are alive and remain until the coming of the Lord." It agrees with his statement, "Brethren, I tell you a mystery, we shall not all sleep" (1 Corinthians 15:51). It agrees with Jesus' promise– his promise to come in the resurrection and destruction of Satan, "Behold, I come quickly, and my reward is with me" (Revelation 22:12).

Of course, as we have seen, efforts are made to water down Paul's statement, "we who are alive and remain until the coming of the Lord," but this can hardly be done. Wanamaker says of Paul,

"He believed that he and many of his contemporaries would still be alive at the time of the Lord's coming, as the phrase *hemeis hoi zontes hoi perileipomenoi ten parousian tou kuriou* (we who are living, who remain until the coming of the Lord") demonstrates. Marshall (127) is unconvincing when he tries to smooth over this implication. Paul could have used the indefinite third person had he not wished to include himself among those who would probably survive to the *parousia*. Instead, he uses the somewhat emphatic first person plural construction *"hemeis...ou me pththasomen* (we...shall certainly not precede" or "have no advantage'). That Paul believed the coming of Christ to be imminent is shown by the way in which his paranetic instruction in 1 Corinthians 7:25-31 is determined by his belief that the adult generation at the time of his writing was the last generation before the end."[316]

Let me drive this point home by making a grammatical point from 1 Corinthians 15. In Paul's discussion he uses the *present indicative, the present passive, and the present indicative middle (voice)* to speak of the resurrection! He not only used the present indicative, he used it ten times to describe the fact that the resurrection was already on-going:

1.) V. 35– How are the dead raised (*egeirontai*– "how are the dead ones being raised")– third person plural, <u>*present indicative middle voice*</u>.
Note Luke 20:37– "Now concerning the dead, that they are being raised (*egeirontai*).
2.) V. 35– "And with what body are they coming (*erchontai*) third person plural <u>*present indicative*</u>. (not *passive* indicative).
3.) V. 36– "What you are sowing (2nd person present tense) is not being made being alive (present passive indicative) unless it dies.
4.) V. 38– "God gives it a body as it has (aorist) pleases Him"– God is giving it a body (*Is Giving,* from *Didosin*– present tense).
5.) V. 42– "It is being sown in corruption" *speiretai*– (third person *singular*, present passive indicative).
6.) V. 42– "It is being raised in incorruption"– (*egeiretai*– third person singular, present passive).
7.) V. 43– "It is sown in dishonor" (*speiretai*– (third person *singular*, present passive indicative).
8.) V. 43– "It is raised in glory"– (*egeiretai*– third person singular, present passive).
9.) V. 44– "It is sown a natural body"– (*speiretai*– (third person *singular*, present passive indicative).
10.) V. 44– "It is raised a spiritual body"– (*speiretai*– (third person *singular*, present passive indicative).[317]

These present tense verbs have perplexed the commentators. This is understandable when the underlying presupposition is that Paul is discussing the raising of human corpses! *With this presupposition* no one can believe the resurrection was on-going when Paul wrote. So, commentators who would otherwise emphasize the grammar of the text, either ignore the Greek or seek to mitigate it. (Significantly, Paul is simply affirming what Jesus said in John 5:24-29. The resurrection had *begun ["the hour is coming and now is "],* but was awaiting *consummation* ["the hour is coming"].)

This is illustrated by an Internet debate I had with postmillennialist Brian Schwertley. Mr. Schwertly notes Paul's use of the present tense of "he must reign" in 1 Corinthians 15:25. He condemns millennialists for ignoring the present tense. In our debate, I noted his appeal to the present tense, and then noted Paul's ten fold use of the present indicatives to speak of the then on-going resurrection. Mr. Schwertly's response was, "That means nothing at all!"[318] When I pressed him to explain why the dispensationalist *must* honor the present tenses, but that he can ignore them he made no attempt to explain, except to exclaim, "This is ridiculous!" He never explained why my appeal to the present tenses was ridiculous but his is valid. Such desperation and inconsistency is all too common.

Another prime example is Gentry. He comments on Luke 22:29 where Jesus said, "I bestow on you a kingdom" Gentry notes: "'bestow is *diatithemai*, which is the present indicative, demanding a present bestowing" (2009, 495). Likewise, commenting on 1 Corinthians 15:25 Gentry insists that the present infinitive, "indicates his ongoing reign (2009, 256). If the present indicative in Luke 22 *demands* a then present tense bestowal of the kingdom, why does the many uses of the present tense in 1 Corinthians not demand the present reality of the resurrection when Paul wrote? If the present infinitive in 1 Corinthians 15:25 demands that Christ was presently ruling when Paul wrote, then how in the name of reason can one say that the resurrection was not in process when Paul wrote? To my knowledge, Gentry makes *no attempt* to address the other present tenses in Corinthians.

My point is that when Paul uses the present passive indicatives to speak of the resurrection in Corinthians this virtually demands that when he said, "those of us who are alive and remain until the *parousia*," he did in fact expect the *parousia* and resurrection in his generation.

So, the evidence is there: "He that has ears to hear, let him hear." Christ's *parousia* was truly near in the first century. There is little doubt that the critical scholars have said– and do say– that Jesus' predictions, and those of his apostles failed. Evangelicals struggle with the language of the Biblical writers, offering up specious, illogical, eisegetic and presuppositional arguments to deflect the issue. But those evasive efforts are of little success especially in the eyes of the enemies of Christianity who literally scoff at such efforts.

The solution to this Gordian Knot is to see what many scholars are now beginning to see– although not following through with what they are seeing-- and that is that Biblical eschatology is not about the end of human history. It is not about the re-creation of planet earth into a utopian society. It is all about the restoration of man to the living presence of a wonderful God who sent His Son – "a second time, apart from sin, for salvation."

We have taken space to present this material so that the reader can see that the New Testament declarations of imminence are objectively meaningful. The New Testament writers were not expressing "timeless imminence," "elastic time," some adverbial "rapidity of action," as opposed to nearness of occurrence, or mere statements of their personal eschatological hopes. They were saying that the times and events foretold by the Old Covenant prophets had arrived: "Yes, and all the prophets, from Samuel and those who follow, as many as have spoken, have also foretold these days" (Acts 3:24). We must take their statements seriously if we want to understand New Testament eschatology.

As the proclaimers of the Old Covenant hope of Israel, the New Testament prophets never, let me repeat that, *never*, speak of an extended prophetic perspective. While they occasionally speak of a "delay" of the *parousia* (Matthew 25:14f) or even speak of the master taking "a long time" to return, those statements are never presented as a delay of millennia, or even hundreds of years. The "delay" and "long time" is invariably posited *within the context of the generation in which they lived*. Gentry's own words demand this.

Addressing the New Jerusalem and the bride of Christ in Revelation 21, Gentry makes this self defeating comment: "The New Testament speaks of the church as Christ's bride (Ep 5:215f; 2 Cor. 11:2f; John 3:29). *The bride totally supplants Israel in AD 70*" (2009, 420, my emphasis).

So, according to Gentry, the bride of Christ totally supplanted Israel in AD 70 in fulfillment of Revelation. But if this is the case, then this means that *Christ came for his bride*– per Matthew 25– in AD 70! Remember that the church was already betrothed to Christ prior to AD 70, per Gentry's own referent to 2 Corinthians 11. This can only mean that since Revelation 19 depicts the wedding at the coming of Christ– which Gentry posits as AD 70, that the coming of Christ was not to betroth the church to himself, but to dwell with his bride! But again, this demands, unless Matthew 25 is a different wedding, that the coming of the groom in Matthew 25 occurred in AD 70. This completely falsifies Gentry's argument that the delay of the groom in Matthew 25:1-13, not to mention the delay of the absent master in v. 14f, spans 2000 years. See our discussion above on the wedding again.

All of this means that we should give Paul's statement, "those of us who are alive and remain until the coming of the Lord" their full force. After all, Gentry claims that the coming (*elthe*) of Christ in Matthew 25 and the parousia in 1 Thessalonians are the same coming. But since Matthew 25 demands, *per Gentry's own view of the wedding*, an AD 70 fulfillment, then this demands that Thessalonians was also fulfilled at that time.

Paul did expect the resurrection and Christ's coming very soon. While he never said that he would personally live to see it, knowing his martyrdom was coming, he nonetheless expressed the true nearness of those climactic events.

It is high time that modern Bible students stop trying to avoid, ignore and deny these multitudinous time indicators in the New Testament. It is time (pun intended) to not only honor the time statements but the covenantal framework of the eschatological predictions. Eschatology is about the end of the Old Covenant world of Israel, not about the material world or the end of the Christian age. It is about the New Creation to be sure, but not a new material creation. I think that, although he still affirms a futurist eschatology, Wright catches the idea of what Paul was actually saying, as he predicted Christ's *parousia* in AD 70: "When Jerusalem is destroyed, and Jesus' people escape from the ruin just in time, that will be YHVH becoming king, and bringing about the liberation of his true covenant people, the true return from exile, the beginning of the new world order" (*Victory*, 364).

THE COMING OF THE LORD WILL BE *AS A THIEF IN THE NIGHT*
1 THESSALONIANS 5:2

Without doubt, Paul's statement that Christ's *parousia* would be as "a thief in the night" is one of the most common arguments given to demonstrate that he could not have the AD 70 judgment in mind. The argument goes something like this:

Christ's coming against Jerusalem in AD 70 would have signs to indicate when it was near (Matthew 24:32f).

But, Christ's coming as a thief would not– because of its unexpected nature– have signs to indicate its imminence.

Therefore, Christ's thief coming cannot be referent to Christ's coming against Jerusalem.

While this argument has a *show* of plausibility, it is actually specious and based on false assumptions. Our purpose is to show that the attempt to dichotomize between *parousias* in the New Testament based on the Thief Coming argument fails.

In my March 2008 public debate with Mac Deaver I made the following argument:

The *parousia* of Christ in 2 Thessalonians 1 is the same *parousia* as in 1 Thessalonians 4:13f. (My opponent agreed with this).

The *parousia* of Christ in 2 Thessalonians 1 was to be in vindication of the suffering Thessalonians and in judgment of their persecutors (2 Thessalonians 1:4f– again, my opponent agreed with this).

The promise of the vindication of suffering and judgment of the persecutors in 2 Thessalonians 1 is the identical promise of the vindication of the suffering saints and judgment on their persecutors as found in 1 Thessalonians 2:15-17.

But the promise of the vindication of the suffering saints and judgment on their persecutors found in 1 Thessalonians 2:15-17 was the promise of the A. D. 70 *parousia* of Christ. (This is how my opponent applied 1 Thessalonians 2).

Therefore, the *parousia* of 1 Thessalonians 4 was the A. D. 70 *parousia* of Christ.

My opponent responded by noting that the coming of Christ in 1 Thessalonians 4-5 was to be Christ's *thief coming* (1 Thessalonians 5:1-3). Christ's thief coming is taken from Matthew 24:42f. In Matthew 24 there is a division between Christ's coming that would be indicated by signs, and his *thief coming* for which there were no signs given, i.e. his coming at the end of time. Since Thessalonians is Christ's thief coming, it therefore cannot be Christ's AD 70 *parousia*. My opponent confidently affirmed that he had overthrown my entire affirmative argument.[319]

The argument offered by my opponent is representative of the amillennial and postmillennial camps (e.g Gentry, *Dominion*, 2009, 437f). The dichotomization of the Olivet Discourse is fundamental to those paradigms. The question is, will an examination of Christ's coming as a thief confirm the traditional claims?

It is my contention that it can be definitively proven that Christ's AD 70 *parousia* was also his thief coming and that all attempts to divide the Olivet Discourse based on the thief coming are misguided. Furthermore, given the perfect parallels between the Olivet Discourse and Thessalonians noted above, if it is shown that Christ's thief coming is his AD 70 *parousia*, then this establishes Thessalonians as predictive of that age ending event.

In spite of my opponent's confident claim, in my response I took note of the following facts about Christ's thief coming.

The *parousia* of Christ in 1 Thessalonians 4-5-- his thief coming-- is the same *parousia* of Christ for his wedding in Matthew 25:1-13 (This is a virtually uncontested tenet).

The wedding of Christ would occur at the time of the destruction of Jerusalem in A. D. 70 (Matthew 22:1-7).[320]

Therefore, the *parousia* of Christ for his wedding– his thief coming– occurred at the time of the destruction of Jerusalem in AD 70.

Matthew 22 irrefutably posits the wedding of the son at the time of the destruction of the city guilty of killing the servants sent to them. Unless Christ was to get married to two different "women," at the end of two different ages,[321] then the correlation between Matthew 22 and Matthew 25 amounts to *prima facie* proof of the unity of the Olivet Discourse. This shows that the argument concerning signs for the AD 70 *parousia* versus no signs of his thief coming are falsified. There is no such contrast in the text.

Furthermore, since Paul is drawing from the Olivet Discourse in Thessalonians, then one is logically virtually coerced to apply Paul's prediction of Christ's coming as a thief to the imminent AD 70 catastrophe.

There is a great deal more we could say about Christ's thief coming but space forbids.[322] Suffice it to say that Paul's appeal to Christ's thief coming, instead of proving that he was writing of some distant event it shows that he was eagerly anticipating the impending termination of the Old Covenant aeon, and the arrival of eternal life in Christ.

What all of this means for the traditional amillennialists and postmillennialists is that since they affirm that Matthew 24:29f applies to A.D. 70, they must now apply Thessalonians to that event as well. What this means for the millennialist is that they can no longer delineate between Matthew 24 and Thessalonians by saying that Thessalonians is the rapture while Matthew is the Second Coming seven years later. Matthew and Thessalonians describe the same time and the same event. And this being so, the rapture theory is destroyed.

WHEN THEY SHALL SAY PEACE AND SAFETY...
1 THESSALONIANS 5 AND JEREMIAH 2-7

As we have noted, there are several Old Testament prophecies that serve as the source of Paul's eschatological prediction. One Old Testament context that is often overlooked as a source of 1 Thessalonians 5 is Jeremiah 2-7. I am convinced that Jeremiah 2-7 serves as the inspiration and source of Paul's prediction in 1 Thessalonians 5 even though the specific terminology of the thief coming is not found there.

Jeremiah 4-7	1 Thessalonians
The Presence of the Lord (4:26; 5:22 from *prosopon*)	The *parousia* (presence) of the Lord
Peace, Peace when there is no peace (6:14)	When they shall say, Peace
Trumpet (6:1, 17)	With the sound of the trump
Sudden report of Calamity, and the sudden coming of the destroyer (6:26)	Sudden destruction comes on them
As a Woman in Childbirth (6:24)	As a Woman in Travail
Judgment for shedding innocent blood (2:30, 34)	Christ's coming in judgment against the persecutors
Judgment for shedding the blood of the *prophets* (2:30)	Judgment for shedding the blood of the *prophets* (1 Thessalonians 2:14f; 2 Thessalonians 1)

| At hand– objectively– The generation of His wrath (7:29) | We who are alive; You are not in darkness, |

Jeremiah was describing the events leading up to the judgment of Jerusalem in BC 586. Jerusalem had become guilty of shedding innocent blood, the blood of the saints, yes, the blood of the prophets. Likewise, in Thessalonians Paul is dealing with a situation in which the church, (including the apostles and prophets of Christ) was being persecuted. That persecution was instigated and driven by the Jews of his day.

We should not think it strange to think that Paul was drawing from Jeremiah. In fact, Paul was constantly alluding to or quoting from Old Covenant examples of judgment on Israel, or prophecies of judgment on Israel, in his speeches and epistles as he spoke either to or about Israel of his day. Take a look at just a few examples.

➡ Acts 13– In response to Paul's gospel presentation– the story of God's faithfulness to Israel in giving to Jesus the "sure mercies of David"– the Jews nonetheless rejected that gospel. In response Paul gave a stern and often overlooked warning: "Beware therefore, lest what has been spoken in the prophets come upon you: Behold, you despisers, Marvel and perish! For I work a work in your days, A work which you will by no means believe, Though one were to declare it to you'" (Acts 13:40-41). This is a direct citation of Habakkuk 1:5 where God's prophet was forecasting the imminent judgment coming at the hands of the Babylonians. (It is worthwhile to note that the scoffers of Habakkuk's day were crying "peace!" when there was no peace, Jeremiah 6:14f). In Acts 13:27 Paul subtly hints at coming judgment on Jerusalem by calling attention to her guilt in Jesus' death.

➡ Acts 18:6– "But when they opposed him and blasphemed, he shook his garments and said to them, 'Your blood be upon your own heads; I am clean. From now on I will go to the Gentiles.'" While there is no citation of an Old Testament text, this passage is a replay and amplification of Acts 13 (Compare Acts 13:51) and brings the impending judgment of Israel clearly into focus. We also hear echoes of Matthew 27:25: "His blood be on us, and on our children" in Paul's warnings.

➡ Acts 28:25-28– In a replay of the earlier chapters Luke records that Paul shares the story of Jesus with the Jewish leaders of Rome, with little to no success. Consequently, he cites Isaiah 6:9f, and says, "Therefore let it be known to you that the salvation of God has been sent to the Gentiles, and they will hear it!"Like Habakkuk, Isaiah's prophecy dealt with the impending judgment of Israel, specifically the ten northern tribes. Paul's citation of Isaiah 6 was a thinly veiled threat of impending national judgment for rejecting the messenger of God.

Not only does Acts record Paul's citation of Old Testament examples and prophecies of national judgment of Israel, but his epistles are permeated with that kind of allusion and citation. We can list only a few of the many that could be given, with only a brief comment.

✦Romans 9:33☛ Isaiah 8, Isaiah 28-- Paul speaks of Israel's disobedience to the gospel of grace and their reliance on justification by Law. Their rejection of the gospel caused him to say: "For they stumbled at the stumbling stone, as it is written, 'Behold, I lay in Zion a stumbling stone and rock of offense, and whoever believes on Him shall not be put to shame.'" This is of course a conflation of Isaiah 8 and 28:16. Both texts predicted the coming judgment on Israel! Isaiah 8 says that those who stumbled would be destroyed, and Isaiah 28 spoke of YHVH's strange work of judgment on Israel when He would destroy heaven and earth. This would be in the day that He laid the foundation stone. The scoffers who rejected that foundation stone would be destroyed. Paul was following the teaching of Jesus in regard to the Rejected Stone by indicating that Israel's rejection of Christ was leading them to national destruction (Matthew 21:40f).

✦Romans 10:20-21☛Isaiah 65:1-2– Paul not only justified his Gentile mission by appealing to Isaiah, he likewise highlighted the recalcitrance of his own beloved people, and the implications for judgment inherent in that rebellious rejection of Christ: "All day long have I stretched out My hands to a disobedient and contrary people." From the context of Isaiah there is no doubt what this meant. National disaster was coming, followed by a New People with a New Name: "The Lord God shall slay you, and call His people by a New Name" (v. 13f).

✦Romans 11:16☛ Isaiah 6– Once again Paul cites from the foreboding context of Isaiah 6:9f to speak of Israel's rejection of the gospel.

✦Romans 11:9☛ Psalms 69– The Psalmist spoke of the rejection of Messiah (Psalms 69:21f) and the consequent judgment to follow: "Pour out Your indignation on them and let Your wrathful anger take hold on them....add iniquity to iniquity and let them not come into Your righteousness. Let them be blotted out of the book of the living" (Psalms 69:24-28). One can't help but wonder if the reference, "Let their table become a snare unto them," is a prophetic allusion to the Passover feast. Jerusalem fell (AD 70) during the Passover feast, as the city was overflowing with pilgrims.

✦Romans 11:26f☛ Isaiah 27, 59– While Paul is focused on the salvation of Israel, he nonetheless quotes from two Old Covenant promises that posited that coming salvation at the time of Israel's judgment. Isaiah 27 foretold Israel's salvation at the time when the altar would be made like chalk stones, and God would reject the people He had created (v. 9f). Likewise, Isaiah 59 said that the promised salvation would be when God would come in judgment for shedding innocent blood.

✦Romans 12:19☞Deuteronomy 32:35– In a context of persecution of the saints, Paul urges the Romans not to retaliate against their persecutors. He promises that vengeance and vindication will come from the Lord: "Vengeance is Mine, I will repay, says the Lord." This is a direct quote from Deuteronomy 32, and the promise that in Israel's last days God would avenge the blood of the saints. (See also Hebrews 10:33-37).

We could multiply these references even more but the point is that in Paul's epistles as he urges his Christian audiences to faithfulness in the face of persecution and speaks of the impending judgment of their persecutors, he invariably cites Old Covenant prophecies or examples of *judgment on Israel*. Go back and read our analysis of 2 Thessalonians 1 where Paul's prediction of the Day of the Lord against the persecutors of the Thessalonians is drawn directly from Isaiah 2-4. Isaiah predicted the last days judgment of Israel for shedding innocent blood (Isaiah 2:2-10; 4:4f).

So, when we read 1 Thessalonians 4-5 and realize that there are so many parallels with Jeremiah 2-7, we see that Paul is once again calling his reader's attention to God's judgment on the persecutors of His saints. Jerusalem of Jeremiah's day had persecuted the prophets (Jeremiah 2:30) and YHVH had judged her. Likewise, Jerusalem of Paul's day was persecuting God's prophets, and judgment– the *parousia* of 1 Thessalonians 4-5-- was about to fall (1 Thessalonians 2:14-16). Thessalonians should not be read in isolation from the *sitz em leben*, the life situation of the Thessalonians suffering persecution. Nor should it be read in isolation from the Old Testament prophecies of God's last days judgment of Israel for shedding innocent blood.

There is a final thought here, and a possible link with what follows. Paul is drawing from Jeremiah's account of the sixth century fall of Jerusalem. In this light, Pitre makes a fascinating observation: "More than any other prophet Jeremiah regularly uses the image of birth pangs to describe the tribulations that will come upon the people of Jerusalem and other cities when they are attacked and destroyed. ... In one case in Jeremiah, five elements of Jesus' prophecy in Mark 13:7-8– wars, rumors of wars, earthquakes, famines and birth pangs"– are all employed in a prognostication in which he predicts the destruction of Jerusalem (and by way of inclusion, its temple; Jeremiah 4:16-31)" (*Tribulation*, p. 251– N. 68).

So, Paul draws from Jeremiah's prophecy of the BC 586 fall of Jerusalem referring to that time of tribulation. Then, Paul employs that imagery of the woman in travail to drive home his point. The connection is, we think, not mere coincidence.

THEN SUDDEN DESTRUCTION COMES ON THEM
AS A WOMAN IN TRAVAIL
1 THESSALONIANS 5:3

Paul's prediction that the Day of the Lord would bring sudden destruction on "them" "as a woman in travail" is a significant interpretive element. It is generally held that this is simply an illustration that Paul used to make a point. Well, of course it *was* an illustration. But this illustration has a concrete, well established usage in the Old Testament. It carried definite connotations of *national judgment*.

Before we explore this however, I would like to make a quick observation about Paul's two illustrations in 1 Thessalonians 5. He says that the Lord's coming would be as a thief in the night and as labor pains on a pregnant woman. We are told that the reference to the thief coming means that there would be no signs. This becomes rather incongruous however, in light of the second illustration.

Does a pregnant woman not know when the birth is about to take place? Are there no signs of the impending delivery? To suggest to any woman that there are no signs of the birth is surely to be met with bemused laughter!

Is it logical therefore, for Paul to give one illustration that means "there are no signs of this event," and then turn around and give an illustration that is universally agreed to have attendant signs? The inconsistency of the "no signs of Christ's coming" argument is self evident in light of these facts.[323] As Wanamaker noted: "For early Christians there was no necessary contradiction between signs of the impending *parousia* of Christ and its sudden occurrence."[324] Let's take a look now at Paul's use of the illustration of the woman in travail.

For brevity let me state three things:
1.) The illustration of the coming of the Lord as labor pains on a woman in travail is a common Old Testament illustration.
2.) The illustration was given to forecast impending national judgment / disaster.
3.) The illustration was given to predict the Messianic Woes leading to the arrival of the kingdom of Messiah.

Point #1 brings us back to an issue discussed often in this work, and that is that Paul's entire theological thought is saturated with the Old Covenant. He is not simply looking around at life's experiences. He is drawing on the well attested use of this illustration in Torah. As Beale notes, "The symbolic or metaphorical use of labor pains is found with great frequency in the OT" (Beale and Carson, 2007, 883). Beale gives no less than 15 occurrences of this illustration.[325] The implications of this for the proper interpretation of Thessalonians are significant.

Point #2– In the OT, the illustration of a woman in travail was given to foretell impending national disaster and judgment. Psalms 48 speaks of the enemies of Zion being in travail as they contemplate YHVH as their enemy. Isaiah 21:3f foretold the destruction of Babylon at the hands of Sennecherib circa BC 703-701. Isaiah 37:3 is the story of the Assyrians before the walls of Jerusalem under Sennecherib. Jeremiah 4:31 anticipated the siege and destruction of Jerusalem at the hands of Babylon, as did chapter 6:24 and 22:23. Jeremiah 48:41 foretold the destruction of Moab at the hands of the Babylonians, and says the leaders of the land would have the heart of a woman in travail at the news. Chapter 50:43 says the king of Babylon would be in travail because of the coming judgment on that kingdom.

Commentators often recognize that the illustration of the woman in travail is intimately linked with a time of national disaster. Pitre says, "the birth pangs imagery was often utilized by the Old Testament prophets to describe the attack and destruction of a city" (*Tribulation*, 251). Wanamaker says the illustration, "is almost always used of the distress experienced in the face of divine judgment" (*NIGTC*, 1990, 180). Wanamaker claims that Paul changes that application in Thessalonians, but he offers no *proof*. In light of what we have seen so far in this study, we find no justification for this claim.

The imagery of a woman in travail carried with it the concept of destruction and death because in the ancient world child birth was extremely dangerous for a woman. Without the benefit of modern maternity wards and medicines the mortality rate among women in child birth was very high. Yet, with the danger and pain came the potential for new life! And this is where the third aspect of the imagery comes in.

Point #3– Paul's referent to a woman in travail brings to mind what is known as the Birth Pains of Messiah that were necessary to usher in the Messianic Kingdom.

There was in Judaism of Jesus day, and well before, a well hammered out doctrine of the Messianic Woes, or, The Birth Pangs of Messiah. This is the doctrine that, to cite Pitre again, "According to the OT, the resurrection itself would be preceded by a period of great tribulation"... Daniel 12, which is the most explicit prophecy of resurrection in the Hebrew books of the Old Testament. Strikingly, this description of the resurrection is preceded by the Great Tribulation" (*Tribulation*, 187). Schurer says that in Jesus' day, "Reference to the last things is almost always accompanied by the notion, recurring in various forms, that a period of special distress and affliction must precede the dawn of salvation...In Rabbinic teaching, the doctrine therefore developed of the birth pangs of Messiah which must precede His appearance (the expression is from Hosea 13:13; cf. Matthew 24:8)."[326] Likewise, Russell notes, "The time period of distress before God's final triumph is 'the travail of the Messiah.'"[327]

Just as Israel of old had been born out of Egyptian Bondage and the travail of the Exodus ("Israel is my son, my first born," Exodus 4:22) in the last days the righteous remnant of Israel had to go through the Second Exodus (Isaiah 11:10f) and the Messianic Woes. As Paul expressed it, "We must through much tribulation enter the kingdom of God" (Acts 14:22). This reality falsifies the millennial paradigm since it is held that Israel is delivered *from* the tribulation, instead of being saved *through* the tribulation. Ice claims: "A key factor in favor of futurism and literal interpretation is that even if one takes the symbolical approach to the text, the fact that Israel is rescued–not judged–in the Olivet Discourse (except Luke 21:20-24) is unavoidable and thus, a fatal blow to preterism."[328] Instead of being a fatal blow to preterism, the Biblical fact that the remnant of Israel had to go *through* the Great Tribulation and be eschatologically transformed into the body of Christ is supportive of Covenant Eschatology.

There is no doubt that the concept of the Messianic Woes is taken out of the Old Testament. Further, as Pitre astutely notes, the Old Testament posits the Great Tribulation *immediately before the resurrection*– which of course would be the resurrection of 1 Thessalonians 4! For both the amillennial and postmillennial views this truth is devastating since both camps posit the Great Tribulation in the first century before the fall of Jerusalem.

In Isaiah 26 the labor pains of Israel result in the resurrection (v. 16-19) at the time when YHVH would "come out of His place to punish the inhabitants of the earth for their iniquity; the earth will also disclose her blood and will no more cover her slain" (Isaiah 26:21). Isaiah 42 actually posits YHWH as in the throes of labor pains, to bring forth the time of the New Song (Isaiah 42:10f) when the Suffering Servant would appear (Isaiah 42:1-4). This likewise would be the time when the Lord would give sight to the blind, light to those in darkness. Yet at this marvelous time, El Shaddai would also lay waste the mountains and hills, dry up their vegetation, etc. (Isaiah 42:15f). So, out of judgment and destruction (even YHVH in labor pains!) comes the New Song, the New World!

This concept of a New World following the birth pangs is brought out in Isaiah 66 where the prophet assured Israel that the New Heaven and Earth would come, but, "The hand of the Lord shall be known to His servants, and His indignation to His enemies," "the slain of the Lord shall be many"(Isaiah 66:12-16). It should not go unnoticed that Paul cites Isaiah 66:15 in 2 Thessalonians 1 to predict the coming of the Lord "in flaming fire." Both texts foretold the judgment of Israel! This is the "refining" of Daniel 12:10 which was taking place when Peter wrote (1 Peter 1:4f).

So, as in Isaiah 65:8-25, the New Creation comes only after the time of judgment and destruction– the birth pangs of Messiah. And it is the destruction of the Old Covenant world that is in focus, not the destruction of material creation.

Micah 4 posits the time of the tribulation when, "Jerusalem shall be plowed like a field, Jerusalem shall become heaps of ruins" (Micah 3:12). The prophet likened her coming destruction to the labor pains of a woman, and said YHVH would give her up, "Until the time that she who is in labor has given birth; then the remnant of His brethren shall return to the children of Israel" (Micah 5:3f). What is interesting in this text is that Micah seems to posit a part of Israel's birth pangs as the Babylonian captivity: "Be in pain, and labor to bring forth, O daughter of Zion, like a woman in birth pangs. For you shall dwell in the field, and to Babylon you shall go" (Micah 4:10f). However, that time of captivity, the time in which YHVH would leave them, is seen as ending with the arrival of the One, "whose going forth is from everlasting to everlasting" (Micah 5:2-3).

The idea of the Messianic Woes is more prevalent in the New Testament than is commonly understood. I suggest that even one of the most common and popular evangelical themes, the New Birth, should be seen within the context of this important Old Covenant theme, at least to a certain degree. When Jesus told Nicodemus, "you must be born again" he used the *plural pronoun* (John 3:7b) indicating that there had to be a *corporate New Birth*. Israel had been born by "water and Spirit" in being delivered through the trial of the Egyptian captivity and Wilderness wandering (Isaiah 63:11-12). Just so, Israel in Jesus' day– the righteous remnant like in Moses' day- had to experience the Second Exodus, and be baptized into Christ, just as Israel was baptized into Moses (1 Corinthians 10:2).

All of this meant of course, that the birth pangs of Messiah, the horrific suffering of the end times that would result in the New Creation[329] had to take place. Israel had to be refined in the fire (See 1 Peter 1, where Peter wrote to the *remnant in the Diaspora*, and said they were being refined in the fire, 1 Peter 1:4f, as they awaited the fulfillment of the prophetic hopes of Israel).[330] The followers of the Second Moses would be revealed as the true people of God (cf. Acts 3:21f). Those who refused to follow His leadership would die in the "Wilderness" (cf. Hebrews 3-4). As the unbelievers heard the story of the end of the temple and their beloved city being preached, they rejected the gospel story of the fulfillment of Israel's promises in Jesus as Messiah. As a result, they cried, "Peace!" when there was no peace. They refused to see the disaster that was about to fall on them from heaven. The Messianic Woes were about to engulf them, "As labor pains."

The reality is that the Birth Pains of Messiah, the Great Tribulation, was indeed present in the first century. Jesus foretold the coming of the Great Tribulation (Matthew 24:15f). He said that the wars, rumors of wars, famines, earthquakes, persecutions, etc. would be "the beginning of birth pains" (Matthew 24:8- *odinon*).

Dispensationalists deny that Jesus was speaking of events for his generation (Matthew 24:34). All sorts of explanations have been given to explain away his straightforward words. And yet, Paul, writing later in Jesus' generation said, "We know that the whole creation groans and labors with birth pangs (*sunodinei*) together until now" (Romans 8:22). That was *Paul's* now, not our's. What Jesus said would occur in his generation was in full swing when Paul wrote. Furthermore, we have definitive proof that the Tribulation was indeed for the first century.

In Revelation 7 and 14, John saw the 144,000 that were out of the twelve tribes of Israel. Furthermore, the angel told John that this number constituted those, "redeemed from among men, being first fruits to God and the Lamb" (Revelation 14:4). This great host is identified as, "the ones who come out (literally, "are coming out" from *erchomenoi*, a present participle) of the great tribulation, and washed their robes and made them white in the blood of the Lamb" (Revelation 7:14). So, here is what we have.

✔The 144,000 were of the twelve tribes of Israel (Revelation 7, 14).

✔The 144,000 was experiencing the Great Tribulation when John wrote Revelation They were, literally, "those who *are coming* out of the Great Tribulation"

✔The 144,000 were "*the first fruit unto God and to the Lamb.*"

✔The 144,000 are the first fruit Jewish Christians– which means, of necessity, that they were *the first generation of Jewish Christians.*

✔This means that the Great Tribulation occurred in the first century.

The *first fruit* does not mean the 50th fruit. It cannot refer to anything other than the *first*.

Here is my argument stated simply:

The 144,000 Jewish Christians would experience the Great Tribulation.
But, the 144,000 were the first generation of Jews redeemed to Christ.
Therefore, the Great Tribulation must have occurred in the first century generation.

The New Testament writers confirm this assessment. James, writing "to the twelve tribes scattered abroad," said, "of his own will He begot us... that we might be a kind of first fruit unto him" (James 1:18). His audience was, when he wrote, undergoing persecution as they lived in the last days (James 5:1-6). Likewise, note Hebrews 12:21: "You have come to Zion, the city of the living God, the church of the firstborn ones." Here, we find the church of the firstborn (i.e. the first fruit) and they had arrived at Zion. Where did the 144,000 of Revelation 7 and 14 stand? Read Revelation 14:1-2; it was Zion.

So, both James and Hebrews were written to the first fruit of Jewish Christians enduring persecution. They were being refined in the fire just as Daniel 12:10 foretold: "Many shall be purified, made white, and refined." They were told that Christ's *parousia* had drawn near, and would be, "in a very, very little while" (James 5:8; Hebrews 10:37).

The Old Covenant prophets utilized the imagery of the woman in travail to speak of the events of the last days, and the coming of the Day of the Lord in His kingdom. Paul clearly understood himself to be living in the anticipated last days longing for the full manifestation of the everlasting kingdom. He well knew that the Messianic Woes would be a horrific time for the unbelievers, those rejecting the Messiah and the message of impending doom on that old world. Yet, it would refine the righteous remnant and reveal them as the true sons of God, recipients of the New Creation promised to father Abraham.

So, when Paul utilized the imagery of the woman in travail he was not simply drawing from an illustration of normal human experience. The illustration was far more than that. The imagery of the woman in travail is packed with concepts of judgment, *national destruction* and eschatological significance. We do ourselves a great disservice when we isolate Paul's statements from this historical, prophetic context. When we honor the repeated Old Covenant use of this illustration, when we honor the prophetic application of the illustration, it is clear that when Paul said, "When they shall say 'Peace and safety,' then sudden destruction comes on them *as a woman in travail*," that he was predicting the national judgment and destruction of those guilty of persecuting the righteous remnant. And this can mean nothing other than the national judgment of Old Covenant Jerusalem in AD 70, that manifested the glorious kingdom of Messiah.

1 THESSALONIANS 4 AND THE END OF THE AGE

We want to look a little deeper at our text in the light of a specific topic, the end of the age. We have already seen that it is assumed by all futurist eschatologies that 1 Thessalonians describes events to take place at the end of the current Christian age.

We have already shown that Biblically there will be no end of the current Christian age (Luke 1:32-33; Ephesians 3:20-21; Hebrews 12:25-28). If the Christian age will never end it is presumptuous to say that Thessalonians describes the end of the Christian age. So, what we want to do at this time is to compare Thessalonians with other "end of the age" passages demonstrating two things, **A.)** That Thessalonians and the other passages are parallel, and, **B.)** That the other passages clearly refer to the end of the Old Covenant age of Israel in AD 70. By establishing these two facts, we will have firmly placed the time and framework of 1 Thessalonians 4 within the first century generation and the fall of Jerusalem in AD 70.

To help us visualize the issues here, we present the following chart.

Matthew 13:30-43– Coming of the Son of Man➝With the angels➝Gathering of the elect/separation➝end of the age
Matthew 24:2-3, 29-34– Coming of the Son of Man➝With the angels➝Gathering of the elect➝ end of the age
1 Corinthians 15 –Coming of the Son of Man (v. 23f)➝gathering of the elect (entrance into the kingdom, v. 50-51)➝time of the end (v. 24)
1 Thessalonians 4:13-18– Coming of the Son of Man➝ With the angels➝Gathering of the elect➝End of the Age

We could certainly include other passages in our study but will confine ourselves to these since they are admitted by all Bible students to be the fundamentally important texts. Let's take a look now at each of these passages in comparison with Thessalonians.

1.) Matthew 13:30-43– There is virtual unanimous consensus among futurists that Matthew 13 and Thessalonians are parallel passages speaking of the end of the current Christian age. The millennialists say that both passages refer to the rapture, and, "The purpose for the rapture is to end the church age" (*Fast Facts*, 158).

Since there is no controversy as to whether these two passages are parallel we will proceed to demonstrate the time and framework of fulfillment. To establish when Matthew 13 was to be fulfilled will establish when 1 Thessalonians 4 was to be fulfilled.

Note that Jesus said his coming with the angels would be "at the end of this age" (Matthew 13:40). Here is one of the simplest, but important questions we could raise, *In what age was Jesus living*? He was not living in the Christian age. He was living in the Old Covenant age of Moses and the Law. Jesus was in fact, "born of a woman, made under the Law" (Galatians 4:4). To deny the temporal standing of Jesus is exegetically and hermeneutically inexcusable.

Keep in mind that the Jews, and Jesus, believed in only two ages. They believed in "this age" and "the age to come." They believed that "this age" was the age of Moses and the Law, and "the age to come" was the age of the Messiah and the New Covenant. They also believed that "this age" was destined to end, while the age of the Messiah was to be *endless*. Note Jesus' words, "Heaven and earth[331] will pass away, but my words will never pass away" (Matthew 24:35). This is an affirmation of the unending nature of the gospel and gospel age.

With this in mind, when Jesus said that his coming with the angels would be at "the end of this age," what justification is there for saying he had the end of the Christian age in mind? Why did he not say, "So shall it be at the end of *the age to come*"? He did not say that because the age to come will never end.

In an amazing admission and affirmation, Gentry admits that the Jewish expectation, and *the Old Testament prediction*, was that the age to come would arrive *at the end of the Mosaic Age*:

"From the linear perspective of the Old Testament, ancient Israel believes that the "age to come' will be the Messianic era *that would fully arrive after their current age ends.* Yet in the New Testament we learn that the 'age to come' begins in principle with the first century coming of Christ. It overlaps with 'this age' which begins in Christ." Thus, we are not only children of 'this age' (present, sin-laden temporal history) but are also spiritually children of 'the age to come' (the final, perfected eternal age). We have our feet in both worlds" (*Dominion*, 2009, 326, my emphasis).

This is an astounding statement. Gentry concurs that the Old Testament prophetic expectation was that the "age to come" *"would fully arrive after their current age ends."* Gentry's eschatology cannot abide this however, for it counters his futurism– and affirms the full preterist paradigm-- so, he inserts that "Yet"! He inserts the non-creedal idea that the age to come "begins in principle" *when it was supposed to*, but the Old Testament expectation and prediction *was not actually realized*! *Do not fail to catch the power of what Gentry has done.* He has adopted (with modification) the dispensational postponement doctrine. Notice the dilemma Gentry has created for himself.

The Old Testament predicted the full arrival of the age to come at the end of the Mosaic age (Gentry).

But, the age to come was only established "in principle"– it did not fully come– at the end of the Mosaic age (Gentry).

Therefore, the Old Testament predictions that the age to come would fully arrive at the end of the Mosaic age failed.

> **Gentry's affirmation and admission that the Old Testament predicted that the age to come "would fully come" at the end of the Mosaic age, *is nothing less than an affirmation of the true preterist paradigm*.**

You simply cannot, logically and exegetically, affirm that the Old Testament prophets foretold something and then affirm that what they foretold did not take place at the time they predicted it to occur, without thereby affirming *the failure of their prophecies*! This is dispensationalism.

Gentry would agree with this if the issue was dispensationalism. He castigates the dispensational world for their "postponement" doctrine that says Daniel foretold the establishment of the kingdom in the first century. However, although that is what the Old Testament foretold, due to the Jewish rejection of Jesus, those prophecies now remain unfulfilled. Gentry says this impugns the scripture, and he insists that the OT scriptures had to be fulfilled on time. We can only say "Amen!"

Gentry categorically rejects the millennial claim that the church was not foretold in the OT. And yet now, he says that although the OT prophets anticipated the full arrival of the age to come at the end of the Mosaic age, we now understand that it will not fully arrive until the end of the Christian age. This means that, just like the millennialists, Gentry is affirming that the OT prophets did not foresee the church age and its end.

If the Old Covenant prophets foretold– as they most assuredly did– that the age to come, the New Creation, the resurrection, etc. would fully arrive at the end of the Jewish age, then to say that the actual fulfillment of those prophecies is yet future means that Israel's Old Covenant remains valid, and Israel remains God's chosen, covenant people. This is simply unavoidable.

Consider Matthew 13 in light of Gentry's affirmation. Jesus said that at the end of the age when the righteous would be gathered into the kingdom at the harvest (the resurrection) "then the righteous will shine forth as the sun in the kingdom of their Father" (v. 43). *This is a direct allusion to Daniel 12:3.*

Daniel 12 is about the end of the age (v. 4, 9, 13) and the time of the resurrection when, "those who are in the dust of the earth shall arise" (v. 2). Matthew 13 is about the coming of the Lord and the resurrection at the end of the age *in fulfillment of Daniel 12*, and 1 Thessalonians 4 is about the coming of the Lord and the resurrection at the end of the age.

In Daniel 12:6 Daniel saw and heard two angels speaking of the predicted events. One angel asked another, "How long shall the fulfillment of these wonders be?" Heaven's response is in verse 7: "When the power of the holy people has been completely shattered, all these things shall be finished."

When was the power of the holy people completely shattered? This cannot refer to the end of the Christian age as Mathison claims, because according to Daniel the kingdom of Christ *will never be destroyed* (Daniel 2:44; 7:13-14).

Keep in mind what we just noted about the two ages. The Old Covenant age was to end. The age of Messiah was *not* to end. Well, we have in Daniel, Matthew 13, and Thessalonians a discussion of the end of the age. But it cannot be a discussion of the end of the Christian age, that is, the complete destruction of the church. It is a discussion of the end of the Old Covenant age of Moses and the Law.

If this is true then since Daniel 12, Matthew 13, and 1 Thessalonians 4 all speak of the same time, the end of the age and the same event, the resurrection, then since Daniel 12 positively places the resurrection and the end of the age as the time when, "the power of the holy people is completely shattered," then this means that 1 Thessalonians was fulfilled when Israel was destroyed in AD 70.

But, what does Dr. Gentry now do? As we have noted above, although Gentry once applied Daniel 12:2 to the "end of human history," he now applies Daniel 12 to AD 70. We applaud his move to the true preterist view of Daniel 12, but it should be noted that by adopting this view of Daniel he has stripped himself of any creedal support or futurist appeal to Matthew 13. Let me put it this way:

The end of the age resurrection of Matthew 13:39f would be when the righteous would shine in the kingdom in fulfillment of Daniel 12:2-3.

But, the end of the age resurrection when the righteous would shine as foretold by Daniel would be fulfilled at the fall of Jerusalem in AD 70 (Gentry, *Dominion*, 2009, 538f).

Therefore, the end of the age resurrection when the righteous would shine (Matthew 13:39-43) was fulfilled at the fall of Jerusalem in AD 70.

Jesus is clear that the end of the age he was anticipating and predicting is the end of the age foretold by Daniel. The connection between Daniel and Matthew cannot be ignored in any positive exegesis. And yet, Gentry ignores that connection, affirming the fulfillment of Daniel in AD 70, while extrapolating Matthew 13 to the end of the Christian age.

Daniel foretold precisely what Gentry said the OT prophets foretold, the resurrection, i.e. the age to come, *at the end of the Mosaic age*, not the end of the Christian age. But again, Gentry will not follow Daniel because of his creedal fidelity.[332] He chooses to create an eschatology unknown to Daniel and the other OT prophets. And, Gentry exacerbates his self contradiction.

Commenting on Acts 3 and "the restoration (*apokatastasis*) of all things" at the Second Coming, Gentry then says, "The Restoration of all things is a reformation that supplants the old order (Hebrews 9:10)" (*Dominion*, 2009, 502). Frankly, we could not agree more with Gentry's position, but once again, he has made a full preterist argument!

Notice what Gentry's argument demands:

The restoration of all things of Acts 3:21-24 is the reformation of Hebrews 9:10 (Gentry).

The restoration of all things is perfected at the Second coming (Gentry).

Therefore, the Second Coming is at the reformation of Hebrews 9:10.

So far, so good, or so it would seem, if one were not familiar with Hebrews 9:8-10. It is vitally important to see what the text actually says:

"The Holy Ghost indicating this, that the way into the Holiest of all was not yet made manifest, while as the first tabernacle was still standing: 9 Which was a figure for the time then present, in which were offered both gifts and sacrifices, that could not make him that did the service perfect, as pertaining to the conscience; 10 Which stood only in meats and drinks, and divers washings, and carnal ordinances, imposed on them until the time of reformation."[333]

Notice that the author says the OT Cultus, that entire system, was imposed, would remain valid *until the time of reformation!* So, let me frame my thoughts utilizing the conclusion that we just made:

The Second Coming of Christ is at the reformation of Hebrews 9:10. (Being the same as the restoration of all things, Gentry).

But, the Mosaic Law and Cultus, the entire Mosaic system, was *imposed until the reformation* (Hebrews 9:8-10).

Therefore, the Mosaic Law and Cultus, the entire Mosaic system remains valid (imposed) until the Second Coming of Christ.

Let me re-frame the argument one more way:

The Second Coming of Christ would be at the time of the restoration of all things, i.e. the time of reformation (Gentry).

But, the time of the reformation was to be at the end of the Mosaic age (Hebrews 9:10).

Therefore, the Second Coming of Christ was to be at the end of the Mosaic age, i.e. in AD 70.

These conclusions are unavoidable, given Gentry's own arguments. It is true that the restoration of all things is the same as the reformation.[334] It is clear that according to Acts 3 Christ's Second Coming would perfect the restoration of all things. But since the restoration is the reformation this demands that Christ's Second Coming was at the end of the Old Covenant system.

So, Gentry admits that the OT prophets predicted the full arrival of the age to come at the end of the Mosaic age. He then affirms that the Second Coming of Christ at the end of the age is the time of the restoration of all things, the time of reformation. But again, Hebrews 9, the text that Gentry himself associates with the restoration of all things at the parousia, says that the reformation would be *at the end of the Mosaic age*. Gentry has made a very powerful- we would say unassailable-- true preterist argument.

Either the Second Coming at the end of the age has occurred, or, the Mosaic Law remains valid.

2.) Matthew 24:29-34 – We have already established in the charts above that Matthew 24 and 1 Thessalonians are parallel. Both texts are concerned about the end of the age. So, Matthew 24 is about the end of the age. 1 Thessalonians 4 is about the end of the age. Therefore, unless each passage is about the end of a different age from the other, we must conclude that Matthew and Thessalonians are both concerned with the end of the same age. This can only mean that Thessalonians is about the end of the Old Covenant age of Israel.

This is confirmed by the fact that the discussion of Matthew 24 is clearly about the end of the Old Covenant age, as we have established. The disciples linked the end of the age with the fall of the Temple. And as we have noted, *the only age associated with the temple was the Mosaic age.*

We have proven that the Olivet Discourse is not about the end of two ages or about two comings of the Lord. It is a united discourse about the coming of the Lord to put an end to the Old Covenant world and to gather to himself the New Covenant people. We have shown that neither Jesus, his disciples, nor the Jews expected the age of the Messiah to end. Therefore, to suggest that Matthew or Thessalonians is about the end of *the endless age of Messiah* is misguided.

3.) 1 Corinthians 15– There is no controversy that 1 Corinthians 15 and 1 Thessalonians 4 are parallel passages. With this in mind we want to establish the framework of Corinthians.

Patently, 1 Corinthians 15 is about the time of the end (v. 24). What is also equally clear, but either ignored or denied, is that Paul said the end of the age was falling on them when he wrote. In chapter 10:11, Paul encouraged the Corinthians to faithfulness reminding them that they were the generation, "upon whom the ends of the ages has come." Paul uses two words that are significant. For the word "end" Paul used *tele*. This word often means termination, as we think of it. *However, telos* also carries with it the meaning of *goal or fulfillment*. This means that if something had reached its *telos*, then it had arrived at its intended and desired *goal*.

So, even when the idea of termination is present there is often another idea present, and that is that the *goal* of that which was being terminated, pointed to and anticipated has been reached. Thus, to say that something was coming to an end indicated that *it was ending because it had reached its prophetic goal*.

Paul said Christ was, "the end of the law for righteousness, to all those who believe" (Romans 10:4). Not only was Jesus to be the end of the Law objectively since he brought that Old Covenant age to its end, but he was the *goal* of that old world. As Galatians 3:23f says, the Law was a guardian of those under that system to bring them to Christ, and "the faith." When that system was fully set in place the Law and everything it represented was *supposed* to end. Thus, the end (*tele*) of the Law was not only the *termination* of the Law but the *goal* of the Law.

Further, when Paul said that the end of the ages had *come* he used another distinctive word. He uses the perfect tense of *katantao*. This word is used twelve times in the New Testament, and it means, "to arrive at something, to arrive at a destination"[335] This word is normally used to speak of arriving at a destination of travel.[336]

What Paul was saying was that the anticipated *goal* of all the previous ages had arrived! What was that anticipated, prophesied goal? To help answer and understand that question, let's ask, *what was the hope of Israel*, since Paul said that his gospel and hope was nothing but the hope of Israel? To re-frame the question a bit, what was it that Israel longed for? What was the hope of Israel, the goal of the ages?

One could make a veritable catalog of elements that constituted the hope of Israel. As a matter of fact, it would be rewarding to do so. For brevity however, we will only list some of the more prominent tenets of the hope of

Israel, the goal of the ages. We will also offer the New Testament texts that comment on that hope.

✣ The *Messiah* was the hope of Israel (Isaiah 11; Haggai 2:7). Peter said that Jesus had been made – not one day would be– "both Lord and Christ" (Messiah!, Acts 2:36f).

✣ The hope of Israel was *her restoration* in the acceptable time, the day of salvation (Isaiah 49:6f). Note that in 2 Corinthians 6:1-2, Paul, *who preached nothing but the hope of Israel found in the prophets,* said, "Now is the acceptable time, today is the day of salvation." Peter agreed that the restoration of Israel was underway. Writing to the *diaspora*, he quotes *verbatim* from the promise of Hosea 1:9f, and says his audience was experiencing what was promised.

✣ The hope of Israel was the *New Covenant* (Jeremiah 31; Isaiah 51; 55; Ezekiel 37; Hosea 2:18). Jesus died to confirm that promised New Covenant (Matthew 26:26f). Paul, *who preached nothing but the hope of Israel found in the prophets,* said that the Old Covenant was passing away (2 Corinthians 3:10f; Hebrews 8:13) and that his ministry was for the transformation from the Old Covenant to the New Covenant (2 Corinthians 3:16-4:1-2).

✣ The hope of Israel was *the Messianic Temple* (Ezekiel 37; Zechariah 6:13). Paul, *who preached nothing but the hope of Israel found in the prophets,* said to the church at Corinth "You are the temple of God, as it is written, 'I will dwell in them and walk among them, I will be their God, and they shall be my people'" (2 Corinthians 6:16). Likewise, he said that the temple of God was, through the Spirit, under construction (Ephesians 2:20f). Peter concurred in this (1 Peter 2:4f).

✣ The hope of Israel was to be *remarried to her God* (Hosea 2:19f). Paul, *who preached nothing but the hope of Israel found in the prophets,* said to the church at Corinth, "I have betrothed you to one husband, that I might present you as a chaste virgin to Christ" (2 Corinthians 11:2). Of course, John agreed with this, and proclaimed that in the imminent destruction of the city of Babylon, the time of the *presentation*, the Wedding, would take place (Revelation 19:6-7).

✣ The hope of Israel, believe it or not, was *the calling of the Gentiles* (Deuteronomy 32:21f; Isaiah 49:6f; 61:1f). *Paul, who preached nothing but the hope of Israel found in the prophets,* was the apostle to the Gentiles and he said that his ministry was in direct fulfillment of the Old Covenant prophecies! *(Romans 10:19-21).*

✣ The hope of Israel was *the outpouring of the Spirit to raise her from the dead* (Ezekiel 37:12f; Joel 2:28f). Peter affirmed in the most unambiguous language possible, "this is that which was spoken by the prophet Joel" (Acts 2:15f) as he described the events of Pentecost.[337] Likewise, Paul said in 2 Corinthians 3:3f, that the work of the Spirit was transforming them from the ministry of death to the ministry of life.

❖ The hope of Israel was the *New Creation* (Isaiah 65-66) and Paul repeatedly taught that the New Creation was a reality–although awaiting perfection-- in Christ: "If any man be in Christ, he is a new creation, old things are passed away, behold, all things are become new!" (2 Corinthians 5:17, see Ephesians 4; Colossians 3, etc.). John anticipated the promised New Creation and posited it as a direct result of the destruction of the city Babylon, the city "where the Lord was slain" (Revelation 18; 21:1f). He said those things were at hand and coming quickly.

Clearly, the New Creation hope of Israel was related, not to the end of time or human history, but to the end of Israel's aeon. According to Isaiah, the New Creation would come only when Old Covenant Israel was destroyed (Isaiah 65:13f). This is the end of Israel's world, not the end of the world. Keep in mind that Gentry agrees that the OT prophetic expectation was that the "age to come" would fully arrive at the end of the Old Covenant age.

❖ The goal of all the previous ages and *God's eternal purpose* was that, "He might gather together in one all things in Christ, both which are in heaven and which are on earth–in Him" (Ephesians 1:10). This was to be accomplished in the "fullness of times." We know from Ephesians 2:11f, that this was *being accomplished*, not in a restoration of national Israel *but in the body of Christ*![338] Jesus appeared in the fullness of time (Galatians 4:4).

❖ The goal of the ages was *the Age to Come* (Luke 20:33f) when "this age" would come to an end (Matthew 13:39-40). For Paul to say, therefore, that the end of the age had come upon them was incredibly significant. For the age to come to be fully in place, "this age" had to come to an end. But, Jesus' and Paul's "this age" was not the material world. It was the Old Covenant world of Israel. See our discussion of Matthew 13.

Note how Paul's statement impacts Gentry's admission above that the OT prophets predicted the full arrival of their hope at the end of the Mosaic age. For Paul to say that the goal of the ages had arrived in the first century belies Gentry's claim that the age to come will not arrive until the end of the (endless) Christian age. What was happening in Paul's day was the *consummation* of those OT hopes, just as Peter said "all the prophets from Samuel forward, yes all who have ever spoken, have spoken of these days" (Acts 3:21f). Gentry's paradigm demands that the OT prophets spoke not only of Peter's day, but of days thousands, perhaps many thousands, of years away!

Paul said the twelve tribes were serving God night and day hoping to "attain" (*katantao*) unto the resurrection (Acts 26:7). The desired destination of the previous ages was *the promised age to come, the age of the resurrection* (Luke 20:33f) wherein sons of God would be produced by resurrection (not by the marrying and giving in marriage as under the Torah) and could never die. Repeatedly, Paul said believers were joined with Christ's death, burial and resurrection in baptism, raised to walk in newness of life, forgiven of sin, and thereby *sons of God by faith* (Galatians 3:26-28; Romans 6:3f; Colossians 2:11-13). He also said that in Christ, "there is no condemnation" (Romans 8:1f) as opposed to existence under the Law–his "This Age"-- where, "I was alive once, without the law, but the commandment came, sin revived, and I died" (Romans 7:7f). The then still present age of the Law was still the ministry of death (2 Corinthians 3:6f) but was "nigh unto passing away"(Hebrews 8:13).

♣ The destination anticipated by the previous ages, and the hope of Israel was, in a word, *the kingdom*, in all of its nuances and elements.

This is critical: Israel as a people, her land, her city, her temple, her cultus, were all *anticipatory*, *types* and *shadows* of better things to come (Colossians 2:14f; Hebrews 9:24; 10:1-3). The better things to come were the goal, they were the things that Israel longed for. This does not mean for one moment that Israel, in Jesus' day, properly *understood* these things, but, that does not alter the fact that these elements were the things foretold by the prophets.

Israel had a noble and royal purpose as the chosen people of God, and that purpose was to point to the inclusive people, the heavenly land, city, temple and worship! YHVH would never leave Israel until He had fulfilled all of His purposes and promises to and through her (Genesis 28:15f). But, when Israel had served her purpose, and *the goal of her existence had been reached*, she would no longer hold that distinctive place. The arrival of the *body*, the *substance* of what she typified meant that the shadow was to pass. While unexpected and rejected by many in Israel (and today!) who wanted to hold onto the Old Covenant form, this was nonetheless God's plan all along.

For our present purposes, it is important to realize that the goal of the previous ages was the end of the old world, and the full arrival of the new. It was the time of the resurrection. Thus, for Paul to say that the end of the ages had come is the same as saying that the time of the resurrection had come! The *end* of 1 Corinthians 15:24 is not a different time of the end from that in 1 Corinthians 10:11. Nor is the resurrection of chapter 15 a totally different anticipated goal of the ages from that in chapter 10. This means, unequivocally, that the time of the resurrection– the *end* of 1 Corinthians 15:19f-- was impending.

Consider again Romans 11:7, a text noted above. Paul said: "Israel has not obtained that for which she sought, but the elect has obtained it, and the rest were blinded." When coupled with Paul's statement that the goal of the previous ages had arrived, it carries incredible force.

Remember that the millennialist does not believe that the church age was anticipated or foretold in the previous ages. According to leading millennialists, the church age established by Jesus through his blood and proclaimed by Paul, *was a total mystery to the previous ages.* Pentecost says, "The existence of this present age which was to interrupt God's established program with Israel, was a mystery (Matthew 13:11)."[339] He goes ahead to say that the church age was not foretold by the Old Testament prophets. On page 137 of the same work, Pentecost says, "The concept must stand that this whole age with its program was not revealed in the Old Testament, but constitutes a new program and a new line of revelation in this present age....It has been illustrated how this whole age existed in the mind of God without having been revealed in the Old Testament."

The contradictions in the millennial world are evident at this juncture. Tim LaHaye and Thomas Ice concur with Pentecost that the church was unpredicted by the Old Testament prophets. At least they say this on some occasions. However, on other occasions they say something totally different! In *Charting* (28) LaHaye and Ice say that when Jesus stood up in the synagogue at Capernaum, and read from Isaiah 61: "The phrase 'proclaim the acceptable year of the Lord' refers to the fulfillment of Jesus' prophecy in Matthew 16:18-19 to build His church." On page 30, again in reference to Jesus' use of Isaiah 61, they say, "That's a reference to the church age."

So, on the one hand we are to believe that the church age was a total mystery, unknown and un-prophesied in the OT. On the other hand, Isaiah 61 foretold the establishment of the church and the church age! This is an unreconcilable contradiction.

Given the millennial view of the church expressed above, consider the following:

The Old Testament prophecies contain the "hope of Israel."
The church, the body of Christ, was not foretold anywhere in the Old Testament (dispensationalism).
Therefore, the church was not- and could not be- the hope of Israel, per millennialism.

The problem of course, is that Paul said that the remnant was obtaining what Israel longed for when he wrote. *But, the remnant was entering into the Body of Christ!* The remnant was entering– *comprising!*– the spiritual temple. The remnant was offering spiritual sacrifices. The remnant had been betrothed to her soon to be husband. The remnant was entering into the New Covenant. The remnant was becoming part of the New Man (Ephesians 2:13f). The remnant was receiving the promised mercy and son ship.

This means that either Paul (and the rest of the New Testament writers) did not understand the true nature of the hope of Israel, or, modern evangelicals do not understand the nature of the hope of Israel as defined by the inspired apostle. Let me put it this way.

Paul preached the church, the body of Christ.
Paul preached nothing but the hope of Israel.
Therefore, the church truly was the hope of Israel, as divinely interpreted by the Spirit in Paul.

Let me put it another way:
The Old Testament promise of the kingdom (with all of its nuances and elements) was the hope of Israel.
The remnant was obtaining the hope of Israel, that for which Israel longed, in the first century (Romans 11:7).
Therefore, the remnant was obtaining the kingdom promised by the Old Testament prophets.

Now, when one considers that the resurrection was, preeminently, the hope of Israel (Acts 26:6f) then Paul's statement that the remnant was already receiving that for which Israel longed is *prima facie* proof not only of the spiritual nature of the kingdom and resurrection, but of the imminence of the resurrection–and the end of the age-- in the first century.

Paul's statement in Romans 11:7 means that it really does not matter what our concept of the kingdom or the resurrection might be. If the kingdom and resurrection was the hope of Israel, and who can deny that, then Paul's affirmation that the remnant was already entering into the hope of Israel demands that we bring our concepts of the kingdom and resurrection into conformity with his statement. *No matter what* the hope of Israel was, it was being fulfilled when Paul wrote.

All of this agrees with what Paul says in 1 Corinthians 15:50. Writing to the same audience to whom he has just said that the goal of the ages had arrived, he then says, "Brethren, I tell you a mystery, we shall not all sleep." This is a euphemistic way of saying, "We will not all die before the resurrection." This makes perfect, although challenging, sense.

With all this in mind, we state again that the end of the age, the time of the resurrection was impending when Paul wrote. Furthermore, Paul believed that the coming of Jesus for the resurrection was near (Philippians 3:20-21; 4:5). The fact that Paul emphasized that Jesus was the "first fruits" (1 Corinthians 15:20) demands that Paul believed that the resurrection was present, although not perfected.

The imagery of the first fruit is taken directly from the agricultural world of Paul's day. When the harvest was ready, the high priest would go into a specially designated field and cut from it a symbolic sheaf of wheat, barley, or designated grain. He would then offer it to the Lord in thanksgiving for the harvest that was now ready to be reaped. Fifty days later, on Pentecost, a sheaf was offered to Jehovah as a "wave offering." The point is that there is no temporal separation, no huge gap of time, between the taking of the first fruit and the harvest. *The first fruit and the harvest are inseparable*. Thus, for Paul to say that Jesus was the first fruits of the dead, was to say in the most powerful of ways, that the resurrection "harvest" was about to be perfected. It is disjunctive to insert a gap of two millennia, and counting, between the gathering of the first fruit and the gathering of the harvest.

Jesus appeared "in the end of the age" (Hebrews 9:26). This was undoubtedly the Old Covenant age (Galatians 4:4). He was, of course, raised in the end of that age as well. This is important.

Remember Daniel 12. The prophet said the resurrection would occur at the end of the age when Israel would be completely destroyed. If Jesus was the *first fruit of the harvest*, and if his resurrection was *at the end of the Old Covenant age*, and if Daniel posited the resurrection as occurring at the end of the age of Israel, then we have proof positive that the resurrection is confined to the end of the Old Covenant age of Israel. This means of course, that since 1 Corinthians 15 and 1 Thessalonians 4 are about the resurrection, that both of these passages must be placed within the framework of the end of Israel's aeon. This is confirmed in 1 Corinthians 15.

Paul tells us that the resurrection, when, "mortal has put on immortality, and when "corruptible has put on incorruptibility," would be when"the law" that was "the strength of sin," and when "the sting of death" was removed, in fulfillment of the predictions of Isaiah 25 and Hosea 13:14. There are two basic questions here.

First, what is "the law" that served as the strength of sin? W. D. Davies helps answer this question, "By 'law' or 'the law' the NT usually means the Law of God revealed in the Old Testament (OT)."[340] He is undoubtedly correct. The term "the law" is used some 117 times in the NT and there are only approximately 10 times when it does not refer to Torah. In each of the exceptions, the context makes it abundantly clear that it is not the Torah in view. What this means is, for Paul, the resurrection would take place when the Old Law, that was the strength of sin, was removed. This agrees perfectly with what Daniel said about when the resurrection would occur.

Second, Paul says the resurrection would be when "the sting of death," i.e. sin, was removed (1 Corinthians 15:56). We must understand that for Paul, faithful Jew that he was, the promise of the removal of sin was the promise of the New Covenant: "this is my covenant with them, when I take away their sin" (Romans 11:26f).[341]

Paul was emphatic that the Old Law could never give life or righteousness (Galatians 3:20-21). The Law was the ministration of death (2 Corinthians

3:6f). It could justify no one (Galatians 2:10f). No matter how many sacrifices a person made, "It is not possible that the blood of bulls and goats can take away sin" (Hebrews 10:1-4). Disobedience to the Law brought only death, separation from God, "I was alive without the Law once, but the commandment came, sin revived, and I died" (Romans 7:9f).

However, Jeremiah promised that the day was coming when God would make a New Covenant and under that New Covenant, "Their sins and their iniquities I will remember no more" (Jeremiah 31:29f). *The New Covenant would provide for the removal of sin, the sting of death!*

Someone might say, "In Corinthians they already had the New Covenant. Paul was still saying that the resurrection was future. Therefore, he is speaking of physical death, whereas the death to be overcome by the New Covenant was spiritual death." This is a false objection because it assumes that there were two kinds of death to be overcome by Jesus. Also, it clearly denies that Paul does posit the resurrection at the time when "the Law," that was the strength of sin would be abolished. That means that whatever our concept of death might be the resurrection has to be placed within the confines of the passing of the Old Law, the Old Covenant age of Moses.

However, the New Covenant was not yet completed and the Old Covenant had not yet passed away when Paul wrote Corinthians (See Hebrews 8:13; 10:12-17).[342] Salvation was not yet perfected. The atonement was not yet consummated. This is proven by a quick look at Hebrews 9.

In Hebrews 9 the writer calls attention to the typological / prophetic nature of the ministry of the High Priest. He says the liturgical services of the Priest were mirrored in the actions of Jesus as High Priest. The old temple was a type of the heavenly Temple, and the High Priestly services were a shadow of Jesus' spiritual services (Hebrews 9:6f, 24f). Thus, Jesus appeared in the end of the age to sacrifice himself (v. 26). He entered into the Most Holy Place to offer himself as sacrifice (v. 24) and he would appear again the second time for salvation (v. 28). The writer then calls attention to the prophetic nature of these actions, "For the Law, having a shadow of good things (about to come, from *mello*) come, and not the very image of the things, can never with these same sacrifices which they offer continually year by year, make those who approach perfect" (Hebrews 10:1). The word "for" is a connective that shows that Jesus' actions were, and were to be, the fulfillment of the High Priest's actions. The process was not yet complete for Jesus had not yet returned.

Consider the typological significance of the High Priestly actions reflected in Jesus' actions. At what point on the Day of Atonement did Israel know that God had accepted their worship? Was it when the sacrifice was killed? No, that was the *initiation* of the process. Was it when the High Priest entered the

Most Holy Place? No, that was the "mid-point' of the process and a time of fearful waiting on the part of the congregation gathered outside the Temple.

So, *when did* Israel know that Jehovah had accepted the sacrifice and service of the High Priest? *It was when the High Priest returned*! This is the point of Hebrews 9-10. Jesus had completed the sacrifice, but he had not yet returned to declare the Atonement perfected.

We must note the correlation between Daniel 9, Hebrews 9, and 1 Thessalonians 4. For succinctness, I will offer an argument on 1 Thessalonians as it relates to the *atonement work of Jesus*. This will build on what we have presented earlier.

1 Thessalonians 4:13-18 is the Second Coming of Christ.

The Second Coming of Christ was to complete the High Priestly atonement service (Hebrews 9:24-28).[343]

The Atonement is confined to the Seventy Weeks of Daniel 9 (Daniel 9:24).

Therefore, the Second Coming of Christ of 1 Thessalonians 4 is confined to the Seventy Weeks of Daniel 9:24.

A correlated argument would run like this:

1 Thessalonians 4:13-18 is the Second Coming of Christ.

The Second Coming of Christ was to complete the High Priestly atonement Service (Hebrews 9:24-28).

But the High Priestly atonement service would be accomplished at the end of the Old Covenant Typological system (Hebrews 9:10).

Therefore, the Second Coming would occur at the end of the Old Covenant typological system.

Take note of the first part of these two arguments. Daniel 9:24 says the seventy weeks were determined, "to make atonement for iniquity." Now if it is true that the Atonement included not only the offering of the sacrifice (i.e. the death of Jesus) but also included the entrance into the Most Holy, *and the return of the High Priest*, then it is *prima facie* proof that the return of Christ had to occur at the end of the seventy weeks of Daniel 9. And the end of the seventy weeks was the fall of Jerusalem in AD 70– "Seventy weeks are determined for...your city" (Daniel 9:24)

To suggest that the return of the High Priest was not included in the Atonement process is false. The Hebrews writer is clear that Jesus' actions were the fulfillment of the actions of the High Priest under the Old Covenant. Thus, to suggest that the Atonement was consummated at the Cross short-circuits the Biblical atonement process. When Daniel 9 says that God would "make atonement for sin" within the seventy weeks this *demands* that Christ's "Second Coming" for salvation, to complete the Atonement process had to occur at the end of the seventy weeks, in AD 70.

We cannot over emphasize how devastating this is to the millennial view. The dispensationalists claim that the seventy week countdown was postponed because of Israel's rejection of Jesus. They claim that the sixty ninth week

> **The Atonement belongs to the 70 weeks. Jesus died to make the Atonement. The death of Messiah, to make Atonement, would occur** *after the sixty ninth week, but in the seventy*! **Therefore, the atoning death of Jesus occurred in the seventieth week! There is no postponement!**

ended at the moment of Christ's Triumphant entry into Jerusalem, and the seventieth week will only begin counting again either at or very soon after the rapture.[344] How important is the gap theory to millennialism? Thomas Ice says, "Without a futurized (i.e. postponed, DKP) seventieth week, the dispensational system falls apart. There can be no pre-tribulational rapture, great tribulation, or rebuilt temple without the gap."[345]

According to the millennial view the Cross does not lie within the seventy weeks. Yet, Daniel was told that seventy weeks were determined *to make the Atonement*, and Daniel 9:26 says that Jesus' death would be "after" the sixty ninth week! If you are counting to 70, *what comes after 69?*

If Jesus' death, which was to make the Atonement, was after the sixty ninth week, but was confined to the 70 weeks, then to suggest that the death of Jesus postponed the countdown of the 70 weeks is a denial of the text. *The Cross of Jesus did not postpone the seventy week countdown, it was an integral part of the seventy weeks.*

Ice's statement is true, without a postponed seventieth week there is no dispensationalism. But the Cross proves there is no gap! Dispensationalism crumbles at the foot of the Cross!

A quick side note here. The fact that the Atonement could not be completed until the *parousia* (Hebrews 9:28) mitigates the view that the fall of Jerusalem actually occurred after the seventy week period. It is claimed that only the "determination" of the destruction occurred within the seventy weeks, but that the actual desolation lay beyond the seventy week fulfillment.

(Gentry, *Dominion*, 1992, 322).³⁴⁶ This is *not* what Daniel says. Daniel was told, "Seventy weeks are determined... on your city." You cannot divorce the fate of the city from the countdown. Since Daniel 9:24 definitely places the making of atonement within the seventy weeks, and since it is the *parousia* that consummates atonement, this *demands* that the *parousia* of Christ actually belongs to the seventy weeks.

This discussion of the Atonement brings us back to 1 Corinthians 15:54-56. The Atonement *parousia* of Christ and the resurrection are synchronous events, and resurrection would be for the purpose of removing the Law that was the strength of sin, and sin, the sting of death. *Atonement is the removal of sin!* Do you see the correlation between the finalizing of the Atonement and resurrection? Jesus' *apocalupsis* was for the purpose of finalizing, declaring and manifesting the removal of sin!

The Old Law could not take away sin, *the sting of death*, but the New Covenant, confirmed by the death of Jesus (Hebrews 9:16f) *does take away the sting of death*, because his New Covenant has been perfected by his *parousia*. To put it another way, if a child of God has the true forgiveness of sin today, through the blood of Jesus, *he has no sin*. But, if a person has no sin, *then death has no sting*, (*no matter how you define "death"*) which means that person has entered into resurrection life! How can a person that is not under "the Law," delivered from its condemning power through Christ (Romans 6:1-10; 7:1-10) and forgiven of sin, be subject to death? Did Jesus not say, "If a man keep my saying he shall never see death"? (John 8:51)

Take a look at our argument in simplified form:

Seventy Weeks were determined to "put away sin" (Daniel 9:24).

The time of putting away sin is the time of the resurrection (1 Corinthians 15:54-56).

Therefore, the Seventy Weeks were determined for the time of the resurrection.

Now notice a corollary argument:

The Seventy Weeks were determined for the time of the resurrection i.e. to put away sin.

But the Seventy Weeks would end with the destruction of Jerusalem in AD 70.

Therefore, the resurrection would occur at or by the time of the destruction of Jerusalem in AD 70.

We just took note of the tremendous implications of these truths for the millennial philosophy. However, the doctrine of the Atonement and the putting away of sin also has incredible implications for the amillennial and postmillennial views as well.

Both of these views believe that the Atonement and the final putting away of sin, *remains in the future, at the resurrection*, the time of the end (1 Corinthians 15:24-28, 54-56).[347] Incidentally, it is fascinating that both the amillennial and postmillennial views condemn the millennialists with vigor because of the "gap theory" i.e. the idea that the countdown of the seventy weeks was postponed. However, in reality both paradigms have just as big a gap in their theology as the millennialists! Here is why.

Both the amillennialist and postmillennialist say that Jesus did die to put away sin. However, they then say that the final putting away of sin lies at the end of the Christian age, when Jesus comes to put an end to human history. *The trouble is that Daniel 9 confines the putting away of sin to the seventy weeks!* Daniel knows nothing of a 2000 year gap between the *initiation* and the *finished work of atonement.* By placing the resurrection in the future, 2000 years removed from the generation when the Atonement sacrifice to put away sin was made, the amillennialist and postmillennialists have joined hands with the millennialists in inserting a gap between the sixty ninth and seventieth week!

We have briefly developed these ideas to show that in 1 Corinthians 15 Paul definitely places the resurrection at the end of the Old Covenant age. He posits resurrection at the time when "The Law" that was the strength of sin was removed, and when the stinging power of sin was destroyed. To suggest that resurrection life is not a present reality in Christ is to suggest that the Law that was the strength of sin is still in effect, and that the blood of Christ does not in reality take away sin from the believer. *To say that resurrection life is not a reality today means that there is no forgiveness of sin today!*[348] What good then is Christ's atonement? Let me develop this briefly from Hebrews 2:14-15:

> "Inasmuch then as the children have partaken of flesh and blood, He Himself likewise shared in the same, that through death He might destroy him who had the power of death, that is, the devil, and release those who through fear of death were all their lifetime subject to bondage."

Notice that Jesus' mission was to destroy the one who had the power of death. We must ask: what is this "power of death" the writer mentions?

Was the power of death the power to actually kill? Probably not, based on the story of Job. This likewise suggests that physical death is not the power of the devil in Hebrews 2.

I suggest that the power of death in the mind of the author is "the strength of sin," and "the sting of death" of 1 Corinthians 15:54-56. *Torah was the power of death!* Through imposition of that which was intended for life, death came (Romans 7:10-12). But in Romans it is very clear that physical death cannot be in view since Paul said that due to "the law" he had died as Adam had died. The fear of death–thus death itself-- was magnified through the legal demands of *Torah* (Romans 5:21). *This* was the power of death!

Vlachos notes that commentators are perplexed about 1 Corinthians 15:54-56 where Paul- seemingly without justification per the commentators- says that the resurrection would be when God would destroy (from *katargeo*) death. This would be when "the law that is the strength of sin" was removed.[349] It is only because commentators fail to honor Paul's concept of death that they are perplexed by this connection, however. For Paul, Torah was the ministration of death (2 Corinthians 3:4f) and could never deliver man from "the law of sin and death" (Romans 8:1-4). Torah could never take away sin which was the sting of death (Galatians 2:10f; Hebrews 10:1-4). So, for Paul the power of death was Torah, because Torah produced sin, and sin brought condemnation, i.e. death (Romans 6:23; 7:4-14).

The question then is valid: Does the Christian genuinely have forgiveness of that which brings death today? Has the Christian been delivered from the power of death? *Is the Christian delivered from the fear of death?*

It must be noted that Paul affirmed that Christ was already in the process of destroying death (1 Corinthians 15:25– "the last enemy that is *being* destroyed (present passive indicative of *karargeo*) is death." Likewise, the apostle affirmed that Christ *has abolished* (from *katargeo*) death, and brought life and immortality to light through the gospel" (2 Timothy 1:12). When a person dichotomizes Paul's discussion into a discussion of spiritual death versus physical death in these verses it presents a host of illogical and unscriptural implications. Paul was discussing the *initiated* work of the resurrection, the *on-going process* of resurrection and the anticipation of the *consummation* of the resurrection. He was not discussing two different kinds of resurrection.

So, if forgiveness and reconciliation is objective today, then it must be true that Christ has destroyed him who had the power of death, just as Hebrews 2 says he came to do.

Unless Christ failed to come "shortly" and crush Satan as Paul said he was about to do (Romans 16:20) then the one who had the power of death is destroyed.

If one says that physical death is the power of the devil then the death of even the most faithful child of God is a demonstration of the failure of Christ, for it is a manifest demonstration that the Devil still has the power of death.

If the Devil still has the power of death then the gospel has not delivered Christians from the law of sin and death (Romans 8:1-3) and is no more effective than the Torah! This means that the gospel has replaced Torah as the strength of sin, and empowers the sting of death. *Did Christ simply replace one condemning law with another?*

The denial of the fulfilled parousia of Christ leads inexorably to the view that Satan still rules, that we remain in "the present evil age" as Gentry affirms (2009, 326) and that Christ has accomplished virtually *nothing*! After all, if the blessings of forgiveness, deliverance from the fear of death, deliverance from death itself is not a reality, and we have to wait until the termination of the gospel age to receive these things as Gentry affirms, then this means that the gospel ages stands between us and our longed for blessings! *But what is wrong with the Christian age that it must end?*

It is commonly objected that the Christian does have the freedom from the fear of death, for Paul said "comfort one another with these words" (1 Thessalonians 4:18). Of course this is true, but Paul said those words in the context of the imminent coming of Christ to destroy the one who had the power of death. He did not anticipate a parousia delayed by two millennia to accomplish that work!

If Christians do not have to fear death, how is it so? Paul's point in Hebrews is that *it would be through the crushing of the one who had the power of death that the fear of death would be destroyed*! So, it is illogical to argue that the Christian has no need to fear death, but then affirm that the one who had the power of death still *has* the power of death.

To reiterate our point then: 1 Corinthians 15 and 1 Thessalonians 4 speak of the same time and event, the coming of Christ at the end of the age to bring resurrection life. This much is agreed to among virtually all Bible students. However, in 1 Corinthians 15 Paul places the resurrection at the time when the Old Law would pass away (when it would be *fulfilled*) and when "the sting of death" would be removed.[350] As we have seen, this agrees perfectly with the prediction of Daniel 9. To suggest that the resurrection has not occurred is to say that the Old Law remains valid today, and to suggest that the blood of Christ does not provide true forgiveness. It is to suggest that the Atonement is not yet perfected.

What we see then is that Corinthians agrees perfectly with all the other evidence we have examined to this juncture. The resurrection of 1 Thessalonians 4 belongs to the end of the Old Covenant age, and that occurred with the fall of Jerusalem in AD 70.

We want to return to Daniel 9 and present a final argument here in regard to the resurrection, Thessalonians, and the end of the age.

Our argument is this:

1.) 1 Thessalonians 4:13-18 is about the resurrection.

2.) The time of the resurrection is the time when the sting of death, sin, would be removed (1 Corinthians 15:54-56).
3.) Sin would be removed by the end of the seventieth week of Daniel 9:24.
4.) The seventieth week of Daniel 9:24-27 deals with the end of the Old Covenant world of Israel in AD 70.
5.) Therefore the resurrection would occur by the end of the seventieth week of Daniel 9:24, i.e. by the time of the end of the Old Covenant world of Israel in AD 70.

No one doubts points #1 and 2. Further, point #3 cannot be effectively denied since Daniel was told that seventy weeks were determined to "put an end to sin," meaning that Jehovah would provide a final solution to man's problem with sin. Thus, point #3 is not contested by anyone.

Point #4 is also virtually un-contestable. The prophecy of the seventy weeks is about Israel, "Seventy weeks are determine on your people and thy holy city" i.e. Jerusalem. As Goldingay correctly notes, Daniel 9, "is not speaking of the end of all history."[351] The passage is dealing with the consummation of Israel's promises. There is *nothing* here about the end of the Christian age.

It needs to be seen that Daniel 9 is clearly *about the time of the end.* There is surely the termination of the seventy weeks. Of that there can be no doubt. And what would be the end of the seventieth week? It would be the time of the Abomination of Desolation, the end of *"the war,"*[352] when desolation would continue "even until the consummation." (It is significant that the millennialist has no place for a total desolation of Israel in the last days. They see a time of trouble to be sure, but they also see deliverance from that desolation. The trouble is that Daniel saw the time of desolation that would lead to total desolation and consummation).

The point is that Daniel 9 deals with the end of Israel's age. The seventy weeks would bring Israel's world to it's anticipated consummation. The end of the seventy weeks would be the anticipated "end (goal) of the ages" discussed earlier. It would be at that time when Jehovah would "bring an end to sin." God would effectively provide a solution to the sin problem!

This brings us to point #5. Since the time of the resurrection, the time of 1 Thessalonians 4:13-18, is when God would deal finally with sin, and since the end of the seventy weeks is the terminus for when God would deal finally with sin, then it follows that the time of the resurrection is linked inextricably with the end of the seventieth week of Daniel. That is, the resurrection is tied to the end of the Old Covenant age of Israel. That occurred with the fall of Jerusalem in AD 70.

The only way to counter the force of this argument is to be able to establish that any one of the premises or statements is false. However, as we have just seen, points #1-4 are incontestable, and are admitted by virtually every eschatological paradigm.

The only way to mitigate our argument is to prove beyond a doubt that the promise of putting an end to sin in Daniel 9 is unrelated to the idea of resurrection. However, Paul said resurrection would become a reality when *sin* was dealt with. Thus, Daniel 9 is dealing with resurrection.[353]

I want to make one final point in regard to the end of the age, the resurrection, Daniel and 1 Corinthians 15. I will keep this as brief as possible by presenting a comparison chart of Daniel 12 and 1 Corinthians 15.

Daniel 12	1 Corinthians 15
Prediction of the resurrection (v. 2)	Prediction of the resurrection
Resurrection at the time of the end (v. 4)	Resurrection at the time of the end (v. 24).
Resurrection to everlasting life (v. 2)	Resurrection to incorruptibility, immortality (v. 55f)
Promise to Old Covenant Israel	Resurrection promised to Old Covenant Israel (v. 55-56) in fulfillment of Isaiah 25 and Hosea 13:14
Fulfillment when Israel shattered (v. 7)- at the end of the Old Covenant era	Fulfillment at the end of the Old Covenant era, at the end of "the law" that was the strength of sin
Far removed temporally from Daniel's day– "You will rest" (i.e. die) (v. 13)	"We will not all sleep" i.e. die (v. 51).

These parallels are clearly more than simple similarity of language. The topic is the same, the theme is the same, the context is the same. But of course, the temporal statements are *radically different*! What was far off when Daniel wrote was now near when Paul wrote (1 Corinthians 10:11[354]). More on that momentarily.

As we have seen above, Gentry now holds to the true preterist view of the resurrection prophecy of Daniel 12. Given the direct parallels between Daniel and 1 Corinthians 15, this logically demands that Gentry now apply the resurrection of 1 Corinthians to AD 70 as well.

Gentry attempts to negate the power of such comparisons however, by simply castigating the true preterists as unorthodox. He claims preterists believe that simple similarity of language proves identity. This is a *blatant misrepresentation* of the preterist hermeneutic. *I know of no true preterists that uses the hermeneutic that Gentry ascribes to us!* Remarkably, and revealingly, Gentry did not cite a single preterist work to support his claim. This is unbecoming and unscholarly.

To support his paradigm, Gentry must prove that there are two different resurrections, of two different natures, at two different times of the end of the age. And yet each of these supposedly disparate resurrections is a resurrection to everlasting life and reward! Gentry makes no effort to provide the evidence in support of such a dichotomization.

SUMMARY OF THIS SECTION

What have we seen ? We have seen that the Bible consistently teaches that the "end of the age" is a referent to the end of the Old Covenant age of Israel that occurred with the fall of Jerusalem in AD 70.

We have shown that the Bible teaches that Christ's coming at the end of the age, the coming of 1 Thessalonians 4, was therefore, at the end of the Old Covenant age in AD 70.

We have shown that Paul emphatically declares that the end– the goal of the previous ages-- had arrived, and that the remnant of Israel was entering into the "end of the age" hope prophesied by the Old Covenant prophets.

We have shown the correlation between Daniel 9, 1 Corinthians 15, Hebrews 9 and Thessalonians, and shown that the completion of the Atonement, the putting away of sin and the coming of Christ in Thessalonians are confined to the seventy week countdown of Daniel 9. That was fulfilled at the end of the Old Covenant world of Israel in AD 70.

Unless a person can show that the coming of 1 Thessalonians belongs to the end of a different age, i.e. at the end of the Christian age (which as we have shown has *no end*) then we are forced to apply Thessalonians to the end of the Old Covenant age.

Unless a person can show that the *parousia* of Thessalonians is unrelated to the putting away of sin and the consummation of the Atonement, then the coming of Thessalonians was fulfilled in AD 70.

I suggest that any discussion of 1 Thessalonians 4 and the end of the world must be kept within the framework of the end of the Old Covenant world of Israel, not the end of the physical cosmos.

SPECIAL STUDY:
DO EXPECTATIONS DEMAND A RAPTURE?
AN EXAMINATION OF THE LITERAL RAPTURE IN AD 70

Having completed the exegetical part of our study, we want to address some related issues. In the preterist community, there is a belief that a literal rapture occurred at the fall of Jerusalem in AD 70. Ed Stevens of the International Preterist Association,[355] is primarily responsible for popularizing this idea, although Russell espoused it in the 19th century. Another book, *Taken to Heaven in AD 70* now espouses a literal rapture in AD 70.[356] Stevens argues that there had to be a literal rapture of the Christians in order to explain the total silence about the fulfillment of the *parousia* of Christ in AD 70. There are no Apostolic or Patristic writers that point to the fall of Jerusalem as the Second Coming. Stevens says this silence demands that there were no Christians with an understanding of the significance of that event left. The faithful Christians had been removed. Those "left behind" were "sleepers" that did not comprehend the event.

Stevens also maintains that the early church expected to be removed from earth at the *parousia* and that this expectation demands that this is what happened. A couple of quick observations.

Stevens is to be commended for attempting to answer the perplexing issue of the silence of the early church authors. Not many in the preterist community have addressed the topic in a substantive way. Whether one agrees or disagrees with his position, and I *do* disagree, it is certainly proper to address such issues. One of the thrilling things to me about the preterist movement is the freedom to ask questions openly, to investigate and to rethink. I think most preterists would agree with me on this. However, there is a tendency, part of our human make-up I suppose, to allow *ourselves* the freedom that we would not give to others. *We must not do this*. Further, there is really no excuse for emotional tirades against Stevens and his view.[357] The issue has to be discussed objectively and openly, based on the merits of the view itself, not on personalities or traditions, likes and dislikes. That is what we will attempt to do here. With these things stated, let us proceed.

First, the silence of the early church about the significance of AD 70 is indeed perplexing. However, to argue that this silence demands that the true Christians had been removed is a *non-sequitur*. Arguments from silence are extremely tenuous at best, and cannot be used as *prima facie* evidence to prove a doctrine. Thus, while troubling, it is inappropriate to attempt to prove a doctrine based on the silence of history.

Second, as Frost has cogently noted, "We do not have what could even be called a representative majority of believers in the early and apostolic church. Charles Hodges wrote, 'Ten or twenty writers scattered over such a period cannot reasonably be assumed to speak the mind of the whole church.'"[358]

Thus, while Stevens attempts to build a case on the silence of the apostolic and patristic writers, in fact, we have so few of these writings that we really do not know what "the church" believed or did not believe. We can only make statements about the writings that do exist, and given the idiosyncratic, often aberrant and erroneous nature of these writings, to place too much emphasis on what they did not say is questionable.[359]

Third, it is presumptive to argue that "expectations demand a rapture." This argument presumes the *nature of the expectation*, and then presumes *the validity of that expectation*. The fallacy of this kind of argument should be more than apparent.

The Jews of Jesus' day expected a literal, national restoration of their Theocracy (Luke 24:25f). Did that expectation demand such a restoration? Patently not. Their expectation did not demand anything. Jesus categorically rejected that expectation.

Modern day "monster hunters" go into the woods of the Northwest "expecting" to find Sasquatch, or Bigfoot, and dinosaur hunters probe the depths of Loch Ness looking for "Nessie." Do their expectations demand the existence of those creatures? Clearly not. On a more theological note, Wright observes, "Christians and Jews would agree the world has not yet become all that the Biblical hope would indicate."[360] His point is that the religious world "expects" a world of physical, geo-political, social transformation. Does that mean that this expectation demands an earthly utopia? Those in the amillennial and true preterist camps would certainly disavow such a view maintaining that this is an unrealistic expectation.

The expectations in these examples are real, sincere expectations. However, those expectations did not and do not mean they would receive what they expected!

What has to be proven is that what is being claimed was expected, was in fact what was expected.

Stevens claims that the New Testament saints were expecting to be removed from earth because of the language of, "shall be caught up together with him," and, "I will come again and receive you to myself." Our exegesis of Thessalonians and John 14 has falsified that view, however. We have shown that John 14 does not speak of a removal of the disciples. Likewise *apantesis*, *episunagogee*, the concept of the Wedding and the Messianic Tabernacle also falsify the idea of a literal rapture.

We have a right to ask, if the saints were expecting a literal removal from planet earth were they not also expecting a literal, visible, bodily coming of Christ? The language of the coming of the Lord on the clouds of heaven is just as literal as the language of the catching away, is it not? What is the basis for claiming that the catching away is literal, while the language of the coming of the clouds is not literal? These events go hand in hand in the language of the texts. If the saints were expecting a literal removal from earth, therefore, were they not also looking for a literal coming of the Lord? Were they not also looking for the destruction of material creation? We are reminded once again of John 14:19f, where the nature of the *parousia*, and the nature of the "catching away" are clearly defined as issues of salvation fellowship *and not a removal from earth*.

WHAT ABOUT SILENCE?

Does the silence of the early church "fathers" prove that the faithful disciples of the first century were raptured from earth? We think not. Make no mistake, the silence of the apostolic and patristic authors concerning the *parousia is perplexing*. However, while silence is perplexing, and even troublesome, silence cannot be used, logically, to positively prove any proposition. Silence may make us wonder, but it cannot be pressed too far. Does silence mean non-fulfillment? Do we really want to argue that we know something happened because no one told us that it did happen?

> Do we *really* want to argue that the reason that we know something happened, is *because no one told us that it happened?*

There is another silence in the patristics, at least a *temporary* partial silence, that is deeply troubling. Setzer tells us that in the patristic writings, Justin the Martyr (circa AD 155) was the very first to mention any association between the fall of Jerusalem and Jewish guilt for killing Jesus.[361] This silence is deeply troubling. How, one might ask, could the early writers have missed such a doctrine as this? Did not Jesus and Paul and the other writers make the connection between Jewish guilt and impending judgment on Jerusalem so clear, so unequivocal that no one could fail to see it? You would think so (cf. Matthew 23; 1 Thessalonians 2:15f; Revelation 11:8f, etc.) Why then did it take 100 years for that connection to be made? A troubling silence indeed!

Frost offers another excellent illustration: "Gentry (Kenneth Gentry, DKP) borrowing from the late nineteenth-century theologian Milton Terry, interprets the Babylonian Whore in Revelation 17 to be Jerusalem in the age of Paul. This is brand new. No father taught this that we are aware of. For nearly two-thousand years this view never breathed, if and only if we are to maintain that all eschatology can be found in these writings" (*Hope*, 154). The point is applicable and powerful.

Stevens believes, like Gentry and myself, that Babylon of Revelation was Old Covenant Jerusalem. Yet, the apostolic and patristic writers are *unanimously silent* about this identification according to Frost. What does Stevens do about this silence? He affirms that although we have no apostolic or patristic support for this view, it is true nonetheless because of the Biblical testimony. We don't need the church fathers to tell us it is true, the Bible affirms it, and that is enough.

To argue that the silence of the Christian writers proves the reality of the rapture proves nothing, and fails to consider the silence of the *secular writers* of the first century and immediately afterward. Here is my point. Stevens argues that since the Christian writers do not mention the fulfillment of the *parousia* that this proves that the faithful Christians had been raptured and those left behind did not realize what had happened. The silence of the early writers supposedly proves the reality of the rapture. However, this fails to consider the silence of the secular writers.

It is well known that the secular writers of the first and second century, both Jewish and Roman, were notoriously superstitious. Josephus records all sorts of signs and portents. Likewise, the Roman historians Dio Cassius, Suetonius and Tacitus commonly wrote of all sorts of signs and wonders as they perceived them. If an owl or eagle so much as landed on one of the prominent buildings in Rome at a time of crisis, this was considered a sign of impending doom or deliverance, and made "front page news."

We must interject here a comment about Josephus. Stevens, in a personal e-mail to me, (12-9-03) stated that he is convinced that, "the *parousia* of Jesus was visible even to his enemies (e.g. Josephus' references to the angelic armies in the clouds)." This is fascinating. How is it possible to argue that the silence of the early writers proves the rapture occurred and then argue that even the enemies of Christ saw that event, and claim that it was recorded by Josephus? This hardly amounts to *silence*! So, while Josephus was not an apostolic or patristic author, to claim that Josephus recorded the reality of the *parousia* is itself destructive to the entire argument built on silence. It might compound the problem of the silence of the *patristics*, for why would a *secular* author record it and not the Christian authors, but the bottom line is that if you take the position that Josephus records the fulfillment of the *parousia, you can no longer argue that there is a total silence concerning that event!*

Furthermore, and this is critical, if Stevens argues that even the enemies of Christ saw the *parousia*, why in the world, other than Josephus, do we not read about it in other secular writings? We are not talking here about just the sudden disappearance of some slaves. We are speaking here about the appearing of the Son of Man, with the angels of heaven, in flaming fire, with the shout of the Arch-Angel!

If the silence of the *patristics– who did not see the rapture, per Stevens*-- after the event demands that the faithful Christians were taken, then does not the silence of the *secular writers* not demand an explanation? The Christian writers say nothing about the disappearance of the faithful saints. This means that the faithful saints were taken and the remaining ones were slow-witted and "sleepers" per our friend. But the secular writers supposedly did see the *parousia*, and were not raptured, but they did not say a thing about it! If they did see the event *why then did they not record what they saw?* This silence is a greater mystery than the silence of the patristics who, according to Stevens, did not see the event.

It is one thing to say that men who did not witness an event did not write about it. It is *another thing entirely* to say that men saw something, something awesome, other worldly and marvelous, and yet did not say a word about it! It seems to me that to argue that secular writers did see the *parousia*, and yet did not write about it, poses an insurmountable obstacle to Steven's proposal.

So the question is, if the secular writers of the time commonly wrote of signs and portents and yet did not mention the sudden disappearance of thousands, perhaps tens of thousands, of people from all walks of life, what does *that* silence mean? If they saw the *parousia* why did they not write about it. Does not arguing from the silence of the Christian writers demand that we also consider the silence of the *secular writers*?

At this juncture, Matthew 24:30-31 is helpful. Jesus said the fall of Jerusalem would be the sign of his presence. He was to come in the glory of the Father (Matthew 16:27-28)[362] and the destruction of the Holy City would be the proof positive of his identity as King of kings and Lord of lords. Notice what Jesus said: "Then the sign of the Son of Man shall appear in heaven." Unfortunately, this is often understood to mean that Jesus would appear in the sky. However, as Chilton cogently notes:

"Most modern translations of Matthew 24:30 read something like this: 'And then the sign of the Son of Man will appear in the sky.' That is a mistranslation, based not on the Greek text but on the translators' own misguided assumptions about the subject of this passage (thinking it is speaking about the Second Coming). A word-for-word rendering from the Greek actually reads: 'And then will appear the sign of the Son of Man in heaven.' As you can see, two important differences come to light in the correct translation: first, the location spoken of is *heaven,* not just the *sky;* second, it is not the *sign* which is in heaven, but *the Son of Man* who is in heaven. The point is simply that this great judgment upon Israel, the destruction of Jerusalem and the Temple, will be the sign that *Jesus Christ is enthroned in heaven at the Father's right hand, ruling over the nations and bringing vengeance upon His enemies*. The divinely ordained cataclysm of AD 70 revealed that Christ had taken the Kingdom from Israel and given it to the Church; the desolation of the old Temple was the final sign that God had deserted it and was now dwelling in a new Temple, the Church."[363]

Gentry (*Dominion*, 1992, 348) and DeMar[364] concur in this rendering. The point is that we are not dealing here with a literal, bodily, visible coming of Christ. We are, as established earlier, dealing with the spiritual presence of Christ in dedicating the new temple. *The "sign" of his coming was not to be the disappearance of the church from the earth, but the destruction of the temple and city.* Contra Stevens' claim that the *parousia* was to be a "seen" event, this passage affirms the direct opposite.

The *parousia* was not to be an event observable with the human eye (John 14:19f; 2 Corinthians 4:16f). The sign of his presence was to be the destruction of Jerusalem.

Consider the significance of the word "sign" in Jesus' statement. To whom, and for whom, would the destruction of the city and temple be a sign, proving that the *parousia* had occurred? We can certainly argue that it would have been, *should have been*, a sign to the unbelieving Jews to whom the church had spoken for a full generation, saying that the destruction was coming. However, do we find any Jewish writings admitting that Christ came in the destruction? Did they acknowledge the "sign of the Son of Man" Patently not. What does their "silence" in this regard mean? Does it mean that the *parousia* did not take place? Does it mean that the Jews were themselves taken and removed, and thus, left no record behind?

For whom then, was the destruction a sign that the Lord had come? Was it not a sign for the Christians? Was it not the sign that the Lord had come in *vindication, in manifestation* as the sons of God and the *glorification* of their status? If this is true, then didn't the Christians have to witness that "sign"?

If the rapture was a physical, observable event, this demands an answer as to why the secular writers–or even why, "all the tribes of the earth"--did not take note of it. The sudden disappearance of masses of Christian slaves and citizens would not have been a localized event confined to Judea. This would have been an event of major proportions, even granting, as Stevens affirms and I concur, that an apostasy of the majority of the church occurred prior to AD 70 (Matthew 24:10-12). But, consider the church in Rome.

Are we to believe that the sudden disappearance of perhaps thousands of people, went unrecorded by those who otherwise wrote about every strange breeze that blew? The list of Christians in Romans 16 informs us that there were some prominent citizens in the church at Rome. Likewise, we know of many prominent individuals throughout the Biblical text. The sudden disappearance of these individuals would surely have caused a stir. So again, if the silence of early church authorities concerning the *parousia* is troublesome, then the silence of secular writers as to an instantaneous disappearance of thousands of people is equally troublesome. Furthermore, Stevens does not sufficiently address the issue of the continuing presence of Christians, faithful Christians, after AD 70.

LEFT BEHIND?

Keep in mind that Stevens insists that only the faithful elect were taken. Marginal Christians, those of little faith and understanding were left behind. Stevens calls these the "sleepers" because they did not comprehend what had happened. More on this momentarily, but for now there is a serious issue to consider.

Stevens is acutely aware of the tradition that John the apostle lived beyond AD 70. He even admits that if this is true his theory of a literal rapture is severely damaged, because no one would question whether John was one of the faithful elect (*Expectations*, 29). If the elect were to be literally raptured, assuredly John would have been raptured. However, tradition says he did not disappear. How does Stevens respond to this troublesome issue?

Interestingly, Stevens attempts to answer this conundrum by calling into question the traditions about John living beyond AD 70. As a matter of fact, Stevens says that preterists, such as myself, who would even appeal to any patristics writings about certain Christians living before and after AD 70, "have just given license to our critics to use the patristic traditions against the preterist view" (*Expectations*, 17).

We could say a bit about this, but will allow this to suffice. It is ironic *to say the least* that Stevens seeks to explain the problem of the apostle John by castigating the testimony of the patristics. He then uses the *silence* of those same writers concerning the *parousia* to prove his case! In other words, for Stevens, what the patristic writers *do not say* is more important than what they *do say*. He discounts what they do say and then demands that we read an entire theological doctrine into their silence. But here is a question. If, as Stevens affirms, and we tend to agree with him to a great extent, that we cannot rely on what the patristic writers say, *why should we believe what they said even if they had mentioned the rapture?* How can you say on the one hand that you do not accept what they say and then demand that they should have said something?

Make no mistake, it is a well known fact even among patristic scholars that those authors were, in many ways, eccentric, and in many places simply unreliable. For instance, Grant says, "Eusebius of Caesarea has found severe critics of his historical reliability, but there is question whether his critics have gone as far as they should."[365] However, granting this fact it is *questionable* as to whether one should build an entire doctrine on what the early writers *do not say*, while totally ignoring what they do say. The problem of John's presence after AD 70 is not the only issue at stake.

In those same troublesome writings, there is the testimony of an unbroken chain of Christians. By that we mean that according to the patristic authors, the apostles personally appointed their successors, and those successors were definitely present at the time of, and immediately following the destruction of Jerusalem in AD 70.[366] Polycarp was "an intimate disciple of the apostles."[367] 'The line of "succession" in regard to Polycarp presents a daunting challenge for Stevens. Polycarp was supposedly the personal disciple of John the apostle and in turn Iranaeus was the disciple of Polycarp. Did Polycarp lie, was he mistaken, or did he just miss the rapture of his master, or was he (Polycarp) after all unfaithful? Wouldn't Polycarp have known if his mentor had simply disappeared one day? Was Iranaeus mistaken about the relationship between Polycarp and John? In addition, Ignatius was "the successor of Peter at Antioch" (Eusebius, *History*, Bk. II, chapter XXXVI, 120). Iranaeus goes to great length to establish an unbroken line of succession between the apostles and those who followed them. Other examples could be given, but these illustrate the problem.

If the patristic writers knew nothing about a "gap" between the apostles and their successors, and if they never said a word about any of the apostles or their successors simply *disappearing*, then *this silence* is as disturbing, perhaps more so, as their failure to say the *parousia* had occurred. What Stevens is asking us to believe is that the early church fathers were dim-witted enough to have missed the rapture–to have not understood why so many living saints had disappeared--and yet, at the same time were so egregiously ignorant as to say the disciples did not disappear at all! How would it have been possible for the early authors to claim that there was an unbroken succession from the apostles onward if in fact (at least some of) the apostles themselves had disappeared and their faithful successors had disappeared as well?

This problem is exacerbated by the fact that according to tradition some of the most prominent, faithful Christians mentioned in the Bible lived well beyond A. D. 70, the time when, according to Stevens they should have disappeared from the earth. According to "tradition" Timothy, Paul's beloved traveling companion, lived well beyond AD 70 into the time of Nerva, when he suffered martyrdom.[368] Was Timothy one of the weak, faithless, dull witted Christians who just did not "get it"? Titus was said to have died at an "advanced age" as well. (*McClintock*, 440). And what about Luke the beloved physician? He was supposedly martyred when he was 84, and this would assuredly mean he was alive after AD 70.[369] Furthermore, the last we hear of Luke in the inspired record is that he was most assuredly faithful (2 Timothy 4).

Stevens says that if the faithful Christians were alive post AD 70 they could not have failed to say something of the fulfilled *parousia* (*Expectations*, 13). He lists Timothy, Titus, Luke, Apollos, Silas, Aquila and Priscilla, Gaius, and Aristarchus as some of the faithful that would have been forced to write something if it had happened. And of course, as noted above, the apostle John is said to have lived beyond AD 70.

So, again, the problem is that in the case of many of these faithful saints tradition says they lived well beyond AD 70. But Stevens discounts the tradition and claims that (at least) John was actually taken. He says that those disciples most intimately acquainted with him actually thought he and his circle of disciples remained, and wrote their histories to that effect. This truly raises the issue of being *dim-witted!*

If in fact, some of the apostles and their faithful successors[370] were still alive and well on planet earth post AD 70, then, in the words of Stevens, "this would certainly bring the rapture view into serious question" (*Expectation*, 29). On the other hand, if the faithful saints had actually been raptured, and then, those writing afterward were unaware of that fact, but wrote that those saints had actually remained on earth until their death they really were *dim-witted* in the worst sort of way! How could they say that those saints had remained and died, either naturally or by martyrdom, if in fact those saints were not even on earth?

AWAKE THOU THAT SLEEPEST!

Stevens contends that one of the reasons we have no record of the literal rapture is because the "left behind" Christians were what he calls "sleepers." They were in reality unfaithful, and dim-witted believers who just did not "get it." However, this stretches credulity to the limit.

For the left behind believers not to have caught onto a literal rapture of the faithful, the following must have been true:

1.) For a full generation, although the doctrine of a literal rapture had been proclaimed in their assemblies, promising that they were going to be taken away, these "sleepers" were, well, *asleep* when that sermon was preached. Are we to believe that they slept through an entire generation of sermons promising their removal from the world?

2.) When the rapture actually occurred and the faithful members of their congregations, which would, we assume, include at least some of the leadership of the congregation, did not show up for weeks, months and years, the sleepers never once made the connection between their disappearance and the message that had been proclaimed for an entire generation. Are we to believe that Sunday after Sunday, day after day, these men and women never once wondered where brother Timothy, or Titus, or Silas, or whoever, had gone? Are we to believe that no one, not one of them, ever said, "Wait a minute, brethren, don't you remember? Brother Paul told us that the faithful would be taken away at the Lord's coming!"

It is legitimate to ask, if the brethren could have been so dull as to have missed the *literal rapture* could they not have been dull enough to have missed *a non-literal rapture*? Would they not have been so dull as to have failed to see the spiritual significance of the fall of Jerusalem? We know for a fact that there was a literalistic mind-set that set in very early. If in fact the early saints were that dim-witted it is easy to see that there was no literal rapture at all, but that the early church simply missed the significance of what had been taught.

At this juncture we need to consider the church at Thessalonica. There were some teaching that the Lord had already come (2 Thessalonians 2:2). Thus, per Steven's view this demands that they were teaching that *the rapture had already occurred* and the faithful had already been taken. *Think about that for a moment!*

If we are to believe that at the *parousia* the faithful Christians would simply disappear by the thousands this text presents some difficult questions.

The foregoing scenario demands that the Thessalonians to whom Paul was writing were the slothful sleepers who did not know what had happened. If that is the case however, *what made those slothful ones think the Day had already occurred?* We have no clue that they believed that the Day had come because of all the missing Christians, so what made these slothful, sleeper Christians think that the Day had already come and gone?

Of course all of this raises a disturbing question about *Paul*. If the Thessalonians thought that the Day had already happened they knew that Paul had not disappeared, didn't they? Does Paul qualify as one of the righteous ones? The Thessalonians knew the following: They knew that *they* had not disappeared. They knew that Paul and his entire entourage had not disappeared. To correct their idea that the Day of the Lord had already occurred Paul did not say, "Brethren, look around, none of the believers have been taken. You were not taken, and by the way, if the Day of the Lord has already occurred, then that means that all of us have been left behind!"

Paul's response to the Thessalonians– to quell their idea that the Day of the Lord had already occurred– was to point out that the preliminary signs of the Day had not yet come to full bloom. But here is the point, if the Day of the Lord was to be when the faithful believers were whisked away, why didn't Paul explain that? Paul does not address the idea of the nature of the Day, and this is important.

If those at Thessalonica believed that the Day of the Lord had already come they must of necessity have believed *that they themselves had been left behind!* Furthermore, if they believed that the rapture had already occurred they should have had *no concern for those taken*, but for *themselves*. After all, the taken are the faithful, the left behind are the unfaithful. Finally, as the left behind, if they were the "sleepers" *they should not have even been aware that the rapture had occurred!* So, what is the situation in Thessalonians?

First, *something* had clearly happened that caused the Thessalonians to *think* that the *parousia* had already happened. They were patently aware of that something, whatever it was! But, that "something" was not the disappearance of the faithful Christians, because as we shall see immediately below Paul certainly had not disappeared.

The bottom line is this: They did believe that the *parousia*, and thus the "rapture" had occurred. There is not the slightest indication that they believed that their loved ones, or Paul and the other apostles had been taken. The fact that they believed that it had happened belies the idea that they were "sleepers." If they were "alert" enough to think that the *parousia* had occurred would they not be alert enough to know who was missing?

Second, those at Thessalonica were not concerned about themselves. They were concerned about their brethren who had died before the *parousia*. (The situation between 1 Thessalonians 4 and 2 Thessalonians 2 is interesting. In 1 Thessalonians they were concerned about their loved ones who had died *before the parousia*. In 2 Thessalonians 2 they now believe the rapture had *already occurred*. All of this confusion within a span of approximately 1-3 years!) In spite of this confusion, the point is that the remaining Christians were not concerned about their own spiritual welfare. They were concerned only with their brethren who had died.

Now, why didn't Paul say, "Brethren, if the rapture had already happened, you should not be concerned about the dead Christians but about yourself! You– *and I!!* --have been left behind! We are the ones in danger!"

It is of more than passing interest how the false teachers could have had any desire to teach that the rapture had already occurred. If the Thessalonians believed that the Day of the Lord was to be when faithful Christians are removed from earth it would not exactly be appealing to be told, "Hey, brethren, the rapture has already occurred, and we have all missed it!" Just exactly where is the benefit for Hymenaeus and Philetus to teach, "the resurrection is past already," when upon Steven's view of the rapture that would mean that Hymenaeus and Philetus were saying that they themselves had been left behind! Personally, I would not find that a very appealing doctrine! (Why didn't Paul argue, when disputing with those who said the Day was past, "Look, you and I are still here. If the Day is passed that means we are unfaithful. We have been *left behind*!" We find nothing even closely resembling this in Paul's polemic.)

Third, it is patently obvious that those in Thessalonica were not sleepers, in the sense meant by Stevens. *They were faithful Christians!* Those saints were very focused on eschatology and believed that the Day had already passed. But, if they were "sleepers" per Steven's definition they should have had no concern. They should have had no suspicions that anything at all had happened. They should not have even been aware that anyone was missing, perhaps even their own loved ones. This clearly will not work.

MATTHEW 19:28 AND THE APOSTLES
JUDGING THE TWELVE TRIBES OF ISRAEL

Stevens believes that Jesus' promise that his apostles would "sit on twelve thrones, judging the twelve tribes of Israel" in the regeneration (Matthew 19:28) demands that they had be physically removed from the earth. However, the evidence points in the other direction. Notice the constituent elements of Jesus' promise and how they are depicted as being fulfilled in the first century, before the fall of Jerusalem.

Jesus said the apostles would sit on *thrones*. On this topic Paul said, "he has raised up together, and made us to sit in heavenly places" (Ephesians 2:6). It might be argued that Paul was speaking here of Christians, all those in Christ, but that does not mitigate the point. What was true of those Christians was all the more true of the apostles.

Paul's use of the prefix "*sun*" (pronounced "soon") when he said they had been raised "with him" means that the Ephesians had been raised "with Christ." Christ had been raised from the dead (Ephesians 1:20) and the Ephesians had been raised from the dead "with him"(2:1). Likewise, Christ had been enthroned "in the heavenlies" (1:20) and the saints had been "co-enthroned with Christ"[371] "in the heavenly places" (2:6). From Paul's perspective, the saints, assuredly including the apostles, *were already on thrones in the heavenly realm.* For Paul, neither he nor the Ephesians had to leave earth to be raised from the dead and to be seated on thrones of glory and judgment.

Was Paul (and the other apostles) judging Israel? Read his words in 2 Corinthians 2:15f: "We are to God the fragrance of Christ among those who are being saved and among those who are perishing. To the one we are the aroma of death to death, and to the other the aroma of life to life." And to whom did Paul bring this message that meant life or death? He went, "To the Jew first, and then to the Greek" (Romans 1:16-17). He likewise called himself an ambassador for Christ (2 Corinthians 5:20- *presbeuomen*). This word means an royal ambassador, one with the full authority of the one commissioning them. They held the power of life and death.

So, as the apostles commissioned to fulfill the World Mission proclaimed the message "to the Jew first" they were, without any question judging Israel. They did not have to be raptured off the earth to sit on the thrones and judge the twelve tribes of Israel. (Notice how Peter wrote that message of "life and death" to "those scattered abroad," and James wrote to, "the twelve tribes scattered abroad" (1 Peter 1; James 1)

Furthermore, as the apostles went preaching the message of judgment they were already in the "regeneration." Paul's statement, "If any man be in Christ, he is a new creation" (2 Corinthians 5:17) can be taken in no other way.[372] The apostles proclaimed "the washing of the regeneration" (Titus 3:5). John the Immerser had begun the work of restoration (Matthew 11:17; 17:11f) and the time of reformation / restoration would be consummated at the *parousia* of Jesus.[373]

So, the apostles were *on thrones* preaching the message of life or condemnation (judgment) to the twelve tribes of Israel during the time of the regeneration, i.e. in the first century, before the fall of Jerusalem. Their mission would be accomplished when the judgment they proclaimed became a reality. Since they did not have to be removed from earth to sit on thrones in the "heavenly places" proclaiming that message of judgment, it hardly seems logically necessary that they would have to be removed from earth to sit on literal thrones, and judge the twelve tribes.

DO WE HAVE ANY REFERENCES TO CHRIST'S COMING IN AD 70?

Stevens is correct to say that we have no apostolic writers or patristic authors who point to AD 70 as the time of Christ's final coming, the judgment and resurrection of the dead. This silence is indeed perplexing, not only to those who accept the preterist view but to all who understand that Jesus posited these events for the first century. There are those scholars who understand that Jesus believed (mistakenly of course, in their eyes) that the end of the world would come at the fall of Jerusalem.[374] However, there are what I will call "echoes" of the significance of AD 70 in the early writings.

Frost has shown that the author of the *Shepherd of Hermas*, (circa 85-140) and the earlier *Pseudo-Barnabas*, although decidedly still futurist looking, expressed the belief that the end was *supposed to have come* in AD 70. (*Hope*, 91+) These apostolic authors undoubtedly linked the fall of Jerusalem with their concepts of the end. The end had been *delayed*, and a delay demands that the appointed time had come and gone.

What this means is that while these authors did not say that AD 70 was the time of the *parousia*, they seemed clearly to have believed that it *should have been the time of the end!* That means that in a back handed sort of way we do have apostolic testimony about the significance of the end of the Old Covenant age. Why would they speak at length of the fall of Jerusalem as a sign that they were in the time of the end if they did not associate the destruction with their eschatological beliefs?

In point of fact, there are in the early writings *echoes of preterist theology*. It would take a separate volume to fully document the statements in the patristics that indicate they saw the events leading up to, and the events of the destruction of Jerusalem as eschatological fulfillment. We will briefly document some of the eschatological predictions made by the Lord that were considered as fulfilled by the patristic authors. The question is, if the patristic writers could clearly see that the eschatological signs had been fulfilled as foretold by the Lord, why could they not see that the end had come? A perplexing question indeed and one for which we have no easy answer. However, because we have no answer does not negate the reality of what they said. With this in mind, let us examine a few of the major eschatological elements that the early writers definitely believed had been fulfilled.

THE WORLD MISSION

Few students of eschatology deny that the completion of the World Mission is eschatologically significant.[375] The question is, how could anyone believe that the World Mission had been fulfilled and not believe the end came as well? Origen saw this connection: "If any one is minded to say rashly that the gospel has already been preached in all the world as a testimony to all nations, he will consequently be constrained to say that the end has already come!"[376] So Origen said that to say the World Mission was fulfilled was to say the end had come. Given this relationship, one can only wonder then at how many of the early writers did indeed believe and teach that the World Mission was completed before the fall of Jerusalem.

1.) Iranaeus (circa 170+ A. D.): Speaking of the 12 apostles, Iranaeus said: "They went out to the ends of the earth, preaching the good things that come to us from God, and proclaiming peace from heaven to men." "The tradition of the apostles, made clear in all the world can be clearly seen in every church by those who wish to behold the truth."[377]

2.) Justin the Martyr, (A. D. 155) in his "First Apology," (Richardson, 269,) says, "In our own time, Jesus Christ, who was crucified and died, rose again, and ascending into heaven, began to reign; on account of what was proclaimed by the apostles in all nations as coming from him, there is joy for those who look for incorruption."

3.) Athanasius, (AD 296- 373)
"But if the Gentiles are honoring the same God that gave the law to Moses and made the promise to Abraham, and whose word the Jews dishonored, –why are (the Jews) ignorant, or rather why do they choose to ignore, that the Lord foretold by the Scriptures has shone forth upon the world, and appeared

to it in bodily form, as the Scripture said. . . . What then has not come to pass, that the Christ must do? What is left unfulfilled, that the Jews should not disbelieve with impunity? For it, I say, which is just what we actually see, - there is no longer king nor prophet nor Jerusalem nor sacrifice nor vision among them, but even the whole earth is filled with the knowledge of God, and the Gentiles, leaving their godlessness, are now taking refuge with the God of Abraham, through the Word, even our Lord Jesus Christ, then it must be plain, even to those who are exceedingly obstinate, that the Christ is come, and that He has illumined absolutely all with His light."[378]

Athanasius does not say only once that the gospel had been preached into all the earth. He says it repeatedly. Furthermore, note his emphatic statement that all prophecy had been fulfilled.

4.) Eusebius, (AD 314-318)

"Moses himself foresaw by the Holy Spirit that when the new covenant was revived by Christ and preached to all nations, his own legislation would become superfluous, he rightly confined its influence to one place, so that if they were ever deprived of it and shut out of that national freedom, it might not be possible for them to carry out the ordinances of his law in a foreign country, and of necessity they would have to receive the new covenant announced by Christ. Moses had foretold this very thing and in due course Christ sojourned in this life, and the teaching of the new covenant was borne to all nations, and at once the Romans besieged Jerusalem and destroyed it and the temple there. At once the whole of the Mosaic law was abolished, with all that remained of the Old Covenant, and the curse passed over to those who became lawbreakers because they obeyed Moses' law, when its time had gone by, and still clung ardently to it, for at that very moment, the perfect teaching of the new Law was introduced in its place."[379]

5.) Chrysostom (AD 347- 407).
There can be no doubt that this influential patristic author believed that the gospel had been preached into all the world, in fulfillment of Matthew 24, and was a sign of the end.

"And it is a plain proof of this, that the word shall surely be preached everywhere in the world, so much shall ye be above the things that alarm you. For, that they may not say, how then shall we live? He said more, Ye shall both live and preach everywhere. Therefore He added moreover, *"And this gospel shall be preached in the whole world for a witness to all nations, and then shall the end come,"* of the downfall of Jerusalem.

For in proof that He meant this, and that before the taking of Jerusalem the gospel was preached, hear what Paul saith, "Their sound went into all the earth;" and again, "The gospel which was preached to every creature which is under Heaven." And seest thou him running from Jerusalem unto Spain?

And if one took so large a portion, consider what the rest also wrought. For writing to others also, Paul again saith concerning the gospel, that "it is bringing forth fruit, and growing up in every creature which is under Heaven."

But what meaneth, "For a witness to all nations?" Forasmuch as though it was everywhere preached, yet it was not everywhere believed. It was for a witness, He saith, to them that were disbelieving, that is, for conviction, for accusation, for a testimony; for they that believed will bear witness against them that believed not, and will condemn them. And for this cause, after the gospel is preached in every part of the world, Jerusalem is destroyed, that they may not have so much as a shadow of an excuse for their perverseness. For they that saw His power shine throughout every place, and in an instant take the world captive, what excuse could they then have for continuing in the same perverseness? For in proof that it was everywhere preached at that time, hear what Paul saith, "of the gospel which was preached to every creature which is under Heaven."[380]

There can be no doubt that Chrysostom related the preaching of the gospel to the time of the end, and the end was the destruction of Jerusalem. Further, he is emphatic that the gospel was preached into all the world in fulfillment of Matthew 24:14.

So, we have seen from the patristic authors that at least some of them did believe that the World Mission was completed. It was completed before the fall of Jerusalem in AD 70, and at least in some instances, the authors related the "end" to that destruction. Why did these authors not see the inconsistencies of their own eschatology? Perhaps for the same reason that many today have the same problem.

THE ABOMINATION OF DESOLATION

Not only did the early writers believe that the World Mission had been fulfilled they also believed that the Abomination of Desolation had been fulfilled. They related that event to the days prior to the fall of Jerusalem.

1.) Clement of Alexander (circa AD 194)

"And Christ our Lord, 'the Holy of Holies,' having come and fulfilled the vision and the prophecy, was anointed in His flesh by the Holy Spirit of His Father. In those 'sixty and two weeks,' as the prophet said, and 'in the one week,' was He Lord. The half of the week Nero held sway, and in the holy city Jerusalem placed the abomination; and in the half of the week he was taken away, and Otho, and Galba, and Vitellius. And Vespasian rose to the supreme power, and destroyed Jerusalem, and desolated the holy place. And that such are the facts of the case, is clear to him that is able to understand, as the prophet said."[381]

"We have still to add to our chronology the following, -I mean the days which Daniel indicates from the desolation of Jerusalem, the seven years and seven months of the reign of Vespasian. For the two years are added to the seventeen months and eighteen days of Otho, and Galba, and Vitellius; and the result is three years and six months, which is "the half of the week," as Daniel the prophet said. For he said that there were two thousand three hundred days from the time that the abomination of Nero stood in the holy city, till its destruction. For thus the declaration, which is subjoined, shows: "How long shall be the vision, the sacrifice taken away, the abomination of desolation, which is given, and the power and the holy place shall be trodden under foot? And he said to him, Till the evening and morning, two thousand three hundred days, and the holy place shall be taken away" (*Stromata*, Bk. I, chapter 21, p. 445+).

2.) Athanasius (fourth century)
"And when He Who spake unto Moses, the Word of the Father, appeared in the end of the world, He also gave this commandment, saying, 'But when they persecute you in this city, flee ye into another" (Matt. 10:23); and shortly after He says, 'When ye therefore shall see the abomination of desolation, spoken of by Daniel the prophet, stand in the holy place (whoso readeth, let him understand); then let them which be in Judea flee into the mountains: let him which is on the housetop not come down to take any thing out of his house: neither let him which is in the field return back to take his clothes' (Matt. 24:15). Knowing these things, the Saints regulated their conduct accordingly."[382]

3.) Eusebius (fourth century)
"Forasmuch as though it was everywhere preached, yet it was not everywhere believed. It was for a witness, He saith, to them that were disbelieving, that is, for conviction, for accusation, for a testimony; for they that believed will bear witness against them that believed not, and will condemn them. And for this cause, after the gospel is preached in every part of the world, Jerusalem is destroyed, that they may not have so much as a shadow of an excuse for their perverseness... For that He intimates this was manifested by what follows. For He brought in also a prophecy, to confirm their desolation, saying, "But when ye shall see the abomination of desolation, spoken of by Daniel the prophet, standing in the holy place, let him that readeth understand." He referred them to Daniel. And by 'abomination' He meaneth the statue of him who then took the city, which he who desolated the city and the temple placed within the temple, wherefore Christ calleth it, "of desolation." Moreover, in order that they might learn that these things will be

while some of them are alive, therefore He said, *"When ye see the abomination of desolation"* (*Homily* 74. P. 948-950).

The implications of believing that the abomination of desolation had been fulfilled are profound and thoroughly eschatological. According to Daniel 12:1-12 the abomination of desolation would occur at the time of the end, the time of the great tribulation, and *the time of the resurrection!* As Pitre says, "According to the OT, the resurrection itself would be preceded by a period of great tribulation"... "Daniel 12 is the most explicit prophecy of resurrection in the Hebrew books of the Old Testament. Strikingly, this description of the resurrection is preceded by the Great Tribulation."[383]

So, the valid question is, if the patristic authors believed that the end time events of the great commission, the abomination of desolation, and of course, the great tribulation, *had already occurred prior to the fall of Jerusalem* then how in the name of reason did they fail to see that the *parousia* had indeed occurred? We must confess puzzlement, but it does not change the fact that they did believe the end time events had already been fulfilled.

To this point we have seen that at least some of the prominent early writers believed that the World Mission and the Abomination of Desolation had occurred before the fall of Jerusalem in A. D. 70. This raises the question as to how they could have believed so firmly that the signs of the end had occurred, and still not believe, or *grasp*, that the end itself had occurred. As we have seen, Origen believed that if you said the Great Commission had been fulfilled you were forced to believe the end had come. Well, these men believed the Commission had been fulfilled, but did not realize the end had come! Why? *We do not know why.* However, while we may not understand why, the fact is that they did see that the signs of the end had come. But these writers were not alone in failing to see the actual significance of that event.

Gaston, *(Stone,* 462f) tells us that many of the early Jews calculated that the 70 years of Daniel 9 ended at the fall of Jerusalem in A. D. 70. The significance of this is incredible. There were some Jews who seemed to see the meaning of this and were perplexed as to why the fulfillment of their Messianic hopes had not been realized. In other words, they saw the fulfillment of Daniel 9 in the events of AD 70 but did not realize that those events were the fulfillment of their hopes!

Bauckham cites later Rabbinic sources (260 AD) that condemn calculations of the time of the end, "Blasted be the bones of those who calculate the end. For they would say, since the predetermined time has arrived, and yet he has not come, he will never come."[384] This is telling since it shows that the Jews believed that the time of the end had come and gone, and they linked that time to the AD 70 catastrophe.

Gaston likewise cites some rabbis who said, "All dates for the end have expired, and the matter now depends solely on repentance and good works"

(*No Stone,* 464). In other words, they knew the time was up, and the signs had been fulfilled, but they could not see that the prophecy was fulfilled! Why did they not see the reality? What does it mean that these authors expressed disappointment that the end did not come? *What does this silence say?*

So, both Christian and Jewish sources from the earliest of times said the time of fulfillment was in the first century. Some even lamented the fact that, *seemingly* the end did not come. To what shall we attribute this? Ignorance? Perhaps. A heart of unbelief? Perhaps to a degree. To an apostasy from the truth? I believe that there is a lot more to this than is generally admitted and allowed (Matthew 24:9-12; Luke 18:6-8).

THE COMING OF THE LORD OUT OF HEAVEN

For those who claim that none of the early writers believed that the Lord came in AD 70, Eusebius dispels that claim. Commenting on Micah 1:2-4; 3:9-12; 4:1-4 he said the Lord *came* in the fall of Jerusalem in AD 70. (*Proof,* Bk. VIII, chapter 3, 140). He says that the time when men would not take up sword against one another anymore, when every man would, "have his own fig tree, according to the prophecy" (Micah 4:1-4) had been realized. He quotes Micah 1:2-4 the prophecy of the coming of the Lord out of heaven and says this occurred with the fall of Jerusalem.(*Proof,* Bk. VIII, chapter 3, 140). Citing Micah's prophecy that Jerusalem would be plowed like a field he says he had seen that with his own eyes.

Likewise, commenting on Zechariah 14 and the prediction of the coming of the Lord with all of His saints and the siege and destruction of the city, he says, "the present prophecy foretells a second siege of Jerusalem which is to take place afterwards, which it suffered from the Romans, after it inhabitants carried through their outrage on our Saviour Jesus Christ. Thus, the coming of our Saviour and the events connected therewith are very clearly shewn in this passage– I mean what was done at the time of His Passion, and the siege that came on the Hebrew race directly after, the taking of Jerusalem, the call of the Gentiles also, and the knowledge attained by all nations of the one and only God" (*Proof,* Book VI, Ch. 18, 26).

Eusebius clearly believed that Jesus came with the angels in flaming fire!
"One might also literally in another way connect fire and chariots with His coming through the siege that attacked Jerusalem after our Savior's Advent for the Temple was burned with fire not long after and was reduced to extreme desolation, and the city was encircled by the chariots and camps of the enemy, after which too the promises to the Gentiles were fulfilled in harmony with the prophecy."

He made these comments in regard to Luke 12:49 and Isaiah 66:18-19. (See also Proof, Bk. VIII, chapter 4, 144f where he says *Christ came,* "with the chariots and horses" to conquer the army of the Jews).

Finally, Eusebius uses the destruction of Jerusalem as proof positive of the coming of the Lord!

"When, then, we see what was of old foretold for the nations fulfilled in our own day, and when the lamentation and wailing that was predicted for the Jews, and the burning of the Temple and its utter destruction, can also be seen even now to have occurred according to the prediction, surely we must also agree that the King who was prophesied, the Christ of God, has come, since the signs of His coming have been shewn in each instance I have treated to have been clearly fulfilled" (Proof, Bk. VIII, 4, 147).

This passage is remarkable, for on any reading Eusebius appeals to the destruction of Jerusalem as proof that Christ had come! There is, therefore, no question that Eusebius believed that the Lord came in AD 70.

Eusebius understood that predictions of the Day of the Lord included "historical" events, and did not demand the end of time. It is remarkable therefore, to read scholars such as Kistemaker claim: "Early Christian literature does not report any belief that Jesus returned to earth at the time of the destruction of the city and temple of Jerusalem. Instead, the universal church repeated the prayer uttered by Christians of the first century: 'Maranatha, Our Lord, come!' There are no indications that anyone believed that Jesus returned spiritually when Jerusalem was destroyed."[385] Kistemaker is clearly mistaken.

THE COMING OF THE LORD AND THE CHARISMATA

Another fascinating and significant fact from the patristics is the confusion that they showed in regard to the charismata, the gifts of the Spirit, and the coming of the Lord. On the one hand certain patristic writers affirmed that the charismata were supposed to endure until the Day of the Lord, (Eusebius, *History*, Bk. V , chapter XVII, 200) while other writers said that the miraculous gifts had ended "long ago," and that, therefore, *the Lord should have returned!*[386]

So, this confusion among the patristics speaks eloquently to us. At least some of them understood the relationship between Christ's *parousia* and the cessation of miracles. They believed that miracles were to end at the time of the end. They acknowledge that the miracles had ended. They are even perplexed that the Lord had not come!

THE NEW HEAVEN AND EARTH / NEW JERUSALEM

Certain early writers affirmed that the church was in the New Heavens and Earth in fulfillment of Isaiah 65. Theoderet spoke of the contrast between Old Covenant Jerusalem and the church: "Let them (the Jews, DKP) show us their Jerusalem delivered from tears. For that city (Jewish Jerusalem) was handed over to many misfortunes, whereas for this city (the heavenly Jerusalem) alone enjoys life without grief and free of tears."[387] We have just seen that Eusebius believed that the time of universal peace that was promised for the New Creation had arrived. In fact, we can show that in *some* way, perplexing as the statements may be, some of the early writers did in fact say that the second coming– and the resurrection-- had occurred!

THE SECOND COMING AND RESURRECTION

Chrysostom, cited above, stated, "Having in remembrance, therefore, this saving commandment and all those things *which have come to pass for us*: the Cross, the Grave, the Resurrection on the third day, the Ascension into heaven, the Sitting at the right hand, *and the second and glorious Coming*" (St. Chrysostom, *Divine Liturgy*, my emphasis). To say the least, this is a perplexing quote, for Chrysostom was undeniably a futurist. However, there also seems to be little doubt that he expresses full preterist theology!

Furthermore, Athanasius, cited above, expressed the belief that the resurrection had occurred, that 1 Corinthians 15 was fulfilled! Read what he says, commenting on the Jew's refusal to believe in Jesus as Messiah:

"Their state may be compared to that of one out of his right mind, who sees the earth illumined by the sun, but denies the sun that illumines it. For what more is there for him whom they expect to do, when he is come? To call the heathen? But they are called already. To make prophecy, and king, and vision to cease? This too has already come to pass. To expose the godlessness of idolatry? It is already exposed and condemned. Or to destroy death? He is already destroyed. **7.** What then has not come to pass, that the Christ must do? What is left unfulfilled, that the Jews should now disbelieve with impunity? For if, I say, -which is just what we actually see, — there is no longer king nor prophet nor Jerusalem nor sacrifice nor vision among them, but even the whole earth is filled with the knowledge of God, and gentiles, leaving their godlessness, are now taking refuge with the God of Abraham, through the Word, even our Lord Jesus Christ, then it must be plain, even to those who are exceedingly obstinate, that the Christ is come, and that He has illumined absolutely all with His light, and given them the true and divine teaching concerning His Father."

Furthermore, commenting on the work of Christ, Athanasius, says this of the resurrection: "Have no fears then. Now that the common Savior of all has died on our behalf, we who believe in Christ no longer die, as men died a fore time, in fulfillment of the threat of the law. That condemnation has come to an end; and now that, by the grace of the resurrection, corruption has been banished and done away" (*Incarnation*, ch. 4 (21)). Just as in Chrysostom, this statement is strongly preteristic, affirming the present reality of incorruption and freedom from death. What is also clear is that Athanasius is citing 1 Corinthians 15! Well, if men today, in Christ, have incorruptibility and are free from the death of the Law– *as promised in 1 Corinthians 15*– then the resurrection has come.

So, what do we make of these and other citations that could be given? It is difficult to know for sure. However, we should not be too quick to dismiss them because we find in them a significant echo of realized eschatology. Athanasius and Chrysostom *were* futurists. How did Athanasius harmonize these contradictory eschatological beliefs in his own mind? We may never know. But the fact remains that we have from his own stylus unmistakable preterist statements. And, the point could be made that virtually every major eschatological element is said to have been present and fulfilled by one or more of the early writers. In spite of this they nonetheless expressed futurist eschatological convictions.

So, the question again presses in on us, how could these early writers say the things they did about eschatological prophecies and not see implications of their own words? And the troubling answer is, we just do not know the full answer. However, because we do not know the answer to this question does not justify us in saying that because they did not say the right things, there had been a literal rapture of all faithful Christians in AD 70. Stevens insists that their silence demands a rapture. Yet he almost totally discounts what they *do say*. Stevens is well aware of the inconsistent, often aberrant, even perverted nature of the patristic writings. He has no reservations about openly rejecting what they *do say* in many instances. Why then build an entire doctrine on their silence?

As you can see from the above, there is some solid evidence in the early writings that echo a realized eschatology. Were these writers consistent with their own statements? No. Did they even fully realize the implications of their beliefs? It certainly seems they did not. Their statements however, are very clear and unambiguous. Perhaps in time to come more light will be discovered that will give us a more comprehensive picture into the beliefs of those early writers. For now, we must continue to ponder.

FACT: WE *HAVE* A *DIVINE* RECORD!

It is my personal conviction that the argument that we have no record of the *parousia* and end of the age is mistaken. This claim overlooks the claims of Revelation.

John was taken in the Spirit to see the events of the Day of the Lord. I would like to suggest that Revelation is, to some degree, distinctive in this regard. Other prophets simply foretold events to come. They were not, so far as we are told, actually projected into the future, to see the events unfold in vision, before they happened in time and history. I am suggesting that John was a true "time traveler," privileged to witness events miraculously. This would help explain why he so often used the past tense to describe events that had not yet happened. He saw them happen because he was taken into the future and he wrote of those things as they happened. Yet, from a purely historical perspective those events had not yet occurred.

What this means is that Revelation, while written before the events it predicted actually transpired, was nonetheless an inspired record of the fulfillment of those events! John saw prophecy as history. So, while we do not have emphatic declarations from the patristic authors concerning the fulfillment of all prophecy we do have the inspired record of the Apocalypse. It is the prophetic, historical record of the fulfillment of God's promises.

WHAT ABOUT THE 144,000?

Although we have discussed the 144,000 already it is relevant here as well. Stevens notes that the 144,000 are depicted as being in heaven, and they, "came out of the Great Tribulation." Since they are depicted as in heaven, and since it does not *say* they had died, they must have been raptured. Once again, this is an argument *ex silencio* (from silence). However, it is only a silence from the immediate context. This argument fails to consider the relationship between Revelation 7,14 and chapter 6.

Stevens claims that those under the altar in chapter 6:9-11are specifically said to have been killed. However, the 144,000 are not specifically said to have been killed. This means that the 144,00 were not martyred. And again, per his argument, since they are depicted as in heaven only a literal rapture explains this situation.

This argument ignores the fact that the 144,000, and the great multitude as well, represent *the completed number* of the martyred saints mentioned in Revelation 6:11. The martyrs under the altar cried out for vindication and vengeance on their persecutors. They were told that what they desired would come, "when their fellow-brethren who should be slain as they were should be fulfilled." Thus, from 6:11 onward we should find some reference to the completing of the number of the martyrs. That is exactly what we find in chapters 7 and 14 in regard to the 144,000.

Who are the 144,000? They are those who follow the Lamb. Bauckham says the 144,000 represents, "an army of martyrs who triumph through their martyrdom, because they are followers of the Lamb who participate in his victory by following his path to death."[388] He continues by saying, "the whole vision of chapter 7, with its play on the idea of numbering (7:4, 9) to be the fulfillment of the promise to the martyrs in 6:11." Likewise, Caird says that the 144,000, along with the great multitude, "are the whole body of martyrs."

Notice the correlation between 6:9-11 and 7:9f. The martyrs were given white robes as a sign of victory and martyrdom. In 7:9f the 144,000 were given white robes because, "These are the ones who come out of the great tribulation, and washed their robes and made them white in the blood of the lamb." It does not say that they were saved *from* the great tribulation. They came out of it by following the lamb. Where had the lamb led? To sacrifice and death. There was no "pre-tribulational rapture." These saints completed the measure of those destined to die for the lamb in the end times. (Cf. 1 Corinthians 4:9; Colossians 1:24f; Revelation 6:11). These saints overcame, *not because they were taken from the world*, but because they were "faithful unto death."

These same saints are depicted in Revelation 12, being, or perhaps having been, persecuted by the Dragon. Satan and his hosts are depicted as being cast out of heaven and the heavenly paeon is sung: "Now salvation and strength and the kingdom of our God, and the power of His Christ have come, for the accuser of our brethren who accused them before our God day and night has been cast down. And they overcame him by the blood of the lamb, and by the word of their testimony, and they did not love their lives to the death."

The language here is similar to that in Revelation 6, 7 and 14. What is clear is that those who overcame by the blood of the Lamb are depicted, not as having been taken from the world *but as martyrs for their faith.*

If there is any relationship between the 144,000 and the filling up of the number of the martyrs then Steven's argument for a rapture of these saints is falsified. If there is a relationship between chapter 6 and chapter 12 then the overcomers are martyrs. There is no way to ignore the prediction of 6:11 that the number had to be fulfilled, or to ignore the direct correlation between the robes, the tribulation and the method of overcoming. As Jesus said to the church at Smyrna, "be thou faithful until death, and I will give you the crown of life (Revelation 2:10). This was not *simply* saying, "Be faithful until you die, someday by and by, of old age." He had told them that persecution was coming and that they were to be faithful in the midst of that persecution even if it meant they had to die. No rapture promise here. And remember, he was speaking to the "faithful." The promise was not that he would remove them from earth. The promise was that if they would be faithful enough to *die* he would give them life.

We find no justification for the assertion that Revelation 7 and 14 speaks of saints removed from the earth at the rapture in AD 70. The connection between the motifs, themes, promises and contexts of chapters 6, 7, 12 and 14 are too similar to allow us to dichotomize between these passages. And that being true, chapters 7-14 tell the story of the filling up of the number of the brethren that should be killed. It is not about a rapture of the church from the earth at all.

2 THESSALONIANS 1 AND THE RAPTURE

Stevens offers 2 Thessalonians 1 as a proof that a literal rapture was necessary (*Expectations*, 12). However, I suggest that this text proves just the opposite.

Stevens says:

"Notice what Paul promises the Thessalonians. Their Jewish persecutors would be repaid with affliction at the *parousia*, when Christ would come from heaven in flaming fire to destroy them. Question: Did the Jews experience that destruction in a tangible and visible way? Did they see it and know it occurred? Or was it some 'spiritualized' fulfillment that was not recognizable by the physical or mental senses? Why wouldn't the first century saints expect their 'relief' from this tribulation to be seen and experienced in a real and tangible way as well?"

I believe the argument is invalid.

First, the Jews did experience that destruction in "a tangible and visible way." However, according to Jesus it was that "tangible and visible" destruction of the city that was the *sign* that he had come "in the glory of the Father." See the discussion above on the language of Matthew 24:30. The Greek of the text does not say that they would see Christ coming on the clouds in a visible manner. It says that the destruction of Jerusalem was to be the sign of His Sovereignty enthroned in the heavens. The "tangible and visible" was a sign of the invisible.

Second, Stevens asks if the first century saints expected their vindication and relief from their persecution to be "real and tangible as well?" In other words, Stevens is arguing that if the vindication and relief were tangible and real then the *parousia* and rapture must be tangible as well. This is an unjustified logical leap. The vindication, like the destruction, was tangible and real. But, like the destruction *the vindication was the sign of the invisible!* Remember, we have demonstrated that Jesus said the kingdom and thus the *parousia*, "does not come with observation" (Luke 17:20f). Paul said of the resurrection, "we do not look on the things that are seen, but unseen" (2 Corinthians 4:16f). They did not walk by sight but by faith (2 Corinthians 5:17) and would never know or see Christ in the flesh again (2 Corinthians 5:16f). This reinforces the argument that the visible destruction of Jerusalem was the sign of the invisible.

Third, the vindication of the sufferers in 2 Thessalonians 1 is directly associated with the vindication of the martyrs in Revelation 6:9-11. The saints under the altar prayed for their vindication to occur "on the earth."

Why, therefore, would the saints have to be removed from the earth to be vindicated? There is not a word in 2 Thessalonians 1 that suggests a removal of the church from the earth. It speaks rather of the vindication of the church *on the earth.* And that would be in response to the prayer of the saints under the altar. Is Stevens suggesting that the church could not praise God–on earth– for their victory over Judaism?

Let's put this in more prosaic terms. Set aside the concept of the rapture for a moment, and focus strictly on the idea of the judgment on Israel for persecuting the saints and killing Jesus. We have already shown that according to Setzer, Justin the Martyr (circa AD 150) was the first Christian apologist to explicitly link the destruction of Jerusalem with the Jews' guilt of killing Jesus. So, we have a 80 year silence in the church writings about the relationship between Christian martyrdom and the judgment on Israel. *Why?*

Does that silence mean that no Christian realized that Israel was judged for killing the Lord? Does the fact that the early church did not mention the relationship between Jerusalem's destruction and God's judgment on her mean that the destruction (and vindication) did not happen?

It would not be appropriate here to say, "Well, those left behind were the sleepers that did not understand the rapture had occurred." The issue here is not the rapture. It is the basic issue of the relationship between the judgment on Israel and the persecution of the saints. Are we to suppose that the post 70 saints were so ignorant that they could not see that connection?

In fact, the Christians are not the only ones silent about the connection between the fall of Jerusalem and the persecution of the church. The post 70 rabbis seem baffled as to why Jehovah allowed the Romans to desolate the city. When they looked back at the judgment in BC 586 they candidly admitted that the reason for that judgment was because their fathers persecuted the prophets and shed innocent blood. However, when discussing the catastrophe of AD 70 they said it came on them for profaning the Sabbath, for not teaching their children the Law, for a lack of shame, etc..[389] But they did not list shedding innocent blood as a reason for the destruction!

How could this relationship have been missed or denied? The early church preached that relationship for a full generation and their blood was spilled for that message confirming the truthfulness of what they were saying. So, why did the early *Jewish writers* never pick up on that and seemingly still have not admitted it to this day? The question therefore, of how both Christians and Jews failed to see the connection between the fall of Jerusalem and the shedding of the martyrs blood is a serious challenge to the rapture doctrine.

The point is that in 2 Thessalonians we have the promise of Christ coming to vindicate the church at Thessalonica and to bring judgment on their persecutors. There is nothing in the text to suggest that Paul was promising a removal from earth or out of the persecution. He was promising relief from that persecution by the act of God in turning the persecutors into the persecuted. Thus, Stevens' argument: "Why wouldn't the first century saints expect their 'relief' from this tribulation to be seen and experienced in a real and tangible way as well?" is actually misplaced. It is identifying their expectation of relief with removal from the earth, not as the judgment on the Israel leading to a cessation of persecution. The *relief* was *cessation from persecution*. Cessation of persecution does not demand a removal from the earth. A quick note in light of what is to follow:

The persecutors of the Thessalonians were to be *gathered*, as we will see, *just like the righteous*. Yet, Paul says the persecutors would become the persecuted at the parousia. But, if the persecutors were gathered, i.e. raptured, how could they become the persecuted?

Fourth, Stevens notes that Christ would be glorified in his saints at the *parousia* (2 Thessalonians 1:10-12) and asks, "Where is the record of this happening?" Did it actually occur?" We might counter with this: Stevens believes the Lord did come in AD 70 though we have no written record of it. So, can we today glorify Christ? Has the church since the *parousia* glorified Christ without a written record of that event? Further, did/does Christ have to be "bodily, visibly present" for the church to glorify him since that Day?

Fifth, moving onto 2 Thessalonians 2:1f, Stevens queries, "Paul mentions their 'gathering together to Him' at His *parousia*. If this isn't a promise of a rapture, what else can we make of it?" (*Expectations*, 12).

We have already answered this question definitively in our study of the distinctive Greek words *apantesis* and *episunagogee*.

The gathering (*episunagogee*) of 2 Thessalonians 2 is the same gathering (*episunagogee*) as Matthew 24:31. Stevens will agree. Since the gathering of Matthew 24:31 *cannot* be a physical gathering (removal) from earth, then the gathering of 2 Thessalonians 2:1 cannot be a removal of Christians from the earth. Unless Stevens can prove beyond doubt that Paul is using the identical word used by Jesus in a radically different way, to speak of the same event, then the rapture of 2 Thessalonians 2:1 cannot be a physical rapture.

MATTHEW 13 AND THE RAPTURE

Matthew 13 and Jesus' parable of the sower, the wheat and the tares has been, up to this juncture, ignored in the discussions of a literal rapture in AD 70.[390] The problems presented by Matthew 13 for a literal rapture in AD 70 are, it seems to me, insurmountable.

Jesus told of a man that sowed the seed. The enemy came and sowed tares among the good seed. As the crop grew, the tares sprang up among the wheat. The servants asked the master if he desired them to go and separate the tares from the wheat. The master said, " Let both grow together until the time of the harvest" (Matthew 13:30). In his interpretation of the parable Jesus explained the harvest is at the end of the age" (v. 39f). But here is the difficulty for the literal rapture in AD 70. It was not just the wheat, i.e. the righteous that were gathered. *The wicked (tares)were gathered at the same time:* "as therefore the tares are gathered, and burned in the fire, so shall it be at the end of this age" (v. 40). In fact they would be gathered *first*!

The conclusion is inescapable. *If the righteous saints were literally removed from the earth in a supernatural event, then of necessity, the wicked were literally removed from the earth at the same time!*

> **IF THE RIGHTEOUS WERE REMOVED (RAPTURED) FROM THE EARTH AT THE *PAROUSIA*, *THEN OF NECESSITY THE WICKED WERE REMOVED AT THE SAME TIME*: "GATHER YE TOGETHER FIRST THE TARES" (MATTHEW 13:30).**

Undeniably, the wicked were *not* removed from the earth in AD 70. Josephus, certainly was not one of the elect, was he? Those inside the city, the rebels against Rome, against the Law and against Christ, were not literally removed in a supernatural rapture, *were they?* The wicked and the saints were both to be "gathered" (from *sullego*); the same word is used to describe the gathering of the elect and the wicked.

The problem here is acute and substantive. And it is not confined to Matthew 13. The identical problem presents itself in Matthew 25:31f, and in fact, *every "gathering" text*. Take for instance Luke 13 and Steven's argument that expectations demanded a rapture, and that the silence of the Christian literature explains that silence.

Jesus told the recalcitrant, unbelieving Jews:
"There will be weeping and gnashing of teeth when you see Abraham, Isaac and Jacob and all the prophets sit down in the kingdom of God *and you yourselves cast out*. Many will come from the east and the west, the north and the south, and sit down in the kingdom of God" (My emphasis).

Based on Steven's argument that since Jesus told them they would see Abraham, Isaac and Jacob, along with all the prophets sit down at the Messianic Banquet in the kingdom, we have the right to ask:

1.) Do we have any record from the unbelieving Jews of any such vision? Josephus' account of the angels and chariots will not qualify here. Jesus said Abraham, Isaac and Jacob, along with all the prophets would be seen at the messianic table.

2.) Was the Messianic Banquet to be a literal banquet table with the patriarchs and prophets gathered round? If the seeing was to be literal why is the banquet table not literal? Was Iranaeus right? He said that the kingdom is not yet present because no one is eating at the banquet table, where, "vines will be produced, each one having a thousand branches, and in each branch ten thousand twigs, and on each twig ten thousand shoots, and on each shoot ten thousand clusters, and each cluster ten thousand grapes, and each grape, when pressed will give twenty-five metretes of wine. And when one of the saints takes hold of a cluster, another will cry, 'I am a better cluster, take me, bless the Lord through me.'"[391] Iranaeus says that Papias, "who was a hearer of John and an associate of Polycarp, a fine old man, bore witness to these things in writing, in his fourth book, for there were five books that he compiled." It is clear that Iranaeus and Papias expected something, something concrete and tangible. Did their expectation, ostensibly based on the authority of John, demand a literal fulfillment?

3.) If the absence of Christians explains the silence concerning that event, and the *parousia*, why is there a total silence among the very men that Jesus said "you will see," i.e. the rebellious Jews? We know those men were not raptured as just noted. So, if Jesus said they would see Abraham at the Messianic Banquet and themselves cast out (did they *see* that casting out, or was that a *perceived* reality?) why did *not one of them* who was "left behind" sit down and write about the incredible things he or they had seen? This is a serious issue.

While several passages focus on the gathering of the saints without specifically mentioning the wicked it is improper to divorce the gathering of the wicked from that time and event. These are synchronous events.

It can hardly be argued therefore, that the saints were miraculously raptured, disappearing suddenly, but that the wicked were not likewise caught away to their doom. No distinction other than fate can be maintained between the nature of the gathering (*sullego*).

If therefore, the literal rapture theory cannot explain how it is that the wicked did not disappear, yet they were to be gathered just like the righteous, then the concept of a literal rapture is falsified. Patently, the wicked, whether Jewish or Roman, did not miraculously disappear in AD 70. However, they were "gathered" if we are to believe the Lord. Likewise, the righteous were "gathered," but that does not demand that they were supernaturally removed from planet earth.

LUKE 19:11f

Our next point is taken from Luke 19:11f where Jesus told the parable of the talents. Jesus told this parable because the crowds believed that the kingdom was about to come immediately. In the parable, a rich nobleman went into a far country there to receive a kingdom, and to return. It is well known that the parable is based on the story of the death of Herod and his son Archaelus. Upon the death of Herod, Archaelus, as Roman authority demanded, traveled to Rome, to receive the investiture. While there, the Jews sent an ambassage to Augustus asking that Archaelus not be enthroned. This naturally enraged Archaelus, who received the kingdom in spite of the Jewish opposition, and he expressed his wrath when he returned as ruler.

The point is this: the king did not remove his citizens from the land when he returned. *He came to rule over them!* There is no removal of citizens. Perhaps this is why Jesus prayed to the Father concerning his followers: "I do not pray that you should take them out of the world, but that you should keep them from the evil one" (John 17.15). Yet, this is *precisely* what the parable should depict if there was to be a removal of the saints from the earth at the *parousia*. Instead, *the king returns to be with the citizens!* This agrees perfectly with what we have seen in regard to John 14.

Our final point to be made is relative to the idea of "expectations." Stevens argues: "The 'EXPECTATION' (sic) statements are too clear about what they would 'see' and 'hear' and experience at our Lord's glorious 'appearing.' The words 'appearing' and 'revelation' and 'manifestation' lose all meaning if there was no conscious, visible, tangible experience of the Parousia." So, because the words "appearing" and other corollaries are used to speak of Christ's *parousia* this means it had to be a literal appearance. This brings up the issue once again that if this is true, why didn't the heathen world witness this "universal" appearance of Christ? Furthermore, the scriptures also affirm that at Christ's *parousia* there was the expectation that the "world" was to be destroyed! The "elements" were to be dissolved and "heaven and earth" was to be destroyed. *That was the expectation of the early saints*. Did the material creation cease to exist? Stevens would of course argue that we must define the "world" and the "heaven and earth" as the Old Covenant world, and the "elements" as the fundamental doctrines of that old world. In other words, he would argue that we must allow the scriptures to define what the word "world" and "earth" and "elements" meant in scriptures. And I would fully agree.

My point is that when the New Testament writers used the words *appearing, manifestation, parousia,* etc. that they were using those terms in the exact same way the Old Testament writers used them to speak of the Day of the Lord. In the Old Testament, Jehovah never literally, bodily, visibly descended from heaven on cumulus clouds, and destroyed literal creation. However, He was seen by the nations. His presence (LXX, *prosopon*, for face, nose) was "in their face" (cf. Jeremiah 4.23-28; 5.21-22).

Christ's *parousia* was to be "in the glory of the Father" (Matthew 16.27). This means it was to be in the same manner as the Father (cf. John 5.19f).[392] In other words, the Old Testament defines the "expectation" of the Day of the Lord, Christ's *parousia*, just like it defines "heaven and earth" as *spiritual* realities, not references to literal, physical realities.

The point is, that if Stevens insists that the Lord had to come literally because the saints expected his "manifestation" and his "appearance," then upon the identical grounds we must conclude that the saints expected the destruction of literal heaven and earth and the burning of the elements. If they did not expect the literal creation to come to an end, there is no justification to insist that they expected Jesus to literally come out of heaven on the cumulus clouds. It is clearly inconsistent to speak of their expectation of a literal rapture and a literal parousia, without at the same time demanding that they fully expected the destruction of the material cosmos. And yet, Stevens does not believe that they did expect such a cosmic destruction.

Mark 9:1 also has a direct bearing on the idea of a literal rapture in AD 70. Jesus told the audience: "Assuredly, I say to you that there are some standing here who will not taste of death till they see the kingdom of God present with power." Unfortunately, the NKJV and not many versions communicate the proper force of the text. As Robertson notes, "Jesus actually says that some standing there would not die before they saw that the kingdom had "already come."[393] The Greek text has the perfect active participle (*eleluthuian*). What Jesus was saying is that some in that audience would live *until* the *parousia*. They would live *beyond* the *parousia*, and look back on it in recognition of what it was. This presents a daunting problem for any literal rapture view.

First of all, this passage precludes the idea of a literal, bodily rapture. Jesus is patently saying that some would *live until* the parousia, *beyond* the parousia, and then look back in time and *realize that the parousia had already happened*![394] It would be the passing of time and the coming to an awareness of events that would lead them to the recognition of the reality of the events that had already taken place. We are reminded again of Isaiah 26 where the wicked and the righteous would both see the same events. The righteous would see God's coming in those events while the wicked would see nothing! If the coming in view was to be a literal, bodily, visible descent of Christ out of heaven this would not be possible.

For some, Mark 9:1 reinforces the problem of the silence of history and why virtually no one wrote about it. *Yet, this silence should not be the ground for formulation of our doctrine.* As already suggested *inspired history* is not in fact silent in this regard, since Revelation is the *inspired historical prophecy* of the fulfillment of Christ's *parousia* prophecies.

There are only so many types of people that would have been in that audience Jesus was addressing and speaking about that day.

1.) Unbelievers.
2.) Faithful believers.
3.) The sleepers, i.e. the weak in faith, the indolent, the ignorant in the body of Christ.

No *matter which group* of people is included in Jesus' statement, *the fact remains that Jesus said some would live through it and look back on it*, with *comprehension*. This presents insurmountable problems for the rapture view.

If Jesus was speaking of unbelievers living beyond the *parousia* and looking back on it, *in recognition that the kingdom had come*, then why didn't those unbelievers write about this dawning recognition that God had acted? Isn't the silence of this group of people significant?

If Jesus had the faithful believers in mind, then they would not live beyond the event and look back in recognition of what had taken place. They would be removed from the scene! Jesus was speaking of a dawning of recognition on those who would live beyond the event. He was not talking about recognition through a removal from earth!

If Jesus was speaking of the "sleepers" then he was saying that the sleepers would finally wake up and realize what had taken place! Thus, they would no longer be "sleepers!" Whoever Jesus is speaking about, they would live beyond the *parousia* and then they would look back on that event and recognize that the kingdom had come with power. Jesus most assuredly did not say that some would live beyond the *parousia*, die, and then in the spiritual realm look down and realize what had happened while they were on earth! He said, "there are some standing here that shall not taste of death until they see that the kingdom had come with power." This is a post *parousia*, *living realization* of the past occurrence of the *parousia*. They would not die until they realized the parousia had occurred. So, if these started out as sleepers, then the ones left behind were supposed to become fully cognizant of what had happened! What about *their* silence therefore?

The fact that Jesus said that some of his audience would live past the time of his coming, and then look back *and realize what had happened*, not only rejects a literal concept of the *parousia*, but defines Christ's coming as a non-visible, non-bodily coming. He was to come in the glory of the Father.

ROMANS 13:11 AND THE RAPTURE THEORY

Finally, I would like to suggest that a passage that is often ignored in almost all eschatological discussions presents a devastating blow to the idea that the faithful Christians were removed– or will be removed from earth– at Christ's *parousia*. That text is Romans 13:11f.

"And do this, knowing the time, that now it is high time to awake out of sleep; for now our salvation is nearer than when we first believed. 12 The night is far spent, the day is at hand. Therefore let us cast off the works of darkness, and let us put on the armor of light. 13 Let us walk properly, as in the day, not in revelry and drunkenness, not in lewdness and lust, not in strife and envy. 14 But put on the Lord Jesus Christ, and make no provision for the flesh, to fulfill its lusts."

While this text is full of significance, notice that Paul was urging his readers to holy living in light of the impending Day. That much virtually all commentators see. What most commentators do not see so clearly is that Paul urged them, "Let us walk properly, *as in the day."* The meaning of this, "as in the Day" is critical to any discussion of the rapture, future or AD 70.

Paul was saying that he wanted the Roman Christians to understand that *the arrival of the Day demanded that they live certain kinds of lives, lives of holiness and purity.* Almost all futurist eschatologies say there will be no temptation, no life on earth, no need for ethical *paranesis* after the end. Yet Paul undeniably posits that life after the arrival of the Day and the passing of the Night would be one in which believers in Christ must live a certain way.

However, if the rapture doctrine, whether futurist or preterist, was true, *Paul's exhortation was given to the wrong people.* After all, the faithful to whom he wrote would be gone out of this world, free from the obligations of ethical standards, free from temptation, free

> Paul was preparing the Roman Christians for life "in the Day" by telling them to live temperate lives in Christ, "as in the Day." That is, *as if the Day had arrived!* But, if the rapture was to take them away his exhortations were meaningless, for those to whom he wrote would no longer be on earth, duty bound to walk honestly "as in the Day."

from earth. This is not life in the Day that Paul envisioned for them, however.

Paul was telling them to live lives beyond moral reproach *in preparation for life after the arrival of the Day.* This demonstrates that he expected them to continue to live on earth confronted by temptation, but living triumphant lives in Christ. This exhortation provides a refutation of the rapture doctrine, *any* rapture doctrine.

THE HOPE OF ISRAEL

I will keep this brief. It cannot be forgotten that if one is going to posit a literal snatching of the faithful from the earth, then they must do so with OT authority. Remember that Paul affirmed that he preached nothing but the hope of Israel, found in the OT prophets. The question is, *where in the OT do we find such a prediction or expectation?* To my knowledge (perhaps I missed it) Stevens makes no attempt to demonstrate the OT source of the rapture doctrine. This is a huge problem, needless to say, for from Paul's perspective, if it was not in the OT it was not in the gospel!

What we do find in the OT is that there would be survivors of the Day of the Lord and they are *the righteous remnant* (Isaiah 4:1-5). Furthermore, after the coming of the Lord in flaming fire the remnant shares the message of the glory of God and comprises a new priesthood (Isaiah 66:15f). The point is that this is the righteous remnant, and they survive the Day of the Lord to continue to spread the Word of YHVH! This hardly suggests that they were snatched off of the earth.

SUMMARY OF THIS SECTION

So what have we seen in our examination of the idea that *"Expectations Demand A Rapture?"* We have shown that unless one can prove that the coming of John 14:1-6 is a different coming from that foretold in John 14:19f, then since Jesus plainly defined the coming of vs. 19f as a fellowship dwelling and not a removal from earth this disproves the idea of a rapture in verses 1-6.

Unless those who believe in a physical removal of believers from earth, either in the first century or in the future, can prove that the Old Testament prophecies foretold a different dwelling of God with man from that promised in John 14, this means that John 14 is not about a rapture of man from the earth. It is about the restoration of the dwelling of God with man.

Further, unless one can prove that the coming of Christ foretold in John 14 is a different coming from that foretold in Revelation 19-21, then since Revelation undeniably posits the dwelling place of God coming down from heaven to man, this demands that John 14 cannot be speaking of a rapture of men from the earth.

We have shown that 1 Thessalonians 4, John 14 and Matthew 24:29-31 all speak of the same time and event. We have shown that the coming of John 14 was the time for the completion of the new temple of God that was to come down from God out of heaven. God's dwelling place was to come to man. Man was not to leave earth.

We have shown that the gathering of Thessalonians and Matthew 24, the *episunagogee*, cannot be construed to speak of a physical removal of man from earth. *It is God gathering man into covenant relationship and dwelling with him.* Unless one can prove that the distinctive Greek word *episunagogee* is being used differently in Matthew 23:37 and Matthew 24:30, and also that the gathering of Matthew 24:30 is therefore a different gathering from that of 1 Thessalonians 4, this nullifies any possibility that 1 Thessalonians speaks of a physical snatching away of living humans from planet earth.

Our analysis of *apantesis* is a virtual falsification of a literal rapture doctrine, or any kind of rapture doctrine. Furthermore, when coupled with the fact that all other passages that describe the purpose of the *parousia* depict it as a coming *to dwell with man*, not a removal of man from the earth, this adds considerable weight to Paul's use of these suggestive technical terms *apantesis* and *parousia*.

We have shown that expectations prove nothing, unless it is demonstrated beyond doubt that *the expectation itself is valid*. We find no support for the idea that the early church actually expected to be removed from earth at Christ's *parousia* in AD 70, or any other time.

We have demonstrated that it is tenuous at best to argue from the silence of the apostolic and patristic writers. While we readily agree that the silence of these authors is perplexing, it should not be the foundation for an entire theological doctrine.

We have demonstrated the logical inconsistency of arguing on the one hand that the early writers would have written certain things, and then turning around and totally discounting their consistent testimony in matters that are destructive to the theory being proposed, i.e. a literal rapture. It is not consistent to disparage the testimony of the patristic authors about the "faithful Christians" remaining on earth after AD 70, and then claim that we should take their silence about the rapture as positive proof that what they did say about the continuing presence of these faithful Christians was false!

We have shown that Stevens actually claims that Josephus records for us the reality of the *parousia* (not in those precise words to be sure) by telling us about the chariots and angelic armies being seen in the sky over Jerusalem. (Wars, 6:5:3) Interestingly, Stevens gives the impression that Eusebius, "also mentions these same kinds of things happening at this time" (*Expectations*, 65). In fact, Eusebius was simply reiterating what Josephus said. Eusebius was not reporting independent or additional information.

Nonetheless, if Stevens argues that what Josephus saw was in fact the *parousia*, as he *seems* to indicate in his personal email to me, then the patristic silence is to a great extent mitigated–although grantedly still puzzling–by the fact that *there is no longer a silence about the parousia!* If Josephus recorded the fulfillment of the *parousia* then there is no longer a silence about that event in early history. The record might not be in the pages of ecclesiastical history, but it is to some degree, emphasized by being recorded by a non-Christian!

We have shown that the testimony of the early church writers reveals that they believed the end was supposed to have come in AD 70 (e.g. Barnabas, Hermas). This "expectation" is clearly expressed not simply implied or extrapolated from silence. This is then testimony to the eschatological significance of AD 70.

Similarly, we have shown that even the Jews of the late first century and later lamented the fact that the end of the 70 weeks had come and gone, the time for the end had expired in the fall of Jerusalem in AD 70, but that they failed to see (or accept) the reality of that event. This too is powerful testimony, and it is not silence.

We have shown that an appeal to 2 Thessalonians 1-2 does not support a literal rapture concept at all. The gathering in 2 Thessalonians 2 is the same gathering as in Matthew 24:31 and we have proven that this was not to be a removal of Christians from the earth.

We have shown that if one demands a literal removal of the saints in AD 70, they must, based on Matthew 13, also believe that the wicked were removed in the same manner, although clearly to a different fate. *To posit a literal rapture of saints demands a literal rapture of the wicked.* This is undeniable and fatal to a literal rapture doctrine.

We have shown that according to Jesus in Mark 9:1 some of that first century audience would live past Christ's *parousia* and look back on it in recognition of what had happened. This means that whether Jesus was speaking of the wicked, the righteous, or the "sleepers," it really does not matter. The point is that Jesus said that they would live beyond his coming, and then look back on it in recognition of what had taken place. We might well ponder as to why no one wrote about it *post facto*, but we cannot afford to formulate our theology on a doctrine of perplexing silence.

We have shown that Paul's moral exhortation to the Romans to live moral lives above reproach, as if the Day had arrived, demonstrates that Paul expected the Romans to live on after the arrival of the Day, on earth, and to live lives of morality and purity. This negates any idea of their removal from the earth at the rapture.

Finally, we have shown that unless one can produce the rapture doctrine from the OT then it is not part of the NT message. Furthermore, we have shown that in the OT, what we do find is that there would be survivors of the Day of the Lord and they are called the righteous remnant. They were not snatched away, they were not sleepers. This is a serious problem for a literal rapture doctrine of any kind.

In summary then we find no evidence that expectations demanded a literal rapture in AD 70, or at any other time. We turn now to our discussion of the dispensational futurist concept of the rapture.

SPECIAL STUDY: A LOOK AT THE DISPENSATIONAL RAPTURE DOCTRINE

It goes without saying that the doctrine of the rapture is a popular doctrine in our world. To listen to men like Hal Lindsey, Tim LaHaye, Thomas Ice, Grant Jeffrey and other popular prophecy pundits, the rapture is an established Bible doctrine.

1 Thessalonians 4:13f is the chief proof-text for the rapture doctrine. However, our examination of that text is an effective refutation of the rapture doctrine. As we proceed, it will be seen that there are several ways to expose the rapture doctrine as false. For brevity we will examine only the most fundamental aspects of the doctrine in comparison with the inspired text.

THE DOCTRINE OF IMMINENCE AND THE RAPTURE

It is somewhat amazing to me that the proponents of the rapture would appeal to the doctrine of imminence as a supportive tenet of their theory. The very idea that an event that was said to be imminent 2000 years ago is supposed to prove that it is near today seems patently specious at the least. It hardly makes sense to say, "Well, it was near 2000 years ago, therefore it is near today!" However, here is where the rub comes in.

The millennialists do not define imminent the way the word imminent is normally defined, either in normal conversation or in the dictionaries. It is important for the reader to understand the subtle, *but extremely important*, shift in definition made by the millennialists when they use the word imminent. Thomas Ice, defines imminent:

"An imminent event is one that is always 'hanging overhead, is constantly ready to befall or overtake one; close at hand in its incidence' (Oxford English Dictionary, 1901, v. 66.) Thus, imminence carries the sense that it could happen at any moment. Other things *may* happen before the imminent event, but nothing else *must* take place before it happens. If something else must take place before it happens then that event is not imminent. In other words, the necessity of something else taking place first destroys the concept of imminency...As I hope you can see by now, 'imminent' is not equal to 'soon'" *(Prophecy, 105+).*

It is specious to say something is *imminent*, but not *at hand*. The Oxford dictionary quote actually says something imminent is, "close at hand!" This is a desperate attempt to make time statements mean nothing. Yet as we have seen in our examination of *apantesis*, Zuber insists that the doctrine of imminent but not near is one of the critical distinctions between the rapture and the Second Coming.

Ice lists 14 New Testament passages that speak of the imminence of Jesus' *parousia* and says, "As we consider these passages, we note that Christ may come at any moment—that the rapture is actually imminent. Only pretribulationism can give a full, literal meaning to such an any-moment event" (*Prophecy*, 106+). However, to cite passages that said Christ's coming was near *2000 years ago* and say they mean *it is imminent now,* is anachronism exemplified. The New Testament writers did not say there was *the possibility* that Christ's coming was near. They affirmed, "In a very, very little while, He that will come, will come, and will not delay!" (Hebrews 10:37).

Notice how Ice changes the reading of the text. He says, "As we consider these passages, we note that Christ may come at any moment." He takes a passage in which the inspired author was writing to living breathing humans telling them the *parousia was near when he wrote*, and applies that statement to a generation 2000 years removed! That is a questionable hermeneutic to say the least. Does audience relevance not mean anything?

It is revealing that Ice does not quote a single verse that says, "Brethren, we shall not all sleep" (1 Corinthians 15:50f). He ignores, "There are some standing here that shall not taste of death till they see the Son of Man coming" (Matthew 16:27-28). He omits, "those of us who are alive and remain until the coming of the Lord" (1 Thessalonians 4:15,17). These are not statements of "hope so," "could be," or "maybe." These are inspired statements made two thousand years ago to living people. The statements affirm that Christ would positively return in their generation.

Ice affirms that the 14 verses prove Christ's coming was *imminent* (but of course, not *near*!) in the first century. However, he also says the necessity for any prophetic event to occur before the imminent event destroys imminence. You need to understand the importance of what he is saying here. According to the millennial paradigm, an event can only be *imminent* (in their definition of the word) if there is absolutely no other prophetic event *that has to take place before the imminent event*. Essentially, what imminent means to the millennialists is, "next on the prophetic calendar," although the next event might be centuries or millennia away. So, the argument is, an event can be *imminent*, only if there are no other prophetic events that must take place before the imminent event. If there are any other prophetic events that must take place before the imminent event, then imminence is destroyed. Let's test that argument.

The AD 70 destruction of Jerusalem was, by Ice's admission, a *prophetic event that had to happen* before the rapture! And yet, Ice cites 14 Bible verses, *every one of which was written before the fall of Jerusalem*, and says that the inspired writers were affirming the imminence of the rapture! The prediction of–and prophetic necessity for–the fall of Jerusalem before the rapture completely destroys Ice's argument about imminence. Either the fall of Jerusalem in AD 70 was not a prophetic event–yet Ice admits that it was--

or Ice's definition of imminence is fatally flawed. The latter is patently correct.

The argument is simple therefore: The necessity for the fulfillment of any prophetic event, before the occurrence of an *imminent event*, destroys imminence (Ice and other millennialists). However, it was *prophetically necessary* that Jerusalem fall in A. D. 70 before the rapture could occur. Therefore, the rapture was not imminent before the fall of Jerusalem in AD 70. Yet, as we have seen Ice says that there are 14 verses, *all written before the fall of Jerusalem*, that affirm that the rapture was imminent before that event! This reality negates Ice's argument on imminence. But that is not all.

According to Ice, the restoration of Israel in 1948 *had to occur* before the rapture (*Prophecy*, 56+). How then could the New Testament writers have affirmed, as Ice claims, that the rapture was *imminent* in the first century? Indeed, how could the church have been (correctly per Ice) proclaiming that the rapture has been imminent for the almost 1900 years since the dispersion in AD 70? If the re-gathering of 1948 was a prophetic necessity,[395] and Ice says it was, then clearly, the New Testament writers were wrong to affirm that the rapture was near, when in fact, not only had the re-gathering not occurred, the *dispersion had not occurred either*! After all, per Ice, the necessity for the fulfillment of any prophecy before the "imminent" event destroys the idea of imminence! According to Ice, the re-gathering of 1948 was 1900 years away, but was *prophetically necessary*. Yet, the NT writers said the rapture was imminent, even though they supposedly knew that there were *several* other prophetic events that had to occur before the rapture could occur! If the authors of the New Testament had the millennial view of imminence, they were clearly being deceptive to say that the rapture was imminent, i.e. next on the prophetic calendar.

Still another example of a prophecy that had to occur before the rapture is the fulfillment of the seven church ages. That is, Ice and most millennialists believe that the seven churches of Asia ,"are prophetical, they represent seven consecutive periods of ecclesiastical history."[396] The seven stages of the historical church are identified by the millennialists as:

1.) Ephesus–AD 30-100 AD
2.) Smyrna–AD 100-313 AD
3.) Pergamos–313-590 A. D.
4.) Thyatira–590-1517 AD
5.) Sardis– 1517-1730 A. D.
6.) Philadelphia– 1730-1900
7.) Laodicea– 1900-? (*Charting*, 45)

Here is the problem. Ice, LaHaye, Jeffrey, Van Impe and others insist that if there are any prophetic events that must transpire before an *imminent* event, then imminence is destroyed. They claim the rapture was "imminent" in the first century. Well, according to their own view, the seven different stages of the church had to transpire before the rapture. That is 1900+, *and counting*, years of prophetic fulfillment! How could the NT writers have said that the rapture was *imminent* if there was 1900+ years of prophetic fulfillment that had to take place? Were the inspired writers actually that confused, ignorant, or deceitful, or, is Ice's definition of imminence wrong? The latter choice is clearly the correct one.

Ice, citing Showers again, continues his attempt to void the objective nature of the time statements of the Bible by claiming, "A person cannot legitimately set or imply a date for its happening. As soon as a person sets a date for an imminent event he destroys the concept of imminency, because he is thereby saying that a certain amount of time must transpire before that event can happen. A specific date for an event is contrary to the concept that the event could happen at any moment" (*Prophecy*, 106).

But wait, the Lord, "appointed a Day," in which He would judge the world (Acts 17:30-31). In light of that appointed Day, He informed His followers that the Day, "has drawn near" (James 5:8). Did that *nullify* or *magnify* imminence? Was the Spirit lying to Peter when He inspired him to affirm, "The *time* (*kairos, appointed time*, DKP) has come for *the* judgment to begin" (1 Peter 4:17)? It is the Father that set the Day, and it is the Father that caused Peter to say the time for the appointed Day had come. Imminence was *not* destroyed, imminence was emphasized!

Furthermore, if setting a date nullifies imminence, what are we to make of all the modern prognosticators? What about Edward Whisenant who said that 1988 was to be the rapture "without fail"? Didn't his predictions cause lots of (misguided) folks to think the event was *near*? According to Whisenant, all of the signs were fulfilled, nothing else had to be done! I think we all know the result of his predictions. Jack Van Impe said that 1999 was the year, definitely. Did his date setting cause the Lord to delay the rapture? John Hagee, in a sermon entitled, "Ten Reasons Why We Are the Terminal Generation,"[397] said the coming of the Lord would be in 2007.[398] If you listen to these men you would think that the appearance of signs and the fulfillment of a plethora of prophecies *emphasizes* the imminence of the rapture, instead of mitigating it.

So, what does all of this mean in regard to the rapture doctrine? It means that when the NT writers said, "The coming of the Lord has drawn nigh" (James 5:8) or, "In a very, very little while, the one who is coming will come, and will not tarry" (Hebrews 10:37) or, "Little children it is the last hour" (1 John 2:18) etc., that they were affirming that Jesus' coming was near! They were not playing word games. All 14 of the passages cited by Ice, to affirm the "imminent but not near" idea, in truth affirm that Christ's coming was actually near in the first century. But if this is true, the rapture doctrine is reduced to rubble.

Plainly, to argue that the time statements of scripture mean "imminent but not soon" is a desperate and specious attempt to maintain a preconceived idea about the rapture. It destroys the meaning of words, and creates meanings unknown in the lexicons.[399] It is unworthy of those who would honor the authority and inspiration of scripture.

WHO'S ON FIRST?

One of the key elements of the dispensational rapture concept is the idea that it is not until the end of the millennium that the wicked are gathered (resurrected). However, in Matthew 13 one of the key texts that supposedly mentions the end of the Christian age Jesus' shows that the millennial doctrine of the rapture is misguided.

Jesus told the parable of the wheat and the tares. What is so important for our purposes is what he says in verse 30. In speaking of the harvest at the end of the age, Jesus said, "Let both grow together until the harvest: and in the time of the harvest I will say to the reapers, 'Gather ye together first (Greek, *proton*) the tares, and bind them in bundles to burn them.'"

So what is the problem? The problem is that the doctrine of the rapture says *the church is gathered first*, while Jesus said the wicked would be gathered *first*. The rapture theory says, in fact, that the wicked are not gathered for judgment until *the end of the millennium* which is supposed to be (at least) 1007 years *after* the events of Matthew 13! The question is, how can rapture advocates appeal to Matthew 13 in support of the rapture when the order of events in Matthew 13 denies the rapture doctrine?

But there are other problems with the rapture view of Matthew 13. In an article entitled, "The Age to Come," Thomas Ice comments on the meaning of the significant eschatological terms *this age*, and *the age to come* as used in the Bible. He notes that these terms were common among the Jews of Jesus' day and that Jesus and Paul used the terms in the commonly accepted manner:

"The Jewish perspective of Bible prophecy views history as consisting of two ages. The first was 'this present age' the age in which Israel was waiting for the coming of Messiah. The second was 'the age to come,' the age in which all promises and covenants would be fulfilled and Israel would enter into her promised blessings."

Ice is correct about this. However, here is the problem. Ice says that Jesus used the terms this age and the age to come in the well accepted context of his times. This means that *this age* was the age of Israel as she waited on her salvation. It is important–critical– to know that the millennialists do not believe that the age of Israel is in any way at all identified with the church age. As a matter of fact, one of the fundamental doctrines of millennialism is the distinction between Israel and the church. The promises of Israel are not the promises of the church, and vice versa. Keep this in mind.

In Matthew 13 Jesus spoke of the end of "this age" (Matthew 13:39-40). This could not be the end of the Christian age because the Christian age had not even begun, and Ice admits this: "I believe that 'this present age' refers to the current Christian age that began almost 2000 years ago *on Pentecost*" (My emphasis). So in Matthew 13 when Jesus spoke of the end of "this age," he was not speaking of the end of the Christian age because: 1.) He used the terms this age and the age to come in the standard Jewish way, which means, per Ice, that it had nothing to do with the church age, 2.) The church age had not even begun and would not be established for a time yet. So, where is the problem, you say?

The problem is this. Ice believes that, "The parables in Matthew 13 survey the church age in terms of God's kingdom on earth, which covers the time between Christ's first and second comings" (*Charting*, 48). But this cannot be! Remember, according to Ice and the millennialist the church age was never foretold by the Old Testament prophets. And yet, Jesus said that the end of the age he was speaking about would be the fulfillment of Daniel 12:3 (Matthew 13:43). So, whatever Matthew 13 foretold it was foretold by the Old Testament prophets.

In addition, when Jesus and the Jews spoke of *this age, and the age to come*, they were thinking in Jewish terms and this did not include the church age according to Ice. Yet, in Matthew 13 we have Jesus using the standard terms of *this age*, and *the end of the age*, and Ice claims that Jesus was speaking about the church age! If Jesus was using the terms *this age,* and *end of the age* in the way that Ice says he was, there is no way in this world that he should have been speaking of the end of the church age, because according to Ice, *this age* and the end of the age were Jewish concepts and had nothing to do with the church![400]

RAPTURE OR SECOND COMING: WHICH IS WHICH?

Another way to demonstrate that the rapture doctrine is false has been examined earlier. We have shown that 1 Thessalonians 4:13-18 is parallel to Matthew 24:29-31. See the chart again and our discussion. Why is this important? Because the millennialists insist that Matthew 24:29-31 is the Second *Coming, that supposedly occurs 7 years after the rapture.* You see, the millennialists say that there are two different comings of the Lord in the future. There is the rapture, and then 7 years later, the Second Coming. As we have seen earlier this is part of the basis for Zuber's rejection of the technical meaning of *apantesis*. He insists that Thessalonians is the rapture, not the

Second Coming. His doctrine of the rapture is at odds with that technical usage. Therefore, he rejects the well documented meaning of that word.

We have proven that this idea of two phases of Christ's coming is false. Matthew 24 and 1 Thessalonians 4 are speaking of the same event. This is devastating to the millennial paradigm for if the two passages speak of the same time and event then their entire house of cards is destroyed. For convenience, we will present the shorter chart again:

Matthew 24:29-31	1 Thessalonians 4:13-18
Coming of the Son of Man	Coming of the Son of Man
With the angels (v. 30-31)	With the angels (v. 16)
With the Trumpet (v. 31)	With the Trumpet (v. 16)
Coming in the clouds (v. 30)	Descend from heaven, in the air (v. 16, 17)
Gathering of the redeemed (v. 31)	Gathering of the redeemed (v. 17)
This generation shall not pass until all these things are fulfilled (v. 34)	"We who are alive and remain until the coming of the Lord" (v. 15, 17)

This chart proves that the motifs, words, terms and time statements as to when those things were to occur are the same. Both Jesus and Paul affirmed that these things would occur in the lifetime of the first century generation. Since this is true this means that Thessalonians does not teach a doctrine of a rapture seven years before the Second Coming.

Per the millennialists the rapture occurs to bring the Christian age to its end. However, in Matthew 24 the Second Coming supposedly occurs at the end of the Jewish age, i.e. at the end of the final seven weeks of Daniel 9. Does it not strike you as strange that we have the end of two *ages only seven years apart?* (How can the Second Coming put an end to the age of Israel, when in fact the millennium is supposed to be the *re-establishment* of Israel?)

The problem this raises is addressed elsewhere in this work. That is, the Bible affirms that *the Christian age has no end!* If the Christian age has no end (Ephesians 3:20-21; Hebrews 12:28, etc.) it is patently wrong to say that 1 Thessalonians 4 describes the rapture at the end of the Christian age. The *only* age that was supposed to end was the Mosaic age. That was the age symbolized by the temple and it was the prediction of the destruction of the temple that prompted the disciple's question about the end of the age. We ask again, how would the prediction of the destruction of the Old Covenant temple of Israel cause the disciples to ask about the end of the Christian age? There is no correlation between these concepts.

Another problem with the millennial posit of two future comings of the Lord is the arbitrary manner in which they assign the different passages to the different comings. For instance, in *Charting*, (111) LaHaye and Ice say that when Jesus told Caiaphas, "You will see the Son of Man coming on the clouds of heaven,"[401] that this was a promise of the Second Coming. However, this shows the, may I say it, sloppy nature of their exegesis. Here is what I mean.

The millennial view of the resurrection is that the wicked are not raised *until the end of the millennium* (*Fast*, 166). In other words, there is the rapture then seven years later the Second Coming. Then there is the 1000 year reign. Finally, at the end of the millennium the resurrection of the wicked takes place. *Now, in the millennial view of things there is no coming of the Lord on the clouds of heaven at the end of the millennium!* Yet, that is where they *must* place the coming of Matthew 26:64!

Caiaphas qualifies as one of the wicked, does he not? Thus, his resurrection, when he would see the Lord per the millennialists, cannot be until the end of the millennium. However, *per Ice and LaHaye* Jesus told Caiaphas that he would see *the Second Coming*! The only way he could see the Second Coming is to be resurrected. But again, per the millennial view his resurrection would not be until the end of the millennium and *there is no coming of the Lord at that time!* This is a major problem to be sure.

Our point is that while it is widely admitted that Thessalonians describes the coming of Christ *at the end of the age*, that passage has been tragically applied to the end of an age *that has no end*. Let me say this again, since the Christian age has no end the doctrine of the rapture is falsified. Furthermore, as we have seen, there is no difference between the so-called rapture and the Second Coming. The arbitrary manner in which the millennialists divide the rapture from the Second Coming is without Biblical support.

WITH OR *FOR*, OR, WITH *AND* FOR?

There is a major problem with the millennial attempt to delineate between Matthew 24 and 1 Thessalonians. It is argued that the two passages must be referring to different events because the Second Coming (Matthew 24) speaks of Christ coming *with* the saints, while Thessalonians speaks of Christ coming *for* the saints (*Prophecy*, 102). This is a false distinction.

Notice that in Matthew 24:29f, it says that at the coming of Christ, "he shall gather together the elect from the four winds." If that is not a coming *"for the saints,"* what is it? By the way, where in Matthew 24 does it speak of Christ coming *with* the saints? It speaks of his coming with the *angels*, but where does it specifically mention the coming *with the saints*? The millennialists totally ignore the fact that Matthew 24 speaks of Christ coming for the saints and make it say he would come *with* the saints!

It is questionable to say the least to draw hard distinctions based on the use of different words and based on elements mentioned in one text and not another. See our critique of Kenneth Gentry below.

To suggest that 1 Corinthians 15 speaks of a different *parousia* of the Lord from that in 2 Peter 3, because Corinthians mentions the resurrection but Peter doesn't is fundamentally flawed. To suggest that 2 Peter is different from 1 Thessalonians 4 because Peter does not mention the coming on the clouds, the Trumpet, the Shout of the Arch-Angel, while it does mention the destruction of "heaven and earth" is equally egregious.

The millennial attempt to delineate between the rapture and the Second Coming based on a coming *with* or *for* the saints is the worst sort of textual manipulation. These tactics smack of an *a priori* paradigm that refuses to be guided by text and context.

Take a look at 1 Thessalonians 4, the foundational rapture text. Does it draw a distinction between Jesus coming *with* the saints and coming *for* the saints? It does not. In fact, it includes both elements. Look at 1 Thessalonians 4:14, "If we believe that Jesus died and rose again, even so, God will bring *with* Him, those who sleep in Jesus" (My emphasis). This has Christ coming *with the saints*, yet this supposedly does not happen at the rapture.

Notice now verse 17, "Then we who are alive and remain shall be caught up together with them in the clouds to meet the Lord in the air." Here is the coming *for* the saints, but again, it cannot be divorced from the coming *with* the saints, for it says they would be caught up "together." Those he would come *for*, would join those he came *with*! There is no distinction between coming *for* and coming *with*.

If you are going to say that when a passage says Christ would come *with* the saints, that this means he would come another time *for* the saints, then it is patently wrong to take a passage (Matthew 24) and say it speaks of Christ coming *with* the saints (and not *for* them) when in fact, it only mentions his coming *for* them! And, you cannot say that Thessalonians speaks only of Christ coming *for* the saints when in fact the passage emphatically says he was to come *with and for* the saints!

Ice insists:

"The movement for the believer at the rapture is from earth to heaven, while it is from heaven to earth at the second advent. At the rapture, the Lord comes *for* his saints (1 Thess. 4:16) while at the second coming the Lord comes *with* His saints (1 Thess. 3:13). At the rapture, the Lord comes only for believers, but His return to the earth will impact all people. The rapture is a translation/resurrection event where the Lord takes believers 'to the Father's house' in heaven (John 14:3) while at the second coming believers return from heaven to the earth (Matt. 24:30). Hindson says, 'The different aspects of our Lord's return are clearly delineated in the scriptures themselves. The only real issue in the eschatological debate is the time *interval* between them.'"[402]

Notice how Ice seeks to delineate between comings. He says: "At the rapture the Lord comes only *for* his saints." Well, take a close look at Matthew 24:30f. The text says the angels would, "gather together the elect from the four winds, from one end of heaven to another." This is clearly the coming "for the saints." According to the millennial dogma this should not be the case. Matthew 24 is supposedly Christ coming *with*, not *for* the saints!

A statement of hermeneutic here. Passages can be delineated from one another if they are truly different[403] and posited in different temporal contexts. However, as we have shown, just because one passage omits referent to a given element or even gives different information does not necessitate a different topic.

For the millennial argument to stand they would have to find passages that speak of the coming of Christ in which the author said that Christ was coming with angels, but in another passage the author made it a point to say that Christ was coming *without angels*. In this case there might either be a contradiction, or, there would be two different comings in view. However, to suggest that every writer has to mention every constituent element and motif that might possibly be associated with the *parousia* imposes a literary impracticality. Most commentators accept this when not arguing against one another. However, in polemics, strange arguments are often birthed that are not only unsound hermeneutically, but patently illogical.

JOHN 14 AND THE RAPTURE

It is often insisted that John 14 must speak of a literal rapture of believers off of planet earth, because Jesus said, "I come again to receive you...so that where I am, there you may be also." The fact is that John 14 is not a "rapture" at all, *but a coming of Christ to dwell with man*. See our discussion of the Messianic Temple above.

It seems to have escaped the notice of the rapture advocates that the disciples inquired about Jesus' promise to come. In verses 19f Jesus continued his discussion of his coming to dwell with disciples:

"A little while longer and the world will see me no more, but you will see me because I live, you will live. At that day you will know that I am in the Father and you in me, and I in you. He who has my commandments and keeps them, it is he who loves me. And he who loves me will be loved by my Father, and I will love him and manifest myself to him."

Jesus reiterates his promise to dwell with his disciples and it is at the time after the sending of the Spirit (vs. 15-18). Jesus promised that his coming to be with them would be in "a little while." Further, he said that the world would no longer see him. Jesus was saying that his "Second Coming" would not be an optical event seen by the world.

Jesus said that at the time of his coming to dwell with them the Father would dwell with them as well. This is parallel to his statement, "In my Father's house are many dwelling places" (v. 2). These are not two different comings at two different times. The issue is being in the presence of Christ and his Father. The nature of that presence is clearly delineated in verse 20f: "You will know that I am in the Father and you in me, and I in you."

Note that Jesus said, "I will love him and manifest myself to him" (v. 21). The word translated as "manifest" is *emphanizo*, the future form of *emphanes*. The word means, "apparent, conspicuous, obvious to the sight." It can refer to things optically visible (cf. Acts 10:40) or to things not optically visible, but perceptually manifested. In John 14, it is apparent that the manifestation of Jesus is not optically visible to the world, but *perceived by the disciples*. How do we know? Because Judas (not Iscariot) asked Jesus, "Lord how is it that you will manifest (*emphanezien*, infinitive future) yourself to us and not to the world?'"

It would have been appropriate, if the literal rapture theory is correct, for Jesus to say, "I will snatch you off the earth." But Jesus did not say that. If a literal catching away from the human experience was what Jesus was promising he could have said at this point, "It will be manifest to you when you leave this world behind." But, he did not say that. Jesus' answer, in describing his coming to dwell with them in fulfillment of verses 1-6, falsifies the concept of a literal rapture.

In response to Judas' question about how Jesus was going to come and manifest himself to them, and not the world, Jesus said: "If anyone loves me, he will keep my word, and my Father will love him, *and we will come to him and make our home with him"* (My emp.).

Jesus patently does not say that his coming would be to remove the disciples from the earth. While the majority of commentators see John 14 as a promise to remove Jesus' followers from earth, in actuality *it is a promise that God would come to dwell with man!* This is critical!

1 Thessalonians 4:17 provides help in understanding that neither John 14, nor any other text, supports the idea of a removal of the church from the earth, either in a literal AD 70 rapture, or in a rapture as perceived by the dispensational school.

2 THESSALONIANS 1 AND THE RAPTURE DOCTRINE

Virtually all dispensationalists assign 2 Thessalonians 1 to the Second Coming. Ice and LaHaye list 2 Thessalonians 1:4f as a Second Coming text (*Charting*, 111). MacArthur,[404] Pentecost,[405] Walvoord and Zuck[406] all agree.

A key element of dispensationalism is that the church is *not on earth at all* during the Great Tribulation. Ice claims, "Not one OT passage on the tribulation refers to the church, nor does the New Testament ever speak of the church in relation to the tribulation" (*Watch*, 108). Ice then lists 2 Thessalonians 1 as a passage that does not speak of the church in relationship to the Great Tribulation. Pentecost is emphatic, "The silence in the epistles (concerning the church and the Great Tribulation, DKP) which would leave the church unprepared for the tribulation argues for her complete absence from that period altogether" (*Things to Come,* 210).

So, according to millennial dogma the church is not on earth during the Great Tribulation and will not be on earth under tribulation at the time of the Second Coming. But let us look at the facts in 2 Thessalonians 1:

√ 2 Thessalonians 1 predicted the Second Coming.

√ Second Thessalonians 1 is addressed to the *church*.

√ Second Thessalonians 1 is addressed to and about the *church* experiencing *Tribulation*.

√ Second Thessalonians 1 promised that the church would be delivered from that persecution at the time of the Second Coming.

Do you see the problem? *Everything Paul says in 2 Thessalonians 1 contradicts the millennial view.* Paul is addressing the *church*, but the millennial view is that what he says is not true of the church. Paul speaks of the church *under tribulation at the time of the Second Coming.* The millennialists says the church is not under tribulation at the Second Coming. Paul says the church would receive relief from tribulation at the Second Coming. The millennialist denies this.

If the church is not on earth during the Great Tribulation she cannot be on earth at the time of the Second Coming. Will the church be experiencing tribulation *in heaven?* If 2 Thessalonians 1 is speaking of the church under tribulation at the time of the Second Coming then that has to be the *Great Tribulation* because that is what is going on at the time of the Second Coming, per the millennialist.

So, by positing 2 Thessalonians 1 as the Second Coming the dispensationalist negates his entire paradigm.

2 Thessalonians 1 cannot be speaking of the rapture according to the millennialists because it is the time of the judgment of the wicked.

It cannot be speaking of the Second Coming because it deals with the *church*, and not Israel (2 Thessalonians 1:1).

However, since 2 Thessalonians 1 is about the church then it cannot be speaking of the Second Coming because according to the millennialists the church is not on earth at the *parousia*! The text denies the millennial posit.

If 2 Thessalonians 1 is speaking of the Second Coming and it is dealing with giving the church relief from tribulation at that time, then patently, the church does go through the Great Tribulation after all. The church is not raptured out before the Tribulation.

The facts are clear. The millennialists almost universally apply 2 Thessalonians 1 to the Second Coming, and not the rapture. However, the millennialists do not believe that the church will be on earth at the Second Coming, and therefore will obviously not be undergoing persecution, and certainly not the Great Tribulation. Therefore, the promise of 2 Thessalonians 1 cannot apply to the church or to the Second Coming in regard to the church at all. Yet, the text is specifically applied to the church and that is even how millennialists understand it.

Furthermore, the millennialists cannot now re-adjust their understanding of 2 Thessalonians to apply it to the rapture. This would demand that at the rapture the ungodly persecutors of the church would be judged and there is no place for that in the millennial paradigm. *There is simply no way for 2 Thessalonians 1 to be a rapture text in the millennial view of things.*

So, the millennialists cannot apply 2 Thessalonians 1 to the rapture without destroying their doctrine. They cannot apply it to the Second Coming without destroying their doctrine. That means that the rapture doctrine is falsified.[407]

2 THESSALONIANS 2 AND THE RAPTURE DOCTRINE

2 Thessalonians 2 likewise delivers a devastating blow to the millennial camp. Remember that paradigm: you have the rapture, a seven year tribulation period, the Second Coming, the millennium and finally the Day of the Lord.

Imagine therefore, how impossible it would be for the Thessalonians to believe that anything remotely resembling this scenario had already occurred.[408] To believe that the rapture had occurred– or, to believe that the Second Coming had already occurred,[409] the Thessalonians would have had to believe the following:

1.) The rapture had already happened. Of course, if they believed that the rapture had occurred, then they must have thought that they, Paul and the other apostles, as well as the leadership of the Jerusalem church, had all been left behind!

2.) They would have to believe that the Christian age had already come to an end! Remember that according to dispensationalism the rapture brings the Christian age to an end. This means that the Christian age had ended only 18-20 years after being established through the blood of Jesus.

3.) The Man of Sin had already signed a peace treaty with Israel according to the millennial view of Daniel 9.

4.) That the temple in Jerusalem had already been destroyed and then rebuilt again all within a brief span of time. According to millennial dogma, which the Thessalonians *supposedly believed*, the temple that was standing in the first century is not the tribulation temple. That temple has to be rebuilt after the rapture when the Man of Sin is supposed to grant the Jews the right to rebuild the temple and: "Judaism is revived, and traditional sacrifices and ceremonies are re-instituted in the rebuilt temple in Jerusalem."[410]

5.) They would have to believe that the 144,000 Jews had been converted, and that the gospel had been preached into all the world.

6.) They would have to believe that the Man of Sin had already broken his treaty with Israel and that he was at that time persecuting the Jews. (Of course, it was not the Jews that were being persecuted when Paul wrote, it was the *Christians!*)

7.) They would have to believe that the Great Tribulation was past.

8.) They would have to believe as some at Ephesus did (2 Timothy 2:18) that the resurrection had already happened.

Ask yourself, could anyone ever be convinced that all of these things so vital to the millennial view *had already occurred*? Could those in Thessalonica have actually believed that every dead person who had ever lived had been raised?

Furthermore, how could the Thessalonians have an idea of the Day of the Lord, thinking it could have happened, and yet not know that the righteous were to disappear in the preceding rapture? Is there the slightest hint from the text that they had looked up to see that the most faithful of their congregation had disappeared? Hardly. The rapture view cannot be sustained in light of what Paul says here.

If the Thessalonians believed that the Rapture had already occurred this means they believed that the Christian age had ended only 18-20 years after being established through the shedding of the blood of Christ. *How is this Possible?*

SIGNS, SIGNS, EVERYWHERE A SIGN...OR NOT?

We want now to examine 1 Thessalonians 4 and the rapture doctrine as it relates to the ubiquitous claims that every where we look today we see the signs of the end.[411] To chronicle the confusion within the millennial camp in regard to signs would demand the production of a separate book. We will try to keep this brief.

To say there is confusion and contradiction among millennialists in regard to the presence of signs of the end is a gross understatement. Jack Van Impe insists, (and the newspapers supposedly prove it!) that we are witnessing more signs of the end of the age than any other generation. Ice and LaHaye agree with this (*Charting,* 119). I heard John Hagee present a lesson entitled, "12 Reasons Why This Is The Generation That Will See the Coming of the Lord."[412] His reasons were the presence of all the "signs." Hal Lindsey was so convinced by the "signs of the end" that he said the Lord was supposed to come in 1988. Remember?

On the other hand, Ice says, "The present age is not a time in which Bible prophecy is being fulfilled" (*Prophecy*, 10). He even goes so far as to criticize Lindsey, Van Impe, etc. for making what he calls, "harmful speculation about the future" (*Charting*, 37) and he then says:

"Since believers today live in the church age, prophetic signs relating to Israel are not being fulfilled in our day. Some prophecy teachers like to talk about how God is fulfilling dozens of prophecies in our day. This is not the case because the prophecies they cite refer to events that will take place during the tribulation" (*Fast Facts*, 197).

So, according to Ice all of the so-called signs of the end being emphasized by Lindsey, Van Impe and others are not signs of the end of the Christian age at all, and their dispensational brothers are guilty of "harmful speculation about the future." Oh, but wait.

In the book *Charting the End Times*, Tim LaHaye and Ice write at length about the signs. In fact, they have a lot to say about *current signs* that supposedly prove that the end of the church age is near. Strangely enough, the signs they give as proof of the nearness of the end are the same signs mentioned by Lindsey, Van Impe, Jeffrey and the others. So, on the one hand, Ice says his dispensational brothers are wrong for applying these signs to the end of the church age, and then he applies them to the end of the church age!

In *Charting* (p. 84) it is said, "Israel's re-gathering and the turmoil are *specific signs* that God's end-time program is on the verge of springing into full gear" (My emphasis). On that same page the heading is, *"Israel: God's Super Sign of the End Times."* On page 119, the chapter headline is: *"The Signs of Christ's Return,"* and we find statements like this in regard to the things happening in this generation:

1.) "The first and most important sign, the re-gathering of the Jews in Israel after nearly 2000 years of wandering, is so highly significant that we have devoted one whole chart on that subject alone" (*Charting*, 119).

But wait, if there are no signs of the end of the Christian age, how can the re-establishment of Israel in 1948 be the "Super Sign of the End of the Age?"
2.) "The rise of Russia to become a world superpower militarily from 1950 to 1995 and beyond is a fulfillment of prophecy" (*Charting*, 119).

3.) "All the strikes and unrest we see in the world today are not just a disruption of society, they are a fulfillment of prophecy of the last days" (*Charting*, 120).

Okay, didn't we just see that Ice claims, "The present age is not a time in which Bible prophecy is being fulfilled"? Yes, the same man said, "This is not an age in which prophecy is being fulfilled." Yet, the strikes we see around the world are "a fulfillment of prophecy of the last days."[413]

4.) "The rise of ancient Babylon in our day constitutes another sign of the times that sets the stage" (*Prophecy*, 72). But remember, there are not supposed to be any signs of the end, right?

5.) "What are the signs of the end times? The first sign Jesus pointed to was war. Not just any war, of which the world has seen over 15k to date, but a special war started by two nations and joined by many other nations on either side until all the world is involved. That occurred with the World War I in 1914-1918. Since then there have been *a parade of "signs*," the most significant one being the re-gathering of the Jewish people back into the land of Israel and the recognition of Israel as a nation in 1948"[414] (*Charting*, 36).

It is obvious from this quote that Ice and LaHaye believe that WWI was one of the key major signs of the end of the Christian age. But here is the problem, Ice is also on record as saying: "Wars, earthquakes, famines, and false christ's *during any part of the church age* would not constitute signs of the times indicating a near return of Christ" (*Prophecy*, 74). So, is war a sign of the end or not?

Do you see the contradictions? From affirming that there are no signs being fulfilled in the Christian age, to affirming that there has been a veritable "parade of signs," the authors of *Charting*, present a confused and confusing doctrine. Be sure to read my book, *The Last Days: Identified*. In that book the identity of the last days is proven to be the last days of the Old Covenant world of Israel, not the last days of the church age. In short, the Bible nowhere teaches the end of the Christian age.

Let's look closer at the issue of signs and the rapture. Ice says, "The rapture is a sign-less event" (*Prophecy*, 11). However, as we have seen, Ice and LaHaye are equally zealous in proclaiming that there has been a veritable "parade of signs in our generation," of the end of the church age.

The normal explanation of this contradiction is to say that there are no signs of the rapture but there are signs of the end of the age. Thus, the re-establishment of Israel in 1948 is the, "Super Sign of the End of the Age," yet it is not a sign of the rapture, because, "If there were signs that related to an event (the rapture, DKP) they would indicate whether it was near or not near. Therefore, the event couldn't happen until after the signs were present. Thus the signs would have to precede the event–which means the event couldn't happen until after the signs appeared. Since the rapture could occur at any moment, it can't be related to any signs at all" (*Prophecy*, 11). Allow me to be blunt, this is theological nonsense.

Let's look at it like this: Again, on the one hand, Ice and LaHaye say there are no signs of the rapture. However, on the other hand, they affirm that the restoration of Israel in 1948 was the "Super Sign of the End of the Age." To say the least, this is a major contradiction!

When do Ice and LaHaye say the rapture will occur? At the end of the Christian age: "The purpose of the rapture is to end the church age so that God may return and complete His program with Israel" (*Fast Facts*, 158).

If the rapture is to end the Christian age, and *if there are signs of the end of the Christian age*, then the signs of the end of the Christian age, are, *de facto, signs of the rapture*! You cannot say that the rapture and the end of the Christian age[415] are *synchronous* (same time) events and say that there are signs for one, but not signs for the other! Thus, we say again, if the rapture is to end the Christian age and if there are signs of the end of the Christian age, then it is undeniable that the signs of the end of the Christian age are *signs of the rapture!*

It should be clear that dispensationalists have some severe problems in regard to their doctrine of the rapture.

They say there are no signs, yet they say there has been a parade of signs.

They say there are no signs of the rapture, but there are signs of the end of the church age, *which happens at the rapture.*

They say wars are not a sign of the end, and then they say WWI is one of the most significant signs of the end.

They say that the necessity for any precursor signs before an imminent event destroys imminence, but they then point to a host of signs (AD 70, 1948, WWI, etc.) as proof of the "imminent" rapture.

And on and on it goes. The confusion never stops. It is time for the evangelical community to reject this contradictory, convoluted dispensational message that continues to foster skepticism and ridicule. Every time the so-called prophecy teachers point to the newspapers and current events and cry, "This is the sign, the end is near," and those prognostications continue to fail, the name of Christ is shamed. Every time our dispensational neighbors point us to 1 Thessalonians therefore, and tell is that the time for the rapture is near, we need to lovingly but forcefully remind them of the inherent contradictions in their paradigm. You cannot (*logically*) say the rapture is a sign-less event and then point to the newspapers as proof that the rapture is near!

TWO COMINGS OR ONE?
WHAT WAS THE EARLY CHURCH EXPECTING?

The dispensational view is based on the idea of two different comings of the Lord. There is the rapture that is silent and invisible and then there is the physical, bodily, visible Second Coming. Commenting on 1 Thessalonians 1:10 Ice and LaHaye claim, "The context of that passage is the rapture, for Christians are not waiting for the glorious appearing" (*Charting*, 107). So, the early church, and even the church today, is not waiting on the Second Coming because that comes 7 years or so after the rapture. The church in the first century was supposedly awaiting only one event, the rapture.

The trouble is, the early church did not believe in two different comings of the Lord as posited by the millennial camp. They believed in one judgment coming of Christ and that it was very near to them. If it can be shown that any of the passages Ice and LaHaye call "Second Coming but not rapture" texts teach that the coming in view was near in the first century, their doctrine is destroyed. Further, if it can be shown that there was to be only one *parousia* the rapture theory is overthrown.

Take a look at Titus 2:13. Paul says those Christians were, "Looking for that blessed hope and glorious appearing of the great God and Savior Jesus Christ." Now remember, LaHaye claims that the early church was not looking for the glorious appearing of Christ back then. They were supposedly looking for the blessed hope, i.e. the rapture. So, the millennialists see two different comings here.

There are many problems for this view, and the main one is the text itself. The Greek grammar of the text forbids an understanding of two comings. According to Granville Sharpe's rule,[416] in order for two comings to be present the text would have to read, "looking for *the* blessed hope and *the* glorious appearing." While some translations provide two definite articles, there is but one in the Greek standing before "the blessed hope." This means that the one definite article controls both subjects. In other words, they were looking for *one thing*, the blessed hope which was the glorious appearing of the great God and Savior Jesus Christ![417] This means that the Second Coming really was near in the first century. The first century church, according to Ice, LaHaye, Lindsay, etc. was not supposed to be looking for the Second Coming, but according to Paul they were not only looking for it they were *expecting* it!

Paul used a distinctive word when he said they were "looking" for Christ's coming. It is from the Greek word *prosdekomai* (προσδεχομαι) and means "expectantly awaiting" (Knight, *NIGTC*, 321). This word controls both the "blessed hope" and "glorious appearing." In other words, it actually does not matter if "blessed hope" and "glorious appearing" were two events, the word "looking" demands that they were eagerly expecting both of them *soon*! Whereas the millennialist says that the early church *was* eagerly looking for the "blessed hope," they were *not* eagerly looking for the glorious appearing, the text says they were eagerly looking for the "blessed hope, the glorious appearing!" You cannot distort the text into saying the Cretan Christians were looking for one event but were not looking for the other. This is a violation of the grammar of the text.

Thus, the first century church was eagerly expecting *one event*, the Second Coming. But, if the first century church was eagerly expecting the Second Coming, which is supposedly seven years after the rapture then the millennial house of cards comes tumbling down.

The grammar of the text not only shows that "the blessed hope and the glorious appearing" are the same event, but it also shows that Titus was predicting what Jesus foretold in Matthew 16:27-28. Jesus said he was coming in *the glory of his father*. That event would be in the lifetime of his contemporaries. Mounce[418] shows that the grammar of the text indicates that Paul was saying that they were eagerly looking for, "the appearing of the glory of the great God," rather than the appearing of the great God. Ice and LaHaye say that Matthew 16:27-28 will ultimately be fulfilled at the Second Coming. Jesus said it would be in his generation. Paul affirms that the Christians at Crete were expecting it.

Another fact destructive to the millennial view is that Matthew 24 gives a major sign of the Second Coming. That sign would be the fulfillment of the World Mission (Matthew 24:14). Remember, the millennialists say the Second Coming was not near in the first century. However, they admit that Matthew 24 is about the Second Coming. Well, Jesus was asked for a sign of the Second Coming (Matthew 24:3). He said the fulfillment of the World Mission would be a sign the end was near (24:14). He told them that when they saw the sign they could know the end was near (24:32).

The New Testament writers are emphatic that the World Mission was fulfilled in their lifetime.[419] Paul said the gospel had been proclaimed to all the *nations* (Greek, *ethne*, Romans 16:25-26). He said the gospel had gone into all the world (*oikoumene*) and into all the earth (*ge*, Romans 10:18f). He said the gospel had been proclaimed and was bringing forth fruit in all the world (*kosmos*, Colossians 1:5). He even said the gospel had been preached to every creature (*ktisis*) under heaven (Colossians 1:23). Significantly, Paul uses *every single Greek word* used by Jesus to predict and command the preaching of the Gospel into all the world, to say it had been done! If the inspired writers used the identical words used by Jesus to say that what he had predicted and commanded to be done had been done, how is it possible to deny that it had been done?

Notice again Titus 2:11-13. Paul said that the gospel had been preached to every man offering salvation. That is a declaration of the fulfillment of the Mission. Jesus said the gospel would be preached to all nations then the end would come. Paul said the gospel had appeared to all men and then said they were "looking (expecting!) for the blessed hope." Paul was clearly building on what Jesus had said. The same thing is done in Romans 16. Paul avers the completion of the Mission (16:25-26) and proclaims that the destruction of Satan-- which is a Second Coming concept–would occur *shortly* (Greek, *en tachei,* Romans 16:20[420]).

In spite of this impressive evidence–and there is lots more-- Ice claims that the Mission was never fulfilled. He claims Paul was using the words that Jesus used in a different way. The problem is that Paul emphatically tells us that he got his gospel directly from Jesus (Galatians 1:11f). Thus, unless Jesus used the words in two radically different ways, then when Paul writes about what Jesus talked about, and uses the identical words that Jesus used, where is the justification for changing the meaning of Paul's words? No amount of rationalization can turn Paul's *"has been preached* to every creature," into, *"has not been preached* to every creature" without doing violence to the inspired Word. The World Mission was completed in the first century, and this proves that the Second Coming was near in the first century.

Finally, we want to quickly examine some of the passages that dispensationalists apply to the Second Coming. If it can be shown that the first century church expected the Second Coming, as we have noted, then the rapture is rejected. Our comments will be brief. Each of the passages listed below are listed by Ice and LaHaye as Second Coming passages that must according to them be delineated from the rapture.

1.) Daniel 2:44-45– In the days of the fourth world empire (Rome) the God of heaven would establish the eternal kingdom. Jesus came, along with John the Immerser and said, "The time is fulfilled, the kingdom of heaven is at hand." This means, without any doubt, that Jesus was saying that his Second Coming would occur in that generation. It is important to note that Ice and the millennialists admit that it was near when Jesus said this. Ice says that because the Jews rejected Jesus, "the kingdom is no longer near but postponed" (*Tribulation,* 115). Well, if the kingdom was near *then*, this means the Second Coming was near then, and if the Second Coming was near *then*, any doctrine of the rapture is impossible.

Do you understand that the millennialists believe *the Second Coming of Christ was postponed?* It is common to hear them say the *kingdom* was postponed. However, to say the kingdom was postponed *is to say the Second Coming was postponed* since the kingdom was to come at the Second Coming (Matthew 16:27-28). Ice is candid in this regard. He says, "the Second Coming of Christ has been postponed until after the current Church age" (*Call,* 19). But wait, if the Second Coming was postponed, then...

✔ *The rapture was postponed.* After all, you can't say that the Second Coming is near without saying the rapture is even nearer. Thus, if the kingdom was near, the rapture was even nearer, but since the kingdom was postponed, the rapture was postponed.

✔The Man of Sin was postponed. This means of course that *he had to have been alive when Jesus said the kingdom is at hand.* Think about that for a long moment. The Bible did not predict many different *"men* of Sin." There was *only one* "man of sin" and he was of necessity alive in the first century according to the dispensational postponement doctrine.
✔The signing of a peace treaty was postponed.
✔The destruction and rebuilding of the temple was postponed (that presents some daunting challenges to say the least!).
✔The breaking of the peace treaty was postponed.
✔The appearance of the Two Witnesses was postponed. Were they alive then? How can you say that the kingdom was near in the first century without saying the Two Witnesses were alive? But if they were already alive, then any appearance of Two Witnesses in the future means that God's original plan had gone awry.
✔The 144,000 virgin, Jewish evangelists to fulfill the Great Commission were postponed. But of course, just like the Man of Sin, if they were postponed this means that the 144,000 *were alive* when Jesus said, "The kingdom is at hand!" What happened to those guys?
✔And, of course, if the 144,000 were postponed this means that the preaching of the Gospel into all the world was postponed. The problem is, as we have just seen, the inspired Word of God says the World Mission was completed in the first century.

A brief word here about the 144,000. Revelation 14:4 tells us these saints, "were redeemed from among men, being the first fruits unto God and the Lamb." It does not say they were or will be the first fruits of the Tribulation. It says they were *the first fruits of these redeemed to God!* This absolutely precludes the possibility that they could be anyone alive today or in the future. *These were the first generation of Jewish Christians.* Thus, James wrote to his first century Jewish audience and said, "Of His own will he begat us with the Word of truth, that we should be a kind of first fruits of his creatures." Here are the first fruits unto God alive in the first century! Further, the Hebrews writer told his (Jewish) audience, "you have come unto mount Sion, and unto the city of the living God, the heavenly Jerusalem, and to an innumerable company of angels, to the general assembly and *church of the first born* (The Greek of the text is in the plural. Thus, "the first born ones." My emphasis).

The point should be clear. Revelation 7 and 14 are discussing events that would happen involving *the first fruit of the redeemed.* Only the first century, *first generation of Christians* qualify as the first fruits unto God and the Lamb. How many generations removed from that first fruit generation are we now? How many generations of those redeemed unto God and the Lamb have come and gone? No other generation could ever be the generation of the first born unto God and the Lamb than that first century generation. This means that any discussion of a future rapture is reduced to rubble by the first century presence of the first fruits unto God.

✔ The Great Tribulation was postponed. Of course, if it was postponed this means it *should* have occurred in Jesus' generation just as Matthew 24 indicates.

You see, you can't just blithely say the kingdom was postponed without saying that every constituent

> **No other generation could ever be "the first born unto God and the Lamb" than that first century generation.**

element associated with the kingdom was postponed as well. Okay, I promised to be brief, so let's take a look at some other passages.

2.) Daniel 12:1-3-- Ice and LaHaye insist that this is a Second Coming text (*Charting*, 111). However, Daniel 12:7 says this prophecy would be fulfilled, "When the power of the holy people has been completely shattered." The power of the holy people was shattered in AD 70. Therefore the Second Coming occurred in AD 70.

3.) Matthew 13:41– Amazingly, Ice and LaHaye list this as a Second Coming text (*Charting*, 111). Here is the problem.

They insist that the *rapture* terminates the church age.

But, Matthew 13 is about the end of the age. (Whatever age it is, it is the age in which Jesus was living at the time, see verses 39-40).

So, what age ends at the Second Coming? It can't be the church age since per Ice and LaHaye the church age ended at the *rapture seven years before the Second Coming.* (See our comments about *Who's On First?*)

The other problem with Matthew 13:41 is that it would be fulfilled, *"When the righteous shine forth as the sun"* (v. 43). This is a quote of Daniel 12:3. As we have seen, Daniel 12 is about the end of the age of Israel, "When the power of the holy people has been completely shattered." Matthew 13 has nothing to do with the end of the Christian age.

4.) 2 Thessalonians 1:6-10– See our discussion of this text above. Paul promised living human beings, suffering the pressure of tribulation that they would receive *relief from that persecution,* "when the Lord Jesus is revealed from heaven" (v. 7). Did Paul's promise to those saints fail? Was he mistaken? There is no doubt, if language means anything, that Paul gave those brethren the belief and hope that Christ was coming back to give them relief *in their lifetime.* The only question is, Did Jesus keep his word, or did he give them a false hope?

If 2 Thessalonians is a Second Coming text, and of course it is, then it is obvious that the first century saints were expecting it in their lifetime. This belies the claim by Ice that the first century saints were not looking for "that glorious appearing."

5.) Revelation 1:7, 22:7, 12, 20– How many times, and in how many ways does God have to say something before we will take Him seriously? The book of Revelation tells us, as a Revelation from the Father, that the events being foretold in the book were "at hand" and, "must shortly come to pass" (Revelation 1:1-3). And yet, almost every futurist paradigm ignores, distorts, or seeks in other ways to mitigate the meaning of those words. If we take these time statements seriously there is no possible way to place that event in the present or future.

If the *parousia*, i.e. the Second Coming of Revelation was near to John it is obvious that futurism is falsified. You cannot admit that the Second Coming was near in the first century and then claim that the NT writers were not looking for it. LaHaye and Ice claim, "The apostles and the church of the first three centuries whole-heartedly expected that Christ would return for His church during their lifetime" (*Charting*, 50). The problem is that the apostles were inspired. Those who came after them were not. To say that the expectation of the apostles failed is to deny their inspiration. Why did they expect the return of Christ, whether rapture or Second Coming, in their lifetime? Because the Holy Spirit said, *"The coming of the Lord has drawn near"* (James 5:8-9) *"In a very, very little while, the one who is coming will come, and will not tarry"* (Hebrews 10:37) *"the end of all things has drawn near"* (1 Peter 4:7) and, *"Behold, I come quickly!"* They not only believed that Christ was coming back in their lifetime, they taught it as Divine Truth. Were they wrong?

Notice something in regard to Revelation 1:7. What would be the purpose of the coming in view? Take a close look. Does it not refer directly to "the tribes of the earth"? The Greek word *phule*, translated tribes, is used about 31 times in the NT, and only a very few times does it not refer to the 12 tribes of Israel. Further, at the coming of Jesus in view, "those who pierced him" would mourn. This is Christ coming in judgment of those who killed him!

When Jesus was on trial, Pilate washed his hands of Jesus' innocent blood. In response, the Jews cried out, "Let his blood be on us and on our children!" (Matthew 27:25). Revelation is the record of God's response to their prayer. Revelation is about the time of the avenging of the blood of the prophets, foretold by Jesus in Matthew 23 (cf. Revelation 16:6-7). The book is about the judgment of the city, "where the Lord was slain" (Revelation 11:8). It is about the time of judgment of the city, outside of which, no prophet could perish (Luke 13:31). It is the city that had killed the apostles and prophets of Jesus (Revelation 18:20, 24).[421] The destruction and judgment of that city was "at hand." It was not 2000 years away. This being true, the millennial rapture theory falls. Here is our argument in succinct form.

If the first century church was expecting the Second Coming of Christ to occur in their lifetime the doctrine of the rapture is destroyed.

The first century church *was expecting the Second Coming* to occur in their lifetime.

Therefore, the doctrine of the rapture is destroyed.

Let me remind you of something. Our millennial friends tell us that this text speaks of the removal of the church from the earth at the end of the Christian age. Furthermore, they tell us that the hope of the church and the hope of Israel are two distinct, even disparate hopes, unrelated to each other.

In the millennial paradigm, 1 Thessalonians is the key rapture text. And yet, a comparison of what we have seen and emphasized in this work so far will dispel the millennial view of the rapture, Israel and the church. Consider the following.

> The millennialists claim that the church was never predicted in the Old Testament, and had nothing to do with the promises to Israel.
> Paul said his gospel was *nothing* but the hope of Israel found in Moses and the prophets.
> This means that whatever else we might think of 1 Thessalonians 4, *Paul found it in God's promises to Israel in the OT!*
> Thus, the millennial view of Thessalonians is falsified.

Paul said that his gospel, his eschatology, was *nothing*[422] but the hope of Israel and he preached that doctrine from the Old Covenant prophets (Acts 26:21f; 28:18f; Romans 16:25-26). This means that whatever else we might think of 1 Thessalonians 4 *it was an expression of the Old Covenant hope of Israel!* If, therefore, 1 Thessalonians 4 is an expression of the "hope of Israel" found in Moses and the prophets then the millennial claim that it deals with the church separate and apart from the promises and hope of Israel are falsified. This deals a fatal blow to dispensationalism.

GAPS IN THE GAP THEORY

The rapture theory that is based on 1 Thessalonians 4 depends *totally* upon a gap between the sixty ninth and the seventieth week of Daniel 9. Read again what Ice says: "Without a futurized (i.e. postponed, DKP) seventieth week, the dispensational system falls apart. *There can be no pre-tribulational rapture* (my emphasis, DKP) great tribulation, or rebuilt temple without the gap."[423] Do you catch that? Without a gap between the sixty ninth and the seventieth week, there is no rapture doctrine. See the discussion again on the atonement and "putting away of sin." At this juncture, I want to present some thoughts on the Gap Theory, to show the falsity of that view.[424]

If there is a gap in the text between the sixty ninth and the seventieth week of Daniel then: Jesus either *did or did not know* about it.

If there is a gap of 2000 years in Daniel 9 and if Jesus knew there was a gap then when he announced the nearness of the kingdom (*i.e. the end of the seventieth week*) he was purposely *giving the wrong impression* to his audience, or, he *did not know how long the gap was to be.* You see, the establishment of the kingdom belongs to the end of the seventieth week. Therefore, if there was a gap in the text of Daniel 9 and Jesus knew of it, but told his audience the kingdom was near even though he knew there was still 2000 years to go, then he was being deceitful.

If there is a gap in Daniel 9 and Jesus knew it, but *did not know* how long it was supposed to be, *his knowledge of Daniel's prophecy is impugned.* Yet, for Jesus to *say* that the end of the seventieth week was near demands that *he thought he knew* what Daniel actually predicted. If he thought he knew but didn't, clearly this impugns his Deity. *Jesus claimed to know what time it was*!

If there is a gap in Daniel 9, and *Jesus knew* of it, he should have known that he could not even *truthfully* offer the kingdom to Israel. If there is a gap of 2000 years and Jesus knew of it, then he had to know that the kingdom was *not near* and he could not truthfully offer Israel the fulfillment of her hope.

If there is a gap in Daniel 9, then even if Jesus did ostensibly offer the kingdom, *Israel could not accept that offer* because the prophecy of the kingdom was not truly for Jesus' generation.

If there is *no gap in the text* of Daniel 9:24-27 and Jesus said the kingdom, which is to come *at the end of the seventieth week*, was at hand then *Jesus was right* to say the kingdom, for the end of the seventieth week, was near.

If there is no gap in the text of Daniel 9, but the kingdom was postponed due to Jewish rebellion, then it must be true that the Lord *created a gap* between the sixty ninth and seventieth that was *not originally in the text* of Daniel 9. This means that Daniel's original prediction *failed*. This also means *Jesus failed* in his prediction of the nearness of the kingdom. This means that God failed since He supposedly sent his Son, "at just the right time" to fulfill Daniel's prophecy.

If there is no gap and if Jesus would have established the kingdom (Ice *Tribulation,* 115) had the Jews not rejected him, this means that *Jesus was right* to say the kingdom, and thus the end of the seventieth week, was at hand. But if there is no gap and Jesus was right to say the kingdom was near, then if God did not establish the kingdom as Jesus promised, Daniel's prophecy failed. Jesus failed. God failed.

As you can see, there can be no gap in the prophecy of Daniel 9, thus the rapture doctrine is reduced to Rubble.

ONE TAKEN, ONE LEFT?

If there is no rapture, what about the passages that say that at the coming of the Lord, "Two men will be in the field, one taken and the other left. Two women shall be grinding at the mill: one will be taken and the other left" (Matthew 24:40-41)? Doesn't this passage and those like it, teach a rapture? These passages do teach a "catching away," but you and I would not want to be part of this kind of rapture!

Notice that the context of the "rapture" in Matthew 24:40f is the discussion of judgment. Just as the flood came and took away the unbelievers of Noah's day, "So also will the coming of the Son of Man be." This rapture was the snatching away to destruction, not a catching away to glory! Even Dwight Pentecost admits this to be the case in the Matthean text.[425] The context in Luke 17 is identical.

So, what does this terminology refer to? As noted, it is the idea of judgment. This comports well with the idea that some being taken while some are left was a perfectly understood idiom in the Biblical world. In describing the invasion of Judah by Nebuchadnezzar, the author of 2 Kings twice took note of the fact that the Babylonians had, "carried into captivity all Jerusalem: all the men of valor...all the craftsmen and smiths. None remained except the poorest people of the land...Nebuzaradan carried away captive the rest of the people...but the captain of the guard left some of the poor of the land" (2 Kings 24:14f; 25:11).

What we are saying is that the terminology "one taken, one left" was from the ancient world. It was a commonly understood reference to the invasion and conquering of a nation when the best of the citizens were taken as slaves while the poorest were left to eke out a living from a desolated land. Lamsa says this phraseology was a common idiom of the first century world: "During the persecutions and wars when a town is conquered by the enemy the young girl at the house and the boy in the field are taken captive, but the old woman and the old man are left."[426] You did not want to be involved in this kind of *rapture*.

So, what have we seen in regard to the rapture? We have shown that the early church looked forward to only *one* coming of the Lord and that it would occur in their lifetime. The repeated, unambiguous statements in the NT that the *parousia* was near cannot be ignore. They prove that the coming of the Lord, however you wish to define it, was not a long time away. This fact alone destroys the rapture doctrine.

We have shown that the attempt to delineate between a coming of Christ *for* the saints and a coming of Christ *with* the saints breaks down on even a cursory reading of the texts. Matthew 24:31, which is supposed to be the Second Coming of Christ *with* the saints says not one word about coming *with* the saints, but his coming *for* the saints. On the other hand, 1 Thessalonians 4, which is supposed to be the *parousia for* the saints contains *both* the coming *with* the saints and the coming *for* the saints. There is no justification for two comings based on a coming for the saints versus coming with the saints.

We have examined the millennial doctrine of *imminent but not near* and shown that it is self-contradictory, illogical, and unbiblical. The idea that the necessity for any prophetic event that must occur before the imminent event destroys imminence, actually destroys the rapture doctrine. There were *many* prophetic events that had to take place before the rapture, and yet *the millennialists admit* that the NT writers say the rapture was imminent. If the NT writers knew that the fall of Jerusalem, the restoration of Israel in 1948, the passing of the Seven Church ages, etc. had to occur before the rapture, and of course they (supposedly) did, then *they could not say the rapture was near*. The New Testament is clear that they did affirm the nearness of Christ's coming. This mitigates the millennial doctrine of imminence. Without this aspect of their doctrine the rapture theory is ruptured.

We have shown that the first century saints were looking for the Second Coming. The millennialists say this could not be true. It is true however, and therefore the rapture doctrine is false.

We have shown that the foundational necessity for the validity of the rapture theory, a gap between the sixty ninth and the seventieth week of Daniel 9, is wrong. Without a gap between the sixty ninth and the seventieth week there is no dispensationalism. We have proven that there is no gap between the weeks. The rapture doctrine is falsified.

COMINGS AND MORE COMINGS:
A BRIEF EXAMINATION OF PARTIAL PRETERISM

There is a group of Bible students that call themselves "partial preterists," who gladly accept the fact that the New Testament writers affirmed that Jesus was indeed to return in judgment in the first century and that he kept those promises when he returned in A. D. 70. However, these same students believe there is a yet future *parousia*, judgment and resurrection at the "last day." 1 Thessalonians 4 is considered a strong fortress in defense of a yet future coming. Gentry says 1 Thessalonians 4, "refers to the visible, glorious, second advent to conclude history" (*Dominion*, 1992, 279). Strimple claims that 1 Thessalonians must be referent to the end of human history, and, "This passage gives hyper-preterists great difficulty" (*WSTTB*, 342f).

We have effectively destroyed that myth. However, we want to examine a fundamental element of the partial preterist view, that in Thessalonians Paul speaks of two different comings. It is held that Paul speaks of the "final" coming of Christ at the end of the current Christian age. He also supposedly speaks of Jesus' coming in judgment of Israel in AD 70.

Our purpose is to show that Paul speaks of only one coming in Thessalonians. With that truth established, the partial preterist fortress for a future coming is stormed and captured. If no text in Thessalonians speaks of a yet future *parousia* and resurrection, then no Biblical text does. I am not aware of any partial preterists that would deny this. We will proceed by examining some of the arguments for multiple comings, and couple that with the evidence we have already presented.

For ease of reference, we will focus our comments on the arguments of Gentry.[427] He is a prolific author and an ardent advocate of the partial preterist movement. In addition, Gentry is vehemently opposed to the true preterist paradigm presented in this work,[428] insisting that since it is not found in any of the creeds it is false. Our investigation will chronicle Gentry's view on each of the major eschatological passages in both Thessalonians epistles. Gentry believes that both the AD 70 *parousia* and a yet future, end of history *epiphany* are taught in these letters. We will examine his reasons for delineating between the "comings" and present our objection to his posit.

Gentry's views on the various passages in Thessalonians follows:
1.) 1 Thessalonians 4:13-18– Gentry says this is the final coming of Christ at the end of human history. (*Dominion*, 1992, 387).
2.) 2 Thessalonians 1:7-10– Gentry says this text refers to a final future coming of Christ, because it speak of, "'everlasting destruction from the presence of the Lord,' being brought against the opposers of Christ."[429]
3.) 2 Thessalonians 2–Gentry applies 2 Thessalonians 2 to Christ's judgment coming in AD 70.[430]

What are Gentry's reasons for delineating between these texts? In *Dominion*, (1992, 388ff) Gentry argues that the coming of 2 Thessalonians 1:10 is different from that of chapter 2 since in chapter 1, "Paul even employs a different word for the coming of Christ (*elthe*) than he does in 2:1 (*parousia*). There the Second Adventual judgment brings 'everlasting destruction from the presence of the Lord:' here the temporal judgment makes no mention of these mighty angels (2:1-12)."

Gentry's arguments are specious, and his newest tome proves it. In his revised (2009) *Dominion* book, Gentry comments on the coming of Matthew 21:40, which he applies to AD 70, and the coming of Christ in Matthew 24:27, which he likewise applies to the Lord's AD 70 coming. Matthew 21:40 uses *elthe*, while Matthew 24:27 uses *parousia*. Per Gentry's hermeneutic on 2 Thessalonians 1 and chapter 2, this should *demand* that Matthew 21 and 24 speak of two different comings of the Lord. Not so, per Gentry, however! He says, "That Mt. 21:40 uses the Greek term *elthe* (from *erchomai*) and Mt. 24:27 use the term *parousia*, does not harm this comparison. Both terms can apply to the second coming of Christ." (*Dominion*, 2009, 353).

According to Gentry, because Paul used *elthe* and *parousia* in Thessalonians this demands two different comings. However, when Jesus used *elthe* and *parousia* we need not see two different comings. Per Gentry's own argument *elthe* and *parousia* can and do refer to the same event, the AD 70 coming of Christ. He has effectively falsified his own argument on 2 Thessalonians 1 and 2.

If the coming of 2 Thessalonians 1 must be different from that of chapter 2 because a different word is used and because angels are mentioned in chapter 1 but not in chapter 2, this creates hermeneutical chaos.[431] Furthermore, *Gentry flatly rejects this hermeneutic when it is used by the millennialists.*

Noted millennialist John Walvoord sought to delineate between Christ's coming in Thessalonians as the rapture, and other texts because Thessalonians contains elements not found in other texts, and because it does not mention elements found in other texts. What does Gentry think of such a hermeneutic? Here is his response to the dispensational hermeneutic:

"But how can this prove a distinction between the rapture and the second advent? Does not Walvoord admit a limited design for the passage: to comfort Christians concerning the resurrection of deceased loved ones? Why would Paul have to provide a whole complex of eschatological phenomena? The dispensational argument is one from silence, based on a preconceived theory" (*Dominion*, 2009, 286).

In response, one might well suggest to Mr. Gentry; "Thou art the man!" The millennialists say that Thessalonians is different from other texts because it does not contain all the eschatological elements. Gentry cries "Foul!" Yet,

Gentry says that 2 Thessalonians 1 is a different coming of the Lord from that in 2 Thessalonians 1 because chapter 1 contains an element not found in chapter 2, i.e. the angels. Might we not ask: "Why would Paul have to provide a whole complex of eschatological phenomena?" Why would Paul have to mention every eschatological element in every text?

Again, the millennialists argue from the silence of certain texts in regard to certain eschatological elements and Gentry says: "The dispensational argument is one from silence, based on a preconceived theory." We concur, but this is *precisely* what Gentry does as well.

The millennialists are simply employing Gentry's own hermeneutic to prove two different comings. Gentry rejects this insisting that there is no rapture distinct from the Second Coming. But if Gentry can dichotomize between comings based on "coming with the angels" versus no angels mentioned, why can't Walvoord, Ice, et. al., delineate between a coming *for the saints* and a coming *with the saints*? Let's look closer at Gentry's hermeneutic.

In Acts 1, the angel told the disciples that Jesus would *come* (*eleusetai*, future form of *erchomai*). *Elthe* is also a cognate of *erchomai*. There is no substantive difference between *elthe* and *erchomai, and Gentry would agree*. This is important as we shall see. In 2 Thessalonians 1, *elthe* is not the same word as *parousia* used in 1 Thessalonians 4. Not only that, in Acts 1 there is not a hint of the destruction of the universe as is found in 2 Peter 3, per Gentry. There is no shout of the Arch-Angel, no sounding of the Trumpet, no raising of the dead as in Thessalonians. There is nothing said about Christ judging the world and sitting on his throne as in Matthew 25:31f. In fact, the *majority* of the constituent elements that Gentry associates with a yet future end of the Christian age *are absent from Acts 1*. And Acts 1 uses a different word from that used in other texts that Gentry applies to the future.

So, Acts 1 and 1 Thessalonians 4 use different words. Acts omits many elements that Thessalonians mentions. Yet Gentry affirms that Acts 1 and Thessalonians speak of the same event. However, he claims that because 2 Thessalonians 1 uses a different word from that used in chapter 2, and because chapter 1 includes an element not mentioned in chapter 2 that this demands that chapter 1 and chapter 2 speak of different events. This is hardly consistent.

Let's look closer. Gentry says 2 Thessalonians 2:1f must refer to the AD 70 coming of Christ because it uses a different word from chapter 1, and because there are elements mentioned in chapter 1 that are not mentioned in chapter 2. Well, 1 Thessalonians 3:13 speaks of the coming of Christ *with all his saints*. This is parallel with chapter 4:13f since that chapter speaks of Christ coming with the saints (4:15-17).

Here is the interesting thing, 1 Thessalonians 3:13 uses the word *parousia*. Chapter 4 also uses *parousia*, and *2 Thessalonians 2:1* uses *parousia*. Gentry says 2 Thessalonians 2:1 has to be the AD 70 coming because it does not use the same word as 2 Thessalonians 1:7f. So, *parousia* in 2 Thessalonians 2:1 is the word for the A. D. 70 coming. However, if *parousia* is the AD 70 event then 1 Thessalonians 4 must also be the AD 70 event. Yet, Gentry says 1 Thessalonians 4 is *not* AD 70.

How can Gentry argue on the one hand that *parousia* in 2 Thessalonians 2 must refer to AD 70 because it is different from chapter 1, but then turn around and insist that *the identical word* in 1 Thessalonians 4 has to mean the same thing that 2 Thessalonians 1 meant after all? If Paul was drawing a distinction between *parousia* and *elthe* in 2 Thessalonians why would he have used *parousia* in his first epistle to refer to an event unrelated to the events of the A. D. 70 *parousia*?

Per Gentry's argument, 2 Thessalonians 1 has to refer to the future because it uses the Greek word *elthe* and not *parousia* as does chapter 2. However, Luke 18:8 and Matthew 21:40 use *elthe* and not *parousia to speak of Christ's coming*. Furthermore, Matthew 24:30 uses *erchomai*, from which *elthe* is taken, and verse 27 uses *parousia*. To what does Gentry apply these texts? *To the AD 70 coming of Christ against Israel!*[432]

Consider now Matthew 13 and the parable of the Wheat and Tares. As we have seen, Gentry applies this parable to the current church age that will supposedly terminate in the end of human history (*House*, 196, *Dominion*, 2009, 247). It is not too much to say that Matthew 13 is one of the kingpins of the postmillennial view. For the moment, we want only to examine Gentry's contention that the use of different words demands different comings. See our discussion of Daniel 12 and Matthew 13 above.

When speaking of the gathering at his coming, Jesus used the word *sullego*. This word is used eight times in the New Testament and six of those times are in Matthew 13. What is interesting is that in Matthew 13:47, Jesus used a cognate of *episunagogee* to illustrate *sullego*. Clearly, *episunagogee* and *sullego* are used synonymously by Jesus. The trouble for Gentry is that he believes *episunagogee* speaks of Christ's coming in AD 70 in Matthew 24:31 *and* in 2 Thessalonians 2:1-2.

If *episunagogee* is referent to AD 70 why did Jesus use it in a passage that Gentry insists can apply only to the end of human history? Further, why did Jesus use a word in Matthew 13, *sullego*, that neither he nor any of the New Testament authors ever use again to speak of the gathering of the elect? Why didn't Paul use *sullego* to speak of the gathering in 1 Thessalonians 4. *Why did he use a different word?*

Furthermore, Gentry's argument about the use or non-use of words falls on hard times in regard to the coming of Christ. Gentry believes that Matthew

13 speaks of the final coming of Christ at the end of human history. Yet, strangely enough, the text says *not one word* about the *coming* of the Son of Man!⁴³³ Jesus did not use the word *erchomai*, its cognate *elthe*, the word *parousia, epiphany, apocalupsis, or any other of the normal words used to describe his coming!* So, if one wanted to "get technical" about the use of words it could be argued that since none of the normal words for "coming" are even used, but instead, the text speaks only of the Son of Man *"sending forth his angels,"* then Matthew 13 must refer to some event that is different even from 1 Thessalonians 4:13f. Yet, Gentry has no problem applying both passages to the same event.

Remember that Gentry argues that 2 Thessalonians 2 is AD 70 while 2 Thessalonians 1 is the "end of the world." He argues this because chapter 1 refers to Christ coming with the angels but chapter 2 makes no such reference. This hermeneutic brings nothing but grief to Gentry in other passages. Matthew 13 is a prime example. Where is the mention of the sounding of the Trumpet? Not there. However, it is in Matthew 24:29-31 a text Gentry applies to AD 70!

Matthew 13 says not one word about the coming on the clouds. Yet, Matthew 24:30 does use this motif as does Matthew 26:64. And yes, Gentry applies Matthew 26:64 to AD 70 as well.

Matthew 13 makes *no mention* of the shout of God or the shout of the Arch-Angel as 1 Thessalonians 4 does. Yet, Gentry insists that Matthew 13 and 1 Thessalonians 4 are parallel.

Finally, 1 Thessalonians 4 says not one word about *the end of the age (sunteleia ton aionion*, a distinctive Greek term). Yet Gentry has no problem affirming that 1 Thessalonians 4 is about the end of the age.

So, in Matthew 13 Jesus uses a very distinctive Greek term *(sunteleia ton aionion)* and Gentry says this *must* be the end of the Christian age.

However, in Matthew 24:3 that identical distinctive term is used and Gentry says that it applies to the end of the Mosaic age in AD 70.

1 Thessalonians 4 does not use that distinctive term. Yet Gentry affirms that Thessalonians is about the end of the Christian age.

Do you see the problem? It is very real. The attempt to delineate between comings based on the use of different words for coming or for gathering is specious. It backfires on Gentry at every turn. This is proven finally by the fact that Matthew 13 cannot refer to the end of human history.

Take note that in Matthew 13:43 Jesus summarizes the teaching of the parable and says that when the gathering occurred, "Then shall the righteous shine forth as the sun in the kingdom of their Father. He who has ears to hear, let him hear." *This is a direct allusion to Daniel 12:3.* Why is this so important? It is because Daniel was predicting the end of the age just as Jesus was. It is important because Daniel was predicting the time of the resurrection just as Jesus was. The point is that in Matthew 13 Jesus was saying that Daniel 12 would be fulfilled at the time of the gathering. So, when would/will this be? As we have seen, Gentry gives two disjunctive, unrelated answers. He affirms that Daniel 12 was fulfilled in AD 70, but that Matthew 13 will be at the end of human history. Unfortunately, Gentry offers no exegetical proof for his claim. It is mere assertion.

The prophet saw and overheard two angels discussing the vision of the Great Tribulation, the resurrection, and the end of the age. One angel asked another when all (not some, or most, but *all*) of these things would be fulfilled. Heaven's answer challenges all futurist eschatologies: "When the power of the holy people is completely shattered, all these things will be fulfilled" (Daniel 12:7). So, the end of the age and the resurrection/harvest predicted by Jesus in Matthew 13 would occur when the power of the holy people was completely shattered.

Who are the holy people? It is undoubtedly Old Covenant Israel. Old Israel is the only people that scripture says would be destroyed and give way to another "new" people (Psalms 102; Isaiah 65:8f, etc.). The "holy people" cannot be the church since even Daniel was told that the kingdom that God would establish would never be destroyed. The church will never pass away (Ephesians 3:20-21). Amazingly however, Mathison suggests that, "'the shattering of the power of the holy people' is likely referring to a persecution of believers prior to the second coming of Christ." (*Age*, 2009, 283). This is a direct contradiction to Daniel's declaration that the kingdom would never be shattered (Daniel 2:44; 7:13-14). Mathison is forced to this view however, because he refuses to accept that Daniel is speaking to and about Israel, and emphatically posits the resurrection at the end of her age. To avoid the preterist view, he takes a position that directly denies the inspired declarations that the church will never be destroyed.

Thus, from Daniel we have *prima facie* evidence that the end of the age and the time of the resurrection is linked with the end of the Old Covenant age of Israel, not the end of the Christian age.

So, what we have is this. Gentry applies Matthew 13 to the end of the Christian age in spite of the fact that the Bible says *the Christian age will never end.* Gentry says that Matthew 13 is parallel with 1 Thessalonians 4 even though Matthew 13 and 1 Thessalonians 4 do not use the same words. Thessalonians does not mention the end of the age and Matthew does not mention the Trumpet of God. Matthew is silent about the Shout of God, the arch-angel and the coming on the clouds, while Thessalonians includes these motifs. Of course, most destructive of all, Jesus said that the end of the age would be the time of the resurrection in fulfillment of Daniel 12 at the end of the Old Covenant age of Israel, not the end of the Christian age.

Consider this: *the fundamental error* of Gentry, Mathison (*Age*, 2009, 361) and most evangelicals in regard to Matthew 13 is that they view the parable *through the eyes of the church*, and not through the eyes of Israel. They see the *harvest* in the context of the harvest of the Gentile world and the church at the end of human history. This sadly overlooks several critical elements.

☛ Jesus' mission was specifically to Israel (Matthew 15:24).

☛ Jesus came to confirm the promises made to the fathers (Romans 15:8) i.e. OT Israel.

☛ Jesus came to gather together (*sunagagen*) the children of God scattered abroad (literally the children of God "having been scattered abroad" (*dieskorpismena*, third person plural, neuter participle passive, John 11:52). This is the gathering (*episunagogee*) of Matthew 23:37, 24:31; 2 Thessalonians 2:1, etc..

☛ John the Baptizer said that the time of the harvest was near, and Jesus already had the winnowing fork in his hand (Matthew 3:10f).

☛ Jesus agreed that the time of harvest was present (John 4:35).

☛ The promise of the harvest was an OT promise made to Israel. Israel, the ten northern tribes, had "sown the wind" and as a result she had "reaped the whirlwind" (Hosea 8:7). The ten northern tribes were sown in the earth as a result of her sin and was destroyed, never to rise again nationally, geo-politically (Amos 5:1-2). Judah was likewise facing a similar "harvest" (Hosea 6:11, i.e. destruction) in the last days. This would be when YHVH would "return the captives" (Hosea 6:11).[434] In other words, the harvest was a good news, bad news issue, just as depicted in Matthew 13.

Just like the ten tribes were destroyed politically, but would be restored in Messiah– see our discussion of Isaiah 49– Judah likewise had to be "harvested" in the end times. She would be destroyed *nationally*, but restored in Messiah. This is the harvest of Revelation 14 in the judgment of Babylon, i.e. Judah / Jerusalem, the city where the Lord was slain (Revelation 11:8; 14:8ff). The Old Jerusalem / Judah was to pass. The New Jerusalem would stand triumphant.

☛ Jesus links the parables, specifically the parable of the Wheat / Tares, to Isaiah 6:9f and the purpose of *hardening the hearts of the unbelieving Jews,* to justify God's coming judgment on them (Matthew 13:34-35).[435] The parables are not, as Mathison suggests (*Age*, 2009, 361) told to harden the hearts of modern man so that God might bring judgment on the world of today. Just as in the days of Isaiah, the message went to Israel and they rejected the message justifying God's judgment on them. Jesus told the parables to Israel of his day, to harden the hearts of the unbelievers,[436] justifying God's impending judgment on them.[437]

> **The parables were not told to the church, about the church, to harden the heart of the church! The parables were spoken *to Israel, about Israel*, to harden the hearts of unbelieving Israel, to justify God's impending judgment. The failure to honor these indisputable facts has led to the creation of a false "Christian" eschatology.**

Much more could be said on this, but, the bottom line is that it is misguided to interpret the parable of the Wheat/Tares through the eyes of the church and a modern cosmology. The story has to do with Israel and her promises. It is about Israel and her last days, and the ushering in of the age to come at the end of her age, as Gentry admits the OT prophets foresaw.

When we interpret Matthew 13 through the prism of the harvest of Old Covenant Israel and the ushering in of the age to come at the end of Israel's aeon, it demands a first century fulfillment and destroys the futurism of Gentry, Mathison, et. al.

Gentry contends, and we agree, that Matthew 13 and 1 Thessalonians 4 are parallel. But, if Matthew 13 speaks of the end of Israel's Old Covenant age (as Daniel unambiguously affirms) then it must be true that 1 Thessalonians 4 is referent to the end of the Old Covenant age of Israel in AD 70, even though Matthew 13 and 1 Thessalonians use several different words and omit several different motifs to describe the same time and event.

Consider Gentry's argument that the use of different words in the same context demands two comings in regard to the Olivet Discourse. Gentry believes that all of Matthew 24, through verse 35 was fulfilled in the AD 70 catastrophe. What then do we have in the Discourse? We have Christ's *coming (parousia*, v. 27) and his *coming (erchomai*, v. 30) with the angels (v. 30-31) and the gathering of the saints. Gentry *agrees* that this coming would be in judgment of Israel for her persecutorial ways.

Does Gentry believe there are two different comings in verse 27 and verses 29-31? No. Even though *the same two different words* are used in Matthew that are used in Thessalonians, Gentry understands that verse 27[438] and vs. 29-31 speak of the same coming. And, although different words are used to describe the same event we have the coming *with the angels*!

Okay, so in Matthew 24 we have *parousia, erchomai, angels*, the gathering of the saints and the avenging of the martyrs. Gentry says this all applies to AD 70. Well, in 2 Thessalonians 1 and 2 we have *erchomai* (*elthe*, 1:10) *parousia*, (2:1) angels (1:7f) and the avenging of the martyrs (1:7f). Every constituent element that Gentry links to the AD *parousia in Matthew* is present in Thessalonians. Yet in Thessalonians he sees two comings separated by millennia.[439]

Not only does Matthew 24 use both *parousia* and *erchomai* (from whence *elthe* comes) but Matthew 24:30 also speaks of Christ coming *with the angels*. Remember, Gentry says 2 Thessalonians 1 is future because it speaks of Christ coming with the angels, but chapter 2 is different because it has no angels. However, in 2 Thessalonians 2:1, Gentry says, "the 'gathering together to Him' Paul mentions in 2:1 seems to reflect Matthew 24:31" (*Dominion*, 2009, 389). But, if 2 Thessalonians 2 is Matthew 24:31, then this means that 2 Thessalonians 2 does in fact include the angels, and Gentry has falsified his own argument.

Notice another use of *parousia* as it relates to the context of 2 Thessalonians. In James 5:7-8, James urged his brethren, being persecuted for the name of Christ to, "be faithful until the coming of the Lord...the coming of the Lord has drawn near." Gentry applies James and 2 Thessalonians to the first century judgment of Israel.[440] Notice that although James says *nothing* about Jesus' coming to destroy the Man of Sin, Gentry has no problem applying James to the same event as 2 Thessalonians 2.

So, since James, and Paul in 2 Thessalonians 2, both use *parousia*, so far so good. But here is what is so significant. James was writing to a *specific audience* being persecuted for their faith. He urges them to *patience*, with the promise of *imminent vindication* and relief at the *coming* (*parousia*) of the Lord. Remember these facts, they are significant in light of Gentry's hermeneutic. In 2 Thessalonians 1, which Gentry applies to the future, Paul was writing *to a specific audience being persecuted for their faith* just like those in James and he promises them *imminent relief from their persecution at the coming of the Lord*. However, instead of using *parousia* like James, Paul used the word *elthe*.

The use of different words in James and Thessalonians clearly does not mean that two different events separated by millennia are in view. In 2 Thessalonians 1 and 2, the theme is the same, persecution and vindication / relief at the imminent coming of the Lord. James uses *parousia*. Paul used *elthe*, but they are both speaking of the same time and event. Patently, a different coming is not in view in each of these texts.

Let's continue our investigation a little further. Gentry believes that 1 Thessalonians 4:13-18 deals with the future coming of Christ. He believes that 1 Corinthians 15 speaks of the same event. However, remember that his premise is that 2 Thessalonians 1 and chapter 2 must refer to different comings because chapter 2 has some elements in it not used in chapter 1, and *vice versa*. Let's test that logic.

1 Thessalonians 4 mentions Christ coming (*parousia*) with the angels, a shout, the clouds and the Trumpet. 1 Corinthians 15 speaks of the coming of Christ (*parousia*) but says *nothing* about the angels, the clouds or the Angelic Shout. It does have the Trumpet. In addition 2 Peter 3 like Corinthians and Thessalonians, does speak of the *parousia*, but has *not a word* about coming with angels, the clouds, a trumpet, a shout *or the resurrection*, but does include the destruction of "heaven and earth." Yet, neither Corinthians nor Thessalonians says one syllable about the destruction of creation. Gentry applies all three of these texts to the future, final coming of Christ. However, here is the problem.

Gentry says Paul's use of *parousia* in 2 Thessalonians 2 has to apply to the AD 70 coming of Christ. Yet, this is *the identical word* used by Paul in 1 Corinthians 15, 1 Thessalonians 4 and in 2 Peter 3. Gentry says in these texts *parousia* cannot refer to the AD 70 coming.

Gentry would surely rejoin that in Corinthians, Thessalonians and 2 Peter, the common elements identify these passages as speaking of the same time and event even though certain elements are left out. In other words, the authors were simply emphasizing different aspects of the same event. Okay, *why does that not apply to 2 Thessalonians 1 and 2?* Is it not possible that although 2 Thessalonians 1 mentions the coming with the angels and chapter 2 does not that the same event is in view?

Likewise, consider this. 1 Thessalonians 4 speaks of the gathering to Christ and Gentry says this is yet future. Yet, 2 Thessalonians 2 also speaks of the gathering to Christ. Why are these different gatherings? We have shown that the gathering of 1 Thessalonians 4 is the same gathering of Matthew 24:31, and Gentry believes that the gathering of Matthew 24 and 2 Thessalonians 2 is the same. But if 2 Thessalonians 2 and Matthew 24 are the same, then 2 Thessalonians chapters 1 and 2, along with 1 Thessalonians 4 all refer to the same gathering. Could the Holy Spirit not use different words to speak of the same event? Is it not possible to use words interchangeably? Furthermore, to delineate between 2 Thessalonians 1 and chapter 2 because in chapter 1 the punishment of the persecutors is in view while in chapter 2 the focus is on the gathering, is myopic at best.

Does not chapter 2 speak of the punishment of the Man of Sin? Does not the Man of Sin *persecute the church*? Well, if the Man of Sin *persecutes the church* and is destroyed at the *coming of Christ* (v. 8) just exactly how is this different from chapter 1 where the persecutors of the Thessalonians were to be punished, "with everlasting destruction from the presence of the Lord"?[441]

The flow of the context in 2 Thessalonians 1 and 2 denies the possibility of two topics being under consideration. The reader of Gentry's work will probably miss the subtle emphasis placed on the chapter division. He appeals to the words in "chapter 2" versus "chapter 1." However, there were no chapter divisions in the original language. One cannot assume a change of topic because we now have the text divided into chapters. Gentry has attempted to create a false division in subject matter.

Gentry emphasizes that in chapter 1 the emphasis is on the judgment of the oppressors, while in chapter 2 Paul discusses the gathering of the saints. However, this overlooks the fact that in chapter 1 Paul discusses the coming of Christ, "When he shall come to be glorified in his saints." Is this not the gathering to Christ in 1 Thessalonians 4? If 1 Thessalonians 4 includes the gathering of the saints and if 2 Thessalonians 2 speaks of the gathering of the saints, Gentry will be hard pressed to draw a distinction between gatherings.

As we close this section, we want to focus on how Gentry's arguments violate his own well stated hermeneutic. In his revised work, *The Beast of Revelation*, Gentry argues against the futuristic application of Revelation on the following grounds:

"Another detriment to the strained interpretations listed above is that John was writing to historical churches existing in his own day (Rev. 1:4). He and they are presently suffering "tribulation" (Rev. 1:9a). John's message (ultimately from Christ 1:1) calls upon each to give careful, spiritual attention to his words (2:7 etc). John is deeply concerned with the expectant cry of the martyrs and the divine promise of their soon vindication (6:10; cp. 5:3-5). He (John, DKP) would be cruelly mocking their circumstances (while committing a 'verbal scam' according to Mounce) were he telling them that when help comes it will come with swiftness–even though it may not come until two or three thousand years later."[442]

This is an *excellent* hermeneutical statement and we could hardly agree more. However, let's apply this principle to the texts in Thessalonians.

According to Gentry, Revelation cannot apply to the future because: **1.)** It was written to specific historical churches, **2.)** Those churches were actually undergoing persecution, **3.)** John calls on his audience to give heed to his words, and, **4.)** John promised imminent relief from their persecution. Okay, let's apply that to 1 Thessalonians 4 and 2 Thessalonians 1.

First, was Paul, like John, addressing a specific historical church? No one doubts that he was.

Second, was the church at Thessalonica actually experiencing persecution when Paul wrote to them? Undeniably. See 2 Thessalonians 1. Paul uses the present participial form of *thlipsis four times* to describe the persecution they were enduring.

Third, did Paul call on the Thessalonians to give heed to his exhortations? Who can doubt he was? After all, he did say, "Wherefore, comfort one another with these words" (1 Thessalonians 4:18).

Fourth, Paul promised imminent relief (*anesis*, see our discussion above) from their persecution. The words of Mounce apply equally well to Thessalonians as to Revelation. If Paul was simply promising that one of these days by and by Jesus would bring relief to them, "He (Paul in this case, DKP) would be cruelly mocking their circumstances (while committing a 'verbal scam' according to Mounce) were he telling them that when help comes it will come with swiftness–even though it may not come until two or three thousand years later."

Were the Thessalonians not as concerned with imminent relief from persecution as those to whom John wrote? Was it any less important for Paul to give the Thessalonians assurance of imminent relief than for John to assure the churches of Asia?

It must be remembered here that 1 Thessalonians 4 belongs to the identical *sitz en leben*, the same *life situation* as 2 Thessalonians 1. There is no change in the historical context. It cannot be argued that in 1 Thessalonians 4 the church was not being persecuted while they were in 2 Thessalonians 1 because Paul emphatically tells us in 1 Thessalonians that persecution was very real and severe (1 Thessalonians 2:16, 3:1f).

So, Gentry's own well stated hermeneutic which he applies in Revelation applies equally well in Thessalonians, and we might add, in Romans 8 and other eschatological texts. The only way for Gentry to counter our argument is to abandon his own hermeneutic.

Gentry's distinctions–the distinctions utilized by virtually all "partial preterists"-- are superficial and place unrealistic literary and journalistic restrictions on the inspired authors. Further, the distinctions violate the very hermeneutic used by the partial preterists to reject dispensationalism. If the hermeneutic employed by Gentry to reject the millennial claims in regard to Revelation is valid why is it not valid when applied to Thessalonians, Romans, Corinthians, and any other eschatological text? Gentry's supposed distinctions will not stand the test. *Partial preterism*[443] will not stand.

Gentry's supposed distinctions will not stand the test.
Partial preterism will not stand.

SUMMARY AND CONCLUSION

We have examined several different aspects of 1 Thessalonians 4:13-18 and shown conclusively that this text cannot be used to teach or to prove a yet future literal, visible coming of Christ at the end of human history. Nor can the text be used to prove a secret, silent, invisible rapture seven years before the end of the church age and human history as we know it.

1 Thessalonians 4 is about the consummation of God's Scheme of Redemption. That is widely acknowledged, but seldom understood. The Scheme of Redemption is about bringing man back into a relationship with God. That process or resurrection was begun in the initial work of Christ, but not completed until the old world, "the ministration of death written and engraven in stone" (2 Corinthians 3:6f) was removed in AD 70. Paul lets us know that the focus of Christ's coming was, *"whether we live or whether we die, we live with him"* (1 Thessalonians 5:10).[444] The focus was not on the removal of man from earth but the restoration of fellowship between God and man. When man was in fellowship with God in the Garden, time was counting, man had a body of dust and he was on earth. When man sinned his biological make-up did not change. The clock did not all of a sudden start ticking and man did not forfeit the earth. Why then, as most eschatological paradigms teach, must God destroy the earth, end time, and remove man from the earth to restore that broken fellowship? Indeed, Revelation shows us that life in the New Creation involves the New Jerusalem "descending out of heaven from God" for the purpose of God dwelling with man (Revelation 21:10). Eschatology, i.e. resurrection, is about *relationship*. It is not about a "tissue issue" to cite Sam Frost again.

We have not addressed every issue that could be raised in regard to 1 Thessalonians 4. However, we have addressed the most important issues of atonement, resurrection, the putting away of sin and what the Bible says about when these events were to happen. We have shown that the Bible is more than clear in placing the redemptive last days events squarely in the context of the end of the Old Covenant world of Israel in AD 70.

While we have not answered every question, this work has addressed the major tenets of the futurist eschatologies that attempt to use 1 Thessalonians as a proof-text. We have shown that every futurist eschatology must ignore the time statements in the text that prove not only did the Thessalonians expect the resurrection in their lifetime, they got that expectation from Paul. Furthermore, to place 1 Thessalonians 4 in the future all eschatologies must place a gap of so far 2000 years between the sixty ninth and the seventieth week of Daniel 9. This is true because Daniel was told that only 70 weeks were determined to accomplish the Scheme of Redemption, i.e. to make atonement for sin and to put away sin. These elements of redemption include *not just the passion* of Jesus, but his *parousia*. To suggest that the atonement was completed, or that sin was completely put away before the *parousia* and resurrection is to short-circuit God's Scheme of Redemption. 1 Thessalonians 4 depicts the consummation of the atonement work of Jesus when sin was finally put away. And this has to be kept within the framework of the fulfillment of God's promises to Israel.

Understanding the typological nature of the High Priest's atonement work is vital to comprehending the *parousia* of Jesus. His redemptive actions of sacrifice, entrance into the Most *Holy and his coming again* are emphatically posited as being the ultimate and final fulfillment of the typological world of Israel. But as we have seen Daniel 9 restricts that redemptive work to the seventy weeks ending with the fall of Jerusalem in A. D. 70.

To counter the arguments set forth here several things must be proven:

1.) It must be proven that the Christian age will come to an end. Every eschatological school of thought says that 1 Thessalonians 4:13f is about the coming of Christ at the end of the Christian age. *However, the Bible affirms that the Christian age has no end!*

2.) It must be proven that 1 Thessalonians 4:13-18 speaks of a different coming from that discussed in every other eschatological text in Thessalonians. We have demonstrated that every other text in the two epistles discusses the AD 70 *parousia*.

3.) It must be shown that 1 Thessalonians 4:13-18 is not parallel to Matthew 24:29-31. The Matthean text is widely acknowledged among amillennialists and postmillennialists to speak of the AD 70 coming of Christ. Every constituent element found in Matthew is found in Thessalonians including the restrictive time element.

4.) It must be proven that the gathering of Matthew and the gathering of Thessalonians are different events.

5.) It must be proven that the coming of Christ in Thessalonians is totally unrelated to the time of the vindication of the martyrs. The time of the resurrection is the time of the vindication of the martyrs. Thessalonians is definitely set within the context of persecution with the promise of vindication and reward. But Jesus said the time of the vindication of the martyrs would be when Jerusalem was judged in his generation.

6.) It must be proven that the events of Thessalonians are unrelated to the consummation of the atonement process.

7.) It must be proven that the consummation of that process is unrelated to the fulfillment of *the typological nature* of the Old Covenant High Priestly atonement actions.

8.) It must be proven that the consummation of the atonement process and the putting away of sin can be divorced from the end of the seventy weeks. Yet, Daniel was told that the destruction of Jerusalem in AD 70 would be the terminus of his vision. To successfully posit the *parousia* of Thessalonians 4 in the future, the seventieth week of Daniel 9 must be postponed.

9.) For those who believe in a rapture of man from earth it must be proven that the coming of Christ in John 14 and 1 Thessalonians 4 to establish the dwelling of God with man is a coming of Christ different from that promised in Revelation 19-21. Revelation posits the *coming down from heaven* of the prepared dwelling. It is not a removal of man from earth.

None of these things can be proven. The emphatic time indicators cannot be mitigated. The framework of atonement, the restoration of fellowship and the time of the vindication of the martyrs of God all prove in a powerful way that the coming of the Lord in 1 Thessalonians 4:13-18 occurred at the end of that Old Covenant typological world.

As a result of the fulfillment of Paul's promise fellowship with God is now a full reality for the believer. The words of Jesus have now been realized and are fully available: "If a man keep my sayings, he shall never see death" (John 8:51). The resurrection work begun by Jesus has now been perfected. What was only in prospect, guaranteed by the Spirit, is now a reality: "Do you not know that so many of us as were baptized into Christ were baptized *into his death*? Therefore, we were *buried with him*, by baptism *into death*, that just like Christ was raised from the dead by the glory of the Father, even so we also should walk *in newness of life*...For the death that he died, he died to sin once for all. Likewise, reckon yourselves to be dead indeed unto sin, *but alive unto God in Christ Jesus our Lord"* (Romans 6:4-10, my emphasis). Those who belong to God are, "sons of God, being sons of the resurrection" (Luke 20:34f) in the unending *Age to Come* brought in by Christ. To be *in Christ* is to be raised from the dead.

We have addressed the leading critics of Covenant Eschatology and demonstrated that the objections being offered are presumptive, specious, illogical and false. The true preterist paradigm has been confirmed as true.

Thessalonians does not speak of a future end of the Christian age. It does not speak of a rapture of living Christians from the earth either in the past or in the future. Thessalonians is about the consummation of God's Scheme of Redemption when man was restored to life, spiritual life and fellowship with God. It is when the new tabernacle of God was anointed and the New Jerusalem, "descended out of heaven from God" (Revelation 21:10). Man can now, by faith, once again dwell in the presence of Him who loves us.

Christ kept his word. He came in the lifetime of that first century generation. Man is, or can be, restored to the Father in him. The purpose of that event was, "Whether we live or whether we die, we live unto him" (1 Thessalonians 5:9-10). "Behold, the tabernacle of God is with men, and He will dwell with them, and they shall be His people, and God Himself will be with them and be their God" (Revelation 21:3). Amen, and *Amen*!

END NOTES

1. Thomas Ice and Timothy Demy, *Fast Facts on Bible Prophecy*, (Eugene, Ore, Harvest House, 1997)58.

2. See my book *The Last Days Identified*, for a fuller discussion of the "time of the end," as opposed to "the end of time."

3. Space forbids discussion of whether the disciples were confused or mistaken to associate the fall of the temple with the end of the age. Sadly, modern commentators believe Jesus' disciples were confused. This is *false*, however. See my *book, The Last Days Identified*, for a full discussion of this. In the book we have a full discussion of the distinctive Greek term, translated as "end of the age," and show that it always applies to the end of the old age of Israel.

4. In July 2008, (7-8, 10-11) in Indianapolis, Indiana, I engaged in a four day formal public debate with John Welch, amillennialist. One of my questions to Welch was if his eschatological hope was based on and taken from God's Old Covenant promises made to Old Covenant Israel. He responded, rather weakly, that yes, his hope of the future was based on the promise of the Garden, and the (unfulfilled) promises to Abraham. Amazingly, however, he then affirmed in the clearest terms possible, that the Old Law, and Israel as a covenant people were terminated at the Cross! Throughout the entirety of the debate I challenged him to explain how it was possible for the New Testament writers to be anticipating the imminent fulfillment of dead promises, from a dead Law, given to a covenantally dead people. He never attempted– not once-- to respond to my challenge. This huge discrepancy in the amillennial paradigm has no solution. MP3s of that debate are available from me at www.eschatology.org.

5. MP3s of that three day formal debate, held in Carlsbad, N. M. March, 2008, are available from me at www.eschatology.org. Deaver changed his position several times in the debate as he was confronted with his self contradictions.

6. In my July 2008 four day formal debate with amillennialist John Welch, I asked if Christ's death was substitutionary. He said it was *not*! He affirmed that Jesus simply died *on the behalf of man*, not in the place of man, and cited the Passover sacrifice in Exodus as proof. He said the Lamb was slain on the behalf of the people, not in the place of, and correlated that with Christ as the Passover (1 Corinthians 5:5). This claim exemplifies the total *desperation* of those attempting to respond to Covenant Eschatology. Was the Passover Lamb not slain *in the place of- instead of- the first born?* What would have happened to the first born if the Lamb was not slain? (The Egyptians *knew* the answer to that, did they not)? While it is true that the Lamb was slain "on the behalf of" the first born, it is irrefutably true that the Lamb was

slain in the place of the first born. So, if Christ was the Passover, then *he likewise died as a substitution!* MP3s of the Preston-V-Welch Debate are available from me, www.eschatology.org.

7. I am not questioning for even one moment whether Jesus died (or arose) physically. I am simply pointing out that the physical reality of his death and resurrection was the visible sign of the greater spiritual reality at work.

8. I am convinced that in Romans 7, Paul is discussing man under Law, not just and exclusively his own personal experience. Paul is speaking of Israel under Torah, and by extrapolation, any and all men who would and did seek justification through Law. Paul is thinking in collective terms, not strictly individualistic terms.

9. It is significant that Paul had experienced the death of Adam, and considered it a *curse*, longing for deliverance (Romans 7:24). Yet, nowhere do we find Paul speaking of physical death as a curse, something to be dreaded! On the contrary, he eagerly expected that his biological demise would be the door way into the presence of Jesus (Philippians 1). Notice that in Romans 7, the death that Paul discusses is the death that came through violation of Torah. Likewise, in Corinthians, Paul's discussion of the resurrection is the deliverance from the law that was "the strength of sin" (1 Corinthians 15:55-56)– the very law that Paul said brought his death in Romans 7! This amounts to *prima facie* proof that the death of Adam, and the focus of the eschatological resurrection could not be biological death, but alienation from the presence of God.

10. Sam Frost, in one of his presentations at the Preterist Pilgrim Weekend, Ardmore, Ok. (July 17-19, 2008) sponsored by the Preterist Research Institute, demonstrated that Paul's concept of the resurrection is not related to the resuscitation of biological *tissue*, but of the restoration of man to the presence of God. MP3s of that conference, *What Does the Bible Say About the Resurrection?* are available from www.eschatology.org.

11. Interestingly, Jesus was both the sacrifice and the scape-goat. He was offered as a sacrifice– the sin offering, the blood of which was taken inside the Most Holy Place for the people. He was also the scape-goat, on whom the sins of the people were laid. Jesus went "far away," i.e. to the Father, bearing the sins of the people!

12. In several public debates, my amillennial opponents have denied that the Second Coming was necessary to complete the atonement. They have claimed that the atonement was finished at the Cross. Occasionally, however, it is admitted, at least initially, that Christ's *parousia* is the consummation of the atonement. In my July 2008, debate with amillennialist John Welch, he argued (correctly) through 7

speeches that the Second Coming was necessary to finish the atonement. However, I pointed out repeatedly that Daniel 9:24f limited the making of the atonement to the seventy weeks, that ended no later than AD 70. Thus, the *parousia* was limited to the seventy weeks, ending no later than AD 70. In an amazing "debate conversion," in his last speech of the debate, Welch said that the atonement was finished at the Cross, and not the *parousia*! His desperation was obvious.

13. Leonard Goppelt, *Typos: The Typological Interpretation fo the Old Testament in the New Testament*, (Grand Rapids, Eerdmans, 1982)135, n. 34.

14. In fact, Mac Deaver, March 2008 formal debate, said this very thing. He argued that while physical death was introduced by Adam, that now, man dies whether he sins or not! Similarly, Welch, July 2008 formal debate (Indianapolis) said that man today does not die physically because of sin, but because he does not have access to the Tree of Life! Of course, this flies in the face of Romans and forces all other futurists to dichotomize the death of Adam. Paul knew of no such division of death. He knew of "the death" of Adam, not "the *deaths* of Adam."

15. Some are now arguing that Adam's sin did not in fact bring about an instantaneous biological change. Rather, we are told, man's body did not change, but it was the loss of access to the Tree of Life that caused man's death. John Welch, in the aforementioned July 2008 debate, argued that sin no longer brings physical death, but failure to eat of the Tree of Life! As I pointed out in the debate, this essentially removes physical death from the entire discussion of resurrection. Furthermore, since the Tree of Life is in the restored Garden (Revelation 22:2f) this demands that man will once again be dependent on that Tree for the sustenance of biological life! (This position also admits that man was created mortal *from the beginning*. He did not become mortal through sin, he was *created* mortal!) But, if the Tree of Life is for the sustenance of *physical life*, what of the idea of the resurrection in an immortal body, that will never die? You cannot make the Tree of Life to be for the purpose of sustaining biological life– i.e. the loss of the Tree as the reason for biological death today-- without causing major theological problems.

16. I recommend William Bell's examination of 2 Corinthians 5, presented at the 2008 Preterist Pilgrim Weekend, Ardmore, Ok. for a challenging and thought provoking study of the idea of the gift of immortality and incorruptibility. The MP3s of that entire conference, the theme being What Does the Bible Say About the Resurrection? are available at www.eschatology.org.

17. As we will see below, the death of Christ did not perfect, i.e. finish, the Atonement, it *initiated* the process. The Atonement involved not only the sacrifice, but entrance into the MHP, and the coming out to

declare the acceptance of the Atonement sacrifice. Furthermore, Daniel 9:24f undeniably limits the making– not just the initiation of the process– but the making of the Atonement to the seventy weeks, that ended no later than AD 70 and the end of the Old Covenant world– the world that could never take away sin.

18. I was raised a fifth generation amillennialist, and one of the most fundamental tenets of that paradigm is that Torah and Israel were removed at the Cross. In numerous formal debates with amillennialists, my opponents have strongly affirmed that view. In the aforementioned Deaver and Welch debates of 2008, both men stated these convictions. When I asked, repeatedly, how it was possible for all of the New Testament writers to be anticipating the yet future fulfillment of dead promises contained in a dead law, given to a covenantally dead people, neither man could or did answer.

19. In reality, Torah was prophecy, and prophecy was Torah, in the mind of the Jews. It is wrong to try to create a dichotomy between these. Paul called Isaiah "the law" (1 Corinthians 14:20f) and Jesus himself said "the law prophesied" (Matthew 11:13). Paul likewise said the Law foretold the resurrection (Acts 24:14f).

20. When we speak of John's gospel, we are of course referring to his record of Jesus' words. Each of the eschatological passages cited herein came from the lips of Jesus. However, this does not negate–but rather reinforces-- the fact that John's gospel is about the fulfillment of God's promises to Israel.

21. See also Malachi 1:12f, where YHVH promised that the time was coming in which He would have men to worship Him anywhere and everywhere. This implies that the geo-centric locus of worship would no longer be required.

22. Jeremiah's statement that the Ark would no longer be "remembered" is incredibly important. The word "remembered" means significantly more than just brought to mental recollection. It means to be remembered *within a covenant context*. So, Jeremiah foretold the time when the Ark of the Covenant, the symbol of the Mosaic Covenant itself, would no longer retain that covenantal significance.
Furthermore, note that Jeremiah likewise said that *the Ark would not be built again!* Well, if the Ark would not be built again, this infers, by logical necessity that the Ark was destroyed, *never to be rebuilt!* So much for all of the modern claims of the so-called re-discovery of the "lost Ark" hidden away in the foothills of Israel, or Ethiopia, or where ever.

23. Most exegetes see in John 5 two resurrections, one spiritual, one of corpses. Yet, there are not two resurrections disparate in nature, separated in time by what is now two millennia and counting. There was

the *initiation* of the resurrection that had begun, and was awaiting *consummation*. This agrees perfectly well with the fact that in 1 Corinthians 15 Paul uses the *present passive indicative* to speak of the resurrection that was– when he wrote– *already in process*! See 1 Corinthians 15:35f. This hardly comports with the idea of corpses rising out of the ground. See Sam Frost's excellent treatment of 1 Corinthians 15, with emphasis on the present tenses. Sam Frost, *Exegetical Essays on the Resurrection of the Dead*, (Xenia, Ohio, TruthVoice Publishing, 2004)59f. Also, see Jack Scott's treatment of the present passive indicatives in 1 Corinthians at the 2008 Preterist Pilgrim Weekend. MP3s of Scott's presentations are available at www.eschatology.org.

24. Sam Frost shares the story that Robert Strimple argued, in a paper attempting to refute Max King, that Paul never uses the word Israel in 1 Corinthians 15, thus, we are not bound to interpret the chapter in light of God's promises to Israel (Frost, *Essays*, 55). Such failure of logic and sound reasoning is part of the problem behind modern attempts to understand Paul's doctrine of the resurrection. This refusal to consider the Old Covenant source of New Testament eschatology is widespread.

25. Thomas Ice, *End Times Controversy*, (Eugene, Or., Harvest House Publishers, 2003)85.

26. John F. Walvoord, *The Millennial Kingdom*, (Grand Rapids, Zondervan, 1975)231.

27. Tim LaHaye and Thomas Ice, *Charting the End Times*, (Eugene, Ore., Harvest House, 2001)48.

28. Dwight Pentecost, *Things To Come*, (Grand Rapids, Zondervan, 1966)137.

29. Lamentably, the dispensationalists deny that the events of Pentecost were the beginning of the fulfillment of Joel. Arnold Fruchtenbaum, cited often by LaHaye and Ice, says: "Virtually nothing that happened on Pentecost was predicted in Joel" From a three page article sent to me by Thomas Ice, "How the New Testament Uses the Old Testament." Ice does not believe that Joel was fulfilled or even began to be fulfilled on Pentecost.

30. See our discussion above on whether there was a gap between the sixty ninth and seventieth week of Daniel 9:26f. Is a theological fabrication with no contextual justification whatsoever. The Old Testament clearly stated that there would be no delay, no failure, no postponement of the kingdom promises. God promised that Israel's unbelief would not thwart or delay His plan!

31. In numerous formal debates with amillennialists, I have asked if their eschatological hope is based on, and taken from the O.T. promises

made to Israel. The invariable response is "No!" Some seek to equivocate, by saying that their eschatology is based on "the whole Bible," but in reality, they do deny that New Testament eschatology is the reiteration of YHVH's O.T. promises made to Israel. In March of 2008, I debated Mac Deaver PhD, and repeatedly made this point. In desperation, Deaver claimed that the resurrection promise of 1 Corinthians 15, *while it does cite Isaiah 25 and Hosea,* was actually made to the church, and *not Old Testament Israel!* In response I noted that if this is so, then since the New Creation would come via the resurrection, and Isaiah and Daniel said that the New Creation (and thus resurrection) would only come when "Israel" *was completely shattered,* that this meant that the resurrection would be when the church was / is completely destroyed! Such is the incongruity of the amillennial paradigm. MP3s of the Deaver-V-Preston debate are available from me, at www.eschatology.org.

32. See the Deaver-V-Preston debate, March, 2008, Carlsbad, N. M.. MP3s available from me. Deaver, in response to a written question, affirmed that God was through with Old Covenant Israel at the Cross.

33. We need to note that the word translated as tabernacle in this text is not technically the normal word for tabernacle. Here, it is *sukkah*, and signifies more of a hut than of a tabernacle. Cf. Leupold, *Exposition of Isaiah*, (Grand Rapids, Baker, 1972)106+. The fact that the normal word for tabernacle does not appear here however, does not diminish the thought. Undeniably, Isaiah anticipated the time, at the Day of the Lord, when man would dwell in the presence of God, and that is the thought of John 14 and 1 Thessalonians 4.

34. For preterists who posit Isaiah, John 14 and Thessalonians in AD 70, and also believe in a rapture of believers from earth at the *parousia*, this is particularly meaningful. Unless Isaiah 2-4 can be proven to speak of a removal of man from earth, as opposed to God dwelling among men, then the idea of a physical removal of man from earth in the AD 70 *parousia* is falsified. Isaiah lies behind John 14 and Thessalonians. Therefore, unless John 14 and Thessalonians speak of a different "dwelling" than does Isaiah, since Isaiah's promise does not teach the idea removal from earth, neither does John 14 or Thessalonians.

35. In Ezekiel 11 the Son of Man saw the shechinah glory cloud, i.e. God's presence, depart from the temple. In chapter 37, and 40f, is the prediction of the return of the Presence of YHVH. Just as the return of God for the re-marriage is the restoration of covenant fellowship, the return of God in the Messianic Temple was to be the restoration of covenant fellowship. See my *Who Is This Babylon?*, 157f for a fuller discussion.

36. I naturally responded that according to 1 Peter 1:9f, Peter's audience was anticipating the fulfillment of *the promises made to Israel*

in the Old Covenant. Neither Peter or his audience were unconcerned with Israel or her promises. Those promises were the *source* and *focus* of their hope!

37. J. N. D. Kelly, *The Epistles of Peter and Jude*, (Peabody, Mass, Hendrickson, 1969)40. Interestingly, Kelly seeks to negate this meaning and claims that the term was being used by Peter to designate the new Israel, as the people of God longing for heaven. However, in light of the fact that Peter was the apostle to the circumcision, and the fact that he appeals directly to the Old Covenant promises of the redemption of Israel under Messiah as being fulfilled in his audience, I think it far more consistent to posit that he was indeed addressing the diaspora of Israel, those responding to the message of fulfillment in Christ. It *was* the diaspora of Israel being addressed. It was their promises being fulfilled. It is just that those promises were being fulfilled in the spiritual sacrifices, spiritual temple, the spiritual *land*!

38. As with so many Biblical words and themes, redemption (*apolutrosis*) carried both positive and negative connotations. God redeemed Israel from Egypt and Babylon. That was truly good news! However, that redemption came at an awful price, "I gave men for you...I will give men for you" (Isaiah 43). When God "gave men" for Israel's redemption from bondage, it refers to the death of their captors. And in light of Exodus 12-14, redemption was a "two-step" program. There was the death / sacrifice of the Passover lamb, and then the death of the power of the enslaving Pharaoh! Consider then that Paul, writing to the Ephesians says that they had been redeemed. (Ephesians 1:7. Further, the Passover lamb had been slain (1 Corinthians 5:7). However, they were still looking for redemption (Ephesians 4:30). The destruction of the power of the enslaver, i.e. *Babylon*, lay in the near future!

39. The fact that like Paul, Peter affirms the fulfillment of the OT promises of Israel's restoration "in the land" as fulfilled in Christ and the church becomes divine commentary on the meaning of "the land" as seen by the NT writers. Peter and Paul indisputably affirmed the fulfillment of key restoration prophecies (Isaiah 49; Hosea; Ezekiel 37, etc.). And, they affirmed the *spiritual fulfillment* (1 Peter 2:4-5). If the temple was spiritual, if the sacrifices were spiritual, if the priesthood was spiritual, *then the land was spiritual*!

40. Mark Dubis, *Messianic Woes in First Peter, Suffering and Eschatology in 1 Peter 4:12-19*, Studies in Biblical Literature, Vol. 33, (New York, Peter Lang, 2002)59. This is the finest discussion of the Messianic Woes and its relationship to Peter's epistles that I have seen.

41. I don't personally care much for the word "transferred" since it might hint at "replacement theology." This is not what Peter affirmed. He was saying that those scattered abroad, *Israel* (again, albeit now

Christians) was experiencing the fulfillment of God's promises to Israel. Peter was *not* affirming the failure of God's promises to Israel or the replacement of Israel with Gentiles. He was affirming God's faithfulness to Israel! It was Israel's promises being fulfilled to Israel scattered abroad.

42. See my extended discussion of the Rejected Stone in my *The Elements Shall Melt With Fervent Heat*. Simply stated, the ones who had rejected the chief corner stone (Cf. Matthew 21:40f; Acts 4:11f) were about to be crushed. They were the "scoffers" of 2 Peter 3 and this means that Peter's discourse of the Day of the Lord was a prediction of the dissolution of old temple, so that the glory of this new temple that Peter is discussing might be revealed. My book is available from www.bibleprophecy.com, or, www.eschatology.org.

43. For a brief but excellent analysis of Ezekiel's temple prophecy, see "The Millennial Post" March, 2003 by Sam Frost. Contact Frost at www.christcovenantchurchfl.com

44. F. W. Farrar, *Commentary on Daniel*, 278.

45. www.BibleGateway.com

46. I am of course well familiar with the millennial view of a so far 2000 year gap between the sixty ninth and the seventieth week. However, this proposed gap is untenable, and I have addressed this issue in both public debate and in my books. In the 2003 formal debate with Thomas Ice and Mark Hitchcock, I presented a lesson on the millennial gap theory, in one of my affirmative presentations. Neither Thomas Ice or Mark Hitchcock offered one word of scriptural rebuttal to the material in their negative presentations. That debate is available in DVD form from me, at my website: www.eschatology.org. In addition, in my book *Seal Up Vision and Prophecy*, I present, in fuller form, the material that I presented in that formal debate.

47. Steven M Bryan, Institute for Biblical Research, BBR, 14 (2004), *The Eschatological Temple in John 14*.

48. There is a remarkable irony in John concerning "place." The Sanhedrin was concerned (troubled) that if Jesus were left alone, the Romans would come and take away their place (John 11:48). The destruction of the temple is implied here. However, the irony is that in John 14 Jesus uses temple imagery and tells his disciples not to be concerned (troubled) for he was preparing that place. One *place* was indeed to be taken away, and give way to the eternal true *place*!

49. Coloe's work (reference below) has some wonderful insights in it, but it seems to me that she has overlooked part of the story of John. She holds that John wrote after the demise of the Old temple, to help the Christians find their identity. I find this misplaced. John's stated

purpose of the gospel is the record of what Jesus had accomplished, "that you might believe that Jesus is the Christ, the son of the living God" (John 20:30-31). Does it not make us marvel that if, as Coloe correctly posits, John's purpose is to show the construction of the new temple, that *John did not write about the past destruction of the Old temple?* Would not his gospel have been all that much more effective by showing that the old was now destroyed? I would suggest that the reason that John did not point to the past destruction of the Jerusalem temple is because it had not yet been destroyed.

50. Mary L. Coloe, *God Dwells With Us: Temple Symbolism in the Fourth Gospel*, (Collegeville, Minn., The Liturgical Press, 2001)163.

51. While the specific term "my Father's house" is, according to Coloe, (2001, 160f) not found in the Hebrew text of the Old Testament, the idea and theme of the "house of the Lord" is a common idiom for the temple (e.g. Isaiah 2:2f). So, Jesus' use of "my Father's house" is itself, a temple referent, albeit, in Christ, it is re-structured and re-identified! It is no longer the Jerusalem Temple, *it is the dwelling place in Christ!*

52. David Instone-Brewer, *Divorce and ReMarriage in the Bible*, (Grand Rapids, Eerdmans, 2002)37, points out that these words constitute, "an ancient Near Eastern divorce formula."

53. The word "remember" as used so often in the O.T. goes far beyond a simple mental recollection. It is to bring the covenant and its provisions, demands and blessings, into focus. So, Jeremiah 3 is not a statement that the Ark or Jerusalem would never be brought into the mental faculty, but that they would lose all covenantal significance! This is an incredibly powerful prophecy, and one that is virtually ignored in modern eschatological discussions, especially by the millennialists.

54. The metamorphorsis would be traumatic and cataclysmic. It would be the complete dissolution of the Old Covenant, *shadow* form of Judah– which is what Revelation is all about. In my work, *Like Father Like Son, On Clouds of Glory*, I fully discuss the shadow nature of Old Covenant Israel/Judah, and the necessity for the dissolution of the typological form of Israel, into the body of Christ. See Colossians 2:14f; Hebrews 10:1-4, etc.

55. I was personally raised as an amillennialist, and had no concept, no hint of a *clue*, that Matthew 25 was about the fulfillment of God's promises to Old Covenant Israel. In my fellowship, Matthew 25 was–and is, tragically-- posited as the fulfillment of New Testament promises to the church at the end of time. God's promises to Israel are never considered as in any way relevant or necessary for a proper interpretation of Jesus' parables on the wedding.

56. It is sometimes difficult for the modern reader, indoctrinated in the individualism of American and modern society, to think corporately as did the ancients. And yet, as Christians, we are given some insight into the corporate by such verses as this: Husbands love your wives, even as Christ loved the church, and gave him self for her... and he is the savior of *the body*." Notice that Christ is the savior of "the body." This is a statement of *corporate salvation*, corporate action on the part of Christ. For more on the corporate nature of Christ's work, as Paul viewed it, see Tom Holland, *Contours of Pauline Theology*, Christian Focus Publications, Geanies House, Fearn, Ross-Shire IV20 1TW, Scotland, UK, 2004).

57. It is critical to remember that Hosea serves as one of the sources for Paul's doctrine of the resurrection (1 Corinthians 15:55f). I have produced a 30 lesson presentation from Hosea, correlating it to 1 Corinthians 15. I am personally convinced that Hosea serves as Paul's working outline for his Corinthian resurrection discourse. This has profound implication for the nature and form of resurrection. The Hosea study is available from my website: www.eschatology.org.

58. Available at www.eschatology.org, or www.Bibleprophecy.com.

59. I must take note of the changing face of postmillennialism, however. Keith Mathison in his massive new tome, *Age To Age The Unfolding of Biblical Eschatology*, (Phillipsburg, NJ, P and R Publishing, 2009)373, "the missionary task (of Matthew 24:14, DKP) has not yet been completed." This is a stunning change from his earlier works, i.e. *Postmillennialism, An Eschatology of Hope* (Phillipsburg, NJ, P and R Publishing, 1999)112f, where Mathison unequivocally affirms the fulfillment of Matthew 24:14. Mathison gives no indication of the radical change in his view of Matthew 24:14 in his newest work. I am sure the dispensationalist will welcome Mathison's "conversion" to their view of Matthew 24:14.

60. I have produced an 11 tape series on the Immerser showing his pivotal role in NT eschatology. In addition, in my book *Who Is This Babylon?* I show how important the Baptizer's message was to John and the Apocalypse. To ignore the message and mission of John is to ignore vitally important aspects of New Testament eschatology. The tapes and book are available from our website www.eschatology.org.

61. N. T. Wright has some insightful comments on this topic that are well worth the read, N. T. Wright, *Paul*, (Minneapolis, Fortress, 2005)56+.

62. See for instance, N. T. Wright, *Jesus and the Victory of God*, (Minneapolis, Fortress, 1996)341, 345-346---"The close of the age for which they longed was not the end of the space order, but the end of the present evil age." Wright is adamant that the "end of time" did not

belong to Jewish eschatology.

63. Jesus' prediction to come "in the glory of the Father" meant that he was to come *as the Father had come*, many times. Patently, Wright understands that JHVH had never bodily descended out of heaven. So, Jesus' *parousia* in judgment was to be in the same mold as his father's comings. But, the Father had never come bodily, but through the manifestation of His sovereignty in history. This means that the *parousia* of 1 Thessalonians 4 must be viewed in that light. See my *Like Father Like Son, On Clouds of Glory* for full explication of this idea. Available at www.eschatology.org

64. See my in-depth discussion of the Transfiguration and its implications for defining the *parousia* in my *Like Father Like Son, On Clouds of Glory*. The Transfiguration unmistakably posits the *parousia* at the end of the Mosaic age. The *Glory* book is available at www.eschatology.org, or www.bibleprophecy.com

65. See my *How Is This Possible?* in which I point out that it would have been impossible for the Thessalonians to have believed that the Day of the Lord, *as traditionally perceived*, had already happened. This simple, yet undeniable fact should give pause to anyone stuck on a literalistic concept of the *parousia*.

66. Eusebius, called the father of church history, says Zechariah 14 predicted, "the final siege of the people by the Romans, through which the whole Jewish race has become subject to their enemies." *Proof of the Gospel*, Vol. I, (Grand Rapids, Baker, 1981)98. See our comments below. Eusebius also believed that the Lord came in that destruction.

67. William Beiderwolf, *The Second Coming Bible*, (Grand Rapids, Baker, 1972)304

68. E. W. Hengstenberg, *Christology of the Old Testament*, (Grand Rapids, Kregel, 1970)381.

69. Merrill F. Unger, *Zechariah: Prophet of Messiah's Glory*, (Grand Rapids, Zondervan, 1974)238-239.

70. Adam Clarke, *Clarke's Commentary*, Vol. IV, (Abingdon)794.

71. Milton Terry, *Biblical Apocalyptics*, (Grand Rapids, Baker, 1988)166f.

72. See my book *In Flaming Fire* for an analysis of 2 Thessalonians 1. The issues raised in that text prohibit any futuristic application. Paul was dealing with first century events, promising first century saints imminent relief. The book is available at www.eschatology.org, or www.bibleprophecy.com

73. Bauer's, Gingrich and Danker, *Greek English Lexicon*, Second Edition, (Chicago, University of Chicago Press, 1979)65

74. E. g. James Frame, *The International Critical Commentary, Thessalonians*, (Edinburgh, T and T Clark, 1960)221+; F. F. Bruce, *Word Biblical Commentary*); Wanamaker, *New International Greek Testament Commentary;* Jeffrey Wiema, *Commentary on the New Testament Use of the Old Testament*, etc. etc. We have found a mere handful of commentators who ask the question, Who were the persecutors?

75. Kenneth Gentry, *He Shall Have Dominion*, Tyler, Tx. Institute for Christian Economics, 1992)380.

76. Adolph Harnack, *Mission and Expansion of Christianity*, (Harper and Brothers, 1961)57+.

77. Moses Stuart, *A Commentary on the Apocalypse*, (Eugene, Ore. Wipf and Stock, Reprint of 1845 work, Vol. II)68f.

78. Cf. Kenneth Gentry, *Before Jerusalem Fell*, (Tyler, Tx. Institute for Christian Economics, 1989)78f. Gentry cites several patristic sources that say Nero was the first Roman emperor to persecute the church.

79. The fact that Paul posits the casting out of Israel in his future, and because she was persecuting the church belies the common amillennial view that God was through with Israel at the Cross. Israel never persecuted the church prior to the Cross. Is that not self-evident?

80. N. Nisbett, *The Prophecy of the Destruction of Jerusalem*, 1787, p. 25. Reprinted by John Bray Ministries. Available from John Bray Ministry, P.O. Box 90129 Lakeland, Fl. 33804.

81. In numerous public debates, I have posed the question: "Did Jesus come, in the lifetime of the Thessalonians, and give them relief from the persecution they were enduring, yes, or no?" My opponents have responded "No, Jesus did not come in the lifetime of the Thessalonians and give them relief!" See the Thrasher-Preston debate, Athens, Alabama, September 20, 2003. Tapes available on our website. Another debate was between Thomas Ice and Mark Hitchcock, and John Anderson and myself October, 2003, in Tampa, Fl.. Anderson posed the question, and Hitchcock responded. Tapes of that debate are also available. Also, in the Deaver-V-Preston debate, March, 2008, Carlsbad, N. M., Mac Deaver openly said that Jesus did not come and give the Thessalonians relief, but that they got the promised relief when they died. This patently is not what Paul promised, however.

82. See my *Can You Believe Jesus Said This?* for an in-depth analysis of Matthew 16:27-28. This book counters the attempts to divide these

two verses in time and topic, and shows that Jesus' coming in judgment was indeed to be in the first century. The book is available from my website: www.bibleprophecy.com, or, www.eschatology.org.

83. Does the fact that the Man of Sin was being restrained not constitute *prima facie* proof that the millennium was present and on-going? This is tantamount to saying that Satan was bound!

84. W. D. Davies, *The Gospel and the Land*, (Berkley, University of California Press, 1974)194+.

85. Millennialists like to claim that Matthew 24:4f describes Israel being persecuted by the anti-christ, during the Great Tribulation period, after the proposed rapture. Well, we would agree Israel is discussed in these verses, but what the millennialists either overlook or ignore is that *it is the Jews persecuting the followers of Jesus, not the Jews being persecuted by the proposed anti-christ!* Matthew 10 and Mark 13, parallel texts, confirm this when it says that Jesus' followers would be brought before "councils." This is from the word from which we get "sanhedrin." This is patently Jewish persecution of the followers of Jesus.

86. Gary DeMar, *Last Days Madness* (Revised), (Atlanta, GA. American Vision, 1994)325. It is more than a little remarkable that DeMar can see the connection between the Olivet Discourse and 2 Thessalonians 2 based on these parallels, and yet fail to see the same connection between Matthew 24:29-31– which he applies to AD 70– and 1 Thessalonians 4. The parallels between the Matthean text and 1 Thessalonians 4 are *even more precise* than those between the Discourse and 2 Thessalonians 2. DeMar's position is hardly consistent.

87. Brant Pitre, *Jesus, The Tribulation, and the Return From Exile*, (Grand Rapids, Baker Academic, 2005)304f.

88. There does seem to be an exception to this concept, however. Jeffrey A. Gibbs, *Jerusalem and Parousia*, St. Louis, MO, Concordia Academic Press, 2000)230, n. 108– cites 2 Maccabees 8:17, to show that the Abomination of Desolation was set up by Antiochus in "the holy place": "And on the fifteenth day of Chislev, the one hundred forty-fifth year, he set up an abomination of desolation upon the altar, and in the cities of Judah surrounding they set up the high places." I am not personally convinced that this example is consistent with the Biblical datum, however. I find Pitre's concept to be solid.

89. Thomas Ice and Timothy Demy, *Prophecy Watch*, (Eugene, Or., Harvest House, 1998)258, "The sacrifices of the millennium will not be a return to the Mosaic Law, since the Law forever been fulfilled and discontinued through Christ (Romans 6:1, 15; 7:1-6; 1 Corinthians 9:20,21; 2 Corinthians 3:7-11; Galatians 4:1-7; 5:18; Hebrews 8:13;

10:1-14)." Of course, just a few pages before this quote, Ice and co-author Demy wrote, "In the millennial temple, all that was prescribed and initiated in the Old Testament ceremonial and ritual activities will come to completion and their fullest meaning." (P. 256). So, the Law of Moses has been fulfilled and removed in Christ, and yet, it still awaits its completion fulfillment in the millennium!

90. One of the reasons underlying the amillennial and postmillennial view is the foundational–but mistaken-- idea that the Torah was removed at the Cross. Furthermore, as a corollary, essential to both views, the amillennial view especially, is that God was through with Israel at the Cross. So, with these presuppositions firmly in place, these two camps cannot allow Paul's referent to the temple to be the Jerusalem temple and the events of 2 Thessalonians 2 to be applicable to a time when Torah would still be in effect. These underlying false presuppositions prevent the amillennial and postmillennial camps from properly interpreting the text.

91. It is easy to chronicle the apostasy throughout the New Testament epistles, and yet, most commentators want to divorce what was happening then from the prophecies of Jesus and the epistles, and extrapolate the fulfillment of those prophecies thousands of years into the future. Yet, passages such as 2 Peter, that foretold the scoffers is undeniably the background for Jude's urgent epistle in which he says that the scoffers foretold by the apostles were already present! Much more could be said about the apostasy, but space forbids.

92. Kenneth Gentry: *Thine is the Kingdom,* (Vallecito, CA, Calcedon, 2003)162.

93. Jeffrey Wiema, in *Commentary on the New Testament Use of the Old Testament*, Greg Beale and D. A. Carson, editors, (Grand Rapids, Baker Academic, 2007)880.

94. Beale gives a list of 13 parallels between the Olivet Discourse and 1 Thessalonians 4:13-5:7–which as will see momentarily, is a very short list of the parallels. Significantly, Beale conveniently omits the direct parallel in the time statements! Jesus emphatically said that all of the things listed would be fulfilled in his generation. Paul said, "we who are alive and remain until the coming of the Lord." Of course, Beale expends considerable effort to show that neither Jesus nor Paul really meant to express the imminence that their words would normally indicate.

95. Greg Beale, *1-2 Thessalonians, The IVP New Testament Series,* (Downers Grove, ILL, InterVarsity Press, 2003)136.

96. See J. Marcellus Kik's, *Matthew XXIV,* (Philadelphia, Presbyterian and Reformed, 1948) for what is generally considered the

representative amillennial and postmillennial view of the Olivet Discourse.

97. Kenneth Gentry, spokesman for the modern Reformed postmillennial movement, has written extensively on the Olivet Discourse, seeking to prove the two-fold division of the chapter at verse 36. However, amazingly, he equivocates by saying that even if it could be proven that the Discourse were a united discussion of the AD 70 events, that it would not seriously impact his futurist eschatology. See his comments at: http://www.reformed-theology.org/ice/newslet/dit/dit09.98.htm This, in a word, is nonsense. You cannot "surrender" Matthew 24:36-25:46 to an A. D. 70 application without surrendering *all* futurist doctrines of judgment and resurrection, it is that simple. Interestingly enough, when writing to refute dispensationalism, Gentry says that the Olivet Discourse is *vitally important* to the study of eschatology. So, on the one hand, it does not matter if the Discourse speaks only of AD 70, but on the other hand, it is fundamental to a proper understanding of eschatology!

98. Kenneth Gentry, *He Shall Have Dominion, A Postmillennial Eschatology*, Revised, (Draper, VA., Apologetics Group Media, 2009)439.

99. Kenneth Gentry, *Before Jerusalem Fell,* (Tyler, Tx. 1989)142.

100. Gentry is patently *redefining "orthodoxy"* to fit his own views. Gentry holds to *many* views that are either not in the creeds, or are at direct odds with the creeds. Yet, he calls himself orthodox and creedal. The same is true of Mathison. It is little wonder that these men do not want to engage in formal polemics with true preterists, for their inconsistencies would be exposed for what they are, a violation of the creeds that they claim are the very *definition* of orthodoxy.

101. Keith A. Mathison, *From Age to Age the Unfolding of Biblical Eschatology*, (Phillipsburg: NJ: P&R Publishing, 2009)379+. As stated, Mathison claims that the creeds determine orthodoxy, and that as a result, preterism is heresy. Yet, Mathison cannot find his views on the Olivet Discourse, or his doctrine of the coming of the Son of Man, in any of the creeds! My thanks to Mike Sullivan for the reference. Sullivan and three other reformed authors have produced a response to Mathison's *When Shall These Things Be? A Reformed Response to Hyper-Preterism.* The book is entitled *House Divided: A Reformed Response to When Shall These Things Be?*, and is available from me.

102. Keith Mathison, *Dispensationalism Rightly Dividing the People of God?*, (Phillipsburg, NJ., 1995)143f.

103. See my *Who Is This Babylon?* for a fuller discussion of the wedding theme in scripture. Simply stated, the Bible knows of only *one wedding*, and it is the wedding of *Israel*, fulfilled in Christ. The idea of two weddings creates a veritable theological nightmare. The millennialists create a doctrine of two weddings. The church is the Bride of Christ, while Israel is married to God. This overlooks the fact that Jesus was sent to Israel, and confirmed the promises made to Israel. Thus, his parables must be applied to the promise of the wedding of Israel. Yet, again, he clearly places this within the context of AD 70, and this is totally destructive to the millennial view.

104. A study worthy of fuller discussion is the theme of the absentee master, and his return. N. T. Wright has done some insightful work in this area (*Jesus and the Victory of God*, Minneapolis, Fortress, 1996). The point is that Jesus told stories about a master entrusting servants to a task, leaving, and returning. Clearly, Jesus never envisioned a long delay before the return. The time of the return was always near.

105. John Lightfoot, *Commentary on the New Testament from the Talmud and Hebraica*, (Peabody, Mass, Hendrickson, 1989 reprint of 1859 work)194.

106. Bruce Wanamaker, *New International Greek Testament Commentary on 1 & 2 Thessalonians*, (Grand Rapids, Paternoster, 1990)116, says Paul's reference to the Jews filling up the measure of their sin, "suggests an ongoing process that cannot be restricted temporally to the time of the Gentile mission, but includes the history of the Jewish people stretching back to the prophetic period of the OT." This is what Jesus said in Matthew 23.

107. The KJV and ASV rendering of "at hand" is mistaken. The proper translation of *enesteken* is "already come." See my book, *How Is This Possible?* for a study of this word and its meaning in 2 Thessalonians 2.

108. It is not hard to see, if one grants the parallel of the Olivet Discourse and Thessalonians, why the Thessalonians could believe the day of the Lord had come. The things Jesus had predicted, persecution, famines (Acts 11) world mission (1 Ths. 1:8) prophets saying Jesus *had come* (Mt. 24:26f) were all to be signs of the end. Those things, especially persecution and mission were very real to the Thessalonians. Thus the sense of imminence in 1 Thessalonians 3-4 and the subsequent conviction that the Day had actually come (2 Thes. 2:1-2).

109. It should be noted that the word *parousia* meant more than the bodily presence of a person: "There were two contemporary uses of *parousia* which might have served as analogies for its distinctive Christian sense. One denoted the manifestation of a hidden divinity by some evidence of his power or in cultic action (this use is borrowed by

Josephus to describe the coming of the God of Israel at various epochs in Old Testament history; (cf. Antiq. 3:80, 203; 9. 55); the other denoted the official visit of a high-ranking personage to a province or city, when he was met on his approach by a deputation of leading citizens who escorted him formally for the remainder of his journey. In view of the near-divinization of some rulers, there can be no hard-and-fast distinction drawn between these two uses of *parousia* in the Hellenistic-Roman world." F. F. Bruce, *Word Commentary, Commentary on 1 & 2 Thessalonians*, (Waco, 1982, Vol. 45)56-57. See also W. D. Davies and Dale Allison, *International Critical Commentary, Matthew 19-28,* (New York, T and T Clark International, 2004)338.

110. As we have seen, it will hardly do to say Paul's "we" is simply "stylistic." He is clearly contrasting his contemporaries with those that have died--their loved ones. His contrast is therefore very direct, between the dead of the brethren at Thessalonica and those still alive-- thus that generation.

111. Wenham examines the Greek in Luke and Thessalonians in this comparison and says, "We find what are probably the most striking verbal links between Paul and the Synoptists." *Paul and the Synoptic Apocalypse*, Gospel Perspectives: Studies of History and Tradition in the Four Gospels, JSOT Press, Sheffield, England, Vol. II, (1981)353.

112. Plummer, *Commentary on 1 Thessalonians*, p. 83 says of the reference to the coming as a thief in 1 Thes. 5:3: "It is almost certainly a reference to the saying which is recorded in Mat. 24:43."

113. In the aforementioned public debate with amillennialist John Welch, (Indianapolis, July, 2008) Welch proclaimed that 1 Thessalonians 4:13f could not be fulfilled because he had attended funerals recently and that all people had to do to know it was not fulfilled was to "read the newspapers!" In response, I produced the comparison chart between Matthew 24:29f and 1 Thessalonians, noting that Welch insists that the Olivet text refers to Christ's AD 70 *parousia*. I then called on Welch to give his hermeneutic for delineating between the topics. He never uttered one word of response.

114. Here is where Gentry's own hermeneutic backfires on him. He claims that we must delineate between 2 Thessalonians 1 and chapter 2 because of the omission of certain motifs, and the use of different words. Well, Jesus utilizes certain words and motifs in Matthew 25:31f *that are not used in 1 Thessalonians 4:13f!* Thus, per Gentry's "logic" Matthew 25:31f must be different from 1 Thessalonians. However, because Matthew 25:31f does contain the exact elements found in Matthew 24:29f, it must be parallel with those verses. This would demand that Gentry now take the united Discourse view. However, he

is then confronted with the direct parallels between Matthew 24:29f and 1 Thessalonians 4:13f which would demand an AD 70 application of the Thessalonian passage. Such is the result of a wrong hermeneutic.

115. Keith Mathison, *From Age to Age The Unfolding of Biblical Eschatology*, (Phillipsburg, NJ, P and R Publishing, 2009)380.

116. There is a great irony here. As we will show below, the millennialists seek to delineate between comings of the Lord on the (false) claim that Jesus would come *for* the saints as opposed to coming *with* the saints at a different time. It is often argued that because a given text does not include tenets that are given in a different text that different comings must be in view. Some postmillennialists make the similar argument as we will see. The irony is that *every constituent element found in Matthew 24:29f is found in 1 Thessalonians 4*. Yet the millennialists claim that these texts speak of different events! So, on the one hand we must see different comings in different texts because certain elements are omitted. On the other hand, we are to see different comings in spite of the fact that *the identical elements are found in both texts*! Both the postmillennialist and dispensationalists are guilty of this strange hermeneutic.

117. We are arguing for far more than *similarity of language* here. Patently, when one examines the Old Testament it is clear that identical language is used to describe the destruction of Assyria, Edom, the 10 northern tribes, Judah, etc. Yet, we would certainly not argue that because the language is the same, that the *time* is identical. We are saying however, that since the identical language is used in both Jesus and Paul, and since both use the identical *temporal indicators*, with the identical themes (i.e. vindication of the martyrs) that this demands identicality of subject. So, while we would be the first to argue that similarity of language does not prove identicality of topic, we would argue that similarity of language, similarity of temporal parameters, and thematic identicality does demand the same topic.

118. The amazing thing is that the millennialist comes closer to understanding the nature of the Day of the Lord in Thessalonians than they would like to admit. Biblically, the Day of the Lord is *never* an optically visible descent of God out of heaven on a literal cloud (Cf. Isaiah 13, 34; Micah 1:2f, etc.). It is an *in time* event wherein God acted to manifest His majesty, and to judge the wicked and vindicate His people. Jesus said that his *parousia* was going to be in the same manner as the Father had always judged (John 5:19f). Thus, the idea of an optically visible, literal, bodily descent of Jesus out of heaven is misguided. I have developed this extensively in my book, *Like Father, Like Son, On Clouds of Glory*. Also, see my book *Who Is This Babylon?* for a fuller discussion of the nature of the Day of the Lord.

119. For an in-depth examination of Ephesians 4 see *Commentary on the Epistle to the Ephesians*, John Eadie, (Grand Rapids, Zondervan, 1883)284f. Eadie disagrees with the view of many of the early church fathers concerning Christ's work at the ascension, but nonetheless takes note of it as a historical view.

120. I believe that Paul is referring, not to a change from a human material body to a spiritual soma, but from the Old Covenant body, the old tabernacle, to the spiritual body of Christ, and the Messianic, eternal temple. William Bell's presentation at the 2008 Preterist Pilgrim Weekend, Ardmore, Ok. is a fine presentation of this idea. The MP3s and DVDs of those two presentations, along with the other speakers, are available from my website, www.eschatology.org.

121. It should be carefully noted that although Paul uses the word "outward man" his discussion is the outer *tabernacle* versus the heavenly *tabernacle*, as is evidenced in chapter 5:1f. In *every other occurrence* of a contrast between an earthly tabernacle "made with hands" versus a heavenly tabernacle "not made with hands," it is a *covenantal contrast* between the temporal Old Covenant tabernacle system, versus the spiritual and eternal New Covenant temple of Christ. See Acts 7:48, Hebrews 8:1f for instance.

122. I fail to see a significant difference between walking through walls, *and walking on water* (Matthew 14) which of course, Jesus did long before his resurrection. If Jesus could defy the laws of physics before his resurrection (having control over space (John 4:46) nature, sickness and even death) why should it be considered strange that he could miraculously appear within a locked room after his resurrection? He could transport an entire large *boat* through space with but a word, (John 6:21)! Would walking though a wall be all that big a deal for him, if he could do *that?*

123. In my book, *Like Father, Like Son, On Clouds of Glory*, I spend considerable time proving this point and showing the fallacy of the arguments claiming that Jesus' resurrected, pre-ascension body was glorified. John knew what Jesus was like before and after the resurrection, *yet, after the ascension*, he did *not* know what Jesus was like (1 John 3:1f). This is important!

124. The importance of what God actually threatened in Genesis 2:15f cannot be overlooked. He said, "In the day that you eat, you will surely die." He did not say, "You will surely die, eventually, if you eat the fruit." He did not say, "You will begin to die." He did say, "In the day that you eat the fruit, you will surely die." That means that they had to die the very day that they transgressed, or else God failed. The problem is that 99% of all eschatologies are focused on physical death instead of spiritual fellowship, and as a result, they have to "re-word" God's threat to Adam and Eve. This is unsatisfactory.

125. The millennialists distort the story of resurrection, dividing it into several different stages, including the resurrection of the righteous at the rapture, the resurrection of the Old Testament saints and martyred tribulation saints at the Second Coming seven years later, the resurrection of the millennial saints and the wicked at the end of the millennium. Thomas Ice and Timothy Demy, *Fast Facts on Bible Prophecy*, (Eugene, Ore, 1997)166 See my *Who Is This Babylon?* for a discussion of some of the problems in the millennial view of resurrection.

126. It is fascinating that James Jordan, my opponent in a two day public debate, Tampa, Fl, October, 2004, has stated that Paul's reference to meeting Christ "in the air" has a theological meaning, the defeat of Satan. Satan is (supposedly) still the ruler of the air, and thus, to meet Christ in the air is a metaphorical manner of speaking of the destruction of Satan. Jordan nonetheless insists that 1 Thessalonians is not only theological but literal. The question is, why? Furthermore, if the defeat of Satan is the meeting Christ in the air, then Romans 16:20 is the *parousia* of Christ in the air but Jordan does not accept this posit. This is an inconsistent paradigm. Jordan's comments can be found in his tape series on Matthew 24, tape 5, side A.

127. James D. G. Dunn, *Word Biblical Commentary, Romans 9-16* (Dallas, Word Publishers, 1988)907

128. Kenneth Gentry, *Before Jerusalem Fell*, (Tyler, Tx, Institute for Christian Economics, 1989)133+.

129. It is a demonstration of the desperation of futurists when Thomas Ice tries to make *en tachei* mean rapidly as opposed to soon, or quickly. In *End Times Controversy*, (103) Ice claims that Acts 22:18, "is descriptive of the manner in which the action takes place" as opposed to when the action was to occur. The context is Jesus telling Paul, "Make haste, and get out of Jerusalem *quickly*" (*en tachei*) because men were seeking to kill him. Now, think about that for a moment. Was Jesus telling Paul not to worry about *when he left town,* but when he finally got around to leaving he was to take the fastest chariot he could find? No, he was to leave immediately because men were wanting to kill him! Rapidity of action is indeed present, but it most assuredly does not take precedent over how *soon* Paul was to leave!

130. Of course, if Paul was wrong in his predictions about when the end was to come, then the inspiration of scripture is destroyed, and no amount of rationalization can justify maintaining a reliance on such untrustworthy testimony. The wonderful thing is that there is no need to question whether or not his predictions came true. They did. It is the traditional concepts about the nature of the resurrection and *parousia*

that need to be challenged.

131. We have not, and will not develop the concept of the resurrection of the dead as the last days work of the Holy Spirit, due to the already large size of this work. To properly develop that critical doctrine would demand its own large volume. Suffice it to say that God would pour the charismatic gifts of the Spirit in Israel's last days (Joel 2:28f). That Spirit would be to raise Israel from the dead (Ezekiel 37:10-12). On Pentecost, Joel's prophecy– and thus, that of Ezekiel– began to be fulfilled. The charismatic gifts of the Spirit served as the *arrabon*, the *guarantee* (not down payment!) of the impending resurrection (Ephesians 1:12f; 2 Corinthians 5:5f). Thus, the presence of the charismata in the early church, as the message of salvation and the kingdom was preached to "the Jew first," was a manifest sign of God's faithfulness to His covenant promises to Israel. It was proof that the last days were present– not postponed. It was the guarantee that the gift of eternal life was about to become a reality. It ensured the delivery of the promised New Covenant, and much, much more! To ignore the charismatic ministry of the Spirit, for the purpose of the resurrection in 1 Thessalonians 4, is to ignore an essential element for the proper understanding of that text. And yet, very few commentators make the link between God's promise to Israel to raise her from the dead through the outpouring of the Spirit in the last days. This is an oversight that is fatal to the proper exegesis of 1 Thessalonians (or of 1 Corinthians 15).

132. At the writing of this book, I am currently working on a series of audio lessons on Ezekiel 37 and Paul's commentary on that great chapter. I hope to have it finished in the not too distant future.

133. N. T. Wright, Paul, (Minneapolis, Fortress, 2005)54.

134. Ralph Martin, *Word Biblical Commentary, Vol 40 2 Corinthians*, Vol 40. Martin realizes that Paul is affirming the "urgency" of his "now" but makes no comment on the fact that Isaiah 49, that Paul is citing as being fulfilled, is a resurrection prophecy. So, on the one hand Martin says Paul affirms the fulfillment of Isaiah 49, and yet he overlooks the implication of what this means. Isaiah 49 foretold the resurrection. Paul was therefore, by saying that Isaiah 49 was being fulfilled, saying that the time for the resurrection was present.

135. Murray Harris, *The New International Greek Text Commentary, 2 Corinthians*, (Grand Rapids, Eerdmans, Paternoster, 2005)462. Like Martin, Harris fails to comment on the fact that Isaiah 49 foretold the *resurrection*, and that therefore Paul's declaration that the acceptable time had arrived meant that the time of the resurrection was present.

136. One could comment at length on the connection between Romans 11 and Romans 15. We have shown that Paul affirmed, "Israel has not obtained that which she sought, but, the elect has obtained it...". Well,

in chapter 15 he undeniably states that the anticipated Banner for the People, had been erected. As foretold, the nations were being gathered to him. So, the hope of Israel was being fulfilled. The truth is that in direct contradiction to the millennial paradigm, the calling of the Gentiles into the body of Christ was not due to the failure or postponement of the promises to Israel, but in direct fulfillment of those promises.

137. We cannot develop it in-depth here, but, Peter is in agreement with Paul that the promised restoration of Israel– i.e. her resurrection was taking place. In 1 Peter he addresses his (*Jewish*) Christian audience as the *diaspora* (1 Peter 1:1-2). He speaks of the time of their sojourning (this is the "wilderness wandering" or, perhaps her "captivity" (1 Peter 1:17). He calls them pilgrims and sojourners (1 Peter 2:12). This period was their time of testing and refining (cf. Daniel 12:10) but would only last for a short time (1 Peter 1:4f). I suggest that this suffering Peter refers to is the period known as the birth pangs of Messiah, the Messianic Woes foretold by Jesus in Matthew 24:8f, and that Paul referred to in Romans 8:18f. (See our discussion below on 1 Thessalonians 5). Peter also says that the promise of Hosea– the promise of the remarriage / resurrection of the ten tribes *was being fulfilled in them* (1 Peter 2:10– cf. Hosea 2:23) and says that they were becoming a special people for God's own possession (1 Peter 2:9)– a citation of Exodus 19:5-6. The anticipated end had drawn near, and the time had arrived for the judgment– the promised resurrection (1 Peter 4:5, 7, 17). Everywhere we turn in 1 Peter we encounter echoes, allusions and citations of God's promises to restore Israel. Peter is emphatic that those promises were being fulfilled in Christ and the consummation was at hand.

138. As Pitre notes, (*Tribulation*, 417) in the Old Testament, "The Exile is only brought to an end by a climactic period of tribulation or affliction in which a key figure, the Messiah/Son of Man, or the Servant, dies, and thereby atones for the sins of Israel that have led her into exile in the first place." This is precisely what we see in Isaiah 49. That is why we can confidently say that the redeemed of the tribes of Israel in Isaiah 49 come out of the tribulation, just as Revelation describes. John did not invent that concept out of clean cloth.

139. Rikki Watts, *Isaiah's New Exodus in Mark*, (Grand Rapids, Baker, 1997)111.

140. Tom Holland, *Contours of Pauline Theology*, (Christian Focus Publications, Geanies House, Fearn, Ross-Shire IV20 1TW, Scotland, UK, 2004)46. Holland is citing C. H. Dodd.

141. Thomas Ice and Kenneth Gentry, *The Great Tribulation, Past or Present, A Written Debate*, Ice (Grand Rapids, Kregel, 1999)98.

142. The parallelism between Isaiah 49 and 61, and Jesus and Paul's positive declaration that the time of fulfillment had arrived, demands that we see the promises of the restoration of Israel "in the land" as fulfilled spiritually in Christ. Both Isaiah 49 and 61 specifically mention the restoration of the "desolate places" and the land. Yet, while Jesus and Paul affirm the fulfillment of Isaiah, neither one even mention the physical land! Paul sets forth the spiritual nature of the fulfillment as the dwelling place "in Christ." We cannot expound on this further, but, it is highly significant and suggestive. See W. D. Davies, *The Gospel and the Land*, for a good discussion of these issues.

143. In my July 2008 debate with John Welch, he repeatedly, and more than a little caustically, asked why the Thessalonians, "hundreds of miles away" from Jerusalem, would be concerned with that destruction and the fulfillment of God's promises to Israel. My response was that distance does not determine importance, or lack thereof, nor does the size of an event determine its significance. The death of Jesus on the Cross was far less known than the fall of Jerusalem! I asked Welch repeatedly why the Thessalonians would have been concerned with the death of a rabble rousing Jew, hundreds of miles removed from them? He offered not one word of response.

144. One of the great tragedies of the millennial view is the desire to restore a physical king on a physical throne, in a physical city, in a physical land. Yet, from the beginning, that kind of Lordship was a sign of *the rejection of the sovereignty of God!* See 1 Samuel 8:6f: 10:17f; 12:17f. This is why Jesus, when offered that kind of kingship and kingdom, "withdrew himself" (John 6:15). Jesus realized that his kingdom was not of this world (John 18:36) and that to accept the Jew's offer of a nationalistic, socio-military-geocentric kingdom would only confirm the rebellion against his Father!

145. The tabernacle of David in Amos is not referent to a literal temple. David never built the temple. The reference is to the fact that the ten tribes had been cut off from the house of David. (See 1 Kings 12:16f; 2 Kings 17:20f). Amos is promising that the Messianic and salvation promises would be extended to them once again.

146. This book is available from my websites: www.bibleprophecy.com, or, www.eschatology.org.

147. R. C. H. Lenski, *The Interpretation of St Paul's Epistles to the Colossians, to the Thessalonians, To Timothy, to Titus and Philemon*, (Minneapolis, Min., Augsburg, 1946)329.

148. A. T. Robertson, *Word Pictures In the New Testament*, Vol. 4, (Broadman, Nashville, 1931)31.

149. F. F. Bruce, *Word Biblical Commentary, 1 & 2 Thessalonians*, (Waco, Word Publishers, 1982)98

150. See James Everett Frame, *International Critical Commentary, Thessalonians*, (Edinburgh, T & T Clark, 1960)167f; Also Greg Beale, *1-2 Thessalonians, The IVP Testament Commentary Series*, (Downers Grove, Ill, InterVarsity Press, 2003)134.

151. See my book *In Flaming Fire* for an in-depth examination of Paul's promise of imminent vindication and relief of the Thessalonians. While Mathison and Gentry seek to deny the indications of imminence in 2 Thessalonians 1, the language is graphic and specific, falsifying any attempt to negate its power. My book is referenced elsewhere in this work.

152. William Lane, *Word Biblical Commentary, Hebrews 9-13*, (Dallas, Word Publishers, 1991).

153. In a sense the question of whether the translation of 1 Thessalonians 4:14 should be "in Christ" or "through Christ," becomes almost immaterial. Here is why. Thessalonians 4 discusses the time of the resurrection. This is the time of Hebrews 11:35. Therefore, 1 Thessalonians 4 is synchronous with Hebrews 11. But, Hebrews is the time of the vindication and rewarding of the martyrs of God. Therefore, 1 Thessalonians is the time of the rewarding (and vindication) of the martyrs of God.

154. Lane (*Hebrews*, 1991, 390) says that, "Only one specific incident of such a stoning is reported in the O.T. Zechariah, son of Jehoiada the priest, had been stoned to death in the temple courtyard by order of king Joash." This is the Zecharias of Matthew 23, per Lane. It is clear that the Hebrews writer is on the same page as Jesus in regard to the martyrs.

155. As noted, the commentators seldom comment on the link between Matthew 23 and Hebrews 11 in regard to eschatological fulfillment. Lane in an otherwise helpful section on the martyrs of Hebrews 11, does *mention* Matthew 23 a few times. However, he says not one word about the significance of that link in regard to the fulfillment of the Abrahamic promises, the *parousia* or the resurrection. This oversight is lamentable for the implications of the connections are profound.

156. To be sure, there is an "already-but-not-yet" eschatology in the New Testament, as almost all scholars agree. However, what Mathison, et. al, fail to honor is that in the NT, the "not yet" i.e. the consummation to which Mathison refers, is *never* posited as far off. It is invariably at hand and coming soon. This is clear in the Hebrew declaration that those first century saints had arrived at Zion.

157. The importance of Zion in Old Testament prophecies of the end can hardly be overemphasized. Virtually all eschatological and soteriological tenets and blessings are linked with the "holy city." Zion would be the capital of the kingdom and from there the New Covenant would flow (Isaiah 2:2f). YHWH would rule in Zion (Isaiah 24:20f) and In Zion the Messianic Banquet would be spread, when death was swallowed up in victory (Isaiah 25:6f). Thus, for the Hebrews writer to affirm in the most unequivocal manner that his first century audience had now come to Zion was a startling, thrilling, and unabashed declaration that the eschatological consummation was now near.

158. It should be noted that just as Isaiah 25 foretold the establishment of the Messianic Banquet at the time of the destruction of the "city of confusion" (Isaiah 24:10f; 25:1-3) when the Temple would be turned over to foreigners, Isaiah 65 likewise predicted the time when YHVH's servants would feast, but OT Israel would be destroyed, and God would form the New Creation (Isaiah 65:13-19). Matthew 8 agrees perfectly that the Kingdom Banquet would be at the resurrection, when the "sons of the kingdom" would be cast out. Gentry's admissions are fatal to his paradigm.

159. See the even more graphic parallel in Luke 13:27f, where Jesus said Abraham would sit at the kingdom with those from the east and west, "and yourselves cast out." There is no question that Jesus was positing the time of the kingdom, the fulfillment of the Abrahamic *resurrection promise*, at the time when Old Covenant Israel would be cast out.

160. There are some commentators, mostly postmillennialists, who see a distinction between 1 Thessalonians 4 and 2 Thessalonians 2. DeMar *Last Days Madness: Obsession of the Modern Church*, (Atlanta, GA. American Vision, 1994)341 applies 2 Thessalonians 2 to the AD 70 judgment, while applying 1 Thessalonians 4 to a yet future coming (p. 186-189). His reasons for such a division are unconvincing however, and in my *Like Father Like Son, On Clouds of Glory*, I demonstrate that his evidence is faulty.

161. Andrew Perriman, *The Coming of the Son of Man*, (Grand Rapids, Paternoster, 2005)155.

162. See my book *Like Father Like Son, On Clouds of Glory*, for an extensive discussion of Christ's coming "in the glory of the Father." Don K. Preston, (Ardmore, Ok. JaDon Management Inc., 2006, 2010). Available at www.eschatology.org.

163. Ben Witherington III, *Jesus, Paul, and the End of the world*, (Downer's Grove, Ill., Inter-Varsity Press, 1992)163.

164. Normally, the connection between Matthew 23, Thessalonians and Revelation is severed by the assumption that Revelation was written after the fulfillment of Matthew 23 and 1 Thessalonians 2:14f. Thus, it is argued that Revelation discusses a different set of martyrs, a different time of vindication. Of course, this is based on the *false assumption* that Revelation was written after the fulfillment promised by Jesus in Matthew 23, i.e. the AD 70 judgment of Jerusalem. See my book *Who Is This Babylon?* for a refutation of the late date of Revelation.

165. The indisputable fact that Paul says that God would give to the persecutors *what the persecutors were giving the saints*, demonstrates that Paul was not speaking of eternal reward. He was speaking of *physical persecution on the persecutors*, and relief from physical persecution for the believers. This is borne out by the fact that 2 Thessalonians 1 draws heavily from Isaiah 66, as virtually all critical commentators agree, but Isaiah 66 is a prediction of the judgment of Old Covenant Israel for her sin.

166. Charles Wanamaker, *The New International Greek Testament Commentary, on 1 & 2 Thessalonians*, (Grand Rapids, Eerdmans, Paternoster, 1990)224.

167. The Abomination of Desolation must be seen as *Covenant Wrath on Old Covenant Jerusalem* for persecuting the saints. This crucial fact is often overlooked in the exegesis of the Olivet Discourse, but is crucial to properly understand the "why" of the Abomination. Covenantally speaking, YHVH never allowed such desecration of the temple or the land, unless Israel was in violation of Torah. This all hearkens back to the Law of Blessings and Cursings, the Song of Moses (Deuteronomy 32) and the fact that in the last days YHVH would "avenge the blood of His saints" (Deuteronomy 32:43). Needless to say, this has tremendous implications for modern dispensationalism, that holds that during the Great Tribulation, Israel is essentially an "innocent victim" of the dreaded man of Sin. There is no *innocence* associated with the Abomination of Desolation, however!

168. It is, in fact, somewhat interesting to see how little attention Paul's reference to the archangel garners in the literature. While many scholars comment on the *fact* of the archangel, and even how Daniel plays a part in the context of the archangel, there are few indeed that develop the *significance* of this the connection. F. F. Bruce, *Word Biblical Commentary*, (Waco, TX., Word Publishers, 1982)100, even doubts that Michael is intended in Thessalonians, noting that in Jewish tradition there were seven arch angels. This hardly negates our point, since it is still the archangel present at the time of the resurrection in Daniel 12. So, unless one can divorce the resurrection at the time of the work of Michael, at the time of the end, from the resurrection at the *parousia* in Thessalonians, our point remains established. Daniel

posited that resurrection at the time when the power of the holy people is completely shattered.

169. A. T. Robertson, *Word Pictures in the New Testament*, Vol. IV, (Nashville, Broadman, 1931)32.

170. In my aforementioned 2008 debate with amillennialist John Welch, his response to my appeal to the O.T. source of New Testament eschatology was to say, repeatedly, "Preston needs to stay out of the Old Testament!" Similarly, in a formal written debate my amillennial opponent emphatically said he had no interest or intention of studying the OT in our debate, and that there is no need whatsoever to explore the OT in order to understand the New Testament teaching on eschatology. That debate is archived on my website: www.eschatology.org.

171. Robert Brimsmead, *The Pattern of Redemptive History* (Falbrook, CA. Verdict Publications, 1979)8.

172. Daniel 10:13; 10:21; 12:1; Jude 9; Revelation 12:7.

173. See my discussion of Revelation 12 and its correlation to the millennium in my *Who Is This Babylon* book.

174. Perriman (*Coming*, 119+) shows that the language of 1 Thessalonians 2:14f suggests that God's judgment of Israel as the persecutor had already manifested itself in several catastrophic events in Jerusalem when Paul wrote, but that the final crushing blow had not yet been dealt.

175. The attempts to negate Paul's straightforward promise of relief for the Thessalonians at the *parousia* are lamentable. In several formal debates, I have made the point that *you cannot give someone relief from something they are not experiencing*. Paul did not say that the Thessalonians would receive relief from persecution through their death. He did not say that they would die, and sometime millennia later, be vindicated. He said they would receive *relief* from their then on-going persecution at the *parousia*. It is a denial of the text to argue otherwise.

176. Jeffrey Weima, *Commentary on the New Testament Use of the Old Testament*, Greg Beale, D. A. Carson, (Grand Rapids, Baker Academic, 2007)880, lists Isaiah 27:13, Joel 2:1, Zephaniah 1:14-16, and Zechariah 9:14, as Old Testament prophecies that link the Trumpet with the end times.

177. Perriman (*Coming*, 74f) while only briefly mentioning the trump, (and Isaiah 27:13) shows that the gathering of the elect was for the ushering in of the New Creation, a New *Covenant people*, not the end of human history.

178. Jon Levenson, *Resurrection and the Restoration of Israel*, (New Haven and London, Yale University Press, 2006)154-155. Levenson goes on to say that he believed that the later prophets did develop the idea of a biological resurrection, but that this was not the original Hebraic view.

179. Naturally, the establishment of the New Covenant world would have direct implications and impact on the biologically dead as well, as Paul promised that they would receive their reward at the *parousia*. This involved the fulfillment of God's promises to Abraham– long dead biologically– that he would receive the heavenly country and city (Hebrews 11:13f– cf. Matthew 8:11f). However, the fulfillment of that aspect of the promise entailed events in the unseen realm, with the visible events serving as the unseen reality.

180. Notice a somewhat parallel thought in John 5:24f. Jesus said that the dead would "hear the voice of the Son of Man" and come to life. Yet, I am unaware of any commentator that would argue that the dead under consideration would all literally hear the voice of Jesus. The idea is that those who heard the call of Christ *through his emissaries* would be hearing his voice.

181. *When Shall These Things Be? A Reformed Response to Hyper-Preterism*, Keith Mathison, editor, (Phillipsburg, New Jersey, P and R Publishing, 2004). (Hereafter *WSTTB*, DKP).

182. Keith Mathison, *From Age To Age The Unfolding of Biblical Eschatology*, Phillipsburg, NJ, 2009)281.

183. *Postmillennialism: An Eschatology of Hope*, (New Jersey, P & R Publishing, 1999)151f.

184. Kenneth Gentry, *The Greatness of the Great Commission*, (Tyler, Tx., Institute for Christian Economics, 1993)142.

185. Interestingly, in his revised *Dominion*, (2009, 495, n. 45) Gentry takes note that dispensationalist Dwight Pentecost had radically altered his views over the years yet had not acknowledged or indicated that change in his later writings. He says Pentecost's "radical shift" in his application of some key eschatological texts, "does not seem to him to compromise his eschatological system." Gentry has made an astoundingly radical shift in his application of one of the key eschatological texts, and yet has not indicated that change in his writings so far as we can determine. He has *done* what he chides Pentecost for doing!

186. William Hendrickson, *New Testament Commentary*, (Grand Rapids, Baker, 2002)117.

187. Beale even equivocates on how literal the *parousia* is, noting that the word *parousia* actually means presence, not coming. He acknowledges N. T. Wright's view that *parousia* does not indicate a downward coming of Christ on literal clouds. What Beale does not note is that Wright, as we will see, sees the language of meeting Christ in the air (v. 17) as reference, not to the church taken from the earth at the end of human history, but of *Christ coming to dwell with man on earth.* Beale takes note of this definition of *apantesis* (see our discussion below) and acknowledges, "It is certainly possible Paul intends such a background imagery to be woven within the broader framework of Jesus' coming" (2003, 140-141, footnote). Beale does not comment on the incredible implications of granting this view.

188. We take this view because even *parousia* is often said to be a technical term. Adolf Deissman, *Light From the Ancient East,* (Grand Rapids, Baker, 1978)368+ said of parousia: "We are able to trace the word (*parousia*, DKP) in the East as a technical expression for the arrival or the visit of the king or the emperor." So, if *parousia* has technical meaning, and if *apantesis* has technical application, logic would seem to suggest that when used *together* that the technical sense is being emphasized.

189. Balz and Schnieder, *Exegetical Dictionary of the New Testament,* Vol. I, (Grand Rapids, Eerdmans, 1978-1980)114+

190. Bauer's Arndt and Gingrich, *Greek-English Lexicon of the New Testament and Other Early Christian Literature*, (Chicago Chicago Press, 1979)80.

191. Ethelbert W. Bullinger, *A Critical Lexicon and Concordance to the English and Greek New Testament,* (London, Longmans, Green and Co, 1908)491.

192. *Kittel's Theological Dictionary of N.T. Words*, Vol. 1, (Grand Rapids, Eerdmans, 1974)380.

193. *Liddell and Scott's Greek-English Lexicon*, (Abridged) (Simon Wallenberg Press, 2007)77.

194. Louw and Nida *Greek English Lexicon*, Vol. 1, item 15.78, (New York, United Bible Societies, 1988)192.

195. James Hope Moulton and George Milligan, *The Vocabulary of the Greek Testament Illustrated from the Papyri and other Non-Literary Sources*, (Grand Rapids, Eerdmans, 1930)53.

196. *Thayer's Greek English Lexicon of the New Testament*, (Grand Rapids, Zondervan, 1973)54.

197. *Vines' Expository Dictionary of New Testament Words,* Vol. III (New Jersey, Fleming H. Revell, 1966)58.

198. Michael R. Cosby, in "Hellenistic Formal Receptions and Paul's Use of Apantesis in 1 Thessalonians 4:17," Bulletin for Biblical Research, (1994)15-33.

199. It is interesting that Cosby likewise rejected his early (dispensational) theological training based on his "new" understanding of Thessalonians and *apantesis* as a technical term. However, in the aforementioned article, he now says that he has come to reject the technical usage of *apantesis*. I do not find his reasons for now rejecting the technical meaning of *apantesis* to be convincing at all.

200. E. Peterson, cited by Joseph Plevnik, "1 Thessalonians 4, 17: The Bringing in of the Lord or the Bringing in of the Faithful?" Biblica 80 (1999)537-546, Joseph Plevnik, S. J. Thanks to David Warren for pointing me to Plevnik's article.

201. Charles Wanamaker, *New International Greek Testament Commentary*, Thessalonians, (Grand Rapids, Eerdmans, Paternoster, 1990)175.

202. James Frame, *International Critical Commentary on 1 and 2 Thessalonians*, (Edinburgh, T and T Clark, 1960)176+.

203. John Eadie, *The John Eadie Greek Text Commentaries, Thessalonians*, (Grand Rapids, Baker, 1979)169.

204. F. F. Bruce, *Word Biblical Commentary, Thessalonians,* (Waco, Word, 1982)102f.

205. Samuel Waldron, *The End Times Made Simple,* Calvary Press, 2003)189.

206. In fact, I fully agree with the idea of vindication and glorification, for we find this in the idea of meeting Christ in the air (*aer*) demonstrating his victory and sovereignty over the principalities and powers.

207. We are not suggesting an "either-or" view of *harpadzo*. As most commentators suggest, Thessalonians is a multi-layered text, with many ideas at work. The text obviously draws on the OT prophecies, on Jesus' Olivet Discourse, on the Marriage theme, the temple theme, the Coming of the King, etc.. So, one cannot simply say that *harpadzo* must be either the catching up in vindication and relief, or, it must be this or that. It is all of these!

208. As a cautionary note, we are not insisting that every aspect of the technical use of a term must be present. However, the question is does the use of *parousia* and *apantesis* normally suggest a simple meeting, or does the imagery suggest a meeting and accompaniment back to the destination. There seems to be little doubt that the latter is what is suggested. Furthermore, when the rest of the New Testament evidence

is that the *parousia* of Christ was not for the purpose of removing the church from the earth, but rather to dwell with man, i.e. "the tabernacle of God is with man," then this is strong substantiating evidence that we should honor the core images of the technical use of *parousia* and *apantesis*.

209. As we have suggested above, the Father's house is the new Messianic Temple established among men for YHVH to dwell with man.

210. Balz-Schneider, *Exegetical Dictionary of N. T. Words*, Vol. III, (Grand Rapids, Eerdmans, 1982-1983)44.

211. See Adolf Deissman, *Light From the Ancient East*, (Grand Rapids, Baker, 1978)368+ for a discussion of *parousia* in the ancient world: "We are able to trace the word (*parousia*, DKP) in the East as a technical expression for the arrival or the visit of the king or the emperor." Cosby likewise admits, "Christians used *parousia* as a technical term for the second coming of Christ, although, as did others in their cultures. They also used it of lesser arrivals" (1994, 21).

212. Josephus, *Antiquities* XI:8:4-5; (Whiston)306.

213. This story in Josephus is controversial among critical scholars, many claiming that it is spurious. However, generally speaking the reason for that claim is that if the story is true, then the "liberal" claims of the late day of Daniel are falsified. I have seen no convincing evidence to either reject the story in Josephus, or to accept the late date of Daniel.

214. Josephus, *Wars*, Book VII:IV:1, Gaalya Cornfeld General editor, (Grand Rapids, Zondervan, 1982)462.

215. Michael R. Cosby, in "Hellenistic Formal Receptions and Paul's Use of *Apantesis* in 1 Thessalonians 4:17," Bulletin for Biblical Research, (1994)15-33.

216. Thomas Ice, "The Meeting in the Sky," CTS Journal, 8 (July-September 2003)64-70.

217. Robert Gundry, "A Brief Note on 'Hellenistic Formal Receptions and Paul's Use of Apantesis in 1 Thessalonians 4:17'," Bulletin for Biblical Research 6 (1996)39-41. In short, Cosby argued that there are five elements absent from Thessalonians that are present in non-Biblical descriptions of *apantesis*. Gundry shows that in fact, *each of the elements is linked with Christ's parousia*.

218. I will be citing page numbers from that article. I printed the article off of the PDF file on CD that I received when I ordered the set of lessons.

219. See Thomas Ice's article, *Pre-Trib Perspectives*, P. O. Box 14111, Arlington, Tx., Vol. VII, Number 3, August 2002, in which he openly admits that the church has (temporarily) replaced Israel. Interestingly, he condemns non-millennialists for teaching Replacement Theology.

220. Cf. John Walvoord and Roy Zuck, *The Bible Knowledge Commentary, New Testament*, (Whitby, Ontario, Canada, Victor Press, 1984)80.

221. www.eschatology.org, or, www.bibleprophecy.com

222. We are using the word "earth" here accomodatively. I am not convinced at all that the global earth is the focus of 2 Peter 3. See my *The Elements Shall Melt With Fervent Heat*, for an investigation of this issue. Available at: www.eschatology.org, or, www.bibleprophecy.com

223. Joseph Mayor, *The Epistle of St. Jude and the Second Epistle of St. Peter*, (Eugene, Or., Wipf and Stock Publishers, 1907/ 2004)162, n. 2: Points out that the dominant view of ancient Rabbis was that the world / creation is permanent and will never pass away. He Cites Ps. 148:4-6 and 104:5.

224. Richard Middleton, *A New Heaven and New Earth: The Case for a Holistic Reading of the Biblical Story of Redemption*, Journal for Christian Theological Research 11 (2006)73-97– "Laying bare (or uncovering)..."As is well know to New Testament scholars, this is not a translation decision, but rather a matter of text criticism. But, whereas the translators of the KJV had only inferior Greek manuscripts available to them, and thus may be excused, many later English translators continued to utilize these inferior manuscripts despite the clear presence of the verb for "laid bare" (or revealed.' 'Uncovered,' or 'discovered') in the main Greek codices that form the primary witnesses used to construct the eclectic Greek text on which modern translations are typically based."

225. See John Eadie, *Commentary on the Epistle to the Ephesians*, (Grand Rapids, Zondervan, 1861)123+.

226. Max R. King, *Spirit of Prophecy*, (Warren, Ohio, 1971)206f.

227. Tyndale New Testament Commentaries, I and II Thessalonians (Grand Rapids, Eerdmans, 1957)88.

228. Leon Morris, *New International Commentary on the New Testament, 1st and 2nd Thessalonians*, (Grand Rapids, Eerdmans, 1991)146.

229. Milton Terry, *Biblical Apocalyptics: A Study of the Most Notable Revelations of God and of Christ*, (Grand Rapids, Baker Book House, 1898)246-247.

230. Marcellus Kik, *An Eschatology of Victory*, (Presbyterian and Reformed Press, 1971)140-141, cf. 142-143.

231. Hank Hanegraaff, *The Apocalypse Code*, (Thomas Nelson, 2007)254, n. 36, 37.

232. George Eldon Ladd, *The Presence of the Future*, (Grand Rapids, Eerdmans, 1974)62.

233. Colin Brown, *New International Dictionary of New Testament Theology*, vol. 2, (Exeter, UK, 1976)35f.

234. David Chilton, *Paradise Restored*, (Ft. Worth, Dominion Press, 1987)104.

235. We cannot develop this here, but the promise of Isaiah 26 hearkens back to Deuteronomy 32:43, where Jehovah said that in Israel's last days he would avenge the shed blood of His servants. The focus is on Israel's last days, not the last days of time, or the last days of the Christian age. Thus, resurrection–and this includes 1 Thessalonians 4:13f-- is clearly posited at the end of the Old Covenant age of Israel.

236. N. T. Wright, *Jesus and the Victory of God*, (Minneapolis, Fortress, 1996)591.

237. Eusebius, *The Proof of the Gospel*, Vol. I, Bk. I, ch. 6, Edited and Translated by W. J. Ferrar (Grand Rapids, Baker, 1981)35.

238. See my article "1 Peter and Israel's Land Promises." While many commentators claim that 1 Peter was addressed to a Gentile audience, Peter is clear that he was addressing the *diaspora*, and he discusses the Old Covenant promises of the restoration of Israel. See my article at: http://www.eschatology.org/index.php?option=com_content&view=article&id=661:1-peter-and-israels-land-promises&catid=116:topical-studies&Itemid=61.

239. Many commentators believe that "anoint the Most Holy" refers to the anointing of Jesus at his baptism. However, the Hebrew words used in Daniel 9 are used some forty-two times in Exodus, Leviticus, Numbers and Ezekiel. The words are used to speak of the Most Holy Place of the tabernacle more than twice the number of times used to speak of any other object. (See Boutflower, *In And Around the Book of Daniel,* (Grand Rapids, Kregel, 1977)188.

240. The fall of Jerusalem was the sign of Christ's *parousia*. They were not to look for a visible descent of a literal cloud. However, the passing of the Old temple was proof positive, the sign of the Son of Man (Matthew 24:30). It is valid to ask, if the coming of Jesus was to be a visible, bodily coming on literal clouds, why would they need a sign of its reality? And yet, this is precisely what Jesus said would be given, "the sign of the Son of Man." The destruction of the Old temple

was to be the sign that the Son of Man was now in his new temple. See Jeffrey A. Gibbs, *Jerusalem and The Parousia*, (St. Louis, MO, Concordia Academic Press, 2000)198f.

241. When Chilton *wrote Paradise Restored*, he was a "partial preterist," and did not see the connection between Matthew 23:37, 24:29-31 and 1 Thessalonians 4. However, by 1997 Chilton had seen that connection, and had become a full preterist. His speech delivered at the Oklahoma City Prophecy Conference, that I helped organize, is available. On the tape, he undeniably states that he had become a full preterist. Tapes of that conference are available from our website: www.eschatology.org It is, incidentally, disturbing that Gentry *misrepresents Chilton's eschatology* in, *Thine Is the Kingdom*, by calling him a postmillennialist. When Gentry wrote *Thine*, Chilton was dead, but it is undeniably true that in 1997 *Chilton was a full preterist*. I have his own words on tape to prove it. Gentry was fully aware of Chilton's beliefs in 1997, and his misrepresentation of Chilton is shameful on this issue.

242. Isn't the time of the judgment of the living and the dead the time of the resurrection (2 Timothy 4:1; 1 Peter 4:5, 7, 17)? So, the time of the judgment of Jerusalem is the time of the resurrection, and the time of the resurrection is the time discussed in 1 Thessalonians 4.

243. There are actually many motifs included in the language of Matthew 24:29f. The idea of *judgment* is strongly suggested by the darkening of the sun, moon, stars, etc.. The imagery of the Danielic *Son of Man coming into the kingdom* (Daniel 7:13f) is present as well, and the sounding of the Trumpet can signify the resurrection motif, the call to the assembly for the dedication of the new temple, and the sounding of the Great Jubilee, etc.. To say that Matthew 24:29-31 is a treasure house of thought is a vast understatement.

244. Although it may not *be definitive*, the word that is translated as "fellow countrymen" (*sumphuleton*, i.e. fellow *tribesmen*) is suggestive that it is referent to the Jews. This is from *phule*, which is used some 31 times in the N.T. and most generally refers *to the tribes of Israel*.

245. In the Deaver-V-Preston debate, March 2008, amillennialist Mac Deaver argued that the persecutors *were not Jews*, and that he had thus undermined my entire affirmative. I countered by noting–for argument sake- that it did not matter who the persecutors were, because Paul promised the then living Thessalonians relief from that persecution "when the Lord Jesus is revealed from heaven." Furthermore, I noted, with no response from Deaver, that the persecutors were to be cast out of the presence of the Lord, and that *only one people* had ever dwelt in the presence of the Lord and could therefore, be cast out of His presence!

246. It is significant that, with the exception of those commentators who believe that 1 Thessalonians 2:14f is a later Christian interpolation, there is almost universal consensus that Paul was predicting what we now know as the AD 70 catastrophe. How is it then that in 2 Thessalonians 1 we find the identical problem, in the identical church, and the identical promise given, and yet 99.9% of commentators see no correlation between the texts? This is an egregious oversight.

247. The millennialists make a distinction between 1 Thessalonians 4 and 2 Thessalonians 1. They apply 1 Thessalonians 4 to the rapture, and 2 Thessalonians 1 to the Second Coming seven years later, to destroy the man of sin. However, that is untenable as we have shown.

248. As noted above, there are two sides of the Day of the Lord, redemption and judgment. 1 Thessalonians 4 focuses on the redemptive side, 2 Thessalonians 1 is focused on the judgment aspect. These are not two different events as some seek to affirm.

249. In my March 2008 debate with Mac Deaver, he sought to deny that the persecutors in 2 Thessalonians 1 were the Jews. He claimed that the "country men" of the Thessalonians were not the Jews, and that therefore, this proves that the *parousia* in judgment of 2 Thessalonians 1 is not the judgment of 1 Thessalonians 2:15f, which he did agree was AD 70. I noted that the Jews were the country men of the Thessalonians, as proven by Acts 17. I noted that only the Jews had ever dwelt in the presence of God, and were therefore, *the only ones* that could be cast out of His Presence (2 Thessalonians 1:9f). Finally, I argued that in the final analysis, it matters not who the persecutors of 2 Thessalonians were, it does not mitigate the fact that Paul promised the Thessalonians relief from their persecution at the *parousia* of Christ!

250. In my March, 2008 debate with amillennialist Mac Deaver PhD, in Carlsbad, N. M., Deaver tried to imply that if Jesus is not coming back in the future that this destroys all hope of heaven and salvation for the Christian. Such an illogical *non-sequitur* is lamentably characteristic of those who do not understand Covenant Eschatology. It is, in fact, *only if Christ has come* that eternal life and life in the presence of God, are realities and the possession of the child of God today. Otherwise, the Torah remains valid, sin still reigns over us, death is still the enemy of *even the child of God!* See my discussion of these issues in that debate, available from my website: www.eschatology.org.

251. John 3:15-16; 5:24; 6:50, 58; 8:51-52; 10:28; 11:26.

252. John 3:36; 4:14, 36; 5:21, 25, 26, 39; 6:27, 33, 35, 40, 47, 50, 51, 53, 54, 58, 63, 68; 11:25; 12:50; 14:6; 17:2, 3; 20:31.

253. It is obvious, is it not, that the coming of Revelation 14 cannot be an "end of time" coming of Christ? The text plainly says that men

would continue to die (physically) after the coming of Christ! Well, if men continue to die after the *parousia*, then undeniably, the *parousia* does not terminate human history on earth.

254. It is sometimes objected that Paul could not be saying that Christ was to return in the lifetime of "we who are alive" i.e. his generation, since he believed that he would probably die, and then be resurrected at the *parousia* (2 Corinthians 4:14). This takes for granted a physical resurrection, which Paul rejected, and assumes that in Thessalonians Paul was *specifying* who would or would not live until the end. He did no such thing. He did not say, "I will remain until the coming of the Lord." He was speaking nonetheless to living human beings of his generation and said, "those of us who are alive (Was Paul alive at the time?) and remain until." It is not an assertion that *he* would, but that his generation would remain until the coming of the Lord.

255. As an amillennialist, I was raised believing that Matthew 16:27 referred to the "end of time," but that verse 28 referred to Pentecost. This is an indefensible position as I prove in my book *Can You Believe Jesus Said This?* Available from our website www.eschatology.org. Christ's coming in glory is his coming in his kingdom. But, Christ's coming in glory is his coming in judgment, therefore, the coming in his kingdom is the coming in judgment (Matthew 25:31f). This patently did not happen on Pentecost.

256. In April, 2002, Ed Stevens (International Preterist Association, Bradford, Pa, 16701) and I had an all day debate with two amillennialists on the issue of the last days. I presented a major affirmative speech based on the argument about the vindication of the martyrs and resurrection. The argument clearly, and visibly, shook our opponents. During the entirety of the debate, they never said one single word in response to this basic argument. Tapes of that debate are available from our website: www.eschatology.org.

257. *Expositor's Greek Testament,* Robertson Nicoll, (Grand Rapids, Eerdmans, 1970)7.

258. Balz and Schnieder, *Exegetical Dictionary of the New Testament*, Vol. 2 (Grand Rapids, Eerdmans, 1981)232.

259. Richard Trench, *The Synonyms of the New Testament*, (Grand Rapids, Eerdmans, 1975)210, 211.

260. "The anaphoric article is the article denoting previous reference. (It derives it's name from the Greek verb *anaferein*, "to bring back, to bring up"). The first mention of the substantive is usually anathrous (w/o the article, DKP) because it is merely being introduced. But subsequent mentions of it use the article, for the article is now pointing back to the substantive previously mentioned. The anaphoric article has

by nature, then, a pointing back force to it, reminding the reader of who or what was mentioned previously. It is the most common use of the article and the easiest usage to identify." Daniel B. Wallace, *Greek Grammar Beyond the Basics: An Exegetical Syntax of the NT*, pg. 218-19. My thanks to Jeremy Lile of Indianapolis for the citation from the Greek grammar on the anaphoric article.

261. See *Bauer's Arndt and Gingrich Greek Lexicon*, Chicago, University of Chicago Press, 1979)182.

262. Blass-De-Brunner, *A Greek Grammar of the New Testament*, (Chicago, University of Chicago Press, 1961)181 Says that "*mellein* with the infinitive indicates imminence."

263. It is to be noted that Balaam was not predicting the Incarnation and personal ministry of Jesus, since the focus of the prophecy was Jesus as *King* and as *judge*. So, in the clearest of terms, Balaam was being told that fulfillment of the eschatological judgment coming of Jesus was not near. This flies in the face of those who claim that God used time statements indiscriminately, or loosely, and that time means nothing to God.

264. For an excellent defense of the early dating of Daniel and a countdown beginning with Babylon and extending to Rome, see John Evan's, *The Four Kingdoms of Daniel,* (2004).

265. Perhaps it would be good to point out that Daniel only had understanding of the vision *after the angel told him what the vision meant* (Daniel 10:10-14)! In addition, Daniel tells us in 12:8f that he did not fully understand (comprehend) the full significance of his vision, for that was reserved for the time of the end.

266. It will, perhaps, be rejoined that the OT prophets do say that *the Day of the Lord* and the end was near, (cf. for instance Ezekiel 7) and of course this is true. However, what must be kept in mind is that there were many Days of the Lord in the Old Testament. Anytime YHVH manifested His sovereignty by using one nation to judge another, it is said that He came, on the clouds, in glory, etc.. See my *Like Father Like Son, On Clouds of Glory*, for a full defense and explanation of this. Available at : www.bibleprophecy.com, or, www.eschatology.org. In other words, the Lord came many times in the Old Testament. However, the end of the age, the last days, and the establishment of the kingdom, at the time of the resurrection were all predictions of the eschatological *consummation*. It is to these things we refer when we say that the Old Covenant prophets never said the end was near.

267. One can hardly fail to hear the echo of Isaiah in 2 Peter 3:12, where Peter said the saints in Asia were "hastening the Day," i.e. the Day of the Lord to bring in the New Creation. Indeed, Beale and

Carson say that 2 Peter 3:12: "ultimately depends on Isaiah 60:22." Greg Beale and D.A. Carson, *Commentary on the New Testament Use of the Old Testament*, (Grand Rapids, Baker Academic, 2007)1060.

268. Deuteronomy 32, the Song of Moses, is a classic example of this projected imminence. In verses 32-35, Moses said that Israel's judgment was near. That is, if we read the text uncritically. However, if we read the text properly, we will quickly (pun intended) discover that Moses is saying that after his death (31:29f) after many generations have passed (32:7) in Israel's last days (32:19-20; 29f) that it would be then, and only then, that their judgment would be at hand. To fail to honor the projection into the distant future is to do a disservice to the text. The Hebrews writer affirms that the judgment *foretold by Deuteronomy* was about to happen in a "very, very little while" (Hebrews 10:35-37).

269. It is generally accepted that Luke was a Gentile. However, this in no way mitigates my point, for while Luke may have been a Gentile, the theme of both his gospel and his Acts, was *the restoration of Israel*! I have produced a study of Acts entitled *Acts and the Restoration of Israel*, demonstrating that Luke is concerned with the fulfillment of God's promises to Israel, from chapter 1 through chapter 28. The 50+ lesson study is available at www.eschatology.org, or, www.bibleprophecy.com.

270. Mark Nanos, *The Mystery of Romans*, Minneapolis, Fortress, 1996)4.

271. Tom Holland, *Contours of Pauline Theology*, (Christian Focus Publications, Geanies House, Fearn, Ross-Shire IV20 1TW, Scotland, UK, 2004)47.

272. Thomas Ice and Kenneth Gentry, *The Great Tribulation Past or Future, A Debate*, (Grand Rapids, Kregel, 1999)117.

273. F. F. Bruce, *The Time is Fulfilled*, (Exeter, Paternoster Press, 1978)15.

274. Richard Trench, *Synonyms of the New Testament*, (Grand Rapids, Eerdmans, 1975)209.

275. The word translated as "ready" is *hetoimos*, and carries with it a strong sense of imminence.

276. Perriman (*Coming*, 121) notes that since Isaiah said YHVH would lay a stone of stumbling *in Zion* (8:13; 28:16; and compare Paul's appeal to this in Romans 9:33) "we should think twice before removing it from that location."

277. See a fuller discussion of this text in my *The Elements Shall Melt With Fervent Heat*. Available on my website: www.eschatology.org,

org, or www.bibleprophecy.com.

278. Dale Allison, *The End of the Ages Has Come*, (Philadelphia, Fortress, 1985)32. Allison cites several Jewish authorities *before AD 70*, that associated the time of the end with the destruction of Jerusalem.

279. Thomas Ice, dispensationalist, says, "It is probably true that the disciples thought of the three events (the destruction of temple, the second coming, and the end of the age) as one event. But as was almost always the case, they were wrong." Cited in *House Divided The Break-Up of Dispensational Theology,* Greg Bahnsen and Kenneth Gentry, (Tyler, Tx. Institute for Christian Economics, 1989)267.

280. See my extensive article on 1 Corinthians 10:11 at: http://www.eschatology.org/index.php?option=com_content&task=view&id=66&Itemid=61.

281. John MacArthur, *The Second Coming*, (Wheaton, Ill. Crossways Books, 1999)206. MacArthur's book is a feeble attempt to defend futurism and refute preterism. Repeated attempts have been made to get MacArthur to engage in a formal debate with me. All attempts have been met with silence.

282. See my point by point refutation of MacArthur's reasons for why Christ's coming must be yet future, in my *Like Father Like Son, On Clouds of Glory*. Available at : www.bibleprophecy.com, Or, www.eschatology.org

283. The Psalms especially contain the lament and inquiry of the righteous under persecution. See e.g. Psalms 6; 13; 35; 74; 80; 89, etc. as just a few examples.

284. To say that Matthew 24:34 is *prophetic* while Matthew 23:36 is *historical* is sophistry borne of desperation. *Was Jesus not prophesying the future destruction of Jerusalem* in Matthew 23? Ice, like all millennialists, realizes that to admit to the force of "this generation" is to abandon futurism. Thus, definitions and doctrines are created out of thin air with no textual or logical justification.

285. Jesus uses the Greek term *en tachei*, that we have examined above. This term never denotes rapidity of action to the exclusion of imminence of occurrence. To deny this is to deny the un-exceptional use of the term in the NT.

286. *Anesis* is *relief*, not vindication and not reward. While vindication and reward may be, and *are, synchronous* with relief, they are not *synonymous* words. In my July 2008 debate with John Welch, I appealed to Paul's promise to the Thessalonians that they would receive "relief" from their persecution. Welch argued that Paul was speaking of vindication, not relief, and that vindication can come at any time and

need not take place on earth. Of course, this redefines *anesis* and denies the text of Thessalonians. Furthermore, it denies Revelation 6:9f where *vindication* (*ekdekeesis*) of the martyrs is clearly posited as taking place "on earth."

287. Greg Beale, *New International Greek Testament Commentary*, (Carlisle, PA, Paternoster, 1999)393.

288. While ignoring the relationship between Jesus' discussion of martyrdom and vindication in Matthew 23, Beale says the time statements in Revelation 6 basically mean nothing since "Time in heaven, which is referred to in 6:11, may be reckoned differently than time on earth" (*Revelation*, 395). Beale offers not a word of evidence to justify his claim. It is mere assertion.

289. See my *Who Is This Babylon* for a full discussion of Isaiah 2-4 as it is utilized by Jesus, Paul, and John. Jesus (Luke 23:28f) cites Isaiah, and applies it to the coming destruction of Jerusalem. Paul likewise quotes from Isaiah– in fact, *he cites the same verses that Jesus cites in Luke*! (2 Thessalonians 1:9f). And he does so to promise the imminent vindication of the suffering saints in Thessalonica. Likewise, John cites *the identical verses used by Jesus*, to speak of the impending judgment of the persecutor of the saints. The perfect correlation and harmonious use of Isaiah by Jesus, Paul and John, demands that we place the vindication of the martyrs, at the Day of the Lord, at the judgment of Jerusalem, not some future, vague, unknown entity, as Beale and others would do.

290. According to Beale (*Revelation*, 928) there is also a direct allusion to 2 Kings 9:7, and Psalms 79:10. Beale fails to see that John was anticipating the fulfillment of God's last days promises to Israel and extrapolates Revelation into an "end of time" paradigm.

291. For an excellent study of Revelation that develops the theme of the avenging of the blood of the martyrs, see Arthur Ogden's *Avenging of the Blood of the Apostles and Prophets*. While in my estimation Ogden stops short of where he should, he nonetheless did a fine job of showing that the dominant theme of Revelation is the fulfillment of what Jesus promised in Matthew 23. The book is available from my websites: www.bibleprophecy.com, or, www.eschatology.org.

292. See my *Can You Believe Jesus Said This?* for a full discussion of the various attempts to avoid the meaning of Jesus' words. What must be kept in mind is that one has to destroy the meaning of words in order to get any other meaning out of Jesus' prediction. For those who insist that the Bible "says what it means, and means what it says," it is somewhat disingenuous to argue that Jesus did not mean what he said! My book is available at: www.eschatology.org, or, : www.bibleprophecy.com

293. One of the most misguided attempts to divide Matthew 16:27 from verse 28 is the amillennial view that the coming of Christ in judgment cannot be the coming of Christ in the kingdom of v. 28. This completely ignores the idea that both in the OT and the New, the arrival of the kingdom is the time of the judgment! See Daniel 7:23f for a prime example. See also Matthew 25:31f; 2 Timothy 4:1; Revelation 11:15f.

294. The motif of suffering and *imminent vindication and relief at the parousia* is dominant in the New Testament writings. See Matthew 23; Luke 18:1-8; Romans 8:18f; 2 Corinthians 4:16f; Philippians 1; 1 Thessalonians 2:14f; 2 Thessalonians 1 (See my book *In Flaming Fire* for an extended discussion of this text); Hebrews 10:32f; 1 Peter 1:4f; 2 Peter 2-3; Revelation 6, 11, 16, etc.. It is refreshing to see a growing recognition of this motif among scholars. See for instance N.T. Wright, *Jesus and the Victory of God*; Andrew Perriman, *The Coming of the Son of Man*, for just two modern examples. What is still often overlooked however, is that this promised vindication would be in fulfillment of God's promises to Israel. See Deuteronomy 32:43; Isaiah 2-4; Isaiah 26:19f; Isaiah 65:6f to name but a few texts.

295. Matthew 16:27-28 needs a lot of unfolding to do it proper justice. Clearly, Isaiah 62, and the promise of Israel's salvation– *at her remarriage to YHVH*– likewise lies behind these verses. Isaiah 49 and its promise of the Day of Salvation, and an entire laundry list of prophecies are echoed in Jesus' short statement.

296. While it is common to believe that the little horn was a Roman emperor, I am convinced, with Wright, France, Caird, and others, that Jesus applied the language that may have been commonly understood to speak of the pagan nations, or enemies of YHVH, and applied it to the leaders of Israel and to the Israel of his day. That is, Jerusalem and her leaders had turned into the enemy of YHVH– she had become pagan! Paul certainly believed that the Jewish leaders of his day had become the enemies of God (Philippians 3:18). Wright (*Victory*, 598) says Jesus, "Made the book of Daniel thematic for his whole vocation. He understood it to be referring to the great climax in which YHWH would defeat the fourth world empire and vindicate his suffering people. He projected the notion of evil empire on the present Jerusalem regime, and identified himself and his movement with the people who were to be vindicated."

297. There is tremendous controversy as to whether Daniel 7 is speaking of the Lord *descending* as it were, *to earth*, or, as Daniel 7:13f seems to indicate, Jesus, as the Son of Man, *ascends* to the Father. However, even verses 10-14 must be seen as a vision of the judgment that is then explained in verses 21f as the coming of YHVH in judgment of the little horn. While this may present some difficulties for

us moderns to think in these terms, if we can see that Jesus, as a result of his coming to the Father, was then to come "in the glory of the Father," this will perhaps help us to grapple with the text a bit better.

298. The identical theme is found in Revelation 11:8-17, where you have the city "where the Lord was slain" as the persecuting power. The city is destroyed, and the kingdom is given to the saints, as YHVH and His Messiah reign forever and forever.

299. See my *Can You Believe Jesus Said This?* for a full discussion and development of this distinctive Greek term. Available at www.bibleprophecy.com.

300. Mathison may have seen this difficulty, and so he claims, *without proof*, that this persecution by the little horn may refer to "the persecution of faithful Jews by the Romans prior to the coming of Christ" (*Age*, 271). However, Daniel is not predicting Roman persecution broadly considered. He speaks of "the little horn," which in Mathison's view of Daniel must be a specific personage. Mathison's suggestion therefore would demand that prior to the Cross / Ascension there was one single distinctive Roman persecutor of faithful Jews. He would be hard-pressed to find such a Roman figure. Mathison avoids offering an identity of the little horn except to offer that it is Rome.

301. Critics of Covenant Eschatology sometimes argue that because Jesus used the plural "graves" that this must refer to the raising of individual human corpses. This is not, however, justified. Jesus is clearly drawing from Daniel 12:2 and Ezekiel 37. Neither passage predicted the raising of human corpses– (and remember that Gentry now agrees with this)– but to the restoration of Israel under Messiah. Furthermore, Ezekiel undeniably says that this spiritual resurrection would be the raising of Israel out of the graves, plural (Ezekiel 37:12f).

302. Lest it be argued that Mathison is arguing against the dispensational view of imminence and that this is different from his view of "imminent," this is mere sophistry. The dispensationalist says "the end is imminent and could occur at any moment." Mathison says "the end is always imminent and could occur at any moment." Exactly where is the substantive difference in these views?

303. Mathison (*Age*, 638, n. 73) appeals to a late date (circa AD 80s or 90s) of John and says, ""John's statement rules out any type of full preterism." The problem is that if one accepts the evidence of the Olivet Discourse as the source of 1 John 2:18, then *the early date of John's epistle is established*, and Mathison's "objection" which is presuppositional and not evidentiary, is falsified.

304. See Perriman's (*Coming*, 136+) discussion of the man of sin in 2 Thessalonians 2. Perriman sees the man of sin as a first century figure,

that defiles the Jerusalem temple, and is destroyed. This certainly agrees with Paul's thought that the restrainer and the man of sin were already on the scene (2 Thessalonians 2:5f).

305. It must be emphasized that the suffering that Paul and the other New Testament writers speak about is persecution for the cause of Christ. It has nothing to do with the mundane experiences of the human existence such as cancer, heart attack, financial stress, etc. To read the normal human experience of life into these texts that speak of tribulation, is to do a tremendous disservice to exegesis.

306. Significantly, this foundational tenet of dispensationalism is being increasingly challenged. I have just been sent (11-23-08) an email relating events at a recent convention of a major dispensational denomination. During a Q and A session, a querist asked a panel of their leading theologians for scriptural demonstration of a gap between the sixty ninth and seventieth week of Daniel 9. The response: "Once asked, the presenter (one of the speakers, DKP) and panel remained stone silent....not one of these men gave one scripture for their gap in Daniel." This is incredibly significant since, as the poster noted, "Without the gap, there is no basis on which to support their eschatological Dispensationalism– none." See my discussion of the gap theory in this work. I utilized the material in a formal debate with Thomas Ice and Mark Hitchcock, and they did not even attempt to give a response.

307. If Daniel 7 does lie behind Matthew 16:27-28 this proves that one cannot divide verse 27 from verse 28 as is common among commentators. Daniel's vision was of judgment resulting in the kingdom. Jesus' prediction was judgment resulting in the kingdom. There is no temporal dichotomy or distinction in Matthew 16:27-28.

308. Mathison's manifest vacillation on the temporal statements in the NT in his newest work is in stark contrast to his past works. In his *Postmillennialism: Eschatology of Hope*, and in his *Dispensationalism, Rightly Dividing the People of God?*, when he critiques dispensationalism, Mathison is very forceful in insisting that we *honor* the imminence texts as AD 70. In his *Age*, however, we find a different tone entirely. Now, it is, "Some say it means this or that, and others say it means something else. It could mean this, or it could mean that..." It seems that for Mathison, he is now willing to grant virtually any definition of "at hand" as long as it gives no support to the true preterists!

309. *The EnglishMan's Greek Concordance*, (Grand Rapids, Zondervan, 1976)804.

310. Romans 16:25; 2 Timothy 1:9; Titus 1:2; Hebrews 4:7. The last referent is questionable.

311. Matthew 25:19; Luke 8:27; Luke 20:9; John 5:6; 14:9; Acts 8:11; 14:3, 28; 18:20; 27:9; Hebrews 4:7.

312. It is amazing that Gentry would seek to find long expanses of time in Jesus' answer to the disciples' question about the establishment of the kingdom. Gentry believes that the kingdom, i.e. the bride of Christ *came in fulness in AD 70!* Furthermore, the context of Acts 1 demands an imminent fulfillment of the kingdom promises. Jesus said it was not for the disciples to know "the times and seasons" for the coming of the kingdom. Nonetheless, they were to go into Jerusalem and wait for the outpouring of the Spirit. But, the outpouring of the Spirit would initiate the kingdom (Joel 2; Acts 2:15f, and Gentry agrees!). So, Jesus' command for the disciples to await the outpouring of the Spirit was an indirect, but powerful affirmation of the imminence of the kingdom!

313. Richard Trench, *Synonyms of the New Testament*, (Grand Rapids, Eerdmans, 1975)209+.

314. Meredith G. Kline, "Death, Leviathan, and Martyrs: Isaiah 24:1-27:1" in A Tribute to Gleason Archer, ed. by Walter C. Kaiser, Jr. and Ronald R. Youngblood. (Chicago: Moody Press, 1986)229-249.

315. Actually, when one examines the entire context of, "The little Apocalypse" i.e. Isaiah 24-29, we find far more than three prophecies of the judgment of Jerusalem at the time of the salvation of Israel. Isaiah 28:20f, and almost the entirety of chapter 29– where we find the destruction of *Ariel*, the city where David dwelt-- foretold the coming judgment at the time of YHVH's work of salvation. The same is true in Isaiah 59.

316. Charles Wanamaker, *New International Greek Testament Commentary*, in loc, p. 171.

317. My thanks to Jack Scott, minister at the Ardmore Family of God church in Ardmore, Ok. for providing this list. At the 2008 Preterist Pilgrim Weekend, July 2008, Scott presented two powerful lessons on 1 Corinthians 15, emphasizing the present passive verbs, and the implications. MP3s of that conference are available from my websites: : www.bibleprophecy.com, or, www.eschatology.org.

318. MP3s of that Internet debate are available from me at my websites:: www.bibleprophecy.com, or, www.eschatology.org.

319. See my, *He Came As A Thief*, that addresses every New Testament passage that speaks of Christ's coming as a thief. The book shows: **a.)** There were indeed to be signs of Christ's thief coming, **b.)** The thief coming was to occur in the first century, **c.)** The thief coming could be known by the faithful, but not by the unbelievers, **d.)** The thief coming was to be at the judgment of Old Covenant Jerusalem. The

book is available from my website: www.eschatology.org, and is the most extensive examination of Christ's thief coming that I know of.

320. In both the Carlsbad debate and the Indianapolis debate my opponent initially appealed to the thief coming argument. When I produced the correlation between Matthew 22 and 25 neither disputant appealed to Christ's thief coming again.

321. The wedding of Christ is one of the most significant eschatological themes imaginable, yet, in the modern eschatological world it seldom receives significant attention. The amillennialist and postmillennialist seem blissfully unaware that the promise of the wedding was *God's Old Covenant promise to remarry Israel* (Hosea 2; Isaiah 62). Tragically, both paradigms divorce (pun intended) these promises from Israel and give them to the church, in spite of the fact that Jesus came to confirm the promises made to the fathers (Romans 15.8) and Paul said his eschatological hope was nothing but the hope of Israel (Acts 24-28). The wedding of Christ at the destruction of "Babylon" in Revelation 18-19 is seen to have no connection to God's promises to Israel, but is instead somehow to be related to the destruction of ancient Rome or even the yet future destruction of the Roman Catholic church! Exactly how the destruction of a pagan, or even apostate Christian entity could be the fulfillment of God's promises to Israel is ignored or never considered. This guarantees a misapplication of the message of Revelation. See my *Who Is This Babylon?* for a fuller discussion of this important issue.

322. I have written a book on Christ's thief coming, *He Came As Thief!*, examining every occurrence of the theme in the N.T. It is easy to show that the thief coming was known to be coming in the first century, in the AD 70 *parousia*. The book is available at : www.bibleprophecy.com Or, www.eschatology.org. In addition to the book, I presented four lessons on the Lord's thief coming, in February, 2009, at the Fulfilled Prophecy Conference in Montgomery, Alabama. Those four lessons, along with the PowerPoint presentations, and a copy of my Thief book are available from my websites: www.bibleprophecy.com or www.eschatology.org.

323. I examine the premise of "no signs of Christ's *parousia*" in a four lesson series delivered at the Fulfilled Prophecy conference held in Montgomery, Alabama, in February 2009. Those four lessons focus on Revelation 3, 16, 1 Thessalonians 5, and Matthew 24. In addition, there is a special lesson on the relationship between Christ's thief coming and the resurrection. The series is available in MP3. Included are the PowerPoint presentations, *and* a copy of my book *He Came As A Thief!* Available from my website: www.eschatology.org.

324. Charles Wanamaker, *New International Greek Testament Commentary, Commentary on 1 and 2 Thessalonians*, (Grand Rapids,

Eerdmans, Paternoster, 1990)177.

325. Psalms 48:6; Isaiah 13:8; 21:3; 26:17-18; 37:3; 42:14; 66:7-8; Jeremiah 4:31; 6:24; 22:23; 30:4-7; 48:41; 50:43; Hosea 13:13.

326. Emile Schurer, *History of the Jewish People in the Age of Jesus Christ, Vol. II*, (London, T and T Clark, 1979)514.

327. D. S. Russell, *The Method and Message of Jewish Apocalyptic*, Westminster Press, 1964)272.

328. Thomas Ice and Kenneth Gentry, *The Great Tribulation Past or Present*, (Grand Rapids, Kregel, 1999)192.

329. Romans 8:18f serves as the foundational text for those, including N. T. Wright, who see a yet future restoration of material creation in the millennium. However, when we allow Isaiah 26 and its definition of "creation" (*ktisis*) as Old Covenant Israel longing for salvation, this becomes an untenable view of Romans 8–and eschatology as a whole. Paul's view of the *creation* and the goal of salvation was covenantally formed and framed.

330. I am convinced that Peter had the Messianic Woes leading to the time of the kingdom fully in mind in his epistle. Everywhere we turn in 1 Peter we encounter elements found in the prophets related to that theme, and resulting in the salvation foretold by the prophets.

331. Jesus' allusion to the heaven and earth in Matthew 24:35 should be seen as a reference to the temple. In my *The Elements Shall Melt With Fervent Heat*, I show that the temple was referred to as 'heaven and earth" by the Jews of Jesus' day. Jesus was not speaking of the destruction of literal creation.

332. Of course the great irony of all this is that Gentry is at odds with the creeds in his new view of Daniel 12:2. He cannot find the AD 70 application of Daniel 12 in his creeds. This does not seem to disturb him too much, however. What is interesting is that Gentry has now adopted the true preterist view of Daniel, all the while condemning the preterists as heretics. The bottom line is that it does not bother Gentry to violate the creeds when he thinks scripture demands it, which is a laudable position. And yet, he condemns the true preterists because we affirm that the scriptures support Covenant Eschatology, even though the creeds are at variance.

333. Although I give the NKJ rendering of Hebrews 9, it should be noted that in the Greek of the text, the author uses the present tense verbs to speak of what "is symbolic" what "is standing" in which "are offered" etc.. The present tense verbs demand that the Old Covenant system was still valid when Hebrews was written.

334. See my extended discussion of the two terms *apokatastasis* (restoration, Acts 3:24) and *diorthosis* (reformation, Hebrews 9:10) in my *Like Father Like Son, On Clouds of Glory*. Available from www.bibleprophecy.com. Linguistically, the words are synonyms. Theologically, they are parallel. The indisputable fact that Hebrews posits the reformation at the end of the Mosaic Law is virtual *prima facie* proof that the second coming of Christ was in AD 70, at the end of that Old System.

335. See Bauer's, *Arndt and Gingrich Greek Lexicon*, (University of Chicago Press, 1979)415.

336. See for instance, Acts 16:1; 18:19, 24; 20:15; 21:7; 25:13; 27:12; 28:13.

337. See my article, "The Significance of the Presence of the Spirit in Acts and the Epistles," at:
http://www.eschatology.org/index.php?option=com_content&view=article&id=666:the-significance-of-the-spirit-in-acts-and-the-epistles&catid=116:topical-studies&Itemid=61.

338. Since Paul said that the church was the prophetic goal of all previous ages, the suggestion of some preterists that the church ceased to exist after AD 70 is falsified. It is illogical to assert that all the previous ages anticipated an entity–that is called endless– and it was to last for only 40 years!

339. Dwight Pentecost, *Things To Come*, (Zondervan, 1966)134+.

340. W. D. Davies, *Jewish and Pauline Studies*, (Philadelphia, Fortress, 1984).

341. It is vitally important to see that for Paul, resurrection was to be when sin, the sting of death, was removed. It is also significant to see that this promise springs not only from Jeremiah, but from Daniel 9:24f: "Seventy weeks are determined...to put away sin." The critical seventy weeks terminated in AD 70. Thus, resurrection, the time of the putting away of sin, occurred in AD 70. See my *Seventy Weeks Are Determined...For the Resurrection* for a fuller discussion.

342. See my book *Have Heaven and Earth Passed Away?* for a full discussion of when the Old Covenant passed. Simply stated, it was not at the Cross or Pentecost. It was in AD 70 with the destruction of the Temple.

343. It is incredible to me that some deny that Christ's *parousia* was essential to complete the atonement. In several formal debates, my amillennial opponents have argued that the atonement was finished at Christ's *ascension*, (e.g. Deaver-V-Preston, Carlsbad, N. M. 2008; Benton-V-Preston, 2007) and that his "second coming" is unrelated to

the atonement! The entire point of Hebrews 9 is to show that Christ's atoning work was the fulfillment of the typological actions of the Old Covenant High Priest. To suggest that the High Priest did not have to come out of the Most Holy to complete the atonement is an overt denial of the typological significance of that praxis. Furthermore, Hebrews 9.28 said Christ must appear a second time. Chapter 10 begins with the particle *"gar"* (i.e. "For") which is explanatory, showing why Christ had to appear the second time: "For the Law, having (present tense) a shadow of good things about to come..." Christ's *parousia* was necessary to fulfill the typological elements of the Law, the very elements of the atonement under consideration!

344. Thomas Ice, Internet Article: www.according2prophecy.org/seventy-weeks-pt2.html

345. Thomas Ice, *The Seventy Weeks of Daniel Part I*) According to Prophecy Ministries Presents: Pre-Trib Perspectives Articles Archive," page 2 of 22 www.according2prophecy.org/seventy-weeks-pt1.html

346. See my critique of Gentry's view of the seventy weeks in my *Seal Up Vision and Prophecy*, available from my websites.

347. For Paul, the putting away of sin was an "already-but-not-yet" reality. Christ began the work on the Cross, but the consummation of his work was to be at the *parousia* (1 Corinthians 15:24-28, 54-56). Note that he said Christ had already "put all things under his feet" (v. 27) but that he was going to finally put sin under him at the *parousia*. He assured the Corinthians that not all of them would die before that was accomplished (v. 50). Thus, since Daniel confines and restricts the putting away of sin and the Atonement to the 70 Weeks, the Cross and *parousia* both lie within the crucial countdown.

348. In the Preston - V - Welch debate of 2008, I asked Welch to define "the law" that Paul said was "the strength of sin." He responded that it is any law that could not take away sin. I noted that this means that the *parousia* of Christ cannot therefore be at the end of the Christian age since *the gospel does take away sin*! The other (negative) alternative is that the gospel is in fact that law that is the strength of sin! In light of Romans 8:1f this is patently false. Finally, I showed that the gospel *will never pass away* (Matthew 24:35). Welch never responded to these issues.

349. Chris A Vlachos, "Law, Sin, and Death: An Edenic Triad? An Examination with Reference to 1 Corinthians 15:56." *Journal of the Evangelical Theological Society*. 47 (2004)277-98.

350. Obviously, if the resurrection became a reality with the passing of the Old Covenant world in AD 70, then truly "life and immortality" became a reality for the believer at that time as well (1 Corinthians

15:54).

351. John Goldingay, *Word Biblical Commentary, Daniel*, (Dallas, Word,1989)258.

352. Prior to Daniel's prediction of "the war" that would terminate in the Messiah's kingdom, Isaiah also predicted that in the last days there would be "the war" when Israel would fall by the sword. This would be in the Day of the Lord, when YHVH judged Israel for her blood guilt (Isaiah 2-4). Jesus informs us in no uncertain terms when Israel was to be judged for her blood guilt. It was to be in his generation, in "the war" that would lead to the utter desolation of Jerusalem (Matthew 23/ Luke 21).

353. We should note that for Paul, the resurrection would be the time of the fulfillment of *the Old Testament prophecies made to Israel*. In 1 Corinthians 15:54f he quotes from Isaiah 25 and Hosea 13:14 as the source for his doctrine and hope of the resurrection. Thus, the harmony between Daniel 9 and Corinthians is established. In both passages the consummation of Israel's age is the time of God's dealing with sin and death.

354. Gentry applies 1 Corinthians 10:11 to the impending end of the Old Covenant age in AD 70 (2009, 408). He never seeks to prove that the end of the age in chapter 10 is a different end of the age from that in chapter 15.

355. Stevens has written a book advocating the literal rapture in AD 70, *Expectations Demand A rapture*, (Bradford, PA, International Preterist Association, 2002).

356. Ian D. Harding, *Taken to Heaven in AD 70,* (Bradford, Pa, International Preterist Association, 2005).

357. Speaking candidly, this applies equally to Ed Stevens as well. I have been a friend of Ed's for many years. Yet, while Ed has asked, rightly so, for the freedom to study any doctrine, he has shown a disturbing tendency not to grant that same liberty to others. For instance, Stevens has stoutly condemned those who are investigating, or have espoused, the "conditional immortality" issue. He insists it is a matter of faith and faithfulness. When I have pressed him to prove this claim, he has consistently failed to do so. Personally, I have not come down on the issue, but in my opinion, it is definitely not a matter of fellowship. So, the bottom line is that if we are going to ask for the personal freedom to keep asking questions and the right to re-open the study of any doctrine, we must grant that same liberty to others without calling their faithfulness into question.

358. Sam Frost, *Misplaced Hope,* (4703 Fontana St, Orlando, Fl, 2002) Frost has done a marvelous job in dealing with the Epistle of

Barnabas, Hermas and Clement especially, and their eschatological expectations. I consider his book a "must read."

359. For more on the problem of the early writers, see John Dallé, *A Treatise on the Right Use of the Fathers*, (Harrison, VA., Sprinkle Publications, 2000. Reprint of 1856 version). Dalle chronicles the tremendous difficulty of determining what the early writers actually believed, because: 1.) We have so few of their documented writings, 2.) What we do have is dubious in many cases, 3.) The documented unreliability of their testimony, and other issues.

360. N. T. Wright, *The Millennium Myth*, (Louisville, Ky, Westminster John Knox Press, 1999)40.

361. Claudia Setzer, *Jewish Responses to Early Christians*, (Minneapolis, Fortress, 1994)133.

362. See my book, *Like Father Like Son, On Clouds of Glory*, for a full discussion of what it meant for Jesus to come in the glory of the Father. Briefly stated, it meant he was coming in the same manner as the Father had come many times before, and the Father had never come bodily, visibly. Thus, Jesus' coming was not to be bodily, visible in the sense of being an optical event. The book is available from our websites: : www.bibleprophecy.com, or, www.eschatology.org. It is also in audio form in cassette, CD, and CD with MP3 format.

363. David Chilton, *Paradise Restored*, (Ft Worth, Dominion Press, 1987)101 Chilton wrote this well before he became a full preterist. In subsequent years, Chilton came to espouse the full preterist view.

364. Gary DeMar, *Last Days Madness,* Revised, (Atlanta, American Vision, 1994)153+.

365. Robert Grant, *Understanding the Sacred Text, John Reumann, editor, Essays in Honor of Morton S. Enslin on the Hebrew Bible and Christian Beginnings,* "Eusebius and His Church History,"(Valley Forge, Judson Press)235+.

366. Eusebius, *Ecclesiastical History*, (Grand Rapids, Baker, 1987)84+.

367. Iranaeus, "Against Heresies," *Early Church Fathers*, Cyril Richardson, Editor, (Philadelphia, Westminster Press, 1953)372+. In Iranaeus we find the eccentricity of the patristics in full bloom.. Richardson speaks of Iranaeus', "weird systems of fantastic speculation," and his, "sometimes startling exegesis," not to mention his historical inaccuracies. (*Fathers*, 344-353).

368. *Cyclopedia of Biblical, Theological, and Ecclesiastical Literature,* McClintock and Strong, (Grand Rapids, Baker, 1970)416.

369. McClintock and Strong, Vol. 5, 551.

370. Here again is a point of controversy worthy of investigation. The question of whether the apostles appointed their successors can be challenged on Biblical, if not historical grounds. The apostolic office was intended to be temporary (Ephesians 4:8-13). Thus, the idea that the apostles appointed successors to take their place, when the time for the cessation of that office (AD 70) had come and gone, is dubious at best. So, we are once again confronted with the questionable nature of the patristic writings. *Indeed we are confronted with the problem of a perceived failed eschatology that resulted in an alteration even in church government.* W. H. C. Frend says the delay of the *parousia* opened the way for the church government to develop as it did in the second century. (*The Early Church*, 52).

371. John Eadie, *Commentary on Ephesians*, (Grand Rapids, Zondervan, reprint of 1853 version)145.

372. Needless to say, preterists all agree that the New Creation, while present, was not perfected and would not be consummated until the *parousia*. The already-but-not-yet is very much present. The "not yet" does not in any way mitigate the fact that the regeneration was on-going, and that the apostles were on "thrones" judging during that period of time. Nor does the "not yet" demand literal thrones, with the apostles removed from earth to sit on those thrones.

373. See my book *Who Is This Babylon?* for a fuller discussion of the regeneration and restoration of all things. I must note one incredible fact, however. After commenting on the restoration of all things, which he posits at the end of the current Christian age, Gentry then makes this rather remarkable, and self contradictory statement: "The restoration is a reformation that supplants the old order (Hebrews 9:10)" (*Dominion*, 2009, 502). The problem for Gentry is that the time of reformation which he equates with the time of restoration, is undeniably posited by the Hebrews author as occurring *at the end of the Mosaic Covenant and Cultus!* That Old Covenant was imposed "until the time of reformation" (Hebrews 9:10). So, for Gentry to (correctly) correlate Acts 3:24 with Hebrews 9:10 is to unwittingly confirm the full preterist position!

374. E. G. Loyd Gaston, *No Stone On Another*, (Leiden, E. J. Brill, 1970).

375. Sadly, the amillennial tradition in which I was raised does not ascribe eschatological meaning to the Mission. Amillennialists generally believe that Jesus' prediction of the completion of the World Mission was a sign of the end of the Jewish world that did come to an end in AD 70. Likewise, many postmillennialists (e.g. Gentry, *Dominion*, 1992, 261+) believe that the World Mission was completed in the first century as foretold, but see a still future fulfillment before

the "real" end. So, while the postmillennialist sees a first century fulfillment of Matthew 24:14, they do see eschatological import to the future fulfillment of Matthew 28:18f. See my book *Into All the World, Then Comes the End*, for a definitive refutation of the postmillennial attempt to delineate between Matthew 24 and 28.

376. Origen in his *Commentary on Matthew 39*, cited in *Ancient Christian Commentary on Scripture*, New Testament, Vol. II, Mark, Thomas Oden general editor (Downers Grove, Ill, InterVarsity Press, 1998)183

377. Iranaeus, *Against Heresies*, BK. III, (*Early Christian Fathers*, Cyril Richardson, editor, (Philadelphia, Westminister,1953)370, 372

378. Athanasius, *On the Incarnation of the Word*, 40:5:6, The Nicene and Anti-Nicene Fathers, The Master Christian Library, Ages Software, P. O. Box 216 Rio, WI. 53960 Taken from CD #1

379. Eusebius, *(Proof of the Gospel*, Bk. I, Ch. 6, Grand Rapids, Baker, 1981)34-35.

380. John Chrysostom, *Homily* 74. P. 948-950; taken from Ages Master Christian Library, CD #1, Ages SoftWare, P. O. Box 216 Rio, WI 53960

381. Clement of Alexandria in *Ante-Nicene Fathers*, Bk. 1, chpt. 21 (Edinburgh, T and T Clark, 1868)434

382. Ages Software, Disc #1, Athanasius, (Defense of His Flight 11, p. 707)

383. Grant Pitre, *Jesus, The Tribulation and the End of Exile, Restoration Eschatology and the Origin of the Atonement*, (Grand Rapids, Baker Academic, 2005)187

384. Richard Bauckham, *Word Biblical Commentary on 2 Peter*, (Waco, Word,)311

385. Simon Kistemaker, in *When Shall These Things Be: A Reformed Response to Hyper-Preterism*, Keith Mathison, editor, (New Jersey, P & R Publishing, 2004)239

386. John Chrysostom, *Homily*, from the Nicene and Post Nicene Fathers, Phillip Schaff, Series 1, vol. 13. Chrysostom, arguing against the view that the restrainer in 2 Thessalonians 2 was the Holy Spirit, argued: "If he (Paul, DKP) meant to say the Spirit, he would not have spoken obscurely, but plainly, that even now the grace of the Spirit , that is the gifts, withhold him. And otherwise he ought now to have come when the gifts ceased; for they have long since ceased."

387. Theoderet of Cyrus, cited in *The Land Called Holy*, (Yale University, 1992)324, n. 1 of chapter 11 heading.

388. Richard Bauckham, *The Climax of Prophecy*, (Edinburgh, T and T Clark, 1999)229

389. Robert Goldenberg, "Early Rabbinic Explanations of the Destruction of Jerusalem," *Journal of Jewish Studies*, 1982 (517f)

390. I have read a good number of the responses to Steven's views on www.PlanetPreterist.com, and unless I have missed it, no one has raised the problem of Matthew 13.

391. Iranaeus, *Against Heresies*, Bk V33:3, in, *The Early Church Fathers*, Cyril Richardson Editor, (Philadelphia, Westminister Press, 1953)395

392. See my *Like Father Like Son, On Clouds of Glory,* work for a full explication. Available at : www.bibleprophecy.com, or, www.eschatology.org

393. A. T. Robertson, *Word Pictures of the New Testament*, vol. 1, (Nashville, Broadman, 1930)338

394. It will hardly do to argue that Jesus is speaking of those who would die, enter heaven, and realize then that the *parousia* had occurred. Jesus' words, "there are some standing here that shall not taste of death until they see that the kingdom had come with power,"powerfully precludes the idea that they would, after they died, look back and realize the *parousia* had occurred.

395. See my book, *Israel: 1948, Countdown To No Where*, for devastating refutation of the idea that the events of 1948 were the fulfillment of prophecy. The book is available from our website: www.eschatology.org, or, www.bibleprophecy.com

396. Gary Cohen, cited by LaHaye and Ice, in *Charting the End Times,* (Eugene, Ore., Harvest House, 2001)45. Isn't it somewhat ironic that the millennialists, who insist so vehemently that literalism is the only proper hermeneutic, are so quick to find an *allegorical meaning* to the seven churches?

397. On Trinity Broadcasting, November, 2003. Hagee's "proof" was that: 1.) A generation, Biblically, is 40 years, 2.) Jesus said that the generation to see the signs would see his coming, 3.) The sign was the re-establishment of Israel, 4.) Specifically, and at odds with Lindsay and others, Hagee said that the 40 year countdown began when Jerusalem came under Jewish control in 1967. Thus, 1967 + 40 equals 2007.

398. I have issued repeated challenges to Jack Van Impe to meet me in public debate to discuss eschatology. This man boasts of his debating experience, and knowledge of the Bible. Yet, he has not had the courtesy to even acknowledge my challenges, except to send me a fund

raising form letter telling me how important my support is to his ministry!!

399. We have not taken the time in this work to cite all of the dictionaries on the definition of imminent. However, I went to the local library and looked in every available dictionary, trying to find even one that supported Ice's definition. Not one even hinted that "imminent" means, "the next order of events however far removed it might be," or anything closely resembling that. Every dictionary consulted, and that was several, says that imminent means "impending, soon to occur, about to occur, overhanging, etc." When Ice cites the dictionaries to support his aberrant definition he is distorting and manipulating the sources.

400. See my article *The Age to Come* at our website: www.eschatology.org under the heading of The Last Days.

401. Jesus did not say that Caiaphas would *personally* see the Second Coming. The Greek text is in the second person plural. In other words, Jesus was addressing the Sanhedrin *as a body*, when he said, "You will see the Son of Man coming." Thanks to Ed Stevens for calling my attention to this.

402. (http://www.according2prophecy.org/rapsec.html)

403. One must be careful even here. Isaiah 65 foretold the New Creation, and in that New World, the realities of death and aging are still present. John quotes from Isaiah (Revelation 21) to describe his New Creation, yet says there would be "no death." These seemingly contradictory motifs have led some to suggest that John anticipated a different New World. This is mitigated by the fact that John is quoting Isaiah, and by the fact that to press apocalyptic language to the finer points is unjustified. Isaiah 11 and Isaiah 35 patently foretold the same time and events. Yet Isaiah 11 said lions and wolves would be present while chapter 35 says they would *not* be present. This is not a contradiction, nor a description of two different worlds. We must not press the details too far when dealing with prophetic language. This is why the literalism of millennialism is so troublesome.

404. John MacArthur, *The Second Coming*, Wheaton, Ill, Crossway Books, 1999)48. I have done a refutation of MacArthur's work in my book *Like Father Like Son, On Clouds of Glory*. I examine each of his reasons why the *parousia* must still be future, and refute each point carefully from scripture.

405. Dwight Pentecost, *Things To Come*, (Grand Rapids, Zondervan, 1980)392, 394.

406. John Walvoord and Roy Zuck, *The Bible Knowledge Commentary*, (Whitby, Ontario, Victor Books, 1984)715f.

407. See my fuller discussion of 2 Thessalonians 1 in my book *Leaving the Rapture Behind*. Available from my websites: www.bibleprophecy.com, or www.eschatology.org.

408. See my book *How Is This Possible? (2009,* revised and enlarged reprint of a 1992 book*)* for an in-depth investigation of 2 Thessalonians 2. When one considers everything that the Thessalonians would have had to believe had already occurred– if the Day of the Lord was past– it makes it impossible to believe that they had a concept of the Day of the Lord even remotely resembling any of the modern futurist views. My book is available from my websites: www.bibleprophecy.com, or, www.eschatology.org.

409. Paul undeniably has the Second Coming in view in 2 Thessalonians 2, even if one allows, *for argument sake*, the millennial view of a rapture followed by the Second Coming. Paul gave two signs that must precede the Day of the Lord under consideration. But, in the millennial paradigm, those signs belong exclusively to the Tribulation period. Since Paul was showing that the Day of the Lord had not occurred by pointing out that the preliminary signs had not yet occurred, and since those signs– per the millennialists– belong to the period after the rapture, it is *prima facie* evident that it was the Second Coming that they were saying had already occurred. Needless to say, this would have been impossible.

410. Thomas Ice and Timothy Demy, *Prophecy Watch*, (Eugene, Ore, Harvest House, 1998)60.

411. I recently had a formal written debate with dispensationalist Dr. Lloyd Olson. In that exchange, he vehemently denied that any of the signs given by Jesus in Matthew 24 were present in the first century, but that the signs of the end of the age are everywhere around us today. This claim, a firm tenet of dispensationalism, falsifies the New Testament authors, since Jesus told his disciples not to believe, or thus, to make, premature declarations of the nearness of the end (Luke 21:8). And yet, clearly the Biblical authors did say– 2000 years ago– that Christ's *parousia* and the end of the age was at hand. So, if Mr. Olson and the dispensationalists are right, the Biblical authors were wrong.

412. This was a different sermon from that cited elsewhere in this book. In November of 2003, Hagee delivered a sermon "Ten Reasons Why This is the Terminal Generation." He says that 2007 is now the year for the *parousia*. And yet, I am writing this book in 2008! I am sure he has recalculated, or will even deny making those claims.

413. Of course, it is certainly *possible* that the quote is from LaHaye and that Ice does not agree that the strikes and social unrest are in fact signs of the end. However, there is no indication in the book that LaHaye and Ice differ on this claim.

414. LaHaye originally predicted that the generation that saw *WWI* would see the rapture. *Beginning of the End*, (Wheaton, Ill, Tyndale, 1972)168f. Like Lindsey, his prediction failed, so he has "re-calculated," and hoped no one would notice.

415. The church age has no end (Ephesians 3:20-21). Thus, for *Charting* to speak of the end of the Christian age is contra scripture.

416. For an extended scholarly discussion of the application of Sharpe's rule and Titus 2:13, see George Knight III, *New International Greek Testament Commentary*, (Grand Rapids, Paternoster, Eerdmans, 1992)321.

417. As Knight observes, (1992, 322) the text can also be rendered as "the appearing of the glory of the Great God." Paul's point is that the *parousia* would be the manifestation of the Deity of Jesus. He was to come "in the glory of the Father." See my book, *Like Father Like Son, On Clouds of Glory*, for an in-depth investigation of this vitally important concept. The book is available from my websites: www.bibleprophecy.com, or, www.eschatology.org.

418. William Mounce, *Word Biblical Commentary*, Vol. 46, Pastoral Epistles, (Nashville, Nelson, 2000)425.

419. See my book *Into All the World, Then Comes the End*, for a full discussion of the eschatological significance of the World Mission, and for more proof that it was indeed fulfilled in the first century. I am unaware of any other work that examines the World Mission in such a manner.

420. See my book *Who Is This Babylon?* for an in-depth analysis of this distinctive Greek term. The term is never used to indicate rapidity of action as opposed to nearness of occurrence. Thus, when Paul said the crushing of Satan would occur shortly, he was saying unambiguously that the Second Coming was near.

421. See my *Who Is This Babylon?* For a full discussion of this vital issue in Revelation.

422. The force of the Greek text in Acts 26:21f is quite powerful. It literally means that Paul did not preach *anything* that was not found in Moses and the prophets.

423. Thomas Ice, *The Seventy Weeks of Daniel Part I)* According to Prophecy Ministries Presents: Pre-Trib Perspectives Articles Archive," page 2 of 22 www.according2prophecy.org/seventy-weeks-pt1.html.

424. I presented this material in public formal debate with Thomas Ice and Mark Hitchcock, in October, 2003, in Tampa, Fl.. Neither Ice nor Hitchcock even attempted to respond to the material. The impact of the arguments was very powerful. See our website to obtain tapes of the

debate. Also, I present this material in my detail in my *Seal Up Vision and Prophecy,* available at: www.bibleprophecy.com, or, www.eschatology.org.

425. Dwight Pentecost, *Things to Come,* (Grand Rapids, Zondervan, 1980)162.

426. George Lamsa, *Idioms of the Bible Explained,* (San Francisco, Harper and Row, 1985)101.

427. Clearly, our refutation of Gentry will likewise apply to other postmillennialists, such as Seriah. In a rather acerbic work, Jonathan Seriah, like Gentry, seeks to delineate between comings of the Lord in the New Testament because some elements are present in some texts and not in others. Jonathan Seriah, *The End of All Things,* Moscow, Idaho, Canon Press, 1999)176, 183. Seriah also claims that you cannot bring time statements from one text into a discussion of the Day of the Lord in another text. He gives no exegetical or contextual support for this claim. It is mere assertion, born of desperation. This is like saying you cannot bring a discussion of the resurrection into a text that discusses the end of the age, and is patently false.

428. Although Gentry is quite vocal in his opposition to Covenant Eschatology, he has been invited to formally debate me on numerous occasions, by many people. To this date, he has either refused to even respond to those challenges, or simply refused to debate me.

429. Interestingly, Mathison and other postmillennialists differ with Gentry on 2 Thessalonians 1. Mathison believes that 2 Thessalonians 1 applies to AD 70. Keith Mathison, *Postmillennialism: An Eschatology of Hope,* (Phillipsburg, New Jersey, P and R Publishing, 1999)224+.

430. Gentry posits 1 Thessalonians 5 in the future. He applies the coming as a thief warning as a parallel to Matthew 24:44 which, in turn, he applies to the future. (*Thine is the Kingdom,* (Vallecito, CA., Calcedon, 2003)168; *Dominion,* 2009, 437f).

431. I must confess that it is rather stunning to me how desperate the arguments of the opponents of Covenant Eschatology often become. Gentry's attempt to create two *parousia*s in the texts of Thessalonians thoroughly demonstrates bad logic. Similarly, in my March 2008 debate with Mac Deaver, I presented the perfect parallel between Daniel 9:24f and Hebrews 9:24-28. Each passage speaks of the putting away of sin, the atonement, the world of righteousness, the Most Holy Place, etc.. Thus, since Deaver holds that Daniel was fulfilled no later than AD 70, then Christ's *parousia* in Hebrews 9 was fulfilled no later than AD 70. In response, Deaver argued that Hebrews 9 is different from Daniel because Hebrews 9 mentions the death of all men! I responded by noting that this "logic" would therefore, prove that 1 Corinthians 15 and

2 Peter 3 must speak of different times and events, since both passages contain elements not found in the other! The same is true of 1 Corinthians 15 and 1 Thessalonians 4– and the gospel accounts of the Olivet Discourse for that matter! The *only* way that the mention of different elements in different texts can demand different topics is if there are discordant and disjunctive elements that establish a different time, and a different subject, or different theme. I called on Deaver to show that the atonement, the putting away of sin, and the world of righteousness foretold by Daniel was indeed different from that foretold by Hebrews, but he never responded. The Deaver-V-Preston debate is available from my websites:: www.bibleprophecy.com, or, www.eschatology.org.

432. On Luke 18, Gentry says, "Christ had in mind the era of His imminent coming in judgment upon Israel" (*Dominion*, 481). On Matthew 21:40, he says, "God's judgment on Israel is taught in parabolic form in Matthew 21:40" (*Dominion*, 274).

433. In a book designed to refute Covenant Eschatology, editor Keith Mathison argues that the Son of Man passages in the New Testament refer to the AD 70 *parousia*. He fails to inform his readers that Matthew 13 and Matthew 25:31, *passages that he applies to the "final end,"* are Son of Man passages! Thus, on the one hand, Mathison affirms that the Son of Man texts are not future, and on the other hand, he affirms that some of them are! (Mathison, *When Shall These Things Be? A Reformed Response to Hyper-Preterism*, (Phillipsburg, New Jersey, P and R Publishing, 2004)180+. Additional note: Mathison now openly applies Matthew 25:31f to the AD 70 parousia (*Age*, 2009, 380). This is a rejection of his former views as well as the creeds on Matthew 25:31.

434. I develop these concepts more in-depth in a paper presented at the 2009 Preterist Pilgrim Weekend seminar that I sponsor in Ardmore, Ok. every year. MP3s of that presentation are available from me at www.bibleprophecy.com, or www.eschatology.org.

435. See Klyne Snodgrass, *Stories with Intent, A Comprehensive Guide To The Parables of Jesus*, (Grand Rapids, Eerdmans, 2008)156+ for a good discussion of the purpose of Jesus' parables. Snodgrass argues that Jesus utilized the parables, serving as a prophet to warn Israel of impending disaster. Likewise, Wright (*Victory*, 147-165) sees the parables as Jesus' instrument of warning to Israel.

436. Note 2 Corinthians 3:15-4:1-4 where Paul says that there was a veil on the eyes of Israel "even to this day" (his day) in the reading of Moses and the Law. He says that the gospel was hidden to those *who did not believe*, and as a result, they were hardened against it. This is a clear echo of Matthew 13 and Isaiah 6:9f and the hardening of Israel.

437. It might be objected that Jesus spoke of sowing the seed into the "world" (Greek, *kosmos*) and that this can only mean the world in the modern sense. This is misguided. The Greek word *kosmos* is often used of the Jewish world / age (cf. Galatians 4:3; Colossians 2:20f, etc.). Furthermore, the gospel was to be preached "to the Jew first" and Paul said that the gospel had been preached in all the world (*kosmos*, Colossians 1:6). Paul seems to be echoing Matthew 13 in Colossians when he says that the gospel had been preached and was "bringing forth fruit" (Colossians 1:6).

438. Greg Bahnsen and Kenneth Gentry, *House Divided*, (Tyler, Tx. Institute for Christian Economics, 1989)273+.

439. *Elthe* is a form of *erchomai*. To make his point, Gentry would have to prove that *erchomai* and *parousia* can be synonyms, but that *elthe* and *parousia* cannot be used interchangeably. This simply cannot be done since *elthe* is just another form of *erchomai*.

440. Kenneth Gentry, *Before Jerusalem Fell*, (Tyler, Tx. Institute for Christian Economics, 1989)235n.

441. For an in-depth discussion of 2 Thessalonians 1, and why it applied to the A. D. 70 *parousia*, see my book, *Who Is This Babylon?* I show that Paul is quoting directly from Isaiah 2, a passage that *Jesus* applied to his coming against Jerusalem.. So, Jesus applied Isaiah 2 to the judgment of Jerusalem. Paul, directly quoting the identical verse, speaks of the coming of Christ against the (Jewish) persecutors of the church. How is it possible to apply Thessalonians to anything other than to what Jesus applied it, without clearly delineating your application?

442. Kenneth Gentry, *The Beast of Revelation*, (Powder Springs, GA, American Vision, 2002)27.

443. Partial preterism may in fact be called "sub-preterism" because it does not rise to the level of true preterism. It is a theology fatally flawed in its inconsistent hermeneutic and logic.

444. See my work "Resurrection Now," on my websites: www.bibleprophecy.com, or, www.eschatology.org for proof that the resurrection work of Christ was indeed a process, and did not involve the raising of decomposed bodies out of the grave. My article is an in-depth analysis of John 5:24-28 showing that there was only one death and only one resurrection that was the focus of Christ's work, and that was sin-death, separation from God. Not biological death.

Scripture Index

(Written and Compiled by Samuel G. Dawson)

Genesis

Gen. 1.14 5
Gen. 2.5 5
Gen. 2.15f 370
Gen. 2.16-17 5
Gen. 3.5 5
Gen. 3.15 101
Gen. 28.15f 260

Exodus

Ex. 4.22 247
Ex. 19.5-6 373
Ex. 30.34 177
Ex. 31.1-7 178

Leviticus

Lev. 16.21 f 15

Numbers

Num. 24.17 200

Deuteronomy

Dt. 30.4 172
Dt. 32.20, 29, 43 112
Dt. 32.21f 258
Dt. 32.32-35 389
Dt. 32.35 243
Dt. 32.19 220
Dt. 32.43 200, 216, 220, 377, 384, 392

Judges

Jud. 5 81

I Samuel

I Sam. 8.6f 374
I Sam. 10.17f 374
I Sam. 12.17f 374

I Kings

I K. 2.36-37 6
I K. 8.10-11 177
I K. 12.16f 374

II Kings

II K. 9.7 391
II K. 17.20f 374
II K. 24.14f 335
II K. 25.11 335

II Chronicles

II Chron. 6.24 61

Psalms

Ps. 18.3-17 182
Ps. 18.11f 167
Ps. 68 81
Ps. 68.4 167
Ps. 69.21f 243
Ps. 69.24-28 243
Ps. 79.10 391
Ps. 97.2 167
Ps. 102 344
Ps. 104.3 167

Isaiah

Isa. 2-4 30, 200, 216
Isa. 2.2-3 31, 376
Isa. 4.2-6 31
Isa. 6.9f 242
Isa. 8 243
Isa. 11 258
Isa. 11.10f 21, 247
Isa. 11.10-12 92
Isa. 11.11f 132
Isa. 21.3f 246
Isa. 24-27 132
Isa. 24.10 227, 233
Isa. 24.20f 376
Isa. 25-26.16f 233
Isa. 25.6f 376
Isa. 25.6-8 132
Isa. 25.6-10 136
Isa. 25.8-9 92
Isa. 26.19 216
Isa. 26.16-19 247
Isa. 26.19-21 122
Isa. 26.21 247
Isa. 27.1 232
Isa. 27.8-9 173
Isa. 27.9-13 21, 234
Isa. 27.12-13 132, 134
Isa. 27.13 133, 135-136
Isa. 28 243
Isa. 28.20f 393
Isa. 28.21 149
Isa. 28.21-22 211
Isa. 29.14 149

Isa. 29.19f 217
Isa. 31.4f 167
Isa. 37.3 246
Isa. 40.10-11 48
Isa. 42.1-4 247
Isa. 42.10 247
Isa. 42.15f 247
Isa. 43.3-7 33
Isa. 48.20 33
Isa. 49 91
Isa. 49.6-8 136
Isa. 49.6-10 92
Isa. 49.20-21 92
Isa. 49.6f 22, 258
Isa. 51, 55 258
Isa. 53.4-6 11
Isa. 59.1-2 132
Isa. 60.22 206, 389
Isa. 61.1f 258
Isa. 61.1-6 95
Isa. 61.2-12 22
Isa. 63.11-12 248
Isa. 64.1f 89, 243
Isa. 64.1-3 155
Isa. 65-66.15f 22
Isa. 65-66 258
Isa. 65.1-2 243
Isa. 65.8f 344
Isa. 65.8-25 247
Isa. 65.13f 243, 258
Isa. 66.15 247
Isa. 66.15f 89
Isa. 65.17f 89
Isa. 66.6 122
Isa. 66.12-16 247

Jeremiah

Jer. 2.30 241, 244
Jer. 2.34 241
Jer. 3.14f 23
Jer. 4.16-31 244
Jer. 4.23-28 303
Jer. 4.26 241
Jer. 4.31 246
Jer. 5.21-22 303
Jer. 5.22 241
Jer. 6.1, 17 241
Jer. 6.24 241, 246
Jer. 6.26 241
Jer. 7.29 242
Jer. 22.23 246
Jer. 31 258
Jer. 31.29f 264
Jer. 31.30f 43
Jer. 48.41 246
Jer. 50.43 246

Ezekiel

Ezek. 26-27 34
Ezek. 30.3f 167
Ezek. 37 133, 258
Ezek. 37.10-12 371
Ezek. 37.10-14 31
Ezek. 37.12 172
Ezek. 37.12f 258
Ezek. 37.15f 31
Ezek. 37.22-27 172
Ezek. 37.26f 31, 90
Ezek. 40-48 35

Daniel

Dan. 2, 7, 10-12 201
Dan. 2.28f 223
Dan. 2.44 2
Dan. 7 223
Dan. 7.8-11 223
Dan. 7.10 224
Dan. 7.13-14 2, 254, 385, 392
Dan. 7.21f 223
Dan. 7.23f 392
Dan. 7.23-25 223
Dan. 7.27 223
Dan. 9.24 178
Dan. 9.24-27 36, 268
Dan. 9.26 34, 178
Dan. 10.14 201
Dan. 12.1-2 126
Dan. 12.1-3 331, 341
Dan. 12.3 253
Dan. 12.1-7 126
Dan. 12.2 254
Dan. 12.4, 9 201
Dan. 12.6 254
Dan. 12.7 341
Dan. 12.10 247, 250, 373

Hosea

Hos. 1-3 22
Hos. 1.6, 9 34
Hos. 1.9-10 33, 258
Hos. 2.14-18 42
Hos. 2.18 43, 258
Hos. 2.19 162
Hos. 2.23 33, 373
Hos. 2.25 34
Hos. 3.4 44
Hos. 5.14-6.1-3 148
Hos. 5.15 42, 44
Hos. 5.15-6.1-3 44
Hos. 6.1-2 42
Hos. 6.1-3 44
Hos. 6.5 42
Hos. 8.8 177
Hos. 13.1-2, 13-14 173
Hos. 13.13 246
Hos. 13.14 399
Hos. 13.14f 44

Joel

Joel 2.28f 258, 356, 371
Joel 2.28-3.21 204
Joel 3.14 203

Amos

Amos 9.11 102

Micah

Mic. 1.3 167
Mic. 3.12 248
Mic. 4.10 248

Mic. 5.23 248

Zechariah

Zech. 14.5 53
Zech. 6.12-13 178
Zech. 6.13 258

Nahum

Nah. 1.3 167

Habakkuk

Heb. 1.5 242

Zephaniah

Zeph. 1.15 168

Haggai

Hag. 2.7 258

Malachi

Mal. 1.12f 355
Mal. 4.5-6 49

Matthew

Mt. 3.2 209
Mt. 3.7-8 48
Mt. 3.10-12 48
Mt. 5.17-18 21
Mt. 8.11f 114-115
Mt. 10.23 290
Mt. 11.17 286
Mt. 13 314
Mt. 13.11 261
Mt. 13.16-17 210
Mt. 13.17f 107
Mt. 13.24-30, 37-43 83
Mt. 13.30 300
Mt. 13.30-43 251
Mt. 13.39 254
Mt. 13.39-40 259
Mt. 13.41 331
Mt. 13.42 341

Mt. 13.43 315
Mt. 16.18-19 261
Mt. 16.24f 223, 227
Mt. 16.27 183, 303
Mt. 16.27-28 59, 196, 222, 230, 311, 328-329, 392-393
Mt. 17.11f 286
Mt. 19.28 285
Mt. 21.40 340
Mt. 21.40f 243, 359
Mt. 22.1-7 240
Mt. 23.29f 120
Mt. 23.29-36 216
Mt. 23.31-37 179
Mt. 23.32 197
Mt. 23.32f 105
Mt. 23.34 55
Mt. 23.34f 122
Mt. 23.34-36 57, 88, 173, 217
Mt. 23.35 197
Mt. 23.36 390
Mt. 23.37 171
Mt. 24.2-3, 29-34 251
Mt. 24.2-3, 34 212
Mt. 24.8 249
Mt. 24.8f 35, 373
Mt. 24.9 52, 223
Mt. 24.9-12 60, 289-292
Mt. 24.10-12 279
Mt. 24.14 175, 328, 361
Mt. 24.15f 122, 248
Mt. 24.22 213
Mt. 24.26f 367
Mt. 24.29 167
Mt. 24.29f 317, 385
Mt. 24.29-31 227, 315, 385
Mt. 24.29-34 253-257
Mt. 24.30 168, 179, 340, 384
Mt. 24.31 172, 340
Mt. 24.32-33 205, 239

Mt. 24.34 390
Mt. 24.35 399
Mt. 24.40-41 335
Mt. 25.1-13 64, 147, 237, 240
Mt. 25.14f 148
Mt. 25.31 301, 407
Mt. 25.31f 83, 184, 393
Mt. 26.26f 258
Mt. 26.64 317, 405
Mt. 27.25 242, 332
Mt. 27.47 13

Mark

Mk. 1.15 209
Mk. 13.7-8 244
Mk. 13.9 55
Mk. 14.13 151

Luke

Lk. 1.32-33 2, 251
Lk. 1.57 232
Lk. 3.1f 223
Lk. 4.16 99
Lk. 4.18f 95
Lk. 11.49f 120
Lk. 13.28f 116
Lk. 13.31 332
Lk. 17.12 151
Lk. 17.25f 105
Lk. 18.1-8 105, 215, 392
Lk. 18.8 88, 217, 340
Lk. 19.11f 302
Lk. 19.12 70
Lk. 19.14 71
Lk. 19.27 71
Lk. 20.33f 259
Lk. 20.34f 351
Lk. 21.8 227, 406
Lk. 21.8 205
Lk. 21.20f 97
Lk. 22.29 236
Lk. 23.28-31 188
Lk. 23.28f 391

John

Jn. 1.14 38
Jn. 2.19f 38
Jn. 3.7 248
Jn. 3.15 13
Jn. 3.36 14
Jn. 4.20f 3
Jn. 4.20-24 43
Jn. 4.21 175
Jn. 5.19f 88, 303
Jn. 5.24-29 235
Jn. 5.25-29 23, 225, 355
Jn. 6.15 374
Jn. 6.50 14
Jn. 8.51 14, 267, 351
Jn. 8.56 107
Jn. 10.28 14
Jn. 10.28-29 181
Jn. 11.25-25 14
Jn. 11.48 359
Jn. 11.52 172
Jn. 12.31 166
Jn. 14 38, 319
Jn. 14.1-3 177
Jn. 14.9f 39, 231
Jn. 14.15-18 320
Jn. 14.19 85
Jn. 14.19f 279, 319
Jn. 16.7 199
Jn. 18.36 374

Acts

Ac. 2.15f 210, 258
Ac. 2.15-17 27
Ac. 3.21f 248
Ac. 3.21-24 22, 107, 109, 255, 259
Ac. 3.24f 175
Ac. 4.11f 359
Ac. 7.48 370
Ac. 8.11 231
Ac. 10.40 320
Ac. 12.7 88
Ac. 13.27 242
Ac. 13.40 149, 242
Ac. 13.40-41 242
Ac. 14.3 231
Ac. 14.22 225, 229, 247
Ac. 14.28 231
Ac. 15.14f 102
Ac. 15.16f 102
Ac. 17.30-31 199, 313
Ac. 18.6 242
Ac. 21.28 28
Ac. 22.18 88, 371
Ac. 24.13f 28
Ac. 24.13-15 91
Ac. 24.14-15 24
Ac. 25.4 88
Ac. 26.5f 24
Ac. 26.6f 261
Ac. 26.7 260
Ac. 26.17-18 172
Ac. 26.21f 8, 25, 333
Ac. 28.15 146, 151
Ac. 28.19f 25
Ac. 28.25-28 242

Romans

Rom. 1.16-17 176, 285
Rom. 2.28-29 102
Rom. 5.21 102, 269
Rom. 5.6f 11-12, 102
Rom. 6.1-10 267
Rom. 6.1, 16 364
Rom. 6.3f 260
Rom. 6.4-10 351
Rom. 6.5 18
Rom. 6.23 14, 269
Rom. 7.1-6 364
Rom. 7.1-10 267
Rom. 7.4-14 269
Rom. 7.7f 260
Rom. 7.7-9 14
Rom. 7.9f 264
Rom. 7.24 353
Rom. 8.1f 260, 399
Rom. 8.1-3 15, 270
Rom. 8.1-4 269
Rom. 8.18f 373, 392, 399
Rom. 8.22 249
Rom. 8.23-9.4 25
Rom. 9.3f 33
Rom. 9.33 243
Rom. 10.4 253-257
Rom. 10.18f 328
Rom. 10.19-21 258
Rom. 10.20-21 243
Rom. 11.1-3 33
Rom. 11.7 102, 260
Rom. 11.7ff 90
Rom. 11.9 243
Rom. 11.16 243
Rom. 11.26-27 173, 243
Rom. 12.1 157
Rom. 12.19 243
Rom. 15.8 76, 223, 396
Rom. 15.8-12 92
Rom. 15.9f 135
Rom. 15.20 232
Rom. 16.20 88, 232, 269
Rom. 16.25-26 162, 328, 333
Rom. 16.25-27 26

I Corinthians

I Cor. 4.9 297
I Cor. 5.7 358
I Cor. 7.29 213
I Cor. 7.31 213
I Cor. 9.20-21 364
I Cor. 10.2 248
I Cor. 10.11 102, 109, 213, 260, 390
I Cor. 15 232, 251
I Cor. 15.17 19
I Cor. 15.19f 260
I Cor. 15.20 262
I Cor. 15.22 4, 86

I Cor. 15.24 253-257, 260
I Cor. 15.24-28 267
I Cor. 15.24-28, 54-56 399
I Cor. 15.25 236, 269
I Cor. 15.45 8
I Cor. 15.50 261-262
I Cor. 15.51 196, 234
I Cor. 15.51-52 194
I Cor. 15.52 136-137, 181
I Cor. 15.54-56 18, 267-269
I Cor. 15.55-56 19

II Corinthians

II Cor. 2.15f 285
II Cor. 3.3f 258
II Cor. 3.4f 269
II Cor. 3.6f 260, 264, 350
II Cor. 3.6ff 102
II Cor. 3.7-11 364
II Cor. 3.15-18 102
II Cor. 3.16-4.2 258
II Cor. 4-5 84
II Cor. 4.4 166
II Cor. 4.14 387
II Cor. 4.16f 279, 392
II Cor. 5.5f 371
II Cor. 5.16 84
II Cor. 5.16f 298
II Cor. 5.17 258
II Cor. 5.20 285
II Cor. 5.21 9, 11
II Cor. 6.1-2 91, 258
II Cor. 6.14-16 32, 90
II Cor. 6.16 172
II Cor. 10.1f 166
II Cor. 11.2 157, 237, 258

Galatians

Gal. 1.11-12 76
Gal. 2.4f 253-257
Gal. 2.7-9 76
Gal. 2.10f 269
Gal. 3.13 9
Gal. 3.20-21 264
Gal. 3.21 192
Gal. 3.23f 257
Gal. 3.26-28 260
Gal. 4.1-7 364
Gal. 4.4 102, 109, 252
Gal. 4.22-32 56
Gal. 4.29 56
Gal. 5.18 364

Ephesians

Eph. 1.7 358
Eph. 1.8-10 102
Eph. 1.10 111, 258
Eph. 1.12f 371
Eph. 2.2 166
Eph. 2.11f 258
Eph. 2.13f 261
Eph. 2.19f 32
Eph. 2.20-21 34
Eph. 3.20-21 2, 251, 258, 407
Eph. 4.8 81
Eph. 4.8f 178
Eph. 4.8-13 402
Eph. 4.16 178
Eph. 4.16f 32
Eph. 4.30 358
Eph. 5.21 237
Eph. 5.23 361
Eph. 6.12 166

Philippians

Phil. 1.1 392
Phil. 1.19f 191
Phil. 3.20-21 261
Phil. 4.5 261

Colossians

Col. 1.5 328
Col. 1.18f 17
Col. 1.23 328
Col. 1.24f 297
Col. 1.27 157
Col. 2.11-13 19, 260
Col. 2.14f 166, 260, 360

I Thessalonians

I Thes. 1.4 126
I Thes. 1.6 180
I Thes. 1.8 367
I Thes. 1.9-10 47
I Thes. 2.12 224, 228
I Thes. 2.14f 128, 385, 392
I Thes. 2.14-16 49, 108, 120, 244
I Thes. 2.15-17 180, 188, 190, 197, 239
I Thes. 3.3-4 52
I Thes. 3.13 53, 340
I Thes. 4 251, 340
I Thes. 4.13 195
I Thes. 4.13-18 251, 268, 273, 315, 337, 349, 370
I Thes. 4.14 81, 104-118
I Thes. 4.15 63-73
I Thes. 4.15, 17 194-225, 311
I Thes. 4.16 118-129, 140
I Thes. 4.17 141-193, 320
I Thes. 4.18 100, 270
I Thes. 5.1-3 239-244
I Thes. 5.9-10 351
I Thes. 5.10 350

II Thessalonians

II Thes. 1.1 321
II Thes. 1.1f 300
II Thes. 1.3-6 55
II Thes. 1.3-10 121
II Thes. 1.4f 180, 217, 224, 229, 239, 321
II Thes. 1.4-10 190
II Thes. 1.4-12 54-57
II Thes. 1.5-6 56
II Thes. 1.6 224
II Thes. 1.6-10 331
II Thes. 1.7-10 337
II Thes. 1.7f 183
II Thes. 1.8 105
II Thes. 1.9 56, 187
II Thes. 1.10-12 300
II Thes. 1.9f 391
II Thes. 2 337
II Thes. 2.1 340
II Thes. 2.1-2 58, 340, 367
II Thes. 2.2 224
II Thes. 2.3f 59
II Thes. 2.5f 224, 228, 393
II Thes. 2.7 59
II Thes. 2.13 126
II Thes. 2.14f 224
II Thes. 3.1-3 224

I Timothy

I Tim. 2.6 102
I Tim. 6.14f 152

II Timothy

II Tim. 1.12 269
II Tim. 2.18 58, 323
II Tim. 4.1 83, 196, 385, 392
II Tim. 4.6-8 121
II Tim. 4.8 191

Titus

Tit. 1.2 191
Tit. 2.11-13 328
Tit. 2.13 327
Tit. 3.5 286

Hebrews

Heb. 1.1-2 210
Heb. 2.14-15 268
Heb. 3-4 248
Heb. 8.1f 370
Heb. 8.13 260, 364
Heb. 9.6f, 24f 264
Heb. 9.6-10 101
Heb. 9.8-10 255
Heb. 9.10 256, 265, 398, 402
Heb. 9.15f 121, 192
Heb. 9.24 260
Heb. 9.24-28 192
Heb. 9.26 262
Heb. 9.28 16, 221, 267
Heb. 10.1-3 260
Heb. 10.1-4 269, 360
Heb. 10.1-14 364
Heb. 10.32f 392
Heb. 10.32-37 108
Heb. 10.33f 112
Heb. 10.33-37 244
Heb. 10.35-39 221
Heb. 10.37 250, 311, 313, 332
Heb. 11.13f 114, 202
Heb. 11.26 107-108
Heb. 11.32 232
Heb. 11.32f 109
Heb. 11.35 116, 375
Heb. 11.36-39 217
Heb. 12.21 249
Heb. 12.21f 110
Heb. 12.22 102
Heb. 12.25-28 251
Heb. 12.28 110

James

Jas. 1.1f 102
Jas. 1.18 249
Jas. 2.4f 221
Jas. 5.1-6 221, 249
Jas. 5.3-8 210
Jas. 5.7-9 221
Jas. 5.8 250, 313, 345
Jas. 5.8-9 332
Jas. 5.9 231

I Peter

I Pet. 1.1 102
I Pet. 1.1-2 373
I Pet. 1.3-5 206
I Pet. 1.4f 35, 247-248, 373
I Pet. 1.5, 20 211
I Pet. 1.9-12 22
I Pet. 1.10f 109, 205
I Pet. 1.17 33, 232, 373
I Pet. 1.18 33
I Pet. 2.4 34
I Pet. 2.4-5 258, 358
I Pet. 2.5 177
I Pet. 2.5f 34
I Pet. 2.9 373
I Pet. 2.9f 102
I Pet. 2.10 33, 373
I Pet. 2.12 33, 373
I Pet. 3.18 11
I Pet. 4.5, 7, 17 206, 373, 385
I Pet. 4.5, 7, 17-19 35
I Pet. 4.7 198-199, 332
I Pet. 4.17 231-232, 313

II Peter

II Pet. 2-3 392
II Pet. 3.1-3, 13 22
II Pet. 3.10 166
II Pet. 3.12 389

I John

I Jn. 2.18 226, 313
3 181

Revelation

Rev. 1.7 332
Rev. 2.10 121, 191, 297
Rev. 3.9 219
Rev. 5.5 164
Rev. 6.9f 81, 218, 224
Rev. 6.9-11 296
Rev. 6.11 121, 231, 297
Rev. 7.4, 9 296
Rev. 7.14 249
Rev. 7.15-17 93
Rev. 10.1 66
Rev. 10.6 66-67, 226, 232
Rev. 10.7 24, 66
Rev. 11.15f 137, 224, 392
Rev. 11.15-18 83
Rev. 11.16f 196
Rev. 11.8 332
Rev. 11.8-17 137, 393
Rev. 11.8, 15f 128
Rev. 12.6ff 127
Rev. 12.7 378
Rev. 12.11 297
Rev. 13 128
Rev. 14 387
Rev. 14.1-2 250
Rev. 14.4 249
Rev. 14.13 192
Rev. 15.8 81
Rev. 16.6-7 332
Rev. 16.15f 122
Rev. 18.20 128
Rev. 18.20, 24 332
Rev. 18.21 258
Rev. 19.2 220
Rev. 19.6-8 67
Rev. 19.7 198, 258
Rev. 19.7-8 70
Rev. 19.14f 152
Rev. 20 232
Rev. 21.1f 258
Rev. 21.3, 10 145
Rev. 21.3 40, 351
Rev. 21.10 350-351
Rev. 22. 7, 12, 20 222, 332
Rev. 22.12 234
Rev. 22.17 179

Topic Index

(Written and Compiled By Samuel G. Dawson)

144,000, Ed Stevens on 296
1948 creation of Israel, supersign of the end 325

A

A Commentary on the Apocalypse, Moses Stuart 55
A Comprehensive Guide to the Parables of Jesus, parables linked to Isa. 9.6f 343
A Critical Lexicon and Concordance to the English and Greek New Testament, Ethelbert W. Bullinger 142
A Greek Grammar of the New Testament, Blass-De-Brunner 200
A New Heaven and New Earth: The Case for a Holistic Reading of the Biblical Story of Redemption, Richard Middleton 163
A Treatise on the Right Use of the Fathers, John Dalle 275
abomination of desolation, the
  and physical rapture
    a review 289-292
    Athanasius on 290
  Clement of Alexandria 289
  and physical rapture
  Eusebius 290
  and physical rapture
    rabbinic sources 291
  Athanasius on 290
  introduced 60
  leads to destruction of the temple 60
  occured at the resurrection 291

Abraham, heavenly city and country promised to 114
Abrahamic promise
  and the Messianic Banquet 115
  are the promises of Thessalonians 110
  in light of Mt. 8.11f 114
acceptable time
  introduced 91
  Isa. 49 and Isa. 61 the same 99
acceptable year of the Lord, Isa. 61.1-6 95
AD 70
  Gentry says at hand must refer to 208
  Gentry says quickly must refer to 208
  Gentry says shortly must refer to 208
Adam
  death of
    could not be physical death 12
    discussed 4
    either Satan or God lied 5
    I Thes. the triumph over 45
    if physical, denies the efficacy of Christ's death 17
    Paul considered it a curse in Rom. 7.24 353
    Rom. 7.7-9 14
    vs. life of Christ 4
    when did he know good and evil? 6
afflictions to some, rest to others, II Thes. 1.4-12 54
Against Heresies, Iranaeus 281, 287, 302

age to come, the
  an element of the hope of Israel 261
  Gentry admits would succeed Mosaic age 252
  Gentry's dilemma on 253
air
  See also heavenly places
  atmosphere or spiritual realm? 165-170
  meeting the Lord in the 141-164
  not about atmosphere or clouds 166
  not literal if planet and stars burned up 166
  Satan ruler of 165
allegory of Hagar and Sara 56
Allison, Dale *The End of the Ages Has Come* 212
already but not yet 375, 399
amillennialism has no use for Old Covenant promises to Israel 45
An Eschatology of Victory, Marcellus Kik 168
angels were preachers in Olivet Discourse but angelic beings in Thessalonians 80
anoint the Most Holy
  Dan. 9.24 178
  Dan. 9.26 178
  Zech. 6.12-13 178
apantesis
  a final objection to technical usage 163
  Ac. 28.15 146
  commentaries on 143-145
    Bruce 145
    Cosby 143
    Eadie 145
    Frame 145
    Patterson 144
    Waldron 145
    Wanamaker 145
  discussed 141
  in the New Testament
    I Thes. 4.17? 146
    virgins went to meet the bridegroom 147
  Josephus on 154
  lexicons on 142-158
  not like meeting for lunch 151
  objections to technical usage 155
  scholars who reject technical meaning do so on presuppositional theological grounds 146
  the official welcome of a newly arrived dignity 145
  theological time bomb 141
  used by Jesus
    Lk. 17.12 151
    Mk. 14.13 151
    Mt. 25.1-13 147
  used by John in Rev. 19.14f 152
  used by Josephus 153
  used by Paul
    Ac. 28.15 151
    I Tim. 6.14f 152
  used with *parousia* of a royal dignitary 152
  virgins went to meet the bridegroom 147
  with *episunagogee* 150
apostasy, chronicling throughout the New Testament 364
apostles
  already in the regeneration 286
  already on thrones 285
  judging the twelve tribes of Israel 285
apostolic succession 402
archangel
  voice of
    Dan. 12.1-2 126
    discussed 125-129
    I Thes. 1.4 126
    II Thes. 2.13 126
    interpretive key in I Thes. 4.16 128
    Michael? 125
ark of the covenant no longer remembered 355
ascension and descent of Jesus 81

ascension with the dead an unseen event 82
at hand, Gentry says must refer to AD 70 208
Athanasius
   on abomination of desolation 290
   on Mt. 24.14 287
   on second coming and resurrection 295
atonement, Christ's
   2000-year gap between initiation and completion? 267
   Col. 1.18f 17
   Col. 2.11-13 19
   consummated at parousia 19
   discussed 14
   Heb. 9.28 17
   I Cor. 15.17 19
   I Cor. 15.54-56 18-19
   included sacrifice and return of High Priest 264
   not complete until parousia 267
   resurrection at the time of removal of sin 19
   Rom. 6.5 18
   Rom. 6.23 14
   Rom. 7.7-9 14
   Rom. 8.1-3 15
audience relevance, imminence and 311
Avenging of the Blood of the Apostles and Prophets, Arthur Ogden 220
avenging the elect speedily
   Dt. 32.19f 220
   Dt. 32.43 220
   Heb. 10.35-39 221
   Heb. 11.36-39 217
   Ice on Mt. 23.29-36 216
   II Thes. 1.4f 217
   Isa. 2.2 220
   Isa. 26.19f links Day of the Lord and the ressurection 217
   Isa. 4.4 220
   Jas. 2.4f 221
   Jas. 5.1-6 221
   Jas. 5.7-9 221
   Lk. 18.1-8 215
   Lk. 18.8 217-218
   Mt. 16.27-28 220
   Mt. 23.29-36 216
   Rev. 19.2 220
   Rev. 22. 7, 12, 20 222
avenging the elect speedily
   Rev. 3.9 219
   Rev. 6.12f 220
   Rev. 6.9f 218
avenging the martyrs, foretold in Dt. 32.43 200

B

Babylon, Gentry identifies as Old Covenant Jerusalem 66-69
Balz and Schnieder *Exegetical Dictionary of the New Testament* 142, 198
Bauckham, Richard *The Climax of Prophecy* 296
Bauckham, Richard *Word Biblical Commentary on 2 Peter* 291
Bauer's Arndt and Gingrich, Greek-English Lexicon of the New Testament and Other Early Christian Literature 54, 142, 199, 257
Beale, Greg *1-2 Thessalonians, The IVP New Testament Series* 63, 140
Beale, Greg *New International Greek Testament Commentary on Revelation* 218, 220
Beale, Greg, and D. A. Carson *Commentary on the New Testament Use of the Old Testament* 207
Before Jerusalem Fell, Kenneth Gentry
   falsifies watchfulness implies delay 66
   inconsistencies in I Thes. 1 and 2 345
   Jerusalem the persecutor of Christians 55
   on imminence statements 87

Beginning of the End, Tim LaHaye 325
Beiderwolf, William, *The Second Coming Bible* 53
believers shall never die 14
Benware, Paul, rapture vs. second coming in dispensationalism 159
better resurrection *See* resurrection, the better
Bible, a Jewish book on God's promises to Israel 159
Biblical Apocalyptics: A Study of the Most Notable Revelations of God and of Christ, Milton Terry 53, 168
biological death *See* death, biological
birth pains of the messiah at the tribulation 248
Blass-De-Brunner *A Greek Grammar of the New Testament* 200
Boutflower, Charles *In and Around the Book of Daniel* 178
bride of Christ, Gentry on 237
brides, dispensationalism requires two, and two weddings 161
Brimsmead, Robert *The Pattern of Redemptive History* 125
Brown, Colin, *New International Dictionary of the New Testament Theology* 169
Bruce, F. F. *The Time Is Fulfilled* 209
Bruce, F. F. *Word Commentary, Commentary on 1 & 2 Thessalonians* 54, 74, 104, 125, 145
Bryan, Steven M., *The Eschatological Temple in John 14* 38
Bullinger, Ethelbert W. *A Critical Lexicon and Concordance to the English and Greek New Testament* 142

C

calling the Gentiles was an element of the hope of Israel 258
Can You Believe Jesus Said This? Don K. Preston 59, 196, 220, 223
captives taken under the altar
 introduced 81
 who saw it? 82
captivity was death of Israel 133
caught up, *harpadzo* and *episunagogee* 181
charismata and the coming 295
Charting the End times, Tim LaHaye and Thomas Ice 26, 99
Chilton, David *Paradise Restored* 171, 279
Christ
 as High Priest vs. Old Covenant one 15
 atonement of *See* atonement, Christ's
 brings dead without observation 85
 death of
  didn't deliver from physical death 19
  gathering of Israel not limited to 22
  if Adam's death physical, denies the efficacy of 17
 died spiritually? 9
 first to rise from the dead 8
 forsaken by the father? 13
 in or through Christ, I Thes. 4.14 104
 no longer known after the flesh 85
 not first to rise biologically 8
 substitutionary death *See* substitutionary death
 suffer allienation from the father? 9
 world would see him no more 85
Christian age

all futurist views of I Thes. 4 see
  end of
  no end to 3
Christology of the Old Testament, E.
  W. Hengstenberg 53
Christ's coming, nature of *See*
  parousia
chronos
  Englishman's Greek Concordance 231
  Gentry on 232
Chrysostom, John
  Homily 289, 294
  on Mt. 24.14 288
  on second coming and resurrection 295
church age has no end 2
church ages, Ice's seven 312
church not forseen per Walvoord, LaHaye, and Ice 26
Clarke, Adam, *Clarke's Commentary* 53
Clarke's Commentary, Adam Clarke 53
Clement of Alexandria
  discussed 401
  in Ante-Nicene Fathers 289
  on abomination of desolation 289
clouds of heaven
  discussed 166-170
  Ezk. 30.3f 167
  historical judgments on men 168
  Isa. 31.4f 167
  Lk. 21.25 168
  Mic. 1.3 167
  Mt. 24.29 167
  Mt. 24.30 168
  Nah. 1.3 167
  Ps. 18.11f 167
  Ps. 68.4 167
  Ps. 97.2 167
  Ps. 104.3 167
  reflects majesty and judgment 168
  three nuances to 168
  Zeph. 1.15 168

Coloe, Mary L. *God Dwells With Us: Temple Symbolism in the Fourth Gospel* 39
coming of the Lord
  as a thief in the night *See* thief coming of the Lord
  expected in Thessalonians' lifetime 47
  Gentry says different in I Thes. and II Thes 338
  God had come in the past 89
  in I Thes. 4 and II Thes. 1 are the same 58
  partial preterists believe still a future coming 337
  patristics expected observable 291
  positive and negative aspects 149
  Eusebius said he had 292
  Mic. 1.2-4 292
  Mic. 3.9-12 292
coming of the Lord out of heaven
  Mic. 4.1-4 292
  patristics on 292-293
coming on the clouds, N. T. Wright on 50
coming with saints
  I Thes. 3.13 53
  Zech. 14.5 53
comings and more comings: partial preterism 337-348
Commentary on Daniel, F. W. Farrar 36
Commentary on Ephesians, John Eadie 285
Commentary on Matthew 39, Origen 287
Commentary on the Epistle to the Ephesians, John Eadie 81, 165
Commentary on the New Testament from the Talmud and Hebraica, John Lightfoot 71
Commentary on the New Testament Use of the Old Testament, Greg Beal and D. A. Carson 63, 207

Commentary on the New Testament Use of the Old Testament, Jeffrey Weima 131
conditional immortality, Ed Stevens on 400
context of I Thes. 4.13-18
  I Thes. 1.9-10 47
  I Thes. 3.13 53
  I Thes. 3.3-4 52
  II Thes. 1.4-12 54-57
  introduced 47
Contours of Pauline Theology, Tom Holland 97, 207
corporate concept of death and resurrection 42
corporate new birth 248
corporate salvation 361
Cosby, Michael R. *Hellenistic Formal Receptions and Paul's Use of Apantesis in I Thessalonians* 4:17 143, 154
creeds
  Gentry at odds with 396
  Mathison says they define orthodoxy 366
cursed, was Christ on the cross? 9

D

Dalle, John *A Treatise on the Right Use of the Fathers* 275
date setting
  1988, Edward Whisenant 313
  1999, Jack Van Impe 313
Davies, W. D. *Jewish and Pauline Studies* 263
Davies, W. D. *The Gospel and the Land* 60, 100
day of atonement
  at what point did Israel know God accepted their worship? 264
  in Lev. 16.21f 15
day of salvation
  Isa. 49.6f 22
  linked to gathering of Israel 22

resurrection on the 90
today is the 91
Day of the Lord, the
  already come?
    discussed 58
    how to convince it had already happened 59
  becomes the parousia of Christ 119
  could escape by fleeing to mountains in Isaiah 188
  final victory over Leviathan 233
  how to convince someone it had happened 59
  II Thes. 1.9 a direct quote from Isaiah 187
  in I Thessalonians 47
  Isa. 26.19f links to resurrection 217
  Isa. 26.21 233
  Isa. 27.9-13 21
  Jesus applies to upcoming judgment on Jerusalem 188
  judgment and salvation 51
  linked to Great Trumpet 21
  Mt. 11.13ff 48
  Mt. 17.11f 48
  new heavens and earth or new creation on 89
  Old Covenant concept 59
  Paul anticipated fulfillment of Isaiah 187
  Revelation is the divine record of 295
  visible sign of 122
  we have a divine record 295
  why Thessalonians could believe had come 367
day of vengeance in Isa. 61.1-6 95
day, the
  Gen. 2.5 5
  Gen. 2.16-17 5
  Gen. 3.5 5
  I Kings 2.36-37 6
  Numbers 30.3ff 7
  used metaphorically 5

days of vengeance
  Dan. 9.26 97
  Deut. 28.49-63 97
  Hos. 8.1-10:15 97
  I K. 9.1-9 97
  Jer. 6.1-6 97
  Jer. 26.1-9 97
  Lev. 26.27-33 97
  Lk. 21.20f 97
  Mic. 2.12 97
  Zech. 11.6 97
dead in Christ
  Christ brings without observation 85
  in Christ or through Christ? 104
  in Hebrews 11 105
  martyrs in I Thes. 4.14 104
death
  biological, resurrection has nothing to do with 4
  corporate concept 42
  Jesus overcame two deaths 264
  physical
    not the death of the Garden 100
    sleep a euphemism for 196
    sting of remained until law taken away 267
  substitutionary *See* substitutionary death
death of Christ *See* Christ, death of
death of Israel linked to her divorce 44
Death, Leviathan, and Martyrs: Isa. 24.1-27.1, Meredith G. Kline 234
decent, Jesus'
  also an unseen event? 83
  and ascension of Jesus 81
defeat of Satan, nearness of..86-87
Deissman, Adolf *Light From the Ancient East* 142
delay, watchfulness implies (Gentry) 65
DeMar, Gary *Last Days Madness*
  distinguishes between I Thes. 4, II Thes. 2 118
  gives nine parallels between Olivet Discourse and II Thes. 60
  on the sign of Christ's coming 279
Demy, Timothy and Thomas Ice, *Prophecy Watch* 61
Demy,Timothy *Fast Facts on Bible Prophecy See Fast Facts on Bible Prophecy*
destruction of Jerusalem
  early rabbinic explanations of 299
  John didn't write about 359
  never allowed unless Israel violated Torah
    II Chron. 6.24 61
    Ps. 41.11 61
  silence of early church perplexing 274
  silence of patristics on viewing as second coming 274-279
  why Gentiles would care 103
die, believers shall never 14
differences, rapture vs. second coming in dispensationalism 159
dispensational rapture doctrine
  See also two comings or one?
  coming of Christ postponed *See* postponement theory
  everything in II Thes. 1 contradicts the millennial view 321
  examined 310-336
  gap theory *See* postponement theory
  I Thes. 4.13f chief proof-text 310
  Ice: without postponement, dispensationalism falls apart 333
  II Thes. 1 321
  II Thes. 2 devastates 322
  imminence and the 310
  one taken, one left *See* one taken, one left
  postponement theory 329
  rapture vs. second coming 315

says church gathered first, but Jesus said wicked would be? 314
signs 323
this age, the age to come 314
who's gathered first? 314
church has temporarily replaced Israel 161
crumbles at the foot of the cross 267
has no place for total desolation of Israel in last days 273
necessity of gap for 399
physical king, physical throne, physical city, physical land a rejection of the sovereignty of God 374
dispensationalism
rapture vs. second coming 159
requires two weddings and two brides 161
Dispensationalism Rightly Dividing the People of God, Keith Mathison holds to unified view of Olivet Discourse 69
on coming of Christ at end of human history 231
Divorce and ReMarriage in the Bible, David Instone-Brewer 42
divorce of Israel, linked to her death 44
dual fulfillment theories, based on dichotomy of last days 240
Dubis, Mark Messianic *Woes in First Peter, Suffering and Eschatology in I Peter 4.12-19* 34
Dunn, James D. G. *Word Biblical Commentary, Romans 9-16* 86

E

Eadie, John *Commentary on the Epistle to the Ephesians* 81, 165, 285
Eadie, John *The John Eadie Greek Text Commentaries, Thessalonians* 145

Early Rabbinic Explanations of the Destruction of Jerusalem 299
Ecclesiastical History, Eusebius 281
end of the age, the
cannot be the end of the Christian age 253-257
Dan. 12.6 253-257
Dan. 2.44 253-257
Dan. 7.13-14 253-257
Dan.12.3 253-257
Eph. 3.20-21 251
Gal. 23.4f 253-257
Gal.4.4 253
Heb. 12.25-28 251
I Cor. 15 251
I Cor. 15.24 253-257
I Thes. 4 251-273
I Thes. 4.13-18 251
Lk. 1.32-33 251
Mathison on 254
Mt. 13.30-43 251
Mt. 13.43 253-257
Mt. 24.2-3, 29-34 251
Mt. 24.29-34 253-257
not end of the age to come 253
Old Testament writers never said it had come 202
parallels in Mt., Cor., and Thes. 251
Rom. 10.4 253-257
end of the ages, the
has come upon us
I Cor. 10.11 213
I Cor. 7.29 213
I Cor. 7.31 213
I Pet. 4.7 214
Mt. 24.22 213
Mt. 24.2-3, 34 212
time remaining had been shortened 213
end of time
did not belong to Jewish eschatology 361
N. T. Wright says Jews didn't contemplate 50

End Times Controversy, LaHaye and Ice's definitive refutation of preterism 25
end, no, to church age 2-3
end, the
    Gentry on end in I Cor. 10.11 vs. I Cor. 15 400
    Gentry vs. Mathison on imminence of..203
Epistle of Pseudo-Barnabas, The (79-135 AD) 401
episunagogee
    and *harpadzo* 181
    and *parousia*
        II Thes. 2.1-2 340
        Mt. 24.31 340
    gathering of Israel *See* gathering
    II Thes. 2 and Mt. 24.31 300
    with *apantesis* 150
eschatology
    already-but-not-yet 375
    not about end of history, but restoration of man to presence of God 236
eternal life *See* life after death
Eusebius
    on abomination of desolation 290
    on Isa. 66.18-19 292
    on Lk. 12.49 292
    on Mt. 24.14 288
    on Zech. 14 292
    said Lord came in fall of Jerusalem 292
    said saw the fulfillment of Micah's prophecy that Jerusalem would be plowed like a field 292
Eusebius, *Ecclesiastical History* 281
Eusebius, *Proof of the Gospel* 53, 176, 288
Evan, John *The Four Kingdoms of Daniel* 201
Exegetical Dictionary of the New Testament, Balz and Schnieder 142, 198

Exegetical Essays on the Resurrection of the Dead, Sam Frost 23
Exodus, Second *See* Second Exodus
expectations demand a physical rapture
    discussed 274-279
    left behind? 280-285
    review of Ed Stevens' position 274
    the problem of John 280
Expectations Demand A Rapture, Ed Stevens, review of 274
Exposition on Isaiah, Leupold 31
Expositor's Greek Testament, Robertson Nicoll 198
Expository Dictionary of New Testament Words, W. E. Vine 143

F

Farrar, F. W. *Commentary on Daniel* 36
Fast Facts on Bible Prophecy, Thomas Ice and Timothy Demy 2, 86
fear of death, Christians delivered from 269
fellowship
    I Thes. about the restoration of 45
    resurrection in the Torah dealt with 134
firstfruits
    and harvest are inseparable 262
    Christ first to raise biologically? 8
    from agricultural world of Paul's day 262
flesh, Christ no longer known after the 85
forgiveness
    linked to parousia 19
    linked to resurrection 19
forsaken, was Christ on the cross? 13
fourth beast, days of the 227

Frame, James *The International Critcal Commentary, Thessalonians* 54, 104, 145
Frend, W. H. C., *The Early Church* 282
From Age to Age the Unrolding of Biblical Eschatology, Keith Mathison 69, 77, 228
From Age to Age, The Unfolding of Biblical Eschatology
  creeds define orthodoxy 366
  defends late date for Revelation 393
  Mathison's change on Mt. 24.14 361
Frost, Sam *Exegetical Essays on the Resurrection of the Dead* 23
Frost, Sam *Misplaced Hope* 274
futurist view of eschatology
  all of I Thes. 4 *See* end of Christian age
  heaven's answer to all 342
futurists
  agree with skeptics that inspiration is damaged 215
  all have kingdom coming with observation 83
  implications for if Olivet Discourse united

G

gap
  2000 years between initiation and completion of atonement? 267
  necessity of for dispensationalism 393
gap theory
  See also postponement theory
  gaps in the 333
  Jesus didn't know about it 334
  Walvoord, LaHaye, and Ice on 26
gaps in the gap theory 333
Gaston, E. G. Loyd *No Stone On Another* 286
gathering

See also episunagogee
  Ac. 3.24f 175
  Ac. 26.17-18 172
  at the time of the resurrection 172
  Christ coming with or for saints? 317
  come unto me 175
  Dt. 30.4 172
  Eph. 2 and Ezk. 37 177
  Eusebius on 176
  Ezk. 37.12 172
  Ezk. 37.22-27 172
  Hos. 13.1-2, 13-14 173
  II Cor. 6.16 172
  in the new synagogue 176
  into fellowship 175
  Isa. 26.20-21 173
  Isa. 27.8-9 173
  Jn. 4.21 175
  Jn. 11.52 172
  Mt. 23.34-36 173
  Mt. 23.38 175
  Mt. 24.14 175
  Mt.24.31 172
  or snatching? 171
  purpose of the trumpet 133
  Rom. 1.16-17 176
  Rom. 11.26-27 173
  time of, is also time of separation 77
  was an element of the hope of Israel 258
  why and what? 175
gathering of Israel
  See also regathering of Israel
  at her remarriage, Hos. 1-3, Isa. 61.2-12 22
  Isa. 49.6f 22
  linked to Day of Salvation 22
  linked to New Creation, Isa. 65-66.15f 22
  not limited to Christ's incarnation or death 22
generation, Gentry on 194
Gentile Christians

their concern about Jewish fate 103
why interested in promises to Old Covenant Israel 100
Gentiles, the
contained ten northern tribes 177
Israel regathered for their salvation 103
Gentry, Kenneth
at hand must refer to AD 70 208
end in I Cor. 10.11 vs. I Cor. 15 400
quickly must refer to AD 70 208
shortly must refer to AD 70 208
accepted hermeneutic of Walvoord 338
admits age to come would succeed Mosaic age 252
affirms true preterist paradigm 253
at odds with the creeds 396
different comings of the Lord in I Thes. and II Thes 338
dilemma on age to come 253
distinctions utilized by virtually all partial preterists 347
elthe and *parousia* 338
falsifies watchfulness implies delay 66
fundamental error on Mt. 13 343
futurist application of Revelation 347
has changed on Dan. 12.2 254
hermenutic backfires 368
I Thes. 4 drawn from Mt. 24 66-69
identifies Babylon in Rev. as Old Covenant Jerusalem 66-69
inconsistent use of the patristics 203
inconsistent view of imminence statements 208
on generation 194
on *chronos* 232
on church as bride of Christ 237
on I Jn. 2.18 226
on I Thes. 4.13-18 345
on II Thes. 2, vs. I Cor.15, I Thes. 4, II Pet. 3 346
on Lk. 22.29 236
on *parousia* 345
on the last hour 226
on the wedding 237
partial preterists believe still a future coming 337
Paul's statements impact his admissions 259
problem with Mt. 13.39f 254
redefines orthodoxy 366
rejected hermeneutic of Walvoord 338
self-contradictions on end of the age 255
subtle emphasis on chapter division 347
vs. Mathison on imminence of the end 203
watchfulness implies delay 65
wedding a first century event 66-69
Gentry, Kenneth *Before Jerusalem Fell*
gathering together of Christians 345
Jerusalem the persecutor of Christians 55
on imminence in Revelation 87
Gentry, Kenneth *He Shall Have Dominion*
See also He Shall Have Dominion
changes view of Dan. 12.2 137
doesn't acknowledge radical changes in his views 379
gathering together of Christians 178
on Nero's persecution of the church 55
on the nature of Christ's coming 168
on the sign of Christ's coming 279

two views of world mission 287
united Olivet discourse wouldn't
affect his futurism 64
Gentry, Kenneth *He Shall Have Dominion* 137, 178
Gentry, Kenneth *The Beast of Revelation* 347
Gentry, Kenneth *The Greatness of the Great Commission* 137, 379
Gentry, Kenneth *Thine is the Kingdom*
  applies II Thes. 2 to 70 AD 337
  discussed 63
Gentry, Kenneth and Greg Bahnsen *House Divided: The Breakup of Dispensational Theology* 212, 344
Gibbs, Jeffrey A. *Jerusalem and Parousia* 61, 178
gifts to the church, Eph. 4.8-16 178
God Dwells With Us: Temple Symbolism in the Fourth Gospel, Mary L. Coloe 39
God, had come in the past 89
Goldenberg, Robert *Early Rabbinic Explanations of the Destruction of Jerusalem* 299
Goldingay, John *Word Biblical Commentary, Daniel* 271
good and evil, when did Adam know? 6
Goppelt, Leonard, *Types: The Typological Interpretation of The Old Testament in the New Testament* 17
Grant, Robert *Understanding the Sacred Text* 280
graves imply resurrection of individual corpses? 393
great tribulation, the
  on Christians by Jews, not Jews by antichrist 364
  postponed if second coming was 331
Greek English Lexicon, Bauer's Gingrich and Danker 54

Greek English Lexicon, Louw and Nida 143
Greek Grammar Beyond the Basics: An Exegetical Syntax of the New Testament, Daniel B. Wallace 199
Greek-English Lexicon of the New Testament and Other Early Christian Literature, Bauer, Arndt and Gingrich 142, 199, 257
Greek-English Lexicon of the New Testament, Henry Thayer 143
Gundry, Robert, on *apantesis* (meeting) 155, 157

H

Hagee, John, set 2007 as date or rapture 313
Hanegraaff, Hank *The Apocalypse Code* 168
Harding, Ian D. *Taken to Heaven in A. D. 70* 274
Harnack, Adolph *Mission and Expansion of Christianity* 55
harpadzo
  and *episunagogee* 181
  demand a literal snatching away? 181
  discussed 381
  I Cor. 15.52 181
  II Thes. 1.7f 183
  Jn. 10.28-29 181
  Jude 23 181
  Mt. 16.27 183
  Mt. 25.31f fits this scenario 184
  Ps. 18.3-17 182
Harris, Murray *The New International Greek Text Commentary, 2 Corinthians* 91
harvest, firstfruits inseparable from 262
Have Heaven and Earth Passed Away?, Don K. Preston 264
He Came As A Thief, Don K. Preston 240, 245

He Shall Have Dominion, Kenneth Gentry
  changes view of Dan. 12.2 137
  doesn't acknowledge radical changes in his views 379
  gathering together of Christians 178
  Jerusalem the persecutor of Christians 55
  on the nature of Christ's coming 168
  on the sign of Christ's coming 279
  two views of world mission 287
  united Olivet discourse wouldn't affect his futurism 64-65
heaven and earth
  reunited in one body in Christ, Eph. 1.8-10 102
  separated with sin of Adam 101
heavenly places, conflict between God and Satan in 166
Hellenistic Formal Receptions and Paul's Use of Apantesis in I Thessalonians 4:17, Michael R. Cosby 143, 154
Hendriksen, William *New Testament Commentary* 138
Hengstenberg, E. W. *Christology of the Old Testament* 53
Hermas, Shepherd of *See* Shepherd of Hermas
Herod the Great, death of in parable of the talents 71
High Priest, Jesus vs. Old Covenant 15
History of the Jewish People in the Age of Jesus, Emil Schurer 246
Holland, Tom *Contours of Pauline Theology* 97, 207
holy people, who are the? 342
Holy Spirit, resurrection and the workd of the 90

Homily, John Chrysostom 295
hope of Israel, the
  and the rapture 305
  elements of 257
  I Thessalonians as the 21
House Divided: The BreakUp of Dispensational Theology, Greg Bahnsen and Kenneth Gentry 212, 344
How Is This Possible?, Don K. Preston 51, 58, 322
Hymenaeus and Philetus, problem of silence 284

I

I Thessalonians 4.17: The Bringing in of the Lord or the Bringing in of the Faithful?, Joseph Plevnik 144
I Thessalonians as Hope of Israel 21
Ice, Thomas
  admits the church has temporarily replaced Israel 161
  claims world mission never fulfilled 329
  doesn't believe Joel fulfilled on Pentecost
  gap theory 26
  on this generation 216
  on Ac. 22.18 371
  on *apantesis* (meeting) 155
  on the seven church ages 312
  on this age, the age to come 314
  says temple service will resume 364
  without postponement, dispensational falls apart 333
Ice, Thomas *End Times Controversy* 25
Ice, Thomas *Fast Facts on Bible Prophecy* See *Fast Facts on Bible Prophecy*
Ice, Thomas *The Seventy Weeks of Daniel Part I*
  defines imminence differently 310

Ice, Thomas *The Seventy Weeks of Daniel Part* I 266, 334
Ice, Thomas and Kennethy Gentry *The Great Tribulation Past or Present? A Written Debate* 98, 207, 247
Ice, Thomas and Timothy Demy *Fast Facts on Bible Prophecy* 86
Ice, Thomas and Timothy Demy *Prophecy Watch* 61, 323
Idioms of the Bible, George Lamsa 335
I-II Thessalonians, The IVP New Testament Series 63, 140
imminence
   audience relevance and 311
   dispensational rapture doctrine and 310
   dispensationalists have a different definition 310
   Gentry's inconsistent use of the imminence statements 208
   Ice's definition 310
   of parousia
      See also end of the ages has come upon us
      Ac. 17.30-31 199
      avenging the elect speedily *See* avenging the elect
      I Cor. 15.51-52 194
      I Pet. 1.3-5 206
      I Pet. 1.10f 205
      I Pet. 4.5, 7, 17 206
      I Pet. 4.7 198
      I Thes. 2.15-17 197
      I Thes. 4.13 195
      I Thes. 4.15, 17 194-225
      II Tim. 4.1 196
      Jn. 16.7 199
      Lk. 21.8 205
      Mk. 1.15 209
      Mt. 13.16-17 210
      Mt. 16.27-28 196
      Mt. 23.32 197
      Mt. 23.35 197
      Mt. 24.32-33 205
      Mt. 3.2 209
      Rev. 11.16f 196
      Rev. 19.7 198
      skeptics and futurists agree on discounting inspiration 214
   imminence passages, Mathison's vacillations on 394
In and Around the Book of Daniel, Boutflower 178
in Christ or through Christ, I Thes. 4.14 104
In Flaming Fire, Don K. Preston 54, 222
inner man from outer man at resurrection 84
Instone-Brewer, David *Divorce and ReMarriage in the Bible* 42
Into All The World, Then Comes The End, Don K. Preston 47, 287
Iranaeus
   knew wicked not raptured 302
   on Mt. 24.14 287
Iranaeus, *Against Heresies* 281, 287, 302
Isaiah's New Exodus in Mark, Rikki Watts 97
Israel
   1948 creation of a supersign of the end 325
   amillennialists have no use for Old Covenant promises to 45
   Bible a Jewish book on God's promises to 159
   death of *See* death of Israel 44
   dispensationalists say church has temporarily replaced Israel 161
   divorce of *See* divorce of Israel
   remarriage of *See* remarriage of Israel 41
   resurrected out of their graves, Ezk. 37.10-14 31
   resurrection body of 227
   room for all twelve tribes in Jn. 14 38

salvation of, Old Testament prophets foretold, I Pet. 1.9-12 22
ten tribes never lost 177
transformed at resurrection 43
two houses reunited, Ezk. 37.15f 31
Israel, Old Covenant, resurrection the fulfillment of promises to 4
Israel: 1948, Countdown To No Where, Don K. Preston 312

J

Jerusalem and Parousia, Jeffrey A. Gibbs 61, 178
Jesus
   ascencion and descent 81
   overcame two types of death 264
   source of his eschatology 21
Jesus and the Victory of God, N. T. Wright 44, 69, 173, 222-223
Jesus' eschatology, source of
   discussed 21
   Mt. 5.17-18 21
Jesus, Paul, and the End of the World, Ben Witherington III 119
Jesus, The Tribulation and the End of Exile, Restoration Eschatology and the Origin of the Atonement, Grant Pitre 60, 94, 291
Jewish and Pauline Studies, W. D. Davies 263
John
   didn't write about the destruction of the Old Temple 359
   problem of for physical rapture 280
John the Baptist
   cites Isa. 40.10-11 48
   messenger to Israel to call them back to the Law of Moses, Mal. 4.5-6 49
   most ignored figure in eschatology 48
John's eschatology, source of 23

Josephus
   Antiquities, on *apantesis* (meeting) 153-154
   Wars, on *apantesis* (meeting) 154
judgment
   See also time for judgment
   and kingdom are synonymous concepts 223
   and salvation on the Day of the Lord 51
   Mt. 19.28 and the apostles judging the twelve tribes of Israel 285
   of living and dead
      at the resurrection 385
      I Pet. 4.5 197
      Mt. 23.36 197
   time of separation and gathering 77
Justin Martyr (150-165 AD), on Mt. 24.14 287

K

Kelly, J. N. D *The Epistles of Peter and Jude* 33
Kik, J. Marcellus, *An Eschatology of Victory* 168
Kik, J. Marcellus, *Matthew XXIV* 63
King, Max *Old Testament Israel, New Testament Salvation* 103
King, Max *Spirit of Prophecy* 165
kingdom, the
   and judgment are synonymous concepts 223
   and resurrection without observation 83
   nature of 91
   Old Testament writers never said drawn nigh 202
   time of is the time of the resurrection
      II Tim. 4.1 83
      Mt. 13.24-30, 37-43 83
      Mt. 25.31f 83
      Rev. 11.15-18 83

was an element of the hope of Israel 260
Kistemaker, Simon, *When Shall These Things Be?* 293
Kittel's Theological Dictionary of New Testament Words 143
Kline, Meredith G. *Death, Leviathan, and Martyrs: Isa. 24.1-27.1* 234
Knight, George III *New International Greek Testament Commentary* 327

L

Ladd, George Eldon *The Presence of the Future* 169
LaHaye, Tim
  gap theory 26
  two comings or one? 327
LaHaye, Tim *Beginning of the End* 325
LaHaye, Tim and Thomas Ice *Charting the End Times: A Visual Guide to Understanding Bible Prophecy* 26, 99
Lamsa, George *Idioms of the Bible* 335
Lane, William *Word Biblical Commentary, Hebrews 9-13* 105, 112
Last Days Identified, The, Don K. Preston 2-3
Last Days Madness, Gary DeMar 60, 118, 279
last days, the
  Ac. 2.15f 210
  dispensationalism has no place in for total desolation of Israel in 273
  dual fulfillments based on dichotomy of 240
  foretold in Isa. 2-4 200
  Heb. 1.1-2 210
  I Pet. 1.5, 20 211
  Isa. 28.21-22 211
  it shall come to pass in the..210
  Jas. 5.3-6 210
  Jas. 5.6-8 211
  Old Testament writers never said arrived 202
last hour, the
  discussed 225
  Gentry on 226
  Mathison on 226
law, the
  Gal. 3.20-21 263
  II Cor. 3.6f 263
  Jer. 31.29f 263
  Rom. 7.9f 263
  usage in New Testament 263
Leaving the Rapture Behind, Don K. Preston 322
Lenski, R. C. H. *The Interpretation of St Paul's Epiesles to the Colossians, to the Thessalonians, to Timothy, to Titue and Philemon* 104
Leupold, H. C., *Exposition on Isaiah* 31
Levenson, Jon *Resurrection and the Restoration of Israel* 133
Leviathan, final victory over when Satan crushed 232
Liddell and Scott's Greek-English Lexicon 143
life after death *See* eternal life
life of Christ vs. death of Adam 4
Light From the Ancient East, Adolf Deissman 142
Lightfoot, John *Commentary on the New Testament from the Talmud and Hebraica* 71
Like Father Like Son, on Clouds of Glory, Don K. Preston
  distinction between I and II Thes. 118
  God had come many times 51
  imminence, Gentry and Mathison on 203
  Jesus' coming in the glory of the father 278

Jesus' coming in the same manner as the father 303
MacArthur refuted on imminence views 214
nature of Jesus' resurrected pre-ascension body 84
parousia would manifest Jesus' deity 327
restoration is same as the reformation 256
restoration is same as the reformation 256
shadow nature of Old Covenant Israel 43
visible coming of Christ 78
little horn, Mathison on 393
living waters at the resurrection 95
Louw and Nida, *Greek English Lexicon* 143

M

MacArthur, John *The Second Coming* 214, 321
man of sin, the
   II Thes. 2.3f 59
   introduced 59
   postponed if second coming was 330
   punishment of 346
   sitting in the temple of God 59
mansions of John 14, room for all twelve tribes 38
Martin, Ralph *Word Biblical Commentary, 2 Corinthians* 91
martyrs
   dead in Christ in I Thes. 4.14 104
   dead of I Thes. 4 probably were 180
   Heb. 11.32f recounts their killing 109
   vindication of at the resurrection 81
   vindication of in Lk. 18.2-8 105
   vindication of purpose of the parousia 104

Mathison, Keith
   admits I Pet. 4.7 refers to AD 70 199
   appeals to progressive revelation 75
   fundamental error on Mt. 13 343
   holds to unified view of Olivet Discourse 69
   on coming of Christ 76
   on I Jn. 2.18 226
   on little horn of Daniel 393
   on Mt. 25.31 407
   on the end of the age 254
   vacillations on imminence statements 394
   vs. Gentry on imminence of the end 203
Mathison, Keith *Dispensationalism, Rightly Dividing the People of God*
   holds to unified view of Olivet Discourse 69
   Mathison now believes in united Olivet Discourse 69
   vacillations in contrast to previous works 231
Mathison, Keith *From Age to Age, the Unfolding of Biblical Eschatology*
   creeds define orthodoxy 69, 366
   defends late date for Revelation 393
   Mathison's change on Mt. 24.14 361
   now holds to united Olivet Discourse 77
Mathison, Keith *Postmillennialism: An Eschatology of Hope* 138, 231, 337
Mathison, Keith *When Shall These Things Be? A Reformed Response to Hyper-Preterism*
   inconsistent on Dan. 12, Rev. 11 137
   on shattering the power of the holy people 342

some "son of man" texts future, some not 341
Matthew Twenty-Four, J. Marcellus Kik 63
Mayor, Joseph *The Epistle of St. Jude and the Second Epistle of St. Peter* 163
McClintock & Strong's *Cyclopedia of Biblical, Theological and Ecclesiastical Literature* 281
meeting
- meaning of 141
- technical sense 141
- then escorting back to their city 141

meeting the Lord in the air
- *See also apantesis*
- church taken off the earth? 141
- discussed 141-164
- earth is the destination 145
- meeting in literal clouds 141
- N. T. Wright on 145
- not like meeting for lunch 151
- statement of triumph over Satan 166
- the official welcome of a newly arrived dignity 145
- the passage teaches the opposite of futurist paradigms 145

messiah, an element of the hope of Israel 258
Messianic Banquet
- and the Abrahamic promise 115
- Isa. 24-25.6-9 21
- linked to resurrection 21
- no literal banquet table 301
- would be spread in Zion 376

messianic temple *See* New Tabernacle 36
Messianic *Woes in First Peter., Suffering and Eschatology in I Peter 4.12-19*, Mark Dubis 34
messianic woes, woman in travail an illustration of 245
Michael the archangel 126

Middleton, Richard *A New Heaven and New Earth: The Case for a Holistic Reading of the Biblical Story of Redemption* 163
Misplaced Hope, Sam Frost 274
Mission and Expansion of Christianity, Adolph Harnack 55
Morris, Leon *New international Commentary on the New Testament, 1st and 2nd Thessalonians* 165
Mosaic age, Gentry admits age to come would succeed 252
Moulton, James Hope and George Milligan, *The Vocabulary of the Greek Testament Illustrated from the Papyri and Other Non-Literary Sources* 143
Mounce, William *Word Biblical Commentary* 328
Mystery of Romans, Mark Nanos 27

N

Nanos, Mark *The Mystery of Romans* 27, 207
new birth, corporate 248
New Covenant, the
- demands remarriage of Israel 43
- resurreection through remarriage 44
- was an element of the hope of Israel 258

new creation
- linked to gathering of Israel, Isa. 65-66.15f 22
- on the Day of the Lord 89
- promised to Abraham 114
- was an element of the hope of Israel 258

new heaven and earth, new Jerusalem
- on the Day of the Lord 89
- patristics on 295
- Richard Middleton on 163
- Theoderet 295

438

New International Commentary on the New Testament, 1st and 2nd Thessalonians, Leon Morris 165
New International Dictionary of the New Testament Theology, Colin Brown 169
New International Greek Testament Commentary on 1 & 2 Thessalonians, Bruce Wanamaker
   filling up sin 71
   Isa. 26.1 233
   no conflict between soon and suddenly 245
   on *apantesis* 144
   on those living and remaining in I Thes. 4.13-18 234
   principle of retribution in I Thes. 4.13-18 123
   who were the persecutors? 54
New International Greek Testament Commentary, George Knight III 218, 332
new name, Isa. 65.13ff 243
New Tabernacle
   Dan. 9.24-27 36
   discussed 29, 31
   Eph. 2.19f 32
   Eph. 2.20-21 34
   Eph. 4.16f 32
   Ezk. 26-27 34
   Ezk. 37.10-14 31
   Ezk. 37.15f 31
   Ezk. 37.26f 31
   Ezk. 40-48 35
   Hos. 1.6, 9 34
   Hos. 1.9 42
   Hos. 1.9-10 33
   Hos. 13.14f 44
   Hos. 2.2 42
   Hos. 2.14-18 42
   Hos. 2.18 43
   Hos. 2.23 33
   Hos. 2.25 34
   Hos. 5.15 42
   Hos. 6.1-2 42
   Hos. 6.1-3 44
   Hos. 6.5 42
   I Pet. 1.4f 35
   I Pet. 1.17 33
   I Pet. 1.18 33
   I Pet. 2.4 34
   I Pet. 2.5f 34
   I Pet. 2.10 33
   I Pet. 2.12 33
   I Pet. 4.5, 7, 17-19 35
   II Cor. 6.14-16 32
   in Ezk. 37 31
   in I Thes. 4 29-30
   in Isa. 2-4 30
   Isa. 2.2-3 31
   Isa. 4.2-6 31
   Isa. 43.3-7 33
   Isa. 48.20 33
   Jer. 31.30f 43
   Jn. 1.14 38
   Jn. 2.19f 38
   Jn. 4.20-24 43
   John 14 38
   Jn. 14.9f 39
   Mt. 24.8f 35
   resurrection when established 90
   Rev. 21.3 40
   Rom. 11.1-3 33
   Rom. 9.3f 33
   seventy weeks 37
   was an element of the hope of Israel 258
   wedding goes with 41
New Temple *See* New Tabernacle
New Testament Commentary, William Hendrickson 138
Nicoll, Robertson *Expositor's Greek Testament* 198
Nisbett, N *The Prophecy of the Destruction of Jerusalem* 56
No Stone On Another, E. G. Loyd Gaston 286
no tears at the resurrection 95

O

Ogden, Arthur *Avenging of the Blood of the Apostles and Prophets* 220
Old Covenant Israel, why would Gentile Christians be interested in promises to? 100
Old Testament citations by Paul 243
Old Testament Israel, New Testament Salvation, Max King 103
Old Testament writers never said
  end of the age had come 203
  kingdom had drawn nigh 203
  last days had arrived 203
Olivet Discourse, the
  DeMar gives nine parallels between II Thes. 2 and 60
  implications for futurists if united 79
  Mathison holds to unified view 69
  not divided 63
  parallel with Thessalonians 72-75
  unity with I Thes. 4.13-18 63
one taken, one left
  background in ancient world 335
  Idioms of the Bible, George Lamsa 335
  II K. 24.14f 335
  II K. 25.11 335
  Mt. 24.40-41 335
  Mt. 24.40-41 depicts a snatching away to destruction 335
Origen, *Commentary on Matthew 39* 287
orthodoxy
  Gentry redefines 366
  Mathison says creeds define 366
outer man vs. inner man at resurrection 84
outpouring of the Spirit, an element of the hope of Israel 258

P

papacy, the, prophesied in II Thes. 2? 61
parables of Jesus
  parable of the talents
  death of Herod the Great 71
  parable of the talents, Lk. 19.12-14 70
  ten virgins, the time of the wedding 64
  told to Israel about Israel 344
  wedding feast a favorite theme of Jesus 44
paradise lost and regained 238
Paradise Restored, David Chilton 171, 279
parallels
  Dan. 7, 10-12 and Revelation 128
  Dan. 12 and I Cor. 15 272
  Eph. 2 and Ezk. 37 177
  I Thes. 4 and Heb. 11 107
  I Thes. 4 and the Garden 86
  I Thes. 4.13-18 and Mt. 24.29 77
  I Thes. 5 and Jer. 2-7 241
  Isa. 25 and Isa. 49 93
  Isa. 26-27 and Mt. 23-24 173
  Isa. 49 and Rev. 7 94
  Mt. 23 and Heb. 10-11 112
  Mt. 23 and Revelation 219
  Mt. 24 and I Thes. 4.13-18 63
  Mt. 24 and II Thes. 1-2 344
  Mt. 24.29-31 and I Thes. 4.13-18 171, 316
  Mt. 25.1-13 and Rev. 19.7-8 70
  Olivet Discourse and II Thes. 2 60
  Olivet Discourse and Thessalonians 72-75
parenthesis *See* gap theory 26
parousia
  and *episunagogee*
    II Thes. 2.1-2 340
    Mt. 24.31 340
parousia, the
  atonement not complete until 267

Christ coming with or for saints? 317
consummation of atonement 19
Day of the Lord becomes the 119
elthe and *parousia* 338
Gentry on 345
I Thes. 3.13 340
I Thes. 4 340
I Thes. 4 and II Thes. 1 are the same 120
II Thes. 2.1 340
imminence of *See* imminence of parousia
in I Thes. 4, Jn. 14.1-6, and Rev. 21 41
interim vs. ultimate? 52
Jesus said world would no longer see him 320
linked to forgiveness 19
Lk.18.8 340
Mt. 21.40 340
Mt. 24.30 340
nature of 88
new temple completed at 177
not observable with human eye 279
of Jesus for the wedding 43
Old Testament prophets foretold salvation of Israel at 22
on clouds of heaven *See* clouds of heaven 166
partial preterists believe still a future coming 337
positive and negative aspects 149
references to Christ's coming in AD 70?
   introduced 286
   Pseudo-Barnabas 286
   Shephard of Hermas 286
Revelation is the divine record 295
same in I and II Thes. 51
sign of 279
silence of
   patristics on viewing destruction of Jerusalem as 274-279
   rabbis 299
some patristics thought fulfilled 304
stated purpose of 118
to vindicate martyrs 104
trumpet audible, but silent for the rapture 80
two comings or one? *See* two comings or one?
used with *apantesis* of a royal dignitary 152
we have a divine record 295
Zech. 14 predicted 53
partial preterism
   discussed 337-348
   Gentry's distinctions utilized by 347
   I Thes. 4.13-18 337
   II Thes. 1.7-10 337
   II Thes. 2 337
   Kenneth Gentry 338
   still a future parousia 337
patristics
   See also church fathers
   believed the end time events had already been fulfilled 291
   expected observable coming 291
   Gentry's inconsistent use of the 203
   have slight record of 275
   insurmountable problem for Stevens 278
   not completely silent
      Athanasius 287
      Chrysostom 288
      Eusebius 288
      Iranaeus 287
      Justin Martyr 287
   not silent on Lk. 19.11f 303
   other issues affected 276
   silence
      not complete 276
      on fall of Jerusalem as second coming 274-279
      problems for Paul 283

problems for Thessalonians 283
problems with 281
problems with Timothy, Titus, Luke, Apollos, Silas, Aquila and Priscilla, Gaius, and Aristarchus 282
some realized parousia had occurred 304
some thought Mt. 24.14 was fulfilled 289
Stevens discounts what they do say 295

Paul and the Synoptic Apocalypse, Gordon Wenham 75

Paul, N. T. Wright 49

Paul's eschatology
Ac. 24.14-15 24
Ac. 26.5f 24
Ac. 26.21f 25
Ac. 28.19f 25
I Thes. 4 25
Rom. 8.23-9.4 25
source of 24

Pentecost, can't apply Dan. 7 to 230

Pentecost, J. Dwight *Things to Come: A Study in Biblical Eschatology* 26, 261, 321, 335

Perriman, Andrew *The Coming of the Son of Man* 118, 129, 131, 211-222, 228

persecutors became the persecuted 122

Peter's eschatology
Ac. 3.21-24 22
I Pet. 1.9-12 22
II Pet. 3.1-3, 13 22
source of 22

physical death
Christ's death didn't deliver from 19
not the death of the Garden 100

Pitre, Grant Jesus, *The Tribulation and the End of Exile, Restoration Eschatology and the Origin of the Atonement* 60, 94, 291

Plevnik, Joseph *I Thessalonians 4.17: The Bringing in of the Lord or the Bringing in of the Faithful?* 144

Postmillennialism: An Eschatology of Hope, Keith Mathison 138, 231, 337

postponement theory
Dan. 2.44-45 329
Ac. 26.21f 333
Dan. 12.1-3 331
Heb. 10.37 332
I Pet. 4.7 332
Ice: without postponement, dispensationalism falls apart 333
if second coming was postponed great tribulation was postponed 331
kingdom was postponed 329
man of sin was postponed 330
rapture was postponed 329
II Thes. 1.6-10 331
Jas. 5.8-9 332
Lk. 13.31 332
Mt. 13.41 331
Mt. 27.25 332
Rev. 1.7 332
Rev. 11.8 332
Rev. 16.6-7 332
Rev. 18.20, 24 332
Rev. 22.7, 12, 20 332
Rom. 16.25-26 333

power of death
discussed 269
one who had is destroyed 270

present passive verb tense, ten passages in I Cor. 15 235

Preston, Don K. *Can You Believe Jesus Said This?* 59, 196, 220, 223

Preston, Don K. *Have Heaven and Earth Passed Away?* 264

Preston, Don K. *He Came As A Thief* 240, 245

Preston, Don K. *How Is This Possible?* 51, 58, 322

Preston, Don K. *In Flaming Fire* 54, 222
Preston, Don K. *Into All The World, Then Comes the End* 47, 287
Preston, Don K. *Israel: 1948, Countdown To No Where* 312
Preston, Don K. *Leaving the Rapture Behind* 322
Preston, Don K. *Like Father Like Son, On Clouds of Glory*
   Christ returning visibly 78
   Christ's coming in like manner as the father 303
   Christ's coming in the glory of the father 278
   Christ's coming in the glory of the father 118
   Christ's coming manifested Jesus' deity 327
   Jesus' resurrection body not his glorified body 84
   many days of the Lord in the Old Testament 203
   refutation of MacArthur's futurism 214
   restoration is same as the reformation 256
   shadow nature of Old Covenant Israel 43
   transfiguration and parousia 51
Preston, Don K. *Seal Up Vision and Prophecy*
   critique of Gentry on seventy weeks 267
   discussed 37
Preston, Don K. *Seventy Weeks Are Determined* 263
Preston, Don K. *The Elements Shall Melt With Fervent Heat*
   global earth not the focus of II Pet. 3 163
   on I Pet. 1.5-12 211
   on the end of the age 252
   on the rejected stone 35
   parousia not optically evident 89

Preston, Don K. *The Last Days Identified* See *Last Days Identified, The* 2
progressive revelation, Mathison appeals to 75
Proof of the Gospel, Eusebius 53, 288
Prophecy Watch, Thomas Ice and Timothy Demy 61, 323
prophecy, New Testament is reiteration of Old Covenant promises to Israel 21
Pseudo-Barnabas 286

Q

quickly, Gentry says must refer to AD 70 208
rabbinic sources
   early explanations of the destruction of Jerusalem 299
   on abomination of desolation 291

R

rapture of the church
   See also caught up
   gathering and snatching 171
   issues of salvation, not removal from eath 276
   Mt. 13 and the 300
   Rom. 13.11 and the 305
   trumpet silent, but audible at the parousia 80
   unknown to Old Testament prophets 45
   vs. second coming 159
   where in the Old Testament? 29
rapture, physical
   abomination of desolation
      Athanasius on 290
      Clement of Alexandria 289
      discussed 289-292
      Eusebius 290
      rabbinic sources 291
   apostles already on thrones 285
   brings Christian age to end 316

Christ coming with or for saints? 317
date setting for a 313
dispensational rapture doctrine *See* dispensational rapture doctrine
do expectations demand a? 274
II Thes. 1 and the rapture 298
John 14 and the 319
John 14 isn't a rapture at all 319
king came to rule, not remove his people 303
Lk. 19.11f 302
Mk. 9.1 and 304
Mt. 19.28 and the apostles judging the twelve tribes of Israel 285
Mt. 24.40-41 depicts a snatching away to destruction 335
new heaven and earth, new Jerusalem *See* new heaven and earth, new Jerusalem 295
patristics not silent on Lk. 19.11f 303
postponed if second coming was 329
rapture and Mt. 13 *See* rapture, Mt. 13 and
rapture and Rom. 13.11 *See* rapture and Rom. 13.11
references to Christ's coming in AD 70?
   introduced 286
   Pseudo-Barnabas 286
   Shephard of Hermas 286
second coming and resurrection *See* second coming and resurrection
seven years before second coming? 315
signs of 323
silence of rabbis 299
Stuart Russell espoused 274
the coming of the Lord and the charismata *See* charismata and coming

the coming of the Lord out of heaven *See* coming of the Lord out of heaven 292
the hope of Israel and the 305
the problem with sleepers 282
the world mission 287
two ages seven years apart 316
two future comings of the Lord 317
vs. second coming 315
we have a divine record 295
what about the 144,000? *See* 144,000, what about the?
wicked not removed in AD 70 301
redemption carried both positive and negative connotations 358
regathering of Israel
   See also gathering of Israel
   Heb. 12.22 102
   I Pet. 1.1 102
   I Pet. 2.9f 102
   II Cor. 3.15-18 102
   Jas. 1.1f 102
   not physical Israel into confines of land 102
   out of alienation 102
   Rom. 2.28-29 102
   so Gentiles could be saved 103
   spiritual regathering into fellowship with God 102
regeneration, apostles were already in the 286
rejected stone
   Dan. 9.26 34
   discussed 358
   I Pet. 2.5f 34
remarriage of Israel
   at time of I Thes. 4 41
   demands a new covenant 43
   gathering then, Hos. 1-3, Isa. 61.2-12 22
   Hos. 3.4 44
   Hos. 5.15 44
   Hos. 5.15-6.1-3 44

resurrection through new covenant at 44
remarriage to God was an element of the hope of Israel 258
remember not just simple mental recollection 360
replacement theology
   dispensationalists say church has temporarily replaced Israel 161
   Ice admits the church has temporarily replaced Israel 161
rest to some, affliction to others, II Thes. 1.4-12 54
restoration of Israel
   at the resurrection 133
   was an element of the hope of Israel 258
Resurrection and the Restoration of Israel, Jon Levenson 133
resurrection body of Israel 227
resurrection of condemnation, Jn. 5.25-29 23
resurrection of the dead, the
   abomination of desolation occurred at 291
   an unseen event 81
   and kingdom without observation 83
   and the work of the Spirit 90
   and vindication of the martyrs 81
   at removal of sin 19
   change from outer to inner man 84
   corporate concept 42
   does graves imply individual corpses 393
   foretold in Isa. 24-27, Hos. 6.1-3, 13.14, Dan. 12 200
   fulfillment of promises to Old Covenant Israel 4
   has nothing to do with biological death 4
   hope of Israel 90
   I Thes. 14 predicted 27
   in the day of salvation 90
   in the Torah dealt with fellowship 134
   in time of Mt. 23.31-37 179
   Isa. 26.19f links to Day of the Lord 217
   Isa. 49 foretold 91
   Israel's return from captivity was depicted as 133
   linked to forgiveness 19
   linked to Messianic Banquet 21
   living waters at 95
   no tears at 95
   of Israel in Ezk. 27 133
   ongoing as Paul wrote I Cor. 15 235
   the better
      of Heb. 11.35 113
      of I Thes. 4.13f 110
   the time of the gathering 172
   through new covenant and remarriage of Israel 44
   time of at the coming of the Lord 196
   time of is the time of the kingdom
      II Tim. 4.1 83
      Mt. 13.24-30, 37-43 83
      Mt. 25.31f 83
      Rev. 11.15-18 83
   was the restoration of Israel 133
   when Messianic temple was established 90
resurrection, physical, of Jesus a sign of something greater 8
Revelation
   cannot apply to the future 347
   Mathison defends late date 393
Revelation, Greg Beale 220
reward and vindication in I Thes. 4, II Thes. 2 119
Robertson, A. T. *Word Pictures of the New Testament* 104, 125, 304
Russell, D. S. *The Method and Message of Jewish Apocalyptic* 246
Russell, J. Stuart, espoused physical rapture 274

S

salvation
    and judgment on the Day of the Lord 51
    corporate concept 361
    resurrection on the day of 90
Satan
    crushed *See* Satan crushed
    defeat of 86
    did he lie, or did God 5
    had power of death but destroyed 270
    meeting the Lord in the air a statement of triumph over 166
    nearness of defeat of 87
    ruler of this world and the air 165
Satan crushed
    final victory over Leviathan 232
    Isa. 24.10 234
    Isa. 25-26.16f 234
    Isa. 27.1 232
    Isa. 27.9-13 234
    Rev. 22.12 234
    Rom. 15.20 232
    when temple was destroyed 234
scheme of redemption, I Cor. 15.22 is the nutshell 86
Schurer, Emil *History of the Jewish People in the Age of Jesus* 246
Seal Up Vision and Prophecy, Don K. Preston
    critique of Gentry on seventy weeks 267
    discussed 37
second coming
    dispensational view occurs seven years after rapture 315
    silence of patristics on viewing destruction of Jerusalem as 274-279
    vs. rapture 159, 315
second coming and resurrection, patristics on
    Athanasius 295
    Chrysostom 295

Second Exodus
    discussed 248
    Isa. 11.10f 21
Seraiah, Jonathan C., *The End of All Things*, partial preterists believe in a future coming 337
seven churches, allegorical meaning to 404
Seventy Weeks Are Determined, Don K. Preston 263
seventy weeks till the New Tabernacle 37
Shepherd of Hermas, The (140 AD) 286
shortly, Gentry says must refer to AD 70 208
signs
    can't signify themselves 8
    confusion among Van Impe, Ice and LaHaye, John Hagee, and Hal Lindsey 323
    Ice vs. Ice 325
    in dispensational rapture doctrine 323
silence of pre-AD 70 Christians
    argument from 276
    Josephus not 276
    not total 276
    of early church on fall of Jerusalem perplexing 274
    of secular writers 276
    other issues affected 276
    patristics not all silent
        Athanasius 287
        Chrysostom 288
        Eusebius 288
        Iranaeus 287
        Justin Martyr 287
    problems
        for Paul 283
        for Thessalonians 283
        in general 281
        of Hymaneus and Philetus 284
        with Timothy, Titus, Luke, Apollos, Silas, Aquila and

Priscilla, Gaius, and Aristarchus 282
sin of Adam, heaven and earth separated with 101
skeptics agree with futurists that inspiration is damaged 215
sleep, a euphemism for physical death 196
sleepers, the problem with 282
Snodgrass, Kayne *Stories with Intent, A Comprehensive Guide to the Parables of Jesus*, parables linked to Isa. 9.6f 343
sound of trumpet *See* trumpet, sound of
spiritual death
    captivity was death 133
    did Christ suffer? 9
    separated from God's presence in the holy land 132
    the death of the Garden 132
Stevens, Ed
    argues from silence, yet discounts what patristics do say 295
    II Thes. 1 and the rapture 298
    on conditional immortality 400
    on II Thes. 1.1f 300
    on II Thes. 1.10-12 300
    the hope of Israel and the rapture doctrine 305
    what about the 144,000? 296
Stevens, *Expectations Demand A Rapture*, review of 274
sting of death remained until law taken away 267
Strimple, Robert B., *When Shall These Things Be?* 194
Stuart, Moses *A Commentary on the Apocalypse* 55
substitutionary death
    did Christ die a? 10
    in I Peter 3.18 11
    in II Cor. 5.21 11
    in Isa. 53.4-6 11
    in Mt. 27.47 13
    in Rom. 5.6f 11

ineffectiveness illustrated 12
Jn. 10.28 14
Jn. 11.25-25 14
Jn. 3.15 13
Jn. 3.36 14
Jn. 6.50 14
Jn. 8.51 14
Psalm 22 and 13
suffering of the saints 228

T

Taken to Heaven in A. D. 70, Ian D. Harding 274
temple of God, man of sin sitting in 59
temple service, Ice and Demy say it will resume 364
temple, the
    destroyed when Satan crushed 234
    new *See* New Tabernacle
    new one and Eph. 4.8f 177
    new one completed at parousia 177
    new one under construction in first century 177
ten tribes never lost 177
Terry, Milton *Biblical Apocalyptics: A Study of the Most Notable Revelations of God and of Christ* 53, 168
Thayer, Henry *Greek-English Lexicon of the New Testament* 143
The Apocalypse Code, Hank Hanegraaff 168
The Beast of Revelation, Kenneth Gentry 347
The Bible Knowledge Commentary, New Testament, John Walvoord and Roy Zuck 161, 321
The Climax of Prophecy, Richard Bauckham 296
The Coming of the Son of Man, Andrew Perriman 118, 129, 131, 211, 222, 228

The Early Church, W. H. C. Frend 282
The Elements Shall Melt With Fervent Heat, Don K. Preston
  global earth not the focus of II Pet. 3 163
  on I Pet. 1.5-12 211
  on the end of the age 252
  on the rejected stone 35
  parousia not optically evident 89
  I Cor. 15.24 and I Cor. 10.11 the same 260
  not near for prophets, was near when New Testament revealed 200
The End of All Things, Jonathan Seraiah 337
the end of the age that has no end 317
The End of the Ages Has Come, Dale Allison 212
The End Times Made Simple, Samuel Waldron 145
The Englishman's Greek Concordance, on *chronos* 231
The Epistle of St. Jude and the Second Epistle of St. Peter, Joseph Mayor 163
The Epistles of Peter and Jude, J. N. D. Kelly 33
The Eschatological Temple in John 14, Steven M. Bryan 38
The Four Kingdoms of Daniel, John Evan 201
The Gospel and the Land, W. D. Davies 60, 100
The Great Tribulation, Past or Present, A Written Debate, Thomas Ice and Kenneth Gentry 98, 207, 247
The Greatness of the Great Commission, Kenneth Gentry 137, 379
The International Critcal Commentary, Thessalonians, James Frame 54, 104, 145

The Interpretation of St Paul's Epistles to the Colossians, to the Thessalonians, to Timothy, to Titus and Philemon, R. C. H. Lenski 104
The John Eadie Greek Text Commentaries, Thessalonians, John Eadie 145
The Method and Message of Jewish Apocalyptic, D. S. Russell 246
The Millennial Kingdom, John Walvoord 26
The Millennium Myth, N, T. Wright 275
The Mystery of Romans, Mark Nanos 207
The New International Greek Text Commentary, 2 Corinthians, Murray Harris 91
The Pattern of Redemptive History, Robert Brimsmead 125
The Presence of the Future, George Eldon Ladd 169
The Proof of the Gospel, Eusebius 176
The Prophecy of the Destruction of Jerusalem, N. Nisbett 56
The Second Coming Bible, William Beiderwolf 53
The Second Coming, John MacArthur 214, 321
The Seventy Weeks of Daniel Part I, Thomas Ice 266, 334
The Synonyms of the New Testament, Richard Trench 198, 210, 232
The Time Is Fulfilled, F. F. Bruce 209
The Typological Interpretation of the Old Testament in the New Testament, Leonard Goppelt 17
The Vocabulary of the Greek Testament Illustrated from the Papyri and Other Non-Literary Sources, James Hope Moulton and George Milligan 143

Theoderet of Cyrus on new heaven and earth, new Jerusalem 295
Thessalonians
  parallels with Olivet Discourse 72-75
  persecuted by Jewish countrymen 49
  what Paul didn't say to the 57
  who persecuting in AD 51? 55
  why concerned with wrath on Jews? 49
  why would Gentile Christians be interested in promises to Old Covenant Israel? 100
thief coming of the Lord
  Ac. 13.27 242
  Ac. 13.40-41 242
  Ac. 18.6 242
  Ac. 28.25-28 242
  discussed 239-244
  Dt. 32.35 243
  Heb. 10.33-37 244
  I Thes. 2.14-16 244
  Isa. 6.9f 242
  Isa. 65.1-2 243
  Isa. 65.13f 243
  Jer. 2.30 244
  Jer. 4.16-31 244
  Mk.13.7-8 244
  Mt. 21.40f 243
  Mt. 22.1-7 240
  Mt. 25.1-13 240
  new name 243
  Old Testament citations by Paul 243
  parallels between I Thes. 5 and Jer. 2-7 241
  Ps. 69.21f 243
  Ps. 69.24-28 243
  Rom. 9.33 243
  Rom. 10.20-21 243
  Rom. 11.9 243
  Rom. 11.16 243
  Rom. 11.26f 243
  Rom. 12.19 243

Thine Is the Kingdom, Kenneth Gentry
  applies II Thes. 2 to 70 AD 337
  discussed 63
Things to Come, J. Dwight Pentecost 26, 261, 321, 335
this age vs. age to come (dispensational view) 314
this generation, Ice's inconsistency on 216
time
  for judgment
    Ac. 14.22 225
    can't apply Dan. 7 to Pentecost 226
    Dan. 2.28f 223
    Dan. 7 223
    I Pet. 4.17 230
    I Thes. 2.12 224
    II Thes. 1.4f 224
    II Thes. 1.6 224
    II Thes. 2.14f 224
    II Thes. 2.2 224
    II Thes. 2.5f 224
    II Thes. 3.1-3 224
    Jas. 5.9 230
    Lk. 3.1f 223
    Mt. 16.24f 223
    Mt. 16.27-28 222
    Mt. 24.9 223
    Rom. 15.8 223
    suffering for the kingdom 224
    vindication and relief from persecution 224
time shortened 213
time, end of did not belong to Jewish eschatology 361
travail, woman in *See* woman in travail
tree of life, sustained biological life? 354
Trench, Richard *The Synonyms of the New Testament* 198, 210, 232
tribulation
  birth pains of the messiah 248
  Israel delivered from 247

of I Thes. 3.3-4 52
of Mt. 24.9 52
woman in travail an illustration of 246
trumpet
   judgment of Old Covenant Israel 137
   Mt. 24.30 179
   resurrection at last 137
   silent for the rapture, audible for the parousia 80
   sound of
      discussed 130-140
      Isa. 11.11f 132
      Isa. 24-27 132
      Isa. 25.6-8 132
      Isa. 27.12-13 140
   was to gather God's elect 133
   with resurrection of Israel 134
Trumpet, Great
   Isa. 27.9-13 21
   linked to Day of the Lord 21
two Adam doctrine 8
two comings or one?
   LaHaye on 327
   what did early church expect? 326
   world mission and 328
Tyndale New Testament Commentaries, I and II Thessalonians 165

U

Understanding the Sacred Text, Robert Grant 280
Unger, Merrill F. *Zechariah: Prophet of Messiah's Glory* 53

V

Van Impe, Jack, set 1999 as date for rapture 313
vindication of the martyrs
   at the resurrection 81
   I Thes. 4.14 105
   II Thes. 1.8 105
   in I Thes. 4 goes with relief and vindication in II Thes. 1 119
   Lk. 17.25f 105
   Lk. 18.2-8 105
   Mt. 23.32f 105
   promised in Mt. 23, Lk. 18, I Thes. 2.14f, Rev. 6.11 121
   purpose of the parousia 104
Vine, W. E. Expository *Dictionary of New Testament Words* 143
voice of an archangel 125-129

W

Waldron, Samuel *The End Times Made Simple* 145
Wallace, Daniel B. *Greek Grammar Beyond the Basics: An Exegetical Syntax of the New Testament* 199
Walvoord, John
   gap theory 26
   hermeneutic accepted and rejected by Gentry 338
Walvoord, John *The Millennial Kingdom* 26
Walvoord, John, and Roy Zuck, *The Bible Knowledge Commentary, New Testament* 161, 321
Wanamaker, Bruce *New International Greek Testament Commentary on 1 & 2 Thessalonians* 54, 72, 122, 144, 234, 245
Wanamaker, Charles *New International Greek Testament Commentary*, on Isa. 26.1 233
watchfulness implies delay (Gentry) 65
Watts, Rikki *Isaiah's New Exodus in Mark* 97
we who are alive, editorial, royal, or covenantal we? 195
wedding feast
   destruction then wedding 64
   favorite parable theme of Jesus 44
wedding, the

dispensationalism requires two weddings and two brides 161
Gentry on 237
Gentry sees in first century 66-69
goes with New Tabernacle 41 of Mt. 22 is not that of Mt. 25 66-69
whose promise is this 161
Weima, Jeffrey *Commentary on the New Testament Use of the Old Testament* 131
Welch, John, on I Thes. 4.13f 368
Wenham, Gordon *Paul and the Synoptic Apocalypse* 75
When Shall These Things Be? A Reformed Response to Hyper-Preterism, Keith Mathison, editor
   inconsistent on Dan. 12, Rev. 11 137
   on shattering the power of the holy people 342
   shattering the power of the holy people 342
   some "son of man" texts future, some not 341
Whisenant, Edgar C., set 1988 as date for rapture 313
wicked
   Iranaeus knew wicked not raptured in AD 70 302
   not removed in AD 70 301
Wiema, Jeffrey *Commentary on the New Testament Use of the Old Testament* 63
Witherington, Ben III *Jesus, Paul, and the End of the World* 119
without observation
   all futurists have kingdom coming with observation 83
without observation
   Christ brings dead 85
   resurrection and kingdom 83
woman in travail
   Ac. 3.21f 248
   Ac. 14.22 247
   at the resurrection 246

birth pains of the messiah 246
corporate new birth 248
Dan. 12.10 247, 250
Ex. 4.22 247
far more than normal human experience 250
Heb. 3-4 248
Heb. 10.37 250
Heb. 12.21 249
I Cor. 10.2 248
I Pet. 1.4f 247-248
illustration of messianic woes 245
Isa. 11.10f 247
Isa. 21.3f 246
Isa. 26.16-19 247
Isa. 26.21 247
Isa. 37.3 246
Isa. 42.1-4 247
Isa. 42.10 247
Isa. 42.15f 247
Isa. 63.11-12 248
Isa. 65.8-25 247
Isa. 66.12-16 247
Isa. 66.15 247
Israel delivered from tribulation 247
Jas. 1.18 249
Jas. 5.8 250
Jas.5.1-6 249
Jer. 4.31 246
Jer. 22.23 246
Jer. 50.43 246
Jer. 6.24 246
Jn. 3.7b 248
Mic. 3.12 248
Mic. 4.10 248
Mic. 5.2-3 248
Mic. 5.3f 248
Mt. 24.8 249
Mt. 24.15f 248
national destruction of eschatological significance 250
Old Testament usage 245-250
period of great tribulation 246
Rev. 7.14 249

Rev. 14.1-2 250
Rev. 14.4 249
Word Biblical Commentary on 2 Peter, Richard Bauckham 291
Word Biblical Commentary, 2 Corinthians, Ralph Martin 91
Word Biblical Commentary, Daniel, John Goldingay 271
Word Biblical Commentary, F. F. Bruce 54
Word Biblical Commentary, Hebrews 9-13, William Lane 105, 112
Word Biblical Commentary, Romans 9-16, James D. G. Dunn 86
Word Biblical Commentary, William Mounce 328
Word Commentary, Commentary on 1 & 2 Thessalonians, F. F. Bruce 74, 104, 125, 145
Word Pictures in the New Testament, A. T. Robertson 104, 125, 304
world mission
  declarations of completion 328
  Ice claims wasn't fulfilled 329
  some patristics thought fulfilled 289
world would see Christ no more 85
wrath to come, Mt. 3.7-8 48
Wright, N. T.
  meeting the Lord in the air 145
  on Mt. 25.14f 148
  coming on the clouds of heaven 50
  Jews didn't anticipate end of human history 50
Wright, N. T. *Jesus and the Victory of God* 44, 69, 173, 222-223
Wright, N. T. *Paul* 49, 91
Wright, N. T. *The Millennium Myth* 275

Z

Zechariah: Prophet of Messiah's Glory, Merrill F. Unger 53
Zion
  importance of in Old Testament prophecies 376
  messianic banquet would be spread in 376

www.ingramcontent.com/pod-product-compliance
Lightning Source LLC
Chambersburg PA
CBHW071233160426
43196CB00009B/1045